North America

North America

A GEOGRAPHY OF CANADA AND THE UNITED STATES

J.H. Paterson
Professor of Geography in the University of Leicester

SIXTH EDITION

NEW YORK   OXFORD UNIVERSITY PRESS   1979

© 1960, 1962, 1965, 1970 by
Oxford University Press
Copyright © 1975, 1979 by Oxford University Press, Inc.

Library of Congress Cataloging in Publication Data

Paterson, John Harris.
  North America : a geography of Canada and the United States.

  Bibliography: p.
  Includes index.
  1. United States—Description and travel—1960–
2. Canada—Description and travel—1951–
I. Title.
E169.02.P33 1979   973.92   78-14360
ISBN 0-19-502484-2
ISBN 0-19-913260-7 U.K.

Cover photo: Wheatfield in Colorado (*David Muench*)

Printed in the United States of America

9 8 7 6 5 4 3

This Sixth Edition commemorates H. J. Dyos,
colleague and friend, 1921–1978.

Author's Note to the Sixth Edition

When in December 1973 I completed the Fifth Edition of this book, I believed that I had probably carried out the task of revision for the last time. No book is immortal, and I expected this one to be superseded, within the lifetime of the Fifth Edition, by something newer and better. Then again, I had been making each successive edition a little more change proof, or less liable to become glaringly out-of-date, and I hoped that the Fifth would be more durable than its predecessors. Surely not even the North Americans, innovators though they are, could modify their geography quickly enough to oblige me to go through the whole process of revision once again?

But indeed they could and lo!—here is a Sixth Edition. For its timing, its pictorial content and some of its emphases I am indebted, as I have been over many years now, to the advice and help of the editorial staff of Oxford University Press, New York. It is difficult for an author who lives outside North America to keep in touch with the needs of the American student or reader, and it is upon the wise counsel of James Anderson and Joyce Berry that I rely for guidance. They possess the charming quality (and perhaps others have ex-perienced it) of making me feel that I am the only author with whom they have to cope.

It goes without saying that, whenever a book is republished, the author should take the opportunity of bringing his facts and figures up to date. This has been done although, as it happens, 1978 is a bad year in North America for doing it; the 1980/81 censuses are almost upon us, and during the late seventies the publication of agricultural and industrial statistics has been lagging badly behind the calendar. Be that as it may, however, the important changes are not in these details—which anyone can, after all, discover by consulting an almanac—but in larger matters.

What the author has to do is to try to decide which issues or developments have, since he last wrote, become critical. Better still, he should be able to predict the *next* development of importance, if his book is to have any reasonable life expectancy at all. This is never easy. When I was preparing the Fifth Edition, for example, I wondered whether to include a section on the redrawing of state boundaries, to take account of various proposals then current for a framework of government more manageable for the United States than a division into fifty states of assorted size. I decided, however, to wait and see if the matter would mature and I am glad that I waited, for so far it has not done so.

The major issues this time around all seem to me to lie in the realm of government involvement with the economy and the environment. The first edition of this book appeared in 1960; that is, at the end of eight years of Republican administration in the United States—and Eisenhower Republicanism at that. With such a starting point, the lifetime of the book has seen a great increase in government participation in everyday affairs. And not all of it has been doctrinaire, mere interference for interference's sake, nor has it necessarily even been political, in the narrow sense of having been programmed by one party or the other. Actually, as we shall see, in many of the matters involved the Administration has followed rather than led. It has responded to the pressure of groups and individuals interested in protecting the environment, or improving the quality of life.

But the outcome has been a steady flow of legislation with a direct bearing on *landscapes*— regional subsidies, land reservation acts, curbs on surface mining, pollution controls—and not only on present landscapes but on landscapes of the future, too. So it has been necessary for a geographer to examine this legislation, all the way from the federal level down to the grass-roots (where it has been fascinating, though confusing, to explore freshly the world of zoning controls and tax assessments), for this certainly seems to me to be an area of American geography which has "gone critical" in the 1970s. It must be given much greater prominence in the new edition, and Chapters 3–5 contain most of the fresh material.

After all that I was relieved, on my last visit to North America, to find how much is still unchanged—relieved because there is comfort in knowing that some parts of my work, at least, have survived the years. Of course, the cities change faster than the country and the coasts, I think, faster than the interior. In the Midwest, the region I know best, it is remarkable and reassuring to rediscover old places and unchanged ways; to find, too, how many survivors there still are of the old generation of real, live pre-1914 immigrants, with their fractured English and their tales of pioneer days; the years go by and they go on, apparently as energetically as ever. My favorite Midwesterner of all is the 96-year-old in Wisconsin who, at the age of 81, decided to fly back to his native Norway—to see his mother.

By these standards, what are the twenty-odd years of the life of this book? Yet it seems to be taking on a timeless character of its own; certainly, I cannot now remember what life was like without it. My conscience, however, is so far clear; to the best of my ability I have kept it up to the minute, and I am grateful to all those helpful readers who have called my attention to changes in the continent's geography which have taken place while I slept. To their vigilance this new edition owes much of whatever novelty it may possess.

J.H.P.
Leicester, England
November 1978

Contents

List of Maps
and Diagrams

North America

The Physical Background

Introduction

The continent of North America has an area of some 8.3 million sq mi (21.5 million sq km). The area with which this book is chiefly concerned is, however, less than that for it excludes Mexico and the countries bordering the Caribbean, and virtually ignores the Arctic Archipelago—the almost uninhabited islands which lie within the Canadian sector of the Arctic. If we deduct those two parts of the continent from the whole, we are left with an area of 6.7 million sq mi (17.35 million sq km), of which Canada occupies 3.1 million sq mi (8.03 million sq km) and the United States, including the huge outlying state of Alaska, accounts for the remainder.

Translated into distances, these dimensions mean that the part of the continent we are considering stretches across almost 50° of latitude, from the Florida Keys to the northern tip of mainland Canada, and across 115° of longitude, from the east coast of Newfoundland to the Bering Strait. The railway distance from Halifax in the east to Prince Rupert in the west of Canada is more than 3750 mi (6000 km); from New York to San Francisco is some 3000 mi (4800 km), and from Brownsville on the United States-Mexican border to the 49th parallel that marks the boundary between Canada and the United States, is 1600 mi (2560 km). Thus Prince Rupert is as far from Halifax as the mouth of the Congo is from London, and New York is as far from San Francisco as it is from Ireland (see Fig. 1-1).

The Physiographic Divisions

For ease of reference the North American continent may be divided, north of the United States—Mexican border, into seven main physiographic provinces, as shown in Figure 1-2.

THE ATLANTIC AND GULF COAST PLAINS

From western Texas to New York the North American continent is bordered by coastal plains. In Texas these plains are 300 mi (480 km) wide; northeastward from the Florida peninsula they gradually narrow or, more accurately, an increasing proportion of them lies submerged beneath the sea. In the neighborhood of New York the plains come to an end, reappearing north of the Hudson only in parts

Degrees of Longitude (Eurasia)

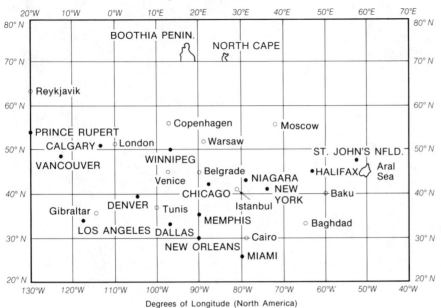

Degrees of Longitude (North America)

Fig. 1-1. North America and Europe: Comparative locations.

of Cape Cod and the islands off the coast of southern New England.

The coastal plains are formed by a series of beds of geologically young materials, dipping gently away from the older rocks of the interior toward the coast. The oldest beds forming the plains are Cretaceous, and lie at the inland margin. The successive layers form belts with low scarp edges facing inland, but the general slope of the plains' surface is so gentle that no true coastline can be formed. Swamps, lagoons, and bars, fronted by almost continuous sand reefs, characterize a transition zone between land and sea. Through it wind rivers that are highly liable to flood.

Not only is this southeastern margin of the continent especially subject to year-by-year changes in its present detail, but it evidently has a long history of changes in level. These are indicated, on the one hand, by the terraces of former shorelines, recognizable more than 250 ft (76 m) above the present sea level, and, on the other hand, by the drowned valleys of Chesapeake Bay and the Virginia shore.

Midway along the coastal plains and separating the waters of the Atlantic from the Gulf of Mexico is the peninsula of Florida, projecting southward for some 350 mi (560 km). It is surrounded by shallow seas underlain by the continental shelf that have probably existed

since Tertiary times; Florida itself, however, became part of the continental land mass only in recent geologic times. Like the plains, Florida is flat (the highest point in the state is only 325 ft (99 m) above sea level), lake strewn, and swampy. In the south an area of over 5000 sq mi (12,900 sq km), known as the Everglades, is composed of swamps only a few feet above sea level. Much of the plateau is underlain by limestone formations, and on its surface, solution hollows and sinkholes are common features. Sandbars and lagoons line the coast, while in the extreme south, coral reefs have formed in the warm waters of the Gulf.

Near their western end the coastal plains spread inland to include the Mississippi Valley south of Cairo. The telltale scarps of the belted plains swing north in a great inverted V to embrace the valley, a structural depression that has been deepened by erosion. The valley bottom is wide, flat, and easily flooded, and through it meanders the Mississippi, carrying the vast silt load that year by year builds its delta further out into the shallow coastal waters of the Gulf of Mexico.

THE APPALACHIAN SYSTEM

In eastern North America, mountain-building processes went on at intervals throughout Or-

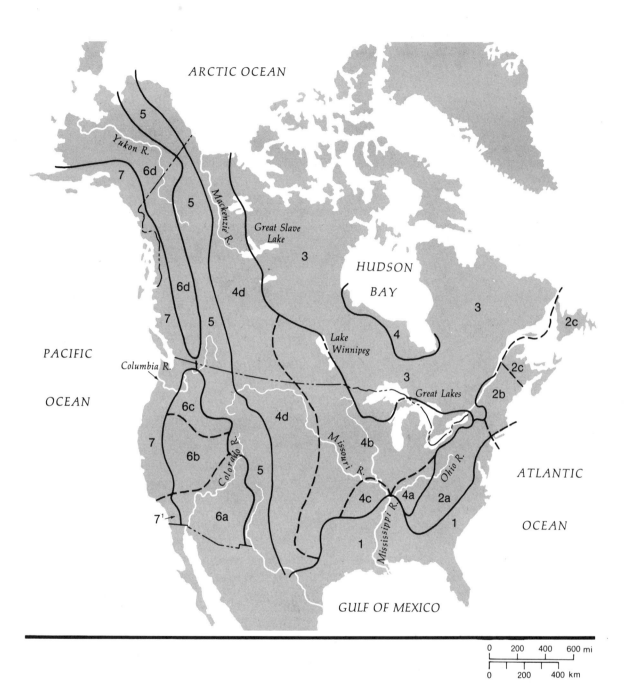

Fig. 1-2. Physiographic provinces of North America: The provinces are: 1. The Atlantic and Gulf Coast Plains; 2. The Appalachian System (*a*) The Southern section, (*b*) New England section, (*c*) Maritimes–Newfoundland extension; 3. The Canadian or Laurentian Shield; 4. The Central Lowland (*a*) The Eastern transition belt, or Interior Low Plateaus, (*b*) The Mississippi-Great Lakes section, (*c*) The Ozark-Ouachita section, (*d*) The Great Plains; 5. The Rocky Mountain Province; 6. The High Plateaus, (*a*) The Colorado Plateau, (*b*) The Great Basin, (*c*) The Plateaus of the Columbia and Snake, (*d*) The Plateaus of British Columbia and the Northwest; 7. The Pacific Coastlands; 7¹. The Angeles Appendix.

dovician, Devonian, and Permian times. The area affected by these processes forms a wide belt, with a marked northeast to southwest trend, from Newfoundland to central Alabama. This area, diverse in present character but unified by its physical history, may be called the Appalachian System. It falls into three sections: a southern section, stretching from Alabama to the valley of the Hudson and including the Appalachian Mountains proper; a New England section, from the Hudson to central Maine; and a northeastern section, covering northern Maine and the Maritime Provinces of Canada.

The Southern Section

In the south the system is formed by two parallel belts. On the east is that of the "old" Appalachians, made up of Precambrian igneous and metamorphic rocks. On the west is a "new" belt, formed by the upthrust edge of the great Paleozoic floor that covers the central lowlands of North America. Each of these belts has an eastern edge different in form from the western, and this further subdivision gives the system four provinces.

On the eastern, or seaward, edge the old rocks have been severely eroded to form a gently sloping, dissected plateau surface known as the Piedmont. From its junction with the coastal plains at the Fall Line (see p. 174) it rises gradually to 1200–1500 ft (365–455 m), where it merges with the wooded mountains. These mountains represent the western half of the "old" Appalachians, an area less heavily eroded than the Piedmont, and so rising in places to 6000 ft (1825 m) or more. In the Great Smoky Mountains and the Blue Ridge of the southern states this mountain barrier is virtually uninterrupted, but it subsides northward, and in northern Virginia and Pennsylvania it becomes low and discontinuous.

When the "new" belt of the Appalachians in the west was upthrust, the Paleozoic strata, which formerly lay almost horizontal, were severely contorted along the line of junction with the older formations to the east. This junction zone now shows a remarkable series of folds running parallel with the trend of the system

and known as the Ridge and Valley Province. This "corrugated" area is 25–80 mi (40–128 km) wide, and through it run the north-flowing Shenandoah and the south-flowing Tennessee with their tributaries, while east-flowing rivers like the Potomac are forced to cut through the ridges in a series of gaps.

West of the fold zone and above a high scarp face (known in Pennsylvania as the Allegheny Front), lies the fourth, or inland, province of the system. It is a plateau section, where the Paleozoic formations retain almost the same undisturbed bedding as they had before the upthrust. The Cumberland Plateau in Tennessee and Kentucky lies at about 2000 ft (600 m), and levels rise to twice that height in West Virginia. Northward the plateau stretches almost to the southern shores of the Great Lakes; westward it drops away to the lowlands. Among its sandstones and limestones lie the vast coal measures of the great Appalachian coal field.

The New England Section

North of the Hudson the Precambrian and Paleozoic belts of the Appalachian System continue into New England. The first of these is represented by the heavily eroded uplands of New England that correspond to the Piedmont. The Ridge and Valley Province of the Paleozoic belt, on the other hand, can be traced running north through the Hudson Valley, and so by way of the Champlain Lowland, to where it merges with the downfaulted St. Lawrence Valley. On the west the Plateau Province terminates in the Catskill Mountains.

The uplands of New England form a plateau surface which drops gently eastward to the sea. They are surmounted by groups of peaks that represent harder masses of rock, which have resisted the attacks of three or perhaps four cycles of erosion. Such peaks have received the name of monadnocks, after Mount Monadnock in New Hampshire. The uplands have two axes, separated by the lowlands that extend from New Jersey north through the Connecticut Valley. The western axis is marked by the line of the Green Mountains and is carried north by

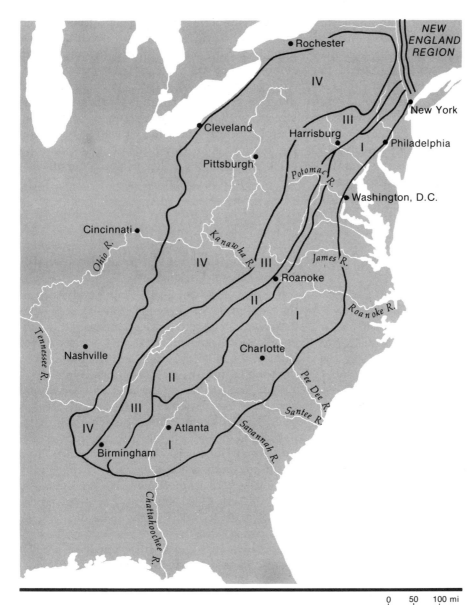

Fig. 1-3. Physical divisions of the Appalachian System: (I) The Piedmont, (II) The Blue Ridge, (III) Ridge and Valley; (IV) The Appalachian Plateaus.

that of the Notre Dame and the Shickshock mountains, which stretch into the Gaspé Peninsula of Québec. None of these is as much as 4500 ft (1370 m) high. The eastern axis runs through the White Mountains [where Mount Washington reaches 6288 ft (1929 m)] and into Canada's Maritime Provinces. The whole surface of New England has been heavily glaciated, and much of the detail of the landscape is due to the action of the ice.

The Maritimes-Newfoundland Extension

While the Appalachian mountain-building processes extended their influence to northern Maine and the Maritime Provinces, and traces of the system persist as far east as Newfoundland, the present structure of the area bears little relation to that further south. Huge igneous intrusions have occured to form the batholiths that constitute the Central Highlands of

5

New Brunswick and the hills of the "arm" of Nova Scotia and Cape Breton Island. Between these old formations in Nova Scotia and the equally old rocks of the Canadian Shield, a wide basin has been formed in which younger beds—Permian and Carboniferous—are found. These beds underlie the lowlands around the Bay of Fundy and Prince Edward Island. On the southern shore of the Bay of Fundy the same feature that forms the Connecticut Valley—a band of young sandstones and shales of Triassic age—occurs again to form the Annapolis Valley of Nova Scotia.

THE CANADIAN OR LAURENTIAN SHIELD

Much of eastern Canada is covered by more than a million square miles of metamorphosed Precambrian rocks that form a vast block known as the Laurentian Shield. Beneath the Paleozoic strata bordering it on the south, on the west, and around Hudson Bay, there can be traced the continuation of the Shield, which underlies much of central Canada and the Great Lakes region as well.

Wide areas of this ancient rock mass have been severely compressed and contorted, and in the zones of disturbance a large variety of minerals is to be found. The present surface of the Shield, however, bears little relation to the previous disturbance. Through a long history of erosion culminating in severe glaciation, it has been converted into an even surface that dips gently away from a level of 1700–2000 ft (500–600 m) along its southeast (or St. Lawrence) edge until it disappears below younger formations just south of Hudson Bay.

The Shield is nearly all Canadian, but two southward extensions into the United States share its main characteristics. One is in the Adirondack Mountains of northern New York State, and the other forms the Superior Upland in northern Wisconsin and Michigan. On the west the Shield sinks beneath later materials along a line that runs through Lake of the Woods, Great Slave Lake, and Great Bear Lake to the Arctic Seas. On the east it includes Labrador, with its monadnock ranges, and it can also be traced to Newfoundland.

The tremendous forces of glaciation scoured the smooth surface in almost unobstructed action. Today the result of this action remains in an absence of soil cover and in a chaotic drainage system. Glacial detritus has dammed and diverted streams, creating a rocky landscape strewn with lakes and swamps. Sometimes, however, these lakes have disappeared, leaving behind them clay-filled beds and offering some prospect of fertility in this otherwise infertile world of the Shield.

THE CENTRAL LOWLAND

Between the Appalachian System in eastern North America and the Rocky Mountains in the West is a vast lowland area. As far as relief is concerned, the Gulf Coast Plains and much of the Laurentian Shield, which have already been described, belong to this lowland also. It is only on geological grounds that they are separated from it, for one is younger and the other older than the region we are now considering.

Even with the coastal plains and the Shield excluded, the remainder of the lowland area is of enormous extent. From the edge of the Appalachian Plateau in Ohio to the foot of the Rockies at Denver is 1200 mi (1920 km). From north to south the dimensions of the region are even more impressive—40° of latitude, or over 2500 mi (4000 km), from the edge of the coastal plain in Texas to the delta of the Mackenzie at 70° North.

Spread across the Central Lowland are Paleozoic beds of great thickness, evenly deposited on the floor of a former sea. In the northeast these beds overlap the Shield, while on the south they are themselves submerged below the later deposits of the coastal plain. In the east, as we have seen, they end in violent contortions against the wall of the "old" Appalachians. In the west they extend, beneath a cover of Tertiary and recent materials, until they terminate against the wall of the Rockies, and on the north they reach the Arctic Ocean.

The Central Lowland comprises several sections. These may be described as the Eastern Transition Belt, the Mississippi-Great Lakes Section, the Ozark-Ouachita Province, and the Great Plains.

The St. Lawrence Valley: The Thousand Islands from the United States shore. Here the old, hard rocks of the Canadian Shield extend southward across the valley to form the Adirondack Mountains of northern New York State. *(New York State Dept. of Commerce)*

The Eastern Transition Belt

Between the Appalachian Plateau, where the paleozoic formations have been upthrust, and the Mississippi Valley, where they lie even and almost undisturbed, there is a transitional area sometimes called the Interior Low Plateaus. As the effects of the Appalachian mountain-building processes spread further afield they became less violent and in the Transition Belt merely created some slight folds and a gentle westward dip away from the moun-

tains. This area has for the most part a sandstone cover underlain by Carboniferous limestone. The latter gives rise to areas of karst topography and to such limestone features as the Mammoth Cave of Kentucky. Of more importance to the economic life of the region is the effect of this folding in creating two domes whose sandstone cover has been removed by erosion, leaving limestone basins—the Blue Grass Basin of Kentucky and the Nashville Basin of Tennessee. Both of these have long been famous for the excellence of the pastures on their lime-rich soils.

The Mississippi-Great Lakes Section

This section constitutes the eastern half of the Paleozoic lowlands. It is a true structural plain whose flatness is emphasized by a mantle of glacial drift as far south as the Ohio and Missouri rivers. Here, as on the Shield, glacial action has affected the drainage system, and the area abounds with lakes. Before the coming of the cultivator, who drained the land, swamps were also widespread. Slight folding accounts for the area's only significant physical features. These are synclines in Ohio and Illinois which contain coal measures, and a basin centered in southern Michigan whose rim is marked by cuestas that form an almost perfect semicircle around it. The best known of these is the Niagara Cuesta, a "rim" of magnesian limestone underlying Niagara Falls that runs northward across a string of islands in Lake Huron, then west and south through Upper Michigan into Wisconsin.

West of the Mississippi the strata dip very gently westward while, equally gently, the land surface rises. The result is a series of east-facing scarps which become progressively younger to the west. The most prominent of these scarps, the Missouri Escarpment, is usually taken to delimit the section on the west. In the Southwest, the Balcones Escarpment provides a similar regional boundary between the Gulf Coast Plain and the Great Plains.

The Ozark-Ouachita Section

West of the Mississippi and near where it merges with the Gulf Coast Plain, the Central Lowland is interrupted by a group of low mountains sometimes called the Interior Highlands. These highlands are formed by two separate features. In the north is a dome flanked by rocks of Carboniferous age and at whose crest Precambrian granites are exposed. This area forms the Ozark Mountains and comprises the Salem and Springfield plateaus and the Boston Mountains. In drainage pattern and landscape it corresponds to the Appalachian Plateau region. To the south, beyond the Arkansas River, lie the Ouachita Mountains, a folded belt that closely resembles in structure

the Ridge and Valley of the Appalachians; indeed, they were created by the same mountain-building movements. The highest point in the Ouachitas is 2700 ft (820 m) and in the Ozarks, a little over 2000 ft (610 m).

The Great Plains

The eastern edge of the Great Plains, in the neighborhood of the Missouri Escarpment, lies at about 2000 ft (610 m) above sea level. The western edge, where the Front Range of the Rockies abruptly rises, is at an elevation of 4000–5000 ft (1215–1520 m), giving an average slope of 8–10 ft per mi (1.5–1.9 m per km) across the area. Yet these plains are structurally part of the Central Lowland. They extend from Mexico northward until, narrowing between the Shield and the Rockies, they reach northern Alaska.

As in the western part of the Mississippi-Great Lakes Section, the strata underlying the Great Plains continue to dip westward toward a trough at the foot of the Rockies. The eastward slope of the land, however, is caused by the recent deposition of a mantle of often quite unconsolidated materials from the Rockies, transported and spread by the east-flowing rivers. This smooth surface mantle is disturbed only by the effects of erosive agents upon it. Wind and water have cut deeply into the soft, loose materials washed down from the mountains. In Nebraska a belt of sand hills have been formed by the force of a virtually unobstructed wind, while in the Dakotas—and to some extent in all the river valleys that cross the plains—water erosion has created the fantastic badland topography for which the plains are famous.

Only one major break interrupts the evenness of the plains—the Black Hills of South Dakota, which rise to over 7000 ft (2130 m). Here the old, crystalline continental bedrock breaks through the surface in a domelike swelling and forms a welcome change from the monotony of the plains.[1]

---

[1] In the granite of this dome, exposed in Mt. Rushmore, is a famous memorial, the gigantic carving of the heads of four American presidents.

THE ROCKY MOUNTAIN PROVINCE

Late in Cretaceous times tremendous mountain-building processes disturbed the western half of the North American continent, where a long series of sedimentary beds lay evenly spread over the ancient continental floor. This disturbance, which was accompanied by volcanic activity, is known as the Laramide Revolution. It resulted in a great uplift of the sedimentary beds, accompanied by folding and faulting, in the areas now known as the Rocky Mountain Province and the High Plateaus.

The uplift led to a much intensified attack by erosive agents in the Tertiary period that followed. From the highest parts of the West, thousands of feet of sedimentary cover were removed, and the Archean floor was exposed. Elsewhere, however, the cover has been preserved—usually by downfaulting—and it is the various strata of this sedimentary covering, with their characteristic horizontal bedding, that give to the landscape of the West many of its particular splendors.

We must now define more closely the nature of the Rocky Mountains. On the eastern (Great Plains) fringe of the area affected, the Laramide Revolution threw up two parallel ranges, running generally from north to south. In their southern section these ranges are mainly granitic, but in their central and northern parts they are formed of towering sedimentaries, many of which have retained horizontal bedding. It is these ranges which form the Rocky Mountains proper and which extend, with some interruptions, from the Brooks Range in Alaska, south across Canada and the United States to about 35° North, with traces of extension beyond this into Mexico. The peaks of these Front Ranges rise abruptly above the Great Plains to heights of from 10,000 to 14,000 ft (3040–4250 m).

The Front Ranges are backed by an area of scattered mountains, interspersed with plateaus. The whole province has an east-west width of between 100 and 300 mi (160–480 km). Most of the mountain ranges follow the general north-south trend of the Rockies, a trend which is accentuated by faulting. Across the boundary between the United States and Canada, for example, runs the remarkable Rocky Mountain Trench, a fault valley 900 mi (1440 km) long, occupied in turn by the Columbia, Fraser, Parsnip, and Finlay rivers. Elsewhere, however, volcanic activity has created great structureless batholiths, like the mountains of central Idaho, where granite forms a wilderness area that rises above 12,000 ft (3650 m) and remains almost impenetrable to the present day.

All through the Rocky Mountains, indeed, the effects of vulcanicity have been great. Lava flows cover much of northern New Mexico, and in Wyoming visitors flock to Yellowstone National Park to watch over 3000 geysers and hot springs that are still active on a 7000-ft (2130 m) plateau in the heart of the mountains.

In the Cordilleran barrier there are few breaches. One of them is in the far north—at the southern end of the Mackenzie Mountains, where the Liard River flows through the break—and is followed by the Alaska Highway. The other is a breach of the utmost importance for transcontinental communications and occurs between the southern and central Rockies where they fall back to form the Wyoming Basin. The old Oregon Trail (see p. 149) made use of this route, on which wagons could be hauled over the Continental Divide without difficulty—without, indeed, more than a distant glimpse of the mountains. Today the railway traveller from Chicago to California glides over the 7000-ft (2130 m) pass without any impression of climbing, and only careful observation will mark the whereabouts of the watershed.

THE HIGH PLATEAUS

West of the Rocky Mountains proper lies an area whose astonishing physical features are the product, in about equal proportions, of crustal faulting, volcanic activity, and intense recent erosion by downcutting rivers. The basic form of the area is that of a series of plateau steps, some of them almost as high as the Rockies themselves and almost all above 3000 ft (912 m). In the southwestern United States, however, the "steps" descend fairly regularly from the Rockies for 500 mi (800 km) westward to the remarkable hollow of Death Valley, 280 ft (85 m) below sea level. Further north the plateau province is narrower, so that its width in British Columbia is no more than 100 mi (160 km).

The development of these plateaus, like that of the Rockies, resulted from the Laramide Revolution, and they form a series from Mexico to the Bering Strait. On the whole their different levels are the result of faulting. For the rest they possess two common characteristics. The first is that the original relief, whether it was based on the old continental floor or on the later Paleozoics, has been smoothed by recent deposits. Over wide areas, notably in the Great Basin of Utah and Nevada, these are ordinary alluvia, but elsewhere lava flows of great extent are found, lying ten or twenty deep in regular horizontal layers. The second common characteristic is that throughout the province there seem to have been great amounts of recent uplift, and the resultant spectacular patterns of erosion are epitomized by the Grand Canyon of the Colorado.

Several parts of the province can be distinguished. In the southeast lie the Colorado Plateaus, developed on horizontal Paleozoics and dropping by cliff steps from 11,000 to 5000 ft (3340–1520 m) above sea level. Through the sandstones and limestones of this sedimentary cover the Colorado and its tributaries have cut gorges up to 5000 ft (1520 m) deep. In the Grand Canyon the river has cut down through the whole Secondary cover and a series of Paleozoics to the Archean floor, thus exposing a giant cross section of the continent's physical history.

The western edge of the Central Rockies is marked by a great fault at the foot of the Wasatch Mountains, and west of this lies the

The Canadian Rockies: The Rocky Mountain Trench. Following the general north-south trend of the mountains, this fault-line valley extends 800–900 mi (1287–1448 km), from Flathead Lake in Montana to the Liard River in Canada. (*British Columbia Government*)

Landforms of the High Plateau Province: A landscape in northeastern Arizona, now the Hopi Indian Reservation. The picture emphasizes that the plateau surface owes its present forms to both desert erosion and volcanic activity—many of the striking features represent volcanic necks, of which there are hundreds. View of Hopi Buttes, looking toward the San Francisco Mountains. *(John S. Shelton)*

Great Basin, stretching for 500 mi (800 km) both from north to south and from east to west. Most of this is an area of inland drainage. The Basin is divided, however, into numerous sections by faulted mountain blocks, a few score miles in length and running, for the most part, regularly north and south. In between the ranges, recent alluvia and lakebed deposits fill the Basin. Great Salt Lake, which today occupies some 2000 sq mi (5180 sq km) at the eastern edge of the Basin, is only a remnant of the former Lake Bonneville, ten times as large, whose shoreline can be traced on slopes 1000 ft (300 m) above the level of the present lake.

North of this "basin and range" country lie the plateaus of the Columbia River and of British Columbia. These are most easily described as lava seas. The surrounding walls of the Rockies and the Cascade and Coast mountains formed "shores" within which the flows were dammed, so that in places they have been built up to a thickness of as much as 2000 ft (610 m). Northward through British Columbia the plateaus become more dissected and interrupted than further south, but the High Plateau province continues, with some breaks, all the way across the Yukon to central Alaska.

THE PACIFIC COASTLANDS

The most westerly physiographic province of North America is filled with a remarkable variety of natural wonders, and it is, indeed, only a common history that links its varied landscapes with each other. In this province are found the highest and lowest points of the continent, some of its deepest valleys and its only remaining (recently) active volcanoes.

On the American shores of the Pacific, the trend of the land features is almost everywhere parallel to the shoreline. These features form three belts, and this triple-banded effect can be traced from Mexico to Alaska, with only a short break in the region around Los Angeles.

On the inland edge of the province, adjoining the High Plateau, is a mountain chain comparable in size and splendor with the Rockies. From southern California this chain, the Sierra Nevada, stretches north to become the Cascade Range in Oregon and the Coast Mountains when it reaches British Columbia. It culminates in the Alaska Range in North America's highest peak, Mt. McKinley, at 20,320 ft (6178 m). Throughout its great length it is cut by only three low-level crossings: the valleys of the Columbia, Fraser, and Skeena river. Formed mostly of old crystalline materials occurring in the shape of batholiths, its crestline is crowned by scores of volcanic cones. These cones, whose lavas lie thick over the ranges, form outstanding peaks like Mt. Shasta and Mt. Rainier (both over 14,000 ft [4256 m]). In Alaska recent uplift has created block mountains like the St. Elias Range, which rises in places above 18,000 ft (5470 m).

Much of the eastern side of the mountains is faulted and very steep. From Mt. Whitney to Death Valley is only 70 mi (112 km) in distance, but the difference in elevation is nearly 15,000 ft (4560 m). The west side of the mountains, particularly the Sierras, is notable for its ice-carved valleys—Yosemite, with its waterfalls and its 3000-ft (912 m) cliffs, and King's Canyon, with its groves of sequoias.

West of the Mountains is a line of depressions—the Central Valley of California, the Willamette Valley, Puget Sound, and the coastal channels of British Columbia. Created in conjunction with the uplift of the mountains, these depressions have been filled at various times with ice, mud flows, and alluvia. Today they are submerged in the north but dry in the south, where up to 2000 ft (610 m) of materials have been deposited to form fertile farmlands, the agricultural heart of the Far West.

Bordering the coast itself is yet another mountain chain. In California it is composed of rolling hills 2000–4000 ft (610–1220 m) high. These enclose the Central Valley on the west, except where the sea breaks through them at the Golden Gate at San Francisco. The coastal chain continues into Oregon, but north of the Columbia it becomes higher and more rugged until it reaches Puget Sound and the 8000-ft (2430 m) Olympic Mountains. North of the Strait of Juan de Fuca the ranges are discontinuous and are represented by Vancouver Island and by the long chain of islands that flanks the coast beyond as far as the Aleutians.

This triple belt of the Pacific coastlands is recognizable everywhere except in the extreme southwestern United States. Here it is interrupted by faulting in an east-west direction, which has created a lowland corridor that links the coast with the southern tip of the Great Basin. The coastal hills and the Sierra Nevada meet and enclose the southern end of the Central Valley of California, and to the south of their junction in the Tehachapi Mountains lies the lowland route to the interior (see Fig. 1-2) dominated today by the great urban area of Los Angeles.

The Glaciation of North America

Of decisive importance in shaping the physical and cultural patterns of present-day North America was the epoch in the continent's history when some three-quarters of its surface was covered by ice. Glacial erosion smoothed its rugged relief and reformed its drainage patterns; glacial deposition covered 1 million sq

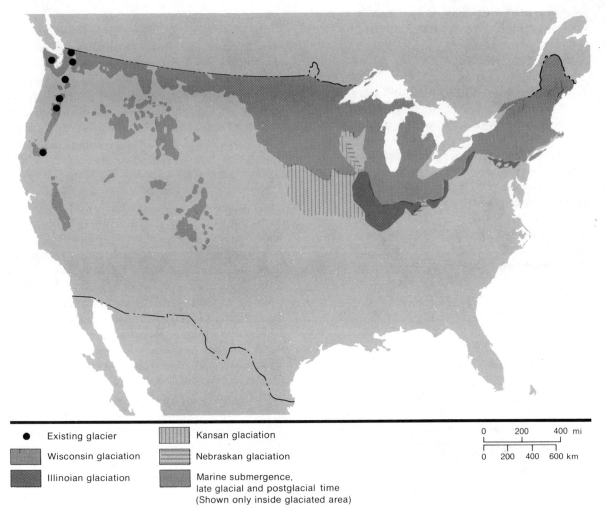

● Existing glacier	Kansan glaciation	
Wisconsin glaciation	Nebraskan glaciation	
Illinoian glaciation	Marine submergence, late glacial and postglacial time (Shown only inside glaciated area)	

0   200   400 mi

0   200   400   600 km

Fig. 1-4. Glaciation of the United States: Extent and nature of the drift covers. The Wisconsin drift, as the youngest layer, overlies the older drifts and masks much of the surface of the northern states. Note the Driftless Area west of the Great Lakes.

mi (2.5 million sq km) with drift, which filled former valleys and provided materials for some of the continent's most fertile soils. On the farmlands of the Midwest it is to the Ice Age as much as to any other single factor that the modern farmer owes his prosperity.

Although the ice was once continuous from coast to coast, it is necessary to distinguish between two separate parts of this great cover. Over the northeast of the continent there spread the vast Laurentide Ice Sheet. In the northwest and west, on the other hand, a separate system of glaciers—usually known as the Cordilleran System—formed in the moun-tains, from which it spread to cover the inter-montane zone. While remnants of this western system are still to be found in the northern Rockies and in the mountains of the northern Pacific coast, the Laurentide Sheet, although much greater in extent, has disappeared en-tirely from the North American mainland and today remains only on the mountains of Baffin and Ellesmere islands.

THE LAURENTIDE ICE SHEET

The ice probably originated in the Hudson Bay or Labrador region. From there it spread across eastern North America almost to the foothills of the Rockies, and at its maximum extent covered some 4.8 million sq mi (12.4 million sq km). It is suggested that it originated in a series of valley glaciers which grew slowly until they became sufficiently widespread to affect the climate; thereafter they would grow with increasing rapidity, expanding in the direction from which most precipitation was being received—in this case, the west. Over so large an area ice would probably accumulate at varying rates, and so domes or "centers" of ice would build up in the areas of most rapid growth. There seem to have been two such centers—the Labrador and the Keewatin—one to the east and the other to the west of Hudson Bay; but these centers may have shifted their position with the passage of time. From them the ice flowed outward in all directions.

Southward the ice spread over New England and the Adirondacks and as far as northern Pennsylvania. But on this all-important southern edge of the sheet, where the force of the ice movement was becoming weaker, the direction of the movement was influenced by the preexisting relief features, such as the Superior Upland and the Niagara Cuesta. Thus diverted, the southern edge of the ice formed a series of southward-moving lobes. Under the influence of climatic fluctuations these lobes advanced and retreated several times during the glacial epoch, so that the southern limit of the sheet varied in position from time to time. On the whole, however, its maximum southward extent is marked today by the line of the Missouri and Ohio rivers, which first developed as streams flowing along the ice front.

Beneath most of the vast area of the Laurentide Sheet the principal action of the ice was erosive. Over most of the area north of the present Great Lakes there was little glacial deposition, but a widespread scouring. Relief was smoothed, soil cover was removed, and a new and sometimes inconsequent drainage pattern was imposed on the area. Today, as we have already seen, the features of this region are an infertile surface and a maze of swamps and lakes.

Along the southern margin of the sheet, however, erosion gave place to deposition,

and scouring to infilling. Here the action of the ice produced a series of highly significant landscape features. Foremost among them is the mantle of glacial drift that covers virtually the whole area. Varying in thickness from a foot or two to 150 ft (50 cm–45 m), the drift has completely reformed the topography of central North America.

It is this drift cover—the ground moraine, or till, left by the Ice Sheet—which serves as the best guide to the advances and retreats of the ice under the influence of climatic fluctuations. Each new advance produced a fresh layer of drift. From the evidence these provide, it is deduced that there were four main periods of southward advance, or "glacial stages," separated by inter-glacial periods. The earliest glacial stage, the Nebraskan (in each case the name is borrowed from one of the states most affected), was followed by the Kansan and the Illinoian and finally by the Wisconsin. As the most recently deposited drift, the Wisconsin overlays the older mantles, which, as the map on p. 14 illustrates, protrude at its edges. Providing as it does the most abundant materials for study, the Wisconsin Stage has been further divided into four substages which seem to correspond to minor fluctuations within the major advance.

The interglacial periods are also not without importance. They were evidently long enough to permit both the development of a vegetation cover and the formation of wide belts of loess. This accumulated on the bare, ice-free surfaces after each retreat and locally, as in the "loess state" of Iowa, it is of the utmost importance to agriculture.

Thus the glacial and interglacial deposits are often interleaved and together form a thick cover which bears no resemblance, either in relief or in soil type, to the earlier surface that can be identified beneath it. While the material of which the till is composed ranges from boulders to fine clays, on the whole it produces excellent soils.

The second main feature of this zone of deposition is the great number of moraines and hills of glacial origin. The edges of most of the drift belts are marked by end moraines. On the map these often appear—especially on the till plains south of Great Lakes—as semicircular ridges that reveal how the ice front consisted of a series of lobes at the limit of its advance. Further east, in New England, these same end moraines are today represented by the islands that fringe the region's southern coast—Nantucket, Martha's Vineyard, and Long Island. Elsewhere, as in Wisconsin, the moraines form long, straight ridges running from north to south. Drumlins abound, especially in the Great Lakes shorelands of Wisconsin, Michigan and western New York; they generally appear in clusters containing dozens together, orientated roughly north-south by the direction of ice flow.

Lying as it does in the heart of the Great Lakes area, the peninsula of southern Ontario possesses these morainic features in very large numbers. The center of the peninsula is covered by glacial drift with drumlins, and this central area is almost surrounded by a horseshoe of morainic hills formed by lobes of ice pressing south into the lake basins on either side of it. Outside this horseshoe lie clay and sand plains; these are relics of the beds of the far larger lakes which formerly occupied the basins of Ontario, Erie, and Huron, surrounding an Ontario "island" much smaller than the present peninsula.

The third feature of note is the effect of glaciation on the drainage pattern. Before the glacial epoch the drainage of most of the midwestern area was probably eastward and then northward toward Hudson Bay. When the ice began to retreat northward the residue of the sheet blocked this route to the sea and meltwater accumulated along the ice front in a series of huge lakes. These reached as far west as glacial Lakes Agassiz and Regina on the Canadian prairies and together covered an area several times larger than that now occupied by the five Great Lakes. The development of the Missouri-Ohio drainage system, while it provided an outlet southward for some of the meltwater, further dislocated the earlier drainage pattern, and widespread damming and river diversion occurred.

As the location of the ice front changed, so the form of these lakes varied. First one outlet and then another was uncovered by the ice, giving a fresh escape route for the meltwater.

As each outlet was cleared and deepened by erosion, the lowering of the water level resulted in the abandonment of an earlier, higher route. At one period or another this great expanse of water seems to have drained away, either southwest and southward to the Mississippi or southeastward into what are now the Susquehanna and the Hudson, or northeastward into the St. Lawrence, when that route was eventually cleared. Today the Great Lakes represent a remainder of this great body of water, whose past presence is attested by the old lake beds which provide the farmers of Illinois, Minnesota, and Manitoba with some of the world's flattest and most fertile farmlands.

Photographs of these lake beds along the Red River or on the Regina Plains often create the impression that the whole of the northern plains and Prairies are plowed in endless straight lines over a uniform surface. The reality, however, is rather different, for over most of the region the effect of ice and drift has been to dot the surface with innumerable kettle holes and patches of swamp. In these, water accumulates in wet weather to form sloughs or "slews." Few Prairie fields are without one or two, however small, and the farmer must take the plow around them. From the air the landscape, for all the regularity of its cultural patterns, including roads that run to the points of the compass, has a pockmarked appearance. In all this drift-covered expanse one small part stands out as an exception—the Driftless Area of Wisconsin. By some trick of relief—probably the sheltering effect of the Superior Upland—this area seems to have been bypassed by the ice.[2] Walled in on two sides by the Wisconsin terminal moraine, its features are water and not ice formed. Its relief is more broken than that of the surrounding areas; its soils are the poorer for being drift free; economically, it shows a marked inferiority to the areas outside the moraine wall.

[2]For a summary of evidence suggesting, however, that the Driftless Area may *not* have escaped all glacial action, see J.C. Frye and others in H.E. Wright and D.G. Frey, eds., *The Quaternary of the United States* , Princeton University Press, Princeton, New Jersey, 1965, pp.54–55.

The Cordilleran System ultimately covered almost the whole of what are now western Canada and Alaska, and isolated ice caps spread over the higher areas as far south as the mountains of northern New Mexico. With its mountains and its heavy precipitation, the northwest, and particularly British Columbia, was a center of accumulation. From the heights of the two main mountain chains the ice tended to flow both east and west, so that eventually the westward-flowing ice from the Rockies and the eastward flow from the Cascades and Coast ranges coalesced to form a complete cover over the intermontane zone.

Further south, where the ranges of mountains were not so close to each other, this did not happen, but with the ending of the glacial epoch the intermontane basins filled with meltwater. As in the east, drainage was dislocated: outflow to east and west was barred by the mountains; northward the remains of the ice blocked all outlets. Only in the extreme south was there an open route to the sea. The Great Basin of Utah and Nevada became the bed of many lakes, the largest of which was glacial Lake Bonneville. It is of this great body of water, ponded between the southern Utah divide and the retreating ice front, that the present Great Salt Lake is merely a relic, its shoreline lying 1000 ft (304 m) below that of its predecessor. Ultimately, Lake Bonneville drained off northward into the swollen Columbia. Although today the Columbia is one of North America's largest rivers (see Chapter 22), it must have been during the meltwater period many times as large as it is now. The Dry Falls in the Grand Coulee of Washington, a water-cut valley representing only one of many of this earlier Columbia's channels, have a brink 3.5 mi (5.6 km) in length.

Of this Cordilleran System, the ice fields of Alaska remain to the present day as substantial reminders. Further to the south, small glaciers still flank the peaks of British Columbia and the state of Washington as far south as Mount Rainier, while a few remnants remain in the Colorado Rockies.

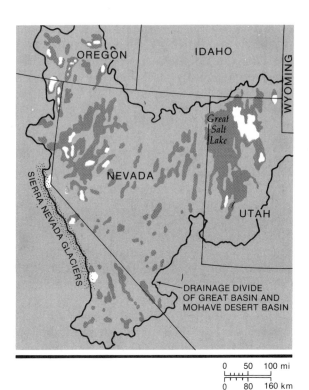

Fig. 1-5. The Great Basin of Utah-Nevada: Extent of pluvial lakes in post-Sangamon (late Pleistocene) time. Surviving lakes are shown in white. The two largest lake areas are (east) Lake Bonneville and (west) Lake Lahontan. The boundary of the drainage basin shown does not precisely correspond with that of the Great Basin of today.

The Climate of North America

The Florida Keys, the southernmost point of the United States, lie just north of the Tropic of Cancer; the northern tip of the Canadian mainland lies at 72° North. With a latitudinal spread of nearly 50°, therefore, the area we are considering has a wide variety of climates. At one extreme are the frostless islands of the Gulf of Mexico; at the other the Arctic conditions of the Canadian Northlands. On the Pacific coast there are stations which record over 200 in. (5000 mm) of precipitation per annum, while a few score miles inland there are areas with less than 10 in. (250 mm). The east-west dimensions of North America are equally significant. There are points in the central plains more than 1000 mi (1600 km) from the sea, and they experience to the full the climatic extremes of a continental interior. On the other hand, within this great land area there is room for a chain of inland seas—the Great Lakes—over 700 mi (1120 km) from east to west and for the 750-mi (1200 km) penetration of Hudson Bay southward from the Arctic Ocean, both of which have specific effects upon the climatic régime of eastern North America.

AIR MASSES

For all its variety, however, the climate of North America is the product of relatively simple controls. Over the greater part of the continent east of the Rockies it is the behavior and interaction of two air masses that is responsible for weather changes. These are the continental air mass centered on the Canadian Northlands and the tropical maritime air mass of the Atlantic-Gulf of Mexico area. West of the Rockies and on the Atlantic seaboard four other air masses play parts of varying importance in weather controls: the polar maritime air of the northern Pacific and of the northern Atlantic, the tropical maritime air mass over the Pacific, and the tropical continental south of the Rio Grande, which affect the southwestern United States and Mexico.

Polar, or arctic, continental air from the first of these air masses spills out from its source area in northern Canada and is associated in summer with cool, clear weather and in winter with cold waves that bring spells of bitter weather to the northern interior and frost danger to the usually milder regions further south. Tropical maritime air from the Gulf, on the other hand, flows northward from its source region over a warm ocean. In summer it is associated with high temperatures and oppressively high humidity over much of eastern North America, while in winter, Gulf air brings mild spells and rain or fog to the cold interior.

As the general position of these air masses shifts with the sun, so they tend to dominate different parts of the continent in summer and winter. There is at all seasons a zone over which they are in conflict; a zone in which the

Utah: The aftermath of glaciation. The etching shows former shorelines of glacial Lake Bonneville, with old cliffs and terraces, on the north end of the Oquirrh Range. *(New York Public Library)*

Alaska: South Sawyer Glacier in the Alaska Panhandle. Alaska possesses most of North America's surviving glaciers. *(U.S. Forest Service)*

effects, sometimes of one and sometimes the other, are dominant. In summer this zone of conflict runs south of the Great Lakes, so that the Midwest experiences alternating warm, humid weather of the type produced by Gulf air, and cooler, less humid weather introduced from the north. In winter, on the other hand, when the whole system shifts south, the zone of conflict lies over the Gulf coast. Then most of the interior is dominated by the cold air flow from the northern high-pressure area, with occasional breaks from the south, which may have the welcome effect of alleviating winter cold, but may also cause fog and brief, dangerous thaws.

This means that in the Midwest there is a period in spring and autumn when the zone of conflict is actually in transit. At such times weather-watchers study the depression tracks rather anxiously, trying to determine whether they will pass by on northern or southern routes. In spring, once the tracks move north of, say, Chicago and its latitude, summer cannot be far behind.

This zone of conflict between North America's two most important air masses is an area where atmospheric disturbances are frequent; consequently it is crossed by an unusually large number of storm tracks, even for a mid-latitude region. Cyclonic storms are generated all along the contact zone between the two air masses, and move across the United States and southern Canada from west or southwest to east. The water expanse of the Great Lakes seems to be a factor in making them converge on the line of the St. Lawrence Valley and the New England-Maritimes area.

It is, then, the interaction of these two air masses that produces the weather experienced by southern and central North America, and so by a high proportion of the continent's population. West of the Rockies, however, the situation is quite different. Penetrations of Gulf air are rare, and the main interaction of air masses is between polar continental from the Northlands and polar maritime air from the Pacific. In winter the Pacific air brings wet and (for these latitudes) mild weather to the coastlands: the amount of precipitation falls off southward. Occasionally the Pacific air penetrates, though cooler now and drier, to the east of the Rockies. In summer the northern Pacific is dominated by a high-pressure system, and the influence of polar maritime air on west coast weather becomes stronger. At this season, however, it is associated with dry, rather cool weather.

The southwestern United States lies within the sphere of influence of two tropical air masses. Tropical maritime air from the Pacific is dominant along the coast of Baja California, where it is associated with the warm, dry conditions along that desert shore. But it is kept from extending its influence far to the north by the strong flow of polar maritime throughout most of the year. Tropical continental air, on the other hand, spreads northward from Mexico during the summer, but affects only a small area of the United States beyond the border.

On the Atlantic coast, in a similar way, the weather is produced by the interaction of three types of air—the polar continental and the Gulf air, as is the case over most of eastern North America, together with polar maritime air from a source area near Greenland. The southward penetration of polar maritime air affects the coastlands of the Northeast, bringing cold and drizzle in winter and lower temperatures with moderate precipitation in summer. Its sphere of influence, however, does not extend southward much beyond Chesapeake Bay.

TEMPERATURE

The wide range of climatic conditions in North America is clearly marked in the temperature statistics. Only narrow coastal areas do not experience extremes of either winter cold, or summer heat, or both. The Gulf Coast and Florida have a seasonal régime of warm winters and hot summers; the mean January temperature is more than 50°F (10°C) and the mean July figure is above 80°F (27°C). At the other extreme, northeastern Canada experiences the cold winters and cool summers (with a mean of less than 50°F [10°C] for all twelve months of the year) of a polar climate. Over most of the land mass, therefore, the chief feature of the

temperature régime is its continentality, with a characteristically large annual range of temperature (up to 80°F or 45°C in northwestern Canada), a wide diurnal range in winter, and alternating cold winters and hot summers separated by only brief transitional seasons.

The majority of North Americans live, therefore, in areas where the mean January temperature is below 32°F (0°C). The January isotherm of 32°F runs from the Atlantic coast just south of New York, past Philadelphia, and then almost due west through southern Indiana and Illinois to southeastern Colorado, while almost all of the Mountain West experiences a January mean well below freezing point. The January mean in Chicago is 25°F (−4°C); in Montreal it is 14°F (−10°C), and at Winnipeg, the coldest of North America's large cities in winter, the mean temperature for the month is −3°F (−19.5°C). The average figures, however, conceal the characteristics of this winter cold which are, first, that during the daytime the temperature will frequently rise above freezing point, only to fall to 10° or 0°F at night (−12° to −18°C), and second, that the means are depressed by extremely low temperatures occurring in periodic "cold waves," rather than by consistently cold weather throughout the winter.[3]

By contrast with the continental interior, the southern and western coastlands—from Virginia to Oregon—everywhere enjoy a January mean of more than 40°F (4.5°C) and the influence of the ocean gives the smaller annual temperature range characteristic of maritime climates. The smallest temperature ranges in North America occur on the coast of central California (where in exceptional locations the annual range is less than 10°F or 6°C), at Key West, Florida (a range of 13°F or 7.5°C), and on

[3]Geography books have sometimes given a false impression that, in a continental interior, the weather is marked by a sameness from day to day, with summers consistently hot and winters unrelentingly cold. Nothing could be further from the truth. Both seasons produce very varied weather. The author will not easily forget two consecutive days in May in Wisconsin, when the noon temperatures were, respectively, 83°F (28°C) and 47°F (8°C). In the intervening 24 hours, 68 people had died in tornadoes in adjacent states.

the coast of Oregon and Washington (14°–16°F or 8°–9°C).

If most Americans spend at least one month of winter at a mean temperature of 32°F (0°C) or below, it is also true that, in almost every major city, they languish through one or more summer months with a mean of 70°F (21°C) or above. The 70°F July isotherm follows fairly closely the boundary of dense settlement across the central Great Lakes; Chicago experiences a July mean of 74°F (23.5°C), and Montréal one of 70°F. Further south July means of 80°F (27°C) or above are general in Oklahoma, Arkansas, and the states lying to the south and southeast of them. Where these high summer temperatures are associated with high humidity—as is the case almost everywhere east of the Mississippi—the resultant summer weather is extremely oppressive, both by day and by night. To find the relief of lower humidity and wider daily temperature ranges, it is necessary to travel either north or to the Mountain West.

In the Mountain West, summer conditions vary with altitude, but days are generally warm and nights pleasantly cool. On the Pacific coast there is a steady decrease of summer temperature from south to north; the July mean at San Diego is 67°F (19.5°C) and at Victoria, B.C., 60°F (15.5°C). The moderating influence of the Pacific extends, however, only a short distance inland; the Central Valley of California experiences July means in excess of 80°F (27°C), while less than 200 mi (320 km) inland lies Death Valley, with its forbidding July average in excess of 100°F (38°C).

PRECIPITATION

The parts of North America which receive most precipitation are first, the mountains of the northern Pacific coast and, second, the southern Appalachians and the southeastern states. If the remainder of the continent is regarded as a rough triangle with its apex in the far northwest, then the southeastern one-third is mainly humid, and the southwestern and northern two-thirds are semiarid or arid. Expressed in other terms, virtually all of the land mass lying east of 98° W longitude and south

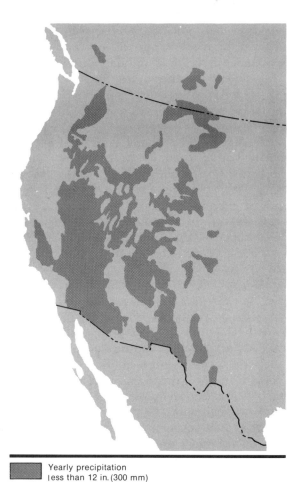

Yearly precipitation
less than 12 in. (300 mm)

Fig. 1-6. The United States: Areas with less than 12 in. (300 mm) annual precipitation.

of the 60th parallel has 20 in. (500 mm) or more of rainfall per annum, while north and west of these lines is a dry belt that stretches to the Arctic and westward almost to the Pacific coast.

Rain-bearing winds reach the continent from the North Pacific, and from the Atlantic and Gulf of Mexico where these seas border the continent on the southeast. The winds of the North Pacific immediately encounter the abrupt rise of the great mountain ranges of the Pacific coast; they shed their moisture in abundance, leaving the greater part of the area between the coastal mountains and the Rockies in the rain shadow. The behavior of the rain-bearing winds of the southeast is governed almost equally by factors of relief, but in this case by the *absence* of any significant mountain

21

barrier to their advance, so that their effect is felt over the whole continent east of the Rockies and south of the Laurentian Shield.

Movement of the pressure systems, on which these rain-bearing winds depend, creates seasonal variations in rainfall. West of the Rockies, in the sphere of influence of North Pacific air, there is everywhere a marked winter maximum. Even in the areas of the British Columbia coast where the annual rainfall is more than 100 in. (2500 mm), July and August have little rain, while further south in California, where the total amount of precipitation is much smaller (it is 20 in. [500 mm] at San Francisco and 10 in. [250 mm] at San Diego), there may be as many as four summer months that are completely rainless, after the familiar pattern of Mediterranean-type climates. Further inland, in the desert basins, while the amounts of rainfall received are even smaller than on the California coast, much the same régime holds good; in the West, summer rains, apart from thunderstorms, are experienced only in the higher parts of the mountains.

East of the Rockies the situation is reversed; here only a small area shows a winter maximum. Elsewhere, as Figure 1-7 shows, if there is a significant maximum, it occurs in the warmer months. It may occur, however, in spring, as in the central Corn Belt, or in early summer, as in the Great Plains, or in late summer, as in northeastern Canada, and this distinction is of great importance to the farmer. In the Agricultural Interior and on the Great Plains, early rains favor the growth of crops. In areas of late summer rain, on the other hand, the maximum occurs too late to be of much agricultural value.

The only area of winter maximum east of the Rockies lies on the eastern coast of Labrador, Newfoundland, and the Maritime Provinces. Over the whole triangle of land lying between the Great Lakes, the St. Lawrence, and the Atlantic, rainfall is plentiful throughout the year because the presence of these water bodies tends to attract to the area depressions travelling on almost all the continent's eastbound storm tracks. Thus New York has 3–4 in. (75–100 mm) of rainfall monthly, and Toronto 2–3 in. (50–75 mm). But where, in addition, the presence of polar maritime (Atlantic) air makes itself felt (see p. 18) along the northeast coast, the winter's rainfall is supplemented from this source and exceeds that of the other seasons.

CLIMATIC REGIONS

Using these details we can now attempt a classification of the climatic regions of North America. The simplest way to consider these regions is to group them as follows:

1. the northern fringe of the continent,
2. the Pacific coastlands,
3. the mountainous West,
4. the Southeast, and
5. the continental interior.

1. The northern fringe of the continent is an area of polar climate which finds its counterpart in northern Siberia. The boundary of this region runs somewhat north of the Arctic Circle through northern Alaska and as far east as the 110th meridian, and then turns southeast across the middle of Hudson Bay and northern Labrador to the Strait of Belle Isle; thus the climatic heart of the North American Arctic is situated over the northern end of Hudson Bay.

2. The Pacific coastlands fall into three climatic regions:

(a) Between approximately the 40th and 60th parallels there is a coastal belt with a cool temperate marine climate which resembles that of northwestern Europe or New Zealand. Yet the summers are drier, so that British exiles often feel that in coastal British Columbia they have discovered an almost idealized version of the climate of their homeland.

(b) Between 30° and 40° N—that is roughly throughout the state of California—is a belt of warm temperate climate of the western margin type usually known as Mediterranean, whose characteristics are a dry summer and moderate winter rain. In other words, the lack of summer rainfall, already noticeable in the cool temperate belt, becomes more marked as the summers become warmer going southward. But it is an overgeneralization, as we shall see in Chapter 21, to describe the climate of California simply as Mediterranean. This it is only in the broad pattern of seasonal variations; in

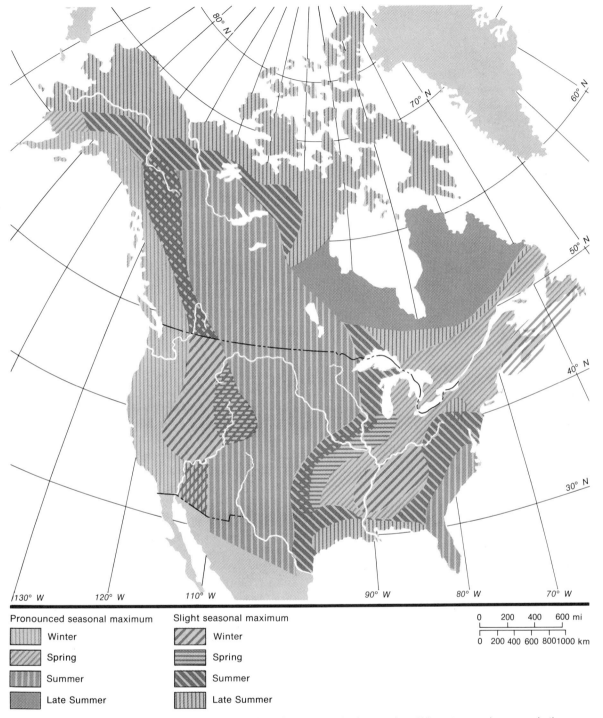

Pronounced seasonal maximum

Winter

Spring

Summer

Late Summer

Slight seasonal maximum

Winter

Spring

Summer

Late Summer

0	200	400	600 mi
0	200 400 600	800	1000 km

Fig. 1-7. The Climate of North America: Seasons of maximum precipitation. The map, which is based on data for some 250 stations, shows the season or seasons having precipitation maxima. Where two maxima occur in the year, this is indicated by crosshatching.

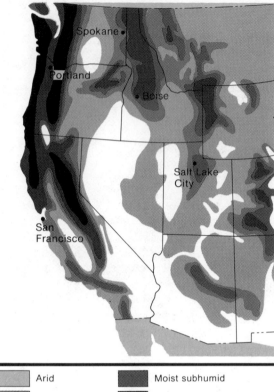

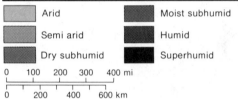

Fig. 1-8. The western United States: The climate west of the Rockies, according to the classification of C. W. Thornthwaite and showing the wide variety of climatic circumstances induced by the varied relief.

Arid	Moist subhumid
Semi arid	Humid
Dry subhumid	Superhumid

0   100   200   300   400 mi

0   200   400   600 km

montane regime at greater heights, where precipitation increases and average temperatures decrease with increasing elevation. Thus most of the continent east of the Pacific coastlands and west of the 100th meridian (that is, including much of the Great Plains) has a middle-latitude steppe régime, modified by altitude, like that of the middle elevations between the Central Asian Mountains and the Russo-Siberian Plains.

4. The southeastern United States as far inland as about the 38th parallel has a climatic régime which can be described as humid subtropical or as warm temperate, eastern margin. It finds its counterpart in southern Brazil and the Plate River region, or, with variations produced by the action of the monsoon, in southeastern China. Winters are mild, summers are hot, and rainfall is distributed fairly evenly among the seasons of the year, with a tendency to a summer maximum that decreases toward the northwest.

5. The climate of the remainder of North America falls, under any classification, into the category of continental régimes; there are the wide annual range of temperatures, the rapid diurnal variations in winter, and the modest rainfall characteristic of a continental interior. Whether this general heading of 'continental' is to be subdivided on a basis of temperature or of precipitation is a matter of personal choice. If the criterion of temperature is used, then the governing factor is the heat of summer, and the interior can be divided on this basis into three east-west belts, with a region of cold continental climate adjoining the polar region in the north, and belts of cool continental and warm continental climate lying between it and the 38th parallel. If the criterion of precipitation is used, then the interior would be classified, in north-south belts, as mostly humid continental, with a subhumid transition belt separating the eastern interior from the steppe (or, as it might be called, the semiarid continental) belt of the West. In either case the climatic analogy is with the western Soviet Union, where there occurs in the same way a north-south sequence based on the northward decrease of summer heat, and an east-west sequence based on precipitation.

detail the local conditions produced by relief are both complicated and varied.

(c) On the coast south of 30°—that is, in Lower California and Mexico—but extending inland to cover much of the southwestern United States is a region of true desert climate which corresponds with the desert regions in similar latitudes in northern Africa, in Australia, or north of the Persian Gulf.

3. Inland from the Pacific coast, relief is too varied to permit the accurate identification of climatic regions, but in general there is a transition from true desert climate at the lowest elevations, in the Lower Colorado Basin and the Great Basin of Utah-Nevada, to semiarid, or steppe, conditions at middle elevations, to a

24

The Soils of North America

Insofar as climate is responsible for soil characteristics, the climatic factors we have just been considering assure the North American continent of a wide variety of soil types. But since a number of other factors are involved in soil formation, the variety is much greater than it would be if determined by climate alone: soil is also a product of different parent materials and of processes such as glaciation. So wide is the variety that its clasification becomes a major problem.

One might assume that the object of a classification system would be to identify as objectively as possible the various characteristics of a soil. This being the presumption, it is curious to find that in the past most systems attempted to classify soils by origin, under categories dictated by climate or parent material, as well as by quality. Perhaps the reason for such an approach was to provide a way in which the soil geography of a continental area could be taught and understood. Classification systems have often, therefore, been in the nature of a compromise between the strict requirements of the professional and the need for comprehension of the non-specialist while, because of the nature of soil formation processes, they have often sought a compromise between genetic and structural categories, and ended by proving satisfactory for neither.

Some attempts at classification made in the past are American in origin and deserve our attention in passing, if only because references to them are still frequently found in textbooks. One such useful generalization, native to North America and bearing an obvious relationship to local conditions, was that made by C.F. Marbut, who proposed a broad classification of soils into *pedocals* and *pedalfers*. Pedocals (the syllable *-cal* is an abbreviation for "calcis" or "calcium") are soils in which carbonate of lime accumulates. Pedalfers (the *-al* indicates aluminium and the *-fer* iron) are soils in which compounds of aluminium and iron accumulate. The factors that decide which of these two processes takes place are mainly climatic. Lime accumulation is a feature of the soil profile of semiarid and arid regions; the depth at which the accumulation takes place varies with the rainfall, so that in the driest areas accumulation takes place near or even on the surface, while with increasing rainfall it occurs at greater depths. In humid regions, however, the process of leaching tends to remove the calcium carbonate from the soil and to lead instead to the formation of a layer of compounds of aluminium and iron. Thus Marbut used the terms pedocal and pedalfer to distinguish the soils of humid regions from those of semiarid and arid regions; in broad terms, of course, this meant in North America a division of the soils into those of east and west, with most of the soils of northern regions falling into the eastern, or pedalfer, group. Although Marbut's classification was oversimplified and has been superseded, it did offer a broad framework for a study of the continent's soils.

Another type of framework is offered by the division of soil types into three categories: *zonal*, *intrazonal*, and *azonal*. This classification presupposes that the basic control of soil is climate, and that soil types characteristic of each climate zone will develop in that zone unless other circumstances intervene. Particular conditions of relief or parent material may modify the zonal soil, giving it a different character from that which might be anticipated within its zone. Such soils are known as *intrazonal*. An example of intrazonal soils is provided by the Rendzinas of central Texas and central Oklahoma and the High Lime soils (or Grey Rendzinas) of eastern Manitoba. These are groups of soils developed on a soft limestone or chalk base which have, in consequence, a high lime content in spite of the effects of leaching; from their chemical composition they appear to have been formed in a drier climate than is actually the case. A second example is provided by the so-called planosols of the Agricultural Interior. These are soils developed on the loess and drift plains of Illinois, Iowa, and Missouri where, in the post-glacial period, deposition has created an exceptionally flat surface and affected drainage; poor soil drainage and absence of surface erosion have created a soil in which there is a gley (sticky clay) horizon, and the subsoil includes a layer of clay hardpan.

In other areas, soils are immature; that is, they are composed of materials so recently accumulated or so lightly bound that no true soil profile has developed. Such soils are classed as *azonal*. Materials in this class cover a significant fraction of North America and include both lands of agricultural value and unimproved areas. For fertility few areas can rival the alluvial plains of the Mississippi Valley and the Central Valley of California, both of which belong to this category. On the other hand, the loose cover of the Sand Hills section of Nebraska is a trap for the unwary cultivator, for the sand, produced by the breakdown of Tertiary sandstones, is entirely unconsolidated beneath a thin layer of grass roots. In the Mountain West azonal materials include the thin, stony cover of the mountains, the alluvia collected in the desert basins, and the most recent of the lava flows on the lava plateaus of the Pacific Northwest.

Beyond these few generalizations, however, most of the earlier systems of classification descend, at their lower levels, into mere description. In any case, they tell little about the structure or potential of the soil: they are too heavily weighted on the genetic side. In the United States, therefore, soil scientists have for nearly thirty years been working on a fresh classification. They have approached the problem by way of a series of *approximations* to a complete solution; the 3rd Approximation, for example, appeared in 1954 and the 4th in 1955. By 1960, they had reached the 7th Approximation and it, with various amendments, forms the present basis of the classification used in the United States.[4] It introduced an entirely new set of soil orders, in accordance with the following propositions:

1. a natural classification should be based on the properties of the objects classified,
2. the properties selected should be observable or measurable, even though instruments may be necessary to observe or measure,

3. properties that can be measured quantitatively should be preferred to those that can be determined only qualitatively.

On this basis, there are recognized 10 soil orders, each with a name ending in -sol. There are then 47 suborders, 185 great groups, 970 subgroups, about 4500 soil families and some 10,000 soil series (or what were formerly known as soil types). The naming of these various individuals in the classification is standardized; each suborder, for example, has a name of two syllables, the second of which identifies its parent order. If one can learn the language, therefore,[5] that person now has access to a system which is designed to depend, at last, entirely upon what the soil is like according to measurable scales of values, and in which the nomenclature is consistently and logically built up. The ten soil orders are given below, together with some familiar names from earlier classifications.

U.S. Soil Survey Order	Includes soils previously named.
1. Entisols	Most azonals
2. Vertisols	Grumusols and some alluvia
3. Inceptisols	Brown forest; *sol brun acide*; humic gleys
4. Aridisols	Desert and desert-saline
5. Mollisols	Chestnuts; chernozems; prairie; rendzinas
6. Spodosols	Podsols; brown podsolic; groundwater podsolic
7. Alfisols	Grey-brown podsols; grey-wooded; some planosols
8. Ultisols	Red-yellow podsols; humic gleys (planosols)
9. Oxisols	Lateritics; latosols
10. Histosols	Bog soils

While the new U.S. classification certainly represents an advance upon the old, haphazard systems of nomenclature it does, however, have its drawbacks. One is that the ten soil orders are so wide as to conceal more than

[4]The relevant documents are: Soil Survey Staff, U.S. Dept. of Agriculture, *Soil Classification, A Comprehensive System, 7th Approximation*, and *Soil Taxonomy: A Basic System of Soil Classification for Making and Interpreting Soil Surveys*, U.S. Government Printing Office, Washington, D.C., 1960 and 1975 respectively.

[5]In itself no light task, although a knowledge of Latin will help. At the third level of subdivision we have, for example, a great group of the order Inceptisol called *Anthrumbrepts* and a great group of Alfisols called *Fraglossudolfs*, after which the student goes on to *Quartzipsamments*, and *Haploxerults*—hardly conversational stuff, but with each syllable telling its own story.

they reveal. To see that this is so one has only to notice, for example, that the Mollisols include what used to be called chernozems *and* chestnut brown soils *and* rendzinas. It is necessary, in fact, to go at least as far as the sub-orders, if not the great groups, before we learn anything very specific about a given soil. A more serious drawback is that while the U.S. Soil Survey has been developing its taxonomy, the United Nations through the F.A.O. has been busily producing an entirely different, international classification. It has not ten orders but twenty-six; its nomenclature is a little less ruthlessly logical (but also less tongue-twisting) than that of the U.S. classification, and only here and there do the American and international schemes coincide. Since the F.A.O. system has already been used to map not only the whole of North America but the rest of the world as well, in the United States the two schemes are in direct competition with each other. It seems unlikely, in fact, that there will be any early ending to the long-standing problem of getting general agreement for any single system of soil classification.

On the basis of the U.S. classification, however, it is possible to make a simple subdivision of the North American continent into five major soil regions:

1. A broad belt of Inceptisols north of 60° N latitude. Inceptisols are wet or frozen according to season and have little or no horizon of accumulation.

2. A northern belt of Spodosols, Histosols, and Entisols, occupying most of eastern Canada south of 60° N and covering much of New England and the Upper Great Lakes area of Wisconsin and Michigan. The Spodosols are the soils of the northern forests (which were formerly broadly classed as podsols); they are generally heavily leached and acid. The Histosols are boggy or peaty, with very slow rates of decay of organic matter; they occupy a broad area around Hudson Bay. The Entisols form the thin and patchy soil cover of Labrador, where glaciation has removed whatever original soils the region may have possessed.

3. The Central Interior (which is also the Agricultural Interior). This region is largely surfaced with soils of two orders:

(a) Alfisols, grading from what were formerly classed as grey-brown podsols and grey-wooded soils to less acid grey-brown types. Alfisols are usually moist and contain lower horizons of clay accumulation. They extend across the southern Great Lakes region, south of the Spodosols, and down the flanks of the Mississippi Valley as far south as Texas.

(b) Mollisols, which underlie the fertile farmlands of the western Interior and the grasslands of the Great Plains, from the Mexican border to the southern Prairies. Rich in organic matter and bases, the Mollisols account for most of the soils formerly classed by their color as black, chestnut-brown, or brown.

4. A southeastern region of Ultisols, stretching from Maryland in the north, west into Kentucky and southern Missouri, and southwest into eastern Texas. Low-latitude temperatures and high rainfall produce a range of soils which are subject to heavy leaching and clay accumulation so that, although they are widely cultivated in the southeast, they are not naturally very fertile; they are basically forest soils. They are often yellow or red in color and some of them have weathered far enough to resemble the tropical laterites or latosols of the Oxisol order.

5. A western belt of Aridisols. As their name suggests, Aridisols are the soils of the deserts, stretching over the Southwest and the intermontane plateaus.

The Vegetation of North America

To the early European settlers, North America was a land of forests. As the French on the St. Lawrence and the English on the Atlantic coast moved inland, they found little break in the monotony of the trees, and their economy became a forest-based economy, like that of the Indians they encountered. Only after settlement from the east coast had penetrated 500–600 mi (800–950 km) inland did the pioneers emerge from the forest into the "oak openings" and small prairies of the area south of the Great Lakes. Since by this time they had come largely to depend on the forest and its denizens for their livelihood, they regarded

1 Entisols   6 Spodosols

2 Vertisols   7 Alfisols

3 Inceptisols (Aquepts)   8 Ultisols (Aquults and Udults)

4 Aridisols (Argids)   9 Histosols

5 Mollisols   10 Mountain and icecap areas; soils often absent

Fig. 1-9. The Soils of North America: Generalized map of
soils classified according to the Seventh Approximation.

the treeless horizons with considerable suspicion, while the true grasslands further west found them, as we shall later see, almost wholly unprepared.

Only in the southwest of what was later to become the United States did the Spaniards, pushing north from Mexico, encounter open country. In southern Texas they entered, at its southwestern corner, a great triangle of grassland whose apex was in the oak openings of the Midwest, and whose base lay along the foothills of the Rocky Mountains northward roughly as far as the 52nd parallel. To what extent, or in what sense, this area could be described as "natural" grassland is uncertain, for it seems clear that occupance by the Indians had altered its character; in particular, that burning had occurred. The coming of the white man produced further changes—the clearance for agricultural use of much of the transitional forest zone bordering the grassland but, to balance this, an end to the burning practiced by the Indian hunters. Through all these changes, however, the basic climatic control of vegetation patterns can still be recognized.

THE FORESTS

Extent and Character

Before the coming of the Europeans it seems that forests covered slightly less than a half of the area of what is now mainland Canada and the United States; that is, some 3 million sq mi out of 6.1 million (7.7 million sq km out of 15.8). In addition rather more than one-third of Alaska was forest-covered. Today this area has been reduced by exploitation and destruction to about 2.5 million sq mi (6.47 million sq km).

This original forest cover was diverse in character but almost continuous in extent over the eastern part and much of the north of the continent. Indeed, it is simplest to state that the forest extended north and west from the middle Atlantic seaboard until it encountered one or another of three limiting circumstances: cold, dryness, or high altitude.

On the north the forest thins out and gives place to the heaths and mosses of tundra vegetation, roughly along the boundary line of the region of polar climate (that is, where all twelve months have a mean temperature of less than 50° F or 10°C). Here the governing factors are the onset of Arctic cold, the lack of summer heat, the dryness of the western Arctic, and the presence of the permafrost layer, which prevents the roots of trees from penetrating to a depth sufficient to support growth. The northern forest boundary runs from the Mackenzie Delta to the middle of Hudson Bay and thence into northern Labrador.

South of this line a belt of forest spreads across the whole breadth of the continent, except in the west, where the cover is broken by the rise of North America's loftiest mountains—those of Alaska and the northern Pacific coast. In Alaska and northern British Columbia, in consequence, the forests are largely confined to the interior valleys and the coastlands. This continent-wide forest cover extends south, with no other serious interruption, until it reaches the tree frontier imposed by increasing aridity in the southwestern section of the continent.

This dry and largely treeless area lies south and west of a line running from southern British Columbia along the 52nd parallel to the Prairies and then southeastward to the apex of the treeless triangle located south of the Great Lakes. Along this boundary, cause and effect are interwoven in the vegetation pattern; on the one hand, increasing aridity, especially seasonal drought, discourages tree growth; on the other, where grassland has become established, young tree shoots compete unsuccessfully with quicker-growing grasses.

From the apex of the triangle in the east, the southern side runs west and south in a broken line to central Texas. Along this line, as on the northern side, the luxuriant tree growth of the eastern Gulf coast and the southeastern states is thinned by diminishing precipitation, increasing evaporation rates, and markedly seasonal rainfall, which favors the growth of grasses against that of trees. Until comparatively recent times thinning of forests in the Southeast was also brought about deliberately by burning.

The remaining forest areas of North America can best be described as three southward

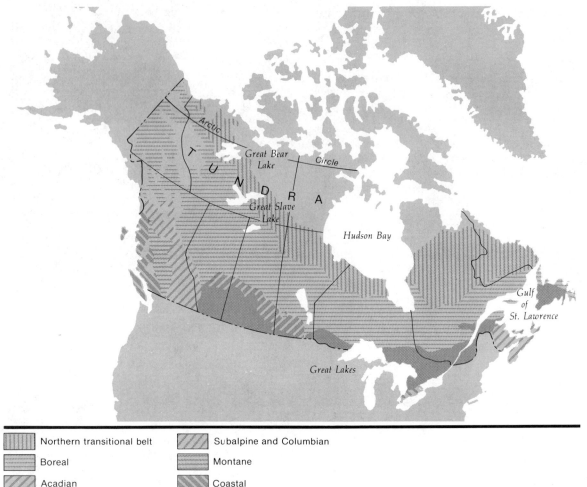

▥ Northern transitional belt	▨ Subalpine and Columbian
▦ Boreal	▦ Montane
▨ Acadian	▨ Coastal
▨ Deciduous	▨ Aspen grove section
▨ Great Lakes-St. Lawrence	▨ Grassland

Fig. 1-10. Canada: Forest regions. The principal species represented in each forest division are: *Acadian*—spruce, balsam, yellow birch, maple; *Great Lakes–St. Lawrence*—pine, spruce, yellow birch, maple; *Deciduous*—assorted hardwoods; *Boreal*—spruce, balsam, white birch, poplar; *Sub-alpine and Columbian*—Engelmann spruce, lodgepole pine, Douglas fir, cedar; *Montane*—ponderosa and lodgepole pine, spruce, Douglas fir; *Coastal*—Douglas fir, cedar, hemlock, spruce.

penetrations of the forests on the northern side of the treeless area. They correspond to the areas of higher rainfall along the Rockies, the mountains of the Pacific, and the coast north of the 40th parallel; together they form an important part of the commercial forest resources of the continent.

The Rockies are, in general, tree covered on their middle slopes. The lower limit of the forest—represented by scattered and bushlike pinyon and juniper—is encountered between 4000 and 6000 ft (1215–1820 m), and the tree-line is, according to slope and exposure, between 9000 and 11,000 ft (2740–3340 m), with alpine meadow and bare rock above it. Various forms of open forest are also found on the higher sections of the intermontane plateaus wherever rainfall is sufficient.

In the great ranges of the Far West are found the continent's largest and most valuable stands of timber. In the Pacific Northwest the forests are continuous from sea level up to the timberline at 6000–8000 ft (1820–2430 m). In California, where precipitation is less heavy, an intermediate vegetation belt, known as chaparral and composed of bushes and small trees, intervenes before the true forest begins, about 2000 ft (610 m) above sea level.

The coastal hills themselves are tree clad roughly as far south as the Golden Gate, and intermittently beyond there. In the Pacific Northwest the coastal forests, like those of the Cascades inland, are composed largely of Douglas fir. But the distinctive feature of the California coast is the redwood belt, the habitat of the continent's largest tree species.[6] In the early days of California's settlement these huge trees were obvious targets for the lumbermen, and one of the continent's first genuine conservation movements sprang up to protect them. Today the finest specimens are preserved, but in the coastal belt, which extends about as far south as Santa Cruz, and which seems to owe its presence to the humid conditions created by coastal fogs, lumbering does take place.

The northern forests are almost entirely coniferous in character. Those of the Great Lakes region and southern New England are mixed; like those of the Appalachians, they mark the transition to the deciduous forests of oak, beech, and hickory found in the southern interior of the continent. In the Mountain West the distribution of species—most of them coniferous, such as spruce, fir, pine, and larch—is governed largely by altitude. Yet no inventory, however brief, can overlook the magnificent stands of Douglas fir that spread densely over the whole coastal belt of the Pacific Northwest and that represent the most valuable single forest resource of North America.

The Forests as Resources

Of the million square miles (2.5 million sq km) of forests remaining in the United States, some two-thirds are classed as "commercial," while in Canada, about 75 percent of 1.6 million sq mi (4.1 million sq km) of forest are said to be

potentially productive. These forest resources have been tapped to supply the needs of a continent which consumes more than half the pulp and paper production and over 40 percent of the lumber production of the world. Both nations began by possessing roughly equal areas of forest, but since both population and demand are ten times greater in the United States than in Canada, it is not surprising to find, first, that after three centuries of exploitation the U.S. has only 70 percent of its cover and 10 percent of its virgin sawtimber left, and second, that it has come to rely heavily on the production of Canadian forests to meet its own gigantic demand for wood products. In fact the annual drain on the sawtimber resources of the United States is 5 percent greater than the annual growth, while in the most valuable part of the nation's forests—the great softwood stands of Oregon and Washington—the drain has been running close to twice the annual growth.

In Canada, by contrast, the annual cut is only about half of the annual growth, if only because half of the potentially productive forests remain to be exploited. The factor that governs their future use is not demand—that may be taken for granted—but accessibility. Exploitation naturally began in the areas of easiest access, along shorelines and the southern edge of the great boreal forest, while tomorrow's reserves lie, to a large extent, either in the western mountains or north of the St. Lawrence-Hudson Bay watershed, whence the rivers on which the logs would be floated run north into the wilderness.

The exploitation of the continent's forests has created industries of great size. While the actual logging operations employ a good deal of labor, much of this employment is seasonal, carried on by part-time farmers or fishermen. It is the processing of the forest products that has become so important. In Canada, wood products—lumber, wood pulp, and paper—form the basis of the country's largest group of industries, a group employing in 1972 some 270,000 industrial workers in Canada, and contributing more than one-quarter of the value of the country's exports. In the United States, the forest-products industries accounted in 1972 for 9.4 percent of the nation's industrial em-

---

[6]There are actually two belts of redwoods, one along the coast, where the predominant species is *Sequoia sempervirens,* and the other midway up the western slopes of the Sierra Nevada, where *Sequoia dendron giganteum* is found. There is very little difference in appearance between the two, but some difference in usefulness as lumber.

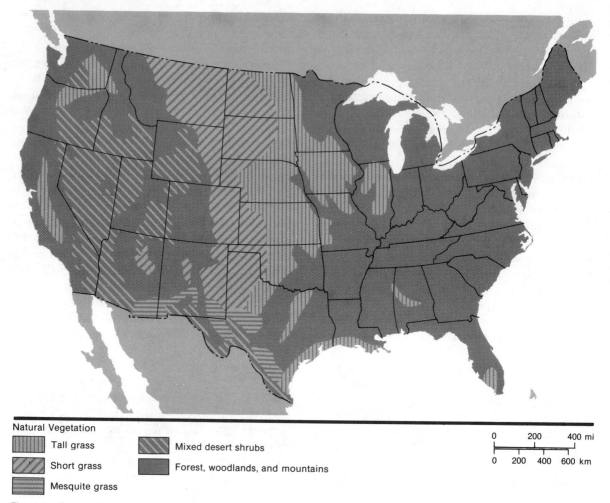

Natural Vegetation

Tall grass	Mixed desert shrubs
Short grass	Forest, woodlands, and mountains
Mesquite grass	

0	200	400 mi
0	200 400	600 km

Fig. 1-11. Grasslands of the United States.

ployees. Locally, of course, these industries play a far more important role than even these figures suggest. In Oregon, for example, they employ nearly 45 percent of the state's industrial workers.

THE UNFORESTED WEST

In the semiarid and arid West the natural vegetation is grass and shrubs. Only on the slopes of the mountains, where precipitation is higher, or along river courses, where moister conditions are found, is tree growth encountered. For the rest it is the quantity of precipitation and its seasonal distribution that govern the character of the vegetation. This

means that there is a sequence of vegetation types that holds good, either between the desert heart of the area and its more humid fringes, or between the lowest levels of the western basins and the lower tree limit on the mountains. Within these sequences it is possible to distinguish four main types of natural vegetation: tall grass, short grass, sagebrush with grass, and desert shrub.

The tall-grass prairies, most of which have now been brought under the plow, occupied the eastern apex of the treeless triangle, where annual rainfall is between 20 and 35 in (500–875 mm) per annum. The vegetation of this region consisted of both tall and short grasses growing together, with such varieties as the bluestems (*Andropogon*) reaching 6 ft (180 cm) or more in height. The dense root network developed by these abundant grasses has produced the deep humus layer that makes the black soils of the tall-grass prairies famous.

As the tall grass is the vegetation of the brown Ustolls of the drier plains, so the dark Udolls, or humid Mollisols, further west are related to the short-grass prairies. Short grass is probably the most extensive, and certainly the most valuable, vegetation type of the unforested West. It is made up of a wide variety of species, among which some of the most common are wheatgrass (*Agropyron*), grama (*Bouteloua*), and buffalograss (*Buchloe dactyloides*). Within this region, which stretches from central Texas and New Mexico to the southern Prairie Provinces, the native grasses grow from 1 to 3 ft (30–90 cm) high; their height is restricted by the shallower percolation of water in the 12- to 20-in (300–500 mm) rainfall zone and the consequent limitation of root development.

While the main area of short-grass vegetation is on the Great Plains, this type of vegetation is to be found in modified form in two other areas of significant extent in the West. One of these is in the southwestern United States, between western Texas and Arizona, where the vegetation is classified as semidesert grass. It differs from the true short-grass prairie in its composition—dominant species are grama, dropseed (*Sporobolus*), and curly mesquite (*Hilaria belangeri*), growing, as on the Great Plains, from one to three feet tall—and in that a scattering of shrubs or even small trees generally accompanies the grass, particularly mesquite and creosote. The existence here of some 50 million acres (20.2 million ha) of semidesert grass is due to the fact that, unlike the areas of true desert adjoining them, these lands receive sufficient summer rainfall (from the Gulf of Mexico) to support grasses; their combination of grass and shrubs thus marks a transition between the true grasslands and the scrub of the deserts.

Short-grass prairies are also found in the Pacific coastlands, especially on the foothills surrounding the Central Valley of California (where they lie below the chaparral in the altitudinal sequence) and in the Palouse region of

Vegetation types of North America: (1) The cactus range of the Southwest. It offers limited grazing for livestock if carefully managed. *(U.S. Dept. of Agriculture)*

Washington and Oregon. These are areas of Pacific bunchgrass, where grasses similar to those found on the Great Plains originally covered some 60 million acres (24.3 million ha). Most of these grasslands, however, have by now been plowed up or have been over-

Vegetation types of North America: (2) Mesquite range of the southern Great Plains. Mesquite and brush have invaded millions of acres overgrazed in past phases of use, and now form a virtually useless cover.

Vegetation types of North America: (3) Sagebrush range in western Colorado. The usefulness of this vegetation as rangeland varies directly with the amount of grass in the understory, and this in turn is likely to reflect the amount of grazing to which the area has been subject. *(U.S. Forest Service)*

Vegetation types of North America: (4) The California chaparral. *(U.S. Forest Service)*

grazed by stock and invaded, in consequence, by sagebrush and shrubs.

The combination of sagebrush and grass is as much a feature of the unforested parts of the High Plateaus as short grass is of the Great Plains. It is a combination estimated to cover 250 million acres (101 million ha) of the West. The intermontane region, as we saw in an earlier section, generally has a winter-spring rainfall. Conditions that favor the growth of woody shrubs rather than grasses occur where annual rainfall is below 20 in. (500 mm). The typical cover is therefore a combination of sage and grass, in which the proportions of the two vary according to the rainfall, the grasses disappearing altogether on the desert margins.

Where the grasses maintain so precarious a hold, however, their disappearance may equally well be the result of overgrazing by livestock. The sagebrush, of which there are a great variety of types, each with wide climatic tolerance, offers little forage to stock (although

game animals feed on it); it flourishes while the grasses decline. Western ranchers resort to spraying and brush-beating to try to keep the scrub down, but only careful management (discussed more fully in a later chapter) will enable the grass cover to flourish.[7]

In the lowest and driest parts of the West, if and where a vegetation cover exists, it is composed of scattered desert shrubs, mostly woody in character. Over most of the dry area, creosote-bush is common, while on the highly alkaline surfaces of salt deserts and old lakebeds, varieties of sage and other alkali-tolerant shrubs are found. In the deserts of southern California and southern Arizona are also to be found a variety of large cacti whose bizarre shapes make them one of the tourist attractions of the Southwest.

[7]It is interesting to note that, while the ranchers generally regard sagebrush as something useless to be eliminated, at the same time western experimental stations are attempting to breed new varieties which will be palatable to stock.

Vegetation types of North America: (5) Alpine flora in the Rocky Mountains. Wild heliotrope and helibore in Glacier National Park, British Columbia. *(National Film Board of Canada)*

Vegetation types of North America: (6) The tundra—a scene on Baffin Island. *(National Film Board of Canada)*

The Population

2

The Indians

The earliest European immigrants to the New World found a native population already in possession. It is not clear how large this "Indian" population was, but it soon became apparent that, as far as North America was concerned, most of the Indians were concentrated on the plateau of Mexico. In the rest of the continent there were probably about one million Indians, of whom some 200,000 lived in what is now Canada.

Among these original Americans, however, there were wide differences of culture and language. Living close to nature, the Indians had adapted their economies to their environment. In the remote North the Eskimos lived by hunting and fishing, while in the East most of the tribes combined hunting with a primitive agriculture that produced corn and squashes. In the Southwest were the pueblos where, by 1500, a remarkable urban culture had reached and passed its climax, while elsewhere roamed tent-dwelling pastoralists or food-gatherers, such as those of the Great Basin of Utah, whom pioneers of the 1830s reported to have the world's lowest standard of living.

These cultural variations, moreover, were not permanent. The pressures of war, famine, or disease would force a tribe to move its hunting grounds, abandon its fields, or adopt new forms of economy. One of the most striking of these changes must have occurred about the year 1300, when a number of the largest pueblos in Utah and Colorado were apparently abandoned, swiftly and for reasons—war or famine—which can only now be guessed at. But the greatest changes of all, both in location and in livelihood, were brought about by the introduction of the horse.

The Great Plains had formerly been the home of a few pastoralist tribes. Across them roamed herds of bison, which were largely immune to the attacks of hunters moving on foot. But about the year 1600, horses—which had been introduced into the New World by the Spaniards—became available to the Indians, making possible for them a new way of life. Travelling on horseback and hunting the bison in groups, the plains Indians became the "new-rich" of seventeenth-century America. So strong was the attraction of this new way of life that other tribes moved into the area. From the eastern woodlands the Blackfoot and Cheyenne tribes trekked west, followed later by the Sioux and others; from the Rocky Mountain foothills came the Comanche; from the Southeast came tribes that abandoned agriculture for the new life of the plains. And hard on the heels of the last arrivals came the white man, to inaugurate the era of "cowboys and Indians" in the West.

From the eastern seaboard the tide of white settlement flowed west. The fate of the Indian tribes whose lands lay in its path was varied. In Canada contact was on the whole peaceful, and a proclamation of 1763 laid down that no Indian could be dispossessed of his lands without his own and the Crown's consent. There were few "Indian wars," and the Indian Act of 1876 insured the status of the Indian people (although it is possible to argue that this was not the result of any special idealism on the part of the Canadian government but simply reflected the fact that destruction of the buffalo herds had already reduced the Indians to starvation and docility before the occupation of the Prairies took place). In the United States conditions were less satisfactory. The westward thrust of the white settlers forced tribe after tribe off its hunting grounds, and while the policy of the government was at most times reasonable, its good intentions were constantly overtaken by the swiftness of the white advance; another war followed and another tribe withdrew, broken, to the west. Lands reserved for the Indians were subsequently "needed" for white settlers. Ultimately, the tribes were assigned reservations in the least desirable—which generally meant arid—sections, and the hunter-nomads were encouraged to become farmers, a change for which nothing in their previous experience had prepared them. Inevitably the extensive system of Indian land use had to give way before the demands of the nineteenth century. But the manner of the change leaves abundant cause for regret.

The Indian population reached a low point at the end of the nineteenth century. Since then, it has expanded again to something over one million, although intermarriage has made definition difficult and in Canada has produced a distinctive population of *métis*, representing the mixture of Indian and European stocks. About 52 million acres (21 million ha) in the United States and 6 million acres (2.4 million ha) in Canada are covered by Indian reservations; that is, lands secured to the Indians by treaty but overseen by the federal governments. On these reservations the Indian culture and life style can be preserved; yet that simple statement itself conceals not one but a whole series of dilemmas for the Indians concerned. For one thing "Indian life style" is often a synonym for poverty—the reservation and its resources are inadequate to support a population at any standard of living resembling Anglo-American norms. The dilemmas then unfold: to leave the reservation or to remain? To preserve the old way of life or attempt an adaptation to that of the white majority? To preserve the old ways for their own sake or as a tourist attraction? To maintain individuality but at the cost of becoming living museum pieces? To pretend that there are simple answers to these questions would be naive in the extreme.

But there is a further complication. On some of the reservations, minerals have been discovered—oil or uranium—in significant amounts. There is a fine irony in the fact that lands which the Indians received because the white man did not want them should now prove to be enormously valuable after all. It is an irony made more poignant by the impact of this wealth on an already weakened tribal structure.

Nor is this all. The treaties made with the Indians by newcomers during three centuries can today be seen to have favored the latter; some lands were grossly under-valued, some rights were simply disregarded, and some treaties were imposed upon the Indians without compensation to them of any kind. In the United States there has existed at least since World War II an official means (the Indian Claims Commission) by which the Indians can claim compensation for past losses. Huge sums of money have been called for, and some much smaller sums have been awarded. Indians have also set in motion legal processes to establish historic title to the ownership of tribal lands, an action which, pending settlement in the courts, calls into question all other land titles within the disputed areas, all the way from Maine to Alaska.

The Immigrants

In the year 1800 there were about 5,500,000 people in the territories now covered by the United States and some half a million in Canada. Immigration from Europe had been proceeding slowly for 200 years, to the French areas along the St. Lawrence, to the Spanish lands on the Gulf of Mexico, or to the Atlantic seaboard, where English culture and institutions dominated a cosmopolitan society that included groups of Germans, Dutch, and Scandinavians.

For the first few years of the nineteenth century the tempo of immigration remained slow. But for the United States, the hundred-year period between the end of the Napoleonic Wars and 1914 was the century of the immigrants—over 30 million of them arrived. In Canada the main phases of immigration came later. The first decade of the twentieth century saw 1,800,000 arrivals, and between 1914 and 1951 the total was about 3 million, most of whom came either in the 1920s or after 1945.

What were the causes of this greatest of modern population movements? They are to be sought largely in the conditions prevailing in the countries of the Old World, both political and social. War, disease, industrialization, agricultural enclosure, religious persecution; all these are mirrored in the rises and falls of the immigration rate. Perhaps the most basic reason of all was the great increase in population which began in Europe about 1800 and which dislocated the agricultural and social systems of the continent. Basic, too, was the

The United States: Immigration. The picture shows European immigrants arriving at Ellis Island in New York Harbor about the year 1900—part of an annual flow at that period of a half a million or more. Ellis Island was the main American entry and control point for this great migration. *(U.S. Immigration and Naturalization Service)*

rapid progress of industrialization, which threw the artisan out of work and created instead a demand for factory labor. Then, as the balance between the continent's economy and its growing population became more delicate, so the effects of crop failure or disease became more catastrophic. Every political rearrangement—the Vienna settlements, the Prussian annexation of Schleswig, or, above all, the Treaty of Versailles—created a new class of refugees. Singly or in groups, driven out or encouraged to leave so that others might remain and survive, the surplus population of Europe found its way to the ports and took ship for the New World.

M.L. Hansen, chronicler of the "Atlantic Migration," has pointed out that there were three main periods in the "immigrants' century." From 1830 to 1860 the movement was largely one from the Celtic fringes of the British Isles and from the middle Rhine, especially Hesse. Scottish crofters dispossessed by the advent of sheep farming joined with Irish peasants dispossessed by their landlords. This movement reached its peak after the terrible famine years of the 1840s. Then, from 1860 to 1890, Englishmen mingled with Germans and Scandinavians in the second great wave. Finally, between 1900 and 1914 (and in Canada between 1900 and the present day), the majority of the immigrants came from the Slavic countries of Eastern Europe, with a strong flow also from the Mediterranean lands. The peak was reached in 1907, when the United States admitted 1,285,000 immigrants.

The war of 1914–18 created upheavals in Europe on a gigantic scale. Immigration to the United States, which had fallen off during the war years, was by 1921 up again to 805,000, and, had emigration been unrestricted, there is no doubt that millions would have left the continent for America. In view of this prospect, the United States felt it necessary to limit by quota the number of immigrants that might be received. The quota, as fixed in 1927, permitted the entry of only 150,000 immigrants each year. Since the quota for each nation was based on the number of persons of that nationality or origin in the United States in 1920, the system favored Great Britain and virtually excluded the nationals of the south and east European countries, whose need for relief and degree of unrest were greatest. Even though the 1927 law was modified, under that of 1952 the quota for the Republic of Ireland, with less than 3 million nationals, was three times as great as that for Italy, with 50 million.

Between the two World Wars, therefore, it is not surprising to find that the stream of emigration to the United States not only dried up but, on balance, was reversed. Only for persons born in Canada, Mexico and the Latin American countries was entrance to the United States unrestricted by quota. After 1945 the arrangement continued in force (with certain concessions to help Europeans displaced by the war) until 1965, when it was finally abolished. In 1975 the United States admitted 386,000 immigrants, of whom 129,000 were Asians by birth. Only 73,000 were Europeans; the remainder were from the American hemisphere, principally from Canada, Mexico, and the West Indies.

In Canada a government policy designed to foster the growth of the population has brought in two main waves of immigrants. The first of these was between 1900 and 1914, when the Prairie wheatlands were being opened up, and it reached a peak of 400,870 arrivals in 1913. It was largely British but contained many eastern Europeans, and by the time it subsided, the most common languages on the Prairies, after English, were German and Ukrainian. The second wave of arrivals came in the years after 1945: up to the end of 1969, this wave had brought into the country nearly 3.3 million immigrants, with a peak of 282,000 in 1957. About a third of this total has come from the British Isles but with the passage of time, the British element is becoming smaller in proportion to the whole; large numbers have come from Italy and Germany, and since 1945 many of the immigrants have been refugees displaced by political changes in Eastern Europe. In every decade, however, a sizeable proportion of the immigrants in Canada have subsequently moved southward, ultimately settling in the United States.

Where, in fact, in the New World were these immigrants to settle? While the ports of entry

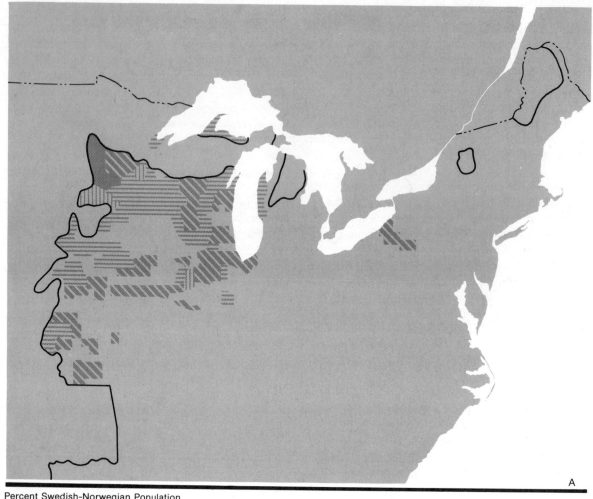

A

Percent Swedish-Norwegian Population

1–4%		Over 25%
4–15%		Limit of Census Area
15–25%		

were filled with a cosmopolitan population in transit, away from the coast there was a tendency for immigrants to settle in "national" areas. West of Lake Michigan, for example, people of Scandinavian stock are in a majority over much of Wisconsin, Minnesota, and Iowa, while other areas are as markedly German or Finnish. In some cases this is simply because the earliest arrivals encouraged their friends at home to join them. In others it is a product of organized, or group, emigration like that of the Pennsylvania Dutch or the Mennonites. In the emigration zones of Europe a system of recruiting existed which provided everything needed for door-to-door emigration. In yet other cases it reflects the *time* of arrival in North America. As settlement extended across the continent, so each decade introduced its own economic frontiers and its own labor needs. The 1860s saw the beginning of the Scandinavian immigration; those years saw also the exploitation of the timber resources of Wisconsin and Minnesota, and the Swedes and Norwegians went there as lumberjacks and frontier farmers. The Ukrainians who arrived in the 1870s were recruited to work in the rapidly expanding coal-mining areas of Pennsylvania; those who followed them in 1900 went west to the Prairies as wheat farmers.

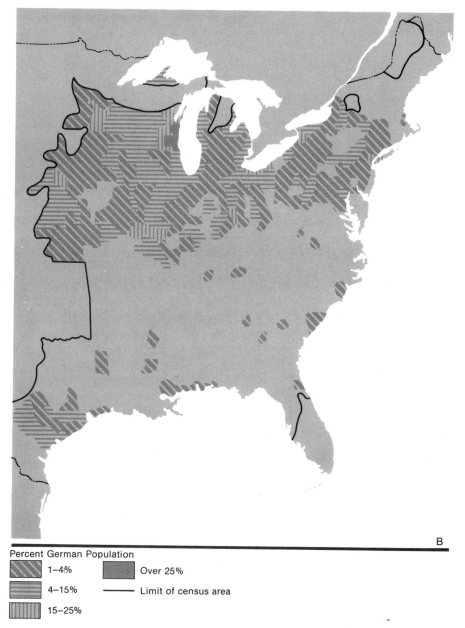

Fig. 2-1. Foreign-born population of the United States at the census of 1870 (opposite) Swedish/Norwegian-born and (right) German-born. These maps, reproduced from the *Statistical Atlas of the United States*, published in 1874 to embody the results of the Ninth Census, clearly show two features of the population distribution at that date: (1) the tendency of the immigrants from Europe to congregate in particular areas, resulting from either the work opportunities available at the time of arrival or the influence of earlier arrivals, and (2) the tendency of European immigrants to avoid the South. Even allowing for the fact that the Civil War had just ended, the complete absence of a foreign-born population (apart from descendants of the French and Spanish settlers) in the region is striking. See pp. 41–42.

B

Percent German Population

	1–4%		Over 25%
	4–15%	——	Limit of census area
	15–25%		

Wherever possible, the immigrants sought work and conditions comparable with those they had left in the Old World. Italians who had raised Leghorn poultry in Italy could start afresh with Rhode Island hens in New England, or establish market gardens and vineyards. Cornish miners worked the lead at Galena, or the copper of Upper Michigan. But the great immigrant problem was that so many of the newcomers were European peasants possessed of a single skill, and that skill in limited demand in a society that was both industrializing and also mechanizing its agriculture. All that many could offer was the strength of their arms, and so they tended to drift into poorly paid labor gangs, often separated from their families. For many, the process of settling in the paradise of the West was hard and long drawn-out.

The one area of the United States where they might have practiced their peasant farming was the South. But in that region the climate

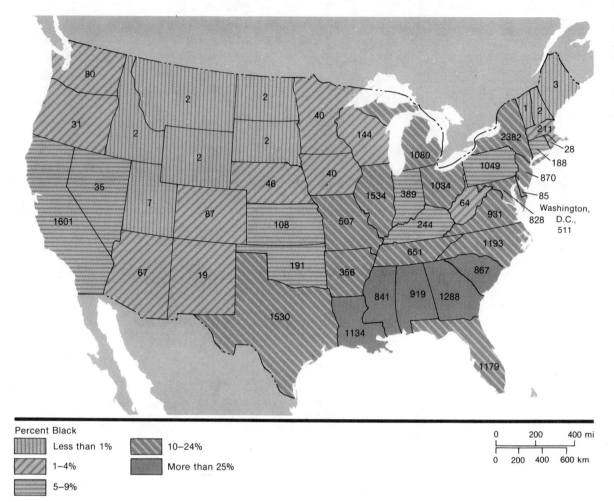

Percent Black

▦	Less than 1%	▨	10–24%
▧	1–4%	■	More than 25%
▤	5–9%		

0   200   400 mi
0   200   400   600 km

Fig. 2-2. The United States: Distribution of black population by states, 1975 estimates. The cross-hatching indicates the percentage of the population of each state which was black in 1975, and the number gives the actual black population in thousands. For the states not shown, the data are: percentages, Alaska—3.0; Hawaii—1.0. Black population, Alaska—9,100; Hawaii—7,600.

was against them, and for laborers the employment question was overshadowed by that of slavery; farm labor was provided by the blacks. For these and other reasons, very few nineteenth century immigrants settled in the southern states. The effect of this virtual exclusion of immigrants from the slave states is graphically illustrated by Fig. 2-1, which is taken from the atlas accompanying the census of 1870.

On the Pacific coast there was another class of immigrant—the East Asian. Chinese labor virtually built California between 1850 and 1880. Japanese market gardeners became

wealthy and successful. But the cry of unfair competition and undermined standards was raised, and in 1882 the United States passed an exclusion law. In certain respects the Asians occupied the place of the blacks as the objects of racial prejudice on the Pacific Coast, at a period when few blacks lived there.[1]

The Blacks

In 1975 there were 24.4 million blacks in the United States, and they formed 11.5 percent of

[1]See D. Caldwell, "The Negroization of the Chinese Stereotype in California," *Southern California Quarterly*, vol. liii (1971), 123–32.

the population. They were the descendants of the slaves brought into North America by the slave traders of Spain and England from 1600 onward, until the trade was outlawed in the nineteenth century.

In the early days of the colonies there was a pressing need for labor. We have already seen that in North America, as opposed to Central America, the native population was sparse; moreover, it was generally hostile, and could not be put to work in the way the Spaniards had conscripted the generally docile natives of the Caribbean. The Spaniards themselves early resorted to importing African slaves, but in the English colonies the process was more gradual. Originally, the labor shortage was met by the *indenture* system. An individual would contract to work for a colonist for a limited period in exchange for his passage and subsistence, and at the end of his term would become a free settler. It was only gradually that this temporary slavery came to be distinguished from that of the blacks, for whom there was no terminal date. The first Africans were brought to Virginia in 1619, but slavery was not made legally hereditary until 1662. For Massachusetts the comparable dates were 1636 and 1641, and in 1705 a law was passed classifying slaves as a form of real estate.

It was in the plantation states of the Southeast that slavery flourished. There, in the hot, humid climate, the plantation owners needed abundant and acclimatized hand labor for the cultivation of tobacco, rice, and cotton. Whatever questions existed in Southerners' minds about the moral legitimacy of slavery were swamped by the demand for labor, as cotton growing spread across the southeastern states in the early nineteenth century. Perhaps the greatest tragedy of all for the blacks was that the South committed itself so completely to cotton cultivation that in the end, in spite of many a voice raised in protest against the system, it *could not* discard slavery and survive.

Civil war and emancipation left the black population solidly concentrated in the Southeast; free, but tied economically to the same cotton lands as before the war. Today, over a century later, there is still a concentration of blacks living in the Southeast, but it is much

less marked. One of the most notable population movements of post-1914 North America has been the migration of blacks from southern farms to northern cities. The beginnings of this movement belong to the period before the Civil War, but the event which may be said to have totally altered its scale was the drying-up of immigration during the First World War, which created a shortage of labor in the expanding war industries of the North. Large-scale urbanization of the blacks dates from this time: in 1920 there were almost a million more blacks classified as urban dwellers than there had been twenty years earlier. The Second World War gave a fresh impetus to the movement, and it has been continuing ever since. By 1970 there were 2.4 million blacks in the New York-New Jersey urbanized area, 1.2 million in Chicago (17 percent of the population of the entire urban area), 844,000 in Philadelphia, 757,000 in Detroit, and 823,000 in Los Angeles. Washington, D.C. became the first major city to record a census population more than 50 percent black, as the federal government pursued a policy of making the maximum number of employment opportunities avaliable to minority workers. And between 1940 and 1970 the black population of Illinois increased from 387,000 to 1,426,000, to give it more black people than Georgia or Texas.

The effects of this movement have been widespread. For one thing, it has reduced the birth rate in the black population as a whole, for the fertility of black farm women is typically well above the average for all black women. The same type of demographic effect has been brought about by the rising level of education among blacks: women with only an elementary education have on average twice as many children each as have black college graduates.[2]

But the most significant aspect of the movement has been to spread the problems of race relations to new areas and to involve the northern states (where in the past people were free to theorize about race) in questions which have long dominated the South: whether blacks can compete for jobs on equal terms with white workers, and whether blacks

[2] R. Farley, *Growth of the Black Population*, Markham, Chicago, 1970, pp. 118, 122.

43

should be free to live on any street where they can afford a home.

We shall have to wait for the next census to discover whether blacks are still moving northward in such numbers as have characterized the last three decades. But there are interim figures for 1975 which suggest that perhaps a peak has been passed and that movement *back from* the north to the south has been increasing, until it may outweigh the south-to-north movement. Certainly, this would fit with a number of known circumstances: a shift in the balance of industrial employment between North and South, making the North less attractive to job-seekers and the South more so; a general rise in economic standards in the South; unfavorable social experiences of blacks in northern cities; some easing of racial tensions in the old slave states. The Civil Rights legislation has given the blacks a legal framework within which they can build eventual equality of status. Their conditions and standing have improved with the years. In 1940, for example, only 4 percent of blacks over 25 had completed 4 years of high school. By 1968 the figure was 20 percent. Still, it remains true that at present they are far from achieving real equality, because real equality is determined not by law, but by social pressure.

The clearest geographical expression of this social position is to be found in the location of black homes. We have recently become familiar with the concept of the urban "ghetto": every city, northern or southern, which has more than a handful of blacks (or, for that matter, Mexicans or Puerto Ricans) has one. Ghetto[3] areas have been known in American cities for many decades, especially in those containing large numbers of immigrants. The new arrivals, many of whom spoke no English, held together for security; in this sense the Italian or Greek ghetto afforded its inhabitants a measure of protection in an unfamiliar environment. But for the European immigrant there was always a route out of the ghetto. Once he had learned English and made some money, he could leave if he wished. The ghetto became simply a convenient transit camp.

When blacks began to arrive in the cities, they gravitated together in the same way. But for them there was seldom a way out of the ghetto. There quickly grew up a pressure from outside that barred them from moving into white areas. Yet, because the move of the blacks to town has been on so large a scale, these ghetto areas have been called upon to house ever-increasing numbers of new arrivals. Thus the pressure of population within mounts until it exceeds the social pressure outside, and the ghetto area gradually expands as the non-black inhabitants of adjacent streets sell out and pull back.[4]

The ghetto is generally situated close to the city center, either in the vicinity of the railway yards or in the ring of inner suburbs which half a century ago housed the upper-class white population. The former single-family homes are badly adapted to the new function of housing several black families, and as more blacks arrive the district quickly deteriorates into a crowded and derelict blight area. In the larger cities the same process will lead to the takeover of commercial as well as residential areas. In their way the black commercial areas are as distinctive as the residential sections.[5]

[3]Maurice Yeates and Barry Garner give the following definition of the word *ghetto* in *The North American City*, Harper & Row, New York, 1971, pp.303–4: "The term *ghetto* originally referred to the Jewish ghettos of eastern and southern Europe. . . . As applied to North America, a *ghetto* is a spatially contiguous area of the urban landscape in which the inhabitants have particular social, economic, ethnic, or cultural attributes that distinguish them from the majority of the inhabitants of the country in which they reside. Because of these differentiating characteristics, the inhabitants are, by and large, not permitted by the majority to reside beyond this well-defined area even if they wished, unless these differentiating attributes change sufficiently for them to be accepted (Rose, 1970). The ghetto is thus a result of external pressure rather than internal coherence."

[4]On this point see H.M. Rose, *The Black Ghetto: A Spatial Behavioral Perspective*, McGraw-Hill, New York, 1971, or his briefer "The Development of an Urban Subsystem: The Case of the Negro Ghetto," *Annals* of the Association of American Geographers, vol. lx (1970), 1–17.

[5]See A.R. Pred, "Business Thoroughfares as Expressions of Urban Negro Culture," *Economic Geography*, vol. xxxix (1963), 217–32.

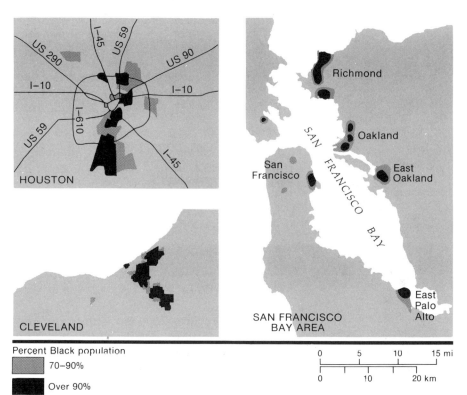

Fig. 2-3. The Urban United States: Examples of areas of black concentration in major urban areas: Houston, Cleveland, and the San Francisco Bay Area. The maps are all drawn to the same scale.

Percent Black population

70–90%

Over 90%

It is a tragic paradox that while the equality of blacks has been legally affirmed on many occasions in recent years, their confinement to all-black areas has actually increased. It is estimated, for example, that in Chicago at the turn of the century about a quarter of the blacks lived in districts that were more than 50 percent black. By 1960 the figure was over 90 percent. It is probably more usual to drive a mile through the South Side of Chicago without seeing a white person than it would be to do the same thing in Lagos or Freetown.

For the black, of course, as for earlier ethnic concentrations in the city, the ghetto fulfils a function: in this case, a political function. The ghetto is the basis of such political power as the black Americans are able to exert. Therefore, in a political sense blacks have a vested interest in the continued existence of the ghetto. Its dispersal might not necessarily work to their advantage. The time needed to disperse a million people and the degree of adaptability this would demand of the dispersed are far beyond present developmental aspirations. In most cities, therefore, the more modest goal is to rebuild the blight areas—to tear down the old structures and replace them, usually with multi-story blocks. Yet this is a solution to the problem of blight which leaves the racial unbalance within the city unchanged.

The magnitude of the problem and the scale of relocation that would have to be contemplated is illustrated by Figure 2-4 and the table which follows. These compare the size of the black element in a dozen adjacent communities along the Passaic River just west of New York City. Newark in the south and Paterson in the north are the two large cities of the group; between them lie a line of suburban communities whose population is totally different in composition.

45

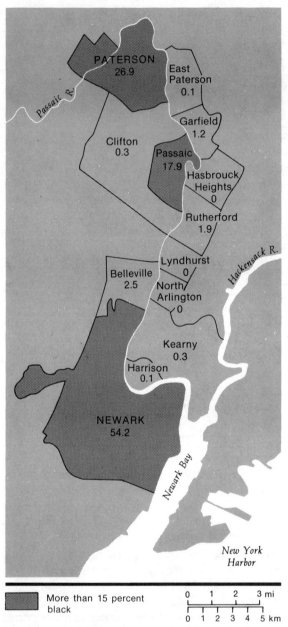

Community	Black Population 1970	Blacks as a percentage of total population
Paterson	38,919	26.9
East Paterson	19	0.08
Garfield	363	1.2
Clifton	267	0.3
Passaic	9861	17.9
Hasbrouck Heights	6	0
Rutherford	402	1.9
Lyndhurst	7	0
Belleville	856	2.5
North Arlington		0
Kearny	121	0.3
Harrison	10	0.1
Newark	207,458	54.2

Fig. 2-4. Communities of the Passaic River Valley, New Jersey. The map shows the location of the communities listed in the adjacent table, which gives their black populations in 1970.

The Melting Pot—Or Not?

The well-worn phrase, "the melting pot," describes the way in which elements of the population of four continents have been set down in the United States and have there merged into one distinctive American society. The phrase rings less true for Canada, for there the melting pot, although real enough, has been devoted to a particular kind of carefully preserved bimetallism—the British and French connections. While the creators of the United States set out deliberately to achieve a society in which political, social, and religious neutrality would produce a new and distinctive way of life, the Canadians have preserved with equal care a link with the culture of those countries which have contributed most to their way of life.

In Canada the numerical predominance of the British and French stocks is marked. In 1971 these two groups made up nearly 75 percent of the population. In the United States, on the other hand, while in 1790 the British element in the young republic represented 80 percent of the population, by 1920, immigration had reduced this figure to less than 50 percent. Germany, Ireland, and the countries of southern and eastern Europe had made their contributions to the melting pot, the contents of which, although largely European in origin, were certainly well mixed. Thanks in large part to the system of public education, with its careful nationalistic emphasis, the American objective had been achieved; the immigrants had been absorbed into the American nation.

There has always been a certain opposition in the United States to the admission of new immigrants. On the whole, however, this reaction has been notably slight, considering how unprepossessing was the appearance of many of the new arrivals, bewildered peasants disembarking after a nightmare Atlantic crossing. At the times of greatest influx it must indeed have appeared that American culture and institutions were in danger of being swamped by aliens. There have in fact been efforts to halt immigration—by old colonial elements fearing the introduction of so much Mediterranean and Slavic blood into Anglo-Saxon America, and, more reasonably perhaps, by those who feared that the introduction of so much cheap labor into the economy would undermine the position of the American worker. That this fear has never become reality is probably because the growth of the United States has been so rapid that labor is usually in short supply.[6] Only in a few depression years has it become redundant; at such times, in any case, the stream of immigration has tended to dry up of its own accord.

Most of the immigrants have readily adapted themselves to American political and social ideals and have been anxious to prove themselves good citizens—some hundreds of thousands did so in the Union armies in 1861–65. At the same time, wherever a group of fellow-countrymen congregated, they kept alive some remnants of the culture of their homeland—a church, a newspaper in their own language, or a group for folk dancing or singing. In general, the larger the alien community, the slower was the process of assimilation and the stronger the nostalgic nationalism. But for the immigrants' children the situation was very different. With no language barrier to overcome they made wider social contacts than their par-

[6]Maldwyn Jones puts the fears of the "old" Americans in perspective by writing, "Indeed, since it was the unskilled labor provided by the "new" immigrants which alone made possible America's phenomenal industrial expansion in the late nineteenth century, it was to them that native Americans and older immigrants were indebted for the increased opportunities available for skilled, white-collar, and professional workers." *American Immigration,* University of Chicago Press, Chicago, 1960, p. 218.

ents. For them the cultural relics of the homeland, like their parents' accent, were largely curiosities. The influence of the school quickly overcame the alien influence of the home and produced, as it was intended to produce, a new generation of Americans.

In the 1970s, however, there is a sense in which this account of the assimilation of the immigrant is already dated, perhaps beyond recall. Once the American nation became consciously united, proving its power in war and diplomacy, and once the flood of foreign newcomers was restricted, the nation could support a greater weight of cultural diversity. The distinctiveness of groups within the whole could be stressed—or tolerated, depending upon the point of view—in a way which, in the nineteenth century, would have been seen as endangering the whole fabric of the nation. A revived ethnicity has become a source of pride. This is seen most clearly in the emphasis today on black and Amerindian cultures, but individual groups of European origin are no less vocal, or less proud of the achievements of their members. And over against all of these is the largest foreign-language minority of all in North America—the 11.2 million persons of Spanish origin, so often overlooked in treatments of the melting pot, but so forcefully present in the lands of the old Spanish empire and in the Puerto Rican quarters of the eastern cities.

The Case of French Canada

To every mention of the melting pot and every suggestion of assimilation to a common cultural denominator, one group has remained doggedly opposed—the French Canadians. United culturally by language and religion and represented politically by Québec, the second most populous province of Canada, they have succeeded as has no other national group in maintaining their distinctiveness through every vicissitude of the continent's political history.

That the French Canadians have achieved this privileged position is due, politically, to their bargaining power—their numerical strength and their concentration in one key province. This power they exerted in 1867 to ensure that the new system evolved for the government of all Canada should be federal, and that the new Province of Québec should preserve intact its distinctive institutions. French Canada, then, is a product of a federal constitution and of the determination of a powerful minority, a minority to whom, as G.S. Graham writes, "national survival had become the dominating passion."

The heart of French Canada, today as in the seventeenth century, is along the Lower St. Lawrence. The area reaches west through Montréal, which is a bilingual metropolis, to a short distance west of the Ottawa River. South of the St. Lawrence, however, most of the settlement was originally British, but this area has now been largely taken over by French Canadians, who have also spread into New Brunswick and over the border into New England. By contrast, the originally French settlements around the Bay of Fundy (Acadia) are now nearly empty of French population. Elsewhere there are clusters and pockets of French Canadians. St-Boniface, for example, across the Red River to the east of English-speaking Winnipeg, retains much of its French-Canadian culture and inheritance, including long lots running down to the river bank which reproduce the landholding pattern of Québec. In northern Alberta, similarly, there are French communities, the product of a series of migrations westward from Québec in the period 1900–1950, many of which were organized and led by the priest of the home parish back in the east. Thirty percent of all Canadians speak French as their mother tongue.

This cultural cleavage at the heart of the Canadian federation is vitally important; it has also widened sharply in the 1970s. We shall consider in the next chapter its relevance for Canada as a whole. For the moment, we need only note that it grew out of the conflicts of colonial days, and was given its dimensions not only by language but by a religious barrier and by a separation between two school systems. Originally, it was a division between a French Catholic rural population and a British non-Catholic population that dominated much of the urban and commercial life of the region. Yet, although the church and the countryside

no longer exercise so strong an influence on the French population, the separatism of the French element is actually growing rather than diminishing.

There are several interesting aspects of this special position of French Canada. One of them is that among the French Catholic families the birth rate has traditionally been high—a good deal higher than for Canada as a whole. (During the period 1910 to 1930 the differential between Québec and the nation was about eight per thousand.) There seemed a possibility that the French population might ultimately grow to outnumber the remainder, and the statistics of population increase have been watched with close attention, especially in the postwar years, when many of the immigrants from Europe were Roman Catholics. However, during the past two decades the Québec birth rate has been falling and since 1961 has been consistently below the national average in every year. By 1973, it was the lowest for any province in Canada.

Militating against this numerical increase is the second factor of change in the situation. In the past the strength of French Canadian culture lay in the rural settlements with their traditional way of life. In the villages of the French *habitants* the two most powerful influences were the church and the family, and there was little to challenge their control. But the increase in population forced sons and daughters to seek employment elsewhere, while the cities offer to them—as to the younger farm population everywhere—a wider variety of interests and prospects than is to be found at home. Today Québec's population is more than 75 percent urban.

So there has been a move to town which has inevitably weakened the ties with the traditional culture. For one thing, the old controls are relaxed; for another, much of the industry of the cities is owned and managed by non-French Canadians.

Nevertheless, there is a third factor whose effect must be taken into account. As the political voice of separatism grows stronger—and whatever the reasons, this is the case—so it becomes important for businesses operating in French Canada to transact their affairs in French. The result is that companies operating all over North America find it advisable to set up branches in Montréal or Québec (where business is carried on in French), and executives whose base is in the industrial cities of English-speaking Ontario spend their evenings learning French.

Distribution of Population—Canada

The census taken in 1976 revealed that the population of Canada at that date was 22,992,604 or 1.4 million more than in 1971. Over 3.8 million sq mi (9.8 million sq km) of territory, however, this represents a very low average density of population. And for vast areas of the country even this figure is misleading, for the Canadian population is gathered in a series of clusters along the southern border, leaving huge northern expanses virtually uninhabited.

From either a strategic or an economic point of view this distribution of population is highly unsatisfactory. The Maritime Provinces are linked to the rest of populated Canada only by a narrow corridor of Canadian territory between the St. Lawrence and the border of Maine. The southward extension of the Laurentian Shield to the shore of Lake Superior virtually cuts Canada in two. Beyond the Prairie Provinces rise the Rockies and the Coast Mountains of British Columbia as further obstacles to movement, while the capital of Canada's newest province, Newfoundland, lies over 1000 mi (1600 km) by sea from Québec and more than 600 mi (960 km) from Halifax.

The Prairie Provinces account for some 16 percent of Canada's population, and the Atlantic Provinces for 9 percent. Over 60 percent of the total, however, are to be found in Ontario and Québec; to be precise, in the southern fringes of these two provinces. Grouped along the St. Lawrence Valley and in the peninsula of southwestern Ontario is more than half of Canada's population.

That these widely separated groups of settlers ever formed the Canadian Federation may be taken as a tribute to skilful diplomacy and as a measure of the fear inspired by the military strength of the United States in 1865. It has often been remarked that it is easier for each of these Canadian population clusters to communicate southward with the United States than with its neighbor on either side; it is certain that up to 1960 the normal highway route from east to west across Canada ran south of the border. Moreover, even when the nation has solved all the problems of communication between its existing parts, there still remains the task of integrating with the remainder of the state the great empty area of the Northlands.

In the east, then, the population has been increasing relatively slowly. Settled early, these areas have been the scene of no striking recent development, and have attracted only a small number of immigrants. Apart from Halifax there is no large city, and today's immigrant almost always makes for the towns, with their industrial and commercial opportunities, rather than for the remote farmsteads of a region such as this.

In Québec a high rate of natural increase in an essentially rural population led, in the period up the the Second World War, to an expansion first into the Eastern Townships, east of Montréal, and then to the northern frontier, where pioneer farmers and lumbermen spread over the Shield in the Lake St. John and Abitibi areas. But in recent decades the cities have been the growth areas: the Québec population has been urbanizing rapidly. In Ontario similar trends are evident. Among recent immigrants one out of every two has made for this province, contributing to the populations of Toronto, Hamilton, and London and spreading from there to the smaller centers. Along the northern edge of the Paleozoic formations, where they adjoin the Shield, there is again a frontier zone, a frontier with outliers in the various clay belts on the Shield further north. But a geological map remains the best key to the distribution of Ontario's population, which is almost wholly concentrated in the southwestern peninsula.

In the Prairie Provinces a steady trickle of workers has been leaving the farms. This migration, as we shall see, has occurred in many other farm areas, especially in the comparable Great Plains region of the United States. While some of the migrants move to the towns, many have left the area to resettle in British Columbia. Between 1941 and 1951, and again between 1971 and 1976, the province of Saskatchewan actually lost population through this rural exodus. In Manitoba and Alberta, however, the loss from the farms has been more than offset by the growth of the Prairie cities, a growth due partly to industrial development and partly to the spectacular rise in oil and gas production.

In the West the population of British Columbia, like that of other parts of the Pacific coast, has increased very rapidly, but outside the metropolitan area of Vancouver it is a population largely scattered over a huge area, in remote valleys and on islands. The Vancouver district has been the goal of many immigrants, but the province also includes a pioneer fringe along the Peace River, whose settlements have contributed to the provincial increase.

Finally, the Northwest Territories and Yukon, which between them comprise nearly 40 percent of Canada's area, possess only 0.2 percent of the population—some 64,000. Half of these people are Indians and Eskimos, the Indians generally to be found in the forested areas of the North and the 16,000 Eskimos on the tundra. The other half of this sparse population is to be found in mining communities and trading posts and on tiny patches of cultivation dotted through a vast wilderness where development has hardly made a scratch. The white population of the Northlands, though it has increased since 1941, is far below the figure for the halcyon days of the gold rushes, 70 or more years ago.

Distribution of Population— The United States

In mid-1977, the United States had a population estimated at 216 million, up from 204.9 million at the census of 1970. The increase in population since the end of World War II had been considerably greater than anticipated: in the early 1950s, it was estimated that the figure of 200 million would not be reached before 1975 at the earliest. For twenty years after the Second World War the U.S. birth rate ran high, after which it began to fall off, and as it did so the share contributed by immigration to

the annual increase in population steadily increased. Today about one-quarter of the annual increase is represented by immigration, a share which has increased from one-fifth in the 1960s. Between 1970 and 1977 two states— New York and Rhode Island—lost population, while all the others gained. The *rate* of gain varied from state to state and was generally greatest in the West and South and least in the Great Plains and the industrial East.

The average density of population was 60 per sq mi (23.2 per sq km), but the density varied from 0.6 per sq mi in Alaska and 3.8 in Wyoming (0.23 and 1.47 per sq km respectively) to 973 (376 per sq km) in New Jersey. The highest overall densities were to be found in the manufacturing areas of the northeastern states; outside the industrial regions the highest densities were in the Southeast. West of the Mississippi and Missouri rivers increasing aridity and mountainous terrain reduced the density of population to 4 to 8 per sq mi (1.54 to 3.08 per sq km) in the Great Plains, and to zero in the deserts of Nevada and California. Beyond these empty areas lay a series of population clusters along the Pacific coastal fringe from Puget Sound to the Mexican border.

While the American population has thus been increasing, its distribution is also continually changing. One of the features of American life that must always impress the European is the mobility of the population. To a degree unknown in older lands, Americans are geographically unattached and prepared to move long distances in search of economic gain or more pleasant living conditions. Out of this mobility have come three great movements of the population in recent years.

The first of these is a movement from the country to the cities, which we have already noted in Canada. Although difficulties of census division and definition mask the precise figures, it seems clear that during the decade 1960–70 there was an exodus from the farms equivalent to one-half of the 1960 farm population. Even allowing for the natural increase of the farm population there was a fall in the total from 15.6 million in 1960 to 9.7 million in 1970. The circumstances surrounding this exodus are examined in Chapter 6; mechanization was a factor, and so, too, was a general increase in the pressure of competition in some branches of agricultural production. By 1970, 73.5 percent of the population was classed as urban.

The second movement is from the centers of the cities to the suburbs. It reflects a rising standard of living and modern housing concepts, and since it brings outside the city boundaries a large population whose interests lie mainly within the city, it tends statistically to counteract the movement first described. To distinguish, therefore, between the farmers and the mere country residents, the rural population is divided into two categories: "farm" and "non-farm." It is the "farm" section which, as we have seen, has suffered such a decline over the past decade; the "non-farm" element has considerably increased.

The best impression of the combined effects of these two movements is obtained from the population figures for the so-called Standard Metropolitan Statistical Areas (S.M.S.A.). These cover the 264 largest cities and comprise not only the city proper but also the suburbs— sometimes several counties in extent. They give, therefore, a fairly accurate impression of the size of the whole built-up area. For each large city, consequently, two population figures can be given—that for the city alone and that for the S.M.S.A.[7] By the mid-1970s, over 70 percent of the population of the United States lived within the S.M.S.A.s.

By far the greatest single metropolitan area in the United States is New York, with a 1975 population of 9.60 million. It was followed at that date by Chicago with 6.97 million and Los Angeles with 6.92, and by 32 other S.M.S.A.s with a million inhabitants or more. Of the 20 S.M.S.A.s with the highest *growth rates* since 1970, five were in Florida, four each in California and Texas, two each in Colorado and Arizona, and one each in Nevada, New Mexico, and South Carolina. The dominance of southern and western states in this list is obvious. If we limit ourselves to the largest metropolitan areas, the impression obtained is much the same: among the big cities with high rates of

growth were Atlanta, Dallas, Denver, Houston, Miami, and San Jose.

On the whole, the big cities of the East and North were to be found near the bottom of the growth list: to be more exact, several of them on the alternative list—that of the S.M.S.A.s which *lost* population since 1970. Heading this second list was New York City itself, with a net annual population loss of around 75,000.

What has happened is, however, to some extent merely a matter of statistical jiggling for on this reckoning Los Angeles lost population, too. Although the S.M.S.A. was originally designed by the Census Bureau precisely to include both the city and its suburbs, the S.M.S.A. has itself become too small to cover the whole built-up area, which may be divided between two or three statistical areas. The urban area around Los Angeles, for example, includes not only the Los Angeles-Long Beach S.M.S.A. (which, as we have seen, *lost* population between 1970 and 1975), but also Anaheim-Santa Ana-Garden Grove, which since 1960 has added no less than one million people to its population, Oxnard-Ventura, with a growth of 250,000, and Riverside-San Bernardino-Ontario, which added 400,000. To take account of these *conurbations,* therefore, the Census Bureau recognizes a Standard Consolidated Statistical Area. The New York S.C.S.A. has over 17 million inhabitants, Los Angeles more than 10 million, and Chicago about 7.5 million.

The third aspect of population movement in the United States is inter-regional. Ever since the first Europeans arrived, there has been a fairly regular shift in the regional balance; in particular, a movement from east to west across the continent. For decade after decade, the main goal of this movement has been California until, midway through the 1960s, it became the most populous state in the union. Draining out of the longer-settled states further east, lesser streams flowed into the Pacific Northwest and Texas. The movement became a tradition, a part of everybody's experience as an American.

The latest figures show, however, that there have been changes. It is no longer a question of a simple westward movement, terminating in California because there is nowhere else to

[7]Throughout this book, population figures given for cities are in every case those for the S.M.S.A., where such a unit exists, unless otherwise noted. In Canada, the equivalent units are called Census Metropolitan Areas.

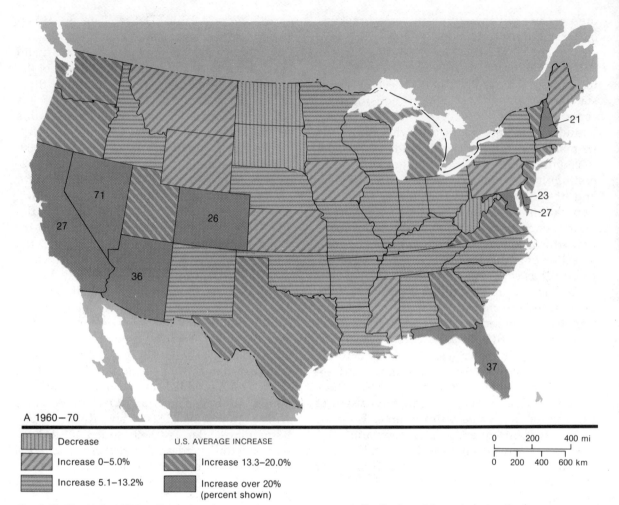

A 1960—70

Decrease		**U.S. AVERAGE INCREASE**	
Increase 0–5.0%		Increase 13.3–20.0%	
Increase 5.1–13.2%		Increase over 20% (percent shown)	

0   200   400 mi

0   200   400   600 km

Fig. 2-5A. The United States: Percentage increase in population by states, 1960–70. The national increase was 13.2 percent. For the two states not shown, the increases were: Alaska, 33.6 percent; Hawaii, 21.7 percent.

go. Between 1970 and 1977, the average annual growth in the population of California (1.1 percent) was less than that of Maine or Arkansas; in fact, it was no higher than the percentage rate for Mississippi, a state in which before 1970 the size of the population had been virtually unchanged for 40 years. Although 1 percent of California's 21 million people still represents a sizeable increase, it is obvious that a fresh analysis of inter-regional movements is called for.

The traditional American incentives to move have been provided by the search for space, independence, and wealth. For many decades, all three of these were to be found in the same region—the West. Space and independence were provided by sparse population and cheap land; wealth by minerals and the thousand opportunities for speculation which a frontier provided. But eventually the frontier was stabilized and the space-seekers began to crowd each other out—which in California, with 21 million of them, is what has happened. So the original movement has been modified in two ways:

1. As the original target areas of the movement filled up, they have been replaced by others. Since the most inviting areas were generally filled first, the new areas may lack one or more of the original qualities, but still compensate for that lack by their present emptiness. In this way there has occurred a switch, for example, from southern California to Arizona—a kind of bounce-back from the Pacific

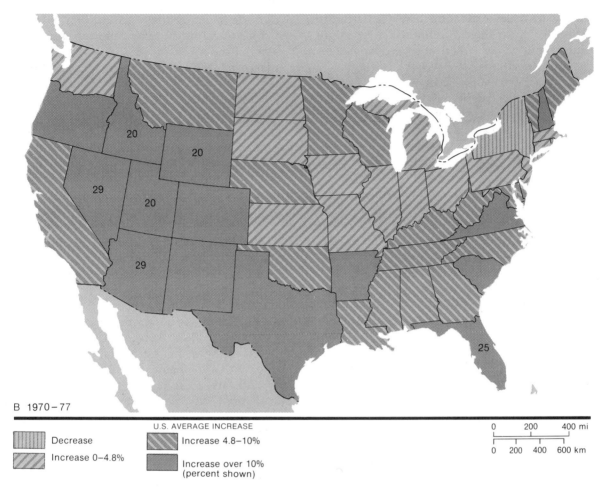

B 1970-77

U.S. AVERAGE INCREASE

Decrease

Increase 0–4.8%

Increase 4.8–10%

Increase over 10% (percent shown)

0   200   400 mi
0   200   400   600 km

Fig. 2-5B. The United States: Estimated percentage increase in population by states, 1970–77. The national increase was 6.4 percent. For the two states not shown the increases were: Alaska, 34.6 percent; Hawaii, 16.2 percent. The pattern of change represented by this map is quite different from that shown by Fig. 2-5A.

Coast. The same kind of rebound may now be happening into Oregon, where the 1970–77 figures show a rising rate of in-migration, which may soon affect the Pacific Northwest as a whole. There are fashions in migration goals as in everything else.

2. To the old incentives to move has been added a new one: amenity. In earlier centuries, when most people were producers of goods, they had necessarily to live where they produced—on their farm or near their workbench. Their choice of home was limited by their work commitments and some of them lived in appalling conditions simply to be near their work. But in North America today, most people are not tied in this way. Seven out of

ten American workers are not producers in the old sense at all: they are employed in service occupations, most of which can be carried on in any place they choose. And they are likely to choose the place for reasons quite unconnected with the occupation itself; in short, for reasons of amenity. There is nothing surprising about this, and no doubt Americans in the past would have greatly preferred, given the option, to stitch garments in pleasant small towns rather than in sweatshops in the slums of New York. The point is that they were not given the option, while today's worker is. He or she has personal freedom of movement, instant information about places to live, a job which can be done anywhere, and sufficient leisure to make recreation a major factor in planning. Under these conditions, as we might expect, millions of Americans have been exercising their options.

There are, of course, economic factors, too. With the steady drift out of farming which North America has experienced, agricultural regions like the Dakotas have lost population. Even more widespread is another economic consideration: that it costs less to live in a warm climate than a cold one—less to heat a house or office, less to buy clothes, less to employ labor where less sick time is taken. If leisure and recreation invite Americans to move to a climate where they can carry on outdoor activities all year around, economic sense reinforces the attraction of such areas.

What America has experienced, therefore, is the development of a Sun Belt. It stretches, in most people's perception, from the Carolinas to California and it contained at the last count almost exactly half of the population of the United States. For all the states contained within it, the figures of population increase are remarkable. Between 1970 and 1975, Florida gained 23 percent, Arizona 25 percent, and Nevada 21. What is perhaps even more striking is that southern states like Mississippi which were previously unfashionable—to put no finer point upon it—with inter-regional migrants have, in the past few years, shared in the increase. Between 1960 and 1970 Mississippi suffered a net out-migration of 267,000. For 1970–75, it showed a net gain and so did Alabama, another former big loser through migration. Texas drew 150,000 net migrants in the whole decade of the 1960s, but 400,000 in the five years 1970–75.

To summarize the factors involved in this regional shift: there is freedom to move and freedom for most people from work-place constraints. There is the economic advantage of avoiding a cold climate (although this is offset to some extent by the probable need for air-conditioning.) There is the attraction of an outdoors accessible and attractive during virtually twelve months of the year. And undergirding all this is the fact of an economy with a sufficient margin of productivity *not* to require every business to be carried on in the absolutely least-cost location, an economy in which

the contentment of the work force is a factor which can be, and is, taken into account.

Most of these considerations apply very particularly to one group of Americans—those who have retired. Welfare schemes and the retirement pension itself are institutions whose coverage has grown greatly in recent years. A worker who retires on a pension can collect payments in Florida as easily as in Chicago; he or she is certainly interested in living cheaply, and has all the leisure time in the world. The drift to the Sun Belt therefore involves great numbers of the retired and, as we shall see again in Chapters 17 and 20, there are communities in the south and west which cater particularly to them.

There is still, therefore, an inter-regional migration from east to west. The new feature is a movement from north to south. For a century past, the South has been a net loser, and in the decade of the 1960s five southern states were among the eight biggest losers in the nation. In the 1970s, this has changed. Not only Florida, with its great resort-retirement centers, but all the Gulf States except Louisiana have shared in the process of in-migration, and so has the whole Southeast and Arkansas.

Urbanization and Urban Problems

All over the world, cities are luring people from the countryside by offering them a fuller range of amenities and a wider choice of occupations than they could enjoy on the land. There can be few areas in the world where the range is wider or the freedom of movement for the individual is greater than in North America. It is here, consequently, that we find the phenomenon of urbanization and its attendant problems developing in what is perhaps its most complex form.

For the concentration into a few small areas of a large population, formerly distributed rather evenly over the inhabited parts of the continent, is bound to be accompanied by problems. One problem is that it involves a reorientation of the whole machinery of supply. Another is that it produces an intense competition for space and site between the various site-using organs of urban life.

The Central Business District (C.B.D.) of a North American city: Five Points, Atlanta. The photograph illustrates clearly the main components of the modern C.B.D.—a concentration of tall office, bank, and hotel blocks contrasting sharply with the generally low building-level of the structures that surround them. There is an intensive search for parking space, often found on the roofs of the central buildings. In this metropolis of the Southeast, banks and financial houses occupy most of the key sites. Atlanta is peculiar in only one respect: its C.B.D. is not laid out on the usual American gridiron of streets intersecting at right angles. *(Atlanta Chamber of Commerce)*

Whereas with a dispersed, rural population these can be—and in practice usually are—scattered, these organs must be arranged both according to their purposes and their site-deserving values. Space has now become precious—too precious to waste on functions that could equally well be accommodated in peripheral locations and away from the center of the concentration, where the value of space is likely to be lower.

Left to themselves these functions of community life—government, commerce, retail sales, residence—will generally sort themselves out into zones or sectors within the city, according to the value or the amenity of various sites. But now a new dimension must be introduced: the change brought about either by technological development or by growth of the urban area. What this means is that the size of the space pre-empted by or for any particular function cannot be constant; it will alter as time goes by. Most American cities today, for example, have large areas, often close to their centers, occupied by railway yards. These yards date from the nineteenth century, when the railway was the dominant carrier; indeed, when the railway was often the creative force bringing the urban area into being (see p. 149) and so took pride of place. Today these yards may well be only lightly used if at all; in any case, there is no technical reason why they should occupy valuable central space rather than be located on the fringe. But unless the railway chooses to remove them they continue to exist as an urban relic, denying the space to other users. In an era when we have grown accustomed to the idea of recycling all kinds of once-used products, we need to think in terms of recycling urban space.

The more common case, however, is that the growing city finds that areas formerly occupied by particular functions are no longer large enough to accommodate those functions when the population of the city increases. The government premises or business districts which served an urban population of half a million are too small for a city of two or three million. So there is a constant pressure by each function for enlargement of its space allotment, a process of continuous change along the boundaries of the functional sectors, and a constant need to adapt the existing pattern to new demands, or habits, or means of transport within the community.

The more rapid the growth of the city, the greater the rate of change within its sectors. In North America growth can be very rapid indeed, at least judged by European norms. In this chapter, for example, we have already noted the existence of urban areas which doubled their population in the past ten years; as it happens, examples of such rapid growth can be found at some place on the continent during most of the decades of the past century, although the actual size of the centers was smaller in the past. Under these circumstances, American cities are in an almost constant state of being rebuilt; a hole in the ground and a half-finished look are not unusual. Sociologists are beginning to discover what this process of constant change does to the inhabitants. Their findings are disturbing.

Before we go on to consider some of the problems that arise from the process of urbanization, we should pause to notice that it has not taken place at a uniform rate all over the continent. The following table shows that in the United States it is a phenomenon of much longer standing in the Northeast than it is in the South and the West, where even in 1970 the urban proportion of the population was in most cases appreciably below the national average. But it is in these southern and west-

ern areas that some very high rates of change have recently been registered. If we exclude the decade of the 1930s, which almost everywhere saw a drift of the unemployed from the cities back to the land during the Depression years, the West South Central region (Texas, Oklahoma, Arkansas, and Louisiana) has recorded decennial increases in the proportion of its population counted as urban of 6.0, 6.8, 9.3, 13.4, 11.5, and 8.0 percent since 1900. The Mountain region recorded increases of 11.3 and 12.7 percent in the past two decades, while the most striking changes in the 1960s came in two regions noted for their traditional attachment to agriculture—the South Atlantic (16.1 percent increase in urban proportion) and the Pacific region (17.7 percent increase), which is now by a considerable margin the most highly urbanized part of the nation. By contrast, urbanization seems to have reached a standstill in New England, where there has been no significant change in the urban proportion since 1910.

Nor has the character of urbanization been precisely the same in all regions: in some, urban growth has led to the creation, in the first instance, of a few very large cities while in others the average size of a city is much smaller. On the whole, the growth of supercities has been most marked (1) in the Middle Atlantic region, where the earliest large cities of Anglo-America grew up, acting effectively as poles of growth and overshadowing their competitors, and (2) on the Pacific Coast, where some 80 percent of the urban population is to be found in S.M.S.A.s with more than one million inhabitants. In some areas of more recent urbanization, however, the process has led instead to the growth of small and

United States: Percent Urban, by Region, 1900–1970

	1900	1910	1920	1930	1940	it1950	1960	1970
New England	68.6	73.4	76.2	77.2	76.1	74.8	75.1	76.4
Middle Atlantic	65.1	70.2	74.6	77.2	79.1	75.6	72.1	81.7
East North Central	45.2	52.7	60.8	66.4	65.5	66.3	67.3	74.8
West North Central	28.4	33.1	37.7	41.8	44.2	49.9	56.0	63.7
South Atlantic	19.2	23.1	28.8	24.1	36.5	41.6	47.6	63.7
East South Central	14.9	18.6	22.4	28.0	29.3	35.5	43.5	54.6
West South Central	16.2	22.2	29.0	38.3	39.7	53.1	64.6	72.6
Mountain	32.2	35.8	36.5	39.3	42.7	49.1	60.4	73.1
Pacific	46.4	56.8	62.2	67.6	65.2	63.6	68.3	86.0

(Source: B. Chinitz and R. Dusansky, "The Patterns of Urbanisation within Regions of the United States," *Urban Studies*, vol. ix(1972), p.292 for 1900–60; 1970 figures added.)

medium-sized cities and has even produced some conscious resistance to the idea that the giant city is—or should be—the inevitable end-product of all urbanization.

Given this background, what are the practical problems that have to be faced? They can be grouped into three or four categories: physical, economic and administrative, and social, or perhaps psychological. Space permits us merely to mention each category here, but later chapters contain a number of references to specific examples of these problems in individual cities.

Physical Problems

The basic physical problems are twofold: how to fit into the available space the right combination of functions and how to provide for the necessary volume of movement into and out of the city. Under "movement" we naturally include the inflow and outflow of people, but we must not overlook as equally vital to the survival of the city the inflow of water supplies and the outward transfer of sewage and urban waste. New York's water supply has been precarious for decades, while both Los Angeles and San Francisco bring in their water from hundreds of miles away. And in closely urbanized areas there is often nowhere to dump waste except on the territory of a neighboring community, which can hardly be considered a solution to the problem.

Theoretically, as the demand for urban functions changes, there should be a process of replacement so that, for example, disused railway tracks become roads, or head offices of national firms replace neighborhood shops. In practice this replacement is never complete: once a city exists no planner, not even those in the bombed cities of Germany and Japan after 1945, has ever had a perfect *tabula rasa* on which to build. Replacement is never total; there are always relics of earlier urban phases. Furthermore, there is always a time-lag in the replacement: there are always zones of transition, in which replacement is not immediate but is a long drawn-out and apparently haphazard process.

Everybody knows that the standard modern solution for a physical lack of space in the city center is to build upward. While this certainly is a solution to the problem of providing more office space in the central city without increasing its diameter, it is a solution that generates more problems in its wake. For all the movement to and from these high-rise buildings is still confined to earth. All the workers—or the groceries—moving into these buildings must do so at ground level. In the so-called "vertical city," the critical point is where the vertical and horizontal planes meet. Sooner or later, building upward will lead to impossible congestion on the ground floor.

It is rather curious that the North American concern for economy in using space is generally confined to the centers of cities, while the suburbs consist of detached homes, only one or two storys high, and stretch for miles. Here the space problem is the opposite of that in the city center: how to provide and support urban services among a very diffuse population (which nevertheless expects services of a high urban quality); how to provide, for example, urban transport when the density of population is so low as to make the bus lines uneconomical to run, or how to dispose of garbage when the city extends for many miles in all directions.

Economic and Administrative Problems

As soon as we speak of "competition" for space within the city, we imply an economic factor, for this kind of competition is normally decided by bids made on the open market; that is, each urban space user, whether as an individual or as an organization, decides what space is worth to him and offers accordingly for it. Space has become a very valuable commodity—so valuable, in fact, that usable space is being sought out and even the air space above a railway line or an old dock can be bought and sold, just so long as it can be linked to earth by some kind of foundation.

But in most cities this competition applies to only *some* of the urban surface and *some* of the urban functions. Alongside the economic life of the city, which produces the kind of competition so far described, there is the administrative life—the necessary services of the community which may not be revenue producing at

Suburban retailing: South Center Shopping Center, King's County, State of Washington, 1976. Opened in 1968, this center engulfed 112 acres (45.3 ha) of prime agricultural land. It is strategically situated close to the intersection of two major highways, Interstates 5 and 405. *(U.S. Soil Conservation Service)*

all. They stand no chance in a system of competitive land values, but the city cannot afford to be without them. Often, the only way to secure space for them is to exercise in some way a government's power of eminent domain—to override the workings of the open property market. This has, of course, become common practice today; cities have zoning ordinances and issue building permits. But it is still very often a complaint in City Hall that the city cannot acquire at reasonable prices the land needed for new hospitals or schools. Compared with the private and corporate individuals who make up its population, the city itself has become a pauper.

The poverty of the cities today stems from another quite different source: the tendency among people who work in them to live, spend, and pay taxes outside the city area. The flight to the suburbs steadily reduces the city's tax revenues; yet its expenditures cannot be proportionately reduced; the streets must still be lit and policed for the sake of the remaining inhabitants (who will nevertheless complain that the services have deteriorated). What is particularly debilitating for the city is that

higher-income taxpayers usually move outside the city and are lost to it, while inside the city there is a growing concentration of the lower-income groups. By this process, the tax base of the city is steadily eroded, while expenditure shows no parallel reduction.

One obvious way to overcome this problem is to allow the city to increase its area so as to include its own suburbs. Cities all over the world have been doing this for decades, to obtain control over fresh space and more taxable property. Equally consistently, the suburban communities fight against annexation: they have no wish to give up local control, or to pay higher local taxes to help subsidize the administration of central slum areas. This is not an American refrain only; it is at least as characteristically European. But the only practical alternative to annexation, if the city is to find space enough and revenue enough to survive, will be the compulsory takeover for public purposes of central areas, where some of the suburban businessmen have their offices, a process which one can only feel would be even less popular to the suburbs than that of being swallowed up by the city. Urbanization today on the North American scale calls for new structures of local government and administration, and some metropolitan areas, such as Toronto, have already experimented with these.

Social Problems

Impressions gained from pictures of slums occupied by ethnic minorities and reports of crime and violence on the streets have made the social aspects of North America's urbanization those most familiar to the outsider. It is not that other cities are free from such problems, but rather that in North America they seem to reach crisis dimensions. It is both interesting and necessary to try to see why.

In North America, the development of these social problems has been powerfully stimulated by a number of factors, peculiar—at least in their combination—to the continent. Several of these factors we have already encountered in this chapter; what now concerns us is their contribution to the problem of the cities. One such factor is certainly the size of the immigrant flow

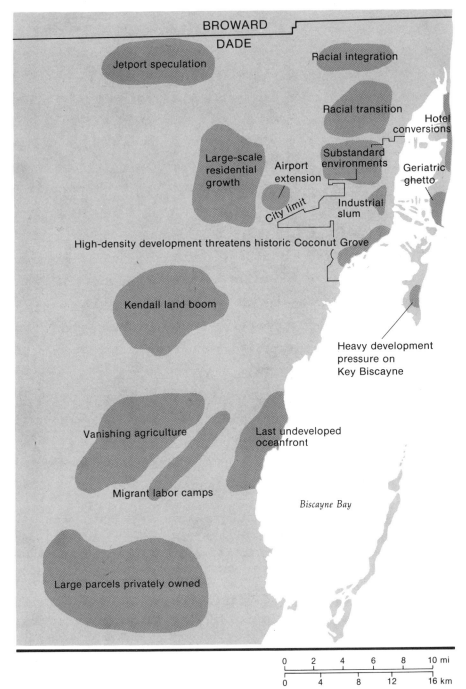

Fig. 2-6. Urban problems of the American city: A sample from Miami that gives an impression of the variety of spatial ills that can overtake a city—even a very modern city. Similar impressionistic maps could be compiled for all the cities of North America, although Miami, perhaps, has more than its fair share of these problems.

and the variety of its origins. We saw how the immigrants tended to stay together for help and security, so forming a whole series of ethnic neighborhood groups and a complex structure of relationships as each group strove to climb the social ladder ahead of newer arrivals—Irish ahead of Italians, or Italians ahead of Poles.

Upon this varied and fragmented urban population we have then to superimpose the effects of (1) very rapid urban growth, which would have created social flux in the most stable of societies, let alone in the circumstances which then existed; (2) the unprecedented freedom of movement created first by suburban transport

Problems of the American city: The Lower East Side of New York, with uncleared garbage and empty buildings. Some of these have been abandoned and some set on fire, while others are in process of being torn down. (Childa Bijur, 1978)

and then by individual car ownership, which freed the population from the formerly inevitable tie between workplace and residence, enabling people to choose their neighborhood and their neighbors; (3) Civil Rights legislation, operating in the economic and administrative spheres, but unable to affect social relationships, so that these latter became a repository for the residue of all the hostilities and prejudices formerly spread throughout the community's life. When we add to these factors the general absence of planning measures typical of most urban growth in North America before the Second World War, we may well conclude that there is nothing surprising about the situation as we see it today.

What appear to be the psychological effects of these urban conditions upon the inhabitants have now become clear. Where rapid change is creating so ephemeral a townscape, where landmarks disappear overnight and are replaced by structures which themselves often have only a very limited life span, the instability of the built environment seems to communicate itself to the population. People lose their sense of association with, or pride in, their city and district and they move frequently, often for no other reason that to acquire a prestige address. Whites become insecure and move because the frontier of the ghetto has advanced too close for their liking, while the black or brown inhabitants across the "frontier" develop a ghetto psychology which inhibits them from moving outside the ghetto to work, even when jobs are available elsewhere. The old concept of a homeplace quickly evaporates in a society where most people are either transients or siege victims.

60

3

Government, Nation and State

The patterns of a country's human geography are shaped not only by the physical factors that govern land use or routeways, but also by the political conditions under which settlement and development take place. In North America there are a number of such conditions whose effects on the distribution of economic activity have been of great importance, and it is the purpose of the next three chapters to call attention to these effects, as a necessary preliminary to the study of the continent's regional geography.

The Nation States

The first and most obvious of these political conditions is that in Anglo-America there are two separate nation-states. They share a common border from the Atlantic to the Pacific, with Alaska as a detached part of the southern nation "behind the lines." Although the two countries are justly proud of their good relations, which today make it possible for them to think in terms of military cooperation rather than military rivalry, the situation has not al-

ways been so happy, nor is the relationship free from periodic tensions. Some of these concern the exploitation of resources which the two countries share. Others arise because each country has given shelter to refugees from the other—the British turned French settlers out of Nova Scotia, and they moved to Louisiana; Loyalists moved north into Canada at the end of the Revolutionary War; draft resisters found shelter in Canada in the 1960s.

But in a deeper sense the very existence of two nations in this one continent can only be explained in terms of a long-standing aversion; an aversion which has kept Canada, with its smaller population and slower industrial development, doggedly unmoved by the apparent advantages it might gain if it joined the United States. And these are quite substantial. Not only would Canadians be able to buy more cheaply those American goods on which they now pay customs duties, but they would be linking themselves with a country where Gross Product per capita is more than 20 percent greater than in their own. In other words, for their independence Canadians are willing to pay an economic penalty that may amount to the forfeit of 20 percent of their potential wealth. The Canadians are, in the words of H. Hardin, "the world's oldest and continuing anti-Americans.[1]

The existence of these two nations therefore raises the primary question: why is there a Canada at all? The existence of any nation presupposes two sets of factors—*negative* factors which deter it from linking up with a neighbor, and *positive* factors which give it, as an independent unit, a reason for its separateness. In the Canadian case, however, the negative factors have been, and still are, much stronger than the positive. Most Canadians are sure that they *do not* want to be Americans; what they *do* want to be or to do is much less clear.

Canada came into existence as a political unit in 1867. The Confederation born in that year grew out of two considerations: (1) the practical need for a working compromise between the French in Lower Canada (Québec) and the British in Upper Canada (Ontario), and (2) fear of the United States, where the Civil War had ended in 1865, leaving the country with the world's largest army and a vocal section of the public suggesting the piecemeal takeover of Canadian territory.

Thus fear played a part in the forming of the Canadian union, and, although the *military* fear of the 1860s soon passed off, the early *economic* fears which led Canada to build canal and rail routes to the West simply to compete with the American routes have never evaporated; rather, they have grown with the threat of economic and cultural domination by the United States. To justify these fears, Canadians can point to their growing dependence on the United States as a trading partner, to the impact of American culture at the popular level, and to the enormous total of American investment in Canadian industry, as described in Chapter 7. It is probably useless to meet these fears by pointing out that, among other things, (1) Canadian-American trade is developing in accordance with trends recognizable all over the world and not only here, (2) the "American" cultural influence may simply be the impact of a standard of living higher than any known before, first attained in the United States and now spreading to Canada, and (3) on a per capita basis there is much more Canadian investment in the United States, and there are many more Canadians working there, than there are American investment or Americans working in Canada. The defensive stance of the Canadian government and people has become second nature. In the words of a wise Canadian:

It must be recognized that the nature of the relations between Canada and the United States is such that explosions of Canadian resentment will occur periodically. The intimacy of the relations of the two peoples and the disparity of power between the two states make it inevitable that American indifference and power will provoke Canadian resentment from time to time. The United States, it is to be hoped, will remove such grievances as can be removed and will suffer the outbursts philosophically, as befits a great power. Canada, it is to be hoped, will avert the accumulation of grievances by dealing firmly and responsibly with grievances as they arise, and so keep the explosions at as long intervals as possible.[2]

In a country the size of Canada the physical obstacles to unity of themselves are tremendous. One would therefore expect that the negative grounds of separateness and the physical barriers to unity would need to be balanced by very strong positive motives for political coherence if the nation were to survive. Yet the striking fact is that in Canada, the positive forces of nationalism—of Canadian nationalism, at least—are hard to discover. The French and British elements (who together make up 75 percent of the population) agree that they do not want to be Americans, but they agree on virtually nothing else, and certainly not on an emotional attachment to the British crown.

This failure to establish national goals and achieve agreement about them is the more striking when we realize that Canada is now playing a most responsible role at the international level. Before the Second World War, Ca-

[1]H. Hardin, *A Nation Unaware: The Canadian Economic Culture,* Douglas, Vancouver, 1974, p. 3.

[2]W.L. Morton, *The Canadian Identity,* Univ. of Wisconsin Press, Madison, 1968, p. 82.

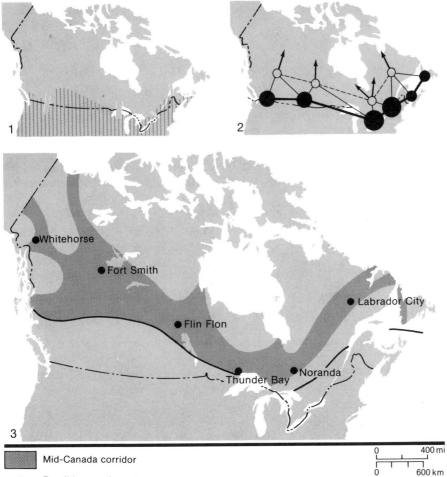

Fig. 3-1. Three views of Canada: (1) Canada as an extension of the United States. This view, which is discussed in the text, sees Canada as constituting simply a part of the settled area of North America detached from the larger (U.S.) section by the political circumstance of the international boundary. Compare (2). (2) Canada as a nation with the national task of occupying the empty Northlands. Like (1), this map is entirely impressionistic: there is little evidence on which to base such an image of Canada's existence and national purpose. (3) Canadian development concentrated within the Mid-Canada Development Corridor, as defined in numerous recent discussions of the Canadian future and as explained in the accompanying text.

Mid-Canada corridor

● Possible growth centers

0   400 mi
0   600 km

nada was a young country with a small population, and little was asked or expected of her except within the British Commonwealth. But the new generations of states born since 1945 have made Canada "middle-aged," and certainly middle-sized. It is now one of the relatively large and mature nation-states, and acts as such: to the Colombo Plan program for southern Asia, for example, Canada has contributed generously. But it has done all this without ever defining clear goals for the nation at home.

To the question, what distinctive role can or does Canada play, Figure 3-1 offers two possible answers. These maps are entirely impressionistic of course; they do not correspond to reality but to two widely held images of Canada. The first, which certainly is fixed in the minds of many Americans, is that the occu-

pied part of Canada (the term Canadian *ecumene* is commonly used) is merely a series of extensions from regions lying south of the border, disconnected from each other and forming natural appendages of the United States. In this view it is pointless to maintain customs barriers that cut off these appendages, or to duplicate factories on the Canadian side, making goods which could be more cheaply shipped in from the United States. In other words, there is no "distinctive role" for Canada to play.

In a rather curious way the Canadian government has encouraged this view of Canada by delegating some of its own powers to the individual provinces. The results have been that (1) in matters of policy the provinces tend to grow apart, so that the idea of a truly national policy or goal becomes more and more remote, and (2) the federal government in its internal policies does little more than help one province or region at a time, by a series of ad hoc measures. Legislation helping the Prairie wheat farmers is followed by subsidies for the Atlantic Provinces or government investment in British Columbia, in a process that has been described as "Political self-bribery."[3] Within Canada, therefore, what counts is not so much a national policy as the strength of regional interests. But systems that promote regional values and consciousness are working against national consciousness, not contributing to it. Only if the nation has something to offer as a nation can feeling on the national level hope to transcend regional sentiment.

The second map in Figure 3-1 offers another view of Canada as a nation—a nation, moreover, with a task worthy of it. This common task which, it is argued, would truly unite all parts of the nation is the mastery of the great, empty Northlands. Just as the advance of the western frontier tended to mold society in the United States and to forge its wildly assorted population into a single nation so, the argument runs, the northern frontier of Canada can influence the country's future by drawing Canadians together in the face of a colossal task. Here is, or should be, the Canadian Heartland.

Whatever logic this view may possess, there is almost no evidence that the nation as a whole is tackling or even considering such a task. If the northern frontier advances at one point, it may well be withdrawing at another; if a new mining community springs up, it merely replaces another which has reached the point of exhaustion and closure. In Trevor Lloyd's words, "Canadians may be a venturesome, northern people at heart, but when it comes to the things that matter they continue to live as far south as their citizenship permits." What they have so far built, he concludes, is simply "a capstone to the American edifice. . . . They have yet to build a nation of their own."[4]

With Figure 3-1 before us as an impression, it is perhaps a suitable moment to introduce the third map, which illustrates a concept that has become widely known and formally recognized in Canada during recent years, the "Mid-Canada Development Corridor." In a certain sense it is a view of Canada and its future which is a compromise between the other two. It looks northward, but not too far north. It asserts a real and distinctive task for Canadian economic development but keeps that task within the bounds of fulfilment (see p. 329). It foresees a concentration of effort along the national axis rather than taking the more ambitious view of developing the whole North. It is a framework for planning and for investment which can and will be modified as the years go by. At the same time it could be argued that it shelves the problem of what to do with the remoter North. That problem will remain to be solved by future generations of Canadians.

In recent years, Canada has been going through an identity crisis unprecedented in its history as a nation. It had no sooner celebrated its centennial in 1967 than the separatists in French Québec stepped up their campaign to take the province out of the federation—to set up an independent nation. It is the same issue as the United States faced in the years before 1861; even the arguments and threats of the two sides sound familiar. In an era when communities of less than a million people are sovereign states and members of the United Nations, there is nothing bizarre about the 6.25 million inhabitants of Québec seeking a separate identity; the questions at issue are rather: how many of the 6.25 million actually want this and, given their particular position and resources, how likely they would be to create a viable state, and not merely to create it but to maintain it without lowering their own standard of living.

We shall return to this question of viability in Chapter 13. In the context of the present section, however, there is one other matter that must be raised: what would be the future of a Canada *without* Québec? What would happen—what *could* happen—to this remainder? How would the Atlantic Provinces survive as part of the nation, given the enormous geo-

[3]Wilson, G.W., Gordon, S., and Judek, S., *Canada: An Appraisal of Its Needs and Resources,* University of Toronto Press, Toronto, 1961, p. xl.

[4]In J. Warkentin, ed., *Canada: A Geographical Appraisal,* Methuen, Toronto and London, 1967, p. 585.

graphical separation between Gaspé and the Ottawa River (not to speak of the considerable French Canadian element in New Brunswick's population)? History's only close parallel to such a national structure is that of the division between East and West Pakistan. The example is not an encouraging one.

We can only wait and see. In the meantime, and whatever its justification as a line of separation, the U.S.-Canadian border exists. Its effect on the movement of goods and people has been somewhat reduced by sensible arrangements made by the two governments, and today it is crossed by oil pipes and power lines, while international agreements cover the movement of tourists and the flow of rivers. But it still has its effects, as we shall see in later chapters, in dividing into two some regions whose interests are at one, and in acting as a kind of strainer on the flow of ideas and even of money from south to north across the continent.

A Federal Constitution

Both Canada and the United States have federal constitutions. The significance of this fact for our present purposes is that while the central government alone possesses authority in such spheres as foreign policy or defence, the local units—the provinces in Canada and the states in the United States—possess wide powers over their internal affairs, including power of taxation. Since in practice each unit pursues its own financial policies, notable differences in economic conditions may occur between adjacent states or provinces.

Some of these differences are large in scale and have important effects on landscape patterns. A state may set out to attract new industries or to lure producers from other states by constructing a tax system that favors manufacturing. State governments are commonly judged by their success in bringing new business to the state through such policies. In a highly competitive economy like that of the United States, unfavorable local legislation may seriously handicap local producers. One of the chief reasons cited by the textile manufacturers of New England, for example, for

their inability to compete with their rivals in the South (see p. 144) was the high level of taxation and compulsory welfare expenditure required by Massachusetts and Rhode Island, and this was a contributing cause to the industry's move southward. By contrast Nevada has built a flourishing tourist trade on an absence of controls, legalized gambling, and the slogan "Anything Goes."

The same differences are to be found, however, on a much smaller scale. Gasoline costs more at the Kentucky or Tennessee end of the Mississippi River bridges (thanks to a higher state tax) than it does at the Missouri end, half a mile away, a fact of which local motorists are naturally aware. Patterns of exploitation on an Alberta oil field are different from those in Texas. In short, although in the United States the erection of barriers to interstate commerce is specifically forbidden in the Constitution, differences in fiscal and resource policies are in both countries sufficient to provide both location incentives and interstate rivalries.

A corollary of the division of powers between the federal and the state or provincial governments is that if the powers of the states are limited, so too are those of the central government, in the United States more narrowly than in Canada. The United States Constitution specified the powers of the federal government and reserved all other powers (Tenth Amendment, 1791) to "the States respectively, or to the people." In order to intervene in any internal affairs, therefore, the federal government must first prove its constitutional right to do so. In any action that has the appearance of a new departure, it can count on the dogged opposition of the states' righters.

A good example of this constitutional problem is to be seen in regional developments such as those in the Tennessee and Missouri valleys. In these areas, which cover several states, what is clearly needed is a concerted, supra-state plan. But all that the federal government may implement is a project for improving the navigation of the Tennessee—or Missouri—since the Constitution gives the federal authority the task of removing barriers to interstate commerce (in this case, river traffic), but gives it no power to plan states' economies for them. This may explain the federal government's apparently misguided pre-occupation with rivers rather than regions. (For a further discussion of this point, see pp. 281 and 336.)

In this kind of backhanded way the federal government tries to do good by carrying out functions of government which its opponents claim that it does not constitutionally possess. The truth of the matter is that a federal authority has two ways, and only two, of overcoming the legal limitation of its powers: example and bribery. Under the first heading, "example," it can create model legislation or codes of practice—for planning, labor relations, conservation, or health. This it can then mail out for information, and it can also apply its model programs to any areas which it owns or controls itself, in the hope that lower levels of government will follow suit—that they will find the example worth imitating. The U.S. government has tried hard to set a good example—by employing numbers of ethnic minority members in its services so as to promote equal opportunities and by producing useful model codes for pollution control and local planning. And since it owns 763 million acres (309 million ha) of public land and controls the District of Columbia, in which the federal capital stands, it has plenty of space, and different kinds of space, in which to follow its own advice. The federal government of Canada owns almost 1 billion acres (405 million ha). The management of these federal lands can and should serve as an example to the states, to local governments, and to individuals.

The second method available to a federal government tied by its constitutional limitations is a kind of bribery. It is to offer money to a state or local authority which will follow a particular course or program, and to withhold it if specified standards are not reached. It pays with federal money to have its will done in spheres where it is powerless to insist. Today the number of such federal programs is enormous. In many of them the principle of "matching funds" is used to enforce standards—the federal government will only share in the cost if it approves the program. The local government or the individual, in order to obtain the funds, conforms to the federal standard.

It is by these methods, as we shall see in Chapter 4, that the federal government has introduced in the 1970s a batch of measures for safeguarding the environment—necessary, overdue, and combining our two principles. By way of example, the U.S. government has bound itself to issue for every project it proposes an Environmental Impact Assessment, which will describe the project's effect, list the alternative strategies available, and alert the public to possible environmental damage before that damage is done. By way of payment, the government has set aside several hundred million dollars for a program of cleaning out polluted lakes and to continue the work begun in clearing out the pollution of slum areas in cities a decade and more ago. By methods such as these a federal government can gradually standardize practices and improve the quality of life, without ever possessing the power to intervene directly.

THE LOWER LEVELS OF GOVERNMENT

Frustrating as it must be for the federal authorities, most of the powers which they would like to exercise—and indeed *try* to exercise by the methods just mentioned—are possessed instead by the states and provinces. It is at this level of government that the reserves of power are to be found. In particular, the all-important police power rests with the states; that is, "the general authority of a government or sovereign entity to take action and legislate in the public interest or the general health, safety, welfare, and morals of the people"; it has to do with "the *regulatory* power of the state."[5]

These powers the states can and do delegate to their own sub-units: counties, cities, or townships. What they will not do is to surrender them willingly to the federal government. But the particular difficulties here are that (1) some states have delegated too much of their power to the lower levels—to governments which have neither sufficient resources nor sufficient scope to exercise them properly,

[5]R. R. Linowes and D. T. Allensworth, *The States and Land-Use Control*, Praeger, New York, 1975, p. 40.

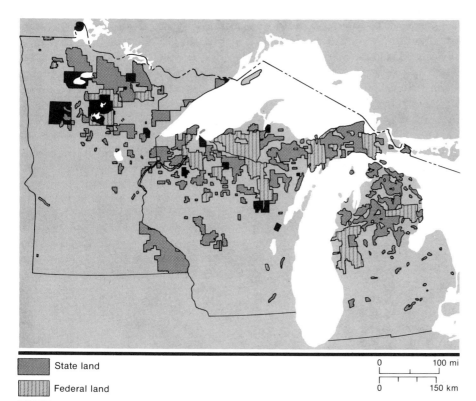

Fig. 3-2. The United States: The mixture of public and special land ownership. The area shown is the northern Great Lakes region of the United States, where there is a characteristic intermixture of federal, state, and special owners; in this case the latter category is represented by the Indian reservations.

State land

Federal land

Indian land

0   100 mi

0   150 km

and (2) some states exercise the police, or regulatory, powers much less than others. This is true of all aspects of government activity, but it is especially true in two areas of particular interest to geographers—the economy and the environment. One of the underlying causes of economic weakness and misuse of land and resources is the reluctance of state governments to enforce regulations which, from a national point of view, are desirable; which the federal government would enforce if it had the power to do so, but which lie outside its constitutional range.

A recent study[6] of the performance of state governments in the field of planning revealed how wide are the discrepancies from state to state. The results showed that the state scoring highest marks in this field was Hawaii. Second was Wisconsin, a state long noted for its concern with issues of environmental management and the "think tank" for much of today's

6A. J. Catanese, "Reflections on State Planning Evaluation," *State Planning Issues 1973* (Council of State Governments, Lexington, Ky, 1973), p. 27.

planning legislation. The Middle Atlantic States scored high, no doubt because the pressure of population and the demands on space have obliged them to face planning issues squarely and so, too, did California. At the other end of the scale, Alabama, Arkansas, and Mississippi had done little in this field; the idea of the state exercising planning powers found only very limited public acceptance, and this was also the case in the home of "anything goes," Nevada.

A number of states have passed their powers on to local governments where special interests can too easily block efforts to regulate: county interests block state plans, and recalcitrant townships block county plans. But in the 1970s, with environmental issues in the news and environmentalist groups doing their best to keep them there, the states seem to be resuming some of the regulatory powers which they too readily handed over. As Bosselman and Callies comment, "states, not local governments, are the only existing political entities capable of devising innovative techniques and governmental structures to solve problems such as pollution, destruction of fragile natural resources, the shortage of decent housing, and many other problems which are now widely recognized as simply beyond the capacity of local governments acting alone."[7]

The state governments, in other words, should govern; they should *exercise* the powers which they have fought so hard to keep in their own hands. If they do not, nobody else can.

Sectionalism

The existence of only two nations within the vast area of Anglo-America means that there is plenty of scope for the development of loyalties more local than the national. To some extent, allegiance to the province or state meets this social need, but the particularly American phenomenon is sectionalism—a unity of outlook and interest within a region.

That this is so is due in the first place to distance and isolation. Over so large an area natural conditions are varied enough to create conflicting needs and interests in the various regions, and to draw together into sectional groups states or provinces with similar characteristics of environment or economies. Secondly, the sectional feeling derives importance from the fact that the boundaries of the states and provinces are for the most part arbitrarily drawn along lines of latitude or longitude, and do not correspond with any geographical reality. Thus the section is the more natural, if informal, subdivision of the nation.

We have already seen how the divergent interests of the various regions and provinces have created sectional interests in Canada—interests which may be so strong that the section commands more loyalty than the nation. This development of Canadian sectionalism follows naturally from the division of the populated areas into four parts, each isolated from the other three by circumstances of physical geography, and with the largest area split again

[7]F. Bosselman and D. Callies, *The Quiet Revolution in Land Use Control*, U.S. Government Printing Office, Washington, D.C., 1972, p. 3.

into two sections by the deep divide between French and British. The long debate that preceded federation in 1867 was not all concerned with the threat of United States expansionism; there was also much discussion of the sectional issues—of tariffs and their effects, of hinterlands for ports, and, above all, of the transcontinental railway links, upon the promise of which the adherence of British Columbia to the federation was ultimately confirmed. That the reconciliation of such conflicting sectional interests should ever have been made possible constituted, as one writer has expressed it, "the miracle of union."

Two other examples of sectional conflicts in North American history call for mention. One is the long-continuing friction, on both sides of the border, between the settled East and the moving frontier. This somewhat over-dramatized aspect of American history may be explained in various terms. It was a conflict between those who, confronted by the apparently unlimited prospects of the empty West, wanted freedom to occupy and exploit it, and those far to the east who wanted to control the occupation. It was a conflict between those who saw the possibilities but lacked the resources to develop them, and those who could finance and equip the expansion—but on their own terms.

In this case the sections moved geographically as the frontier advanced; St. Louis or Winnipeg, once full of the pioneer spirit, became conservative and "Eastern" by contrast with Denver or Edmonton. But of the whereabouts of the sections in the other great conflict there could be little doubt, for the dividing lines were crystallized in secession and battle. Sectionalism—or a "form of regional persecution complex" as it has been called—found its classic expression in the American Civil War of 1861–65.

The Civil War, as Lincoln constantly emphasized in his efforts to preserve the Union, represented a clash between sectionalism and nationalism. Southern feeling—the regional persecution complex—was fostered on the economic side by federal tariff policies unfavorable to southern exporters, and on the political side by the swelling antislavery campaign.

And quite apart from these threats to southern interests was another sectional issue which was resolved by the war: would the great new West become tributary to the North or to the South?

In the event, sectionalism was defeated but not eliminated. (Indeed, in the South it has achieved both an aura of romance and a solid monetary value in the form of a tourist traffic.) After the war a "three-way" sectionalism replaced the "two-way" prewar split between North and South. In due course the West, for all its wealth of natural resources, found itself in a relationship with the Northeast, not much more favorable than did the defeated South. The Northeast had the financial power and the political skills; it controlled the railways and the principal market outlets. We shall consider further some of the economic legacies of this relationship in Chapter 9. For the moment we need only note that the habit of "thinking Western"—or Southern, or Midwestern—is deeply engrained in American culture, and that to each of these sections popular fancy attaches certain stereotypes of custom, dress, diet, and habits.

4

Government,
Land and Water

Public Land and Private Land

One of the earliest problems to confront the infant republic of the United States of America after its formation during the war of 1776–83 was the creation of a land policy. No branch of the small federal government was more active than its Committee on Public Lands; none contributed more documents to those early records of government activity which today fill the volumes on library shelves entitled *Statutes At Large*.

There were excellent reasons why this should be so. There was, in the first place, the undeniable *political* fact that the United States, though now independent, shared the continent with four other powers. To the north lay Canada, retained by the British when thirteen, but only thirteen, of the American colonies opted for independence. To the west lay the French territory of Louisiana, claimed for France in the most grandiloquent but vaguest terms by seventeenth-century explorers who had little idea where they were, let alone what they were claiming. Immediately south of Georgia the Spanish Empire began, an empire

which stretched west to the Pacific and, for that matter, south to Cape Horn. Far away in the northwest the Russians were active, small in numbers but feeling their way down the coast into what is now northern California. Whatever decisions were taken about land, they were going to have international repercussions.

Then there was the *economic* consideration. It was one thing to set up, even on a modest scale, the machinery of a federal government; it was quite another to pay for it. The War of Independence had cost enormous sums, and the only sources of revenue available to the new government were (1) customs and excise duties which, since most colonial trade had been with the ex-enemy power of Great Britain, might well take time to amount to anything, and (2) the sale of whatever assets it possessed. There was in practice only one such asset—land. The sale of land would have to see the government through its early years.

The third reason why the land question occupied so much government time in those first two decades we may call *ideological*. For here was a situation without precedent. In Europe, from which most of America's colonists and institutions had come, there was no such thing as land that belonged to nobody. There were small areas of common land to which traditional rights of use existed, but even including these, all land ultimately had its owner, a landlord who held from an overlord, who in turn held from the king. The concept of land owned by a government rather than by an individual was a novelty. The Spanish empire, for example, was the personal estate of the king of Spain. All grants of land originated with him. But now a republican government had taken possession, in the name of the people, of a huge area not included in the original thirteen colonies (now states)—an area calculated in 1790 at 888,685 sq mi (2.30 million sq km), to which were added by the Louisiana Purchase of 1803 a further 827,192 sq mi (2.14 million sq km), and at various dates between 1819 and 1853, over a million sq mi (about 2.60 million sq km) of the former Spanish empire.

Apart from the precedents set by the land policies of the former colonies—policies which had been very diverse in character—there was nothing to guide the new government at all; no example to follow; nothing but the ideals of the Constitution and the practical constraints of money, counterclaims, and defense. It is not surprising that mistakes were made: what is surprising is that in these circumstances policy was formulated as quickly as in fact it was, mistakes and all.

Eighty years later, the land question also played an important role in the negotiations over Canadian federation. West of the developed areas in Upper Canada—the peninsula of southern Ontario—there was a great wilderness barely marked by the settlements on the Red River of Manitoba and the gold fields of British Columbia. This land had been the preserve of the Hudson Bay Company, whose interest in furs had done nothing to encourage the human occupance of the area. At confederation or shortly afterward, most of the area passed into federal hands, a small government overseeing a very large area, but with one advantage —that it could learn from the mistakes of the United States. The Canadian government could, and did, formulate a land policy

marginally more suitable than that of its neighbor, while imitating it in so many ways, just as the American system was imitated, with local amendments, in the Australian settlements and the Argentinian colonies as the years went by.

Original land titles in British North America were European in character: the Crown granted land to individuals or to chartered companies and they in turn made grants to settlers. There was no shortage of land: there were differences in the size of a grant, but from the earliest days there was a clear distinction between lands already granted and lands still vacant; a distinction which in due course became that between private and public land. Each colony evolved its own policies about size of grant, conditions of sale, pattern of holding or survey, and attitude to squatting (that is, the occupance of public land by private individuals who had no legal title, but who claimed title by right of priority.)

The new federal government, steering a middle course between its belief that the public lands should be distributed to as many of the public as could benefit from them and the undeniable emptiness of the public purse, formulated an initial land policy which rested on two propositions: (1) Land should be sold, at a fixed price, to raise revenue for the government; (2) No land should be opened for sale before (a) Indian title to it had been extinguished by treaty (by which it was hoped to put an end to the long series of Indian wars), and (b) it had been surveyed by the government. The latter principle of "prior survey" was something of a novelty in the northern states; whereas, however, it existed in an embryonic form in New England, in the South it was almost completely new. In the southern states the land claimant normally went out, staked his claim, and then hired a surveyor to map it. The idea that emerged from the Committee on Public Lands was that not only the *location* of available lands would be predetermined by the survey, but also the *shape* and *size* of the unit.

The problem was simply stated: how to carry a survey across unknown lands inhabited by often-hostile Indians, given a shortage of

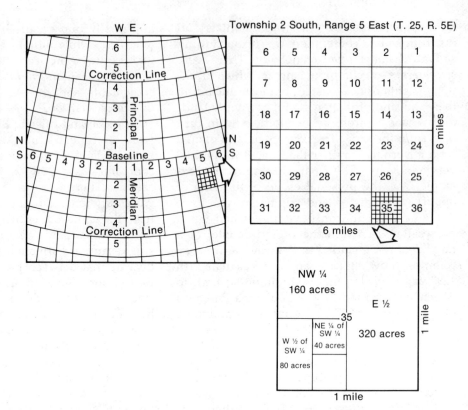

Fig. 4-1. The rectangular survey system of the United States, adopted in the last years of the eighteenth century and continued in its essentials to the present day on all lands of the United States disposed of subsequent to that date. The same rectangular system was adopted by the Canadians for the survey of their own West.

trained surveyors and a lack of money. The solution adopted was to become, in the following century, one of the most formative of all influences on the North American landscape. It was to survey the public lands in 6-mi (9.6 km) squares, forming a *township* of 36 sq mi (93.2 sq km), and later individual square miles (2.59 sq km) within the township, which were known as *sections*. Later still, the sections were divided into halves, quarters, eighths, and even sixteenths.

The Committee's reasoning was clear and logical. The simplest and quickest operation a surveyor could be called upon to perform was to lay out a straight line, from east to west or north to south. This yielded a cheap survey, within the competence of the available surveyors.[1] The only serious problem was that caused by laying out a rectangular grid on a spherical surface, and the surveyors were given detailed instructions about making allowances for this.[2] Besides the benefits of speed and cheapness, the system also had the advantage that it could always be rechecked by astronomical fix. It was hoped, too, that its regularity might reduce the amount of litigation about boundaries which arose wherever the casual southern system of "metes and bounds" was in force, and history has proved the expectation valid. Only where the gridiron of squares ran into patterns of previous French or Spanish landholdings did it cause problems (Fig. 4-2). These exceptions apart, the pattern of survey initiated in 1785 in the lands immediately beyond the Pennsylvania state line marched from there, westward across the continent, in an endless succession of squares that stretched all the way to the Pacific Ocean or eternity, and

[1]Anybody who imagines, however, that a straight line is something that even a child could lay out needs only to consult the 1:24,000 U.S. topographic maps today to see into how many different shapes a mile square can be missurveyed. In defense of the very first surveyors, however, it can at least be argued that they had to start work in the hilly, forested terrain of what is now southeastern Ohio, a peculiarly difficult area in which to see where they were going.

[2]The story of the survey is well told by W. Pattison, *Beginnings of the American Rectangular Survey System, 1784–1800*, Univ. of Chicago Dept. of Geography Research Paper No. 50, Chicago, 1957, and particularly by Hildegard B. Johnson, *Order Upon The Land*, Oxford Univ. Press, New York, 1976.

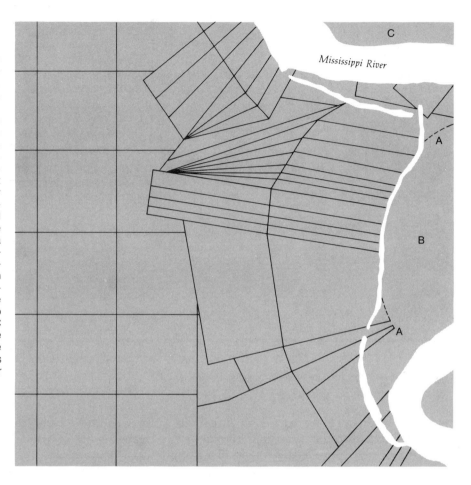

Fig. 4-2. A clash of survey patterns. In this area on the lower Mississippi, the old French survey pattern of "long lots" perpendicular to a river frontage antedates the American rectangular survey pattern. Lands disposed of by the French prior to the Louisiana Purchase of 1803 have been brought into the overall pattern; this legal maneuver occupied a great deal of time in the early years of the republic, before the two systems could be harmonized. At A the dashed line represents a former course of the Mississippi (which has constantly shifted its bed in the past 300 years of European occupance), and the property lines run down to this old course. B and C are two areas which have come into existence since the French survey was made, as the river changed course.

northward in due course to cover the Canadian prairies in their turn.

That the surveyor's checkerboard has imposed itself on the landscape of western North America is evident from one's first flight across the country. That it provided a framework for subsequent land policies of the American and Canadian governments we shall see in the next section. But one thing which has not been so immediately recognized by geographers or historians is its impact upon the growth of settlement. It turned it into a kind of lottery. For every one of those several million squares had exactly equal locational value, and four identical corners where it adjoined the neighboring sections. Which of those squares would prove to be the most important? Which of the section crossroads had the best hopes of becoming the focus of a metropolis? The questions are as unanswerable as if we were asking them about a chessboard. In practice, any one

of several million crossroads *might* be the site of a future Chicago—and a good many of them, as we shall see again in Chapter 14, aspired to be just that. In other words, the survey system provided for virtually unlimited competition since no one point had an advantage over any other.[3]

Whether or not the system worked to the benefit of the West would be hard to say. It may, for example, have encouraged the growth of too many central places in the formative years. What *is* clear is that the gridiron had other drawbacks. One was that it tended to maximize the length of roads needed to supply and serve a population settling the surveyed lands. Another was that travel was

[3]In the humid eastern sections covered by the survey, this statement would need to be modified by admitting that river and lakeshore sites had a clear advantage over the other squares. But further west the absence of navigable waterways removed even this element of choice.

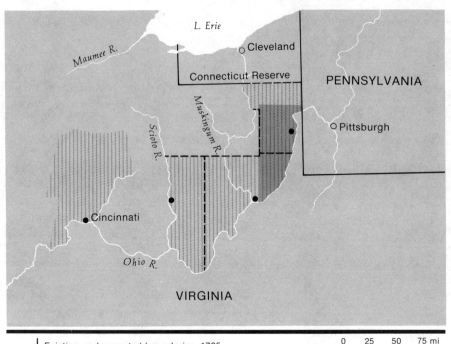

Fig. 4-3. Origins of the United States public lands survey. The system of rectangular survey began in what is now southeastern Ohio, in the so-called Seven Ranges. From there it spread across the continent to the Pacific.

☐ Existing and accepted boundaries, 1785

▨ Initial survey—The Seven Ranges, begun 1786

▥● First federal land districts and land offices, 1800

```
0    25   50   75 mi
├────┼────┼────┤
0    40   80   120 km
```

easy in north-south or east-west directions, but often to this day it is tedious to make diagonal journeys since all the roads run along the survey lines: one has to go around two sides of a triangle. A third drawback was that such a regular system left no gaps which could serve later as reserves of land; settlers were packed in, cheek by jowl, which was admirable in the early days when it prevented the frontier from fragmenting, but which poses immense problems today, when farmers are desperately seeking extra acreage in order to maintain the efficiency of their farm operations (see Fig. 6-6). But this brings us to our next topic—the distribution of land to the settler.

Land Disposal and Land Law

Driven by its own poverty, the U.S. government was in the land business from its earliest days. Only by disposing of its holdings could it obtain revenue, and in the disposal process

it was in competition with the individual states, most of which had lands within their own boundaries that they were anxious to have settled.

From the first, there was an idealistic hope that it might be possible to give away public lands in small quantities to penniless but worthy applicants who would be "actual cultivators" (the phrase recurs in early debates; clearly, the Americans had not forgotten the absentee landlords of Europe and the early colonies). It was an ideal eventually realized some 80 years later in the Homestead Act of 1862. But for the moment idealism had to bow to the necessity of placing a value on land (1) to raise revenue by selling it, and (2) to enable the government to pay off its ex-soldiers with land since it could not pay them with money. If land had no value, the soldiers would receive nothing for their service.

The first federal land law offered land at $2.00 an acre, cash ($4.95 per ha). The blocks offered were large, for the surveyors had not progressed beyond some initial six-mile squares, and there were few buyers. Land in the states was equally available and generally cheaper. With these beginnings, alterations in that first law of 1785 can best be understood as modifications to suit changing times and conditions.

1. The government was obliged to offer smaller units for sale. This implied, of course, an increasingly detailed—hence more expensive—survey. But it was the only way to create demand. In 1804, when Indiana was being settled, the federal government first began to deal in units which, for better or worse, came to figure in nearly all subsequent land laws— the quarter-section of 160 acres (64.8 ha). Further subdivisions came later, but the quarter-section achieved a kind of sanctity, which made it virtually impossible to dislodge it from congressmen's minds even decades later, when the frontier of settlement lay far out in the arid West and a quarter-section had about the same economic value as a small field back in the humid East.

2. The price had to be lowered and graduated. To offer all land, regardless of quality, at $2.00 an acre was nonsensical, especially in competition with the states. The price quickly fell to $1.25 an acre ($3.10 per ha). There was later added the principle of graduation whereby land which still had no buyers after years on the market, could be offered at progressively lower prices down to 12½ cents an acre (31 cents per ha). Seen in this light, the Homestead Act of 1862 represented the ultimate price reduction—to zero.

3. The original intention of selling land strictly for cash was modified to allow credit sales. At that point the revenue consideration in U.S. land policy was, for practical purposes, lost. The credit terms were progressively weakened, and the revenue from land fell off. Fortunately for the government, its income from customs duties proved unexpectedly buoyant, so that early in the nineteenth century the revenue factor in land policy began to diminish in importance, giving way on the one hand to the original streak of idealism about free distribution and, on the other, to the far-from-idealistic concern of the country to settle its public lands as quickly as possible to ward off potential claims by Britain, Spain (later Mexico), or Russia.

4. The principle of "prior survey" survived until 1841. In that year Congress passed the Preemption Act, the effect of which was to legalize squatting. A settler who had gone ahead of the surveyors could, when they caught up with him, now lawfully purchase a quarter-section of the land on which he had settled.

By the middle of the nineteenth century, a new principle effectively governed U.S. land policy, and was to govern that of Canada. Land was no longer seen primarily as a source of revenue but as a truly public asset which should benefit as many citizens as possible. Political and economic considerations alike favored the rapid settlement of the empty lands. The federal government became increasingly generous with the public domain. It gave away millions of acres to newly-formed states. At the other end of the scale, the 1862 Homestead Act (copied by the Canadians in 1872, but with slightly easier conditions) offered the individual settler title to a quarter-section for the cost of the registration fee alone, if he would settle it, improve a part of it, and remain on it for five years. In between these two extremes, the main category of disposals consisted of those for "internal improvements." Recognizing the need for transport routes in opening up the continent, the U.S. government began, and the Canadian government continued, a system of granting land to companies which would construct canals, roads, and especially railroads. The government had not the funds to subsidize construction, so it granted land along the proposed right-of-way. The idea was that the construction company would sell this land (land whose value would be increased by the provision of transport routes) and use the proceeds to finance construction. It was in theory a sensible enough scheme; that it left enormous opportunities for fraud and oppression of individual settlers might have been foreseen but was, for the most part, overlooked in the general haste to open up the territory. The big land grants under this head of disposal began with an award to the Illinois Central Railroad in 1856 and culminated in the 1881 land grant to the transcontinental Canadian Pacific, which was to receive 25 million acres (10.1 million ha; later reduced to 18 million acres, or 7.3 million ha) as its subsidy for building across the empty west. Moreover, the company was free to pick and choose lands "fairly fit for settlement" as the U.S. railroads had never been able to do—they generally received alternate sections on either side of the line, no matter what the character of the land.

By one means or another, therefore, the U.S. government divested itself of a great part of its public land. It reserved some areas, such as the forest and mineral lands of the West, but generally only after it saw the private fortunes that could be accumulated by obtaining title to these lands. One of the most far-sighted reservations ever made, however, dated from the very beginnings of public land policy: that of two sections out of every 36 in a township for educational purposes. But on the whole the public domain, at the end of this period of disposal, consisted of the driest and most worthless parts of the original public lands—the parts nobody else wanted. Excluding for the moment Alaska, which occupies 375 million acres (152 million ha) and which became a state only in 1959, the public domain today represents just under 400 million acres (160 million ha) out of a starting area of 1,900 million acres (766 million ha).

There were good reasons why the federal government appeared to be in such a hurry to divest itself of its public lands (and why the Canadian government acted more cautiously). But one side-effect was important: the impression was created that what was so easily disposed of was of little value. If the nineteenth century saw, as it did, a huge wastage of natural resources in the United States with land, grass, and forest squandered on an unprecedented scale, then some of the blame attaches not only to the individuals who exploited the resources but to the government which seemed to care so little for their fate.

Carelessness can in part be explained by the inability of the federal agencies to keep a close watch over the whole enormous area of settlement. There were too few land officers to travel around verifying claims; consequently, many claims were fraudulent. Perhaps harder to ex-cuse was the second weakness of federal policy—inflexibility. Despite mounting evidence that in the dry West a quarter-section was a pathetically small unit, Congress moved at a snail's pace to modify the land laws. Clinging to a legacy of pre-Civil War belief that anything more than a quarter-section was in effect a plantation (with all the connotations of slavery that term had once carried) the legislators condemned hopeful but ignorant homesteaders to slow bankruptcy by the thousand. In Canada, although the homestead of the period was of similar size, it was made as easy as possible for the homesteader to buy an adjoining quarter-section (and so effectively to double his holding), while an alternative in the form of a pastoral lease was usually available in areas too rugged or too dry for cultivation.

Around the world at this period other governments were grappling with the same policy decisions about the occupance of empty, or near-empty, lands—on the Pampas, on the South African *veldt*, in the various settlements in Australasia, and on the Russian steppes. It is safe now to say that none of these achieved any near-perfect solution, and some of them did much worse than the North Americans. The United States was first in the field, and made the pioneer's mistakes. The rest had the opportunity of profiting from the lessons learned and, on the whole, the Canadians did so. But the basic question and the one to which we must now turn, was the *degree of control* over land use which should be, or could be, built into the policies of the central government.

The Control of Land Use

In the days when the young nation was creating its constitution and its land policy, there was one simple criterion by which to decide whether land was being "used": it was either being farmed or it was not. With the trifling exceptions represented by the few cities, all land use was agricultural in character. And apart from any purely local restriction which might be applied by the community or the town meeting, the individual farmer decided how best to use his own land.

If today we draw up a list of land uses, the difference is at once obvious: the list is much longer. Apart from agriculture, land is required for housing, for industry, for routeways (some of them, especially airports and freeways, very large space-users), and for recreation, to name only the major competitors. We might also add space needs for waste disposal, defense installations, water catchment, and mineral workings. Such is the competition for land, in fact, that it comes as something of a surprise to learn that the area in agriculture in North America today is about the same as it was in 1940, to such an extent have we come to think of farming as a kind of residuary legatee of land uses. The farms of today occupy the same *amount* of space as they did forty years ago, but not the same spaces; farms have been swallowed up by suburbs and parking lots, but so far these losses have been made good by new lands elsewhere.

We shall consider American agriculture in Chapters 5 and 6. For the moment we need only note that, once two or more users are competing for land, the conflict can only be resolved in one of two ways: by the price mechanism, which secures the space for the user who will pay most for it, or by some form of regulation, which will impose a use regardless of price. Such regulations, by whomever they are imposed, constitute land use *control*.

The control of land use forms part of the police power which in North America, as we saw in the last chapter, reposes in the state or province. If arbitration among conflicting land uses is needed, then it is from the state that it must come. In practice, however, the states have generally been rather inactive about this power in the past. Insofar as anything has been attempted, it has been by delegating power to local units of government, like counties or cities—that is, to units often too small to plan comprehensively or to cover the most important problem areas.

The problem is actually more specific. It is that the control of land use in *cities* has been a feature of North American life almost from the first settlements, with *urban zoning ordinances*

applying very generally in the twentieth century. But control of land use *outside* the city is not only in many areas non-existent, but is looked upon with genuine hostility by many Americans. In other words, land-use control is considered a necessary feature of urban life but an undesirable one in rural areas—the very areas where, needless to say, so many of the present-day use-conflicts are focused.

To explain this paradox would involve a book in itself, and we have space here for only a very brief summary of the position.[4] Why should zoning or control be acceptable in the city but not in the country?

THE POSITION IN THE CITY

Zoning in its modern form was introduced in American cities in the early 1900s. It prohibits particular land uses in a given area and as such provides sensible safeguards to health and amenity, like keeping the glue factory or the oil refinery away from residential areas. Yet this is only the beginning of the story. It can also be used as a discriminatory device to prevent particular *kinds* of residential development, even within a residential area. Low-cost housing, for example, may add little to a city's tax base but a good deal to its school population. On the other hand, if the city zones an area for development in large, single-house lots of, say, 2.5 acres (1 ha) minimum, a city can ensure at a single stroke that it will attract wealthy residents, that they will put up expensive, high-tax houses, and that the need for new school places will be limited at worst to one family per 2.5 acres (1 ha). A block of apartments on the same site might produce 50 or 100 school pupils and wreak havoc with the educational budget.

It is such use of the zoning power which leads to complaints that zoning is basically a matter of politics and not of planning; that it is a discriminatory power rather than a proper application of the police power as we earlier defined it. Nevertheless, all the major cities in

---

[4]For the sake of those interested, especially bewildered Europeans, the author has listed a number of reference works in the Suggestions for Further Reading.

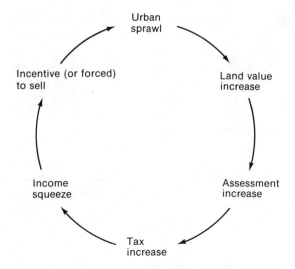

Fig. 4-4. Land use on the urban fringe. The diagram illustrates the vicious circle of land-use changes described on this page.

the United States employ it, except Houston, Texas, which has steadfastly maintained its faith in a free land market, and which claims that by so doing it has benefitted its less well-to-do citizens by providing more low-cost housing than would have been built under zoning arrangments.[5]

THE POSITION IN THE COUNTRY

Once we cross the city boundary, however, a quite different situation exists. We may understand it best by visualizing a farm located just beyond the fringe of the present built-up area. In the absence of any intervention or control, the farmer can confidently expect that, within one to five years, he will be approached by builders, supermarket chains, and restaurant owners, all of whom will bid up the price of his fields until he decides to sell out and retire a rich man. But now let us suppose that the county or township in which he lives declares that his land is zoned for agriculture alone or lies within a "green belt" which is to be preserved from built-up uses. Immediately the procession of would-be buyers to his door will stop, and immediately the farmer will claim

that under the terms of the Constitution of the United States (Article 5) he has been deprived of his property without due process of law. For his right to the property (which in most cases he holds in fee simple) includes, as he sees it, the right to sell to the highest bidder; that is, he claims the right not only to own the land but also to make the most of it. And if necessary he will go to court to maintain this right. He will argue that a green belt, which is merely one of a number of planning devices that limit the range of uses to which land may be put and that are in common use in Europe, is unconstitutional.

However, this is only one-half of a complex whole. The other half of the drama is being played out in the offices of the local tax assessor. It is the task of this official to set a value on all property, including the farm in question. But this value is normally based not on the farm's output or sale price *as a farm*; it is based on what the builders or supermarket chains would offer the farmer to sell out. As the fringe of the city creeps nearer, therefore, the farm produces what it has always produced but the assessed value, and so the tax bill, rises sharply. At a certain moment, the farmer can no longer meet his tax obligations, even though he may wish to remain a farmer; high taxes have driven him to sell out. We thus have, on the urban fringe, the vicious circle shown in Figure 4-4. Whereas originally it may have been the farmer who opposed the idea of a green belt because it limited his freedom of sale, he is now joined in his opposition by the tax assessor, who counts on increasing the tax revenue simply because the city's edge is approaching, and who will be equally opposed to any land-use control which has the effect of halting it. It is a simple and infallible recipe for urban sprawl and, to judge by present indications, it is what a majority of American governments at all levels want.[6]

Before such reasoning, the non-American can only bow in awed silence. Nevertheless,

[5]B. H. Siegan, *Land Use Without Zoning*, D. C. Heath, Lexington, Mass., 1972, p. 122.

[6]To justify this last statement, one might cite R. G. Healy, *Land Use and The States*, Johns Hopkins, Baltimore, 1976, who reports that, out of 38,000 county and lower government units in the U.S., only about 14,000 regulate land use in some way.

there are steps that *could* be taken, if anybody wished to do so, to break the vicious circle in both city and country, and there are scattered indications that this is occurring. In the city an immediate reduction in the political use of zoning could be achieved if the cost of education could be transferred, to a substantial degree, from the local government to the state. Education at present accounts for so large a share of local taxes that the temptation to zone schoolchildren out is very strong. If the incidence of school costs on the local taxpayer could be reduced, the temptation might be removed.

In the country there is an equally simple device for arresting urban sprawl, given only the will to do so. It is to assess farms for tax purposes *as farms,* so long as they continue in that use, and to increase the assessment only when their use changes. To assess them as potential supermarket sites is to ensure that, sooner or later, supermarkets are what they will become. A number of states already have made such tax provisions: California led off in 1965 with its Williamson Act, which allows local governments (but does not oblige them) to tax farms as farms, on the basis of income produced, provided that the farmer undertakes to keep his land in agricultural use for at least ten years. Other states followed suit even though some of them, like Wisconsin (whose Farmland Preservation Act was signed in 1977) had to alter their constitution (the so-called tax "uniformity" clause) to do so.

In both city and country, it is evident from what has been written here and in Chapter 3 that the burden of responsibility rests with the *states.* The local government unit is too small and self-centered; the federal government can do no more than exhort. The states have the necessary power and some, if not all, of the funds. We have already noted that the level of enforcement of land-use controls varies widely from state to state, but in general terms there is a drift toward greater state involvement. By 1974, for example, 23 states had taken legal powers to regulate the siting of power plants; 27 to regulate surface mining. This is somewhat short of marking a new American revolution. But it certainly represents a change of viewpoint on the part of some American legislators.

Government and Water

The involvement of the North American governments with water resources has been slower to develop than that with land, but it nevertheless has a considerable history. It first became explicit when settlement penetrated into the dry areas of the West, and water became no longer a universal presence but a resource in short supply. Even then, the settlers might have resolved their difficulties without recourse to law had it not been for the emergence of two activities which used water on a far larger scale than hitherto and which led to bitter disputes among users. These activities were irrigation agriculture and placer mining.

Most of the early immigration into North America was from northern Europe—the British Isles, France, and Germany—where rivers flowed for the most part year around and the accepted basis of water use was that any property owner whose land included a water course had the right to reasonable withdrawals. There were no uses so large as to appreciably affect the stream flow. But southern Europe (the Mediterranean lands and Spain) knew of such uses; specifically, of irrigation. As we shall see in Chapter 6, the quantity of water involved in irrigation agriculture is so large that, in the dry West, it was possible for a settler beside a stream to enjoy a water supply one year and before the next growing season find that diversions for irrigation upstream had left him literally high and dry. Placer mining was less demanding of water in the sense of absolute withdrawals, but the water returned to the stream was likely to be choked with sediment, because the whole idea was to wash the earth away to get at the gold particles.

It was the introduction of these two water uses which forced upon the West a change in custom and eventually in law, so that today the subject is one of the most complex and regionally variable in the whole legal field.[7] Water rights are a subject of endless litigation, up to and including the international level, as we shall later see. The governments of all the western states and provinces are involved.

[7]In evidence of this, see T. A. Garrity and E. T. Nitzschke, *Water Law Atlas: A Water Law Primer,* New Mexico Bureau of Mines and Mineral Resources, Socorro, N.M., 1968.

The federal government in the United States became involved in water resources originally through its efforts to control floods and to improve navigation; it built the locks at Sault Ste. Marie and virtually rebuilt the Mississippi River south of Cairo through the efforts of its Corps of Engineers. From here, as we noted in Chapter 3, it moved into other aspects of river basin control, using the interstate commerce clause of the Constitution to justify its operations: it was removing barriers to commerce. As early as 1902 it entered the field of irrigation, when the Bureau of Reclamation was set up with the responsibility of bringing irrigation water to such sections of the public domain as could be assisted in this way. But after World War II an increasing shortage of water in some areas led to a presidential commission which examined the whole water resource pattern. Meanwhile, treaties with Mexico and Canada and joint action on the rivers concerned involved the Colorado and the Rio Grande, the St. Lawrence, and the Columbia.

The 1960s and 1970s have brought Americans to a realization that water is not to be taken for granted, but is a valuable resource. Before we consider, however, the conservation of resources in the next section, let us be clear as to the nature of the problem. Taking the continent as a whole there is, of course, no absolute shortage of water. There are *local* shortages, as in the lower Colorado Basin, or west Texas, and there are important shortages of *clean* water, especially in the eastern states. There are problems caused by competition among *states* for water since, once again, it is to the states that the main legal powers over resources belong, and states today are sensitive about water as they have *not* always been about land. We shall later refer to interstate rivalries for the waters of the Delaware in the East and the Colorado in the West. And then there are, as we have already noted, *international* overtones to the water problem—the ex-

pectation of Mexico that the United States will not drain the Rio Grande or Colorado dry before they reach the border, and the expectation of Canada that works built on the lower Columbia will not affect the upper, or Canadian, section except in accordance with treaty.

If these are the three levels—local, interstate, and international—at which there is a water resource *problem,* is there a level for *solution?* So far as the government is or might be involved, there are two:

1. The river basin approach. The natural unit of water planning is the river basin. In almost no case does a major basin fall within a single state, so that interstate rivalry must be overcome before there can be a practical solution. This is, of course, precisely what the federal government achieved in the Tennessee Valley (see Chapter 15) and might, given the opportunity, have achieved elsewhere. But there has been no second Tennessee. In the other major basins, the states have preferred a more informal arrangement and have kept the federal government at arm's length.

2. The continental approach. Far transcending all other projects for harnessing the water resources of North America is a plan which was designed not by government but by private enterprise, although its fulfilment would certainly involve the continent's governments up to the hilt.

The most water-conscious area of North America is the Pacific Southwest; specifically, southern California and Arizona. And it is precisely from this area that the plan emerged. It is based on the fact that within the continent there is one area of abundant water supply where pure water, in an economic sense, is running to waste. It is the Canadian Northwest. The Mackenzie, a river with a mean annual flow only slightly less than that of the St. Lawrence, discharges 343,000 cu ft (9710 m³) into the Arctic Ocean every second. The plan, which is illustrated in Fig. 4-5, and which is known by the title of the North America Water and Power Alliance (NAWAPA), calls for the "wasted" supplies of northern water to be tapped, stored, and reversed. By a series of canals, old river beds, and tunnels they could then be brought southward to the thirsty areas of the Southwest, with a subsidiary feeder to

Hydraulic mining in California: A destructive practice which persisted from the earliest days of mineral exploitation in the American West until the end of the nineteenth century. Before the coming of the bulldozer, it was the quickest method of removing unconsolidated materials like river alluvia, but its erosive effect was appalling. *(U.S. Geological Survey)*

Hoover Dam on the Colorado River: The highest and one of the most impressive of the federal dams in the West, 726 ft (221 m) from lip to lower outlet level. The picture shows the penstocks fully open, but this is a very rare occurrence, for the water is escaping rather than driving the generating turbines. *(Las Vegas News Bureau)*

the Great Plains and something left over for Mexico. It would be a great north-south transfer forming, in effect, a water grid for the continent exactly like that for electricity. Nor is that all. Northern water could also be sent eastward, to flush out the pollution from the Great Lakes (which for all their size have a very small catchment area) and so restore life to the dead or dying lower lakes.

The plan seems to be quite feasible. It is expensive, of course, but that is not its main drawback. The main problem is political: the water in question, which would save southern California, help the Mexicans, and bring bathers back to the U.S. shore of Lake Erie, is Canadian water.[8] We have already commented

on Canada's reluctance to join the United States in thinking in continental terms—at least when the resources are Canadian and the users of these resources would, under the plan, be foreigners. One has to try to visualize what the price of the water might be; what Canada might expect in exchange for taking part in such a scheme.

It is not easy to think of anything. On the whole, it may be simpler to keep on with the developing technology of turning seawater into fresh water than to attempt the political exercise of turning Canadian water into American.

Conservation of Resources

There is one further topic to be considered in this chapter on the relationship of government

[8]Lest anyone should miss this point, Canada's federal Northern Inland Waters Act of 1970 proclaims it with all the splendor of a royal command: "3(1) . . . the property in and the right to the use and flow of all waters are for all purposes vested in Her Majesty in right of Canada."

Fig. 4-5. Water supply: The NAWAPA scheme of the Ralph M. Parsons Company of Los Angeles, originally made public in 1964 and shown here in a later, more elaborate form. Water from the north and northwest of the continent—mainly water from Canadian sources—would be used to fulfill a variety of purposes in other parts of the continent, such as supplying the arid southwestern United States and the east coast of Mexico and "flushing out" the Great Lakes.

to land and water resources, but it might be argued by some enthusiasts that it does not really belong here at all. The conservation of resources in North America, they might argue, owes little to the government, and much more to private initiatives which have goaded it into

action or taken it to court; which have carried out the educational processes necessary to alert the nation to the true realization of what it possesses and what it must do.

It is true that private groups have played an important part in the conservation movement

Destructive exploitation of resources: A section of privately owned California redwood forest near Prairie Creek State Park after logging over. *(Philip Hyde)*

and continue to do so. But the record of government is by no means negligible, and for any program to have teeth it must ultimately have the force of law. We shall therefore consider this subject before going on in the next chapter to some of the specific issues, such as energy policy.

One of the major decisions facing the population of any area is the *rate* at which its resources shall be used. Many of them are irreplaceable; others are replaceable only by slow processes such as soil formation or forest regeneration. To use these assets more rapidly than they are replaced, or to use more of them than current need justifies, is wasteful exploitation; a rate of use which is adjusted to speed of replacement and to current need represents conservation. Experience on almost every new frontier of settlement supports the general statement that waste and exploitation accompany the first settlers, and that regulation of use is the only alternative to a rapid deterioration of the area's natural resources. Upon a community's willingness to accept such regulation depends the future of its supplies of minerals, timber, water, or food. Of the existence or absence of these policies of regulation the landscape will often contain visible evidence; there is a landscape of conservation and a landscape of waste.

Throughout the first three centuries of European settlement in North America the continuing impression made upon the settlers was one of inexhaustible natural riches. In a land where space was unlimited, where the forest seemed to go on forever, where fish and game abounded, the early generations of Americans can be excused for feeling that they need never fear a permanent shortage of the materials necessary for a livelihood. If they exhausted the possibilities of one area, they could always move on. Imbued with this spirit they did move on, until there stretched across the continent a series of frontiers littered with the debris of exploitation and abandonment. In the north the fur men cleared the forests of fur-bearing animals. In the Great Lakes area the lumbermen passed through with all the devastating effect of a forest fire, cutting out only the species of timber they could market, and leaving behind the tangled remnants of the forest cover as useless slash. In the south farmers grew cotton or tobacco until the soil had lost its virtue, and then abandoned their farms and moved west to repeat the process on newly cleared lands.

Every nineteenth-century frontier saw this kind of bonanza—the wasteful consumption of resources far beyond any scale of present need. But in North America the technical means of spoliation were more available, and the consequent waste probably greater, than anywhere else. The government's land disposal policies cannot have helped: what was so freely handed over could be assumed to possess little intrinsic value.

But already before the end of the century there were signs of change. Individuals and groups fought to preserve particular treasures—Yosemite Valley, or the Yellowstone Plateau, created as a national park in 1872. In the last years of the century the government moved over to a policy of land reservation; late in the day it began to conserve what was left of its lands. This policy meant the withdrawal from further public entry of lands whose resources—in the first place timber—made them of special value to the nation. National forests were set up and in them the federal government undertook to regulate land use. Later, control was extended also to the open grazing lands of the public domain.

In the meantime the situation had been de-teriorating back in the eastern states. The pressure of an increasing population on land and resources used with traditional American freedom had made deforestation, soil erosion, and diminishing crop yields common. The vicissitudes of business during and after the First World War, which culminated in the Great Depression of 1929–33, made it clear that a new approach to the problem of resource conservation must be made. As if to underline this, the droughts of 1934 and 1936 produced the famous dust bowls in the southern Great Plains. In 1936, therefore, the Soil Conservation Service was established, with the task of organizing farmers into district groups for the development of anti-erosion measures, and of instructing them in more scientific methods of land use.

In Canada, government control of national resources has been somewhat closer than in the United States. For this fact the decision to hand over control of the public lands to the provinces may have been responsible. In certain respects the contrast is marked. In the northwestern forest states of Washington and Oregon, for example, the rate of timber cutting has until recently far exceeded the rate of growth. In British Columbia, however, where some 90 percent of the forest is owned by the province, it has been possible to keep the annual cut to a figure lower than the total annual increment. Again, when the big Alberta oil fields came in after 1947, the government took immediate steps to regulate development and, profiting by the unhappy experience of some of the oil regions south of the border, to avoid wastage by restricting competitive drilling. On the whole, then, the time-lag between the development of the United States' West and that of Canada gave the latter time to profit by the former's mistakes, and the allocation of all crown lands to the provinces gave local governments an immediate stake in the orderly development of their resources.

One of the major problems in creating a successful conservation program in the United States is the division of responsibility between several agencies, federal and local. As we shall see later, the federal domain is not administered by a single government department, while over private lands there is almost no di-

These pictures show the development of a gully in Woodbury County, Iowa. The advancing gully head reached the bridge in 1948 and rendered it unusable. By 1956, when the first picture was taken, the head had advanced a further half-mile. In the second picture, dated 1960, stabilization measures had been taken, although the loss of topsoil and plowland was irreparable. Iowa, although a part of the prosperous Corn Belt, has suffered severely from soil erosion. *(U.S. Soil Conservation Service)*

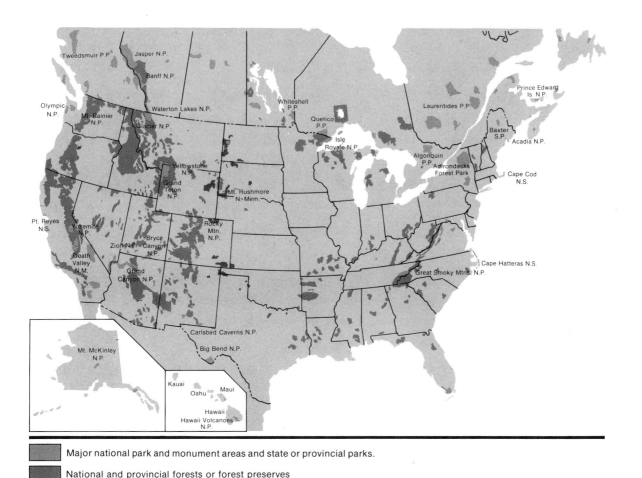

	Major national park and monument areas and state or provincial parks.
	National and provincial forests or forest preserves
	National grasslands (U.S.)

Fig. 4-6. North America: Major parks and forests. Besides the areas shown on the map, it should be noted, there are many smaller parks, national monuments, and recreational areas in both federal and state/provincial ownership. For an impression of these multiple ownerships, see Fig. 3-2.

rect control. Consequently some of the threatened land resources are well administered and others are not. It is almost always possible to tell when one leaves or enters a national forest, for example, even without the help of the neat wooden signs which the Forest Service puts up and which seem to imply that anything may happen outside the forest limits, but the Service is not to blame. From the conservation point of view, there would be a good case for making the Forest Service responsible for the entire public domain, although from the point of view of those wanting to promote development this might be a far from welcome solution.

If conservation has been a twentieth-century theme in North American life, there is no question that it has grown much louder in the past decade. Indeed, to read the literature of the early 1970s one might get the impression that the North American nations, having been the world's wealthiest, had been bankrupted of their resources and become poverty-stricken almost overnight. At the same time, the focus of attention has shifted rather abruptly from the familiar problems of the last half-century, of which the best known was that of soil erosion, to a different sphere—that of water pollution. The dramatic focus of the new interest was Lake Erie, which was described as a new

Pollution of the environment: A disturbing scene from one of the most sparsely populated states in the U.S.—Utah. In this largely empty area oil, acid, and rubbish fill a pond. It is consoling to be able to report that this particular eyesore, at least, has since been cleaned up. *(Docuamerica)*

Dead Sea, but the problem was and is a general one, a problem which, like those of forest destruction and soil erosion, was a long time in the making before it forced itself upon the attention of the public.

Pollution resulted from untreated wastes, domestic or industrial, being released into rivers and lakes. It resulted from an enormous increase in the use of chemical fertilizers on American farms; the chemicals were then washed out into the water supply. Closed bathing beaches and polluted oyster beds were the warning signs. It is, of course, possible to reduce pollution levels greatly by insisting on the treatment of wastes before they are discharged, but treatment costs money, and the question is, who pays for it? Unless, for example, a very strong law made treatment of a particular waste obligatory in every state or province, the manufacturer who treated his waste merely out of public conscience would simply add to his costs and place himself at a competitive disadvantage over against his less scrupulous competitors.

If such measures were to apply nationwide in either the United States or Canada, they had to originate with the federal government, constitutional limitations notwithstanding. Following its normal practice, the federal authority would have to bribe or cajole its citizens into complying with the standards it set in its federal codes. Firing the first shot in the campaign, the National Environmental Policy Act of 1969 opened with the words, "The Congress . . . declares that it is the continuing policy of the Federal Government, in cooperation with state and local governments, . . . to use all practicable means and measures, including financial and technical assistance, in a manner calculated to foster and promote the general welfare." The tone is, generally speaking, one of pious hope. However, the Environmental

Quality Improvement Act of 1970 then followed, and after it came a series of acts in 1972 and 1973 aimed at producing clean water: "it is the national goal that the discharge of pollutants into the navigable waters be eliminated by 1985."

Other legislation set standards for noise abatement (1972), coastal zone management (1972), and clean air (1973). In the meantime, and in the realm where practical measures can actually be enforced—that is, by the action of the states—these years brought some notable achievements: the California Coast Commission of 1973, given a popular mandate to control coastal development up to 1000 yd (1 km) inland; the Vermont Environmental Control Act of 1970, to subject all large developments to planning control; the Environmental Land and Water Management Act of 1972 in Florida, a state whose natural resources were under the heaviest pressure of all as population increased faster than anywhere else.

The early 1970s were equally productive of legislation in Canada. In 1970 alone, four important measures were placed on the statute books: the Arctic Waters Pollution Prevention Act, the Canada Water Act, the Northern Inland Waters Act, and the Oil and Gas Production and Conservation Act covering the federal northern territories and offshore areas. The year 1972 brought the Great Lakes Water Quality Agreement with the United States, an agreement about which, incidentally, Canada has done a good deal more by way of implementation than its partner. The Environmental Protection Ordinance of 1974 rounded off this avalanche of legislation. Suddenly, environmental safeguards had become politically fashionable.

We might summarize the change in outlook in this way: when the conservation movement began in the late nineteenth century, its first objective was to halt the attacks on American nature that had been so numerous in the preceding decades; in other words, it was a backward-looking effort to put an end to the gross carelessness of the past. By the time that the 1930s brought the Dustbowl and soil erosion to public attention, the conservation movement was dealing with contemporary, urgent problems, reflecting concern about damage occurring before the eyes of farmers and ranchers.

Then, as time passed, the focus of interest shifted to the future. If it is sensible to arrest damage to the environment as it occurs, it is even more sensible to forestall it.

It is this latest phase of the movement which finds its expression in the U.S. government's acceptance of the Environmental Impact Statement (see p. 88). It is a commitment to weigh the effects of every federal project or proposal and to consider alternative strategies in advance. It offers the opportunity for public appraisal of the side-effects of building, or damming, or installing a nuclear plant, and at that point it can count on the Statement being examined under a magnifying glass by the powerful environmentalist lobby, that cluster of groups which represents the interest of thousands of Americans in their continent's future. Court actions and counterproposals may then hold up the project for months or years, until an acceptable scheme has been evolved. But it is the federal government itself which has voluntarily tied its own hands in this way.

The rate of use of the world's natural resources has greatly increased in the first half of the twentieth century. This is a result partly of the tremendous increase in world population and partly of the technical revolution which, particularly in the western world, has so markedly enlarged the productive capacity of the individual. Crudely put, this means that man can now overwork his soil and strip his forest land more swiftly and thoroughly than ever before. What is at least encouraging in these conditions is that awareness of environmental damage, hazard, and possible disaster is also now at a higher level in North America than it has ever been before. "Ecology," "ecosystem," "environment" have become household words. Pressure groups favoring conservation measures have multiplied, and every legislative action is reviewed and criticized by those who fear further destruction. This is not to say that the situation is firmly in hand. But certainly a heightened level of awareness exists. Controls of air pollution, water pollution, and land use; controls over the activities of fishermen, forest industries, and mining companies become more necessary—but also more feasible—as the years go by and the magnitude of the problem increases.

Government and Economic Activity

The involvement of the North American governments in the national economy has been developing gradually over a long period. Some of this involvement was explicit in the U.S. Constitution, which assigned to the federal government such tasks as levying customs duties, establishing post roads, or regulating foreign commerce. Some of it was implicit, such as the responsibility "to promote the progress of Science and Useful Arts . . . ," a phrase that may be taken to have covered, say, the setting up of the U.S. Department of Agriculture in 1862. Some of it was, to say the least, unexpected, such as the way in which the Interstate Commerce Commission, a regulatory body with considerable powers, emerged in 1887 out of the apparently innocent wording of Article 1, Section 8 of the Constitution, authorizing the federal government "To regulate Commerce with foreign nations, *and among the several States . . . .*" Today, this involvement is taken for granted: government and economy have grown to overlap each other to such an extent that their separation is impossible.

This chapter will review some of the principal economic areas in which the federal governments of both Anglo-American nations are active. Expressed in geographical terms, they represent the distortions in spatial patterns of production brought about by the intervention of government in a theoretically free economy.

Government, Transport, and Freight Rates

In all economic activity the cost of transport is an important factor. The greater the distance involved in assembling or selling goods, the more important it becomes in the final cost. But in North America it gains additional significance from the way that freight rates are structured, and the government exercises control over them.

To weigh a shipment of goods and calculate the charge for carrying it a given distance does not at first sight appear complicated. To the transport company, the cost of carrying freight is represented by the graph in Figure 5–1. It costs something to load goods aboard a train, truck, or plane; thereafter, the cost increases with distance but, on a long haul, the terminal costs form a smaller proportion of the total and the cost *per unit of distance* is less than on a short haul.

However, neither all haulage nor all freight is uniform, and the actual slope of the graph depends upon a number of factors. Some kinds of goods, such as precision instruments or fish, require more care in transit than others, like coal or sand, and for each type of goods the carrier fixes a *class rate*. Then again, the cost of transport is higher in mountain or desert areas than in level, well-settled regions. Again, the cost is less when a large amount of any one kind of goods is being carried between two particular points. Large shipments, and especially *regular* shipments, are for several obvious reasons cheaper to handle than small loads that need sorting in half-empty trucks. For large quantities, the carrier can reduce his costs and offer a lower *commodity rate,* applicable between the points he specifies.

For the complications that follow from these simple facts, two things are responsible. One is competition and the other is the policy of the Canadian and U.S. governments of using freight rates to influence economic development. In short, the American rate structure is governed not merely by *cost* of service, but also by *value* of service, both to the shipper and the consumer.

Each transport company, whether dealing in land, water, or air freight, wants to offer acceptable terms to shippers of goods and to capture their business. A century ago, when canals and railroads were being built in North America by the score, it was often a matter of life and death to the carrier to capture the traffic of a city or area from his rivals. In these circumstances savage "rate wars" developed which frequently led to the ruin of all those involved; and the freight rate "structure" became simply a series of special arrangements between carriers and shippers, reflecting their relative bargaining strengths. Already in the 1850s a number of states had set up govern-

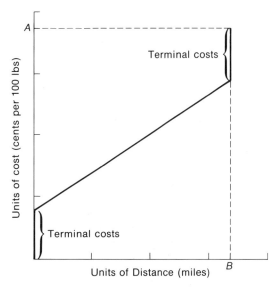

Fig. 5-1. Freight rates: Basic cost diagram, to indicate a cost, A, for moving a unit quantity of freight B miles. Compare with Figure 5-2.

ment bodies to safeguard the public interest in efficient transport service, and inevitably the federal governments were drawn in to check what had become a scandal. In 1887 the United States established the Interstate Commerce Commission (I.C.C.), and in 1903 the Canadian Government provided for a Board of Railway Commissioners (renamed the Board of Transport Commissioners in 1938 and, in 1967, the Canadian Transportation Commission).

But, while these controls checked the worst abuses of the system, the freight rate structure remained basically unchanged, a mass of millions of separate agreements between carriers and shippers. The commissions merely act as referees, and by enforcing certain rules of the business, they see to it that a reasonable degree of competition is maintained. Indeed, if a local market is in the undisturbed possession of one set of producers, the commissions may *create* competition by allowing producers from elsewhere an exceptionally low rate into the market. To do this, they sometimes have to break their own golden rule: if there are two points on the same line, the rate to the more distant one must not be less than that to the nearer one. The commissions' basic aim is to ensure that the public is provided with efficient service and safeguarded against costly

Railroads and farmers: A cartoon of 14 August 1873, which appeared in a New York newspaper and symbolized the power which the railroads were able to exert upon the farmers whose goods they carried, thanks to their influence over the government in Washington. The artist was Thomas Nast, a cartoonist who rose to prominence through his repeated pictorial attacks on the corrupt politicians involved with "Boss" Tweed of New York and Tammany Hall. *(Library of Congress)*

monopoly. To achieve this they support the bargaining power of the shipper against the carrier, and of the carriers against each other.

Some of the best-known special rates have been the transcontinental commodity rates, approved by the I.C.C., that have been agreed between the railways and the California fruit growers. Some of these rates are as low as one-half the standard class rate for the distance. The rate on oranges may serve as an example (Fig. 5–2). Oranges are grown both in California and in Florida. But California is twice as far from the great markets of the northeastern states as Florida is, and there is little possibility of the California oranges competing in these markets unless they can be cheaply transported to the East. To the western railways, therefore, the alternatives are cheap transport or no transport at all; thus they set up a low commodity rate on California oranges to New York, a rate so favorable, in fact, that

the California growers can hold their own with their Florida competitors.

On a much broader scale, the Maritime Provinces of Canada put forward the claim that, owing to their geographical isolation from the rest of the country, they were entitled to a lower level of rates than other sections in order to be able to place their produce on the home market on competitive terms. The Canadian government accepted this argument in principle, and by an act of 1927 reduced the railway rate level for goods moving either within or westbound out of the Maritimes by 20 percent. This subsidy to the region was extended to road haulage in 1968.

With the passing of time the nature of the competition among the carriers has changed. Under increasing pressure from truckers the railways have stopped fighting each other and have instead banded together to preserve their interests. In certain limited spheres water routes also provide a challenge that forces a special reduction in freight rates by rail. Instead of bidding separately for traffic, therefore, the railways negotiate their rates through regional committees of their representatives, watched over by the I.C.C., the C.T.C., and the state commissions.

But the functions of the commissions are not purely preventive. It was early realized that the freight rate structure could have an important positive influence on the development of a country or region: in economic terms, that the difference between *cost* of service and *value* of service could be manipulated by either the carrier or the government in a highly creative manner. The Canadian government has been very sensitive to this fact, particularly since it became the owner of one of Canada's two great railway systems. Its chief concern was to assist the outward movement of Canadian raw material exports and the forward movement of settlers' necessities into the frontier zones. Thus in 1897 it concluded with the Canadian Pacific Railway the Crow's Nest Pass agreement, whereby in exchange for a subsidy, the railway agreed to fix low rates on a number of commodities from the western frontiers, particularly grain. This favorable rate on grain has remained to the present, justified on the ground that, as the 1951 Royal Commission on

Transport stressed, production of grain for export is for Canada "an industry requiring special consideration as in the national interest." In economic terms, therefore, this low rate, secured by the government, acts as a subsidy to the grain producers.

Once the government starts to subsidize freight rates, however, it is not easy to stop. The western grain farmers were helped in the way just described: it was now the turn of their customers. The Canadian government offered Feed Freight Assistance to livestock farmers in other provinces—a system of subsidies planned to make sure that the freight cost of obtaining animal feeds outside the grain-growing areas should be held down to an acceptable level. Meanwhile, the railways themselves were in need of assistance, especially at the point where the transcontinental lines had to cross the great empty, unproductive stretch of the Shield. To help carry the costs of running these "bridge" lines, a so-called "Bridge Subsidy" was paid to the two companies involved.

The Canadian government has been careful to maintain a general level of rates comparable with that of the United States, since over many routes, especially the transcontinental ones, the Canadian and United States services compete with each other and with the sea routes through Panama. A higher rate level in Canada, added to the greater physical obstacles on the Canadian side of the border, would be certain to divert business to the American carriers, at the expense of the Canadian.

With the passage of time, a number of these special rates have been eliminated, either because they were seen by the government concerned as a purely temporary form of subsidy or because some, like the rates on grain and settlers' effects established under the Crow's Nest Pass agreement, had been low to begin with and were maintained unchanged for decades. In fact the Canadian Pacific is still losing revenue through its obligation to haul its important grain traffic at these artificially low rates. But in the meantime the after-effects remain: the influence of the millions of separate bargains which together constitute the American freight rate system and which have guided locational decisions and choices in the past.

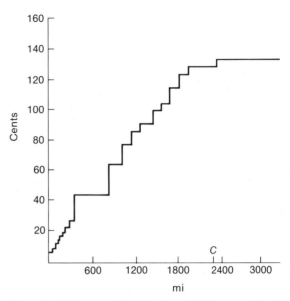

Fig. 5-2. Freight rates: The structure of the transcontinental commodity rate on citrus fruit from California to New York, the rate which opened the big eastern markets to the California producers. C marks the location of Chicago on the distance scale.

Government and Agriculture

We have already considered the government's attitude to land in North America, and this section deals with an extension of the same topic: its influence upon the *agricultural use* of land. This is a sphere where the government has gradually moved from a peripheral to a central role as its involvement has increased.

In the nineteenth century, the federal government was involved in agriculture in two main ways: in an advisory capacity and as landlord and user of the public domain. In the United States the year 1862 saw the founding not only of a federal Department of Agriculture but also of a program for land-grant colleges in the West where the farm population could receive further education. From these beginnings, the advisory functions of the government grew to cover experimental farms, on-the-farm counselling, and a huge range of publications. The public lands, for their part, were in due course placed under the care of various government services, which became responsible for controlling their use: the National Forest Service,

93

the Bureau of Land Management, The Bureau of Reclamation, and in Canada, the Department of Northern Lands.

Then in the twentieth century both the Canadian and U.S. governments abruptly found themselves in the position of having to rescue farmers from depression, shrinking markets, and bankruptcy; mere advice or example were no longer sufficient. They organized programs to save the farmers, and kept those programs in being for several decades, during which the original causes of disaster were lost to sight and farm fortunes rose and fell. Some parts of the programs, in fact, remain to the present day. In this way, government involvement in agriculture became direct; it continued to advise (those years saw, for example, the founding of the U.S. Soil Conservation Service), but it also paid farmers to plant, or *not* to plant, particular crops.

In the most recent period—since about World War II—it has been influential in agricultural *planning;* its policies help to decide which lands shall be used for agriculture and which types of farm shall flourish. Without giving up its old functions, the federal government has come to possess a series of new ones.

The turning point in this development came in 1929-33. After the First World War and throughout the 1920s, agricultural demand and prices had fallen off, only to be struck a catastrophic blow by the onset of the general depression. At the same time, decades of carefree land use had produced serious problems of soil erosion by water in humid areas, and decades of unwise cultivation had brought on dustbowl conditions in dry areas. With the farmers desperately trying to raise unwanted crops on worn lands and sell them to non-existent buyers, the government stepped in.

In the United States, it was the New Deal legislation of 1933 which brought in the new program. Its object was to raise both demand and farm prices, and to do so it had first to reduce supply—to get rid of the unmarketable surpluses that had built up. The method adopted was to pay farmers a subsidy based on the number of acres planted to the particular crop in surplus. Each farmer was given a quota acreage, and assured of a fixed price for the produce of those acres but no others. In

that way, one set of measures simultaneously reduced the area under the crop—cotton, wheat, tobacco—and boosted the price received by the farmer. By adjusting the price which it guaranteed to the farmers (and which it expressed as a stated percentage of a "parity" price each year) the government could, theoretically at least, fine-tune the economy and divert production from crops in surplus to crops in shorter supply.

The system had its advantages and its disadvantages. One of the *advantages* was that the land on which the farmers did *not* obtain a quota was taken out of the traditional crops— crops which, incidentally, may well have been grown for generations and been responsible for serious soil depletion—and used for other plantings, like pasture or peanuts. As various crops were placed on acreage quotas, shifts took place to non-quota crops, generally to the benefit of the land. One of the *disadvantages* was that a quota system which limited acreage rather than output was undermined by the constant rise in agricultural productivity. This simply meant that the surpluses (which the whole scheme was designed to eliminate) were produced from a smaller acreage than before, but were produced just the same.

Another disadvantage was that, once the farmers had become accustomed to the idea of government support prices, they were most reluctant to forego them, even when times were good. Surpluses continued to pile up, only this time the problem of disposing of them was the government's, and not the farmer's. The 1950s were a period of embarrassing overproduction, and saw the introduction of another type of restraint: the "Soil Bank." Under this scheme, the government made payments to farmers to take their land out of cultivation altogether, and rest it. The land was benefitted and the area under crops reduced, both without loss to the farmer, whose problem has always been that of carrying the initial costs of land conservation measures over the period when production is reduced.

So in the period of the forty years after 1933 the U.S. government played a role which the Constitution never foresaw for it—that of farm salesman and grain wholesaler. It is true that after the Second World War government-to-government sales of farm produce greatly increased, and remain an important feature of the present world market. Yet it was too much, perhaps, to expect that a series of measures conceived in the emergency of depression would serve equally well, through good years and lean, for the next four decades, and their success was in practice very uneven. Not until the market became much tighter, with increasing world demand, in the early 1970s did U.S. agriculture again begin to operate in a fairly free market. But if conditions change once more, we can expect to see the return of the same mechanisms.

Why *did* the U.S. government continue with this structure of supports for so long a period? One reason, already mentioned, was the reluctance of the farmers to see it disappear: to them, it represented the guarantee of a continuing government commitment to their economic welfare, and they used their political influence to see it perpetuated. But there may well have been another factor: the wish of the government to support farm incomes and so slow down the drift of Americans, especially the young, from farming into other occupations. This would support the American commitment to the ideal of the family farm, to which we shall return in Chapter 6. Inevitably, workers were leaving the land for better-paid employment elsewhere, but the support program might do something to check the flow by raising farm incomes.

Perhaps it did. But although the idea was to encourage the survival of the *small* farmer with his marginal income, the effect was to benefit most the *large* farmer. Support prices naturally do most for those who have most to sell—bushels of corn or bales of cotton. The government was therefore keeping a certain number of small farmers in business by making a few large ones rich. The motivation, in this case, was clearly ideological rather than economic. It was a measure of the American commitment to the image of the small family farm.

In Canada as in the United States the 1930s marked a turning point. The Prairies provided a dramatic focus for the troubles of agriculture: as a region, they were suffering from drought, and dependent as they were on exports for their livelihood, the Prairie farmers were in an even worse situation than the Americans, many of whose markets were at home. So it was in the Prairies that the principal relief measures were instituted. There were two. One was the establishment in 1935 of the Canadian Wheat Board. Ever since 1912, there had been a Board of Grain Commissioners, whose powers included the control of grain prices and quality, but the 1935 Act gave the Board control over all grain exports from Canada; it relieved the Canadian farmers of at least some of the problems of finding markets for their crop, and in doing so it set a price for each year's crop which acted as a guaranteed floor for grain prices (although a very low one) upon which the farmers could rely.

But the Board had first to find its markets, and in this respect we may notice a difference between the Canadian and U.S. systems of support. Canada in the 1930s was a nation in whose economy agriculture played a very large part, and the rest of that economy was not strong enough to subsidize the farmers on, say, the American scale. If everybody is a farmer, nobody is left to subsidize him. The Wheat Board only paid for what it could sell; it did not buy up surplus crops in the American fashion. It was not, in fact, until 1958 that the Canadian economy had matured enough to sustain agricultural support on something approaching the U.S. scale. In that year the Stabilization Act introduced a system of guaranteed prices similar to that of the United States, and applying to other products besides grain, although the difficulty of disposing of the great Prairie crops year after year continued to be the focus of the problem.

The second Canadian measure of 1935 was the passing of the Prairie Farms Rehabilitation Act. Under it, the government took wide powers to restore prosperity to the region. Soil erosion was checked, marginal lands were taken out of cultivation, scientific farming was encouraged, irrigation schemes were assisted or developed to bring security to farmers on the dry margins, and grazing reserves were gradually acquired to support stock in emergencies. Over the years, the P.F.R.A. has been used in so many different ways that it has become a kind of governmental Aladdin's lamp for the Prairies.

Governments all over the developed world have been sensitive in recent years to the well-being of their farmers; in this respect, the Canadian and U.S. governments are following along some distance behind, say, their counterparts in the European Economic Community. Government policy will certainly influence the future pattern of agricultural land use even though in the late 1970s North American agriculture is probably freer of direct government intervention than it has been at any time since the early 1930s. But with wheat nowadays an instrument of foreign policy and farmers a loud-voiced minority in national legislatures, there is little danger of agriculture being overlooked by government in the future.

Government and Industry

The involvement of government with industry in North America has been a series of fits and starts. On the whole, industry was left to itself until its own condition brought the action of the government down upon it. When it threatened to develop monopolies, it became the target of antitrust action. When it neglected the basic rules of health and safety, either for its employees or its products, it was subjected to federal inspection. But on the whole the "fits and starts" are readily identifiable; they correspond with periods when the government itself became industry's customer, and most of these periods have coincided with times of war or emergency.

Both the First and Second World War years saw North American industry swiftly adapting itself to the production of armaments. Korea and Vietnam maintained the connection, and in between the war periods the government has remained a big customer—in certain industries the biggest, in some industries the only one—for the output because of its involvement in space flight and other pioneering technical developments. Plants exist today—steel mills, aluminum smelters—in locations which, had it not been for military requirements, would never have attracted them. At the end of World War II, defense planners encouraged the dispersal of industry away from the traditional, crowded areas in the northeast of the continent, where it was felt that it formed too easy a target for missile attack: even in that period of comparatively unsophisticated weaponry, something like a third of all U.S. industry was within range of missiles fired from submarines lying off the coast.

But the major impact of government on industry in the 1970s has certainly been through its role as customer. In 1973, for example, the U.S. government was the customer of "defense-oriented industries" for products with a value added by manufacture of $91.3 billion, and these industries gave employment to 3.9 million workers.

This government demand may take the form of supplying capital and plant for a government-operated factory, or it may simply mean that industry is producing *for* the government. In either case it is likely to play a significant part in regional development, particularly in areas where the accumulation of investment capital would otherwise be difficult. A great deal therefore depends on how the government distributes its contracts. In wartime, governments have usually been in a hurry to obtain results and have tended to rely upon existing plants or industrial regions for added production. But in peacetime, when results can be planned for on a longer-term basis, the regional balance of government investment may well favor previously non-industrial regions. This is, in fact, what has happened in the United States, as the following table shows:

Distribution of Military Prime Contract Awards, Fiscal Years 1941–45, 1951–53, 1961 and 1971; By Regions

Region	Annual averages 1941–45 (World War II)	1951–53 (Korea)	Fiscal year 1961	Fiscal year 1971
New England	8.9	8.1	10.5	9.5
Middle Atlantic	23.6	25.1	19.9	18.5
East North Central	32.4	27.4	11.8	10.4
West North Central	5.6	6.8	5.8	5.9
South Atlantic	7.2	7.6	10.6	15.8
South Central	8.8	6.4	8.2	14.7
Mountain	1.2	0.7	5.7	2.6
Pacific	12.3	17.9	26.9	21.2
Alaska and Hawaii	–	–	0.6	0.8
	100.0	100.0	100.0	100.0

(Source: For figures up to 1961: "The Regional Impact of Defense Expenditures." Symposium, *The Western Economic Journal*, vol iii, 130. 1971 percentage calculated from *Statistical Abstract of the United States, 1972*).

So large is the scale of the government's involvement in industry for defense purposes that some areas of the continent depend very heavily on government contracts and spending for defense (see pp. 202 and p. 393). This dependence can be calculated as a so-called "defense-dependency ratio," which expresses the relationship between employment of civilians in defense-generated industries and defense installations on the one hand, and total civilian employment on the other. If to the 3.9 million workers in defense-oriented industries referred to above we add the 1.06 million civilians who worked in federal defense-related agencies, these 4.98 million workers represented 5.7 percent of the total U.S. labor force in 1973. For some states, like Alaska and Utah, the dependency ratio was much higher. If we turn to another index of government activity, that of federal contracts outstanding in 1975, California was in the lead by a long way (almost $8 billion worth); New York state was a poor second, and Connecticut third. So far as distribution among the states is concerned, therefore, there is a random element in government spending, especially on defense.

What is true of government contracts for industrial *production* is perhaps even more clearly true of the related and very important activity of *research*. In 1976 the federal government of the United States was carrying obligations under this heading (usually referred to as R and D) of $21,600 million, as compared with an expenditure on R and D by all other bodies of $16,400 million. The federal government was therefore paying for 55 to 60 percent of all R and D, but the actual work was largely carried out by non-government agencies—about 70 percent of it by industry and another 13 to 15 percent by the universities. Up to now most of the federal allocations for R and D have been made not on a geographical basis but in accordance with what has been called "a decided bias in favor of excellence, wherever it existed." The result has been that federal funds have become concentrated in a few states and, indeed, in a few institutions: California, for example, in a recent year received almost 40 percent of the total, while among the universities and institutions, the twenty leaders received one-half of all federal expenditures under this head, and most of these twenty were on either the Atlantic or the Pacific coast. In view of the size of these expenditures, we may expect in the future to find political pressures building up for a change in policy for their allocation.

The relationship of government and industry in Canada has a special quality, and it is one to which we shall return in Chapter 7. In a sense this relationship belongs as much to the realm of foreign policy as it does to that of economics. Because so much of Canada's industry is financed and directed from the United States, the Canadian government must be constantly on the alert to safeguard Canadian interests while at the same time maintaining good relations with its neighbor. As a balancing act, this calls for considerable political skill.

Government and Energy

The entry of the government into the field of energy policy is the most recent of the developments which we are reviewing in this chapter. It is true that for some decades now the U.S. government has kept a general watch over the petroleum industry, and that in the so-called Tidelands dispute it has claimed as federal property the offshore oil fields which lie more than 3 mi (5 km) out. But most of the day-to-day regulation of the industry is left to the oil states themselves. It is true, too, that the first nuclear energy was produced by a federal agency set up for that purpose in World War II; the story is well-known. But in the broader field of energy as a whole the idea of a *policy* is new. Individual energy sources might be regulated, but only in the past few years has the federal government intervened in the decision about priorities which is implicit in the term "policy."

There is little doubt about when this change of heart occurred. It followed the decision in 1973 by the oil-exporting countries (OPEC) to raise the price of oil, a decision which led to turmoil in the world petroleum market. In that year, petroleum and natural gas together accounted for 77 percent of energy consumption in the United States, which in turn was using

Energy and the future: The alternatives. The photographs show (left) the Tennessee Valley Authority's Paradise steam generating plant on the Green River near Greenville, Kentucky, the largest thermal power station in North America. Around the coalburning plant, with its tall smoke plumes, are areas of strip mining from which coal is fed to the plant. (right) Brown's Ferry nuclear power plant near Athens, Alabama. Both types of power plant have their opponents, but once available hydroelectricity potential has been fully exploited, the choice for the future appears to lie between these two. (Billy Davis Aerial Photography; T.V.A.)

about one-third of the entire world energy production. More than one-third of the U.S. consumption of oil was imported from overseas, and since 1973 the figure has crept upward to more than 40 percent. It was therefore no surprise to find that crisis followed the price increase.

The federal government was faced by the need for an immediate reappraisal of the energy position. The United States, for so long the world's largest producer as well as consumer of petroleum products, was unaccustomed to the feeling of being dependent upon the whim of foreign suppliers, particularly since foreign oil fields had in a majority of cases been opened up by American companies. Oil could usually be exploited more cheaply overseas than in the United States, and since the depreciation allowances granted to

the companies by the government were the same in both cases, the oil companies had tended to concentrate on overseas fields and to neglect home exploration. With one-third of the world's petroleum consumption, the United States had by 1974 only six percent of the world's known reserves. And overseas the oil companies were faced by demanding governments, which no longer treated them as equals or looked on them as benefactors, but as foreigners exporting national resources "on the cheap."

The response of the U.S. government was to launch Project Independence in 1974. It was to cost $11 billion and was a five-year program designed "to take us to the point where we are no longer dependent to any significant extent upon potentially insecure foreign supplies of energy." It had two aspects. One was to cut

down the consumption of energy in everyday American use, and the other was to find fresh energy sources. Some of these sources would represent technical breakthroughs, like harnessing the energy of sun or wind on a new scale. Other finds might, it was hoped, add to the known reserves of conventional fuels: more oil in the Arctic or on the continental shelf; a fuller exploitation of the mid-continental oil shales, like those of Colorado (see p. 348). A major role was assigned to nuclear power. By 1977 there were 60 nuclear units on line, with a capacity of 43 million kw. The Project represented a serious attempt to think of energy for the first time as a whole rather than as a series of separate power-producing industries.

It is as yet too early to pass judgment on Project Independence. Some things, however, are clear. One is that dependence on imported oil has not been reduced, but rather has increased, in spite of the bringing on stream of Alaskan oil from the North Slope (see p. 425). Another is that the plans for replacing the imported fuel have run into strong opposition from environmentalist groups. The *quickest* ways to reduce dependence on imported oil are (1) to press ahead as rapidly as possible with nuclear developments and (2) to revert to the use of the other hydrocarbon source, which is available in quantity but has for decades now been overshadowed by petroleum; that is, coal.

Neither way is easy. The construction of a new generation of nuclear plants is fought at every step by groups hostile to the use of radioactive materials, or fearful of accidents at the power plants. The new plants should already be under construction if they are going to contribute their planned share of future energy requirements, but they are not. On the other hand, the use of coal has fallen foul of so much new legislation that it, too, is of limited usefulness. Clean air is the order of the day. In California, for example, coal-fired power stations have been outlawed, and even oil-burning plants must use a specified grade of fuel. The largest traditional sources of coal supply, in the Appalachians, happen to have a high sulphur content, and their use is banned in many states and communities on grounds of air pollution. Meanwhile, environmentalist pressure has been building up against strip mining, at least in the form that a coal state like Kentucky has known it in the past (see Chapter 15); yet in 1972, strip mines accounted for nearly one-half of total U.S. coal production. There *is* low-sulphur coal which can be readily strip-mined. Most of it, however, is out in the West, much of it on or under federal land, and the government has so far moved very slowly to lease the mining rights to interested companies.

We can best summarize all these developments in a few simple sentences: (1) A national economy, the world's leading consumer of energy, has become highly dependent upon one energy source—petroleum products. (2) This energy source is now in short or uncertain supply. (3) Alternative sources exist, given freedom of action on the part of the government and the power producers, (4) But at this precise point in time, freedom of action is denied by a newly vocal section of the American community which is highly critical of what such "freedom" has meant in the past. (5) Stalemate ensues.

Meanwhile, the Canadians look on. Their own energy situation is relatively favorable: they have been developing hydroelectricity for decades, and they have oil from conventional fields and tar sands from which oil can be extracted. They have constructed nuclear plants on the shores of the Great Lakes. Now their concern, in this as in so many other matters, is not to become involved in a crisis of the Americans' making. Yet their own oil companies float on American capital, and, as with water, they are being urged to take the continental view with energy—to contribute their resources to a common pool.

Percentage of Energy Inputs in the U.S., 1976 and Later Estimates

	1976	1980	1985
Coal	18.7	19.6	20.5
Petroleum	47.2	47.0	44.0
Natural gas	27.3	23.6	19.4
Nuclear power	2.7	5.0	11.4
Hydroelectricity & other	4.1	4.0	3.7

Agriculture

The Agricultural Regions

Few maps of North America are more familiar to the eye than Figure 6-1. Based on the county statistics of farm activity, it reveals the basic generalization that North American agriculture falls geographically into a series of belts or regions, in each of which one type of farming, and in some cases one crop, predominates. Indeed, apart from the size of the entirely blank areas (which cover some 92 percent of the total area of Canada), perhaps the most significant feature of the map is the relative smallness of the sections labelled "general farming"—those regions whose agriculture is assorted enough to defy more detailed classification. Everywhere else the main agricultural emphasis is clear.

It must at once be understood, however, that these agricultural regions are not permanent divisions. They represent simply the present state of development of a pattern which has been evolving for three hundred years, and which has, in fact, changed quite significantly even in the short period since the Second World War. It now seems likely that the pattern of belts—Cotton Belt, Corn Belt, and so on—with which the geographer has become so familiar will prove to be no more than a passing phase. The cartographer of the future will almost certainly have to map smaller and more numerous agricultural regions, for while specialization in agriculture is increasing rather than diminishing, today it is specialization by the individual farmer rather than by a whole region. General farming is dying out in face of this individual specialization but so, too, is the old region-wide concentration on a single crop.

The Formative Factors

What are the forces that have brought into being an agricultural pattern such as this, and that are now changing it once again? For the sake of convenience, we may divide them into three groups, historical, environmental, and economic.

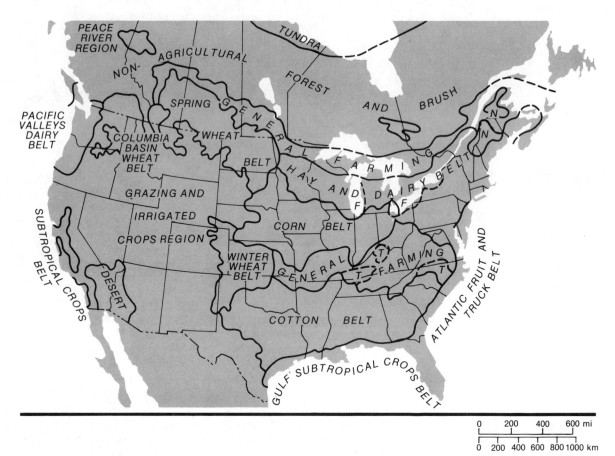

Fig. 6-1. North America: Agricultural regions. (F = Fruit regions of the Great Lakes' shore, N = Non-agricultural lands within the northern General Farming Belt, T = Sections of the southern General Farming Belt specializing in tobacco.)

HISTORICAL DEVELOPMENT

Much of the story of American agriculture takes its character from the fact that the continent was settled by agriculturalists spreading westward from the east coast. The earliest settlers on the Atlantic seaboard had to be as nearly self-supporting as possible. They brought with them wheat and livestock, learned the use of corn (maize) and squash from the Indians, and imported little but sugar. Hemmed in along the coast and the St. Lawrence by mountains, forests, and Indian opposition, they had to make the best of the available lands, unsuitable for cultivation though they often were, since the state of communications made it virtually impossible to transport food beyond the confines of the individual community.

As time went on, the problem was modified in two ways. First, the gradual improvement of communications did away with the need to produce every requirement in each settlement, and made possible a regional division of labor. Areas particularly suited to the production of one crop began to specialize in it. The new situation also meant that intensive forms of farming could be practiced nearest to the settlements, where land was in greatest demand, and that extensive forms, such as the growing of cereals and the raising of sheep, were relegated to the fringes of the settled area, where space was no problem. Provided that transport facilities were satisfactory, this represented the most economical form of land use.

The second modifying factor was the discovery, made as the frontier of settlement moved westward, that beyond the mountain barrier

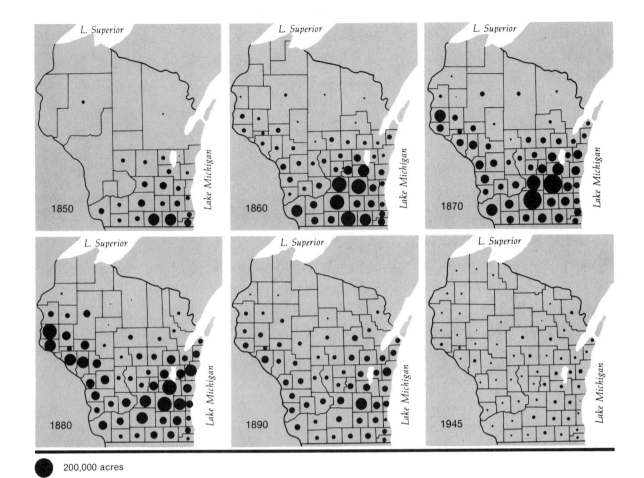

200,000 acres
80,000 acres
25,000 acres

Fig. 6-2. The Wheat Belt moves west: A series of maps of Wisconsin, showing how the Belt traversed the state during the period 1850–90, as it moved toward its present location in the Dakotas.

were wide expanses of the continent which were more fertile and easier to farm than the original agricultural lands along the east coast. To the hill farmer of New England or the western Piedmont, the level grassland of Kentucky and the forest openings of Ohio or southern Ontario seemed a paradise indeed. Once the interior was settled and linked by river, canal, or railway with the Atlantic seaboard, the high-cost, marginal farming which had been forced upon the east coast states could not hope to compete with that of the favored interior.

The effects of these two processes have been most marked.

1. *Geographically*, the effect has been that the centers of production have moved westward, their position dictated by the availability of transport facilities. The clearest example is that

afforded by wheat, and is illustrated by the maps in Figure 6-2. Before 1825 most of North America's wheat crop grew in the Atlantic coast states, between Vermont in the north and Virginia in the south. In 1825, however, the Erie Canal was opened, linking the Hudson River with the eastern Great Lakes region. This event brought about such a revolution in transport costs that the center of wheat production promptly moved from New England to the open lands on the Lake Erie shore of western New York. Through the period 1830–40 the wheatlands spread further westward, this time into Ohio and southwestern Ontario. The next decisive step was the development of a railway network throughout the Great Lakes region. This occurred during the 1850s—New York and Chicago were linked in 1852—and made

Harvesting corn, old style: A print reproduced from a nineteenth-century geography text. *(From* Harper's Introductory Geography, *1896)*

available for wheat-growing the grasslands of Illinois. Through the 1860s and 1870s the process continued, with the centers of production moving on westward across Wisconsin and Iowa. The 1880s, marked as they were by the construction of the Northern Pacific and Canadian Pacific railways and a number of shorter lines, saw the end of the process—the establishment of the Wheat Belts which appear on the present map in Kansas, the Dakotas, and the Prairie Provinces. Here aridity brought to a halt a movement that had covered 1200 miles (1900 km) in seventy years.

In much the same way, further south, wheat-growing spread from Maryland and Virginia to Tennessee and Kentucky, and from there across the Mississippi into Kansas and northern Texas. The southern crop, however, did not figure prominently in the nation's markets until Kansas began to produce; until that time much of it was consumed within the subsistence farming economy of the southern states.

2. *Economically,* the effects of these processes have been no less striking, and it is interesting to notice that there is a close parallel with the agricultural situation of Great Britain over the same period. For eastern North America, as for

Britain, the opening up of fertile and extensive agricultural lands meant severe competition for the farmers of the older areas. At the same time, moreover, as the railway network was spreading westward, there occurred a parallel technical advance in the manufacture of agricultural machinery, which brought further advantages to the farmers of the level interior lands and further increased the handicap of the less-favored eastern regions.

What happened was that the Easterners were forced to retreat from one form of agricultural production to another. Except in a few specially favored areas, the eastern farmers could profitably produce only what could not easily be shipped into the region from outside. Their farming had to fulfil two conditions: that production should be intensive, and that it should be concentrated on commodities for whose sale closeness to market, the Easterner's one solid advantage, was of prime importance. In these circumstances, a concentration on dairy products and fresh vegetables could safely be predicted, and this prediction is largely borne out by facts. Yet even with this limited range of output, the eastern farmer depends on first-class communications for his ability to sell. Without them, as we shall later see, he is likely to be deprived of a market altogether.

The early settlers on the Pacific coast found themselves confronted by a situation not unlike that of the seventeenth-century immigrants to the Atlantic seaboard. In the 1840s their supply route lay round Cape Horn, or at best crossed the Isthmus of Panama; their penetration inland was shallow, and the settlements had necessarily to be self-supporting. So there occurred in the isolation of the West an agricultural development on much the same lines as that already described in the older settlements of the East. Local self-sufficiency gradually changed to regional specialization. Today the West Coast has its Wheat Belt in eastern Washington, and its Hay and Dairy Belt in the Willamette-Puget Sound Lowland. Recently it has even developed its Cotton Belt in central California, although it bears little resemblance to its older eastern counterpart. Only the midwestern Corn Belt, product of a unique combination of physical and economic circumstances, has no replica in the West.

As the mining booms of the 1840s and 1850s brought prospectors and camp followers to the West Coast, the early farmers enjoyed a seller's market so profitable as to lure many an unsuccessful Forty-Niner away from mining to the safer business of feeding his more persistent partners. So long as western agriculture fulfilled this limited function of local supply, its problems were few. But with the passage of time two changes took place. First, in spite of the region's phenomenal population growth, the total agricultural output quickly grew to exceed western demand. Second, the Pacific coastlands developed a series of specialty crops which are produced not for the local but the national market. The combined effect of these two changes is to make today's western farmer dangerously dependent on outside markets, and so also on his means of transport to those markets. Here his isolation beyond the mountains counts against him. Before they can begin to sell in the main markets of the continent, California oranges must travel 1600 mi (2550 km) from Los Angeles, and Washington apples a similar distance from the valleys of the Cascades. British Columbia's farmers are, if any-

thing, worse off in this respect than those further south. For many western products the Panama Canal offers a better route to market, even to the North American market, than do the transcontinental roads and railways.

In the meantime, what is to be said of the great intermediate region that divides East from West—the Agricultural Interior? Between the Ohio and the Missouri rivers and the Canadian Shield are to be found some of North America's most favored farmers. They possess all the advantages of their fellow farmers to both east and west of them, and yet escape most of their problems. Farmers in the East have the advantage of a large urban market close at hand, but lack wide stretches of fertile farmland. Farmers further west have space and fertility in plenty, but have the problem of getting their produce to distant markets, as well as the hovering threat of climatic variability. The Midwesterners, on the other hand, have both fertile drift plains to cultivate and excellent markets in the cities of the Manufacturing Belt; they have at their disposal, moreover, a communication network which is probably unrivalled throughout the world. The area produces no major export crop, and markets or processes a large proportion of its output within its own boundaries. With a remarkable degree of balance between crop and livestock production, and also between rural and urban population, it is not surprising that this largely self-contained region possesses the highest average of farm prosperity in the continent.

West and south of this region of what might be called agricultural equilibrium, the situation of the farmers becomes less favorable. Westward across the Great Plains, this decline can be explained in terms of increasing distances to market and of climatic hazards. Prosperity in a single year, or in a series of as many as ten years, may be equal to that of the Midwest, but there can be little security. Drought, dust, or grasshoppers will redress the balance. Southward, beyond the Ohio, there are neither the urban markets which are basic to the midwestern equilibrium nor the same midwestern fertility in the soils. Furthermore, the pattern and, in the long run, the prosperity of southern agriculture has been distorted by its historic loyalty to King Cotton.

Only since the Second World War, as Chapter 16 describes, has any semblance of a midwestern type of equilibrium emerged.

ENVIRONMENTAL FACTORS

The preceding paragraphs have outlined some of the historical circumstances responsible for the present pattern of North American agriculture. They have been presented first because all too often they disappear behind the physical factors of climate, relief, and soil, which are much more accessible to the geographer in search of explanations. It must now be recognized, however, that the ultimate control of this pattern is not human but natural; and, on the continental scale we are considering, the principal environmental influence is climatic. Thus the migration of the Wheat Belt from the Atlantic coast to the western plains, which has already been described, was the outcome of economic change, but it was confined within limits set by climatic factors—on the north by temperature and on the west by aridity. Again, in the Southwest, the spread of slavery as an institution was checked not merely by political force (for it was legal in areas it never touched) but by the climatic limits of the region in which cotton, its economic accompaniment, could be grown. Where the Cotton Belt could not reach, slave-owning lost much of its purpose.

In general, where the boundaries of the agricultural regions run from east to west, they are determined by temperature, and where they run from north to south, by rainfall.[1] The northern limit of successful cotton cultivation is governed by the diminishing length of the frostfree season. The northern limit of the Corn Belt depends upon the amount of summer heat required to ripen the corn, and its boundary with the Winter Wheat Belt in the Southwest upon the prevalence in that quarter of dry summer winds, which parch the corn. The northern limit of the Spring Wheat Belt is a product not only of poor soils and distance to market but also of diminishing amounts of summer sunshine and increasing frost hazards.

[1]The one major exception is the southern limit of the old Cotton Belt, which was governed by the heavy summer rainfall on the Gulf Coast, and not by temperature.

The rainfall control of the longitudinal boundaries is most clearly seen on the Great Plains. The cultivation of cotton, corn, and hay in the south, center, and north respectively of the Agricultural Interior, give way along the 20 to 25-in. (500–625 mm) isohyet to wheat growing, and this in turn is abandoned in favor of range livestock farming further west, where the precipitation drops to 12–15 in. (300–375 mm) annually.

Thus the major agricultural divisions reflect climatic influences. On a smaller scale, relief and soil account for local differences. The ruggedness of the Mountain West, the lack of soil over much of the Canadian Shield, the sandy character of the southern Pine Barrens, and the inadequate natural drainage of the low-lying Florida Everglades all serve to illustrate the limiting effects of the natural environment on the North American farmers. So, too, do the ravages of various crop and animal diseases. Of these perhaps the best known is the cotton boll weevil; a U.S. Department of Agriculture publication commented that "it has encouraged diversification of crops in the Cotton Belt more than has any other single factor" since its appearance in the 1890s.

A further comment in this section must be devoted to the blank parts of the map of agricultural regions. A combination of the factors we have been considering, both natural and economic, makes them unsuitable for farming under present conditions. In the United States these empty areas appear to be relatively small and scattered. The largest of them are in the western states: the desert of southern California and Arizona, where average rainfall is below 5 in. (125 mm), and the rugged and in part snow-covered terrain of the Sierra Nevada-Cascade chain and the central Rockies. But the map of this western region is misleading, for over much of the Range Livestock Belt farming is very extensive indeed. The difference between the apparently "farmed" and "unfarmed" areas may be no more than the difference between complete emptiness on the one hand and stocking at the rate of one head of cattle to every 100, or even 200, acres (40–80 ha) on the other. Furthermore, in the mountains and on the desert margins such stocking is only seasonal, and the sum total of agricultural activity in any area may be represented by the presence of a few sheep which find summer grazing in the open forest or above the tree line. Thus the map gives an exaggerated impression of the "agricultural" West.

In the East, non-agricultural lands are found in the swampy and sandy areas of the Southeast and in the forested uplands of northern New England. Here as in the Canadian provinces across the border, remoteness from market combines with poor soils and the cost of forest clearance to militate against the development of agriculture. Indeed, as we shall later see, the farming frontier has tended to withdraw rather than advance in this area over the past 50 to 70 years.

In Canada the non-agricultural areas cover the greater part of the country. Over much of the empty north, physical conditions of climate and soil are too harsh for successful farming, but even where some form of cultivation is possible, distance from market limits expansion along the agricultural frontier. There are, in fact, considerable stretches of these empty spaces which could be farmed, given the necessary demand for their products. But with the present Canadian population, the need to compete with farmers located far closer to markets and ports, and the cost of clearing or draining these lands, their development must await, for the most part, an unpredictable future.

ECONOMIC FACTORS

We have considered the historical and environmental influences which have gone into the making of North America's agricultural pattern. But farming is a business, and we must now turn to the third set of factors which influence that pattern—the economic considerations.

Since 1914 the fortunes of American agriculture have undergone tremendous fluctuations. The wars created a worldwide demand for agricultural produce, which resulted in high prices and prosperity for the farmers. But this demand also encouraged a dangerous over-expansion, both of area cultivated and of output achieved, and in the postwar periods it was necessary to adjust production to the conditions of peace and of renewed world competition.

After the First World War the farmer's fortunes rapidly declined, and they had already reached a low level when in 1929 the great business depression began that stifled foreign trade, reduced domestic demand, and threw hundreds of thousands out of work. Following upon these disasters, a series of bad seasons for the Agricultural Interior during the 1930s came as an added blow. To the outside world the cumulative effect of the farmers' misfortunes was dramatically illustrated by the ravages of soil erosion. Unable to bear the expense of conservation farming at such a time, the farmers watched helplessly while the wind of the Great Plains blew out the dustbowls and the heavy rains of the Southeast washed away topsoil that had lost its virtue through the cultivation of the same crops for decades at a stretch. Drastic government action, as we saw in Chapter 5, was necessary in the United States and in the Canadian Prairie Provinces to reestablish even moderate prosperity for the farmers, before the outbreak of the Second World War in 1939 brought them back into their own.

Once again the war raised prices and output; once again the war's end in 1945 left the farmers' future uncertain. This time, however, there were two factors which eased the position and insured the farmers, at least temporarily, against rapid price declines. One was the tremendous postwar need for agricultural produce in the devastated areas of Europe and Asia. To the North American farmer this meant that the high wartime level of demand continued for several years, while his government shipped relief supplies to countries in need. Only gradually did the old problems of overseas trade and competition reappear. The second relieving factor for the farmers was that their political position was much stronger in 1945 than in 1919, and consequently they were able to secure by political pressure a continuation of wartime price supports to insure themselves against another rapid fall of prices like that of the 1920s.

Through all these fluctuating fortunes, however, certain permanent features of North American agriculture are evident.

Low Intensity of Land Use

The European's first impression of rural North America probably is the amount of unimproved

107

land, even in areas of relatively dense settlement. Such was the speed of the westward movement in the nineteenth century that, except in some parts of the Atlantic seaboard, settlement was never compact, at least by European standards. The land policies of both governments encouraged a loose and generally careless occupance of the land. At the same time the knowledge that there was more room further west encouraged the pioneers to move on as soon as they considered that the older regions were becoming too crowded or too civilized. Long before all the lands east of the Mississippi were occupied, the restless pioneers were opening up the Great Plains and the Pacific coast. With land to be had virtually for the taking, there was no point in being crowded. On the other hand, the low cost of land west of the Appalachians and the Canadian Shield meant that there was no point in costly improvement schemes either; the obvious course was to pick the best lands, avoiding those that needed money spent on them. It was cheaper and easier to move to the oak openings of Illinois than to stay and clear the forest in Kentucky, and there was no useful purpose in staying to drain a few swampy acres in Ontario when miles of fertile prairie were open to occupation under the Homestead Act in Manitoba.

The cheap land policies of both governments were thus responsible for the diffusion of settlement across the continent. Even when land values began later to rise, many of the former uncultivated areas remained, and to this day have never been considered worth the cost of improvement.

Capacity For Producing Surpluses

In order to understand this last feature of American agriculture, however, another factor must be borne in mind: Americans can *afford* wasteful land occupance because their overall agricultural output has generally been much greater than their needs. Despite the tremendous population increases of the present century (in 1900 the United States had a population of 76 million), it is not scarcity but recurrent surplus that has most often been the problem of the American farmer. In these circumstances the question of recovering land left unimproved in the rush of western settlement has remained largely academic.

This persistent tendency to overproduce has had two causes. The first of these, in point of time, was the constant development of new farm lands in the West, whether in the initial expansion, or later by irrigation. Generally speaking the opening of these lands was not a product of need for food but of settlement policy; the principal motive was to provide homes where agriculture could yield an income, rather than farms to meet a national need for expanded output. The encouragement of farming was thus unrelated to either present surplus or predicted shortage.

The other cause of overproduction is the entirely worthy one of increasing efficiency. Not only have new lands been brought into production, but a greater output has been secured from the old. The effect of this increase in efficiency has been striking. In the United States between 1930 and 1960, the population increased by roughly a half, and the index of agricultural output by 70 percent. Yet the acreage under crops in 1960 was actually 8 percent *less* than in 1930. Each unit of land in 1960 was feeding three people, where thirty years before it had fed two.

In Canada, with its low population density and its imperial connection, the production of an agricultural surplus for export is basic to the national economy. Its farmers produce regularly for export markets, chiefly in Great Britain and the United States. But in the United States a number of the main farm products appear only irregularly on the international market; the exports represent the surplus, if any, after home market demands have been met. In the depressed thirties, for example, the United States exported 123 million bushels of wheat in 1931 and 106 million in 1938, but was a net *importer* of wheat over the years 1934–36. The 1950s were the period when farm surpluses reached their highest levels; no matter how much the American exporter sold or the American government gave away, the farmers still seemed to pile up further supplies, which they expected to be paid for but which nobody wanted.

The days of those huge surpluses are now

over, at least temporarily. Demand has caught up with supply: there have been drought years and changes in standards of living and big movements on the international market, such as huge sales of American grain to the USSR. It would be surprising, however, if a free market in agricultural commodities did not occasionally produce periods of shortage as well as surplus: there is after all no question of giving orders to several million American farmers, or of providing in advance for such contingencies as flood or drought. Consequently, the 1970s have produced by far the tightest conditions of agricultural supply that America has experienced for many decades past; perhaps, indeed, in all the country's history since the earliest colonists starved. The *capacity* to produce surpluses remains; the surpluses themselves come and go.

A Land of Small Farms

While American agriculture has been so successfully producing more food than the continent needs, its social side has been dominated by two ideas that have taken a remarkably strong hold on the American mind. One of these is that the "right" farm is the family-sized farm, operated by the members of one family, with perhaps a little hired help at peak times. The idea can be traced back to the early days of settlement in the New World and the determination to avoid the situation that drove so many Europeans to emigrate to other lands—a situation in which one man owned a vast estate (but might never even visit, let alone cultivate it) and a hundred others were landless. The early land legislation was full of references to "actual settlers," and the "family" size of 160 acres (64.8 ha) of land came to be accepted, as we saw in Chapter 4, as the proper amount for a government to allocate to an individual. These governments in fact went to great pains to keep the land out of the hands of speculators, although they were largely unsuccessful in doing so.

So strong has this sentiment been in favor of family-scale farming that some states carry on their statute books a law forbidding corporations to engage in farming, and others are considering passing such laws, an astonishing fact of American life in the 1970s, when in industry or commerce the family-sized unit is virtually extinct.

The amount of land that constitutes a family farm—that is, the amount one family can manage—has of course increased over the years. In 1935 the average size of farm in the United States was almost exactly 160 acres (65 ha). In 1972, it was 394 acres (159 ha); yet over 85 percent of the nation's farms were family units, if considered as operating on the labor of one family with little outside help. The area which a family can operate depends, of course, upon the type of farm activity it undertakes. Under the engaging title "One Man Farm is Hard to Beat," a Department of Agriculture writer picked as an optimum size for sample farms in various regions the following areas:[2]

	Acres	Hectares
Montana wheat-barley farm	1960	793
Kansas wheat-grain sorghum	1950	789
Indiana corn-soybean	800	324
Louisiana rice-soybean	360	146
Delta cotton-soybean	600	243
California irrigated cotton	400	162
California vegetable farm	200	81

What is at stake, obviously, is not a particular size of operation but a principle; one for which the U.S. government has consistently stood and consistently legislated since the Homestead Act, if not since the beginnings of the republic. The family farm is seen as the antithesis of the huge collectives of socialist countries, and so far it has outproduced them by a handsome margin. The U.S. government has gone to a great deal of trouble to keep speculators from engrossing lands (not always successfully, however), and it is still dangerous for a North American politician to question the rightness of family farming, except perhaps in California: to be against the family farm would be unthinkable.

It was this same train of thought which led from the Homestead Act of 1862, with its 160-acre (64.8 ha) limitation, to the 1902 act that set up the Bureau of Reclamation. The act

[2]See *Farmers Digest*, vol. xxxvii, No. 10 (April 1974). The same article made a point to which we shall have to return (p. 113), that the average investment in land and other equipment represented by these "optimal" farms ranged from a low of $158,000 to a high of $610,000.

charged the Bureau with the task of bringing water to any parts of the public domain which proved to be irrigable, but went on to specify that no individual might *receive federal water* for more than 160 acres. If the individual farmer owned a larger area within the project that would benefit from the irrigation water, then he was required to divest himself of the excess within a reasonable period.

This is a clause of the act, a phase of family-farm policy, which has so far been honored more in the breach than in the observance. The area where it has most obviously *not* been enforced is in California, where some of the nation's largest irrigated farms occupy the nation's leading agricultural counties, and benefit from federal irrigation water. If the 1902 law were ever applied to this area, these great farm units would have to be split up. Before that happened, however, it is safe to assume that the legal battles would eclipse the San Francisco earthquake in magnitude and ferocity.[3]

The second idea is that the family should own the farm it operates; that tenancy is a social evil. This is an attitude that hardly fits today's facts, but perhaps we can explain it by again recalling the background of so many emigrants to the New World. For them a grasping landlord was their hereditary enemy, his demands the chief reason for their emigration, their fondest hope some day to own land for themselves.

This dislike of tenant status could be justified thirty years ago by pointing out that in two major regions of agricultural distress—the

Old South and the Great Plains—tenancy figures were high. But the argument then has to take account of the fact that during the past three decades, while tenancy has been diminishing in the South, it has been *increasing* in such a prosperous farm area as the Corn Belt, where the farmers have been trying by all means possible to enlarge their holdings, and where land for sale is both scarce and expensive. It has become common practice in such areas to enlarge the farm one owns by renting additional land. In the Corn Belt state of Iowa, for example, the 1970 figures showed that virtually half of all land in farms was being operated under some form of tenancy. But as an arrangement, it is still far from being regarded as an acceptable part of the American way of life.

The Farm Income

In North America, just as in Great Britain, the farmers have had to struggle to obtain a fair share of the prosperity enjoyed by their nation. Despite their efforts the income from agriculture has been consistently lower than that from industry or commerce, and most townspeople tend to assume that it is predestined by nature to be so, and protest at the featherbedding of the farmer.

In Britain one of the main causes of depression in agriculture was the low tariff policy adopted in the 1870s in order to help the nation's industries. By an interesting contrast, the farmers in the United States—whose position before 1939 was just as unfavorable as that of British farmers—also suffered from the country's tariff policy, but in this case from the *high* tariffs the United States imposed. Ever since the Civil War, the country had maintained a high level of tariffs, in order to help American industry by excluding foreign manufactures from the American market. But foreign countries retaliated by imposing tariffs in their turn, and this closed to the American farmers the overseas markets which, as we have already seen, they need as a "safety valve" for their surpluses.

Burdened with these surpluses the American farmers have fought hard, through their politi-

[3]No one took this prospect too seriously until September 1977, when the Secretary of the Interior (under whose jurisdiction the Bureau of Reclamation operates) announced his intention of applying the 160-acre rule to California. How seriously this should be taken, time alone will tell. However, the scale of the infringement, if such it be, of the acreage limitation rule can be judged from evidence given before the Senate Select Committee on Small Businesses, under the published title, *Will The Family Farm Survive In America?* (U.S. Senate, 94 Cong., 1 Sess., Part I, Hearings of 17 and 22 July 1975). It was there claimed that on one section of California's Central Valley Project alone—the Westlands Water District—70 percent of 600,000 irrigated acres (243,000 ha) should have been ineligible under the law, and that the value of agricultural production involved was some $200 million.

cal organizations, to obtain their share of the nation's prosperity. In particular they have campaigned—and successfully—for the system of price supports begun in the 1930s to be continued. Thanks to these supports and to technical progress, it has been possible for the farmers in some favored areas, such as California and the Corn Belt, to close the gap between rural and urban standards of living. But in spite of continued subsidy by the government, the 1960s were a decade of only patchy prosperity on the farms, and this has made the farm income one of the hottest political issues in the American arena in the 1970s.

The situation of the Canadian farmers has been rather different from that of the American. It was not until settlement of the West got under way after 1850 that agriculture emerged as a business in its own right in Canada. Before this time it had generally been treated by successive governments as important, not for itself but as a means of feeding fur traders or settling unoccupied areas—subservient, that is, to the main branches of the economy or the main policies of the politicians. But the opening of the Prairies brought Canada into world trade with a major export crop, and since that time no Canadian government could possibly overlook the country's agricultural interests or the importance of primary production. Canadian policy has accepted the nation's role in international trade, and, although since 1939 Canada has made a vast amount of progress as an industrial power, its raw material exports remain an important element in the national economy. It has been unable, as we saw in the last chapter, to aid its farmers on the American scale, but it certainly has never forgotten them.

American Agriculture in the 1970s

So far we have been concerned with some of the long-standing realities underlying the agriculture of North America. But no feature of the American farm business is of longer standing than rapid change. Technical developments bring with them economic and social changes, and these in turn affect the distribution and character of the farm population.

If we examine these changes, we find that the progress on the farms is due to two basic processes. One is mechanization and the other is the increasing application of science and research to agriculture.

Mechanization began in earnest with the automatic harvesters of the 1830s, took a long step forward with the introduction of the tractor, and is today in evidence all over the farm—in the cotton picker, the combine, and the belts which carry food into the barn and carry refuse out. And mechanization is linked in turn with other developments:

1. It released for other uses millions of acres formerly needed to provide feed for horses and mules.

2. It has had the effect of greatly enlarging the area that one man or one family can farm. In theory, therefore, mechanization should lead to fewer and larger farms. But in practice this can only happen if holdings are amalgamated and some of the farmers find other work. In North America, although the average size of farm more than doubled between 1940 and 1975, this increase has still not been rapid enough to give the farmer the full advantage of his machines. Although many farmers have left the land, those who remain are constantly achieving higher output: in fact there are still too many of them.

There is, however, a side effect of mechanization which is not a benefit at all. It is that the use of machines may enable a farmer to make a living by cultivating a large area of poor land with a very low return per acre. Without machines it would not yield a livelihood, and very probably it ought not to be cultivated at all.

3. Mechanization has altered the character of farm work by raising the level of technical skill required for it. The old casual laborer is no longer in demand; his place is taken by the machine, and such labor as is required usually demands training and education.

Scientific agriculture, thanks to the work done in the laboratory and on the seed plot, is obtaining higher yields per acre, and at the same time taking less out of the land, than at any time since European settlement in North American began. In economic terms the drain

Mechanization of American agriculture: (1) Cotton picking. The two pictures give an impression of the changes mechanization has brought in a region where hand labor was formerly of vital importance (*see* p. 294). The first, a painting entitled *Cotton Pickers, Georgia*, by the noted painter Thomas Hart Benton *(Metropolitan Museum of Art, George A. Hearn Fund, 1953)*, remained a valid picture of labor in the cotton fields until after the Second World War. The second picture shows the machine that has replaced the gang of pickers. *(National Cotton Council)*

on the capital asset—the land—is lower and the interest rate is higher in today's conservation farming than they have ever been before.

How has this come about? There are three main ways:

1. Probably the most important single factor has been the breeding of new strains of crops. Half a century ago the main problem was to produce strains that would withstand the rigors of drought and frost. More recently the emphasis has been on breeding to raise yields. An outstanding example of this has been the

development of hybrid corn. In 1937, when the new hybrids were just becoming available, the average American corn yield was about 25 bushels to the acre (61 bu per ha). In 1972, the national average reached 97 (240 per ha); it is regularly over 80 (200 per ha). The case of sorghum is even more remarkable—the average yield actually doubled during the single decade of the 1950s. Higher yields naturally mean that the crop can be concentrated on the best lands, and the inferior lands can be used in other, more suitable ways.

2. In part the progress is due to a greater input of fertilizers. For the American farmer, fertilizer use is a recently acquired habit; the more old-fashioned habit was to move on to new land when the old soil was exhausted. But there is no longer space to do this, and fertilizer use has doubled since 1955.

3. In part, too, progress has come with the development of selective weed killers and insecticides. Insofar as they both reduce labor needs in weeding and give the cultivated plants a better chance, the effect of these chemicals is to increase the all-round efficiency of the cropping, to combat the spread of worthless plants that readily invade overworked fields, and to increase the stock-carrying capacity of the land.

The scope of this technical improvement has already been stated: agricultural output increased by 70 percent in the 30 years from 1930 to 1960, and by nearly 50 percent in the period 1950 to 1970. It can undoubtedly be raised still higher, merely by applying to more farmland the lessons already learned. Meanwhile, profound economic and social changes have accompanied these advances. The greatest of these has certainly been the migration away from the farms. Mechanization has been responsible for a part of this movement, since it cuts labor requirements; but the opposite is also true: the drift to the cities has made farm labor expensive and thus encouraged farmers to employ machines. In Canada, in spite of an increase of more than 100 percent in total population during the period, the farm population was smaller in 1961 than in 1911. In the United States in 1970 it was actually less than one-third of the 1911 figure, and during the

single decade of the 1960s the farm population fell by almost 8 million; in the 1970s, the fall has continued at about 200,000 a year. Yet as late as 1962 the U.S. Department of Agriculture could assert that "underemployment is a serious problem in agriculture" and concluded that "if such underemployment were suddenly ended, 1.4 million workers would be added to the list of unemployed."[4]

For those who remained, however, other changes were taking place. If technical aids are making farming as a profession more profitable and more attractive, they are also responsible for increasing the capital investment necessary for success. In order to succeed in the competitive, surplus-producing agriculture of today, it is necessary for the farmer to make use of every labor-saving device available. But so great a capital investment does this involve that many a farmer's son, who in a previous generation would have set up in his turn as an independent farmer, is unable to afford such a step, and must leave the land to seek work as a wage-earner instead. It would seem true to say that whereas the formative factor in the American farm economy was once cheapness of land, it is now the high cost of equipment.

It is not only between the country and the cities that there has been a movement of population; the pattern is changing within the farm areas themselves, and that in three ways:

1. Use of the automobile encourages increasing numbers of farmers to live not in isolation on their holdings, but in a nearby village or town, from which they drive to work each day.

2. The needs of today's farms are more varied than in the past; they include spare parts for farm machinery, chemicals and fuels, and the widening range of consumer goods that accompany a rise in the standard of living. The effect of this is that the farmer who once could satisfy his day-to-day needs at a local general store now tends to transact his business at the nearest urban shopping center, where a wider range of shops and services is available. In consequence the smallest form of rural settlement is moribund, and is being replaced in

[4]U.S. Department of Agriculture, *After a Hundred Years* (U.S.D.A. Yearbook), U.S. Government Printing Office, Washington, D.C., 1962, p. 510.

importance by the local supply centers, with their greater capacity for catering to the modern farmer's needs. We shall return to this subject in Chapter 14, when we come to consider the pattern of service centers in the Interior.

3. While the rural population is leaving the farms, there is a reverse movement which, particularly in the vicinity of the big cities, is doing something to balance the trend. City people move out into the old farm homesteads, which become country residences. In many cases the newcomers practice a little farming, without either needing or attempting to make a living from it. In New England and elsewhere on the marginal lands of the East, such part-time farming occupies a considerable area.

If the patterns of production have changed, so also have those of demand. As the standard of living within a country rises, there occur changes in the kinds of food the population consumes. In North America these changes have resulted in a decline in the consumption of bread and potatoes, and an increase in that of the higher-priced livestock products—meat, milk, and eggs. It is partly in response to this changing structure of demand and partly as a consequence of the modern stress on scientific land use that there emerges one further trend of which we must take note. It is a trend away from the old regional specializations of the agricultural "belts" (with their unhealthy tendency to monoculture) toward diversity within regions. This diversity usually takes the form of an increase in the area under fodder crops, and the development of livestock farming. While the trend is most marked in the old cotton and wheat areas, it is interesting to notice that the plans for the development of reclaimed lands in the Columbia Basin and the Central Valley of California were equally emphatic about the part it was hoped livestock farming would play. In all these regions a rising demand for livestock products was assumed, although in some areas it appears to have been overestimated.

Whether or not this is the case, however, the laying down to fodder crops of overworked

Mechanization of American agriculture: (2) The fruit crop. These three pictures of the California grape crop show the extent to which mechanization of fruit picking has become possible. In the first picture, the vineyards are laid out with the rows of vines far enough apart to accommodate machinery. In the second, the grape harvester passes over the vines, plucks the grapes, and deposits them either in a truck or on a paper carpet laid alongside. In the third picture, the grapes are spread in the sun to dry for raisins. (California Wine Institute; Up-Right Harvesters, Selma, Calif.; U.S. Department of Agriculture)

fields, and the encouragement of livestock farming as a restorative for the land, must certainly be approved by all those who are concerned for the best interests of North American agriculture.

Farming the Dry Lands

Over much of western North America the rainfall is too slight or too unreliable to permit the growing of crops by the ordinary methods adopted further east. This vast, dry West has for long, therefore, been a region of extensive grazing, much of it useful, even so, for only a few months in the wetter season of the year. In these circumstances the region produced in the 1920s an average annual output equivalent to only 35 cents per acre (86 cents per ha), or roughly the cost of keeping one head of cattle on the ranges for one month. The basic problem of the region, then and now, is somehow to increase this dismally low figure.

Higher output per acre can be obtained either by planting crops or by increasing the numbers of stock carried on the range. Since neither of these things can be done under natural conditions, special methods must be introduced. The two methods which are most widely adopted are dry farming and irrigation.

DRY FARMING

On millions of acres too dry for ordinary cultivation cropping is, nevertheless, carried out by the use of techniques known collectively as dry farming. The principles underlying these techniques are simple. They are (1) to conserve by every means possible the scanty amounts of moisture available in the soil, and (2) to practice the form of cropping that will make the least demand upon these scanty supplies.

To achieve these objects the farmer generally plants crops with low water requirements, and spaces them more widely than would be normal in the wetter East. The land is usually cropped only in alternate years, and the fallows are so treated as to conserve the moisture of the fallow year for the following crop-year.

When we come, however, to the question of how the fallows should be treated, we find that even since the 1930s there has been a marked change of opinion as to the methods to be adopted. The earlier method is well reflected in W.P. Webb's book *The Great Plains*, published in 1931, and dealing with the adaptations of farming technique that were forced on the early settlers of the region. Briefly, this method consisted of reducing the surface of the fallow land to a "dust mulch"—a finely powdered surface layer which, it was argued, would reduce loss of water through evaporation. But the drought years of the 1930s showed all too effectively that there was little point in retaining the moisture while losing the soil, which blew away in clouds. Today a different method is commonly used. The field surface is left rough, not powdery, and while the fallows are weeded to ensure that no water is lost to worthless vegetation, the soil is covered with a layer of trash and straw to protect it from the action of both sun and wind.

That moisture can be conserved and crops grown by this means seems clear. A large proportion of all North American wheat and sorghum is grown in this way. However, the main question raised by dry farming is one not so much of technique as of desirability. The fact that crops *can* be grown beyond the margins of ordinary cultivation may merely encourage farmers to rash expansion into the climatic danger zones; in other words, it may simply make dangerously possible what ought not to be done at all.

IRRIGATION

The alternative and much more spectacular method of extending the farm frontier into dry lands is by irrigation. By 1969 there were some 39 million acres under irrigation in the United States and over a million in Canada, the bulk of them in Alberta. In the eleven western states of the United States this irrigated area represents some 30 percent of the acreage under crops, and thus plays a part of real importance in the region's life.

The normal method of irrigation in North America until recently has been by canal and furrow. Such a method requires that the land be levelled and the channels maintained if it is to work efficiently. These requirements have tended both to limit the irrigable area and to raise the cost of the operation. Today, how-

Fig. 6-3. Western North America: Principal irrigated areas.

Areas containing irrigated lands, existing or projected

| 0 | 100 | 200 | 300 | 400 | 500 mi |

| 0 | 200 | 400 | 600 | 800 km |

ever, the method of irrigating by sprinkler is becoming increasingly popular; on the Columbia Basin Project, for example, it now accounts for almost a half of the whole operation. Sprinkler irrigation is cheaper to install by perhaps one-third, and it does not demand the same amount of ground preparation. The sprinklers are usually mounted along a pipe stretching across the field and carried on wheels, so that the pipe can be moved at whatever speed the farmer wishes. The system does not demand upkeep of the same field channels as furrow irrigation, and therefore saves both space and labor inputs (keeping the channels clear demands large amounts of fairly skilled labor) as well as making it possible to irrigate on uneven surfaces.

Not all of the irrigated area, however, is land

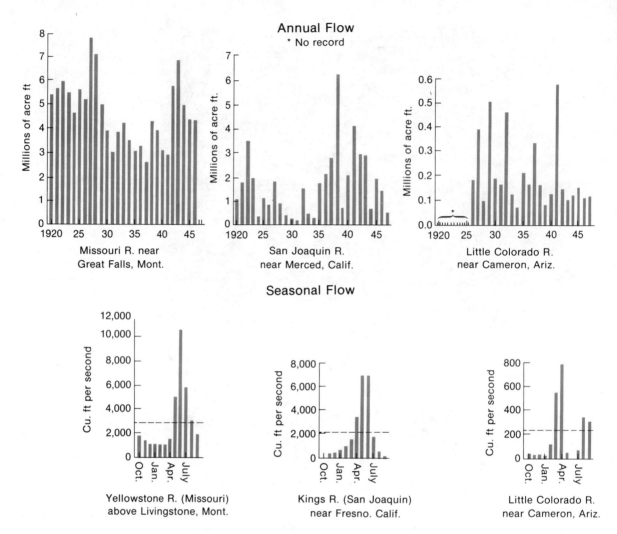

Annual Flow
* No record

Missouri R. near
Great Falls, Mont.

San Joaquin R.
near Merced, Calif.

Little Colorado R.
near Cameron, Ariz.

Seasonal Flow

Yellowstone R. (Missouri)
above Livingstone, Mont.

Kings R. (San Joaquin)
near Fresno. Calif.

Little Colorado R.
near Cameron, Ariz.

Fig. 6-4. The dry West: River flow, showing annual and seasonal variations, illustrated by examples from the San Joaquin, Colorado, and Missouri river systems at the points indicated.

reclaimed from desert or semidesert. In fact irrigation has been applied in three quite different situations: (1) to bring into use unimproved or arid areas; (2) to increase crop yields in areas where cultivation is already possible, but where scanty rainfall limits growth; and (3) to give security to farmers in areas where rainfall is unreliable and drought is a menace. Making the desert blossom is only one of the functions of irrigation and therefore, as the next section of the chapter suggests, it is probably an overrated one. Irrigation is of vital importance outside the desert areas, but in a *supplemental* role, giving security to the agriculture already carried on there. One of the most spectacular recent expansions of irrigation, for

example, is not in the dry lands at all, so far as rainfall is concerned, but in the Central Sand Plains of Wisconsin, where beans and other vegetables are being raised on an altogether new scale by the use of sprinklers.

Great as has been the contribution of irrigation farming to the development of the West, those who pioneered its use envisaged for it a still wider application. With 36 million acres (14.5 million ha) of the West already irrigated, the present estimate of the additional irrigable area amounts to some 12 million acres (4.8 million ha). But early estimates were at least double this figure. That a scaling-down of the estimates has been necessary over the past 70 to 80 years is due to a growing appreciation that irrigation is not a panacea for all the ills of a dry region, but a specialized technique of limited usefulness and limited application.

The limitations are first a product of physical conditions. Apart from the obvious consideration that only the reasonably level areas of the dry West are irrigable, there are three principal factors that restrict the usefulness of this solution:

1. The soil must be suitable for applying irrigation water. If it is too porous or too light, the water will drain through it too rapidly. On the other hand, a heavy, badly drained soil (or an area so level that there is no natural slope to carry the water off) may become waterlogged. In a number of western projects this has in fact happened. The result is serious; not only does the soil become difficult to work, but in areas such as these where the evaporation rate is high, the moisture is drawn up to the soil surface and there deposits a salt layer—a "black alkali" crust—that ruins the land for crops. Often the crust can only be removed by expensive flushing with fresh water.

2. Another physical limitation on the size of the area that can be irrigated is the large amount of water needed, either pumped from wells or diverted from streams. Since most irrigation projects are in hot, dry areas, the water requirements of the crops grown on them are at a maximum. Furthermore, owing to losses that occur through seepage from the irrigation channels or through evaporation, only about one gallon out of every three that are diverted or pumped to the fields actually reaches the crop roots, although by using sprinklers a more favorable ratio can be obtained.

It was this factor of loss en route that was overlooked by the early planners, and that led to overestimates of the irrigable areas. Sometimes they found themselves with canals but with no water to fill them. Downstream users might find the entire flow of a river diverted to supply irrigation projects further upstream. In other areas, pumping of underground water for irrigation has so lowered the water table that once-fertile lands have become sterile. In Arizona, in California, and in parts of the Dakotas, the water requirements, even of the irrigated lands so far developed, greatly exceed the rate of underground replacement.

3. The third factor is that irrigation possibilities are governed by the *nature* of the water supply. To be serviceable the supply must be available during the season of greatest need—generally from April to August. But the majority of projects depend on the flow of streams, and few of the western rivers have a régime that meets these requirements. Not only does their flow vary widely from year to year, but in most cases it reaches its peak in the spring, dwindling away by the late summer to little or nothing.

It therefore becomes inevitable that if these rivers are to be used for irrigation they must be controlled. Storage must be provided, both to counter the late-summer shortages and to eliminate year-to-year fluctuations. The necessity for storage further reduces the number of areas to which irrigation can be applied. It also brings into consideration a new and more drastic limiting factor—cost.

The earliest American irrigation projects were simple stream diversions, constructed by a few farmers and costing little but their own labor. Today's projects involve dams, reservoirs, and canals; and the cost may run into billions of dollars as more elaborate schemes involving a million acres (0.4 million ha) or more are constructed. Since the simplest projects were generally undertaken first, it is probable that any further extensions of the irrigated areas will involve higher rather than lower costs.

This change in the nature of the typical irrigation project was given expression when the North American governments recognized that irrigation had become a matter too big to be left entirely to individual initiative. In 1902 there was founded within the U.S. Department of the Interior a Bureau of Reclamation, charged with bringing into use suitable dry lands on the federal domain. Although in quantitative terms the bulk of the irrigated acreage is still in private projects, it is the huge Bureau of Reclamation schemes of recent years that have caught the public eye. In Canada the federal government was drawn into the field of irrigation finance by the distress of the Prairie farmers in the depression-and-drought years of the early 1930s, from which resulted the Prairie Farms Rehabilitation Act of 1935.

Not all the costs involved in a new project arise directly out of the irrigation works, but it seems fair to say that costs ran at $1000 per acre ($2500 per ha) on the last generation of the large-scale projects which have added most to the irrigated acreage of the West in recent years. For the future it is in terms of this kind of project and this level of expenditure that the West must think.

As has already been suggested, the financing of such projects is almost inevitably a matter for the government, which undertakes the development of a whole valley or region at a time. But even if the government provides the capital and does so interest free, the farmer is still burdened by the tremendous cost of repayment and of maintenance. This burden can in practice be reduced by adopting the solution of the multipurpose project, in which irrigation is not developed alone, but in combination with waterpower, recreation, or flood control. Part of the cost of constructing the irrigation works can then be set against the other users, either to be paid for by the consumers of electricity, or to be absorbed as a social cost by the public who benefit from the parks or the flood control. On the Columbia Basin Project, for example, the Department of the Interior decided in advance on the following allocation of costs and repayments:

Total costs (estimated)—$455 million[5]

Costs attributable to irrigation	$342 million
Costs attributable to power plants	$113 million
	$455 million
But repayment called for from irrigation users	$86 million
But repayment called for from power users	$369 million
	$455 million

Such a method of developing the dry lands raises questions of first importance, and some of these are discussed in the next section. For the moment let us return to the original problem—how to raise the basic output of the dry ranges from its pathetically low prewar average. That this can be done in places by cultivation, using either dry farming techniques or irrigation, is apparent. But most of the dry West will never be anything but rangeland, and the particular value of the cultivated patches is not so much that they grow exotic crops, but that they provide a firm agricultural base for the extensive ranching that must always be the dominant agricultural activity of the area. In other words, the simplest and almost certainly the cheapest way of increasing western productivity is by using the arable lands not to produce export crops, but to guarantee the well-being of a greatly increased livestock population. But this generalization must now be related to a wider consideration of an agricultural policy suited to the needs of the North American nations as a whole.

Agriculture and the Future

CANADA

Up until the Second World War, twentieth-century Canada had experienced a rapid increase in the area in farms. The great Prairie boom occurred in the first years of the century, and, in the course of the boom, settlers carried the frontier of farming far beyond the limits of safety imposed by drought and frost. But since the Second World War, immigration to Canada's farms has been slow; today newcomers make for the cities, where they are joined by large numbers of young farm-born Canadians who have left the land. The tide of farm settlement has ebbed and the area in farms began to fall off—by some 4 million acres (1.62 million ha) between 1966 and 1971. The following census period, however, saw a renewal of the expansion; 5.5 million acres (2.3 million ha) were added between 1971 and 1976. But this increase was regionally concentrated on a limited area. Along much of the agricultural frontier, retreat continued. The big increases came in the northwest, where the Peace River country of Alberta and British Columbia attracted settlers once again, as it has done almost continuously since it was opened up in the first years of the century. Alberta's census division 15 (which covers the Peace country) had 6603

[5]The actual costs were, as might be expected, much higher than this by the time the scheme was opened. Almost the whole extra burden of cost was either allocated to power users or absorbed by the federal government, so that the final share of irrigation users has been little more than 15 percent.

farms on 5.17 million acres (2.09 million ha) in 1971; five years later, there were 8128 farms on 6.15 million acres (2.49 million ha). In British Columbia, all but three census divisions gained in number of farms during the period, while the area they occupied increased by 640,000 acres (259,000 ha). For Canada as a whole, by contrast, the number of farms remained virtually unchanged, while for the United States it fell by about 150,000 over the same period.

Why this should be so we shall have to consider in Chapter 23. But certainly one reason for the continuing expansion is the survival of Homestead legislation (see p. 75), applied now not just to the historic quarter-section but in most cases to a whole section. This makes the Peace River a genuine frontier in the nineteenth-century sense; it remains open for settlement by anyone willing to take a chance on surviving for long enough to prove his title.

Should the provincial governments encourage this expansion? The fact is that the chances of a homesteader making good today, starting from scratch on a new holding, are statistically poor: it could well be argued that he should be discouraged from making the attempt. But there is a steady flow of applicants (800 to 1200 a year in Alberta alone) and there is, at least, a growing variety of alternative employment to fall back on if the homesteader abandons the attempt after a few years, as seems almost inevitable. The tradition of letting a man prove himself on the public lands is a long-established one in North America, but for the country as a whole it seems fair to say that the decline in farm area is likely to continue and that investment in new lands, whether cleared of forest or watered by irrigation, should be extremely cautious.

This was certainly the view taken by the federal task force on agriculture that produced the report *Canadian Agriculture in the Seventies*.[6] The report recommended that ways should be sought of moving farmers *out* of agriculture, because only in that way could those who remained be assured of the space necessary to remain competitive. It took the view that prob-ably only one in every three of Canada's farms is large enough for what it called "long-run viability" and was particularly concerned with the phasing out of farms in the "low-income sector"—those farms which cannot, at least in the near future, yield a living wage to the operator.[7] It proposed on the one hand incentives for younger farmers to retrain in non-agricultural occupations and on the other the improvement of services and welfare for the older generation of marginal farmers to enable them to remain on their farms and end their working lives in some measure of comfort instead of at the bare survival level which otherwise was the best they could hope for.

For the farm industry as a whole, the report called for measures to improve management techniques and to reduce surpluses. This latter group of recommendations called, in effect, for the same measures that the United States has adopted over recent years, such as land retirement (through a kind of soil bank), and for more flexible supports and subsidies, which would have the effect of encouraging rapid switches in production according to short-term need. Obviously Canada can profit by U.S. experience in this field of incentives and controls: there are at least some of the American experiments Canada will be careful not to repeat. The major problem is likely to be a financial one: whether a country in which the agricultural sector forms so large a part of the total economy as it does in Canada can afford the kind of agricultural policy for which the Americans, for their part, have long been paying.

THE UNITED STATES

In the U.S. the farm industry has been undergoing great structural changes, as we have already seen. Such changes make it difficult to answer, but necessary to ask the questions: which lands will produce the agricultural supplies needed by the next generation of Americans, and what will be the character of the farms that produce them? On the whole, the first fifteen years after World War II were occupied by debate about the *lands* to be used, while since 1960 there has been a

[6]*Report of the Federal Task Force on Agriculture*, Ottawa, December, 1969.

[7]*Canadian Agriculture in the Seventies*, pp. 409–27.

shift of interest to the question of what the *farm* of the future will look like, and how it will be organized.

Which lands?

The population of the United States is increasing rapidly. During the past three decades the additional farm supplies needed by this population have been provided not by increasing the area in farms but by raising yields. But in practice we may take it as certain that *some* new lands will be brought into use in the future. It is certain, firstly, because new lands are needed to replace worn-out or marginal farmlands, which should be retired from cultivation. It is certain, secondly, because today's higher yields generally involve concentrating on the best areas available, and some of these may not at present be under cultivation. And it is certain, in the third place, because of the way in which farmland is being swallowed up every day for non-agricultural purposes—housing, roads, airports, and factories.

The first and second of these points need no special comment: what they amount to is a *rearrangement* of the nation's agricultural areas. It is estimated that there are probably 40 million acres (18.4 million ha) of farmland which should be withdrawn from cultivation, and the soil bank offers farmers an incentive to retire them. They can be replaced by areas more favored in their topography and soils but at present needing irrigation, drainage, or clearance of forest cover. On these favored lands farming will be efficient and productive.

The third point calls for fuller comment. In the ten years from 1966 to 1976, the United States lost 47 million acres in farms (19 million ha). Judged even by the standards of 20 years ago, today's developments in housing, commerce, and transport—the homes, the parking lots, even the crossroads—all consume space on a gigantic scale. And most of this "space" represents agricultural land now converted to other uses. Of course, only in a very large country could such a rate of loss be sustained. Not only does the United States sustain it, but it does so without any particular concern for the farming displaced by the new highways or factories.

To understand this attitude of unconcern, we must recall not only the traditional American confidence that there is plenty of room for all, but also the hard fact that in the scale of land values almost any other form of land use—say a parking lot for a supermarket—stands higher than farming. Acre for acre, most areas yield a higher return when they are converted from agriculture, regardless of what they are converted to. With so much space available in the United States we find, therefore, that areas which *can* be used for anything but agriculture will be developed for those other purposes, and that there is in progress in the United States what might be described as a game of "Last-one-in-the-water-grows-food-for-the-rest."

This is easily seen in the way in which the eastern seaboard has left the business of food supply to the less crowded lands further west. As a matter of fact, the Northeast is rapidly getting out of the farm business altogether, as Chapter 10 explains. But it comes as something of a shock to find that it is now being seriously suggested that California, the largest food producer among the fifty states, should do the same: that since so many people want to live there, agriculture, already being driven away from several hundred thousand acres each year, should take a subordinate place in the state's economy. In other words, the business of agricultural supply, having moved westward from the crowded East, now promises to rebound from the crowded West Coast into the area where, after all, it most naturally belongs—the Agricultural Interior.

For all these reasons we can assume that new land will be required for agriculture. It can be brought into use by two main methods: reclamation by irrigation in the dry West, or reclamation by other means in the humid East and Northwest.

Of these two methods it is undoubtedly irrigation that has occupied the limelight, particularly during what economist John Kenneth Galbraith has described as "the vast postwar boom in our great nationalized industries of dam-building and ditch-digging."[8] As a method it has the advantage of producing spectacu-

[8] J.K. Galbraith, *American Capitalism*, Houghton Mifflin, Boston, 1956, p. 187.

lar results. But in view of the enormous cost of recent schemes, it is necessary to overlook the spectacular, and to be quite clear that this is the most economical way of adding to the food reserves of the nation.

That Westerners are themselves enthusiastic about federal irrigation projects need surprise no one, for the local benefits conferred by such a project are great. The government makes the community what is in fact a large interest-free loan; taxable values are much enhanced; and the basis is provided for compact, intensive land use, with all the advantages of concentrated settlement, such as lower cost of services. But on the national level the advantage may be much less distinct. There seems some reason to fear that the decisive factor in government reclamation planning may have been not a clear concept of *national* need, but rather a sectional political influence. This is particulary likely when irrigation is linked with the development of electric power, for power supplies in their turn can provide a basis for industrialization, by which the whole region will be enriched.

According to present government estimates, increased crop acreages for the future could be provided by 15 million acres (6.1 million ha) of irrigable lands, 20 million acres (8.1 million ha) that could be made productive by drainage, and 42 million acres (17 million ha) which, if cleared of forest or brush, would provide good (Class I or II) arable land (see Fig. 6-5). In addition there are large areas at present under grass that could be cultivated. If the national need is simply for more cropland, then there are millions of acres in the humid East which either are lying idle or could yield much larger returns if improved. One comparative study made at the time suggested that for every acre of cropland reclaimed by irrigation in the Columbia Bend, not less than 7.5 acres (3 ha) could have been reclaimed in the southern Piedmont at the same cost. While it is true that many of these idle acres in the East need both drainage *and* clearance, and while it is reasonable that a *part* of the additional cropland required should be obtained by irrigation in the West, it has long been true that, in the words of a Department of Agriculture bulletin, "more of the physically feasible irrigation projects in the West than of the physically feasible drainage works in the South and East are now authorized."[9] And this preference is very probably reinforced by the existence of a government agency—the Bureau of Reclamation—whose whole purpose is to plan and execute the "physically feasible irrigation projects" on the federal lands of the West. Here, clearly, is a matter involving the use of federal resources that should be decided by national considerations alone. Where the benefits derived from reclamation works are local benefits, then taxpayers elsewhere are entitled to argue that the financing of such projects should be local too.

The two arguments that can legitimately be advanced in favor of western rather than eastern development are (1) that in view of the marked growth of population there, the West is where additional food supplies are likely to be needed, and (2) that since the West needs to exploit its waterpower reserves in any case, irrigation may as well accompany the development and be subsidized by power users. To both these arguments, especially if they are used to justify federal participation, there are clear rejoinders. Upon the merits of each side of the case, and not upon political sectionalism, must depend the future policy of the government.

Which farms?

Years of homesteading, accompanied by years of speculation in land and followed by decades of technological change, have left the United States with a wide range of farm types and farm sizes. As we have already seen, one type—the family farm—not only predominates numerically but has been the object of special solicitude on the part of governments and politicians. In fact the preservation of the family farm has become a goal of *social* policy, quite independently of its virtues or failings as an *economic* unit. In particular it has been extolled as a form of organization in a period when it serves politically to highlight the distinction between America with its individual freedoms and the Communist world with its collective farms.

[9]U.S. Department of Agriculture, *Agricultural Land Resources in the United States*, U.S. Government Printing Office, Washington, D.C., 1955, p. 89.

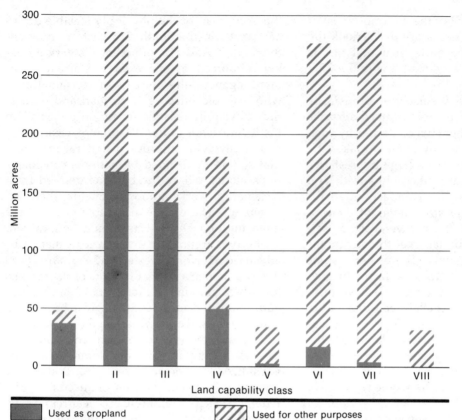

Fig. 6-5. The United States: Land used as cropland and for other purposes, by land-capability class. Note the large amount of land which, although designated Class I or Class II, is not at present under cultivation. This land represents a reserve of fertility, and should be taken into account when schemes are proposed for increasing the cultivated area by expensive methods such as irrigation of the desert. There may be cheaper ways of attaining the same end.

Now, as it happens, the *economic* record of the family farm is good, so that it has been possible to reconcile the social and economic arguments for this type of unit without too much difficulty. But having said that, we must note that the family farm can only remain efficient if it can steadily be enlarged; that is, if a constant input of labor (which is the criterion for defining this type of unit) can be accompanied by an increasing input of land, to take account of technical advances.

Some idea of the extent to which enlargement of the original, quarter-section ideal has become necessary has already been given by the figure on p. 125. In practice, few family farms occupy the optimal acreage for their operations, not because the operator cannot manage the work, but because he cannot obtain the land. Land only becomes available, in the settled areas at least, if a neighbor retires or a younger farmer gives up farming for some better-paying job off the land.

The number of farms in the United States reached a peak of 6.8 million in the 1930s. To-day, the figure is about 2.8 million, but in round figures 1 million of these produce 85 percent of the agricultural output. More than a half of the farms that exist, in other words, are commercially irrelevant. Yet this tremendous decline in the number of farms has in a sense been insufficient. It has not prevented a scramble for land, with farmers willing to travel 20–30 mi (30–50 km) to outlying parcels if they can rent them as extensions to their base-farm.[10] They must enlarge to survive.

Of the million-odd farms which contribute 85 percent of the nation's agricultural output, many are family farms—those which have managed to maintain an economical size. But size is not the only problem; there is also the capital investment which a farm of optimal size represents. For most types of farming, in order to stay in contention a farmer must

[10]See M.D. Sublett, *Farmers on the Road: Interfarm Migration and the Farming of Non-Contiguous Lands in Three Midwestern Townships, 1939–1969*, Univ. of Chicago Dept. of Geography Research Paper No. 168 (1975).

Fig. 6-6. Farm size and farm fragmentation: The problem of enlargement. Nineteenth-century settlement of the American Interior in series of quarter-section farms has left a legacy of problems for today's farmers, who need to expand the size of their operating units in order to remain economical producers. Extra land is seldom available adjacent to the original farmstead, and the scattered unit thus becomes commonplace, with farmers driving many miles between their fields.

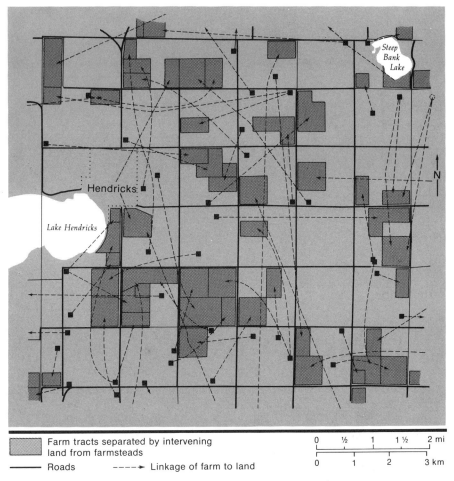

Farm tracts separated by intervening land from farmsteads

——— Roads   - - - -➤ Linkage of farm to land

reckon on an investment of at least half a million dollars—a million for a Class I farm. This figure is financially light years away from the free homesteads with which the grandparents of today's farmers began. What is more, whereas those grandparents operated in almost complete self-sufficiency, today's farmer is closely tied to a whole complex of "agribusiness," which involves buying in such inputs as fertilizers and shipping out virtually his whole product for processing off the farm. There has been a change of function; the farmer has become a producer pure and simple, and much of the old independence has gone.

Alongside the family farm, the postwar period has seen the rise of another type of unit, corporate in ownership, massive in scale, and industrial in organization. These giant farms are sometimes held by companies with no obvious connection with agriculture. They employ a labor force, often on a seasonal or contract basis, with which the relationship of the management is the same as in industry. Some states, as we have already seen (p. 109), have banned them out of hand. But nationwide, the competitive pressure in the future is going to be intense. The family farm has done well for America—and for hungry Europe, too, for that matter—in the past. But it will make little sense to cling to the past in planning and policy, no matter how emotive the concept of the family farm may be, if this particular form of organization cannot supply the growing nation with its requirements in the future.

7

Industry

Introduction

In 1961 the United States and Canada between them produced just one-third of all the world's manufactured goods in terms of value added. In the world outside the U.S.S.R. and Eastern Europe, their share in value added by manufacture was 47.7 percent.[1] That North America should have taken over the role of nineteenth-century Britain as world manufacturer is to be explained only partly in terms of rich natural resources. Great as these are, another part of the explanation must be sought in outlook and in organization, without which the resource base might have lain as valueless as in the days when the Indians roamed the continent.

There are certain impressions of Americans industry traditionally held by Europeans—that it is made up of huge combines operating equally huge plants; that the American have invented a machine to do everything in life. Although few aspects of American life are more widely misunderstood, these crude impressions do serve at least to call attention to the factors that have been decisive in establishing North America's industrial power.

Size of Units

While there are thousands of plants in both Canada and United States that employ only a handful of workers, it is true that in most industries output is dominated by a few large corporations and that these tend to spread between the two countries without much reference to the international boundary. Far from finding such a situation undesirable, most Americans contend that there is no reason to be afraid of bigness as such, and that the ever-increasing complexity of modern industrial processes, together with the need for more costly research, absolutely requires the creation of larger industrial units. Further, it may be pointed out that it is only in the past few years that the control of such huge business units has been made possible—by devices like the electronic calculator, or by telephone and radio communication—and that the larger units are merely taking advantage of these advances. Only when the leadership of an industry falls into the hands of *too* few firms does the equally strong, and often conflicting, American fear of monopoly overcome the

[1]U.N. Department of Economic and Social Affairs, *The Growth of World Industry 1938–1961*, New York, 1965, pp. 230, 236.

126

widespread belief that bigness and goodness are somehow allied. Then the antitrust laws are invoked against the monopolist, but often in a manner sufficiently uncertain to emphasize rather than resolve this basic dilemma in the American mind. Meanwhile the industrial corporation, with its billions of dollars in capital assets and its vast expenditures on scientific and social work, has become a profoundly influential element in the life of the nation.

Mechanization

The widespread mechanization in both factory and home in North America is perhaps best accounted for in two ways. On the one hand, the general level of American labor costs has always been high enough to encourage manufacturers to seek ways of replacing men by machines. On the other hand, a high standard of living makes available surplus income that can be spent on removing the drudgery from life by the use of machinery. To these two considerations may be added a third; the size of the North American market is sufficient to encourage large-scale production techniques, based upon the classic American industrial device of assembly-line construction and the more recently established control methods of automation.

There are, however, other factors involved: the generally high standard of managerial ability and the huge expenditures on research into both the technical and the human aspects of industry. And such elaborate and costly research programs are only made possible by the basic condition that underlies all American industrial development and multiplies whatever advantages of technique or skill the American workers may possess—the great size of the internal market. The manufacturer who anticipates sales in terms of millions can spend far more on research—or for that matter on any other overhead—than the manufacturer whose sales will number only thousands, without incurring extra cost per unit. Here then lies another secret of American industrial success.

All these circumstances have their effect on the changing geographical patterns of the con-

tinent's manufacturing, and it is now time to make a brief survey of the industrial areas.

The Distribution of Industry

While one of the features of modern industrialization in North America has been the tendency for industry to spread into rural districts, there remain certain major concentrations. These are:

The Middle Atlantic Region

This stretches along the Atlantic coast from New York to Baltimore and inland to such towns as Reading and Bethlehem. As a "funnel" for many of the United States' imports and exports, this well-established area attracts a major share of the nation's processing, with a full range of industries from the heaviest to the lightest.

The Northern Appalachians

In the valleys around Scranton and Wilkes-Barre there is a small industrial area located on the Pennsylvania anthracite field. Declining demand for anthracite (see p. 131) and comparative inaccessibility have posed many problems for this region since the Second World War, but present low figures for unemployment suggest that it is gradually recovering a measure of prosperity.

Southern New England

In the three states of Massachusetts, Rhode Island, and Connecticut, where manufacturing is widespread, lies North America's oldest industrial area. There are local specializations, among them textiles and leather goods, with a growth of new industries introduced to relieve dependence on older ones whose fortunes have declined. Boston is the largest manufacturing center and the commerical hub of the area today, as it has been throughout New England's era of industrial development.

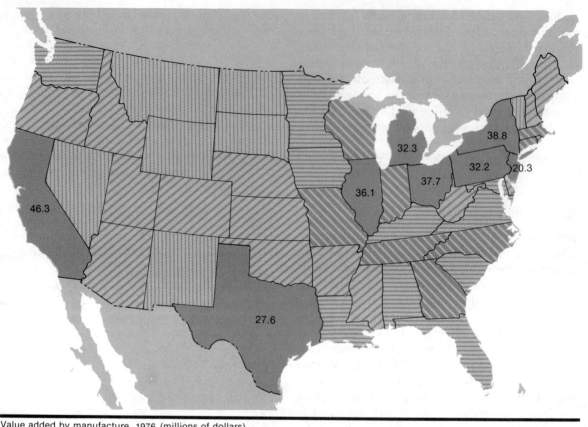

Value added by manufacture, 1976 (millions of dollars)

- Less than 1,500
- 1,500–5,000
- 5 000–10,000
- 10,000–20,000
- More than 20,000

Fig. 7-1. The United States: Value added by manufacturing, by states, 1976.

The Mohawk Valley

This is a linear industrial belt stretching from Albany to Rochester, New York. Benefitting by their unrivalled location on one of North America's natural "connecting links," a number of manufacturing towns have grown up, each with its own specialities.

The St. Lawrence Valley

For long it has been the industrial core of Canada. This area is focused upon the great center of Montréal, which has over 10 percent of Canada's manufacturing workers and a wide range of industries. Elsewhere the processing of forest products predominates. The use of hydroelectric power is basic to the valley's industrial development.

The Industrial Eastern Interior

Throughout a wide region that includes the Ohio Valley, the eastern Corn Belt, and southwestern Ontario, industry has everywhere penetrated into what is still basically an agricultural section, creating such large industrial centers as Toronto and Cincinnati. While industry's original business in this area was the supply of farm requirements and the processing of farm products, the region has attracted many other industries from the more crowded parts of the old manufacturing regions.

Geographically a part of the *Eastern Interior,* but functionally distinct, are three of the most intensively industrialized areas of the continent:

The Pittsburgh-Lake Erie Region

It stretches along the coal and iron routes of the Great Lakes and Appalachian area from Toledo to Hamilton, Ontario, and southward into Ohio and western Pennsylvania. This is the core area of American heavy industry.

The Chicago-Lake Michigan Region

This has many of the characteristics of the Lake Erie steel area, but it also fulfils the supply and processing functions typical of the Eastern Interior as a whole. In both roles Chicago dominates the Interior, with more than four percent of United States industrial employment.

Michigan

Although Michigan, too, is geographically a part of the Industrial Eastern Interior, it is treated separately here because the state's manufacturing is so dominated by the automobile industry. Nearly 30 percent of Michigan's industrial workers are associated directly with it, and in Detroit this figure rises to over 30 percent. Branches of the industry are to be found scattered widely throughout the state.

The Cities of the Western Interior

Among these, the most important are Winnipeg, Minneapolis-St. Paul, Omaha, Kansas City, and St. Louis. These cities and scores of lesser centers perform in nearly every case the same double function. They serve as regional supply points, and they participate in the Midwest's basic industries—meat packing, flour milling, and the production of agricultural machinery.

The Southeastern Region

A wide horseshoe around the southern end of the Appalachians and an area of scattered industry rather than of great manufacturing centers, it has been the scene of much recent development. It is powered by hydroelectricity and Southern petroleum and has specializations in cotton textiles, tobacco, chemicals and plastics.

The Texas and Gulf Coast Region

This industrial area is of recent growth, and its resources and facilities have already attracted a wide variety of plants to the coast and to the inland oil field regions, which are dominated by Houston and by the Dallas-Fort Worth conurbation respectively.

The Pacific Coast

Here industry is concentrated in four or five nodes—the Vancouver area, the lowlands of Puget Sound and the lower Columbia, the San Francisco Bay Area, and the Los Angeles-San Diego lowland. As an industrial area, the Coast has developed a wide range of products for both local and national markets with a long statistical lead for three types of industry: food processing, lumber manufacturing, and the manufacture of transport equipment, especially aircraft and aerospace vehicles.

Of the factors of location that influence this industrial pattern, some—the classic forces of proximity to water supply, to means of transport, or to markets—are common to all industrial communities. But what may be regarded as a peculiarly North American phenomenon is the influence on distribution of the force of local competition.

In a great free-trade area like Canada or the United States, where space is usually plentiful and both resources and markets are widely scattered, the manufacturer generally has the choice of a number of equally suitable locations for his plant. Where this is the case, he can base his final decision not merely on broad considerations of markets or transport but on a detailed study of social conditions in the rival

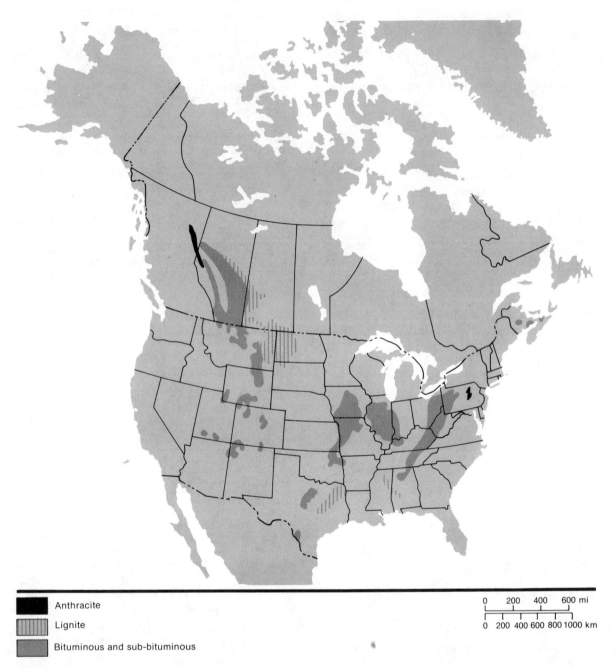

Anthracite

Lignite

Bituminous and sub-bituminous

0   200   400   600 mi

0   200 400 600 800 1000 km

Fig. 7-2. North America: Coal fields.

locations he has in mind. That is to say, being assured of a number of reasonably suitable sites, he can pick the one which will give to his plant and his workers the pleasantest possible surroundings and the richest community life. The kind of factor upon which he will ultimately make his decision may well be: what recreational facilities will this community af-

ford the workers? Are the schools good? Does the appearance of the town show the citizens to be progressive and proud of their homes? How efficient are the public services? That these social considerations should bulk so large in the manufacturer's mind may upset the geographer's explanations, but the prominence given to them betokens a high standard of living, a mobile labor force, and a concern for the industrial worker that would have been welcome in earlier phases of industrialization.

The opposite side of the matter—the community's approach—is equally significant. State with state and city with city, the communities of North America compete with each other to attract new business, business that will increase their tax revenues and provide new sources of employment. Most self-respecting communities want to expand, and in doing so will seek to maintain a balanced employment structure and to attract desirable forms of industry—those that will be clean to live with or that will bring to the community a skilled type of worker with high wage rates. If a manufacturer is planning for this type of industry, he will probably be wooed by the local chamber of commerce; he may perhaps be offered bargain tax rates as an added inducement. If his coming would harm the social environment of the community, he will be discouraged.

This form of competition has been particularly evident where the federal government has been building industrial plants for military purposes. Government investment of this kind is usually a valuable addition to the assets of an area, and competition to secure contracts is keen. What atomic power has meant to Tennessee, or missiles to California and Florida, can never be fully assessed, but it amounts to hundreds of millions of dollars of additional income for the state.

Coal, Iron, and Steel

COAL

The backbone of North American industry is formed by a continental coal production of 550–650 million tons and a steelmaking capacity in excess of 150 million tons. Upon the movements of these huge quantities of primary industrial materials depends the pattern of an industrial structure of unparalleled magnitude.

By far the greatest part of the coal output comes from the Appalachian region. Virtually all of North America's anthracite is produced on the Pennsylvania fields, where today's output of this once-popular fuel (less than 6 million tons) is far below the 1916 peak of 98 million tons. Of the continent's bituminous coal, some 75 percent of the annual production is mined in the great Western Appalachian field. Underlying the plateau section of the Appalachian System, this remarkable gift of nature provides wide areas of good coking coal that are often aligned in thick horizontal seams which outcrop on valley sides and afford the easiest possible conditions for mining. The earliest development occurred in the northern end of the field, in southwestern Pennsylvania, and with the passage of time, mining has spread south through West Virginia and into eastern Kentucky. Meanwhile, far to the south, the field has been developed around Birmingham, Alabama, where it is partnered by iron ore deposits.

For almost a century Appalachian coal has supplied a continent-wide market, moving not only north to the steel mills but east to the ports of Hampton Roads (Norfolk and Newport News, Virginia), which handle 90 percent of export shipments, and west to the Great Lakes, for distribution by water. This coal is still the major supply within the continent, but its popularity has waned. For one thing, the old categories of "coking" and "non-coking" coal have been rendered largely obsolete by advances in the technology of steelmaking, so that the importance of this quality no longer has the effect of reserving particular markets for Appalachian coal. For another thing, growing concern over pollution led to restrictions on the burning of fuel with a high sulphur content—such as Appalachian coal. The past decade has therefore seen a change in the relative importance of coal sources, with a decline in that of Appalachia and a rise in that of some previously insignificant producers, such as the western states of Wyoming and Montana.

In the western half of the continent there are vast if scattered coal reserves, many of them low grade. Saskatchewan and North Dakota produce lignite; Alberta and Montana produce both lignite and bituminous coal, and coal is also mined in Wyoming, Utah, Colorado, New Mexico, and Washington. Exploitation has generally been restricted by two factors: (1) there is no large market within economic range of these deposits, and (2) as we shall later see,

Coal in western North America: A strip mine in Montana. The picture calls attention to two trends: one is the increasing proportion of American coal won by stripping the surface rather than sinking deep shafts, and the other is the expansion of production of coals with a relatively low sulphur content to replace high-sulphur supplies from the Appalachian field. The coal is sub-bituminous, with low heating value, but the seam here is 23 ft (7.3 m) thick, and the 120 ft (36.5 m) of overburden are removed by a huge electric shovel, so that the operation is fully economical. *(Bureau of Reclamation, U.S. Dept. of the Interior)*

in these western and southwestern parts of the continent, coal is climbing the economic gradient of competition against oil and natural gas. Early coal production was generally related to local needs, especially to supplying fuel for railway locomotives, and was small in scale. Today, however, with a search for low-sulphur coals forced upon the industry and a large and growing market for North American coal in East Asia, prospects for the western branch of the industry look better than they ever have. The only other field of importance within the continent is the Eastern Interior, the bulk of whose production comes from southern and western Illinois.

Production and consumption of coal in North America have fluctuated widely in recent years. In 1975, for example, the United States produced 640 million tons of bituminous coal, whereas in 1961 the output was only 420 million, with an additional 10 million tons produced in Canada. These fluctuations are largely the result of competition from other energy sources and the consequent need to search continually for new markets.

Consequently, the coal industry has been an industrial battleground for the past two or three decades. It has modernized itself, and turned in part from shaft mining to strip mining, and replaced men with machines. The result has been an industry of varying fortunes, employing 415,000 workers in 1950, 125,000 in 1969, and almost 200,000 in 1975, in the aftermath of the dramatic rise in the price of oil (see p. 97). In times of slack demand the smaller, often independent mines close down; there were 7228 mines in 1965, but only 4744 in 1973. When demand revives, the big companies move in with their machines and quickly increase production. Caught in the middle of these wild economic gyrations are the miners themselves. It is no coincidence that in the years since 1950 one name has come to be synonymous with poverty and depression in the United States, and it is the name of a coal field—Appalachia. As Chapter 15 explains, Appalachia has replaced the Deep South in the nation's consciousness as the pauper in the North American family of regions.

IRON ORE

Over the past hundred years North America's iron ore production has been just as markedly dominated by a single source as has its coal production. This source is on the shores of Lake Superior—vast ore bodies first made accessible to industry by the opening of the Soo Canal in 1855, and reaching full development with the opening up of the Mesabi Range in the 1890s. From this wilderness area, where the main ore bodies are almost ideally accessible for working, there has flowed a century's supply of high-grade ore for Canada and the United States alike.

The future prospects for Superior ore, however, are less encouraging. The tremendous drain of the past decades, and especially of the period since 1940, has removed the most accessible and most valuable ores. Huge quantities of low-grade ore remain, but the situation confronts the steel men with two alternatives. One is to process, or "beneficiate," the low-grade ore at plants in the vicinity of the mines, in order to reduce the bulk of material to be carried across the Lakes, and to supply the industry's furnaces with the same grade of material they are now adjusted to consume. Such plants have already been established on the Lake Superior shore, and low-grade taconite deposits

are being treated in this way. Inevitably, however, a new item of cost is involved in this extra processing stage. The other alternative is to seek new sources elsewhere.

Around Birmingham, Alabama, there are deposits of ore that have been worked for a century. In conjunction with the adjacent Appalachian coal, these deposits form the basis of a well-established and low-cost steel industry. But for the quantities of ore they require, the northern steel men are now looking to two other sources—Labrador and Latin America.

The story of the discovery of iron ore in the forested wilderness of Labrador, 300 mi (480 km) north of the St. Lawrence—of how the concession holders battled with the elements and of how at length the ore fields were linked by rail with tidewater—has lost nothing in the telling. More prosaically, the companies involved—in which Great Lakes interests are prominent—have pushed production ahead toward the mark of 50 million tons a year. Some of the ore is low grade, and it must be beneficiated like that from Lake Superior. Labrador ore is nowadays available to replace Mesabi ore throughout the Lake Erie-Pittsburgh area and on the Atlantic coast. About half of it moves west by the St. Lawrence Seaway (p. 152); with the present freight rate structure, the costs of moving it to Pittsburgh via the Seaway and via the Atlantic coast ports are roughly equal.

Imported ores from Venezuela are widely used by the East Coast steel mills, and both the largest companies—United States Steel Corporation and Bethlehem Steel—have made big investments in Venezuela. In view of the prospects for Mesabi, it is significant also that in the early 1950s, when U.S. Steel was seeking a site for a new integrated steel mill, it chose an Atlantic seaboard location—Fairless, near Trenton, New Jersey—where it uses Latin American ores almost exclusively. But because the Venezuelan ores are high grade, they can be economically carried as far inland as blast furnaces in Ohio. Thus the dependence of the American steel industry on imported ores, either from South America or from Labrador, is tending to increase as the Mesabi supplies run down. In 1951 only eight percent of the ores received at U.S. plants were foreign in origin. Today the proportion is one-third.

THE STEEL INDUSTRY

The assembly and dispatch of the great quantities of heavy materials with which a modern steel mill deals are problems of such dimensions as to make the steel industry "transport orientated." In terms of quantities involved the ore presents the biggest problem, but in terms of cost the most expensive item is the shipment of the finished product. In practice, therefore, the decisive location factor in the modern industry is likely to be proximity to markets. However, such is the capital investment represented by an integrated mill that another feature of the industry is its high degree of inertia. The giant corporations, which alone can afford to compete in such circumstances, will accept higher costs for a period, in unfavorable locations, rather than have to build afresh.

Bearing in mind these factors, we can now briefly consider the industry's distribution. First, there are several plants on the Atlantic coast. They receive most of their ore from abroad and their coal from the Appalachians; the coal generally travels by rail to Hampton Roads and by water from there. The strength of their position lies in their access, by water or by land, to the great Middle Atlantic market area. It is, in fact, a position strong enough to enable them to supply New England as well and to give to the oft-proposed New England steelworks (which would be much further from its coal supplies) only a slender chance of competing successfully.

The largest part of the steel industry, however, is to be found in the central region between Chicago and Milwaukee in the west and Buffalo and Hamilton, Ontario, in the east. The center line of this region is the Great Lakes waterway, by which Superior ore—in recent years, some 60 to 70 million tons per annum—moves eastward (see Fig. 14-6). Originally the movement was a simple one: ore from Superior was carried to meet Appalachian coke at Pittsburgh. Since the 1890s, however, the pattern

has grown more complex, for a reverse flow of coal shipments has developed, amounting to 20–30 million tons per annum; with coal and ore moving in opposite directions between Duluth and West Virginia, the flow could clearly be interrupted not only at Pittsburgh but at almost any other point en route. In practice the most suitable place at which to interrupt the flow is at the lakeshore ports where transshipment takes place. Thus the industry has spread from its Pennsylvania-Ohio nucleus back along the center line, with concentrations at the ports along Lake Erie and at other Great Lakes ports such as Chicago and Hamilton, which are not on the direct Duluth-Pittsburgh route but are equally accessible to the ore carriers. Indeed, the industry spread the whole distance to Duluth, where a steel mill was opened in 1915 under pressure from the state of Minnesota (which wished to obtain some industrial benefit from its ores) but against the better judgement of the steelmakers. The location at Duluth is remote from any major market and represents in reality an overextension of the industry along its center line.

From the point of view of the steelmakers, it was fortunate that when the Lake Superior ores began to run out, their replacement source—the Labrador ores—was accessible by the same route through the Great Lakes. It was therefore unnecessary for the industry to relocate in order to take advantage of these new supplies: the shores of the Lakes remain in the new phase of the industry as good a location for a steel mill as they have been ever since the 1890s.

Three other groups of steelworks must be briefly mentioned. One is that around Birmingham, at the southern end of the Appalachian coal field. Here the juxtaposition of fuel and ore makes for low production costs and gives the industry a dominant position in the expanding markets of the South and Southwest. The second location is in the Maritime Provinces of Canada, where local coal supplies are used in conjunction with ores imported from Labrador. Output is small, and remoteness hampers development.

The other group consists of the scattered plants of the West. While a few of these, such

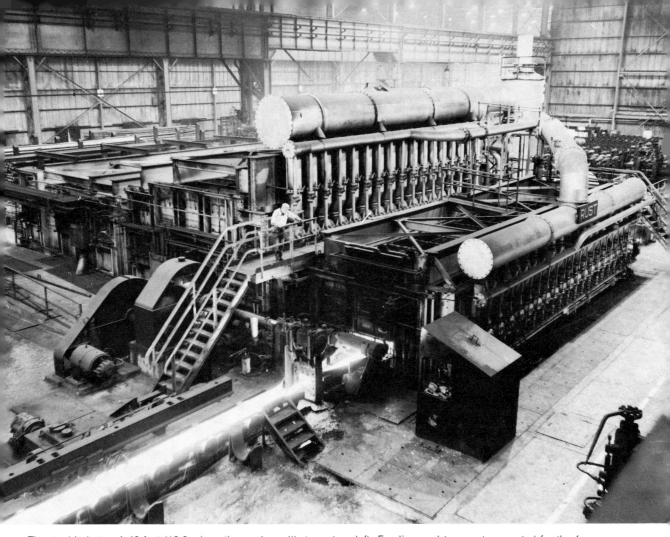

The steel industry: A 40-foot (12.2 m) continuous bar mill at the Fairless Works, with a billet leaving the mill at the bottom left. Feeding and temperature control for the furnace are automatic. *(United States Steel Corp.)*

as that at Pueblo, are of earlier date, most of them are a product either of military supply programs in the Second World War or of postwar expansion by eastern firms into the new western markets. Thus each of the major industrial centers of the Gulf and Pacific coasts—Houston, Los Angeles, San Francisco-Oakland, Seattle—is a steel producer, although not one of them is well situated in terms of raw material supply. In addition the U.S. government constructed, and U.S. Steel now owns, the Geneva Works near Salt Lake City, a plant with reasonable access to ore and coal (100–200 mi [150–300 km] of movement in each case), but remote from the Pacific coast market it was built to serve. In one way or another, therefore, all these western plants operate under considerable handicaps.

This distribution pattern of the steel industry was for a long time stable. Before the Second World War it was maintained by a number of factors, among them the power of the great corporations, which found expression in the price system known as "Pittsburgh Plus." Under this system, all steel sold was, by agreement within the industry, priced as if it had been produced in Pittsburgh and shipped from there, even though the purchaser may have fetched it himself from a mill in his own city. The object of this device was to discourage the spread of production into outlying market areas and thus to protect the steelmakers' huge investments in the central region. It was a kind of stage-managed industrial inertia, enforced by the overwhelming power of the U.S. Steel Corporation.

But the pattern has now changed. In 1924 Pittsburgh Plus was declared illegal, and in 1948 its successor, the basing point system, was also abolished, freeing the industry from artificial restraints upon relocation. At the same time other, technological, changes have taken place. The industry is using less iron ore and more scrap metal in its furnaces. To the extent that this occurs (and on the West coast 85 percent or more of the furnace material is scrap), it lessens the importance of access to ore and increases that of access to scrap—which is found in areas of greatest steel use; that is, in the market areas. The industry is using less coal too, as plant efficiency increases, and especially because of the tendency to integration, by which the metal is heated only once and goes through all the stages of production in one continuous process. To these changes in technology and pricing must be added the effects of replacing ore supplies from Lake Superior by those from Labrador and Latin America. All these influences must be weighed against the impact of changes in demand; in particular the growth of the automobile industry as the steel industry's prime customer. With these developments in demand for steel, the industry has tended in the latest period to increase its capacity in Michigan and in the Far West, while the relative importance of the old steel heartland around Pittsburgh has diminished.

Petroleum and Natural Gas

We must now consider briefly North America's other sources of power for industry. The first of these are petroleum and natural gas, of which the United States is both the largest producer and the largest consumer in the world. In 1975 its output was 3050 million barrels of crude petroleum but the country was, nevertheless, a net importer.[2] The production of natural gas was 21,900,000 million cu ft.

[2] An interesting commentary on the changing position of the U.S. in world petroleum supply is offered by the fact that, when the first edition of this book was published in 1960, the United States produced 2575 million barrels of crude, and this was 33 percent of the world total. In 1975, its 3050 million barrels represented just 16 percent of the world output.

The rise of the United States petroleum industry has been one of the great economic phenomena of the past century. It is only about a hundred years since an oil strike in western Pennsylvania ushered in the era of commercial exploitation. The early days of the industry were marked by savage competition, from which John D. Rockefeller's Standard Oil Trust emerged in 1882 with a virtual monopoly of the continent's refining and pipeline facilities and so a stranglehold upon the producers who depended on these facilities. The early Pennsylvania fields were soon eclipsed by those of California, opened in the 1890s, and much more so by the southwestern fields, which came in after 1901. New fields were discovered and new wells were drilled in such numbers that production far outstripped demand and untold wastage occurred. Under the mining law of the United States, the holder of the mineral rights is entitled to anything he can extract from the area covered by his lease, an arrangement suited to mining for gold or silver, but not to drilling for something so mobile as oil or gas. The result was that drilling became competitive; it paid to sink as many wells as possible. The resulting pattern is illustrated by Figure 7-3, which shows an area of the western suburbs of Los Angeles now adjoining the "Miracle Mile" along Wilshire Boulevard. Not only was such a large number of wells quite unnecessary to extract the oil, but under these conditions the natural pressure, which forces up the oil once it is tapped, is very quickly lost, so that it becomes necessary to pump, which increases the cost for all concerned. It is small wonder that the cost of producing oil on most of the American fields is many times higher than on those of the Middle East, where a single large concession enables the holder to drill in the most rational and economic way possible.

The wastage and accompanying fluctuations in price gave both to the oil states and the oil companies an interest in controls, and in the 1930s, quota systems were introduced. In the Second World War the federal government intervened in the national interest with a nationwide quota scheme, which the industry voluntarily applied after the war. Thus, after eighty years of competitive exploitation, a self-im-

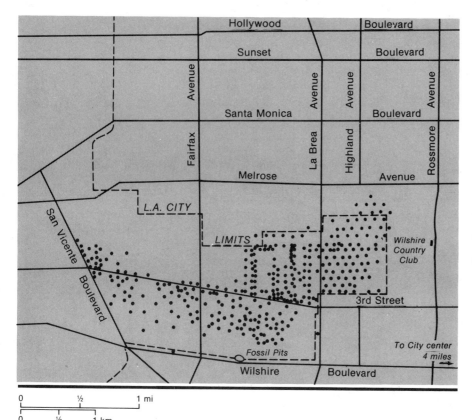

Fig. 7-3. The pattern of competitive exploitation on an American oil field. The map covers an area in western Los Angeles, which includes part of Wilshire Boulevard and the La Brea fossil pits as they were in the 1920s. Note the dense clusters of oil wells and their relation to the city limits. Such clusters result from conditions explained in the text and still survive on some American fields, although little trace of this particular field remains beneath the luxury apartments which today occupy the area.

posed sobriety had come to mark the industry. Today the leading producer-states are Texas, California, Louisiana, and Oklahoma, while Kansas, Illinois, Wyoming, and New Mexico play a smaller but still significant part.

As the petroleum industry has grown over the past century, so too has its market. In the early days the product in demand was kerosene, for lighting and heating. Then at the turn of the century the advent of the internal combustion engine created an entirely new market, which was the prime cause of the great increase in exploration and production in the period 1900–40. Today over 80 percent of the total petroleum output is converted into motor and aviation fuels and oils. The next development was the emergence of the petrochemical industries, which provided a market for the by-products that had formerly gone to waste in the process of gasoline production. Finally, there has been the growth of a market for natural gas as a fuel. This gas, present in many oil wells, was for long regarded as a nuisance and was either burnt or allowed to escape. Only

recently has natural gas come to be appreciated as a fuel in its own right; it is now piped away to the factories and homes of almost the whole continent. Since 1940 natural gas has cut deeply into markets formerly held not only by coal but also by petroleum and oil, both in the domestic and in the industrial fields. Thus the industry has achieved an ever fuller use of its raw materials and reached a widening circle of market outlets.

In Canada the industry's development is far more recent. As lately as 1936 the country produced only one and a half million barrels of oil. The comparable figure for 1974 was 595 million barrels. A long period of intensive but almost fruitless search was crowned by the strike at Leduc, near Edmonton, in 1947. This was followed by a series of other discoveries in Alberta and later in Saskatchewan.

The petroleum industry has three phases: production, transport and refining. The three can be, and sometimes are, organized separately from one another. But, because of the nature of the product and the need either to

137

Oil field development in the United States: (1) The early years. This picture was taken in 1865 in Pennsylvania, not far from the site of the 1858 strike, which ushered in the modern era of the petroleum industry. Note the closely packed wooden derricks in the barely cleared forest valley. Compare this scene with the next. *(Standard Oil Company of New Jersey)*

store or to move the oil as soon as it reaches the surface, the producer is usually dependent on a means of transport. This is especially the case when oil is flowing under natural pressure, and it was also especially true in the early days of the industry, when the oil was collected in anything available, such as empty whiskey casks, and the barrelmakers and carters held the producers to ransom by asking exorbitant prices for their services. It was by appreciating the relative weakness of the oil producer vis-à-vis the transporter that Rockefeller scored his first success in the petroleum industry; he would have nothing to do with the producing end of the business. Today the big oil companies—the "majors," which include parts and branches of the empire Rockefeller himself founded—still adopt something of the same caution toward the actual production business: in 1970, for example, the top 20

Oil development in the United States: (2) A later phase. The kind of competitive drilling which produced the forest of derricks in the 1865 picture, and which is illustrated by the map in Figure 7-3, gradually gave way to a more rational type of exploitation with individual, well-spaced derricks, such as those seen in this picture of Wheeler Ridge, southern California (right). But there is a further phase still, in which the derrick is eliminated altogether after drilling is completed, and is replaced by a pumping device known as a "Christmas tree." (below) *(Exxon)*

producers were responsible for only 69 percent of crude production, but for 87 percent of the refinery runs and 80 percent of the pipeline mileage. Even this figure of 69 percent represented a recent increase; in 1955, the proportion was 55 percent.[3] They had been drawn into the business of production by the need for more sophisticated techniques of prospecting and development, techniques which demand larger capital outlays than those the individual in the past could afford.

The network of transmission pipelines for various petroleum products that has grown up over the years now forms a vitally important element in the continental communication system. While the trunk lines run from the Southwest to the Middle Atlantic region and the Chicago and Detroit areas, few settled parts of the continent are today isolated from the network. Alternative routes to northern markets are provided by the pipelines to the Pacific and Gulf coasts, from which a fleet of tankers

[3]*Project Independence,* U.S. Government Printing Office, Washington, D.C., 1974, p. 16.

carries both crude and refined products to the Atlantic coast and to foreign ports. In Canada, the Prairie fields are connected by pipeline with both the East and West coasts. Edmonton and Calgary possess refineries, but by far the largest part of the country's refinery capacity is to be found in the Montréal area, with a smaller concentration at Sarnia, on the Great Lakes waterway.

The refining phase of the industry may in principle be located anywhere between the well and the market, but for technical reasons the refineries are usually either in the market areas or at the ports of shipment. Refinery towns are dotted along the coastlines of Texas, Louisiana, and southern California; important concentrations are also to be found on the New Jersey-Chesapeake Bay shore, adjacent to the great eastern cities, and at points along the Great Lakes and Mississippi waterways, such as Detroit and St. Louis.

Since the Second World War, North America has been living through a technological era dominated, as the table on p. 100 suggests in the case of the United States, by power supplies derived from petroleum and natural gas, which together now account for more than three-quarters of all energy consumed. This period has seen the conversion of the continent's railways from steam to diesel traction and the disappearance of coal-fueled municipal gasworks: both private homes and factories now use natural gas. Some of these developments can be traced to the genuine advantages of using petroleum rather than coal in powering vehicles or in reducing heat loss. But they can also be attributed to the cost advantage that oil and gas have enjoyed over other forms of power, which has encouraged conversion to their use and built up demand. These developments have also, however, led to a very rapid depletion of reserves, which first alarmed the oil-producing states and then began to threaten the nation as a whole. Quite suddenly, as it appeared, North America was facing an energy crisis.

Because so much has been said and written about this energy crisis in the past few years, we need to be clear about its character. In a sense it is merely coincidental that the crisis has come to national attention during the oil-gas period of America's technical development: what produced it was the very sharp rise in energy consumption—on the order of 29–30 percent overall during the six years 1965–71, or over 20 percent per capita. The strain of providing for such rapid increase falls naturally on whatever power source is supplying the largest share of energy at the time; in this case on oil and natural gas. With an economy so thoroughly converted to the use of these fuels, it is little comfort to know that there are huge coal reserves remaining, or that nuclear power is steadily enlarging its share of the energy market: the question is whether there will be fuel for the family car tomorrow.

The danger of dependence on a single type of energy source has been preached for years. The United States government initially responded to this situation by a rather paradoxical move—by restricting imports of petroleum products. The restriction was intended (1) to hold back the competition of cheap imported oil and (2) to force the American oil industry to keep up a high level of exploration for new domestic supplies. In the early 1950s the effect of this policy was to hold the U.S. imports of crude and refined petroleum products combined to 15 percent or so of domestic production, and this proportion remained fairly constant through the big production increases of the following decade. By 1970, however, the United States was in the position of having to import more than one-third of its petroleum products (35.5 percent in that year), and fears about the depletion of domestic reserves were being more widely expressed than ever before. Unless some dramatic change in policy soon makes itself felt, the import proportion will shortly reach a half.

It was in these circumstances, as we saw in Chapter 5, that the U.S. government was confronted by the need for an energy policy. For one thing, the initiative in price setting in the petroleum industry had passed from its domestic oil companies (operating at home or abroad almost without price distinction) to foreign governments. For another, it would be suicidal for a superpower like the United States to depend too heavily upon imported fuel supplies. Project Independence (see p. 98) therefore

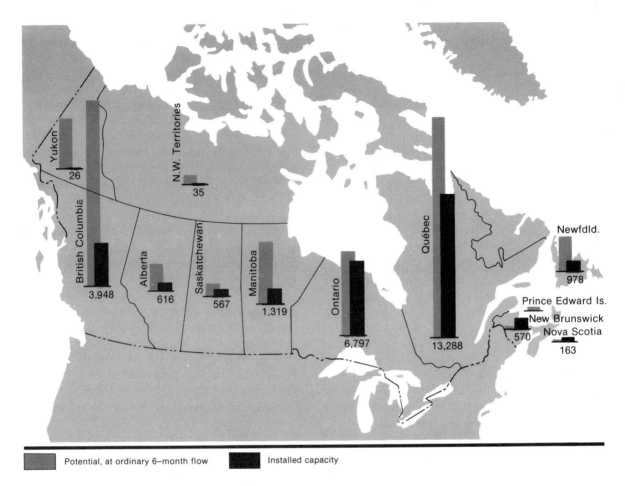

Fig. 7-4. Canada: Hydroelectric resources and development, by provinces, 1971.

proposed all the obvious measures: reduction in oil use, search for fresh reserves, switch to alternative energy sources. One sure consequence of all these actions is to raise the price of energy, but that may not be a bad thing: the whole difficulty of the present is caused by the relative cheapness and competitive marketability of petroleum in the past. It has been offered too cheaply for rational exploitation.

We can expect intensive prospecting by the American oil industry in the coming years, especially offshore, and some pressure on the Canadians to share their supplies. But part of the answer lies in the area to which we must now turn—the alternative energy sources available at present, especially hydroelectricity and nuclear power.

Electric Power and Nuclear Energy

The rivers of North America provide the continent with a valuable potential source of power. This the two nations have exploited to such good purpose that the United States and Canada rank with the USSR as leaders among the countries of the world in terms of installed hydroelectric generating capacity.[4] Even so, the present development represents only about one-quarter of the continental potential.

[4]It must be added, however, that while three-quarters of all Canada's generating capacity is in hydroelectric plants, in the United States, hydroelectricity accounts for only 15 percent of capacity and (in 1971) 16 percent of production—a proportion which, incidentally, had fallen from 20 percent in 1955.

The United States is favored by huge power resources—in New England and in the Mississippi Basin, but especially in the remote Mountain West and on the Pacific coast. Canada's potential is concentrated in two areas—the southern half of the Laurentian Shield and the mountains of British Columbia. In the first of these areas, it is well placed to power the industries of the St. Lawrence Valley and has played a vital role in their development. A good deal of the potential, however, is in remote areas, and its use involves either long-distance transmission or the location of plants at the power sites, as in the case of Kitimat (see p. 426).

Almost every major river in the United States has now been "put to work," though not all of them as spectacularly as the now-famous Tennessee. Of the potential remaining undeveloped—some 110 million kilowatts—over half is in the Mountain and Pacific regions, with about one-sixth in the state of Washington alone. Here it is the Columbia River system, already harnessed by such giant works as the Grand Coulee and Bonneville dams, that represents the principal source for future development.

The three areas of the continent in which hydroelectricity has been particularly important in industrial development are the Pacific Northwest, the Tennessee Valley, and eastern Canada. The first of these, remote from supplies of either coal or oil, could never have responded as it did to the demand created by war in the Pacific without drawing upon its one local source of power. The Tennessee Valley, although close to the Appalachian coal fields, has found an altogether new prosperity in power development and has been the scene of a now-familiar type of rural industrialization, made possible by the use of electrical energy. In the St. Lawrence Valley and southern Ontario, another area situated none too favorably in relation to coal and oil, electric power supplies have been sufficient not only to support Canada's industrial core but also to permit a considerable export of power across the border to the heavy-consumption areas of the northeastern United States. Completion of the St. Lawrence Seaway made a further two million kw of generating capacity available for the expanding industries of the valley.

Despite the rapid increases in generating capacity brought about by the construction of large numbers of dams in recent years, many parts of the continent are suffering from shortage of power. Even the Pacific Northwest, for all its Columbia Basin development, suffers in this way and the T.V.A. now produces far more electricity from thermal power stations it has had to build than from turbines at the dams for which it is famous.

Apart from the material problems to be met in increasing capacity to meet present demand, there has been another, political, hindrance to expansion in the United States. The question is whether the new power schemes should be in government or in private hands. The emergence of the T.V.A., followed by the Bonneville Power Administration, as federal agencies selling electricity in competition with private companies, touched off a political dispute that is still a burning issue wherever new construction is projected, be it on the Columbia, the Snake, the Colorado, or the Missouri. While the coordinating role of the government is generally accepted, there seems no need for the government therefore to assume responsibility for all construction, nor indeed any likelihood that Congress would vote the funds necessary. Yet the government has not always encouraged private development, with the result that the rivers have flowed on unharnessed between the two contestants.

A new dimension was given to the production of electricity when it became feasible to replace waterpower or steam by nuclear energy. Considering, however, the lead the United States took in atomic developments, its application of the new energy source to power production was rather slow.[5] But it is now playing its part in electricity generation, and is scheduled to increase its share as the years go by. Since one of the principal locational requirements of a nuclear station is a very large

[5]In evidence of this fact, the *Statistical Abstract of the United States* as recently as 1967, in classifying prime movers for generating electricity, included nuclear fuel only in a footnote, along with "wood and waste." This curious anachronism has now disappeared, or rather shifted: the 1976 *Abstract* duly records that nuclear power was responsible for 8.9 percent of electricity generation in 1975, and lumps the "wood and waste" in with coal.

supply of cooling water, the new stations are sited in appropriate places like the shores of the Great Lakes and the banks of major rivers, including the Tennessee, which becomes the first region to produce electricity by all three of the main methods so far introduced—hydro, thermal, and nuclear. Since nuclear stations require neither coal nor waterpower, there has been a tendency also for them to be built in areas lacking these two resources.

A further generation of nuclear plants has reached the planning stage. That they do not already exist is due to the hostility which the use of nuclear power has provoked, not only in North America but in Europe also, on grounds of environmental hazard. While the nation seems reluctant as a whole to curb its energy consumption, it seems equally reluctant to permit the most direct course toward solving its energy problems. Decisions are now long overdue.

Two Sample Industries— Automobiles and Textiles

It is clearly impossible to describe here all of the major industries of North America; space permits the discussion only of samples. In choosing these samples, we may well turn our attention to the manufacture of automobiles and of textiles. Not only have these two industries undergone interesting recent changes, but they represent the two sides of consumer goods production—the durable and non-durable categories—and so, taken together with the steel industry (the backbone of capital goods production) they form a small but balanced cross section.

THE AUTOMOBILE INDUSTRY

Although it is barely 75 years old, this is a record-making industry. In the United States it ranks first in terms of value of output among all industries making a single product. It is the largest customer of the American steel industry. It contains the world's largest manufacturing corporation—General Motors of Detroit. Although its output of vehicles fluctuates considerably from year to year, there is no ques-

tion as to the magnitude of that output: in 1973 it produced 9.6 million private cars and some 3 million trucks and buses. Throughout the continent it employed 900,000 workers.

A strictly geographical explanation of the fact that nearly half of these were concentrated in Michigan, and a quarter of them in the Detroit area alone, would be difficult to supply. The state has little mineral wealth to attract industry and lies midway between the two older, established industrial areas of Pittsburgh-Lake Erie and Chicago. While it might have been predicted that an industry using so much steel would be drawn to a location somewhere on the Great Lakes coal and iron route, and while the main market in the early days was in the Midwest, the decisive location factor seems to have been the whereabouts within this general zone of a few successful producers, and especially the whereabouts of Mr. Henry Ford.

To understand what has happened to this industry, it is necessary to recall its early history. In its beginnings, it was an industry of hundreds of small, independent producers, and each car was regarded as a separate construction task; indeed, many of the early car manufacturers were former coach-builders, with the mentality of their earlier trade still unaltered. But between 1908 and 1914 came the vital change in the industry's character. Henry Ford of Detroit applied to car manufacture the techniques of standardized parts and the assembly line, and so ensured that in the future all the advantages would lie with the mass producer. The effect of this change from small-scale to large-scale production has been to reduce the number of manufacturers from hundreds to half a dozen, and to give the "Big Three"—General Motors, Ford, and Chrysler—all but 1 or 2 percent of the total output.[6]

Both the changing organization of the industry and the nature of the finished product, which is an assembly of thousands of parts—metal, cloth, plastic, and glass—have their effect on the location pattern of car manufacturing. Around the main Detroit assembly plants there has

[6]Output, not sales. In the year ending 1977, for example, the U.S. car market was shared as follows: General Motors, 44.9 percent; Ford, 20.6 percent; Chrysler, 11.4 percent; American Motors, 1.2 percent; imported cars, 21.9 percent.

grown up a ring of industrial towns in which vehicle parts are manufactured. The great corporations, each controlling numbers of these parts producers, can distribute their activities in the most economical way, and it is by this process that the whole of southern Michigan has become involved in the industry.

On the other hand, vehicle assembly is not confined to Michigan. All the firms now producing do so for a national market. But to distribute such bulky objects as complete cars to all parts of the continent from one small producing area is clearly uneconomical, and there are now assembly plants in outlying market areas in half the states of the United States (although the Canadian industry has until very recently been concentrated almost exclusively in Ontario). Only the essentials of the vehicles are shipped from Michigan, which greatly reduces freight costs; the accessories are produced and the car is assembled in the market area. Thus there grows up around the assembly plant, in California, or Georgia, or New Jersey, a ring of parts producers supplying the branch plant just as the suppliers in Michigan serve the main works at Detroit.

THE TEXTILE INDUSTRY

For many years after the introduction of factory production, the bulk of North America's woolen and cotton cloth was made in southern New England, and the manufacture of garments from the cloth was centered in much the same area—the northeastern states. The cotton used came from the southern states, and the wool largely from the Far West, to be processed in the Northeast and sent on its long return journey to the consumer—in much the same way as England herself was drawing upon the raw material supplies of her colonies and exporting her manufactures to them. The strength of New England's position lay in its early interest in commerce and industry and in its waterpower, capital resources, and labor force. The Northeast, with the mainstream of immigration running through it, was able to maintain a cheap yet skilled supply of tailors and garment makers.

Today the Middle Atlantic region still retains a large share of the nation's clothing industry; a quarter of the industry's workers are to be found in the New York-New Jersey metropolitan area alone. But New England has lost its dominance in textiles to the South.

It was in the 1880s, the period of major industrial investment in the South following the chaotic Reconstruction Era, that the textile industry grew to significant size in the southern states. It began, naturally enough, as a cotton textile industry in a cotton-growing region, and by the early 1920s it had caught up with that of New England. Since then the South's share of the cotton industry has become overwhelming: in 1973 the cotton-growing states possessed 9.8 out of the 9.9 million active cotton spindles in the country and accounted for 99 percent of the industrial consumption of raw cotton, the two Carolinas possessing by far the largest share in each case.

The woolen textile industry is considerably smaller, and at present it is rather evenly divided between North and South. But that the South has captured any of it is significant and suggests that further shifts may take place. Then again, the newer, man-made fibers, whose share in total consumption was a mere 8 percent in the mid-thirties, claimed 34 percent of the market in 1962 and 70 percent in 1975, and they are produced mainly in the South. It possesses 75 percent of the looms and abundant supplies of most of the raw materials, whether these are forest products for making rayon or petroleum by-products for nylon and other synthetics.

The general decline of New England's industrial advantages is discussed in Chapter 11, and the recent industrialization of the South in Chapter 16. These accounts provide the background, and we are concerned here only with the migration of a particular industry. Among the many possible causes of the movement, those most commonly cited are (1) the greater enterprise of the southern mill owners, (2) the greater efficiency of southern labor, based primarily on the use of modern machinery, (3) restrictive legislation in New England governing conditions of employment, shift working, and so forth, (4) the structure of taxation, and

(5) though given less prominence than might be expected, the southern advantage of proximity to raw materials.[7]

It seems probable that in time the woolen industry, like the cotton industry, will desert New England—if only because of the increasing competition offered to both these long-established industries by the new fabrics, whose history and whose production belongs to other parts of the country. With the departure of textile manufacture, the Northeast's clothing industry may also be affected, but, although this industry has indeed grown up in numerous market areas further west, the great concentration in the Middle Atlantic region seems, at least for the present, to be maintaining its importance.

American Industry: The Latest Phases

North American industry has undergone considerable changes in recent years, and it is the purpose of this section to call attention to some of them. They comprise changes in type of industry, total employment, nature of employment, and distribution.

Changes in Type of Industry

Once the overexpanded war industries of the 1940s had contracted to peacetime size, there were three main factors responsible for changes in the type of industry being carried on in North America. One of these was the introduction of new materials, some of which replaced older materials—as in the case of nylon, plastics, and light metals—while others were re-

[7] In 1948 the closing down of a textile mill in a New Hampshire town represented so serious a threat to the city's employment that an official investigation was made of the necessity for so drastic a step. The reasons given by the mill owners were: that southern plants could produce more cloth per hour with less workers; that New Hampshire law prohibited the working of a 3-shift system; that power costs were much higher in the Northeast than in the South; that freight rates increased the cost of cotton used above the southern level; and that property taxes per spindle were five times as high as in the South.

sponsible for the creation of whole new industries; perhaps the best example of these is the group known as petrochemicals. Such changes in raw material base naturally result in changed industrial locations, and so in the growth of new industrial areas.

The second factor was advancing technology, which meant that some types of manufacturing were growth industries on a big scale. Chemicals and electrical engineering are probably the best examples of this trend; they have expanded as the research frontier advances.

The other main influence has been the rising standard of living, which has increased demand for some types of goods—cars, household gadgets, newsprint—without much affecting others. In today's affluent society it is the "durable consumer" goods which have become the mainstay of industrial demand—these, and the military equipment produced by private industry for the government.

In this situation, American industry has enjoyed almost unbroken prosperity since the war, but it is a situation which has its dangers. Changes in military policy and demand may have serious effects on areas (such as southern California) where defense spending is high. And the demand for durable consumer goods such as cars and household appliances inevitably varies with the prosperity and the whims of the whole nation; to a large extent, it is a social demand that industry has itself created by its own salesmanship.

Changes in Total Employment

Total employment in industry in North America has fluctuated considerably since the Second World War, reaching peaks in 1956, 1963, 1969, and 1973. During this period, however, the index of output has steadily risen. That industry is producing more with less labor is explained by the spread of automation—the replacement of workers by machines. The numbers employed in a particular industry give, therefore, a less and less precise guide to its growth. Some of the largest industrial plants today, such as the oil refineries, operate with only a handful of men to control them.

Changes in the Nature of Employment

This second type of change leads to a third, in the kind of work for which labor is required. This is a change from blue-collar to white-collar work, and it is reflected in the fact that the ratio of "production workers" to total employees is steadily falling; that is, more and more of the employees are office, planning, or sales staff. In today's industry the demand is more for training and less for either stamina or manual skill than in the past. In 1927, the ratio of production workers to other employees in U.S. industry was 10:1.6. In 1957, it was 10:2.9 and by 1973 it was 10:4.0.

Changes in the Distribution of Industry

All these changes have contributed to shifts in the location of industry and so, too, have other forces in North American life which we must recognize. Among these are:

1. The dispersal of industry. Manufacturers have moved out of the older, crowded industrial areas. This has been, in part, a move to new sources of power: electricity, oil, and natural gas. Just as the old Manufacturing Belt was an expression of the influence of coal upon industry and transport, so there are growing up new industrial areas whose character is a product of the newer fuels.

Here it is worth noting that, compared with coal, all of these newer power sources tend to exercise a "liberating" effect on industry. For several decades the motive power in factories was supplied by coal-produced steam, and the movement of goods was based on railway transport. The effect was to crowd plants together around their boiler-houses, and to tie them to sites along the railways. From these technical circumstances emerged the "dark satanic mill" landscape of nineteenth-century industry.

Today such a layout is unnecessary. Use of electricity or natural gas permits the dispersal of plant operations, while the coming of transport trucks has reduced the significance of the railside location. Moreover, what has become technically possible has also become socially desirable. In a continent where labor is notoriously mobile, and where it is axiomatic that

the worker will usually move rather than put up with unsatisfactory working conditions, it is not surprising to find that new industrial communities have sprung up—generally small by contrast with the great concentrations of the steam age, but less crowded and better adapted to the living standards of the modern American worker.

2. The influence of freight rates. The changing structure of both the Canadian and U.S. freight rate systems has already been mentioned in Chapter 5. Both governments are committed to a policy of making freight charges standard throughout all regions of the country, and of eliminating the differentials which formerly placed a city or an area at an advantage in relation to its neighbors. Like the abolition of the basing point system (see p. 136), this policy will free industry from artificial restraints on its location and allow manufacturers everywhere a chance to compete with each other.

3. Government contracts. It is unnecessary to repeat here what has already been written in Chapter 5 about the importance of the federal government as a customer for the nation's industrial output. Let us simply notice that while the government may be a very large customer, it is one with notoriously changing tastes, as federal programs are promoted or cut back. At any given moment, it is likely that part of the government-oriented industry of the nation is in mothballs, awaiting the next policy decision, or the next administration.

4. New markets. The most basic cause of recent changes in distribution has been the growth of new market areas. Formerly both population and purchasing power were heavily concentrated in the old manufacturing regions themselves. Owing, however, to the general westward drift of the population, to the prosperity of some farm regions, to the minimum wage legislation, and to such local factors as the development of the Texas and Alberta oil fields, the purchasing power or potential market for the manufacturer in the outlying regions has greatly increased.

Manufacturers who cater for the national market have responded to this situation by establishing branch plants in the new market areas. While this trend is perhaps most marked in the automobile industry, it applies equally to agricultural machinery or soft drinks. Thus a growing industrial maturity characterizes the Pacific coast, the Canadian Prairies, Texas, and the Southeast.

What has been occurring has been described as a process of "import substitution" in the sphere of manufacturing. Since this term is normally employed in connection with the growth of manufacturing in underdeveloped countries in the Third World, it is worthwhile to stop and consider the use of the term in the present context. Like the underdeveloped lands of Latin America or Africa, peripheral regions of North America used to depend on an external source for their supplies of manufactured goods: they "imported" them from the Manufacturing Belt and paid for them, generally, with raw material shipments. The clearest example was one already considered in this chapter: that of cotton, which was grown in the South, shipped to New England, and in due course received back in a manufactured form. But there was no particular *reason* why the cotton should make this double journey, other than the fact that the cotton textile industry had originally located itself in New England. On the national scale, an obvious saving in transport costs would be made if the cotton processing took place on the spot, in the South. This, today, is the case. In the same way, other regions and other products have been affected by a growing rationalization of the movement of raw materials and finished goods, each region tending to manufacture for itself and thus to cut down the need for "imports" from other regions.

All these factors have produced a movement of industry into *rural areas* and into *the West and South*. They have led to a decline in the relative importance of the older industrial towns of the East and to a distribution of industry more in keeping with the distribution of population. A spectacular new "manufacturing belt" has grown up along the Gulf Coast, an area which offers oil, gas, labor, capital, and space for expansion. Southern California is now a great industrial area, and so, in their way, are the Appalachian Piedmont and southwestern Ontario, all of them basically different in character from the older manufacturing areas. Of the new jobs in manufacturing created in the United States during the 1960s, it is estimated that nearly 40 percent of them were in eight states of the formerly poor and industry-deficient Southeast. Today, in terms of percentage of labor force employed in manufacturing, North Carolina with 37 percent and South Carolina with 34 percent are the most heavily industrialized states in the United States.

CANADA'S PROBLEMS

Canada's industries have their special problems. One of them is that there has been a serious gap in efficiency between Canadian and U.S. industry; in 1957 the Royal Commission on Canada's Economic Prospects estimated that real output per man-hour in secondary manufacturing was 35 to 40 percent below that in the United States. The existence of this gap was not in itself a surprise; the same kind of gap, if not a wider one, separates the United States from other countries besides Canada. What was noteworthy was that, despite this gap and the ease with which American goods could be imported, Canada continued to develop her own industries behind a tariff wall. The result was, of course, that Canadians paid more for their manufactured goods than they need have paid.

We have already seen in Chapter 3 the importance to the continent of Canada's insistence on her separate identity. In the industrial sphere it has led to the development of plants and firms that serve only the small Canadian market, merely duplicating much larger industries in the United States, which have ample capacity to supply both countries' needs. From this point of view, it is easy to argue that Canada has become overindustrialized: in practical terms, the manufacture of automobiles in Detroit makes it unnecessary to manufacture them also in Windsor, Ontario, a mile or two away across the river.

But in developing her own industries Canada is only following the example of many other nations, in declining to depend on a foreign power for her requirements of manufactured goods. Any sovereign state has the right to choose this course, and in the years since the 1957 report just quoted, the efficiency of Canadian industry has certainly increased. What gives the situation a rather ironic twist is the way in which much of this increase has been achieved. Canadian efficiency is coming closer to parity with United States efficiency because a large share of Canadian industry is owned or controlled by American interests.

Either by share purchase or by the establishment of branch plants in Canada, individuals and corporations from the United States have come to hold or control a share in the capitalization of Canadian industry that stood, in the mid-1960s, at 97 percent for the motor-vehicle industry, 90 percent for rubber goods, 66 percent for electrical apparatus, and 54 percent for chemicals. At the same time, foreigners owned nearly two-thirds of the petroleum industry in Canada and, in the preceding five years, had taken out 95 percent of all patents registered in the country. The situation was not in itself new, but the concentration of foreign control in the newest and most promising sectors of manufacturing was striking.

In such an arrangement there is much that is beneficial; the U.S. corporations can apply in Canada the fruits of research financed by their much larger American operations, and can afford costs of modernization or automation which might lie beyond the resources of a small, all-Canadian firm. At the same time, the arrangement has effects which have made the Canadians react defensively, as they so often have in their relations with the United States (1) because the dividends paid out by Canadian industry are leaving the country in such quantity—over $1000 million a year; (2) because it is felt that such an arrangement denies to Canadians full access to the higher technical positions in their own industry and encourages a steady flow of trained Canadians southward into the United States; (3) most basically, perhaps, because of the challenge presented at the emotional level to a nation by the foreign ownership of nearly half its industry. In spite of differences of location and form, Canada shares with the older lands of Western Europe a common problem: that of living with the United States. The problem of ownership or control, which is particularly acute in Canada, has also become so in Western Europe, where the influx of American capital has produced precisely the same kind of defensive reaction that the Canadians (with, let it be said, a good deal more justification) have shown.

8

Transport

Introduction

The most important early routes into the North American interior were along the waterways. It was by means of the St. Lawrence, the Great Lakes, and the Mississippi that the French made the swift westward penetration in the years before 1763 that almost succeeded in closing the ring round the English colonists further south and east. It was by the water routes that the English thrust more slowly west through the mountains until, crossing the portages, they reached the Ohio River and made of it the main road to the west. And it was largely by water that Mackenzie made the first transcontinental journey, from Upper Canada to the shores of the Pacific, in 1793. There were few land routes, and those that existed—the Wilderness Road to Kentucky via the Cumberland Gap, and Zane's Trace through Ohio, for example—were so full of hazards that, until the opening of the Erie Canal (1825), the safest and most economical freight route to and from the interior was a one-way circuit, whereby goods travelled down the Ohio with the current and returned by way of the Mississippi, the Gulf, and the Atlantic to the East Coast cities.

Only in the lands beyond the Mississippi, where the rivers are mostly unsuitable for navigation, did land routes from the first possess a comparable importance. Here the historic trails struck out across the plains and mountains—the Santa Fe, linking the East with the Spanish settlements in New Mexico; the Gila, the Spanish route to California; the Oregon Trail that carried the early emigrants to the Northwest, and its branch, the California Trail, leading (after 1848) to the gold fields. Later, when the first railways came to the West, they followed much the same routes.

If the opening of the Erie Canal as a two-way route for freight revolutionized travel in 1825, the changes brought about by the railways were even greater. In determining the regional balance of power within the continent and in the settlement of the West, the role of the railways was of the utmost importance. It was in the late 1840s that a crude network of lines reached as far west as the Mississippi. Before that time the all-important river traffic on the Mississippi had linked the new Midwest with the South. With the coming of the railways, this link was replaced by a far stronger one between the Midwest and the Northeast, whose significance was quickly demonstrated. As J.T. Adams writes: "When civil war at last came, and the South counted on the West joining with it on account of their being bound together by the arms of "Ol' Man River" and an outlet on the Gulf, it was the newly completed railways between West and North that enabled those sections to hold together, instead of South and West."[1]

But it was west of the Mississippi and on the Canadian Prairies that the railways exerted their maximum influence. We have already seen in Chapter 4 how both the United States and Canadian governments made the railway companies their agencies for settling the West, giving them in return land grants with which to finance their operations. Equipped with millions of acres for disposal, the railways set out to colonize the lands along their right-of-way, and in doing so became the greatest single factor in fashioning the cultural landscape of the West.[2]

For the western railway was so much more than just a pair of tracks. It was a whole economic system in itself. It had first to find its settlers. To do this, it conducted recruiting campaigns throughout Europe and eastern America and indulged in propaganda sufficiently fanciful to earn the name of "the Banana Belt" for one company's lands. It then carried the settlers and their goods, free of charge, to their new homes and established them with tools and grain or stock. In years of drought it gave relief supplies to tide the farmers over, and it maintained agricultural advisory services to increase output. It was buyer and shopkeeper to the settlers, and

sometimes it abused its monopoly. Finally, the railway was responsible for the location and layout of the towns and villages, itself deciding which cluster of huts and tents should become a city, and which should disappear from the map. Along the western railways today, it is common to find that, while one-half of the settlements may have Spanish or Indian names, the other half are either named after railway engineers, or were named by them.

In eastern North America the heyday of rail transport lasted until the First World War; in the West until the 1920s, for there the network of all-weather roads is of very recent date. (In the North are areas where transport has from the first been based on the airplane, where neither railways nor roads have penetrated.) Not long after road transport came to challenge the railways' monopoly of heavy freight haulage, the commercial airlines began to capture the railways' business at the other end of the scale—the conveyance of mails and packages. In the field of passenger traffic, while the bus provided alternative transport for the less well-to-do traveller, the airplane catered to the more wealthy, both at the expense of the railway.

From 6.4 percent of the passenger-miles traveled in the United States in 1950, the railways' share in passenger-carrying fell away in the mid-1970s to less than three-quarters of 1 percent. Busses, with 1.9 percent of the traffic, were not faring much better. The airlines, on the other hand, were steadily increasing their share—from less than 2 percent in 1950 to 10.5 percent in 1973. For all other journeys, the automobile was sufficient: it accounted for 85–90 percent of all passenger movement.

The position regarding freight movement is rather different, and is set out for the United States in the table which follows. In the movement of freight, railroads still play the largest part, and although their percentage share in the total has fallen, the ton-miles of movement for which they are responsible have increased in almost every year since 1961 and are today more than double what they were in 1940. This is not surprising when we recall the great increases in agricultural and industrial production which have taken place in the intervening years.

---

[1] J.T. Adams, *The Epic of America*, Atlantic Monthly Press, New York, 1931, p. 244.

[2] By 1914 Canada had more miles of railway line per capita than any other country in the world. In 1961 the Royal Commission on Transportation was moved to comment (Vol. II of its report, p. 93): "Historically, the transportation system in Canada was used so extensively as an instrument for the pursuit of broad national policy objectives that the character of the system as a system tended to become a matter of secondary concern. As a result, national transportation policy has often been a great deal more preoccupied with the question of how effectively the transport system was functioning as an instrument to fulfil national policy objectives, than with the question of how well it was functioning as an economic enterprise."

The Canal Era: Building the Erie Canal. The scene is at Lockport near the western terminus. Lithograph from *Memoir of the Completion of the New York Canals*, 1825, by C. Colden. *(New York Public Library)*

see p. 336

United States—Domestic Freight Traffic, Selected Years, 1940–74
(Unit—1000 million ton-miles [T-M])

	Railways		Motor Vehicles		Inland Waterways		Oil Pipelines		Airways	
	T-M	%	T-M	%	T-M	%	T-M	%	T-M	%
1940	411	63.2	62	9.5	118	18.1	59	9.1	0.014	0.002
1950	628	57.4	172	15.8	163	14.9	129	11.8	0.318	0.029
1960	594	44.7	285	21.4	220	16.5	228	17.1	0.778	0.058
1970	768	40.0	412	21.4	307	16.0	431	22.4	3.400	0.176
1974	860	38.9	495	22.4	348	15.8	506	22.9	3.900	0.175

Waterways and Ports

North America possesses a system of extensive and well-integrated waterways, thanks to a century of engineering improvements. In 1974 some 350,000 million ton-mi (560,000 million ton-km) of freight were carried over this system. Its two major components are the Great Lakes and the Mississippi River with its tributaries, which together account for about 85 percent of the freight movement mentioned.

Although its relative importance in the nation's transport system has greatly declined since the riverboat era before the Civil War, the Mississippi System has been much extended and improved since that time. From the ocean traffic terminals at New Orleans and Baton Rouge, 9-foot (2.74 m) channels now extend up the main stream as far as Minneapolis, up the Ohio and Monongahela beyond Pittsburgh, and up the Tennessee to Knoxville. The Missouri, perennially a navigator's nightmare, has a 9-foot channel as far as Sioux City, and fulfilment of the Missouri Valley Project (see p. 336) will mean that this can be extended. The Arkansas River has a 9-foot channel into eastern Oklahoma—450 mi (720 km) of river, with 18 dams and locks.

The whole system connects at New Orleans with the Intracoastal Waterway and, by way of

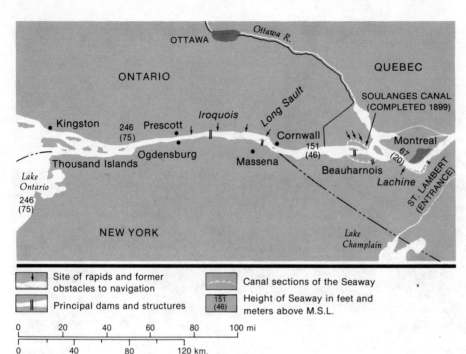

Fig. 8-1. The St. Lawrence Seaway.

Site of rapids and former obstacles to navigation

Principal dams and structures

Canal sections of the Seaway

151 (46) Height of Seaway in feet and meters above M.S.L.

0   20   40   60   80   100 mi

0   40   80   120 km.

the Illinois River and a canal across the low divide south of Lake Michigan, with the Great Lakes at Chicago.

The St. Lawrence and Great Lakes provide a natural route to the heart of the continent, but one whose present usefulness is based on improvements made by the governments of both the United States and Canada. To the west is the Sault Ste. Marie (Soo) Canal, opened in 1855 to clear the way from Lake Superior to Lake Huron and now the continent's busiest artificial waterway. While significant amounts of western grain and timber are shipped through the canal, the bulk of this tremendous movement is represented by iron ore on its way from the Superior mines to the steel regions. To the east the Welland Canal, completed in its present form in 1933, serves to bypass the Niagara Falls on the Canadian side and shares the strategic importance of the Soo Canal, although at present it carries a smaller weight of cargo.

As a result of these improvements, most of the Great Lakes route was open for ships 600 ft (182 m) and more in length and with a draught up to 30 ft (9.1 m). The weak link in the chain,

however, was the section of the St. Lawrence itself between Kingston, Ontario, and Montréal, where there were still only a shallow channel and short locks up to 300 ft (91 m). To open the great deep-water system further inland to ocean-going vessels was the object of the St. Lawrence Seaway, opened in 1959. Begun jointly by the Canadian and United States governments in 1955, the scheme provides, besides hydroelectricity for both countries, a 27-ft (8.2 m) channel from the Lakes to the sea, thus making Chicago and Duluth as truly ocean ports as Montréal or New York.

The St. Lawrence-Great Lakes route is available for only seven to eight months in the year, owing to winter ice in the canals and along the lakeshores. However, this navigation season is gradually being extended through improvements to the channels and the ships using them. The main effect of seasonal use has in the past been felt by the steel companies and other processing industries on the lakeshores, which have been obliged to stockpile iron ore or other lake-borne raw materials in order to continue operating during the closed period. Freedom from the necessity to stockpile would, among other things, release a large area of lake frontage in each of the port cities where the stocks are now kept.

After the Seaway was opened in 1959, traffic built up rather slowly at first, but from 1961 onward there has been a steady rise—from 20 million net tons of freight in 1960 to 51 million in 1970 and 71 million in 1976. Of this, about one-quarter is movement to and from countries outside North America, foreign trade that is largely handled by two ports—Chicago and Toronto. Of the cargoes carried on the Seaway, grain from the West and iron ore from the Lower St. Lawrence make up two-thirds of the total. This grain traffic, which formerly came down the Lakes and then moved overland to the Atlantic coast ports, represents the Seaway's one major "capture" so far. It is possible that others may follow (see Fig. 14-7).

In terms of tonnage of goods carried, no other section of the waterway system can compare with the Great Lakes and the Mississippi. Nevertheless, some other rivers and canals have great local importance, especially those of the Gulf Coast. A number of the manufacturing and refining cities of the coastlands—Houston, Beaumont, Lake Charles, New Orleans—are linked with the sea by ship canals, and cross-linked, in turn, by the Intracoastal Waterway, a route designed, when complete, to provide a sheltered 12-foot channel from New Jersey to the Mexican border. Some parts of this waterway are canals in the accepted sense, while others make use of the lagoons and sheltered water behind the long line of offshore sandbars in the Gulf. The Intracoastal has become a lifeline for the booming industries of the "golden crescent" on the Gulf Coast; it now carries as much traffic as the Ohio River, and the number of industrial plants choosing a location on its banks is continually increasing.

In the Northeast, water transport plays an important part in the movement of goods between the great manufacturing cities. This water movement, however, is now essentially coastal, making use of such "shortcuts" as the Cape Cod Canal or the Chesapeake and Delaware Canal between Baltimore and Philadel-

phia. The historic canals of the interior, such as that from the Hudson to Lakes Ontario and Erie, whose opening revolutionized transport a century and a half ago, have greatly declined in importance in comparison with the railways and roads that now parallel their course.

Along the great inland water routes of North America, port cities have grown up to handle the river and lake traffic. The largest of them, however, are those which combine internal with external traffic, or river craft with ocean-going ships. As we have seen, the St. Lawrence Seaway has made foreign-trade terminals out of the Great Lakes ports, while a river port like Baton Rouge, 150 mi (240 km) above the mouth of the Mississippi, is accessible to foreign craft and handles over 20 million tons a year of overseas trade.

The foreign commerce of the North American countries was once directed overwhelmingly toward Europe, the source area of their immigrants and their capital for investment, and the market for their primary produce. New York was by far the greatest port in the continent, with Philadelphia, Baltimore, and Montréal playing subordinate roles. New Orleans, with its river-sea connections, had a great past but had also known lean times, while the ports of the Pacific were few in number, and trade with Asia was spasmodic and unreliable.

Much has changed since the early part of the present century. The New York-New Jersey port region still handles the largest flow of traffic—123 million tons of cargo in 1974, compared with 111 million for Philadelphia and the Delaware. But both the direction and the nature of the traffic have changed. Canada's leading trade partner was once the United Kingdom; now it is the United States. For its part the United States still exports more by value to Western Europe than to any other destination, but imports more from Canada. However, the big changes have come with the shift of U.S. trade toward Latin America and Asia. The first of these has greatly increased activity in the ports of the Southeast, led by New Orleans. The second has strengthened the links between Japan and San Francisco and

Vancouver; Japan now supplies nearly 12 percent by value of U.S. imports, the same figure as the whole of Latin America. In Canada, the rapidly growing ports, apart from Vancouver at the "back door," are to be found on the north shore of the St. Lawrence: most of them handle a single commodity, such as iron ore.

All over the continent the fast-growing ports are those which have made the swiftest adaptation to the new character of ocean traffic and especially to the ships that serve it—the container ship and the bulk carrier. Old port facilities are no longer suitable (see p. 184); what is needed nowadays is space to handle containers ashore rather than warehouses, and deep water and rapid unloading facilities for big bulk carriers of petroleum, coal, or iron ore. This revolution in cargo handling has given the opportunity to some ports to break back into business which they had lost to the old, dominant ports. Boston, for example, is experiencing a new lease on life and so, too, are some smaller ports which for long were overshadowed by New York. Along the Gulf Coast, a relatively new chain of ports handles a bulk traffic in petroleum and much else besides; in 1974, the ports along the Gulf between Tampa and the Mexican border handled a total of 360 million tons of cargo—considerably more freight than all the ports from Boston south to Baltimore.

Railways

Anglo-America has a railway mileage almost identical with that of Europe-with-USSR—260,000 mi (416,000 km), of which some 207,000 mi (331,000 km) are in the United States and the remainder in Canada. The standard (4 ft 8.5 in. or 1.43 m) gauge prevails over almost the whole of this system, the only important exception being the 700 mi (1120 km) of 3 ft 6 in. (1.06 m) track in Newfoundland.

While the system of railway-operating in the two countries is virtually identical, and traffic movement takes place freely across the border,

subject only to customs check, the patterns of railway ownership are quite different. In the United States no less than 360 companies operate parts of the system, of which 74 are Class I railways (defined as railways with an operating revenue of more than $1,000,000 per annum). In Canada, on the other hand, the bulk of the system is controlled by two great companies—the Canadian Pacific and Canadian National. The Canadian Pacific is the product of private investment backed by a government land grant (see p. 75); the Canadian National represents a consolidation, made in 1923, of a number of earlier companies and is operated by the government. Since the Canadian National was in reality formed to save a number of financial lost causes, it is considerably handicapped in competing with its privately owned rival.

The railway network as it appears today is a product of intense competition in the great railway-building era of the second half of the nineteenth century. On the one hand, cities fought to secure railway connections and, having succeeded, to use them to extend their spheres of economic influence. On the other hand, the railways fought among themselves to attract the traffic. A large part of the struggle was financial rather than technical, and by the time that the scandals of the Railroad Era had brought down on the railway promoters the attention of federal and state governments, the continent had been crisscrossed with lines, many of which could never be economically justified or, even if they could, had been built under conditions that crippled the line's working, wasted the investor's money, and enriched no one but the promoter. It has been suggested[3] that by the 1880s the United States had twice as many railways as the economy of that period could support. It is known that in 1876 two-fifths of all railroad bonds were in default, and it is estimated that between 1873 and 1879 investors—mainly in Europe—may have lost as much as $600 million through bankruptcy and fraud.

A new foreign trade route for interior North America: The St. Lawrence Seaway, showing an ocean freighter passing through the St. Lambert lock at the Montréal entrance to the Seaway. (National Film Board of Canada)

[3]By J. Moody, early historian of the American railways. Quoted in M. Josephson, The Robber Barons, Harcourt Brace, New York, 1962, p. 292. Josephson also supplied the other figures.

The Railway Era: Railway construction on the Great Plains—a woodcut from *Harper's Weekly* for 17 July 1875. Note the "town on wheels," which formed a mobile rail-head, following the advance of construction and catering to the needs of the work crews. *(The New-York Historical Society)*

In North America today, as in Europe, the railways are suffering from the competition of other transport services—road, air, and water. And as in Europe, they have attempted to meet this situation by two means: to get rid of services which do not pay, and to improve those which do.

For most North American railways, the least profitable part of their operations was their passenger service. They therefore concentrated their economies on it, closing stations and abandoning services whenever they could gain authorization for doing so. North America became in the 1960s the only continent in the world in which there are cities of more than one million inhabitants not served by a single passenger train. In a number of cities where the old passenger station occupied a valuable site in the center of the city, the ground was sold and the small remaining business trans-ferred to a suburban station, where it usually became smaller still.[4]

So far did this decline in passenger services go that the federal government eventually felt it necessary to intervene, to preserve at least a skeleton service linking major cities. The Rail Passenger Service Act of 1970 brought into being a National Railroad Passenger Corporation, which then offered to relieve each rail-

[4]This does not exhaust the list of measures taken (or, more accurately perhaps, thought to have been taken) by the American railways to shake off their passengers: they have done it quite literally—for example, by replacing rolling stock with ancient cars which give a rougher ride. For a list of this and similar charges against the railways, see the colorful account in R. Fellmeth, *The Interstate Commerce Omission* (The Ralph Nader Study Group Report on the I.C.C. and Transportation), Grossman, New York, 1970, Chapter 10. From a historian's viewpoint, see also R.B. Carson, *Main Line to Oblivion: The Disintegration of New York Railroads in the Twentieth Century*, Kennikat Press, Port Washington, New York, 1971.

Technical modernization of the railroad: The Seaboard Coast Line's freight yard at Waycross, Georgia, is completely automated to speed handling and sorting of the freight cars. *(Seaboard Coast Line Railroad Company)*

road of its remaining obligations to run passenger trains. Most of the railroads quickly accepted, and the Corporation began in 1971 to ensure connections between 21 pairs of cities designated by the Transportation Secretary as forming the nodes of a basic network. Under the name of AMTRAK and with an initial allocation of federal funds, the Corporation is therefore now providing virtually all main-line passenger services within the United States. It has launched an extensive publicity campaign to attract travelers back to the railroads and its stress on service, comfort, and punctuality made at least an initial contrast with the last years of the old passenger trains. To relieve overburdened highways and air routes makes excellect technical sense; whether the public response will be sufficient to enable the Corporation to turn it into sound financial sense remains to be seen.

In Canada, the Canadian National, at least, did not give up without a struggle, and introduced some interesting experiments with cheap fares and new types of vehicle, particularly on the corridor run between Toronto, Montréal, and Québec. But in Canada, as in the United States, the government has had to step in to maintain the services: the Canadian equivalent of AMTRAK is called VIA Rail.

To keep their freight services, by contrast, the railways have fought hard and well. They have accepted the fact that road and pipeline transport have come to stay, and have produced integrated services—as in the piggyback trains that carry trucks by rail. They have switched completely from steam to diesel for greater speed and efficiency (although a few sections of line are electrified). And the railway companies themselves have sought—by mergers for greater efficiency and by financing

157

their own road transport and pipeline operations—to beat their competitors by joining them.

The density of the railway network corresponds very fairly with the distribution of population, with the same marked change, about the 98th meridian, from a closely covered East to a sparsely covered West, that we have already noted in other connections. Crossing the emptier West there are nine transcontinental routes, two in Canada and seven in the United States. The focus of the United States' seven routes and the unchallenged railway center of the country is Chicago. While other cities may be more exclusively concerned with railroading, none can rival the tremendous concentration of 22 major railways and 7800 mi (12,480 km) of track that characterize the Chicago "terminal district."

From both Canada and the United States, railway ownership and operation extend across the border into the neighboring country. The Penn Central Railroad, whose main line runs south of the Great Lakes from Chicago to Toledo and Cleveland, has an alternative, Canadian route via Detroit and the northern lakeshore to Buffalo, over which its trains pass in bond. From the Canadian side, in order to reach an ice-free port for winter use, the Canadian National Railways own a line that cuts across the United States to the Atlantic coast at Portland, Maine.

Roads

As North America has taken the lead in the production of motor vehicles, so it has been also the first continent to create a network of roads designed specifically to take advantage of this new form of transport. With vehicle registrations in the two countries reaching a total of over 130 million, the task of providing for and controlling this huge volume of traffic becomes a problem of the greatest national importance. Its proportions can best be judged by the fact that in 1974 more than $20,000 million were spent on road construction in North America.

Responsibility for this great network and its maintenance is divided, as in Europe, among various bodies. In Canada virtually the whole responsibility lies with the provinces, or, in the case of city streets, with the municipalities. In the United States, however, the federal government has established a basic network of principal routes for which it is responsible—some 200,000 mi (320,000 km) in all. The states develop their own systems within this framework, and, as in Canada, the municipalities are responsible for the upkeep of their streets.

The establishment of this network has been no easy task, considering the natural hazards involved—the lakes and muskegs in the North, the mountains and deserts in the West, the swamps of the southern coasts, and the extremes of heat and cold that break up road surfaces. There could be no better expression of the economic meaning of federalism than the hundreds of miles of expensive roads that crisscross the empty West and Great Plains, roads that have little local use, but that are justified by and built for the through traffic they carry across the nation.

The network is not yet complete. There are still several links missing in the United States network, and in Canada there is much to be done. The Trans-Canada Highway was only completed in 1962, and in the North the "Roads to Resources" program (p. 429) has a wilderness to conquer. Besides this, only a small proportion of Canadian roads are surfaced with asphalt or concrete.

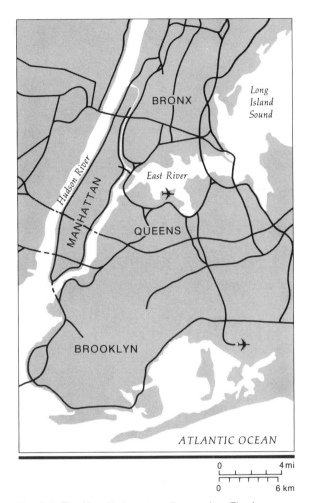

Fig. 8-3. The New York metropolitan region: The freeways, status in 1978.

But in a wider sense this road network is incomplete because the volume of traffic is constantly overtaking the rate of construction. Highways built a decade ago are already superseded by superhighways with double the traffic capacity. Around such cities as New York and Los Angeles, the congestion of arterial roads is becoming intense, and finding space for these broad highways is a problem that is often solved by carrying the new artery above or below the old street level. But to a visitor returning to America after an absence of ten or fifteen years, the progress of road building during the interval is quite the most striking feature of the landscape.

159

Recognizing this situation, the U.S. government undertook the building of a completely new network of Interstate expressways, 41,000 mi (65,000 km) in length. In the meantime the car has placed its mark on North American life, and especially urban life, to which we referred in Chapter 2. Its two main effects can best be labeled *destruction* and *reorientation*. In this context, destruction is the process whereby the centers of cities are increasingly given over to throughways and parking spaces: more and more of the available area is pre-empted by the motor vehicle and less space, in consequence, is available for all the other urban functions. In Los Angeles, which is usually regarded as the city offering the most outstanding example of this process at work, almost one-half of the surface area of the city center is dedicated to motor vehicles, moving or parked. Not only spatially, but also socially, this type of land use is disruptive. The modern, limited-access freeway, which is barred to pedestrians and of no use for purely local movement, may represent a barrier as socially uncrossable as the Great Wall of China, isolating sectors of the city and generating blight areas along its course.

Fortunately, at a certain point in this process of disintegration the opposite tendency—reorientation—begins to make itself felt. The more congested the city center becomes, the greater is the incentive for businesses to move out to suburban locations. In any case, with so much of the downtown space devoted to motor vehicles, there is a perceptible thinning out of business premises. So the last two or three decades have witnessed a transfer of some of the activities formerly concentrated in the city center—especially retail trade—from the downtown area to the suburbs where, after all, a majority of customers now live, where access is easy and so, too, is parking.[5] In some cities, especially the smaller centers where there is no great demand for alternative uses like office space, the reorientation of retail trade toward the suburbs has gone so far as to leave a serious question over the future of "downtown": it is simply not clear that anybody needs it any more.[6] To adapt to the motor age, the layout of cities and the distribution of economic activities has been, over the past three decades, one of the most formidable tasks confronting the peoples of North America.

Airlines

From the time that air travel first became a commercial possibility, conditions in North America have favored its development. This method of travel is well suited to two countries whose area is enormous and whose parts are separated from each other by considerable natural barriers, but whose administrative and commercial structure makes rapid communication between regions essential. Once a network of principal routes had been created, no city of any size could afford to be isolated from it, so that municipal airport construction was pushed ahead, and "feeder" lines to the main routes were developed.

Today more than one-third of all the world's air traffic flies within North America. The number of passenger-miles flown on domestic

The American highway traffic problem: A view of the West Side Highway on Manhattan Island, New York, which forms part of a shoreline freeway around the island (see Figure 8-3). The view here is north from about 150th Street along a heavily overloaded section of the highway which, despite the fact that it has always been closed to heavy truck traffic, is saturated at peak period with private cars. Further south, this same highway has been closed for years because of maintenance difficulties. (The New York Times)

[5]In what is perhaps the best-known study of this suburbanization of retail functions, *Commercial Structure and Commercial Blight: Retail Patterns and Processes in the City of Chicago,* University of Chicago, Department of Geography Research Paper No. 85, 1963, p. 9, B.J.L. Berry writes, "Only fifty years ago the central business district provided almost all the goods and services demanded by the residents of Chicago. Since 1910 a complex array of outlying business centers and commercial ribbons has developed to serve these residents, however. The 1958 Census of Business reported that all but 14.6 percent of Chicago's retail transactions were completed outside the CBD in that year."

[6]Observant shoppers can also notice that, even when large retail stores retain stores in the city center as well as branches in the suburbs, the quality of goods offered in the suburban outlets is usually higher, and the range wider, than downtown.

flights is increasing by as much as 20 percent each year. What this means in relation to the control of air traffic around major centers can readily be imagined. What it means in terms of airport construction and enlargement must also be taken into account, since not only does it mean that more planes arrive and take off, but, in practice, that the planes themselves are larger and occupy more runway and more standing space at the terminals.

Within North America there has grown up a hierarchy of airline service centers, with a group of primary foci 500 to 1000 mi (800–1600 km) apart, and a number of ranks of airports below them which can be graded by frequency and direction of service. Of the ten airports in the world which at present handle most passengers, nine are in North America: they include not only New York, Chicago, and Washington, as one would expect, but also several of the other first-rank foci: Atlanta, Miami, and Dallas. If it does nothing else (and even if it changes with time, as it is bound to do), this list shows that air travel has created a hierarchy of centers which is very different from that of the railway era.

Air transport, both passenger and freight, has become a factor of considerable importance in the location decisions of business and industry. For passenger movements, "several flights a day direct to Chicago"—or Toronto, or Dallas—has become a powerful argument for choosing a city as home base, while the attraction of air transport for freight movements is seen by the way in which most of the larger airports are surrounded by a zone of light industry and, even more, by warehouses.[7]

Apart from these general traffic movements, air transport plays a particularly important part in North American affairs in two special areas:

1. In the opening up of areas of the remote Northlands, both the initial surveys of the region and the supply of pioneer settlements have been entrusted to air services. Before the opening of the railway to Seven Islands, for example, the whole development of the Labrador iron ore field was based on air supply. And on the basis of per capita miles flown, Alaskans use air travel far more than does the average American. As one indication of this habit, in 1974 Alaska possessed no less than 545 public airports, nearly twice as many as either California or Texas.

2. In industry, use of company planes has become commonplace, especially where a firm has established branch plants in several regions. And on the farm, aircraft are used not only to spray crops and to sow seed but also to carry the farmer from point to point to control operations. To the 20 percent annual increase in scheduled passenger traffic, therefore, must be added a comparable rise in private plane movements, and these latter more than double the total number of plane-hours with which American traffic control has to try to cope.

[7]An interesting example of this situation is found in Winnipeg, where there is a new warehouse zone around the airport and an old warehouse zone around the railway stations in the city center, the latter now largely either derelict or converted to the uses of textile and clothing trades.

Regions and Regionalism

9

In every book on regional geography there comes a point where the writer must commit himself to a scheme of regional subdivision and justify his choice. That point has now been reached, and this chapter is designed to serve as an introduction to the studies of individual regions which follow. There is, however, one question that should be asked before we decide on a way to divide up North America for study: Why is there regional diversity in the first place? Is it inevitable and, if so, what causes it? We shall first consider this question and then go on to evaluate various criteria which might serve as a basis for the subdivision.

Bases of Regional Diversity

Regional diversity is a universal phenomenon. No amount of legislation or cultural mixing will eliminate it, even in countries with a highly centralized and very extensive apparatus of government, such as those of the Communist bloc or, in Western Europe, Sweden. If we concentrate for the present on North American examples, it seems reasonable to suggest that this diversity is the product of a number of factors.

PHYSICAL FACTORS

First and most obviously, it is a product of physical variety; of the circumstance that lati-tude and aspect control climate, and that fertile soils and smooth relief are distributed unevenly over the earth's surface; of the fact that resources such as minerals, forests, and water-power occur in specific locations rather than in a uniform cover. In some cases, possession of one resource compensates for the absence of another: the Canadian Shield has minerals and forest cover but little soil, while the American Southwest has minerals but little rainfall. But there is nothing assured about these compensating resources; in fact, some regions are hopelessly disadvantaged in particular technological eras by having nothing of immediate use to their populations at all.

POSITIONAL FACTORS

Once society has organized itself and, in particular, once the nation-state has become the basis of that organization, another factor comes into play—the position of an individual region in relation to the whole national unit of which it forms a part. We are, of course, accustomed to thinking of ease of access as an important geographical variable, but we need to ask, "access *to* or *for* what?" In general, position and access are important insofar as they define the relationship of the part to the whole political or economic unit. If a region is situated at the periphery of such a unit, it is likely to have higher transfer costs to and from the remainder of the unit than a centrally placed region. We have already noted (see p. 91) the official recognition of increased transfer costs when the Canadian government granted the Maritime Provinces a 20 percent subsidy on freight rates to compensate for peripheral location.

We must then take note (as we shall in later chapters) of how positional factors alter with time and with changes, either in the shape of the political unit or in the location of markets. When European settlement was confined to the Atlantic Seaboard, the position of New England was central to the British colonies. But with the opening of the West, the nation's center of gravity moved away: the once-central location became peripheral. On the other hand, the Pacific Northwest—Washington, Oregon, and British Columbia—once isolated beyond its mountain barriers, and with a permanent grievance about transfer costs to and from the rest of the continent, has been steadily increasing its positional advantages as trade between North America and Japan has mounted to unprecedented levels in the last twenty years.

CULTURAL FACTORS

Since the Anglo-American realm of today was settled and developed by at least three major European powers, operating within a continent which already possessed its distinctive culture and bringing in from Africa (through the slave trade) yet another group of a totally different cultural background, it is not surprising that some of these cultural traits have persisted to form the basis of regional identities. Indeed, the past two decades have seen a conscious strengthening of these regional traits, through the media of language, race, and politics: we have Black Power, Brown Power (see Chapter 20), and Red Power, as well as the movement for the liberation of Québec. The Spanish influence in architecture or the French influence in law and education are quite sufficient of themselves to generate diversity in the landscape, even without their being consciously fostered by culture-based groups.

Cultural distinctiveness, in fact, can be either deliberate or enforced. It was enforced upon the American Indians by their being confined to the reservations and upon the black by every policy which tended to segregate him in a racially distinct minority category. But it is the commoner case today that cultural distinctiveness is sought and magnified, even by those groups on whom it was originally enforced. Making a virtue out of past necessities, the minority cultures have asserted themselves: the last thing they desire is to merge and disappear into a unified Canadian or American culture. Here, then, is a factor that tends to increase rather than to diminish cultural diversity with the passage of time.

AMENITY FACTORS

The fourth basis of regional diversity is the consideration of amenity, but this needs explanation. In a community living near the level of subsistence and threatened by periodic famine, there is little opportunity for the individual to choose either life style or occupation; generally, there is only one way to stay alive, and this is forced upon the members of such a community. By the same token, the individual usually has little choice as to where he may live. But in a community grown prosperous enough to have built a safe margin of surplus between itself and starvation, choice becomes possible: the productive capacity of only a fraction of the population is absorbed in providing the basic necessities of life, and a wide range of choices is possible for the remainder of the community as to what they will do and where they will do it. In practical terms, given such facilities as telephones, cars, and retirement pensions, a considerable proportion of all North Americans can choose where in the continent they will live. Even though they may not maximize their earning power by their choice, they can maximize amenity—by settling in a pleasant climate, or in an uncrowded location, or where their hobbies can best be carried on.

In this way, in societies with a high standard of living, high-amenity areas tend to attract and low-amenity areas to repel. Since the Second World War, as we have already noted in Chapter 2, millions of Americans have expressed their amenity preferences by moving to areas of sunshine and mild winters: Florida and the Southwest and coastal British Columbia are today high-amenity areas. More recently, amenity considerations have been leading people to settle near or in the mountains (growth of interest in winter sports has been phenomenal); for example, in Colorado. As it happens, the Colorado Rockies adjoin one of the areas of lowest amenity estimation in today's America—the Great Plains. In consequence, the Plains have been losing population steadily, and so offer us the curious paradox of empty plains and peopled mountains in close proximity to one another.

Use of a term like "amenity estimation" or "amenity perception" reminds us, of course, that what we are considering are individual choices, made by people free to move and on the basis of their individual assessment of where their values may best be satisfied. Consequently, we are measuring not objective but perceived qualities: the perception in fact becomes more important than the reality. It may also vary with the passage of time.[1] Once a region has established a reputation for high amenity, it will attract individuals and may continue to do so (if southern California is anything to judge by) long after the influx of newcomers has gone far toward destroying the very amenity that was the original source of attraction. It is these perceptions, or "mental maps," that have been explored by geographers with increasing thoroughness in the past ten years.

ECONOMIC FACTORS

The first four points in this section are in a sense preliminary to the fifth one, for it tends to reflect the influence of them all. Income levels vary from region to region; some regions are advancing economically while others stagnate; rich and poor regions react upon one another. But when we come to the question: *how* do rich regions and poor regions affect each other, we find a hotly debated and imperfectly understood subject.[2] It is out of this debate that the so-called "geography of poverty" has arisen.[3]

It is relatively simple to correlate regional income levels with other variables. Perloff and his associates identified five such correlations:[4] they found a high degree of significance in the relationship of regional income to (1) the proportion of the population classified as urban (high regional income corresponding to large urban populations), (2) the percentage of the non-white population (minorities show significantly lower income levels than whites), (3) size of place and, especially, existence of metropolitan centers, (4) relative importance of manufacturing (industry commonly raises income levels), and (5) the *type* of industry represented (fabricating industries support higher income levels than processing industries).

But this is clearly begging the question as to how these circumstances came about in the first place, and why there should be more urbanization or industry in one region than another. The range of variation, after all, is very large: the average per capita income in Alaska is twice that in Mississippi.[5] Given the existence of freedom from internal barriers to trade or movement of labor, and of government policies applied at national levels, why should such discrepancies persist?

Any attempt at an explanation should take account of two groups of factors, which we may call *legacies* and *stimuli*. Among the legacies that may be responsible for holding back regional prosperity are environmental poverty, limiting the range of options open to a region; past failure to invest sufficient social capital, especially in education; and a tradition of seg-

[1]For an example of such variation, see K. Thompson, "Insalubrious California: Perception and Reality," *Annals* of the Association of American Geographers, vol. lix (1969), 50–64.

[2]Quite a good point of entry into the debate would be D.L. McKee, R.D. Dean, and W.H. Leahy, *Regional Economics: Theory and Practice*, Free Press, New York, 1970.

[3]R.L. Morrill and E.H. Wohlenberg, *The Geography of Poverty in the United States*, McGraw-Hill, New York, 1971.

[4]H.W. Perloff et al., *Regions, Resources and Economic Growth*, Johns Hopkins Press, Baltimore, 1960, pp. 600–7.

[5]Figures for 1970, which were indicative of the general contrast, were: Alaska, $4644 per capita; Mississippi, $2626. In 1975, at a time when Alaska was full of oil drillers and pipeline builders, the gap had widened to: Alaska, $8815; Mississippi, $4041.

regation or discrimination, which may artificially depress living standards for a minority group. In the Old South, as we shall see in Chapter 16, there was no environmental poverty (or if there was it was induced only after settlement began), but the other two conditions were certainly present: educational spending was low and the black community was not exposed even to the little education the South could provide, nor was it given the opportunity to raise its own standard of living.

Yet, other regions with similarly unfavorable legacies from the past have succeeded in "taking off": indeed, the New South itself has done so. They succeed because their economies receive a powerful stimulus—or, if the region is fortunate, a whole series of stimuli—from which they gain a regional momentum. The initial stimulus may be of several kinds. One kind would be an abrupt lowering of transfer costs within or across the region; for example, by the construction of an Erie Canal or a railway into Labrador. Export and exchange may then be stimulated; processing and servicing develop, and incomes rise. Or the stimulus may be the emergence of a single industry, but an industry of the kind some economists describe as "propulsive"; that is, an industry large in scale, fast growing, and related to a number of other industries by the need to supply parts or to service the resultant product. In North American experience the two great propulsive industries of the past, both of which fulfilled these conditions, have been the motor vehicle industry and the petroleum industry. What the latter has done for Texas and the Gulf Coast by way of regional "take-off" we shall consider in Chapter 17. Today, the aerospace industry is doing for some regions—particularly southern California—much the same things that the automobile industry did for Michigan at the turn of the century. Or again, the stimulus may consist simply of the organized and large-scale export of a region's single resource—timber, or coal, or wheat—provided that capital is attracted to the region and reinvested in the further exploitation of the resource.

There is, of course, nothing to prevent a government from creating an artificial stimu-lus. Within a region which lacks, say, a propulsive industry it is possible to create a "pole of growth"—a center at which investment is concentrated and around which new occupational or industrial opportunities may form. In a sense this is a "propulsive place" rather than a propulsive industry, but the impact can and should be much the same in both cases.[6]

Some regions seem fated to be immune to all such stimuli. In that case, they become regions of relative poverty. What, then, will be the relationship between the poverty region and the progressing one? What does it do to a region to have a rich neighbor? The question is anything but academic, and it certainly concerns other people besides the North Americans. What, for example, will be the impact of joining the European Economic Community on the west of Ireland, remotest of all the Community's regions from the prosperous heartland? What has been the impact on southern Italy, at the opposite extremity of the Community? It is from the few available case studies that a small body of empirical evidence can be built up.

The reaction between regions of different prosperity levels has been studied by numerous economists, among whom we may cite Hirschman[7] as an example. He postulated the existence of two regions which he called North and South.[8] Then the relationship which develops between them will depend on the relative strengths of two sets of effects, called by Hirschman "trickling down" and "polarization." Trickling-down effects are those generated by the progressive region in its neighbors because of its own surge of activity—for example, an increased demand for raw materials, or the migration out from it of overspill activity. By these means, prosperity will spread from North to South and there will be a tendency to pull South into economic motion, too.

[6]The preceding paragraphs are, in the main, simply a summary of McKee, Dean, and Leahy, *Regional Economics*.

[7]A.O. Hirschman, *The Strategy of Economic Development*, Yale University Press, New Haven, Conn., 1958, Chapter 10.

[8]Since Hirschman is American, it is no surprise to find that North is assumed to be more prosperous than South. But he points out that the same relationship exists between north and south in some other countries, e.g., Italy.

Polarization effects are those which draw into the advancing North even the limited economic potential possessed by South. Typically, young and intelligent Southerners will leave their region and migrate to North in search of better opportunities. Southern raw materials are drawn off, unprocessed, to North (see p. 289 for an example) so that the value added by manufacture accrues to North, and South is left as an unindustrialized producer of raw materials alone.

Which type of effect predominates will obviously depend on a number of factors, such as the quality of communication between North and South and the time period involved. In the short term, polarization is likely to be marked: there is only a limited amount of development capital available, and it has to be applied somewhere specific to begin with. The longer the term, however, the greater becomes the probability that South will begin to benefit from North's activity—unless (which has often been the case) the activity in North responds in the meantime to a new stimulus and the differential between them widens again. A few regions—California is the best example—seem to have been affected by a whole series of stimuli, beginning with the Gold Rush and continuing to the present day and the aerospace boom.

Where the general level of economic activity is high, as it is in North America, the survival of regions whose economy is stagnant offers a challenge to governments and planners. The government can alleviate poverty to some extent by such measures as minimum-wage legislation and a campaign against racial discrimination. But these things do not of themselves create prosperity. Something can be achieved by offering incentives to businesses to locate in depressed areas—there is hardly a country in Europe which does not maintain such a program—but the end product may simply be poorly located, high-cost activities. In the end, South must advance by the same means as North; that is, by a genuine growth of native industry and services.

Field evidence in North America suggests that the critical point where growth is born is the city, especially the medium-sized metropolitan area. A region does not need a New York to grow, but unless it has a Dallas, an Atlanta, or a Winnipeg to generate new activities, it is seriously handicapped. Hansen comments, "It is the metropolitan growth that determines regional growth rather than the converse."[9] The smaller cities do not generate a sufficient range of demand, or skills to meet it. There is today a broad concensus among planners in North America that if poles of growth are to be selected, then they should be chosen from among the middle-rank metropolitan areas.

Government and Regions

The lagging region is a challenge to the government not simply because of the underprivileged voters it contains but also because of the strongly entrenched belief that a lagging region holds back the whole nation. Consequently we find that even in North America, where the federal government's powers do not explicitly cover regional planning (see p. 65), the government has been increasingly active in this sphere, first by way of a series of ad hoc arrangements and more recently, by a series of relatively non-controversial assistance schemes.[10]

The first of these ad hoc arrangements was the Tennessee Valley Authority of 1933. It remains one of a kind and only became a reality at all in face of ferocious opposition, as Chapter 15 describes. It has been remarkably successful, but proposals to repeat the pattern on the Missouri and Columbia met with defeat. So the Missouri basin was provided with a committee rather than a plan (see p. 336). But early in the 1960s the United States government passed the first of a series of acts which began to verge upon real regional planning: the Area Redevelopment Act of 1961, the Economic Development Act of 1965, and, as the

[9]N.M. Hansen, *Rural Poverty and the Urban Crisis*, Indiana University Press, Bloomington, 1970, p. 21.

[10]A good, brief discussion of these schemes as a whole is contained in Robert C. Estall, *A Modern Geography of the United States*, second edition, Penguin Books, London, 1976, Chapter 14. See also his "Regional Planning in the United States," *Town Planning Review*, vol. xlviii (1977), 341–64.

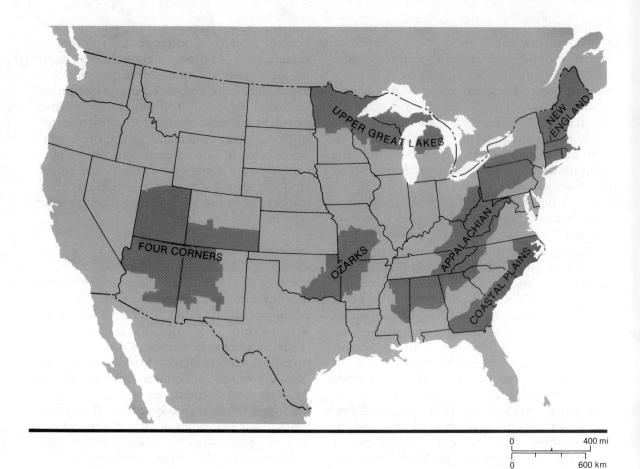

Fig. 9-1. The United States: Redevelopment areas of the 1960s. These areas were designated under the Area Redevelopment Act of 1961 and later legislation, such as the Appalachian Regional Development Act of 1965. Later on, however, as more counties qualified for special treatment under the criteria adopted by the federal government, the map became much more confused; today the map is of historical interest rather than providing an accurate guide to the areas qualifying for aid.

first specific regional application of the new principles, the Appalachian Regional Development Act of 1965, the working of which is reviewed in Chapter 15.

The idea embodied in these acts was that specific criteria would be used to determine which areas were lagging—criteria based on income level and unemployment rate. It is, perhaps, a mark of the inexperience of the United States in the field of regional planning that in applying these criteria the government produced not one program but two, and that a conflict developed over goals and methods. One program identified specific Economic Development Regions (of which the one that attracted most attention was Appalachia) as needing regional assistance. Under the other, any

area, any county, where the economic indicators fell below the specified levels could qualify for Redevelopment Area status. The effect of the first arrangement was to categorize some quite prosperous areas as eligible for assistance solely on the grounds that they lay inside one of the designated regions. The effect of the second was to qualify a great number of communities for aid—so many, in fact, that by 1973 the 1818 designated Redevelopment Areas contained over 100 million people; that is, the ratio of those inside receiving to those outside paying was one to one.[11] It was a case of "everybody develop somebody."

Inexperience (or political pressure) also showed itself in uncertainty about how or

[11]Estall, *A Modern Geography of the United States*, p. 352.

where to spend the development funds. There are certain basic decisions which planners everywhere have to take: whether to concentrate their efforts on a few projects or to diffuse them as widely as possible; whether to help the poorest areas first, or rather to look for areas close to the economic borderline between poverty and prosperity, where a small amount of help may be enough to tip the balance. The planners must also decide whether to develop long-term projects or give short-term relief (and in the United States the manner in which development is funded usually leads the planners to opt for the shorter term). They must decide whether to concentrate on infrastructure, or make-work projects, or health and welfare.

None of these uncertainties have been resolved and, given the federal system of financing the programs, it was perhaps too much to hope that they would have been. In Estall's view, "the indications are that inter-regional rivalries will sharpen" as the competition for funds continues, and "the next few years are unlikely to be a fruitful time for the vigorous promotion of federal programs designed specifically to further the interests of selected regions of difficulty."[12]

In Canada, the Regional Development Incentives Act of 1969 set up a government department with the same name and with a program of development incentives designed to attract industry into specified areas. The system of loans and grants under the act is graduated: the largest incentives apply to the Atlantic Provinces, while a broad belt of territory with somewhat lower incentives stretches from eastern Québec to the Rockies, excluding only the peninsula of southern Ontario. Beyond and within these areas are specially designated pilot projects—for example, at Goose Bay in Labrador or at Lesser Slave Lake in Alberta, where the program is trying to come to terms with the problem of unemployment in a population 45 percent Indian.

In Canada as in the United States these programs are giving a new dimension to locational decisions in the 1970s. Designed as they are to iron out regional differentials in income

[12]Estall, *A Modern Geography of the United States*, p. 363.

levels (and we should note that in Canada these have been very marked, in spite of the absence of conditions like those in the American South, with its big minority group), they cannot fail to create, given time, a new geography of economic activity in North America or to reduce those regional distinctions that have been so prominent in the past.

Criteria of Regional Subdivision

The geographer is not alone in confronting the problem of dividing a large area into smaller units: every government department and almost every business with a national market is engaged in the same exercise. It will make a division into regions to suit its own functions and purposes, and the resultant divisions are usually referred to as functional regions. But such a subdivision is frequently only valid for the single purpose or single criterion adopted. The geographer, whose task is to present a broad and balanced picture of inter-regional differences, therefore has a much more complex task to perform. In practice, he is limited to about five possible types of framework for his subdivision:

1. A system of physical regions. There is much to be said for a system of regions based on physical factors, whether of relief, climate, or some sort of combined criteria, which will yield a so-called "natural region." Such schemes have been popular with geographers at least since the end of the eighteenth century, when they were introduced by a number of writers as an alternative to the systems of political regions then in vogue but disrupted by the wars of the French Revolution. Physical criteria have the advantage of being relatively stable and objective; a further value is that they have repercussions on human activity—climate on crops, or vegetation on forest-based industry.

But they also have the *disadvantage* that, in North America at least, they can be overridden with increasing ease. Mountain barriers no longer possess their old significance in separating communities; they can be flown over. Artificial climates in homes and, for that mat-

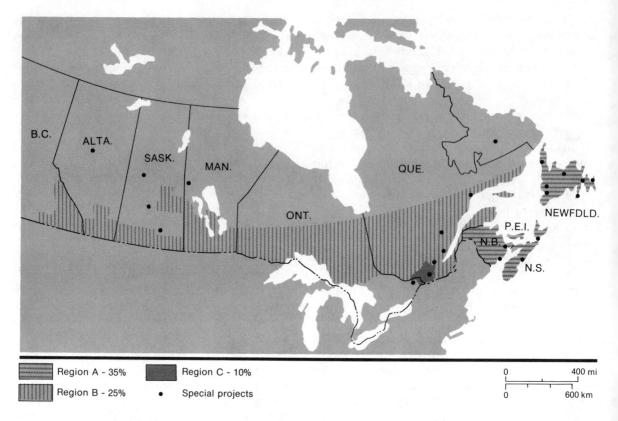

Region A - 35%	Region C - 10%
Region B - 25%	• Special projects

0 ——— 400 mi
0 ——— 600 km

Fig. 9-2. Canada: Development regions as defined by the Regional Development Incentives Act of 1969. In the key the percentage figure shown in each case represents the maximum incentive grant payable within the region as a proportion of the capital cost of new plants introduced to the region.

ter, in fields make people less and less aware of physical conditions. It is true that Americans have become increasingly aware that they can escape the winter by moving south, but this simply tends to give us a twofold division of North America into regions—warm winter and cold winter. In other words, the scale is too gross. In fact, the problem of scale in general makes physical subdivisions difficult to use in looking for a consistent pattern of regional units.

2. A division into major economic types. Another possibility is to identify and use divisions based on the principal economic activity and its characteristics. Figure 6–1 represents a subdivision based on a single such criterion: types of agriculture, classified on the basis of farm income. The major components of that map—Corn Belt, Wheat Belt, Cotton Belt—have in the past often been used for the pur-

pose we are discussing; that is, to identify regions of North America.

The problem here, however, is twofold. First, if we adopt a division by economic type it may be acceptable to use the agricultural map in, say, the Great Plains, but further east we must acknowledge that manufacturing is far more important to the economy than farming and that the concept of a Manufacturing Belt should override the agricultural subdivision. But in some smaller areas of the East and generally in the cities, tertiary activities are more significant (in income terms) than manufacturing. Thus our Manufacturing Belt is interrupted by an Insurance Belt or a Finance Belt, and we have a whole series of economic belts superimposed on one another.

The other problem about using economic types in this way is that they change with time. All the regional textbooks that once con-

170

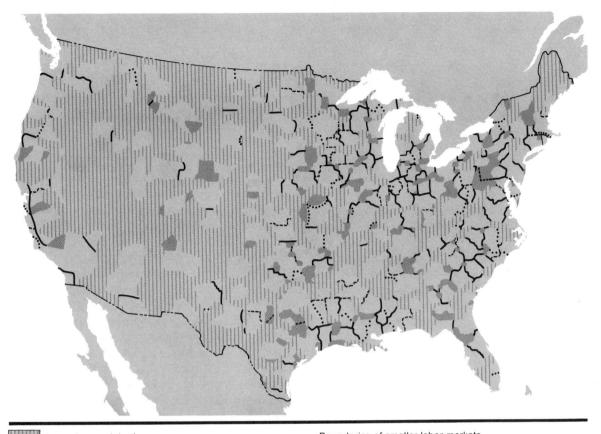

▦ Interurban peripheries	– – – Boundaries of smaller labor markets
▨ Boundary zones in which there is interpenetrating urban influence	⋯⋯⋯ Boundaries of smaller television markets
▬ Simultaneous commuter and television-sheds separating urban regions	

Fig. 9-3. The United States: Daily urban systems. By 1960 all but 5 percent of the population of the United States lived within these "daily urban systems," or commuting areas of the larger cities. The remaining 95 percent were distributed throughout the "inter-urban peripheries."

tained a section on the "Cotton Belt" should by now have been called in for repair and re-writing: if there is a Cotton Belt at all today, it is certainly not in the area those textbooks were describing.[13] This type of subdivision was generally acceptable at the time when most areas of North America were associated with a single activity—wheat-growing on the Prairies or ranching on the Great Plains—but this is a pattern that no longer exists as we have already seen in Chapter 6.

3. A division into metropolitan hinterlands. We noted in the last section of this chapter a

[13]See, for example, M.C. Prunty and C.S. Aiken, "The Demise of the Piedmont Cotton Region," *Annals* of the Association of American Geographers, vol. lxii (1972), 283–306.

measure of agreement among geographers and planners that the critical component of American life today is the metropolis; that as the metropolitan area goes, so goes the region. It has been pointed out that in the metropolitan areas and their daily commuting hinterlands—what are being called the "daily urban systems"—were to be found, in 1960, 95 percent of the population of the United States.[14] It can therefore be argued with a good deal of justification that a subdivision of the continent into metropolitan hinterlands represents the most

[14]B.J.L. Berry, "The Geography of the United States in the Year 2000," Institute of British Geographers, *Transactions* 51 (1970), 21–53. There is a great deal more in the article, besides this; it is recommended to all readers.

appropriate contemporary method for the regional geographer to adopt.

In fact, it is not. Although we shall make use of this concept of metropolitan spheres of influence in a number of places in the regional accounts which follow (Chapters 10–23), it does not provide a satisfactory basis for a complete regional subdivision. In the first place, we should have to exclude and separately cater to various neutral areas which are not effectively within the hinterland of any metropolitan area. They are not merely a part (in the current terminology) of the interurban periphery; they form what might be called the extraurban neutral zone. In the second place, the distribution of metropolitan centers is so uneven, with a marked clustering in the east center of the continent, that to attempt a regional analysis of this cluster zone on a hinterland basis would lead to untold confusion. The regional geography of Ohio would have to be presented in three secions at least, starting with the metropolitan centers of Cleveland, Pittsburgh, and Cincinnati, a division which corresponds to nothing else in Ohio's geography and, in any case, eliminates other important centers such as Columbus and Dayton from the system. Meanwhile, Winnipeg or Phoenix would reign in solitary splendor over huge hinterlands in the West several times the size of Ohio. In the third place, as the last comment implies, there are hierarchies even among the metropolitan areas, the sphere of influence of the larger overlapping those of the smaller. A mining community in the Canadian North may depend on supplies from Winnipeg, but it will obtain its financing from Toronto: if it comes to that, the New York Stock Exchange handles some 75 percent of all trading within the United States. For all these reasons a system of hinterland regions is ill suited to the purposes of the regional geographer.

4. A division on the basis of community of interest or community of problems. If we discard each of the previous possibilities when we consider it in isolation, it may still be possible to bring them all together in some way by noting that physical, economic, and locational factors often combine to give the inhabi-

tants of a particular area a common concern, usually economic in its nature but sometimes either political or cultural. As Chapter 22 points out, there can be few gainfully employed inhabitants of the Pacific Northwest who are not conscious of the problem of marketing the region's products from a position so peripheral to the continent as a whole. The French Canadians in Québec have gone to periodic extremes to express their own political and cultural community of interest. In the two cases mentioned we might reasonably draw the regional boundary in relation to this awareness of community.

In practice, however, we soon encounter difficulties. There is no reason why every inhabitant of the continent should share a community of interest with others. In some regions there is *no* unifying factor, economic or political. With a diversified economic structure or a racially mixed population, there may be no common cause. Once again, therefore, we confront the difficulty of the neutral areas—those sections of the continent which do not fit into any particular region. And once again we must recognize that if the problem is *solved* the community of interest may well evaporate.

5. A system based on regional "personality." We are left with one other possibility of regional subdivision, which is to accept that in the end the geographer will make an empirical choice of regions, on the basis of his own, unified perception of all the characteristics involved. He will select those features which appear to him to distinguish an area from its neighbors; which give it individuality or personality. The *application* of the criteria may, of course, be carried out on a fully objective or quantitative basis, but the *selection* will be his own. In his pioneer study of the United States South, Odum used over 700 criteria to delimit the region.[15] In a later, smaller-scale exercise within the same region Zelinsky used as criteria such factors as diet, house structure, and

[15]H.W. Odum, *Southern Regions of the United States*, University of North Carolina Press, Chapel Hill, 1936.

[16]W. Zelinsky, "Where the South Begins," *Social Forces*, vol. xxx (1951), 172–78.

distribution of farmsteads.[16] The geographer will adopt whatever criteria, in his judgment, best express the region's personality. Cultural origins, climate, space relationships, and livelihood are all likely to be involved, and are given coherence by the writer's perception that they compose an entity.

In effect, this is the basis of regional subdivision used here. In part, the continent is simply divided areally, into north, west, center, and so on. This helps to reduce, although it does not eliminate, the problem of neutral zones. But some of these areal divisions have a meaning of their own. New England is much more than just the northeastern peninsula of United States territory: it has "personality" which makes it regionally distinctive. The Canadian Northlands form a geographical location: they also represent a way of life, a challenge, and a great many common problems. By stressing first one criterion and then another, the geographer makes his personal decisions about what is regionally distinctive in North America today.

The Middle Atlantic Region

Introduction

That a survey of the regions of Anglo-America should begin with the Middle Atlantic region is entirely appropriate. Whether judged by its share of the population, industry, or foreign trade of the continent, or by its wide control of the nation's business, this region's primacy is abundantly evident. In this small section of the continent are found the world's greatest urban concentration and three other metropolitan areas with populations of over a million. Its ports handle a high proportion of all the United States' foreign trade and it has—partly as a result of this fact—a wide range of manufactures, from the heavy industry of Trenton or Baltimore to the luxury goods of New York City. From its beginnings as an assortment of English, Dutch, Swedish, and German settlements, the Middle Atlantic region has achieved its primacy with the help of few geographical advantages other than the all-important one of position.

For present purposes, we shall consider the region to stretch from the Hudson River in the north to the Potomac in the south. Its inland edge is indefinite, for much of the region lies west of the Fall Line and some of it to the west of the Blue Ridge, the only major physical

boundary. Although we shall be considering the Appalachian hinterland of the region again (in its appropriate context, in Chapter 15) it will be useful to give it a place in the present discussion, in order to point out how the regional characteristics of the Middle Atlantic region fade and change as one moves westward.

Defined in this way, the region divides into several physical subsections. In the east lies the Coastal Plain, cut by the deep indentations of Delaware Bay and Chesapeake Bay, and diminishing rapidly in width as it stretches northward. In character much of it is a sandy, infertile area, covered in large part by pine barrens. The long line of coastal sandbars and lagoons that extends north and south from Cape Hatteras and Pamlico Sound continues all the way to Sandy Hook at the entrance to New York Harbor, and fringes the coast of Long Island; but to compensate the sailor for this inhospitable shore the drowned valleys of Chesapeake and Delaware bays and the lower Hudson carry shipping far inland to magnificent natural harbors.

On the landward side the plains end at the Fall Line. Along this line the recent formations of the Coastal Plain meet the older rocks of the Piedmont, and there are falls in the rivers flowing off the Piedmont. Representing as it did both head of navigation and source of waterpower for early industries, the line became the site of a string of settlements stretching from Trenton, New Jersey, southward into Alabama.

West of the Fall Line lies the Appalachian System, with its four component parts. But in this middle section of the system altitudes generally decline from south to north, and indeed in southern Pennsylvania the Blue Ridge virtually disappears for a short distance, to reappear in muted form in northern New Jersey. Elsewhere, the mountains are pierced by water gaps—notably those of the Potomac, Susquehanna, and Delaware—as well as by dry gaps like that at Manassas that presumably result from river capture. In peace as in war, to the railway engineers as to Robert E. Lee and Stonewall Jackson, the position of these gaps has been a matter of constant and decisive significance. Beyond them lies the Great Valley of the Appalachians, important both for its fertile farmland and as a route giving access, through further gaps, to the interior.

Between the Susquehanna and the Hudson the Piedmont also changes its character somewhat, thanks to the presence among its hard, crystalline components, of a belt of softer Triassic formations (which incidentally reappear both in New England and in the Maritimes). The Triassic area lies, on the whole, well below the Piedmont surface level, but included in it are several bands of trap rock—igneous intrusions that form ridges in northern New Jersey.

Throughout this region, soils that encourage the farmer are found in only limited areas. The climate, however, is a factor generally in his favor. The presence of the ocean, here warmed by the Gulf Stream, and the deeply indented coastline give the area a long growing season and serve to moderate temperature extremes. On the other hand, the farmer's gain is the city dweller's loss, for in the region's great urban centers the hot, humid summer weather makes heavy demands on the workers.

Agriculture

Like the settlers of New England and of Virginia, the early inhabitants of the Middle Colonies had to look to the land for most of their needs. They were, however, more favored by natural conditions than the New Englanders and were, on the other hand, free from the commercial link that tied early Virginia's economy so firmly to tobacco production. There were Dutchmen on the Hudson, Swedes on the Delaware, and Germans in Pennsylvania, besides the British colonists who quickly became the dominant element. Each group developed its own agricultural methods, and farming was more mixed than in the colonies to the north and the south.

The semifeudal conditions of land tenure in some of the early settlements, and the pressure on the land of an increasing immigrant population soon produced a drift westward toward the mountains. Here in the rougher terrain of the upper Piedmont and later of the Appalachian valleys, independent farmers carved out their holdings, accepting the handicaps of infertility and remoteness in exchange for liberty of action. To the eighteenth-century farmer the exchange seemed a reasonable one; his twentieth-century descendant, occupying the same hill farm, suffers the handicaps without the same compensation.

The present agricultural pattern of the Middle Atlantic region is the product of one overwhelmingly important factor: the rise of the seaboard cities. Paradoxically, this factor accounts at one and the same time both for the *presence* of such agriculture as exists, and for its *absence* from large parts of the region, where it is squeezed out in the competition for space by cities, suburbs, parks, and country estates which may once have been farmland but are certainly no longer farms.

In the general discussion on agriculture we saw how western competition has limited the range of products with which the eastern farmer can succeed and how, even so, he needs excellent transport facilities to market in order to compete. In the Middle Atlantic region these circumstances combine to create a dairying and truck-farming area based on the supply of milk and vegetables to the huge urban populations of the region, and marked by wide differentials in farm prosperity between the areas adjacent to the cities and the remoter hill farms.

The importance of cattle rearing, especially in Pennsylvania and New York, is clearly revealed in the agricultural statistics. In Pennsylvania the crops of the classic "Pennsylvania Rotation"—corn, oats, wheat, and hay, most of which are fed to cattle—occupy almost 90 percent of the state's cropland, and one out of every two farms is classified as a dairy farm. In New York State the figure is 65 percent. It is mainly to the urban demand for fluid milk that the region caters.

On the sandy soils of the coastal plains, however, dairying is unimportant. Its place is taken by truck farming. Among the pine barrens of New Jersey and the Delmarva Peninsula,[1] and on Long Island, there has developed the world's largest concentration of this intensive and highly specialized type of farming. The whole range of kitchen vegetables is grown, and one crop follows another on each plot throughout the long growing season.

Within the coastal region, potato growing is concentrated in two areas: eastern Long Island and the southern tip of the Delmarva Peninsula. Here, the distinctive potato barns show that the farmers specialize in the crop. Potatoes have, in fact, become increasingly a specialist crop through the years. The days are long gone when every farmer in the East grew them; today, there are four or five specialist potato areas in the United States which account for almost the whole crop.

This remarkable concentration of truck farming is due partly to the genuine suitability of the light soils for fruit and vegetable production, but partly also to the fact that these crops grow in a topsoil that is so largely man-made that the nature of the subsoil is relatively unimportant. Thus the otherwise almost useless pine barrens find in truck farming an ideal function. Lying close to New York or Philadelphia, and possessing an unrivalled road network as well as various rail and water routes, the northern end of the coastal plains provides the truck farmers with an unassailable position from which to market their output. So intensive is production that, in spite of the huge urban demand within the region, a large proportion of the output is sold under contract to

[1]The peninsula enclosing Chesapeake Bay and forming parts of Delaware, Maryland, and Virginia.

the numerous canneries and freezing plants for shipment elsewhere—and even so, the truck farming by no means occupies all the space available to it. Many of the crops are grown under sprinkler irrigation.

No other farm product has the region-wide importance of milk or truck crops, but several are of local significance. Poultry raising, like vegetable growing, is well adapted to the pockets of agricultural land that lie between the cities: it requires little space and caters for the urban markets, so that in Delaware, New Jersey, and Long Island it plays an important part in the farm economy. In Delaware, where the broiler-fowl industry began, no less than 40 percent of the farms are classified as poultry operations. Two other specialities belong to the lower Piedmont, where on the better soils the farmers introduce a cash crop into their rotation—generally either apples or tobacco and sometimes potatoes. The main tobacco areas lie further south: in terms of acreage North Carolina is by far the largest producer. But both Pennsylvania and Maryland, as well as Virginia, market fine tobaccos. Apple growing similarly has its main centers further south, in Virginia, but production is concentrated in the Great Valley and extends north into Maryland and Pennsylvania.

From a survey of the chief farm crops, we may now turn to the pattern of agricultural subdivisions within the region. They are listed in sequence as they would be noted by a traveller making a traverse from the coast to the Great Valley, and then either west to Pittsburgh or north to the shore of Lake Ontario. On the coastal plains, as we have seen, truck farming covers a large part of the agricultural land of Long Island, Delaware, and eastern Maryland, and all that of New Jersey except its northwestern edge. Inland across the Fall Line the lower Piedmont reveals a marked contrast. Here, with its focus in southeastern Pennsylvania and its heart in famous Lancaster County (which produces one-seventh of the entire agricultural output of Pennsylvania), is one of North America's most prosperous farm areas. The farms average only 75–100 acres (30–40 ha) in size, but their handling by successive generations of the Pennsylvania Dutch (the best farmers of whom were German Men-

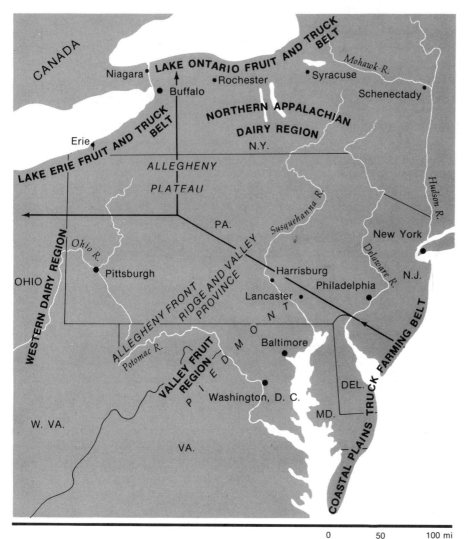

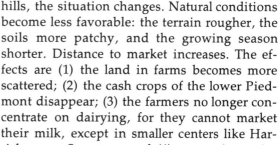

Fig. 10-1. Agriculture in the Middle Atlantic region: The arrows pointing inland from the coast indicate the approximate line of the traverse described on pp. 176–78.

nonites by origin) has been scrupulously careful. It is indeed the skill of the farmers together with the proximity of the Philadelphia market that underlies this remarkable prosperity; for, although tobacco, mushrooms, apples, and poultry are all raised as money crops on the good soils of the area, it is the same unspectacular[2] four-year rotation and the same dairying as is practiced elsewhere that form the basis of the farm operations.

As the traverse continues across this prosperous lower Piedmont and approaches the

[2]The countryside in Lancaster County is unspectacular, too; it is well wooded and rolling, with numerous hedges and a familiar look for Europeans. The only spectacular features are the barns, which are enormous.

hills, the situation changes. Natural conditions become less favorable: the terrain rougher, the soils more patchy, and the growing season shorter. Distance to market increases. The effects are (1) the land in farms becomes more scattered; (2) the cash crops of the lower Piedmont disappear; (3) the farmers no longer concentrate on dairying, for they cannot market their milk, except in smaller centers like Harrisburg or Scranton; and (4) prosperity varies markedly with access to such local centers.

Beyond the Great Valley, with its fertile bottom lands and orchards, these tendencies become rapidly more pronounced. They reach their endpoint in the deeply dissected forest country of the Appalachian Plateau, in the hill

Lancaster County, Pennsylvania: An Amish barn. The particular features of these barns are (1) their size, which is in part a token of the intensity of farming in southeastern Pennsylvania, and (2) their decoration with traditional and stylized designs. The Amish are one of the groups known as the Pennsylvania "plain folk"—the descendants of various sects of German Protestant immigrants who arrived in the early decades of the colony's settlement. They dress distinctively and tend to shun modern machinery, preferring to work with traditional implements. *(Library of Congress)*

farms whose isolation and meager natural endowment prevent the practice of anything other than subsistence farming. Each year that passes now sees the abandonment of more of these plateau farms and the return of the land to the forest that used to cover it.

Beyond this agricultural "dead heart" of eastern North America (which lies at the heart of Appalachia also, and which will be considered again in Chapter 15), we can trace in reverse much the same sequence as that seen on the Piedmont, whether we go westward from here or northward. To the west the market for milk recovers with the approach to Pittsburgh and the coal and steel towns, while on the north side of the plateau the industrial cities of the Mohawk Gap and the lakeshore provide a similar stimulus. Thus in western Pennsylvania and New York State there are dairy regions similar to, if less prosperous than, that of the Piedmont. On the north, indeed, there is even a counterpart of the coastal truck-farming belt, where market gardens, vineyards, and orchards extend along the Niagara Peninsula and the slope south of Lake Ontario.

In all the states in this region the area in farms is steadily decreasing, even though the figures for the latest period show that the area *under crops* has risen slightly; the farmers are evidently making better use of such farmlands as remain. Between the censuses of 1969 and 1974, Pennsylvania lost 714,390 acres (289,226 ha) of land in farms, while in New York State the current loss is running at nearly 150,000 acres (60,720 ha) a year.

What are the causes of this decrease? The first is the expansion of urban and industrial settlement over former farmland. This is a natural result of population growth, but a result intensified by today's social concepts and ideals—the concepts of building "out" rather than "up," which tend to spread the suburbs of cities over huge areas of low-density housing. Many American communities have by-laws enforcing a *maximum* housing density of

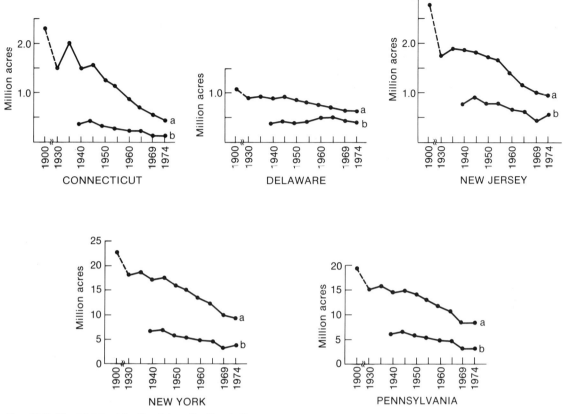

Fig. 10-2. The Middle Atlantic states: Decline in the areas (a) in farms and (b) of cropland harvested, for selected years, 1900–1974.

two acres per house. Small wonder, then, that the cities of the Atlantic seaboard have overrun both agricultural land and smaller towns and villages many miles from their original centers.

The second cause of decline, however, is due to the action of the farmers themselves in abandoning marginal lands. In some sections, such as the Tug Hill Plateau in upper New York State, and very generally above the 1000-foot (300 m) contour, farming has ceased altogether. In today's farming the poorer and remoter lands simply will not yield a worthwhile living. So strongly is the trend toward farm abandonment running that the planners can forecast closure and replan land use even before the farmer has actually made his decision to give up. Only the better farmlands, such as the Pennsylvania Piedmont and the truck areas of the coastal plain, have held their own, agriculturally, in the national setting.

The landscape of farm abandonment is an interesting one and is actually far from uniform. Around the outer suburbs of the cities there is characteristically (in both North America and Europe) a belt of total farm dereliction, where the farmers, foreseeing the spread of the city and the arrival of the developers, are simply waiting to sell out and retire on the proceeds; there is no point, meanwhile, in backbreaking labor. Outside this belt there is often a kind of agricultural aureole—an area of manicured lands, white rail fences, and elegant paddocks. This is the domain of the city businessman and his country estate. Beyond this again, prosperity and its appearances fall off with distance from the urban center. In none of these zones is commercial agriculture being carried on, yet in all of them the farm homes are occupied, at least part of the time.

What has happened (and again there is a parallel with conditions in Europe) is that in the vicinity of cities and in areas of particular rural quality, the farmhouses have been bought up by city people who in many cases use them as second homes and occupy them only periodically. Farming as such is not their concern, and often they allow the land to become grown over and prefer it that way. But as they renovate the farmhouses and bring capital into rural areas, it seems clear that the habit will spread further afield.

What of the future? To all appearances, all these trends will continue. In New York State it is expected that the urban areas will more than double their population in the next fifty years. An extra 15 million people will be wanting homes, mainly on the fringes of the present suburbs. To provide these will mean extending the New York built-up area eastward on Long Island (the eastern half of which is at present an area of scattered suburbs and weekend or vacation homes) and into the hills to the north and west. The cities of the Hudson-Mohawk lowlands and the Lake Ontario shore will spread further, to overrun some of the best of the state's remaining farmland.

From an economic point of view, as we saw in Chapter 6, there is little reason to regret the passing of low-value agricultural land. However, there must be some sensible limit imposed on the spread of built-up areas, and so there arises the question of other uses for abandoned farmland. In the Middle Atlantic region there are two such uses. One of these is forestry. The original farmers, when they cleared the land, left patches of forest which they used in relation to their fields—for fencing-timber or as shelter for their stock. Today forests are planted for their own sake, either to control runoff and improve the catchment areas of the big city reservoirs, or to produce commercial pulp for the ever-expanding newsprint market. In this way, rather ironically, the land acquires a new value when man plants new forests and completes the cycle that began when he first cut down the old forests 200 years ago.

The other use for these lands is recreational. The enormous urban population of the region must find an outlet, and as the land empties of farmers, much of it is enclosed in state forests and parks, and so is secured as open space in perpetuity. In this way, New York state has set up a planning agency to oversee the rational development of the Adirondack area, which at present includes two million acres (810,000 ha) of forest preserve. The Catskills contain another 200,000 acres (81,000 ha) of preserve. In face of the advancing tide of urban sprawl, the states will be well advised to make many more reservations, so that the cities of the future may be able to provide their inhabitants with space in which to breathe and relax.

Industry

The growth of industries in the Middle Atlantic region has been favored by circumstances of both location and history. When the revolt of the colonies threw the United States, in a new sense, upon its own resources, it gave a powerful stimulus to industrial production in the communities of the Atlantic seaboard. Local deposits of iron ore in eastern Pennsylvania and charcoal from the Appalachian forests formed the basis of early ironworking, and skill in a host of crafts that later became factory industries was brought into the coastal cities by immigrants from Europe. This immigrant stream also ensured that there was a constant supply of cheap labor when the factory phase of industry opened. Then, as the settlement of the West began in earnest, the East Coast states served as a supply base, providing the migrants with manufactured goods for their westward penetration—much as Europe had served as a supply base for the earliest colonists. Throughout three centuries during which North America's most important connections, both cultural and economic, were with Europe, the Middle Atlantic region profited by the constant passage of people and goods between the Old World and the expanding frontier of the New, to secure for itself a large share of the processing and shipping services required by both East and West.

Today the strength of the region's industries depends partly on a continuing exploitation of this position in relation to foreign trade, and partly on the huge size of the local market

180

which the position has in turn created. This has permitted the development of a full range of manufactures, and 95 percent of the 500 types of manufacture recognized by the census are represented in the state of New York alone.

In relation to industrial employment, however, two materials are of special significance. One of these is cloth. The two industrial groups of textile mill products and apparel account for a quarter of the industrial employment in the New York-New Jersey metropolitan area, and for one-sixth of that of Philadelphia. Although the region possesses numerous woolen textile mills, it is overshadowed in this respect by New England and concentrates rather on knitting mills and the manufacture of clothing. Although it is commonly found in any large city, the clothing industry has its focus in a remarkable area occupying only a few city blocks between Twenty-fifth and Fortieth streets on Manhattan Island, where several thousand small establishments employ some 25 percent of the nation's garment makers. Nearly a half of all the concerns making women's clothing are located here. 3·4o

The region's other principal industrial material is steel. Before the Civil War the center of the nation's iron industry was in eastern Pennsylvania, where local ores were smelted, first by charcoal and later by anthracite from the Scranton area. After the war, however, the greatly increased demand, the change to steel production and the introduction of new furnace techniques meant both that the Pennsylvania ores were quite inadequate to supply the industry, and that access to coal became relatively less important than access to ore and to market. The result was that the bulk of the steel industry moved westward to Pittsburgh and the Great Lakes. Part of it, however, either remained in eastern Pennsylvania, where there are still a number of small mills, or else moved eastward from the mountains into the coastal plains. Here, coal that had come by rail over the Virginia mountains to the ports of Hampton Roads and from there by water could meet ore from South America, and the seaboard cities provided an unrivalled market. This eastward movement was initiated by the transfer of the Bethlehem Steel Corporation's main plant from its former interior location in the Lehigh Valley to Sparrows Point, Baltimore, where a small mill was acquired, enlarged, and reopened in 1916, as the first American steelworks to rely almost exclusively on imported ores. The advantages of a tidewater location were re-emphasized in 1950 by the decision of the U.S. Steel Corporation to build its great Fairless Works (see p. 133) on the Delaware south of Trenton.

Accompanying the primary steel production of the region are a host of steel-using industries—shipbuilding in the port cities, construction of railway stock and machinery, and the manufacture of cans for the canning industry. Apart from these, two other groups of manufactures deserve mention. One is the chemical group, well represented in both its heavy and light branches, in both agricultural chemicals and in pharmaceuticals. Apart from numerous plants in the New York-New Jersey area, the region contains the headquarters, though by no means all the components, of the great Dupont concern at Wilmington, Delaware.

The other, and closely associated, industry of note is oil refining, whose presence here is related both to regional markets and to export. By pipeline and by tanker, the crude or semi-refined products are brought from the Southwest to the Middle Atlantic coast for processing and distribution. Since sea transport is involved in both receipt and shipment, most of the refinery sites are on tidewater, frequently on reclaimed marshlands that afford the most suitable sites for this industry within the vicinity of the cities. 4·oo

The Middle Atlantic region is one of the great industrial areas of the continent. Its preeminence has, of course, been reduced by the development of newer regions in the West and South, and by the policy of industrial decentralization, but since it still provides manufacturers with their most highly concentrated market, it is not likely to suffer from neglect. Industry, which was initially to be found near the center of cities or along their waterfronts, has spread outward to suburbs and to tidewater areas everywhere, in rather the same way as plantation agriculture was attracted to tidewater frontages in the colonial era. It has spread up the valleys of the Hudson, the Delaware, and the Susquehanna, and there linked together earlier centers or pockets of industry which were products of colonial enterprise or coal field growth. Not only the cities and coastal inlets, therefore, are highly industrialized, but also the hinterland, across which flow some of the main currents of North America's economic life.

Region and Nation

To suggest that the importance of the Middle Atlantic region should be measured simply in terms of its diminishing farmlands or its weight of industry would, however, be to understate seriously the role that it plays in the nation's life. Only three American workers out of ten, after all, are engaged in agricultural or industrial production: they are clearly outweighed by workers who serve, educate, finance, direct, or govern. And in these categories of employment the Middle Atlantic region is particularly rich. It has been commercial from the start and industrial for nearly two centuries, but rather than thinking of it today as a trading region or as a part of the Manufacturing Belt (and it is both), it is more appropriate to consider it as a *control area*—a decision-making region.

Industry and transport and enterprise elsewhere in the United States are directed from this core, which is a kind of general headquarters of Enterprise America, the national economy, even when the actual production processes are carried on in other regions. This region makes decisions not only as to when and on what terms finance shall be provided, but equally what the nation shall read (for it dominates the publishing business), and how American goods shall be advertised or presented. While much of this control is obviously exercised from Washington, as the seat of the federal government, or from New York, as the financial capital of the nation, the rest of the region plays its part, too, as lack of space in the central cities forces offices, research laboratories, and government agencies to disperse to quieter out-of-town locations, where they are linked electronically with their head-

quarters. Not milk nor steel nor chemicals, but decisions are the chief output of the Middle Atlantic region.

The Seaboard Cities

This is, before all else, a region of great cities. Over 15 million people live in the urban area that sprawls across the mouth of the Hudson and has its dramatic focus on Manhattan Island, New York. To the south, and dwarfing such intermediate centers as Trenton (319,000) and Wilmington (513,000), are Philadelphia, which has some 4.8 million inhabitants within its metropolitan area, Baltimore with 2.1 million, and Washington, D.C., the federal capital, with 3.0 million. Diverse in character, all four of these great centers have their distinctive functions, the first three as ports, manufacturing cities, and commercial centers, the fourth given over to the business of government.

When the end of British rule in the United States and later, the Louisiana Purchase opened the era of widespread settlement beyond the Appalachians, there rapidly developed among the Atlantic coast ports an intense rivalry to secure a share in the lucrative supply and transit business with the West.[3] From the first the decisive factor was transport; as communications developed, stage by stage, so the advantage swung from one city to another. In the first stage, up to 1825, Baltimore held a slight advantage. It was the newest of the ports, but it lay closest to the eastern end of the first main route across the Appalachians— the National Pike, authorized in 1806. Then, dramatically, the situation changed: in 1825 New York was linked by the Erie Canal with the Great Lakes. Both Philadelphia and Baltimore responded with canal projects, but it was one thing to cut through the low Mohawk-Lake Ontario divide, and quite another to

[3]Although in this section of the book we are concerned primarily with the competition between cities within the United States, it should not be forgotten that the Canadian port city of Montréal was also a very active competitor with the American cities. On this, see R.I. Wolfe, "Transportation and Politics: The Example of Canada," *Annals* of the Association of American Geographers, vol. lii (1962), 176–90.

The rivalry between the seaboard cities in the Canal Era: Canal connections with their hinterland played an important part in this rivalry, and when New York secured access to the west by the Erie Canal, Philadelphia interests responded with a canal up the Juniata River. But to cross the Appalachians it was necessary to build a portage railway from Holidaysburg to Johnstown, and the southern cities were unable seriously to compete by water with the low-level Hudson-Mohawk route. The picture shows the portage railway in 1840.

cross the main Appalachian barrier, with the Philadelphians reduced to hauling their canal boats up a cable incline to climb the Allegheny Front. Baltimore interests turned to other expedients, and in 1828 began work on America's first railway, the Baltimore and Ohio. A new phase in the struggle opened. Philadelphia responded with the Pennsylvania Railroad, New York with the New York Central and some lesser lines. The southern routes were shorter, but the northern were less heavily graded, and construction went ahead much faster. Competition was intense, and the last stage of the rivalry developed as a struggle for advantageous freight rates. This was won by Baltimore. With its shorter route to the interior, it secured in 1877 an advantage over New York and Philadelphia which it held almost up to the present time. Since the freight rates on most commodities being shipped to Europe are the same for all ports between Hampton Roads and Maine, Baltimore was able to use this rail differential to good effect in building up its export trade, especially in grain.

Yet New York outstripped its rivals in the end, for, although the canal era passed, the Hudson River proved a permanent and deci-sive advantage to the city at its entrance. To this advantage of strategic location New York could add that of its splendid harbor, opening directly on to the Atlantic (both Philadelphia and Baltimore face southeastward down their bays) and its maritime and commercial links with Europe. Once New York established its leadership, it grew with increasing momentum, until today few American concerns doing business on a national scale can afford *not* to have a New York address.[4]

To this story of intercity rivalry on the Atlantic coast there is a tailpiece to add. In 1959 there appeared a new threat to the trade of all these cities—the St. Lawrence Seaway. Ever since 1825 the main trade route from the Great Lakes eastward had run overland to these Atlantic ports. Midwestern grain exports in particular were handled there, especially at Baltimore. But the Seaway has cut very deeply into this transit trade, and grain handling facilities at the Atlantic ports now stand idle, in spite of reduced rail rates granted by the Interstate Commerce Commission. The Seaway has done

[4]In the less academic language of the advertising agency, this comes out as "New York is New York. Is there anywhere else?"

183

for Montréal, Toronto, and Chicago what the Erie Canal did for New York and Buffalo in the early days of the rivalry between the Atlantic coast cities, and this time on a far larger scale.

NEW YORK

The mouth of the Hudson seems a place fore-ordained by nature as the location of a great city. As we have seen, its position here enabled New York to outdistance its nineteenth-century rivals. Yet paradoxically, it is far from providing an ideal *site* for the kind of city that has grown up there. Few of the world's major centers can be so surrounded by geographical restraints as New York. Its core is on an island—Manhattan, 12 mi (19.2 km) long, but in general only 2 mi (3.2 km) wide—which, while it more than served the purposes of the original Dutch settlers, is today hopelessly over-crowded. Its suburbs lie either on adjacent Long Island or on the mainland, and formid-able water barriers interrupt the movement of workers and goods on all sides except the north. Furthermore, it is essential to New York's port function that these waterways be left free of obstructions. Especially is this so on the west (Hudson River) side of Manhattan, where the largest vessels dock. But it is precisely from this western side that most of the freight movement into New York occurs. Even beyond the Hudson, the roads and railways approaching New York from the west have to cross a series of inlets and marshes, and these form further constrictions, hampering the development of an adequate transport network.

Manhattan's links with east and west consist of six or seven bridges and four road tunnels. Of the half-dozen railways that approach the Hudson from the west only one, the Penn Central, penetrates (by tunnel) to Manhattan, and even so, its main freight terminal is west of the Hudson. The terminals of the other rail-ways line the New Jersey shore and, in the days when the city was served by the pas-senger trains of these companies, travelers be-gan their journey by ferryboat. Only to the north, across the narrow Harlem River, is it relatively simple to leave New York. This fact of geography goes some way toward explain-ing the important part in the life of the city

played by the subway network, which tunnels under the physical barriers to movement.

But the same water barriers which impede movement by land have contributed to New York's rise as a port. With waterfront available within the harbor area, with deep channels and a small tidal range, the port grew to domi-nate the Atlantic coast in terms of tonnage handled but, even more markedly, in value of overseas trade. The immigrant traffic of the nineteenth and early twentieth century was funnelled through the notorious Ellis Island terminal while, in the heyday of the North At-lantic passenger ship, the world's largest liners tied up at piers on the west side of mid-Man-hattan specially built to accommodate them.

In 1977 the port of New York handled 121 million tons of freight, and a little more than half of that volume was overseas traffic. No other port in the New World can rival this fig-ure. Nevertheless, much of what one writes about the port must be written in the past tense, for underneath the bare statistics there have been many changes. Most visibly, the passenger liner has virtually disappeared from the North Atlantic route; the waters that sur-round Manhattan appear deserted by contrast with the scene they presented only a decade or two ago, and many of the piers surrounding the island are in a state of chronic disrepair. The reason for this last change, at least, is clear: it arises out of changes of technique in handling cargoes and out of the demand for space in Manhattan. The piers on the island and the adjoining waterfronts offered no "backup" space for assembling cargoes and for storing them: all this had to be done on the pier itself. In particular, the advent of the freight container created a demand for assem-bly space occupying hundreds of acres rather than the narrow waterfrontage of the old har-bor. Much of the activity of the port has there-fore moved to outlying sections, particularly to new facilities like the container terminal at Port Newark.

It is not too much to claim, in fact, that these new facilities on the New Jersey side of the harbor have been the salvation of New York as a modern port. Only a decade ago, traffic fig-ures were declining; pilferage and strikes were

New York City: The World Trade Center, near the southern tip of Manhattan Island, looking south toward the Statue of Liberty (right) and the open sea (left background). Note the area on the right of the picture where old wharves have been replaced by an infill which effectively increases the island's area and provides space for up-to-date uses; many of the old wharves handled ferry services to the New Jersey shore that stopped running long ago (see p. 184). *(The Port of New York Authority)*

Port development in New York Harbor: Container terminal at Elizabeth, on the New Jersey shore. The terminal, whose basic requirement is a huge backup space behind the dockside for stacking the containers, is constructed on reclaimed marshland. *(The Port of New York Authority)*.

discouraging shippers and driving business away to smaller rivals; Philadelphia and the Delaware harbors were overhauling New York in tonnage handled. It was one more phase in the maladjustment of facilities to traffic which, Carey suggests, had been taking its toll at least since 1914.[5]

At this point, the port saved itself by using the formerly unused wetlands west of the Hudson, around Newark Bay. By excavation,

[5]G.W. Carey, "The New York–New Jersey Metropolitan Region," *Contemporary Metropolitan America*, Ballinger, Cambridge, Mass., 1976, vol. i, pp. 163–67.

dredging, and reclamation it created a new container port on the New Jersey shore, well placed for service by road and rail (since it was unnecessary for most traffic to cross the Hudson to get to it) so that it has been able to participate fully in the transport revolution which the container has brought about.

Nevertheless, in the years when New York grew to dominate the continent as a port of entry, it did so also in relation to manufacturing. Within its S.M.S.A. there are over 1.1 million industrial employees. The pressure on space in the central districts of the city, of which the skyscraper is the expression, has driven all but the lightest industries (such as garment manufacturing, which has already been mentioned) down to the waterfronts and out to the fringes of the urban area. It has been calculated[6] that in 1910, 75 percent of the manufacturing employment in New York City was to be found in Manhattan and, of this amount, two-thirds was in establishments situated south of Fourteenth Street; that is, in roughly the most southerly one-sixth of the island. Today much of the heavy industry is to be found on the New Jersey shore, while for newer or expanded industries, sites have been provided by reclaiming the marshes and inlets west of the Hudson, in the Jersey City-Newark area.

Space on Manhattan has become far too valuable to devote to such big space-consumers as heavy industries. The area south of Fourteenth Street is now world famous as the Wall Street financial district, although the actual area occupied by the finance houses is little over half a square mile. The district is easily recognizable by the cluster of skyscrapers that stand on the southerly tip of Manhattan. Then there comes a gap in the skyline until one reaches the prestige areas of Midtown Manhattan—another, and very rapidly enlarging, cluster of tall buildings from Thirty-fourth Street northward to the edge of Central Park, which serve both commercial and residential purposes.

Within metropolitan New York the zonal differences in land use are a source of constant interest to the visitor. Along a single street running for twelve blocks from east to west across Manhattan it is possible to find a complete range socially, from the poorest to the richest and economically, from port function on the West Side, through garment industry and transport terminals, to high-quality residential on the East Side. In culture and even language, too, New York is a series of cities within a city. For a century and half it has been the funnel through which has flowed the greatest tide of immigration known to modern history, and it has acquired in the process a huge foreign-born population.[7] Since these immigrants so often arrived with little knowledge of the ways of the New World, and without even the rudiments of its language, it is not surprising that groups of the same nationality have tended to congregate in specific areas of the city, in Little Greece or Little Italy, where they could do business in the language of their homeland and find the reassurance of at least some vestiges of a familiar culture. Within the narrow limits of Manhattan Island, these cultural divisions are clear and quite often very abrupt. As in most large American cities, the most clearly demarcated is the city in which the blacks live. The word *city* is used deliberately, because the black area contains a range of services just as complete as that of New York as a whole. In New York, the focus of everything black today is in Harlem, north of Central Park. How this came about is a long and fascinating story,[8] the point of which for present purposes is that this has not always been so. New York City, perhaps because of its long history of immigration, shows with particular clarity the workings of the principle of residential succession. When blacks first began to arrive in New York in considerable numbers, early in the nineteenth century, they congregated in the area around the present City Hall. Then between 1830 and 1860 a transfer occurred: the blacks congregated in what is now Greenwich Village and were replaced in their older quarters by Irish immigrants. In the 1890s another shift took place: the blacks moved uptown to the area of the present Penn Station and beyond, and Greenwich Village became Italian. Meanwhile, Harlem was becoming the most fashionable residential section of the city. Linked with what was then the distant city of New York on lower Manhattan Island by the first electric railways, Harlem ex-

[7]The 1970 census recorded that within the S.M.S.A. there were 4.5 million persons who were either foreign-born, or born in the United States of a foreign-born parent: 1.0 million Italians, 512,000 Russians, nearly 400,000 Poles, 340,000 Germans, and 300,000 Irish. Puerto Ricans are U.S. citizens; otherwise they would have swelled the numbers by 845,000.

[8]It is told with very ample documentation in G. Osofsky, *Harlem: The Making of a Ghetto*, Harper & Row, New York, 1966.

[6]By A.R. Pred, in "The Intrametropolitan Location of American Manufacturing," *Annals* of the Association of American Geographers, vol. liv (1964) 169.

perienced a property boom that first inflated values and then abruptly lowered them. It was in the wake of the property speculators and in the years 1904–5 that housing in Harlem began to attract blacks. By 1914 there were 50,000 of them in accommodations originally designed for wealthy white New Yorkers: "Negro tenants, offered decent living accommodations for the first time in the city's history, flocked to Harlem."[9] They started in the north of Harlem and moved south toward Central Park in a veritable "On To Harlem" movement which drew blacks from all over the New York area. Indeed, they were drawn from far beyond the city and in particular from the South, where Harlem was looked upon as a promised land.[10] And so the present Harlem of the blacks came into being.

Around the Central Business District on southern Manhattan Island stretch the suburbs, interrupted and elongated by the water barriers that surround the city. As Carey points out,[11] these suburbs increasingly contain not only the residential areas but the factories, offices, warehouses, and shopping centers of the metropolis, so that the former simple, periphery-to-center trek of the daily work force to Manhattan has been replaced by a much more complex pattern of movement; it has, in fact, been partially reversed as employment has migrated outward. In its outward spread, New York has overrun or overshadowed other cities, such as Newark (2,019,000) and Paterson (456,000), which, in a different setting, would be sizeable in themselves and which had their own origins.[12] The only way to slow down this outward spread is to build upward—to increase the number of skyscrapers and apartment buildings within the

central areas and, of course, to increase the congestion there by doing so.

Although the canal link between the Hudson River and Lake Erie, which wrought such a revolution in transport in 1825, has now faded into insignificance, the Hudson-Mohawk route as such has retained, in the railway and road eras, its importance both to the city of New York and also to the series of towns that lie along it. Followed by the Penn Central Railroad and by a multiple road link, this route has been the main channel by which the output of the Midwest reaches its markets and is an admirable location for industries which tap this flow of goods to obtain their materials. At the eastern end of the corridor, where the Mohawk joins the Hudson, lies the Tri-City area of Albany, Schenectady, and Troy, with a population of about 799,000. Schenectady, "the electric city," is the home of General Electric Corporation, and the district also manufactures railway stock, machinery, and textiles. Then on the low Mohawk-Erie watershed and in the neighborhood of Lake Oneida are the three cities of Utica, Rome, and Syracuse, each with a considerable range of manufactures and with a combined population of one million. Further west again lies Rochester (966,000). Rochester is a canal town: even though it lies not far from the shore of Lake Ontario it is not one of the cities of the Great Lakes (see Chapter 14) for it has no port function worth speaking of. It grew up, like Paterson, at a waterpower site—the falls of the Genesee—and the Erie Canal crossed the river just above the falls, giving the city what for the early nineteenth century was an ideal situation. Today, however, Rochester is better known as a cultural center and as the home of the Eastman Kodak Corporation.

Besides these major cities there are a number of smaller ones strung out along the route-

[9]Osofsky, *Harlem,* p. 93.

[10]Osofsky, *Harlem,* p. 128.

[11]Carey, *Contemporary Metropolitan America,* pp. 146ff.

[12]Those of Paterson are of particular interest: the town grew up at the falls of the Passaic River after Alexander Hamilton visited the site, was impressed by the waterpower potential of the falls, and promoted development through his Society for Establishment of Useful Manufactures. As a result, a mill town grew up which attracted a population of workers just as cosmopolitan as those of New York City across the Hudson.

Much of the later growth of the city can be traced in William Carlos Williams's fascinating epic poem *Paterson.* For anyone who has been in Paterson lately, the most surprising details revealed by the poem are probably that (1) in 1817 the local lads captured a seven-and-a-half-foot sturgeon in the basin below the falls, and (2) one of the world's finest pearls was found in a mussel taken from a tributary of the Passaic about the year 1860.

way. But in spite of their location these are less prosperous. It seems as if the Hudson-Mohawk route has, in fact, encouraged an unfortunate type of urban development here—a linear development creating a series of towns, several of them dependent on a single industry, and none of them large enough to raise itself to the rank of a major service center or to achieve regional prominence. While the larger cities on the routeway are relatively prosperous, the smaller ones are declining. This phenomenon of metropolitan "shadow" is sufficiently noticeable in the Northeast to have prompted the comment that "in New York State it appears that there is a threshold size of approximately 100,000 for substantial manufacturing success."[13] Manufacturing alone, in other words, does little to guarantee the growth or prosperity of a city; that depends on the service functions it develops in relation to its hinterland.

PHILADELPHIA

Owing to the configuration of the river gaps to the north of the city, New York's sphere of influence extends far inland. Moreover, New York draws off, as we shall later see, a large part of the traffic of southern New England. By contrast, the hinterland of Philadelphia is more circumscribed. The city itself, carefully sited and planned by William Penn on his arrival in 1682, lies between the Delaware and Schuylkill rivers just above their junction. This site gives the modern city advantages of location far beyond either the purposes or the imaginings of its founder: 40 mi (64 km) of navigable waterfront on the two rivers, deep channels, and room to expand. On the other hand, the lack of a natural route to the continental interior, of which Penn took little account, is a permanent problem. The Penn Central, Philadelphia's main link with the west, winds its tortuous way up the Susquehanna and the Juniata until with a final contor-

[13]John H. Thompson, ed., *The Geography of New York State*, Syracuse University Press, Syracuse, NY, 1966, p. 250. See the general assessment of "economic health" offered in this volume.

tion it conquers the Alleghenies by means of the famous Horseshoe Curve. Of recent years the situation has been improved by the construction of the Pennsylvania Turnpike, a through route from Harrisburg to Pittsburgh, as the principal highway across the Appalachians. But the pronounced southwest to northeast grain of the country behind Philadelphia, with its influence on the direction of railway routes, has the effect of bringing within the sphere of New York much of the industrial country of eastern Pennsylvania which would otherwise be tributary to Philadelphia.

As a manufacturing center, Philadelphia has a range of industries second only to that of New York, with machinery and textiles as leading groups. Among the city's specialities are radios, children's clothes, and knitgoods, while across the Delaware, in the east-bank suburb of Camden, products from the truck farms of the coastal plains are canned.

As a port, also, Philadelphia ranks only a little behind New York. It possesses major shipbuilding and ship repair industries, and both banks of the Delaware are lined with piers and wharves. In the business of the port the receipt of crude oil for refining and subsequent reshipment and, in recent years, of iron ore plays a large part. The Delaware River terminals have been receiving as much as 25 million tons a year from Labrador and Latin America, and it is here that the first impact has been felt of the United States' increased dependence on foreign ore (see p. 133). While some of the ore is carried up the Delaware to Trenton and the Fairless Works (the river has been specially deepened to permit the ore carriers to operate), this has also become an inlet for ore supplies to the Pittsburgh steel region.

Philadelphia is a stately city—in some ways more so than Washington, which was created with urban stateliness in mind. Although statistically it has fallen behind New York, its self-assurance is striking (as is that of Boston) when confronted by the mere statistics of New York's primacy, for it was in Philadelphia that the republic had its beginnings, and there that the first federal capital was established. Consequently, there is probably no eastern city which has done more than Philadelphia to create an urban landscape worthy of its history, both by restoring its historic buildings and by clearing and redeveloping central blight areas.

Behind the city, across the gently rolling Piedmont, stretches a virtually continuous spread of suburban settlement, from Trenton on the northeast to Wilmington on the southwest. Beyond the suburban ring, between 40 and 80 mi (65–130 km) from Philadelphia, lie a number of smaller industrial centers such as Reading, Lancaster, and the Lehigh Valley towns of Allentown and Bethlehem, each possessing significant manufactures, with steel goods and textile groups generally most prominent. All these cities lie within the orbit of Philadelphia and so, too, thanks to improvements in the highway network, do Scranton and Wilkes-Barre, the cities of the Appalachian anthracite coal field. After a long period of depression brought on by the declining demand for anthracite (see p. 131) and the loss of Scranton's major steelworks to a site near Buffalo on the Lake Erie shore, these cities' fortunes are beginning to recover as improved communications move them effectively closer to Philadelphia (and, for that matter, New York), enabling them to share in the overspill effects of industry and business activity generated by the two metropolitan cities.

BALTIMORE

Baltimore, the third and smallest of the Middle Atlantic region's port cities, lies at the head of one of the branches of Chesapeake Bay, where the mouth of the Patapsco River provides a fine natural harbor. Although founded only in 1729, Baltimore had by 1800 become the third port of the United States. As "the most southern of the northern ports and the most northern of southern ports," it has always drawn upon a wide hinterland for its traffic, and suffered in consequence when the Civil War cut off its important southern trade area. Recovering rapidly after 1865, Baltimore exploited to the full, as we have seen, its connections with the interior in the era of railway competition, but its function as a port was nevertheless hampered until the 1930s by the necessity of routing all but the smallest ships down Chesa-

peake Bay and around the Virginia capes, 170 mi (272 km) to the south of the city. With the enlargement of the Chesapeake and Delaware Canal across the Maryland-Delaware Peninsula, however, a short cut 35 ft (10.03 m) deep has been created for northbound traffic out of Baltimore.

With its freight-rate advantage and good rail connections to the coal and steel regions, Baltimore's chief port function has been the bulk handling of goods to and from the interior, with a particular interest in grain exports, although these have suffered from competition through the opening of the St. Lawrence Seaway. Imports are mainly ores and petroleum for local use, and the coastwise traffic consists largely of receipts of petroleum either from the Gulf ports or from the Pacific coast by way of the Panama Canal.

As an industrial center, Baltimore is usually regarded as the southeastern outpost of the Manufacturing Belt. Its industrial employment structure, which is dominated by the manufacture of primary metal goods, transport equipment, and clothing, is characteristic of the Middle Atlantic region, while the southern cities that lie beyond it reveal different patterns of both employment and layout (see Chapter 16). Its metal-working industries include both copper refineries and the Sparrows Point works of Bethlehem Steel Corporation, situated on the shore of the bay some 10 mi (16 km) from the city center. It shares with Philadelphia the East Coast shipbuilding industry. As a city Baltimore, although the smallest of the Atlantic Coast giants, has plenty of individuality, even in its architecture: indeed, considering the many parallels in the history of New York, Philadelphia, and Baltimore, and the basic similarity of the roles they all three now play, perhaps the most interesting observation to be made about them is that no one who knows them could possibly mistake any one of them for the others.

WASHINGTON

There is a sharp contrast between Baltimore and its neighbor to the south, Washington. Baltimore is an industrial city: one person in

The Atlantic Coast: Oyster fishing in Chesapeake Bay about 1880 (From *Harper's Introductory Geography*, 1896). In 1975, 53 million pounds of oyster meat were taken by U.S. fishermen, mainly in Chesapeake Bay and the Gulf of Mex- ico. In other sheltered waters, first over-fishing and then pollution had closed or reduced the accessible beds: in the Middle Atlantic states, for example, oyster fishing had almost ceased. The typical craft used is still small.

every ten of the population is engaged in industry. In Washington the proportion is one in 75 and only reaches this level by the inclusion of employees in the printing and publishing trades, who make up half of the "industrial" total. The business of Washington is government; the city was founded for this purpose and government accounts for nearly 40 percent of the employment of the S.M.S.A. Its only other significant business is to cater for the thousands of tourists who come each year to visit the city.

The site of Washington, on the banks of the Potomac, was chosen for reasons of political equilibrium rather than for its geographical advantages. Much of the area now covered by the city was marshland, unhealthy and liable to inundation. On this unpromising base was

imposed one of the most grandiose settlement plans of modern history, the fruits of which, after a century and a half of reclamation and construction, are to be seen in the broad vistas and carefully aligned buildings of the capital.

In order to free it from any pressure from the states, the seat of the federal government was established in an area—the District of Columbia—carved out of Maryland, which ceded the territory. For the small affair which was the eighteenth-century federal government, this was lavish provision. Its gigantic modern counterpart finds the District (which has an area of 69 sq mi [179 sq km]) all too small, and, especially in times of national emergency, overcrowding of both offices and workers is a serious problem. The modern expansion of Washington (its population in 1975 was

Megalopolis: The problem of surburban sprawl. This picture, taken on the outskirts of Washington, D.C., is one of a series by the U.S. Department of Agriculture entitled "Land Use Crisis in Suburbia," and calls attention to the effects of suburb-building on the natural environment—the destruction of vegetation cover and consequent danger of erosion. *(U.S. Dept. of Agriculture)*

716,000 within the Federal District) dates from the New Deal of 1933 when, under President Franklin D. Roosevelt's administration, the federal government enormously increased its field of operations. Events since that time have merely emphasized the trend. The District of Columbia itself has been *losing* population since 1965 (when it had 797,000 inhabitants). Like all these cities, Washington has been emptying out from the center into the suburbs—suburbs which now stretch far out into Virginia and Maryland and give the S.M.S.A.

a population of over three million, eighth largest in the nation.

With so great a concentration of city dwellers enduring the summer climate of the Atlantic coast, escape from the city has become a major seasonal operation. The coast is lined with resorts, of which the most famous is Atlantic City, and a series of east-west routes through the pine barrens link the cities with their summer annexes by the sea. Some of these resorts are also fishing ports. The sheltered waters of Chesapeake and Delaware bays support extensive fisheries, and the region's shellfish catch is particularly valuable, although pollution from urban sewage is a problem.

This last comment brings us to the concluding point of our survey of the Middle Atlantic region. The coastal section of the region has become well known to both geographers and general public in the past twenty years under the name given to it by Jean Gottmann—*Megalopolis*. This sprawl of urban areas along the coastal plain certainly deserves some distinctive name, if only because of its enormous length, its total population, and its distinctive problems. Furthermore, since Gottmann first publicized the name Megalopolis in 1961, urbanization has continued and the built-up areas have grown appreciably. For one thing, the interurban spaces—for example, that between Baltimore and Washington—are increasingly filled in by suburban development or by the kind of overspill activity, such as research and educational institutions, which are related to the cities but actually do not need to be in the central areas. For another thing, Megalopolis is extending north and south of its former end points. We shall refer to the growth on the northern fringe in the next chapter. To the south, there is a good case nowadays for regarding both Richmond and the port cities of Norfolk and Newport News as part of the urbanized seaboard too.

Megalopolis has its special problems. Among those to which Gottmann drew attention three particularly should be mentioned. They are (1) water supply, (2) sewage disposal and pollution in general, and (3) political and administrative splintering.[14] The first and second of these are obviously linked with each other. All of the major rivers of the region—Connecticut, Hudson, Delaware, Susquehanna, Potomac—must provide for the needs of large urban populations and what is more, for populations living in two or more states, so that plans for each of these catchment areas require interstate agreements—not the easiest thing to achieve in the United States, at least when a scarce resource is involved. The Delaware, in fact, is within measurable distance of becoming the Colorado River of the East Coast (see p. 357), as New York, New Jersey, and Pennsylvania bargain for its waters. In a conurbation of such unique shape and size, it is vital to coordinate public services and plans for the future. Megalopolis provides a test case which is probably the most pressing, and certainly the most complex, in the Western Hemisphere today.

The lesson of Megalopolis is perhaps best summarized in this way: for many centuries, we have thought of the distinction between town and country as consisting mainly of the fact that the space between the towns was used to grow food for the urban populations. We must now recognize that this is not the only or the most important function of non-urban space. In Megalopolis the chief function of space is simply to keep the cities apart—to provide not food, but water, air, elbowroom, and recreation for the huge concentration of people which is to be found in the cities.

[14]Vol. viii of the *New York Metropolitan Region Study*, published in 1961, was entitled *1400 Governments*.

New England

11

Introduction

The northeastern corner of the United States, lying between the Canadian border, the sea, and the Hudson-Mohawk line, is occupied for the most part by a rolling upland, forested, lake strewn and agriculturally uninviting. The gentler relief and greater fertility of the southeastern section of the region are offset by the barren emptiness of much of the north. The indices of population density and industrial concentration in eastern Massachusetts and Rhode Island are among the nation's highest, but decline northward across the region, almost to the opposite extreme in central Maine and upper New York State.[1]

The main mass of the New England Upland proper is divided into two by a north-south line of lowland, which is occupied today by the Connecticut River. This is the same Triassic lowland that we have already encountered in the Pennsylvania Piedmont and shall meet again in the Annapolis Valley of Nova Scotia,

[1]The Adirondack Mountains of Upper New York State do not, properly speaking, belong to the New England region: they are separated from the latter by the corridor of the Champlain lowlands, and little economic contact exists between the two upland areas. However, their character and problems are sufficiently similar that almost anything said about upper New England applies to the Adirondacks too.

and nowhere is its significance for agriculture and industry greater than here in southern New England. West of the valley lie the Taconic Mountains, the Berkshires, and the Green Mountains of Vermont; east of it are the White Mountains, which stretch away northeastward through Maine, to where the Upland is broken along the Canadian border by an area of softer rocks that underlie the valleys of the Aroostook and the Saint John.

If glacial erosion has been the decisive natural influence in northern New England, smoothing relief and diverting drainage, glacial deposition has played a role of equal significance in the south. This is a region of outwash plains and moraines. At its seaward edge, the frontal moraine of the ice sheet, deposited on the barely submerged northern extremity of the Atlantic Coastal Plain, has given rise to a chain of islands—Long Island, Nantucket, Martha's Vineyard—and to the peninsula of Cape Cod. The presence of abundant loose, ice-borne material has made this a coast of sandbars and spits under the action of the waves. Inland spreads the drift cover, here sandy and there stony, and dotted with drumlins or marked by the lines of eskers. In the valleys terraced clays and gravels remain as a product of the action of either ice or meltwater; much of the lower Connecticut Valley was

The New England fishing industry: The harbor at Gloucester, Massachusetts. (Ellis Herwig/Stock, Boston)

filled by an ice-front lake, whose legacy takes the form of a clay bed into which the present river has cut a series of terraces. It is in these southern valleys, together with the lowlands around Lake Champlain and along the Maine-New Brunswick border, that there are found the region's most fertile farmlands.

New England has no coal or petroleum and little iron ore. To offset this meager natural endowment of minerals, however, the region does possess three types of resources that over the years have brought it prosperity—forests, fisheries, and building stones.

The splendid stands of New England timber early caught the attention of the British Admiralty, and throughout the colonial period the region's forests were one of the prime assets of England's transatlantic possession. Today, after three centuries of settlement and commercial use, while much of the forest cover remains (some 75 percent or 33 million acres (13.36 million ha) of New England are classi-fied as forest land, and forests cover the greater part of the Adirondacks), its value has greatly diminished. It is almost entirely second growth that has developed after the cutting and clearing of earlier years. The best of the timber has long since gone; the main forest products the region yields are wood pulp and maple sugar. For all its acres of forest, New England imports sawtimber from Oregon and Georgia.

The region's fisheries have fared somewhat better over the years. In 1974 New England's 27,000 fishermen were responsible for 10 to 11 percent by weight of the total United States catch. The principal species landed are flounder, haddock, ocean perch, and cod, while in some years there is a big haul of herrings. The shellfish catch, although small in weight, brings in over half the returns by value. Among the fishing ports scattered along the coast, Gloucester, Boston, and New Bedford land by far the greatest share of the catch.

Some of these places, such as New Bedford, are effectively living through their third career as ports: they began with the transatlantic trade in the great days of New England commerce in the eighteenth century, then they turned to whaling, and now, having abandoned that business, they are fishing ports for the coastal and Banks fisheries.

The upland interior of New England yields a variety of valuable building materials. Vermont's granite and marble are famous, and the state is the leading United States producer of these stones and asbestos. Elsewhere in the region granite, marble, slate, and limestone are quarried, together with a variety of lesser-used materials, such as mica and quartz.

The New England Economy

No part of the North American economy has been so frequently and critically analyzed over the past forty years as the regional economy of New England. Most of the statistical temperature-taking has resulted in gloomy diagnosis, and indeed, to some observers outside the region, the patient's case has seemed hopeless. While the New Englanders themselves are far from accepting this verdict, they are nonetheless conscious of the serious problems that confront them.

The explanation of this flurry of interest is not far to seek. There was a time when, in terms of population, industry, or wealth, New England possessed a high proportion of the national totals. Its history went back to 1620; its people were industrious and turned early to commercial pursuits; it was here that factory industry in North America began. But the thirteen colonies on the Atlantic Coast gave place to a nation stretching across the continent, and inevitably the relative position of the East within the nation declined.

But this was not all. The *relative* decline applied to all parts of the East alike. What has marked New England out for special attention is that it has also suffered, in some respects, an *absolute* economic decline. The well-publicized fact that textile firms have left New England for the southern states is taken as a symbol of failure. For in the climate of United States opinion, and in the light of the nation's long history of successful expansion, failure to go on expanding is in itself bad enough; actually to lose ground is to incur a sort of social stigma.

Yet this absolute decline by no means applies to all aspects of the economy, and even if it did, it would still only represent a logical and, for the most part, beneficial redistribution of the nation's population, when better-endowed and more productive lands lie further west. The present size of New England's population and the character of its economy are not primarily the outcome of the region's natural attractions, but of historical chance—that it was from Europe that the great immigrant stream into the New World flowed. It is one of the main strengths of the American economy that, within a great free-trade area, possessing enormously variegated resources, the effects of such an historical coincidence can be adjusted with the passage of time. It is this process of adjustment which has been under way in New England ever since the First World War.

New England's problem has been primarily industrial in character but industry is not, of course, the be-all and end-all of economic development, and certainly the long-established and technically unsophisticated industries New England has lost would be really out of place in the region today. A far more accurate guide to progress is given by the growth of sophisticated industries and by the volume of tertiary or quarternary employment generated within the region.[2] And in this respect New England, far from feeling shame at the closure of old textile mills, can point with pride to its ability to adapt to the changing economic circumstances of the times.

Let us pause for a moment to restate this proposition in another form. We have become

[2]The distinction between tertiary and quaternary is Jean Gottmann's, the same geographer who suggested the name *Megalopolis* for this whole urbanized Atlantic seaboard. "Tertiary" he applies to transport and trade: "quaternary" to employment in research, government, education, and "decision-making."

familiar, not only in North America but in all advanced, industrial communities, with the way in which land use and employment structure within a city change as economic activity increases. The factories that may have formed the core of the original settlement are displaced from its center, and their place is taken by commerce and other central functions of the community or its region. The displaced manufacturing may be relocated in the suburbs or in new and specialized communities elsewhere. Within the city, employment shifts from secondary activity (manufacturing) to tertiary occupations. All that we have to do to appreciate the New England situation is to transfer this concept from a single city to a *group* of cities; indeed, to a whole region. In New England there has taken place a transition in function; that is, a change in the economic relationship between this region and the other regions of the United States. Within this region a concentration of tertiary and quaternary functions serving a far wider area than the region itself has developed. In relation to insurance services, for example, or to education and research, New England possesses resources of national importance.

In short, success or failure for New England should not be judged solely by the size of its industries or the dilapidation of its farms, but by the volume of its bank deposits, by its output of science graduates, or by its allocation of government research contracts.

How this situation has arisen must now be briefly explained.

Rural New England

European settlement in New England began with the establishment of the Massachusetts Bay Colony in 1620. From the early centers in the coastal lowland the newcomers spread westward; but here, even more than in the middle and southern colonies, the westward movement was hampered by obstacles, both physical and human. On the one hand, the forested slopes and rock-strewn surface of the interior made progress painfully slow, and on the other, there was the recurrent menace of

hostile Indians, who, with the sponsorship of the French in Canada, ravaged the borders of the settled area.

Behind this double barrier, cut off for the first 150 years of its history from the great safety valve of the empty areas to the west, New England experienced serious pressure of population. The result was an expansion of settlement, into remote and forested upland margins, where the means of livelihood were meager. With the great new immigrant waves of the early nineteenth century, expansion continued, and indeed was hastened, because of the rise of New England's industrial cities and the resultant demand for food supplies—supplies which, in this period before the coming of the railways, had of necessity to be provided from local sources.

The amount of cleared farmland in southern New England reached a peak in the 1850s and somewhat later in the north. Agricultural production was varied and, although the growing of grain had already declined (in consequence of the opening of the Erie Canal in 1825), sheep and beef cattle were plentiful in the northwest, while the southeast concentrated on the supply of vegetables and dairy produce to the towns.

In the second half of the century, however, a general agricultural decline set in. It manifested itself in the first place by the fact that after 1850 there was little increase in the rural population. On the contrary, as the century wore on, a reverse flow developed—from poor farms to expanding industries, from the isolation of the uplands to the fuller life of the towns. Highwater mark had been reached by the tide of settlement. Far to the west, in any case, the Pre-emption and Homestead acts were making it a simple matter for the would-be farmer to acquire quarter-sections of land that made New England's rocky margins look like a wilderness by contrast. Meanwhile, the westward-spreading railway network brought ever closer to the eastern cities the produce of this new Agricultural West.

These changes had two effects. First, they brought about a gradual retreat of the farmers from the margins of settlement. Farms were abandoned and scrub crept back to cover the cleared pastures. Essentially it was an abandonment of the remoter and higher regions to concentrate on the better soils of the valley terraces and drumlin slopes and on the more accessible farmlands. It was a retreat from lands that would never have been farmed at all if the lands to the west had been opened earlier, and it was a move to lands that offered the New England farmers at least the advantages of fertility and accessibility with which to meet western competition. The process of abandonment was not continuous; there were fluctuations of the frontiers of settlement, but in general it began earliest and has gone furthest in the vicinity of the cities, while in the north of the region the story of advance and retreat has unrolled with a time lag of twenty to thirty years behind the south. There are areas in New England which were once as much as 70 percent cleared and farmed, but where today there is no break in the forest, and the only evidence of the former occupation of the soil is found when, among the trees, one stumbles into the cellar hole of a vanished farmhouse.

New England Land Use, 1880–1974

	Percent of New England land in farms	Land in farms (thousands of acres)	Land harvested (thousands of acres)
1880	52.3	20,725	5,053
1910	51.8	20,566	4,790
1930	38.2	15,142	3,890
1945	34.5	13,948	3,800
1954	27.6	11,121	2,493
1964	19.5	7,745	1,929
1970	13.9	5,559	1,607
1974	11.9	4,800	1,451

The figures in the accompanying table tell a part of this story. Second, New England's changed circumstances meant a change from the diversified farming of the 1850s to a concentration, under the pressure of western competition, on a few staples like dairy products and poultry.

New England seems to have reached its agricultural nadir after the First World War. Since then, its farmers have been actively seeking a solution of the problems created by position and by poverty of natural resources. In this search for a new role the New England farmers

have had to reckon with three main physical limitations:

1. Over much of the upland interior, the growing season has a length of only 90 to 100 days, as against 160 to 200 days on the coast and 130 to 150 in the Champlain area. One particular aspect of this handicap is that the season in the interior is too short for corn to be grown.

2. Snowfall is heavy—well over 100 in. (2.5 m) per annum in the mountains. This represents a factor in accessibility which, as always in the eastern United States, is a matter of the utmost importance to the farmer.

3. The soils are often thin and stony, and are generally heavily leached. Where the hazard of glacial action has left the poorest soil cover, the process of farm abandonment has usually begun; the influence of the soil is generally decisive.

Circumstances, as we have seen, have long been forcing upon the farmers the "solution" of abandonment. There is, however, still need for further withdrawal, and especially for planned withdrawal, in the sense that the abandoned fields should be planted back to forest, rather than be allowed to revert to scrub. This would mean that the farmers were not merely cutting their losses, for such a withdrawal should enhance rather than reduce the value of the uplands. Forestry and recreation create new values, and the "yield per acre" from timber and tourist facilities should exceed that from marginal agriculture. But the scrub that spreads over farmland which is simply abandoned is neither scenic nor useful, and yet it is this scrub that, at least from the air, is the most prominent feature of the rural landscape today in the northeastern United States. Flying out of Boston over the New England countryside, one has the curious impression not that the cities are spreading across the empty landscape, but rather that the forest is creeping stealthily in to extinguish the city, a sort of silent invasion that has penetrated to the very gates of Boston.

A variant of the solution provided by abandonment is seen in the widespread development of part-time farming. This means either that the farmer, recognizing his farm alone cannot support him, supplements his farm income by other work during the slack season, or else that city dwellers have taken up vacant farms as year-long or vacation homes as we saw in Chapter 10. Many a farmstead has become a "summer home," and often these part-timers from the city have brought a welcome infusion of capital into the countryside.[3]

But the abandonment of the margins has been accompanied by a greater concentration of effort on the better lands. Here the farmer's solution involves picking the right lands and then picking the right products to take advantage of the one circumstance squarely in his favor—the existence of a large urban market almost on his doorstep.

Over most of the region the importance of dairying is unchallenged: in Vermont 85 percent of the commercial farmers are classed as dairymen. Only in the urbanized southeast is this situation modified. Here, land values are for the most part too high to support a relatively extensive form of farming like field dairying; more intensive land use is necessary, and poultry production dominates the output, with local specializations in vegetables and fruits resembling those of Pennsylvania and New Jersey. Where dairying does penetrate the "inner ring," it is with the aid of concentrated feeds brought in from the Midwest.

Dairying developed in New England as the earlier forms of farm production declined, in the second half of the nineteenth century, before the competition of areas to the west. Today Vermont is the leading dairy state of the region, with a dense concentration of dairy farms all through the lowlands east of the Richelieu-Champlain line, and there is a second concentration in eastern Connecticut. Because of the limitations imposed by soil and climate, the New England farmer relies, to an extent probably greater than anywhere else in the United States, on simple grass feeds for his cattle.[4] Yields are likely, therefore, to be low, unless the farmer supplements with expensive concentrates, and, although there has been a steady rise in milk yields, a further program of pasture improvement would seem to be one of the region's pressing needs.

The other main group of farm products in New England come from poultry farming. This type of activity has shown a considerable development since the First World War, especially around the cities of southeastern New England, for it is well suited to the suburban fringe areas, and can often be carried on in farm buildings no longer needed for other types of agriculture. From being a widespread secondary source of income on dairy and general farms, it has gradually become a specialized type of production, and the chief areas in which it is now concentrated are in eastern Connecticut and around Bangor in Maine.

Besides these two principal farm activities, New England has a number of crops of local importance to which reference must be made. The chief of these is potatoes. A century ago potato growing was widespread throughout the region. But, as in other parts of the continent, recent years have seen a concentration of potato production in a few areas which specialize in this one crop. What has happened is that with the force of competition, the cost of labor, and the appearance of new crop diseases, potatoes have become a specialist farm crop which can only be produced commercially where yields are at a maximum and where production can be profitably mechanized.

As a result of this change, potato acreage has shrunk everywhere in New England except in the extreme north. Here, by contrast, production has intensified until four-fifths of New England's commercial crop is grown in Maine, and the bulk of it in a single area—the lowlands of Aroostook County, on the Maine—New Brunswick border.[5] Glacial ac-

---

[3]In New England the landscape impact of this tendency is curious: one sees mile upon mile of abandoned fields, with brush invading them and every appearance of neglect, and often containing barns in the last stages of disrepair, but with the farmhouses themselves maintained in a state of such splendor as they can never have known during their life as working farmsteads.

[4]Except in the Aroostook Valley and on Cape Cod, hay represents more than half the cropland harvested all through New England. In Vermont and New Hampshire it represents more than three-quarters.

[5]In most years, the area planted to potatoes in Maine represents about 10 pecent of the United States total.

tion has provided soils well suited to the crop, production is extensively mechanized, yields are high, and the farmers of Aroostook grow potatoes with a single-minded zeal that amounts to dangerous monoculture. For not only are output and price notoriously variable in the potato market, but the remoteness of Aroostook forces the farmers to devote a great deal of energy to marketing. A large part of the crop travels to the coast and then by boat to Boston, New York, or markets as far away as Philadelphia. Yet in spite of transport difficulties and periodic slumps, Maine late potatoes continue to supply a wide range of markets throughout the whole of the Northeast.

Other local specialties are the blueberries of the Maine coast and the cranberries of Cape Cod. Both of these crops, although occupying only a small area of the coastal sands and marshes, supply a national market and profitably utilize land that would otherwise have little value. Elsewhere in southern New England a wide variety of tree fruits and berries is grown, especially apples, pears, and peaches, but the orchards have declined in number in recent years. Tobacco is grown in the Connecticut Valley.

New England's agricultural situation might be summarized as follows: in a region of meager natural endowment there is concentrated a dense population whose presence is related not to food supply but—as in Old England—to position, history, and industrial development. As long as the keynote of agricultural production was regional self-sufficiency (that is, until the coming of the railways and canals made movement of goods in bulk possible), New England necessarily expanded its farmlands as its population increased, and the farm frontier was forced far into the uplands. But once the compulsion for self-sufficiency was gone, and the region became merely part of a larger, competitive complex, such marginal agriculture was unnecessary; nor could it hope to survive economically. It has therefore been necessary, largely by a painful process of trial and error, to contract the region's agriculture to more modest proportions, to accept and concentrate on limited objectives, and to discover how New England's farmers can survive and prosper in a nation that includes so many better-endowed regions. In all these difficult tasks, the evidence suggests, a real measure of success has been achieved.

Industrial New England

The Revolutionary War opened an era of great industrial opportunity for the United States. The old restrictions on native manufacturers which had been a feature of the colonial period (and indeed a contributing cause of the Revolution) were gone; and the United States was estranged from Great Britain, its principal source of manufactured goods. The revolution, too, was followed by the beginnings of large-scale westward movement, a movement on which the Louisiana Purchase of 1803 set the seal; and as the nation's territory expanded, so too did the demand for the means of conquering the wilderness.

In this era of opportunity New England emerged as America's first industrial region. This resulted partly from the fact that New England's interests had long been commercial rather than agricultural, which in turn can be attributed to the lack of opportunity offered by the region's farming. Partly it was the product of New England's labor situation; not only was there a surplus to be tapped in the poor farm areas, but there was also an immigrant stream that brought to the ports of the Northeast a supply of skilled craftsmen from Europe. And when the age of factory industry created a need for power, New England's rivers provided an abundant supply, and their falls became the sites of the earliest mills and factories.

From these early beginnings, the industrial history of New England has run remarkably parallel to that of Old England. Both set out to be "workshops" supplying non-industrial areas; both lost their early lead through the competition of newer rivals and through changes in the source of industrial power; both find themselves today with a wealth of experience in manufacturing, but with out-of-date industrial equipment that places them at a disadvantage in relation to their rivals. Both, too, have made strenuous efforts to remedy their situation.

Southern New England is still one of the most highly industrialized regions of the continent. Connecticut and Rhode Island have 32 percent of their labor force employed in manufacturing, a proportion exceeded only by that in the Carolinas. But changes have taken place which have turned most of New England's earlier advantages into handicaps. The industries that once made it famous have been faltering, and their very concentration in this region has proved a source of weakness, for as they have contracted, whole cities and areas have been robbed of the mainstay of their employment.

The leading industry of southern New England up to the First World War was textile manufacture; at the end of that war the textile mills employed nearly 450,000 workers. The second of the traditional industries was leather-working and shoes. Both of these old industries were rather narrowly localized; the main areas were northeastern Massachusetts, Boston, and the Merrimack Valley in southern New Hampshire, together with a district comprising Providence in Rhode Island and the Massachusetts cities of New Bedford and Fall River.

But from the First World War onward, New England's position as a manufacturing region was clearly weakening. Changes had taken place which left it at a comparative disadvantage after its early start. Among them were:

1. A change in industrial materials. New England's industries developed in a period when a large proportion of all manufactured goods were made of cloth, wood, or leather, all of which were available in quantity. But industry became increasingly metal-based and more recently has come to depend on a whole range of synthetic materials, none of which New England produces itself.

2. A westward shift in the nation's "center of gravity"—both in production and markets—which has left New England on the periphery. This was particularly damaging to a region which must import not only its food but also its fuel and raw materials, as well as export its manufactures.

3. A change in sources of industrial power. Great Britain's supremacy in manufacturing was made possible by her coal, and her industrial advantages have dwindled with the coming into use of newer fuels. But New England's asset—waterpower—belonged to a yet earlier phase of industrialization: the phase passed and the advantage to a region which had neither coal nor petroleum was short-lived (although with the coming of hydroelectricity it has, of course, in some measure returned). The outcome was that fuel had to be imported and became a high-cost item in the region's manufacturing. (As a consequence, the utilization of energy in New England industry is on the average less than half as much per employee as it is for the nation as a whole.)

4. A change in social conditions. The trade unions in New England grew strong; the state governments brought into force a body of law designed to protect the workers, and the region became unattractive to plant owners, who hoped to find more amenable workers and less restrictive legislation elsewhere. At the same time, working conditions in the old mills were unattractive, so that there developed a double exodus from the traditional New England industries—an exodus of firms from the region in search of more favorable operating conditions, and an exodus of workers from the industries in search of other employment.

New England had, in fact, two problems superimposed on one another. One was that from 1919 onward it was losing ground generally as an industrial region.[6] The other was that its leading industry, textiles, was particularly subject to competition, both from other areas (among which, as we saw in Chapter 7, the South was by far the most serious rival) and from new technologies—there were newer mills and newer synthetic fibers to cut into New England's business. And the combined impact of

[6]"For about twenty years prior to 1939, manufacturing industry in New England was declining in both relative and absolute terms." R.C. Estall, *New England: A Study in Industrial Adjustment*, Praeger Publishers, New York, 1966, p. 17. It would be impossible to write on this subject without being in some degree indebted to Dr. Estall and his work, and the present writer readily acknowledges the debt.

these forces was felt most acutely in the areas where the old industries were concentrated.

In 1939 the textile and leather goods industries between them still accounted for over 40 percent of New England's industrial employment. But after the Second World War, numbers employed in the textile mills fell off rapidly—to 280,000 in 1947 and a mere 76,000 in 1972. Employment in the leather industry held up rather better. But within the region the industry migrated, so that the losses in the oldest leather manufacturing areas were very serious.

What could New England do in the postwar years to reform its economy and recruit its industrial strength? Clearly, two tasks lay before it. One was to develop other industries which could replace the older and faltering groups. Given the circumstances of the region, the most suitable type of new industry would be those that require large amounts of skilled or at least semi-skilled labor, but little fuel or bulky raw material. This kind of industry already flourished in southwestern New England: the problem was to establish it in the hard-core area of industrial decline, in Massachusetts and Rhode Island.

The other task was to expand alternative employment, in order to reduce the region's dependence on manufacturing. In New England, with its declining agriculture, this could only be done by concentrating on such activities as commerce and research to serve a national market.

How successful has this adaptation of the regional economy been? In spite of the loss of so many jobs in the textiles industry, total industrial employment rose from 1939 to 1963 by 26 percent, and by a further 9 percent between 1963 and 1969, although after that date there was a fresh fall. The principal replacements for the older industries appeared in New England during the Second World War, and have taken root there very firmly in the years since 1945. They are the manufacture of transport equipment (which in this case mainly means things that fly) and of electrical machinery. New England has plunged into the space age with all the vigor at its command, backed by its long industrial experience and the resources of its unrivalled collection of universities and technical institutes.

These industries are ideally suited to New England's situation. For one thing, they require minimal amounts of raw material in relation to the value added by manufacture, so that total costs of assembling materials and of shipping goods are cut down. For another, they demand a combination of high-grade research and skilled assembly, which are the two things the region is best qualified to provide. In particular, the electronics industry provides plenty of opportunity for the employment of female labor with a background training in factory work, such as the old textile industry offered to so many New England working women. Furthermore, it is part of the character of these industries that the presence of one tends to attract another, so that once the process has started, there is every chance of it continuing through its own momentum.

Undoubtedly, the changeover will go further: the textile industry will contract still more, and electrical engineering will increase as each new research frontier is opened. However, there is a danger here, in that already the region is becoming sensitive to a new pressure: at least half of the output of electronic equipment is for the government's defense program and so is susceptible to changes in budgetary policy. Southern California (see p. 393) has already experienced the economic seasickness that this may lead to. Having successfully thrown off one form of industrial overdependence, it would be unfortunate if New England were to succumb to another, however sophisticated.

But in some parts of New England the new industrial activity has brought salvation, and it is unwise to look a gift-horse in the mouth too closely. The principal location of the new electronics firms has been in the outer suburbs of Boston, and especially along its ring road, the now-famous Highway 128. From here, there has been during the past decade a spread northward into smaller centers—in some cases into the very towns (indeed, the very premises)—which the textile industry had previously abandoned—places like Nashua, New Hampshire. Meanwhile, the surviving elements of the textile and leather industries have shown a tendency to migrate northward into Maine, where labor is cheaper and less hard to find than in the competitive labor market of the Boston hinterland.

In fact, this area north of Boston has undergone striking development in the past ten years.[7] Industrial revival is only one reason for a sharp increase in population in the Merrimack Valley, southern Maine, and southern and western Vermont. Other contributing factors have been the growth of tourism, especially winter sports, and the expansion of the "second home" habit, already well developed among New Englanders. Thanks to the expansion of the freeway network, the effective commuting range of the Boston metropolis now extends well up into New Hampshire and Maine, and so in the 1970 census this area shows population-growth figures the like of which have not been seen in New England since the late nineteenth century.

But there remain old textile areas in southeastern New England which have not experienced this industrial replacement. For them, the need has been to expand alternative, non-industrial employment. At this they have been quite successful, but there has been a considerable out-migration from New England to other regions of the United States. In the years before the First World War, this was masked by the flow of immigrants from Europe entering the region, which in many years reached a quarter of a million and sometimes more. But the habit of moving on from New England is a long-standing one: after all, it was New Englanders who led the way westward through New York and into the Great Lakes area, and when in the 1850s the question arose as to whether the newly forming state of Kansas (admitted to the Union in 1861) should be a slave state or free, it was from New England that the antislavery campaigners drew a swift tide of settlement to tip the balance in the emergency.

There remain local variations in the character and well-being of the region's economy.

The industrial cities of southwestern New England, among which the largest are Springfield-Holyoke (590,000), Hartford (721,000), New Haven (411,000) and Bridgeport (402,000), contain a very wide range of light industries, mostly metal goods of various kinds.[8] Northeastward across New England, the importance of the older industries tends to increase. In centers like Providence (910,000) and Worcester (372,000) there is a rough balance between older and newer industries. For example, in Providence, the capital of Rhode Island and second only to Boston among New England's cities, textiles account for some 25 percent of the industrial employment, but there are also a famous jewelery industry and important manufactures of hardware and machine tools. Beyond this intermediate zone lie the old one-industry cities: the textile centers like Fall River-New Bedford, Lawrence, and Lowell, or the shoe towns of Lynn and Haverhill. The core and headquarters of this industrial area is to be found in metropolitan Boston, which contains 2.9 million people, a sixth of the region's industrial workers, and half the manufacturing plants of Massachusetts. In terms of employment the most important industry is the great new electrical engineering group. It is followed by machinery, apparel, and leather, so that the Boston area reproduces in miniature the industrial dilemma of transition from old to new and the hopes of the region as a whole. It has "one of the largest concentrations of electronic and scientific firms anywhere in the United States" (*The Financial Times*), but it also has the problem of maintaining these plants and their skilled workers in full employment, seeking contracts with private industry when govern-

[7]See G.K. Lewis, "Population Change in Northern New England," *Annals* of the Association of American Geographers, vol. lxii (1972), 307–22.

[8]In the first (1960) edition of this book, the writer commented on the fascinating variety of light metal-goods industries which could be seen when traveling by rail from New York to New Haven, and listed his observations. Returning to this route in 1977, he was glad to find that the variety was, if anything, greater than before, and compiled a long list of manufactures, including lipstick cases, gas meters, weather instruments, castors, and kinkless chain. The latter, as every American reader will recognize, represents a technical breakthrough comparable only with that of the "ouchless band-aid."

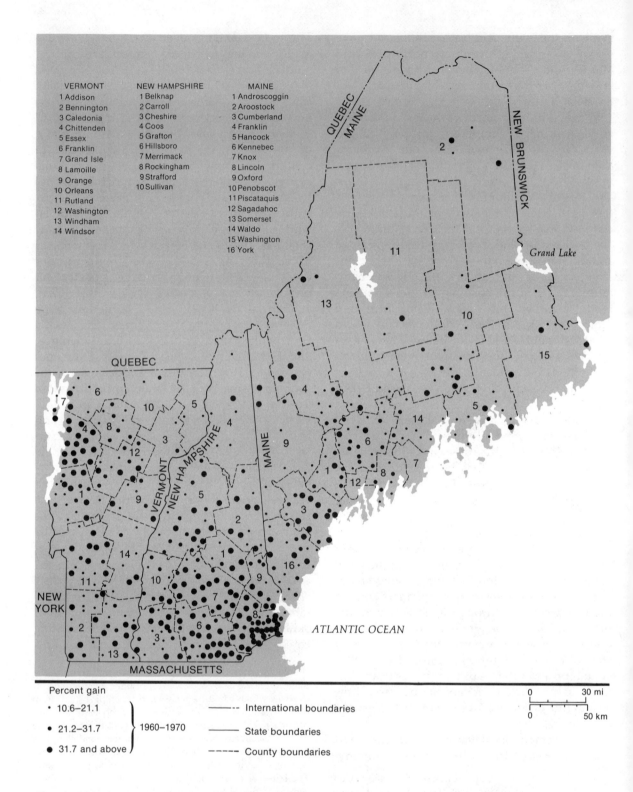

VERMONT
1 Addison
2 Bennington
3 Caledonia
4 Chittenden
5 Essex
6 Franklin
7 Grand Isle
8 Lamoille
9 Orange
10 Orleans
11 Rutland
12 Washington
13 Windham
14 Windsor

NEW HAMPSHIRE
1 Belknap
2 Carroll
3 Cheshire
4 Coos
5 Grafton
6 Hillsboro
7 Merrimack
8 Rockingham
9 Strafford
10 Sullivan

MAINE
1 Androscoggin
2 Aroostock
3 Cumberland
4 Franklin
5 Hancock
6 Kennebec
7 Knox
8 Lincoln
9 Oxford
10 Penobscot
11 Piscataquis
12 Sagadahoc
13 Somerset
14 Waldo
15 Washington
16 York

Percent gain

· 10.6–21.1
● 21.2–31.7   } 1960–1970
● 31.7 and above

——— International boundaries
——— State boundaries
------- County boundaries

0   30 mi
0   50 km

Fig. 11-1. Northern New England: Population changes,
1960–70. Cities and towns experiencing population growth
between 1960 and 1970.

Boston: The harbor from the southeast, with the international airport on the right. This fine and historic harbor was long overshadowed by New York's further south, but the past few years have seen a remarkable upsurge in its fortunes, thanks to good labor relations, low pilferage rates, and the adoption of new techniques of freight handling. *(Massachusetts Dept. of Commerce and Development)*

ment contracts have periodically run out, to avoid the melancholy sight of lines of out-of-work scientists.

Boston is the undisputed regional capital of New England—for finance and for the media—as well as the capital city of the state of Massachusetts. Its original site—on a peninsula separated at certain states of the tide from the mainland—was even more circumscribed than that of New York but reclamation among the low morainic hills and along the sandy shores of Massachusetts Bay has been far simpler than on Manhattan Island. So the city has been able to enlarge its site as it increases its population, and both to spread inland and to reclaim the Bay with a minimum of physical difficulty. The early constrictions of its site, however, have given central Boston a pedestrian-scale size which is attractive among modern American cities: its Common is a scaled-down counterpart of New York's Central Park, and most of its important buildings are within walking distance of the Common. Socially, Boston shares the character of other port cities of the Atlantic coast, with its immigrant quarters and its black ghetto, Roxbury. Its immigrants include perhaps the most famous of all such groups in the New World—the Boston Irish.

Whereas in New York, with its greater ethnic variety, no single group can be said to have attained dominance, the Irish had done so in Boston by the end of the nineteenth century:

Acquaintance with the Irish in these districts [of the city] leaves one with a distinct sense of admiration for the accomplishment of the nationality. They are the ranking national group. Their institutions are at once the largest, strongest, and best managed that one comes upon.[9]

[9]R.A. Woods and A.J. Kennedy, "The Zone of Emergence: Observations of the Lower Middle and Upper Working Class Communities of Boston, 1905–1914, in S.B. Warner, Jr., ed., *Planning for a Nation of Cities*, The M.I.T. Press, Cambridge, Mass., 1965, p. 36.

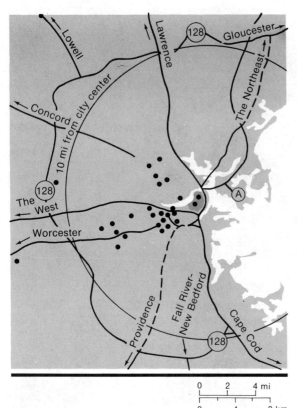

Fig. 11-2. Boston and Highway 128 (also known as the Circumferential Highway and Interstate 93 and 95), along which modern industry and research organizations have settled. Highways shown are interstate highways and other routes of comparable quality; status in 1978. Also indicated are the locations of higher education institutions (omitting junior colleges) in the Boston area.

chapter, for example, Boston took little part. Most of its interests were maritime; its railroad building was less vigorous than that of its neighbors, and although the Taconics are a much narrower obstacle than the Appalachians, in an economic sense they seemed to shut Boston off from the interior. Southern New England tended to ship its goods via New York, and the equalization of freight rates to Europe from all the northern Atlantic ports robbed Boston of the advantage it might have enjoyed through its position on the great circle route to Europe.

All these limitations seemed, until recently, to be epitomized by its port. Despite its splendid harbor and good equipment in the early 1970s it was handling a mere 25 million tons of traffic a year, or less than a quarter of New York's business; what is more, the bulk of the freight movement was simply the coastwise receipt of fuel supplies needed by a fuel-less region.

If the port symbolized the city then, it may perhaps do so in the future, too. For the port of Boston (or Massport, as it is now known) has staged a remarkable revival. The secret has been twofold—good labor relations giving strike-free operation, and whole-hearted commitment to "containerization" and the facilities it requires. Boston now claims to be the fastest-growing container port on the Atlantic Coast and has pitched into battles with the I.C.C. for more favorable freight rates. Remarkably, it seems as if the northeastern United States has room and business both for a resurgent port of New York (as we saw in the last chapter) and a revitalized Boston.

As a delightful bonus, Boston has not only increased its port *traffic,* but has succeeded in renovating its port *buildings.* The old warehouses of the waterfront, grim, ugly, and massive, were until a few years ago an apparently immovable, but quite useless, reminder of the port's earlier functions. The waterfront area was derelict. But if the warehouses were too solid to remove, they were not beyond conversion, and converted they have been, to form a shore area of apartments, shops, restaurants, and marinas which has become a sought-after residential setting, the focus of Boston's life on summer evenings, and a major tourist attraction.

Originally concentrated in the areas of dense and low-grade housing of the inner ring the Irish, as has been the way with other successful immigrant groups, have followed dispersion paths throughout the conurbation, and today no single area contains a marked concentration. But they were followed by the Italians and the latter, as more recent arrivals, are still congregated very strikingly in a Little Italy in the city's North End, on the tip of the old peninsular site.

Important though Boston has always been throughout New England's history, it has usually been overshadowed in its functions by New York, and has sometimes seemed aloof from the concerns of the other Atlantic Coast cities. In the rivalry between the Middle Atlantic cities which we reviewed in the last

Urban renewal: The Boston waterfront. The old wharves and massive stone warehouses of Boston's port were an unpromising subject for urban redevelopment, but the task has been carried out with spectacular success (see p. 206). The warehouses have become shops and apartments, and the old Quincy Market (right side, just beyond the freeway) has been restored. The Customs House is the building with the pointed roof; the financial district is beyond it. *(Massachusetts Dept. of Commerce)*

New England, like any other region, has its strengths and its weaknesses. Most of the regional surveys carried out over the past decades have concentrated on the weaknesses, such as the aging industries and the high cost of fuel and power supplies compared with levels faced by competitors elsewhere. But there are strengths, too, in the regional economy, and these were brought out by Eisenmenger in one of the more recent in the succession of gloomy prognoses: in fact, his optimism struck

an unfamiliar note.[10] He pointed out that, although per capita incomes in New England were above the average for the United States as a whole, labor costs to the employer are *below* national averages, in part because of the low turnover and high skills levels that characterize the region. "The cost of trained labor is the only major cost that is lower in New En-

[10]R.W. Eisenmenger, *The Dynamics of Growth in New England's Economy, 1870–1964*, Wesleyan Univ. Press, Middletown, Conn., 1967.

gland than in most other regions."[11] If electricity is more expensive than elsewhere, then New England's labor-intensive industries use less of it per employee than those of other regions. If some industrial areas are crowded and lack development space, then this drawback is counterbalanced by the economies of agglomeration—the advantage of being close to suppliers or sources of labor.

In summary, the New England region possesses a marked individuality, which is the product as much of its history as of its geography. It dates from the time when the New England colonies formed the most wealthy block on the Atlantic Coast, and when the Atlantic Coast was America. If other Americans feel that New Englanders should awaken to the fact that times have changed, none would deny the vast contribution made to the economic and cultural life of the United States by New England's men of business and letters. Less and less does the New England tradition represent the American norm, yet the region occupies in the United States today a position not unlike that of the senior member of some club, overtaken in accomplishment and sometimes outvoted by the younger members, but still wielding the influence that his prestige warrants over the conduct of business.

[11]Eisenmenger, *The Dynamics of Growth*, p. 76.

12

The Maritime Provinces and Newfoundland

General Situation

Although the history of European settlement in the Maritime Provinces of Canada and in Newfoundland is as long and as distinguished as that in Massachusetts or Virginia, in economic development this region has lagged far behind the newer lands to the west and south. The physical handicaps of the area—which in any case are shared by much of New England—cannot by themselves explain this economic difference. Such an explanation must also take into account the position of the region, in relation both to the rest of Canada and to the continent as a whole.

The Virginians and New Englanders of the colonial period found their progress westward from the Atlantic coast obstructed by the mountain and forest barriers of the Appalachians and the New England ranges. Against these barriers, as we have seen, the flow of migrants was dammed for long enough to produce a relatively dense population and to promote the early growth of cities and industries. Further north, however, the barriers were outflanked by the St. Lawrence route, which led directly to the continental interior. The Mari-

time Provinces lay not astride the main line of westward movement but to one side of it; and their forested and often infertile lands offered little incentive to costly clearance and settlement, when contrasted with the vastly superior areas of Lower Canada that lay within easy reach to the west. There was, in other words, not the same geographical compulsion about the occupance of the Maritimes—and still less of interior Newfoundland—as there was about that of the coastlands further south. The early settlements in many cases looked seaward to the fishing grounds rather than landward, and, significantly enough, the earliest agricultural areas were not forest clearings but coastal marshes reclaimed by diking.[1]

The position occupied by the Maritime Provinces has further drawbacks. Projecting far to the east as they do, it might be expected that the provinces would be particularly well placed to participate in foreign trade, especially in winter, when the St. Lawrence is

[1] " . . . the dyked marshes of the Bay of Fundy gave somewhat the same grudging tolerance to primitive animal husbandry as the St. Lawrence region did to cereal husbandry." V.C. Fowke, *Canadian Agricultural Policy*, University of Toronto Press, Toronto, 1946, p. 3.

frozen. In reality, however, although the winter transit trade is considerable, it forms an insufficient basis on which to develop regional industries. Furthermore, it has become apparent (and not only here, but in other continents also) that in foreign trade, as distinct from passenger traffic, the greatest advantage lies usually not with the area that projects furthest oceanward, but with that which surrounds the deepest penetration of the sea inland. It is at the head of deep-water navigation that both manufacturing and foreign trade concentrate. This head of navigation on the St. Lawrence was at one time at Québec, later at Montréal, and now, with the Seaway giving access to the Great Lakes, it is at Thunder Bay.

But perhaps the most influential factor in molding the outlook and the economy of the Maritimes is the international boundary. The provinces are connected to the rest of Canada only by a narrow corridor, 30 mi (48 km) wide, where the state of Maine reaches almost to the St. Lawrence. Through this sparsely populated corridor run a road and two railways that form a slender and somewhat roundabout link between east and west. But the shortest route from Montréal to the Maritimes (that of the Canadian Pacific) passes through the United States. Indeed, the "natural" connection of this region, insofar as it has any, is with the northeastern United States rather than with Canada, and here the border intervenes. This is a fact whose significance we must later consider.

In physical character the Maritime Provinces form a continuation of the New England system, which is related in turn to the older, eastern half of the Appalachians. The grain of the country still runs from northeast to southwest, with two upland areas separated by a lowland which structurally is a geosyncline. The coastline is deeply indented, with numerous drowned valleys. Inland the relief is nowhere impressive; the mountains of Gaspé rise above 4000 ft (1215 m), but in the Maritimes proper there are few areas of the ice-smoothed surface above 1000 ft (300 m). The main relief features are determined by a number of granite batholiths and other igneous intrusions. One of these underlies the mountains of north-central New Brunswick, and others are found in the "arms" of southern Nova Scotia and Cape Bret-

on Island and along the north shore of the Bay of Fundy. For the rest, the upland areas in the north are based upon formations of Silurian age or earlier, while the lower-lying southeastern part of New Brunswick, much of central Nova Scotia, and the whole of Prince Edward Island are underlain by Carboniferous limestones and sandstones. Coal measures occur in Cape Breton Island, in the vicinity of Pictou in western Nova Scotia, and around the head of Chignecto Bay. Finally, in southwestern Nova Scotia appear formations of Triassic age; the curious form of the southern shore of the Bay of Fundy is produced by parallel bands of Triassic trap rock and sandstone flanking the Nova Scotia granites.

The effect of this pattern on the economic balance sheet is that, in general, the areas of younger, sedimentary rocks are farmed, while the areas of older crystallines are not. The value of these non-agricultural lands lies in their forests and, to a lesser extent, in the building materials they yield—granite, marble, and slate.

The Maritimes, as their name would imply, have a climate much modified by proximity to the Atlantic. Summers are cool; winters in the hills and along the St. Lawrence are cold. Precipitation is ample and well distributed throughout the year. The chief climatic handicap of the region, however, is its lack of sunshine in summer. The southern coasts are often fog bound (for some seventy days in the year), and consequently the moderating influences of the sea on this long, indented coastline are offset by the fog. Inland the governing factor becomes the danger of frost: the growing season shortens by as much as 100 days between the coast and the interior, and indeed in some upland areas of New Brunswick no month of the year is frost free. From this combination of climatic circumstances derive the region's two main natural resources—its forest cover and its abundant supplies of waterpower.

Land and Livelihood

In its origins the population of the Maritime Provinces is thoroughly mixed. The earliest

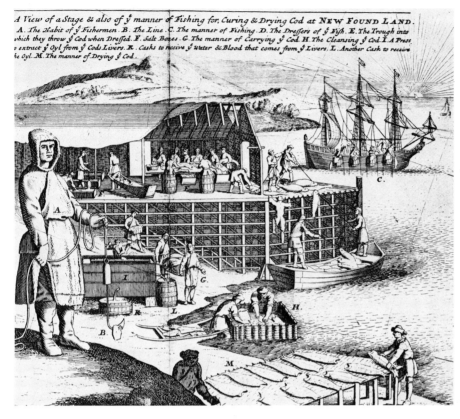

A View of a Stage & also of ŷ manner of Fishing for, Curing & Drying Cod at NEW FOUND LAND.
A. The Habit of ŷ Fishermen. B. The Line. C. The manner of Fishing. D. The Dressers of ŷ Fish. E. The Trough into which they throw ŷ Cod when Dressed. F. Salt Boxes. G. The manner of Carrying ŷ Cod. H. The Cleansing ŷ Cod. I. A Press to extract ŷ Oyl from ŷ Cods Livers. K. Casks to receive ŷ Water & Blood that comes from ŷ Livers. L. Another Cask to receive he Oyl. M. The manner of Drying ŷ Cod.

The Atlantic Provinces: Early days in the fishing industry. An illustration from a map of North America appearing in the atlas *World Described*, dated 1709–20. *(New York Public Library)*

mainland settlements were made early in the seventeenth century by the French, in order to provide shore bases for the Grand Banks fishing fleets; they were situated at Port Royal (the present Annapolis Royal) and on the shores of Chignecto Bay and Minas Basin. The region was then known as Acadia. The main period of British immigration began with the founding of Halifax in 1749, and in 1775 several thousands of French Acadians were deported for security reasons. There followed influxes of Germans, of British loyalists who chose to move north rather than remain in the new American republic after 1783, and of Scots and Irish who, entering in their thousands in the nineteenth century, accepted the hardships of the pioneer life in preference to the famine and evictions of the homelands. Today, about one-third of the population of the three provinces is of English origin; the French account for about one-fifth, largely concentrated in northwestern New Brunswick, and the Scots and Irish for perhaps one-eighth each. By comparison with the Canadian average, this is a population with a much larger rural component

than in the other provinces, although the *farm* element of this rural population is actually smaller than for the nation as a whole.

Yet, perhaps the most enlightening statistic about the Maritime Provinces is that after three centuries of occupance by this population, some 70 percent of their land surface is under forest cover. Farmland occupies 10 percent of total area. Only on Prince Edward Island is the proportion of land in farms significantly higher: there, it is about 60 percent. If we then consider *improved* farmland, the ratio of improved to total farmland is about 40 percent for New Brunswick and Nova Scotia, and 70 percent for Prince Edward Island.

Agriculture, in fact, stands well down the list of sources of income in the Maritimes. But it cannot be overlooked on that account: in the export trade of the region, at least, it makes up a 35 to 40 percent share. Yet only in a few coastal and valley lowlands (but these include much of Prince Edward Island) would it be realistic to speak of an agricultural region. Over the rest of the provinces the farmlands are scattered among forest and scrub and, with

211

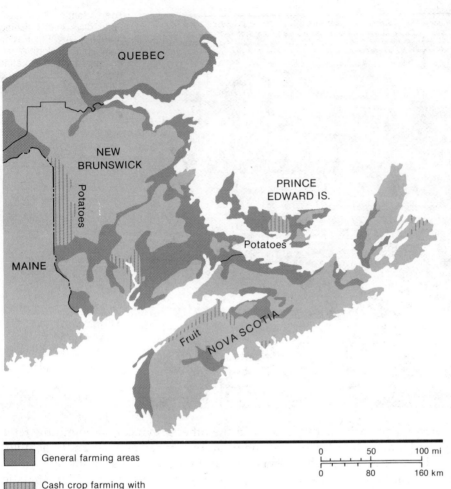

Fig. 12-1. The Maritime Provinces: Agricultural land use.

General farming areas

Cash crop farming with particular emphasis

| 0 | | 50 | | 100 mi |
| 0 | | 80 | | 160 km |

QUEBEC

NEW BRUNSWICK

Potatoes

PRINCE EDWARD IS.

Potatoes

MAINE

Fruit

NOVA SCOTIA

the farm frontier retreating, the scrub is gaining on the fields. Of the remaining farming, a good deal is part-time in the sense that the farmer relies on seasonal work in forestry to supplement the farm income. And gradually the small farmers are giving up and turning full-time to other employment or, in some cases, ceasing to work their holdings because they can now claim the old-age pension or some other type of welfare payment. This is happening even in such a relatively prosperous farming area as Prince Edward Island. The small holdings are either merged into larger units or are left to nature.[2]

[2]Illustrating these tendencies, the 1976 census of agriculture in Canada revealed that, for the nation as a whole, the number of farms classed as "non-census" (those with sales of less than $1200 per annum) fell from 66,260 to 38,460 in

The reasons for this situation are partly physical and partly economic: physical, in that soils and climate limit the range and output of farm products; economic, in that the overriding problem is that of markets. Throughout the whole area, hay and oats easily outrank all other field crops—in New Brunswick and Nova Scotia they occupy 65 to 70 percent of the cropland. They form the basis, as we might expect, for dairying and stock raising, for which natural conditions are quite favorable. But where are the markets for these products? With only three centers of any size within the region—Halifax, Saint John, and the steel

the period 1971–76. In the Maritimes, the next smallest farm class (those selling less that $5000 worth of produce p.a.) made up 44 percent of all farms in Nova Scotia and 41 percent in New Brunswick.

Potato fields near Hartland, New Brunswick. Hartland is in the St. John River valley, across the Canadian border from its U.S. counterpart, the Aroostook. *(National Film Board of Canada)*

town of Sydney—the Maritimes' market for fluid milk and meat is small, so that the dairy farmers must enter the competitive business of butter and cheese manufacture and sell outside the region. The only real alternative to dairying is one that New Scotland has copied from Old Scotland, and that is to concentrate on stock breeding—the sale of animals rather than their products. This has been developed, but it is interesting that it is based largely on imported processed feeds rather than improved pasture within the region.

Besides this basic hay-oats combination, the Maritimes have two cash crops: potatoes and fruit. Potatoes are grown on Prince Edward Island and in the upper Saint John Valley, across the border from the Aroostook potato lands of Maine (p. 199). Fruit growing is widespread, but the chief producing area is the Annapolis Valley of Nova Scotia, with its apple orchards. These two crops, once again, are well suited to physical conditions in the Maritimes—and wholly unsuited to the conditions under which they have to be marketed. Both must be sold outside the region, yet both are bulky and perishable. Prince Edward Island potatoes, for ex-

213

ample, must begin their journey to market on the mainland by travelling in heated vans on a train ferry. Maritimes' apples compete directly, inside Canada, with Québec apples grown nearer to the centers of population; their other main market is in Great Britain. Eggs and poultry have to some extent replaced fruit in the income structure, and during the past decade Prince Edward Island has begun to do well with tobacco.

Just as the cattle farmers have tried to overcome their disadvantages of position by specializing in a quality product—pedigree stock—so, too, have the potato and fruit farmers. The potato growers (and here there is an interesting parallel with the situation in Northern Ireland, whose positional problem is rather the same) specialize in seed potatoes, supplying half the Canadian market and exporting a considerable amount. But quality increases costs, of course, and the market for potatoes in North America is a contracting one: consumption per person is steadily falling.[3] The apple growers have tried various forms of processing and canning as a solution to their own problem, but this can never be more than a partial answer: most of the demand for apples is for the fresh fruit.

Since agriculture is limited by the conditions we have been considering, and there are few large towns, the Maritimes depend heavily on non-agricultural and non-industrial employment—mining, fishing, and forestry. Of the three, mining or quarrying is limited to a few locations but had an output value in 1973 of over $220 million. The most valuable deposits in the Provinces at present are a group of ores around Bathurst in New Brunswick which have been brought into production in the past twenty years and yield zinc, lead, silver, and copper. Gypsum and salt are mined in Nova Scotia, and so is coal. But coal production has fallen off sharply in recent years and in 1974 amounted to only 1.8 million tons, most of it

coming from mines around Sydney on Cape Breton Island. It is coking coal and has formed the basis of a steel industry at Sydney, where the coal was formerly combined with iron ore brought across 400 mi (640 km) of sea from Newfoundland. The latter operation has now been closed, although there is the readily available alternative of Labrador ore, which can be brought in at the same Cape Breton terminals. Coal output has fallen far from its 1940 peak of nearly 8 million tons, and employment has fallen with it. The steelworks were saved from closure in 1968 only by being taken over by the provincial government, which acted to avert a further fall in the level of economic activity and employment. More recently, however, demand for coal for generating electricity has led to the sinking of new mines, and this brings some hope of a revival to the coal fields.

Fishing is important everywhere on the coast. There are in effect two fishing industries, inshore and ocean going. Traditionally the fishermen of the Maritimes have fished the inshore waters. They operate in small boats from small ports: lack of capital has prevented them from making the larger investments required for deep-water fisheries. In any case, fishing is often combined with work onshore, on a farm, or in the forest.[4]

A modern fleet using large boats and fishing the offshore banks is only slowly coming into being, in part because (1) pollution is a growing problem inshore and (2) Canadian and New England fishermen are competing on their own fishing grounds with foreign crews equipped on a massive scale and using factory ships. In 1973 the fisheries yielded $155 million, with lobsters the most valuable item and cod and herring bringing in the greatest weight. Processing employs several thousand workers and raises the value of fish *products* to over $400 million. It takes the forms of canning, freezing (especially on the eastern coast of Nova Scotia and the Burin Penninsula of

---

[3]Except for the various forms of prepared—usually frozen—potatoes which have appeared on the market in recent years, and which are proving popular with the housewife. Producing these, of course, requires processing plants in the growing areas. The Pacific Northwest has done well with them (see p. 414). Perhaps the Maritimes could, also, given the necessary capital.

[4]It often has to be, because of the low value per fisherman employed of the catch, at least in the inshore fisheries. For details see W.A. Black and J.W. Maxwell, "Resource Utilization: Change and Adaptation," in A.G. Macpherson, ed., *The Atlantic Provinces*, University of Toronto Press, Toronto, 1972, pp. 77–84.

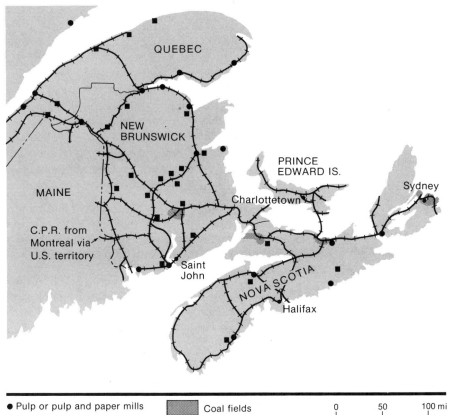

Fig. 12-2. The Maritime Provinces: Railroads, coal fields, pulp and paper mills.

- ● Pulp or pulp and paper mills
- ■ Saw mills, capacity in excess of 6 million board ft.
- ▨ Coal fields
- +++++ Basic railway network

| 0 | 50 | 100 mi |
| 0 | 50 | 100 | 150 km |

Newfoundland), and drying salted fish (concentrated in southern Nova Scotia and eastern Newfoundland). That a part of the catch still has to be disposed of by salting and drying—the method of the original French fishermen three centuries ago— emphasizes once again the marketing problem of the Maritimes. Today, salted and dried fish serves only a limited, low-income market in distant South America and the Caribbean. The obvious market for either the fresh or frozen products is the urbanized northeastern region of the United States—but it has its own fisheries and its own problems of scale and capitalization.

Forestry plays a vital part in the regional economy: there are 25 million acres (10.15 million ha) of productive forest in the three provinces, about one-third of which consists of hardwoods and the remainder of softwoods. Seasonal work in logging gives winter employment to many farmers, and the rivers provide power and transport. Within the industry there has been a gradual shift from the production of sawtimber to that of pulpwood. In part this represents the decline in the quality of the forest cover which followed a period of heavy cutting, but much more directly, it reflects the change in the demand structure for forest products. In any case, the pulp and paper industry, representing as it does a processing of the raw material beyond the simple felling and slicing of timber, is an industry that carries a much higher index of value added by manufacture, and so is of greater benefit to the region as a whole. The manufacture of pulp and paper, dependent as it is on huge quantities of both water and power, is concentrated at a few large plants close to the principal rivers and at tidewater—at Dalhousie, Saint John, and Chatham in New Brunswick, or at Port Hawkesbury on the Strait of Canso. The sawmills, on the other hand, vary greatly in size and are to be found wherever logging is carried on: some of the largest are deep in the interior of New Brunswick.

Most of the industries of the Maritimes are based on the activities already mentioned—food and fish processing, paper and lumber. What the provinces lack is a pyramid of other industries built on the base of these processing activities; the kind of pyramid that evolves in a thoroughly industrialized region and, in particular (as we saw in Chapter 9), is generated by the presence of a city of metropolitan size and function. Halifax, the largest city of the Maritimes, hardly qualifies. Its population of a little over 250,000 makes it small by North American standards, while its one traditional supra-regional function, that of serving as port of entry during the winter months when the St. Lawrence is closed to shipping, has been progressively eroded by the lengthening of the navigation period on the St. Lawrence and by the manifest advantages of using the river for as long as possible each year in order to gain access to the Seaway and the interior. In any case, Halifax's seasonal traffic was not such as to attract footloose industries. For all these reasons the industrial pyramid is truncated not far above its base. The region's problem is to try to build it upward to some kind of apex.

The Prospect Before the Maritime Provinces

The North American Century, the hundred years of amazing development which have fashioned the present geography of the continent, has been a discouraging era for the Maritimes. The indices of population increase and industrial expansion lagged far behind those of the rest of Canada. The region gave an impression of becoming economically stunted after its early start. The opinion was sometimes voiced that federation was a mistake; that the Maritimes exported more, in brains and energy, to the rest of Canada than they received in federal help; that perhaps a political connection with the United States would have served them better.

Since the war, the Maritime Provinces have clearly shown that they do not intend to resign themselves without a struggle to second-class status within the nation. Led by such regional bodies as the Atlantic Provinces Economic Council (A.P.E.C.), they have taken stock of their resources and laid plans for their use.

What can be done to improve the region's economic position? The common thread that seems to run through all discussion of the Maritimes' livelihood is that of the weakness of small-scale operations struggling to compete within a national and continental economy geared to large-scale production:

Fragmentation of the environmental resources has been a critical factor in the use of natural resources in the Atlantic Provinces from the time of the first settlement to the present day. In farming, mining, forestry, and in the fisheries, small operations developed that were highly individualistic. . . . This legacy from the past has hindered the formation of larger economic units compatible with the modern competitive demand for primary resources.[5]

As we survey the various sources of income available, it seems clear that the key to the position in each case is the supply or availability of capital: that given investment, farming, fishing, or forestry can be made to yield better returns. The raising of pedigree stock can have this effect: the problem is to find the capital for improvement of pasture and purchase of the first stock. The fishing industry can prosper: the problem is to modernize the fleet, finance larger boats for offshore work, and extend the facilities for freezing and canning. Forestry confronts an ever-growing market for newsprint and pulp in the United States: the problem is to create the huge mills which form the basic units of the industry. In every sphere of the economy the critical factor is the size of investment necessary.

It may well be that this capital investment would have been easier to obtain if the Maritimes had become a part of the United States, with its immensely greater financial resources.[6] On the other hand, the idea of the

[5]W.A. Black and J.W. Maxwell, "Resource Utilization," p. 73.

[6]This possibility is raised by Andrew Clark in his fine essay "The Roots of Canada's Geography," in J. Warkentin, ed., *Canada: A Geographical Interpretation*, Metheun, Toronto, 1967, pp. 13-53.

Maritimes forming a kind of Ultima Thule, lying out beyond even northern Maine, may equally well chill the blood of Canadians in those parts. For better or worse, the provinces must depend principally on their own efforts.

It is therefore the first task of the A.P.E.C. and the provinces to obtain this capital. Various federal schemes already provide a groundwork—payments to farmers for land improvement, and loans toward the building of fishing vessels. Beyond these, however, the region must find its own sources, by attracting to itself more transit trade and more industries; using the capital these generate to develop by its own research fresh uses for its products, and exerting itself to sell them in new markets. After so long a period of frustration, there is plenty of welcome evidence that the worst is over and that the regional effort of the Maritime Provinces is bearing fruit.

Newfoundland

As a political unit, the province of Newfoundland consists not only of the island of that name, with an area of some 43,000 sq mi (111,000 sq km), but also of 110,000 sq mi (285,000 sq km) of Labrador, the great eastward projection of the Canadian mainland.

The island, with which we are here concerned, was Great Britain's earliest colony. It was for long, however, no more than a base for fishing fleets. Underlain in large part by old igneous and metamorphic rocks, its surface—part forested, part swamp and barrens—has never offered encouragement to the farmer, except in a few sheltered valley locations.[7] Summers are cool and precipitation is high, so that the physical handicaps of the Maritimes are here reproduced in severer form. Ice closes all but the southern coasts in winter and fog replaces it, as a sailor's hazard, in summer.

On an island where so much of the life is bound to the sea, it is not surprising that the population (557,000 in 1976) is mostly found in coastal settlements. Since the coasts are closed in winter by ice, and overland communications are poor away from the road and from the rail axis that runs from east to west, the population lives in isolation for much of the year.

Today, as throughout the island's history, fishing remains the principal occupation of its people. Because of its remoteness from both the American and the European consumer, the staple product of Newfoundland has long been dried cod. With the development of fish processing, however, whether by canning or freezing, it has been possible to place on the market other types of catch. In 1973 Newfoundland landed $47 million worth of fish through the efforts of about 14,000 fishermen.

The old style of fishing, however, which was carried on in small boats based in tiny, scattered settlements is hardly suited to twentieth-century conditions. Recognizing this fact, the government of the province set in motion a process of "centralization" (or, as it has now been renamed, "household resettlement"). The inhabitants of coastal settlements were encouraged to ask to be removed to larger communities, where they could enjoy better services and where, incidentally, it would cost the province less to provide those services while forming parts of larger fishery units. The government has subsidized the moves which, between 1945 and 1971, closed down some 300 communities. Since 1971, the program has continued and has affected on the average about 24 small settlements each year, or perhaps 5000 people.

Since the days of the early fishing settlements, only two other forms of employment for the population have arisen as serious rivals to the original occupation. One of these is mining, for the island possesses a variety of minerals, such as iron ore and copper. Recent years, however, have seen the closure of all but a few of these mines. The other main occupation of the island is forestry. The forest cover on the island's bleak surface is less extensive than that of the Maritimes, but it nevertheless constitutes a major resource and is largely in the hands of two big pulp and paper companies, which ensures efficient exploita-

---

[7]Among the 43,000 sq mi (110,000 sq km) of the island, only 38 of them (98 sq km) are classified as improved agricultural land. In 1976 there were 8694 acres (3520 ha) of cropland, mostly under hay and potatoes.

Newfoundland: A fishing settlement on Placentia Bay. This is the type and size of settlement which is being closed under the Centralization Program (see p. 217). *(National Film Board of Canada)*

tion. The paper industry is largely responsible for the interior settlements of Newfoundland; Grand Falls and Corner Brook, for example, are company towns which form two of the only centers of any size outside the capital, port, and processing center of St. John's.

In the course of a varied political past, Newfoundland has possessed at different periods the status of both colony and dominion within the British Commonwealth. In 1948, however, the islanders voted by a slender majority for confederation with Canada. The majority vote was almost certainly swelled by appreciation of the services made available by the Ottawa government to the provinces, in federal grants for social security and welfare schemes. This recognition that Newfoundland would receive from the federal government more than it could give probably touches the heart of the island's problem—its perennial poverty.

To past generations of islanders, Newfoundland offered a rough, lonely life between the sea and their small farm plots; even so, that life was adequate in the sense that it was better than the one they had left in England or Ireland. But today's standard of comparison is not the Old World environment their ancestors left, but that of the New World they might have reached by going on a little further. The limitations of the environment make it as difficult for Newfoundland to support its population at a "modern" American standard of living as it would be for the Outer Hebrides or Connemara to become as prosperous as the English Midlands.

If the concentration of resources within an area is—as in all the cases mentioned—too thin to support a high standard of living, the only alternative solution to emigration lies in introducing to the area sources of wealth from outside that are independent of the natural poverty within. One such source, either in Europe or in Canada, is government payments and this is, of course, precisely the effect of confederation on Newfoundland—the wealthier provinces of the Dominion contribute to the support of the less prosperous.

For a time during and after the Second World War, it seemed as if Newfoundland had discovered another such source—in its strategic location. Placed as it is on the North Atlantic transit routes, it had profited enormously from the presence of military bases and had built after the war a great civil airport at Gander. Here again was income independent of resources. But the prosperity has proved ephemeral. With the coming of the jet plane, Gander has become little more than an emergency stop, an unnecessary stepping stone in waters that are now narrow enough to be crossed at a single bound. Perhaps for a land which had yielded over the centuries so grudging a livelihood as Newfoundland it was, after all, too good to last.

Better prospects for the future do, however, exist. The decision by the British Privy Council in 1926 to incorporate in the colony of Newfoundland (as it then was) the eastern half of the Labrador peninsula presented the colony with a treasure chest whose contents were, at that date, largely unknown. It has now become clear that the treasure is diverse and valuable, particularly with regard to mineral deposits, while the Churchill Falls hydroelectric development, with its 5,225,000 kw capacity, has by its completion become one of the largest power installations in the World. While it is unlikely to produce any extensive growth of secondary industry within Labrador itself, the Churchill Falls electric power will be fed into the Québec grid (see Fig. 13-2), and the power sales should benefit the whole province of Newfoundland.

The Lower St. Lawrence Valley

Introduction

The region of North America whose focus is the Lower St. Lawrence Valley is small but very distinct. On the one hand, it possesses a physical separateness which leaves it with few connecting links with the remainder of the continent. On the other hand, and more significantly, it has the cultural distinctiveness proper to an area in which some 80 percent of the population speak by preference a language different from that of the other 230 million inhabitants of Anglo-America. This is French Canada.

A map of population distribution shows the extent to which this region is isolated by natural barriers from its surroundings. On the north shore of the St. Lawrence, population density thins rapidly up the slope to the plateau surface of the Laurentian Shield, and there are few communities more than 50 mi (80 km) from the shore; beyond lies the immense emptiness of northern Canada. On the west the Shield encloses the St. Lawrence and Ottawa valleys, swinging south to cross the former at the Thousand Islands Bridge. Here

there is, on the population map, only a slender "connecting link" of settlement to join Lower Canada to Upper Canada; and the traveller between Montréal and Toronto is conscious that he has crossed an economic and cultural no-man's-land, even though the Shield presents no relief obstacle. On the south, settlement spreads across the broad plains of the St. Lawrence and Richelieu valleys until it ends rather abruptly along the edge of the Adirondacks and the mountains of northern New England. There the map reveals the one major link with settlement in other regions, where the Champlain Lowland cuts across the international boundary, and Vermont adjoins southern Québec. Finally, on the east, settlement becomes progressively sparser as the river widens into the Gulf of St. Lawrence, until nothing but a string of fishing and logging villages lines the narrow corridor that joins Laurentian Canada to the Maritime Provinces.

Yet for all its separateness, this region plays a vital part in Canadian life. It contains over 25 percent of the nation's population, including Montréal, its largest city, port, and manufacturing center. Its railway links across the adjacent empty areas are good enough to enable it to handle a major share of Canada's foreign trade. And in the 1970s, in the era of the St. Lawrence Seaway, it has acquired a "back door," an international routeway through it that does something to reduce its isolation.

It is 400 mi (640 km) from the Thousand Islands Bridge to the end of continuous settlement on the north shore of the St. Lawrence beyond Québec; some 650 mi (1040 km) from Ottawa to Gaspé. At their broadest the lowlands stretch for 120 mi (192 km) from northwest to southeast. Only in the junction area between the Richelieu-Champlain Lowlands and the St. Lawrence Valley are there wide stretches of fertile soils. There, however, much of the land is of excellent quality, as a result of the deposition of marine sediments in postglacial times, when the lowlands were submerged beneath a gulf known as the Champlain Sea. It is this junction area which forms the economic heartland of Québec, dominated by the spreading agglomeration of Montréal; a fertile plain out of which rise abruptly a series of volcanic "islands," their lower slopes planted with apple orchards but now increasingly being used as the sites for new homes.

Climatic conditions in the valley are also distinctive: winters are severe, snowfalls are heavy, and weather changes are frequent. These conditions reflect, as we noted in Chapter 1, the convergence of storm tracks on the Great Lakes-St. Lawrence line. The passage of the depressions is responsible for the variability of conditions and for the considerable winter precipitation, which brings snowfall of 100 in. (2.5 m) per annum or more to many valley stations, even at sea level.

Over most of the valley, precipitation is more than 35 in., evenly distributed throughout the year. The January mean temperature is 14°F (−10°C) at Montréal and 10°F (−12°C) in Québec City, and it falls rapidly, on the slopes above the river, to 0°F (−18°C) in the Laurentide Mountains. The St. Lawrence River and the Seaway have both normally been closed to shipping between December and mid-April, but in the past few years the river itself has been kept open for a limited amount of winter

traffic as far upstream as Montréal. The frost-free period available to farmers in the valley is usually limited to 120 or 130 days. July mean temperatures fall from 70°F (21°C) at Montréal to 58° or 60°F (14°-15°C) downriver opposite Anticosti Island. In spite of its long coastline the Gaspé Peninsula has the wide annual temperature range (50° to 55°F or 28° to 30°C) typical of eastern continental margins in these latitudes—Bangor, Maine, for example, has a range of 48°F (27°C) and Vladivostok in the U.S.S.R. has one of 63°F (35°C).

Severe climate and heavy snowfall affect life in Québec in a number of ways. One is to restrict winter employment opportunities, especially in outdoor occupations, thus adding a problem of seasonal unemployment to the difficulties of a region which already has a year-long unemployment level well above the Canadian average (in 1973–74 a rate of 7.8–8.0 percent against 5.4–5.6 for Canada as a whole). Another more pleasant impact of the climate is upon urban services, for in the past decade Montréal has created for its shoppers a whole city underground, where one can wander among stores and services without ever being aware of the weather outside. With the reconstruction of transport terminals and the building of the Metro lines, there is little that the city cannot now provide in this world underground.

Settlement and Landscape

For geographers the St. Lawrence Valley has long provided a useful illustration of the maxim that to interpret the landscape of a region, it is necessary to be familiar with its settlement history. The valley was settled by the French in the seventeenth and eighteenth centuries, and, although by the end of French rule in 1763 there were only some 65,000 of them (whereas the British colonies further south in the continent had more than a million inhabitants), they nevertheless created by their presence a landscape whose distinctiveness remains to the present day. Not only the place names of the Lower St. Lawrence, but also the rural settlement pattern, reflect the legal and

Québec: The legacy of France. Long lots on the north shore of the St. Lawrence near Québec City. *(National Air Photo Library of Canada)*

social arrangements of the French colony which later became Lower Canada and, on federation in 1867, the province of Québec.

French settlement in Canada may be dated from 1608, when Québec City was founded by the man whose leadership dominated the whole enterprise—Samuel Champlain. Although Champlain planned to establish the colony on a firm agricultural basis, it was from the first the fur trade which attracted the French, and the fur trade to which their main efforts were devoted. The permanent settlements on the shore of the St. Lawrence languished, while the French pioneers spread over the interior the peculiarly impermanent form of occupancy and control that fur trading implied. Officials, missionaries, and freelance fur traders—the coureurs de bois—pushed swiftly inland, becoming embroiled in intertribal Indian wars; adopting Indian modes of life and travel; constantly seeking new fur supplies as they pushed westward across the northern Great Lakes to the Upper Mississippi. In 1670 French sovereignty was proclaimed at Sault Ste. Marie. In 1682 La Salle followed the Mississippi to the sea and claimed a vast Louisiana for the King of France.

In the meantime the neglected settlements on the St. Lawrence had achieved by 1660 a population of about 3000. They had spread along the river and were later to spread along its tributary, the Richelieu, in a single line of waterfront settlement. This pattern developed partly because movement by river was simpler than ashore; partly because of the importance of fisheries in the early colonial economy; and partly because the river verges offered unforested patches, where the initial labor of forest clearance might be avoided. Holdings were laid out in long, narrow strips, at right angles to the river frontage, with the homestead close to the water's edge, so that, as one writer has expressed it, "at the end of the French régime, a traveller could have seen almost every house in Canada as he made the canoe trip along the St. Lawrence and Richelieu."

On the inland side the limit of the holdings was usually only a distant line toward which clearance of the forest slowly progressed. But as the population of French Canada increased, not only were the holdings subdivided into still narrower frontages, but a second line (or *rang*) of settlement was laid out parallel to that along the waterfront. Here the process of parcelling out and clearing the narrow strips was repeated, the rural road replacing the river as the base line. Thus there developed a pattern in marked contrast to that of the areas further to the west and south, where survey based on mile-square sections produced the familiar "gridiron" settlement pattern of the American interior. The French pattern has survived in Québec to the present day; indeed, in a modified form it has been used in the most recent expansions of settlement in the province—the Abitibi and Temiscaming areas.

At no time during the period of French rule did agriculture develop real strength: it was carried on merely as a support for the fur trade and the local population which served that trade. Periodically it failed even to fulfil this modest task, and famine resulted. This agricultural weakness was almost certainly one of the causes of the French loss of Canada, for France was competing with a rival very differently placed: "of . . . fundamental importance in the final French withdrawal from St. Lawrence and Cape Breton was the agricultural backwardness of New France as compared with New England. The New England colonies early developed agricultural resources more than sufficient to provision the British staple trades. France could scarcely withstand an opponent upon whom she continuously relied for foodstuffs."[1]

At the end of French rule in Canada in 1763, the settled areas still extended only a short distance back from the shores of the St. Lawrence and Richelieu. The period of British rule that followed, and especially the early nineteenth century, saw an expansion of the settled areas, first into the broad lowland south of the St. Lawrence and east of the Richelieu, which is known as the Eastern Townships. Here the original settlement was predominantly British, and the place names sturdily Anglo-Saxon. But since the population of the older French areas increased rapidly in the nineteenth century (by 1830 it had risen to about 400,000) it overflowed into the Eastern Townships. Today the French-speaking population of the Townships is six times as numerous as the English speaking, and such place names as St-Germain de Grantham and Ste-Anne de Stukely reflect the changing cultural affiliation of the area.

The French Canadians continued to increase in numbers and, owing in part to the agricultural weakness of their "home base"—the St. Lawrence lowland—were obliged to seek other outlets for their excess population.

These they found to the north, south, and the east. Northward they spread up onto the Laurentian Plateau, carrying their subsistence agriculture with them and pushing forward the farm frontier. In most of these areas north

[1]V.C. Fowke, *Canadian Agricultural Policy,* University of Toronto Press, Toronto, 1946, p. 6.

of the St. Lawrence the agricultural acreage reached a maximum about 1920. The area of all land in farms in the province reached a peak in 1941 of 18.1 million acres (7.33 million ha). By 1966 it was down to 14 million (5.67 million ha), and by 1976 it had fallen to 9.03 million acres, (3.65 million ha). These figures are a commentary on the thrust into the north of the Québec pioneers and their subsequent withdrawal as they abandoned the thankless and unrewarding task of farming on the fringe and sought work in cities and industries (from which, as it happens, quite a number of them had originally come.)[2]

Eastward, French Canadians increased in numbers all along the south shore of the St. Lawrence and into New Brunswick, although they have never recolonized in any strength the original Acadian settlements in Nova Scotia. Southward, expansion of French Canada was only possible by crossing the border into the United States. But this proved to be no obstacle to movement as pressure mounted in the St. Lawrence Valley. The industrialization of New England was in full swing, and there were plenty of jobs available in its factories, while back in the Valley crop failures were recurrent. Between 1840 and 1900 it is estimated that French Canada lost about 600,000 people to the United States, the great majority of them to New England. In 1900 in fact, there were 573,000 French Canadians within the region, with the largest concentrations in Providence, Worcester, Fall River, New Bedford, and the cities of the Merrimack Valley. The chief draw was the textile industry, in which developing technology had reduced the level of skill required of operatives, and so reduced its attractiveness for the local American workers, who sought better jobs elsewhere. By 1900 in most

textile towns, a third of the operatives were French Canadians.[3]

The special relationship between Québec and New England has been a two-way thing which has continued through many vicissitudes. While Québecers were moving south to the mills, the Eastern Townships in particular were attracting New England vacationers and, more recently, there have been many buyers of land and summer homes. The market has risen with the construction of freeways that have brought the cities of the two regions effectively closer, and has fluctuated with the availability of land in the upper New England states, or with restrictions on its use, like rural zoning, on both sides of the border.

The agriculture of modern Québec makes this region part of the Hay and Dairy Belt, with 60 percent of the crop acreage under hay and a further 20 percent under oats. The cities of the St. Lawrence Valley provide markets for fluid milk, and butter and cheese are manufactured in large quantities; Québec accounts for more than a third of Canada's butter and cheese output. In addition to this basic farm activity, however, the valley's agriculture includes the production of a number of special crops. The presence of Montréal and its suburbs has encouraged the rise of market gardening in their vicinity. Small fruit crops are numerous in the valley, and Québec produces more than a quarter of Canada's apples, as well as strawberries and a large part of the country's output of maple syrup and maple products.

As is the case everywhere along the northern fringe of the Hay and Dairy Belt—in northern New England, for example, or in northern Michigan and Wisconsin—there is a marked falling-off in the intensity of land use and activity on the remoter fringes of Québec's farmlands. Even in the long-settled Eastern Townships only about a half of the farmland is improved. Away from the valley markets and the creameries, agriculture slips toward a sub-

[2] "It has been estimated that, of every ten farms opened by the Department of Colonization in Abitibi, nine are no longer operational. . . . Certain planners anticipate the eventual disappearance of agriculture from virtually the entire Abitibi region. . . . " P.B. Clibbon, "Evolution and Present Patterns of the Ecumene of Southern Québec" in F. Grenier, ed., *Etudes sur la géographie du Canada: Québec*, University of Toronto Press, Toronto, 1972, p. 24. See Figure 13-1.

[3] The foregoing figures are taken from R.D. Vicero, *Immigration of French Canadians to New England, 1840–1900*, University of Wisconsin, Madison, Ph.D. thesis, 1968.

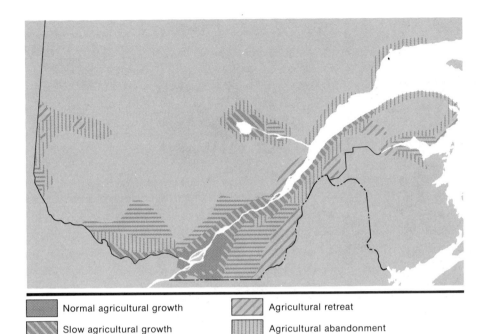

Fig. 13-1. Québec Province: The state of agriculture in 1969. There is a very obvious withdrawal from the margins of agriculture along the northern edge of cultivation and also along the lower St. Lawrence Valley.

▨ Normal agricultural growth		▨ Agricultural retreat	
▨ Slow agricultural growth		▨ Agricultural abandonment	
▨ Agricultural stagnation			

sistence level, and the farm income is supplemented to an increasing extent by fishing, or by work in the forests or in industry.

Power and Industry

The St. Lawrence Valley possesses no coal and no petroleum. It does, however, have two resources that are important on a world scale: it is the world's leading producer of asbestos, and it possesses almost a half of Canada's installed hydroelectric generating capacity. The asbestos is mined in the Eastern Townships in the neighborhood of Thetford Mines and Asbestos, and 1973 production was about 1.5 million tons, the bulk which was exported to the United States. The hydroelectric power is produced mainly on the southern edge of the Laurentian Shield. There, conditions for power development approach the ideal on the rivers that descend through chains of lakes from the elevated southeastern corner of the Shield to the St. Lawrence. Of these rivers the early power producers were the Saguenay, flowing

out of Lake St. John past the great Shipshaw power stations; the St. Maurice, on which the development around Shawinigan accounts for half a million horsepower of generating capacity and other works above and below the falls for a further 1.5 million; the Ottawa with its tributary the Gatineau, and the St. Lawrence itself. These rivers, affording suitable sites within easy reach of the St. Lawrence Valley power users, have been exploited first, and a large part of their potential has been realized. Since, however, demand has continued to rise, more remote reserves have been tapped, such as those of the Bersimis and Manicouagan rivers, 200 mi (320 km) below Québec on the empty north shore of the St. Lawrence. But the remoter potential of the Shield is more than adequate for the foreseeable future—the province is at present using less than half its potential at ordinary six-month flow, [4] and in any case the construction of the St. Lawrence Seaway presented the valley with a huge hydroelectricity bonus produced at the very doorstep

[4]I.e., the volume of water which can be expected to be available for generating purposes for at least six months in the year.

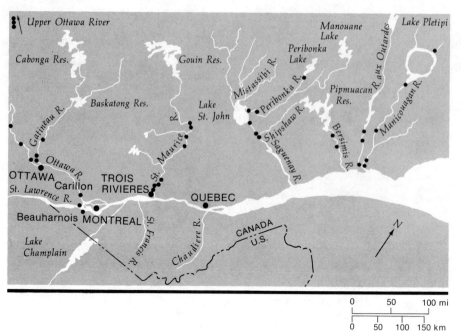

Fig. 13-2. Québec Province: Hydroelectric power development, December 1972. The stations shown are those with an installed capacity of 50,000 kw or more.

of Montréal, a bonus which Québec shared with Ontario and New York State.

Alongside these two major resources of the Valley, we should now place a third: the iron ores of the Québec-Labrador belt. They are not located in the Valley, but they acquire value only when they are brought down to tidewater, at Sept Iles or Port Cartier. In this sense they belong to the region, and the more recent of the mining developments are unquestionably in Québec.[5] The opening of Québec's Wabush Mines in 1965 was as significant, in output terms, as the original development around Schefferville. In 1973 the belt yielded nearly 50 million tons of ores.

As a location for industry, the St. Lawrence Valley thus enjoys the advantage conferred by its power supplies, to add to the advantage of its position as the funnel through which goods leave and enter Canada's eastern side. Although this latter advantage is limited in

winter by the closure of the Seaway, the Valley exerts sufficient attraction upon industry to account for almost one-third of Canada's industrial output by value.

Its industries fall into two main categories. One of these is made up of the wide variety of manufactures found in the Montréal area; that is, the consumer goods industries commonly found in the metropolis of a nation. Among these (and the parallel with New York is evident), the clothing and textile industries form the largest group: the clothing industry employs almost 50,000 workers in the metropolitan area, and textiles over 10,000. Another 12 percent of the total is accounted for by the food products industry. But Montréal also possesses a wide variety of "national" capital goods manufactures. Among these the most recent arrival is the automobile industry, concentrated (within Canada) in Ontario until recently. Its arrival has compensated for the decline of the aircraft industry which, founded during the Second World War, has fallen upon hard times. Then Montréal has become Canada's leading centre of oil refining, with a capacity in its refineries of 30 million tons a year. The crude oil is brought in both by water and by pipeline from Portland in Maine, and

[5] The writer uses what may appear a curious phrase because the original strikes were made in the area which has been in dispute since 1927 between Québec and Newfoundland. In 1927 the Privy Council in London fixed the border between Québec and what was then the separate colony of Newfoundland, but this boundary was never recognized by the province of Québec.

the products feed a chemicals industry now employing over 13,000 workers. In all, Montréal's industries employ over 270,000 workers, a sixth of Canada's industrial labor force.

The other category of industries in the valley comprises those attracted by the availability of electric power. Of these, two are outstanding: the manufacture of woodpulp and paper and the smelting of metals, especially aluminum. Some 80 percent of Québec's power consumption is accounted for by these two industries.

The Laurentian Shield is not merely a rich source of hydroelectricity; it is also a great forest area, and these two resources combine in perfect partnership to produce the pulp and paper industry. While this industry represents only a part of the total forest products output of Québec, the whole of which gives full or part-time employment to many thousands of workers, nevertheless it consumes about two-thirds of the annual cut from the forests and ranks as the province's largest single industry. The industry is located in close proximity to the power sources, along the Saguenay, the St. Maurice, and the Ottawa rivers, and large mills are situated in Montréal, Trois Rivières, and Québec City. The province of Québec accounts for nearly 40 percent of Canada's output of pulp and paper. These form the nation's principal exports, the item of greatest value being the sale of newsprint to the United States. Since the demand for this is likely to increase rather than to decline, it seems probable that Québec will experience a gradual northward shift of the lumbering frontier away from the St. Lawrence and into the vast and at present largely inaccessible areas of timber reserves that cover the Shield.

Aluminum smelting, another power-hungry industry, is carried on at three main locations, Arvida on the Saguenay, Shawinigan on the St. Maurice, and at the mouth of the Bersimis. The fact that Canada itself produces no bauxite, so that all the raw materials for the smelters must be imported, and the additional fact that a large part of the smelter output is exported again, is evidence of the attractive force of the power factor to this industry. The

same attraction will doubtless continue to draw new industries, such as chemical manufactures, to this area at the edge of the Shield, as fresh power supplies become available.

With the launching of the St. Lawrence Seaway project, already referred to in Chapter 8, it was at once apparent that changes would take place, not only in the geography of the upper St. Lawrence, once it became accessible from the sea, but equally in that of the lower valley, where these changes were viewed with some apprehension. The last time that the effective head of St. Lawrence navigation was moved upstream was in 1870, when the channel was deepened to Montréal. As a result Québec City, the older settlement and political capital, found itself at a disadvantage; since it possesses little productive hinterland in its own right and lies more remote than Montréal from the source areas of St. Lawrence trade, its industrial and commercial functions have tended to languish, and, although its communications and its harbor are good and are used in winter, it is as a cultural and political center that the city has developed.

The question naturally arises whether the transfer of the head of navigation to Chicago and Duluth has diminished the importance of the Montréal area in the same way. Up till now the city has carried on a considerable transshipment business, with all the opportunities for local manufacture that transshipment brings. To a limited extent, it remains in this business, since the St. Lawrence channel has a depth of 35 ft. (10.6 m), while the Seaway is constructed as a 27-ft. (8.21m) channel. But it seems clear that, as use of the Seaway increases, Montréal must expect to lose some of this function. However, any loss sustained in transshipment has been more than balanced by the increase in total traffic volume. What is also significant is that an increasing proportion of the traffic to and from the Great Lakes is being handled by Canadian vessels, which presumably represents a factor in Montréal's favor. To exchange the role of terminus for that of gateway need not be regarded as a hardship. In any case, the city's economic base is very broad and its advantages of position are

Montréal: The central business district and part of the harbor. *(National Film Board of Canada)*

great. It is the largest center of land communications in Canada, and one of the two financial centres of the nation. It is a natural focus of routes—which Québec City never was—running northwestward to Ottawa, the federal capital, and southward to the Hudson and New York as well as east and west along the St. Lawrence.

Rather than fear for Montréal's prosperity it might be considered more legitimate to complain that it has grown too big and powerful in relation to the remainder of French Canada. It has become a commonplace to contrast the metropolis with the "desert" which makes up the rest of Québec. Montréal earns two-thirds of all personal income within the province, and it tends to drain its hinterland of productive activities and skilled manpower. Yet it can with equal justice be argued that without Montréal, French Canada would be little more than a cultural curiosity—a backward, rural area in which were preserved the relics of a culture and a community that belonged to a past era. That French Canada is a force to be reckoned with can be largely attributed to the fact that it has at its core a city of world standing, offering a complete range of employment opportunities and services and equipped, educationally and financially, to hold its own in the competitive economic conditions of North America today.

Montréal has for a long time been resisting challenges from its rival city in Ontario, Toronto. It has had to concede to Toronto the larger share of the nation's industry and banking but it could still claim, in 1971, a bigger population. Thanks to the establishment of census metropolitan areas (see p. 51), however, it has now lost the right to this claim, too. It is admittedly only a piece of statistical sleight of hand, but the 1976 census gave metropolitan Toronto a lead over Montréal of 2,803,101 inhabitants to 2,802,485.

Beyond this innocent statistical rivalry, however, much more is at stake. The province of Québec has committed itself to a separatist course: to the eventual severance of links with the federation and, in the shorter term, to such measures as the compulsory use of the French language in businesses and factories, and the reduction of English-language education. The political and ideological issues only Canadians can decide. But the two questions which can be raised here are: (1) What chance has independent Québec of economic survival? and (2) What is the short-term economic or locational effect of the sort of measures just described?

The economy of the present province of Québec is far from buoyant. The expansion of employment in the 1970s has been painfully slow—slower even than in the Maritimes. The agricultural base, as we have seen, is shrinking, although forest and power resources are huge. Perhaps, Québec could live on exports of power and pulp, but Montréal's industries would lose their national markets. Tourism and the traffic on the international Seaway would bolster the economy, but the traffic would be passing through rather than originating or terminating. These do not sound like the makings of an economy that could hold its own, at least by Anglo-American standards of living.

In the short term, measures like compelling firms to use French in their transactions have a direct effect—that of frightening them off. It is not, after all, as if the French-speaking market represents the major share of the Canadian market; on the contrary, it is less than one-third. We can already observe the effect of this type of language law in use—in Belgium, where at least the Flemish-speaking politicians who carried through the law represented a majority of the total population. But the Belgian example is not an encouraging one; it is not by this means that *new jobs* are created. All that happens is that firms that are footloose move away, as finance houses and insurance companies—whose business does not involve any material ties—have already moved from Montréal to Toronto. It is difficult to see the economic profits of separation; easy to count up the losses.

The Interior

General

That part of the great Central Lowland of North America which lies between the Appalachian foothills, the Ozarks, the Great Plains, and the Laurentian Shield is an area which, for all its size, defies satisfactory subdivision into smaller subregions. So closely interdependent are the patterns of its life and economic activity that distance, variety of physical setting, and even the international boundary must not be allowed to hinder the geographer from viewing the region as a whole.

Two basic reasons underlie the decision to treat this area as a single region. The first is found in its agricultural and industrial patterns. Shorn of its details, the agricultural pattern takes the form of a series of concentric circles focused on the central Corn Belt. The industrial pattern, on the other hand, reveals a distinction between a heavily industrialized eastern half of the region and a less heavily industrialized western half; that is to say, the agricultural pattern grades out from the center, while the industrial gradient is from east to west. Furthermore, drawn across the region from northwest to southeast is the great diagonal slash of the Great Lakes, whose presence profoundly modifies the other cultural patterns, and upon whose shores are the homes of so large a part of the region's population. To subdivide the region inevitably means to destroy one or more of these patterns.

The second reason is that to subdivide the Interior means to break up one of the greatest realities in American life and thought—the Midwest. To delimit this cultural Midwest by means of precise boundaries is, of course, impossible. As Graham Hutton pointed out,[1] it includes the states of Ohio, Michigan, Indiana, Illinois, Wisconsin, Minnesota, Iowa, and Missouri, but in the cultural sense it can be said to include much of the area of heavy industry in Pennsylvania and West Virginia. "In other words, the real Midwest, the Midwest of the midwesterners, is the core composed of most of the area of these eight states; but beyond that core you will still find a Midwest, thinning out into something else the further you go from the center.[2]

[1]G. Hutton, *Midwest at Noon*, Harrap, London, 1946, p.4.

[2]Hutton, *Midwest at Noon*. The Midwesterners themselves, of course, do not by any means agree upon the limits of the Midwest. In general, those in the heart of the region would tend to draw its boundaries around themselves and would be suprised that those of the outer fringes regard themselves as belonging at all; thus, for example, an inhabitant of Kansas City might well think of himself as a Midwesterner, while a man from St. Louis would consider it self-evident that he lived far beyond the pale. A postal survey revealed that there are people in rural areas of

What underlies this midwestern sectionalism? To explain it, we might refer to such economic factors as the firm midwestern balance between industry and agriculture; to the farmers' freedom from the marketing problems of East and West that were reviewed in Chapter 6; to the wide range of midwestern manufactures, all making for a high degree of regional self-sufficiency. We should necessarily take account, too, of the historical factor—the uniformity of the conditions under which, in the first half of the nineteenth century, this vast tract was rapidly occupied. Much of this explanation lies outside the scope of the present volume: suffice it to say that there results from these factors a marked degree of economic and cultural individualism within the region.

On the Canadian side of the border, a different set of factors creates a regional distinctiveness no less definite. The term *midwestern* is not in common Canadian use, but the part of Canada over which the geographical patterns of the Interior spread is easily defined. It is that section of Ontario which is cut off from the rest of the country, to the north and east, by the empty barrenness of the Laurentian Shield. In geological terms it is Paleozoic Ontario, and in a historical sense Upper Canada—the area which consciously balances the Frenchness of Québec; the area which, it is sometimes remarked, keeps Canada British.

The Agricultural Interior

The farmers of the Interior are generally favored by natural conditions. The region possesses vast, smooth plains, which make cultivation easy, and wide areas of remarkably fertile glacial drift. It has an adequate rainfall (30–40 in. [750–1000mm], of which one-third to one-half falls in the months May to August inclusive) and hot summer weather to offset the short frost-free period of a continental interior. If the city dweller finds cause for complaint in the stifling summer heat, the icy winds of winter, and the all-too-brief "in between" spring weather, these things cause little inconvenience to the farmer, whose methods are adapted to the climate, who will delight to "hear the corn growing" during the hot summer nights when the cities are sleepless, and whose chief fear is the occasional thunderstorm or hailstorm that may spring up suddenly on a hot afternoon and lash down with tropical violence on his crops. This hazard apart, he has little cause for complaint in the natural conditions.

The effect of this favorable combination of circumstances is to produce an agriculture of intensive land use, with high land values, a high percentage of the farm area under crops, and the conversion of much of the output of the fields into livestock products. Because of the historical circumstances under which the area was settled, all this is typically associated with family farms, where hired labor is at a minimum and the average farm size, until well after World War II, was still close to 160 acres (64.8 ha)—the historic quarter-section which, as we saw in Chapter 4, dominated land legislation throughout the nineteenth century.

But if these are the general characteristics of Interior farming—high land values, intensive land use, widespread cropping, and a dense livestock population—it must at once be added that over so vast an area all of these circumstances do not by any means apply everywhere. Natural conditions limit and modify their application in various parts of the region, creating the local differences that will be described later. But the area where they are most fully developed, where most of them apply most of the time, where lies the heart of this great agricultural region, is the Corn Belt.

THE CORN BELT

The Corn Belt is one of the best-known entities in American geography, its fame enhanced by Russell Smith's classic phrase, "The Corn Belt is a gift of the gods."[3] Yet to define it is almost

North Dakota who considered themselves Midwesterners, an astonishing proposition for anyone from Indiana or Illinois to accept, to whom the Dakotas are little less remote than the moon. See J.W. Brownell, "The Cultural Midwest," *Journal of Geography*, vol. lix (1960), 81–85.

[3]J.R. Smith and O. Phillips, *North America*, Harcourt Brace, New York, 1942, p. 360.

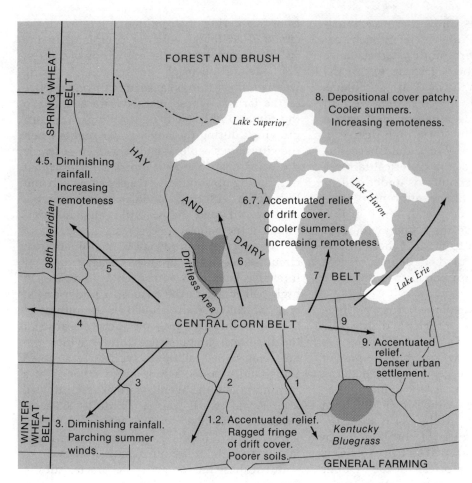

Fig. 14-1. The Agricultural Interior and its subdivisions: The map represents diagrammatically the transition between the central Corn Belt and adjacent regions, which is described on pp. 236–45.

Map labels:

FOREST AND BRUSH

SPRING WHEAT BELT

Lake Superior

8. Depositional cover patchy. Cooler summers. Increasing remoteness.

4.5. Diminishing rainfall. Increasing remoteness

HAY

98th Meridian

AND

DAIRY

Lake Huron

6.7. Accentuated relief of drift cover. Cooler summers. Increasing remoteness.

Driftless Area

5

6

7 BELT

8

Lake Erie

4

CENTRAL CORN BELT

9

9. Accentuated relief. Denser urban settlement.

WINTER WHEAT BELT

3

2

1

3. Diminishing rainfall. Parching summer winds.

1.2. Accentuated relief. Ragged fringe of drift cover. Poorer soils.

Kentucky Bluegrass

GENERAL FARMING

---

as difficult as to set limits to the Midwest itself. There is an area where corn is the first-ranking crop in acreage, and this emphasis on corn gives place to an emphasis on hay or soybeans or wheat on the outskirts of the area. But such a definition will hardly do justice to the reality. Perhaps the best definition is obtained simply by saying the Corn Belt is that area of the Interior where the agricultural characteristics we have already listed are found in the most marked conjunction. In other words, a definition of the Corn Belt involves a criterion not merely of type, but of intensity of land use.[4]

[4]W.E. Akin, in *The North Central United States*, Van Nostrand, New York, 1968, makes use of a definition of intensity of Corn Belt land use which identifies those areas that produce more than 12,000 bushels of corn per square mile. These areas are found in most of northeastern Illinois, northern and eastern Iowa, and south-central Minnesota.

The existence and character of the Corn Belt are to be explained in the first instance by a fact of physical geography: that in the heart of the Interior, south of the Great Lakes, is a belt of the Central Lowland where conditions for farming approach the ideal. Large parts of this area are former lake beds and are perfectly level. Elsewhere a mantle of drift, product of the continental glaciation, has smoothed local relief and provided fertile till plains for farming. In other areas, notably in Iowa, a mantle of loess fulfils the same functions. Once the forests that covered the eastern half of these plains were cleared, and once the numerous swamps were drained, there was no major obstacle in the way of the plow for hundreds of miles. Away from this fertile core area, on the other hand, whether north into the lake and drumlin country of Wisconsin, south into the Ohio Valley and beyond, or east into the Appalachian foothills, the terrain becomes more broken and the soils more patchy.

For the second stage of our explanation, we must enter the field of agricultural economics. In terms of output per acre the crop which yields the best returns in the Interior is corn. It is also the most reliable of the crops introduced either by the Indians or by the early settlers in this environment; it can be depended on to do well year after year. It is also a fact that the American consumer has been conditioned to react favorably to the label "corn fed" when buying meat. Given these realities, it is generally more profitable to market this corn "on the hoof," by turning it into livestock products, than to sell it as grain. The Corn Belt is the area where, thanks to natural advantages and the excellent markets nearby, this sequence can be most profitably followed. The Belt extends as far as conditions of marketing, terrain, and especially climate permit, and beyond that the corn crop is replaced as pivot of the farming system by an alternative crop—wheat or alfalfa in much of the western Interior, hay or oats in the north.

For the Agricultural Interior a particular importance therefore attaches to the climatic limits of successful corn growing within the region. In general terms these are (1) on the western edge of the Corn Belt, the point beyond which summer rainfall becomes inadequate (less than 8 in. (20 cm) in the three summer months) or at which the hot, dry winds off the Great Plains would parch the corn; (2) on the northern edge, the line beyond which summer heat, so necessary for the ripening of the crop, is insufficient (although, as we shall see, corn is grown further north nevertheless and is cut green); (3) on the southern edge, the point beyond which growing season temperatures are *too* high, and corn is replaced by cotton or rice.

This pattern did not, of course, immediately form itself by natural logic when the area was settled in the first half of the nineteenth century.[5] Its first export was cattle, and it was tra-

versed between 1840 and 1860 by the westward-moving Wheat Belt (see p. 103). Nor was its fertility at once appreciated; much of it was swampy, and in any case the first settlers, emerging in Illinois from the forests through which they had traveled all the way from the Atlantic Coast, were suspicious of land that would grow only grass. The present pattern is an outcome of the growth of midwestern cities and communications—that is, of the existence within the region of a virtually insatiable market.

Let us now consider some of the features of this pattern. They are:

1. The high percentage of the total area in crops. Over large sections of the Corn Belt, notably in Iowa and Illinois, the figure is in excess of 70 percent. The forest cover, originally extensive in the eastern part of the Belt and patchy in the west, has been almost entirely cleared, and in the Corn Belt landscape the presence of trees usually implies planted windbreaks—straight lines on the edges of holdings or clusters around farmhouses. There is little permanent grass either; pastures are planted as part of the crop rotation. It is not difficult, indeed, to argue that cultivation has been carried too far—an outcome of great fertility, high land values, and the ease of plowing in long, straight lines.

2. Farms are generally small. Much of the area was occupied in the first half of the nineteenth century under a series of land acts designed to make land available in family-sized units, and virtually all of the area was covered by the rectangular grid of sections and quarter-sections which shows so clearly in the pattern of roads and field boundaries to this day. In the settlement period this arrangement had a number of advantages: the survey was quick and cheap to run, disputes over property boundaries were reduced to a minimum, and the 160–acre (64.8 ha) unit was a suitable size for a family to settle. But under modern conditions this system of occupance is something of a straightjacket; in these days of mechaniza-

[5]See A.G. Bogue, *From Prairie to Corn Belt*, University of Chicago Press, Chicago, 1963; D.R. McManis, *The Initial Evaluation and Utilization of the Illinois Prairies, 1815–1840*, University of Chicago, Department of Geography Research

Paper No. 94, 1964, and J.E. Spencer and R.J. Horvath, "How Does an Agricultural Region Originate?" *Annals* of the Association of American Geographers, vol. liii (1963), 74–92.

Soybeans growing "on the contour" at Melvin, Illinois. Soybeans have invaded the Interior in the past two decades, and now rival corn in Corn Belt acreage, as described on p. 235. *(U.S. Dept. of Agriculture)*

tion a 160–acre farm is far too small for a Corn Belt farmer to operate efficiently: an area three times as great would be more realistic. But since each of his neighbors is likely to be under exactly the same pressure to enlarge, the farmer will not find it easy to obtain additional land. The price of land in the Corn Belt, reflecting as it does this pressure to enlarge, is very high, and the best that most farmers can hope for is to rent the extra acres. In the Corn Belt state of Iowa in 1970 no less than 47.5 percent of all farmland was operated under rental: in northwest Iowa the figure was over 60 percent. A majority of the leases in the Corn Belt call for payment in the form of a share of the crop, which is liable to hamper the farmer who wishes to experiment with new methods or rotations, and few leases offer the kind of long-term security of tenure which the British farmer, for example, has come to take for granted.

3. The actual place of corn in the farm operations. It is important not to be misled by the name Corn Belt into visualizing a sea of standing corn stretching from horizon to horizon. The Belt is in reality an area of genuinely mixed farming, with a notable diversity of crops and stock on most holdings. Of the total farmland within the Belt, corn occupies in any given year about one-quarter. In relation to the

area under crops, throughout most of the central Corn Belt the proportion exceeds 40 percent, and rises above 60 percent in some small areas. Corn is usually grown in rotation with at least one other grain and a hay crop. In this respect, however, rotations have tended to become more simple in recent years, partly because of technical improvements in corn, fertilizers, and so on, and partly because of the most striking land-use change of the past twenty years in the Corn Belt—the increase in the acreage under soybeans. By 1975 this crop had so increased in the Corn Belt states as to begin to challenge the regional title. In Missouri, soybeans occupy a larger acreage than corn. In Illinois, their acreage is 70 percent of that under corn, and the proportion is not much less in Minnesota or Indiana. Nationally, the area under soybeans increased from 23.65 million acres (9.57 million ha) in 1960 to 53.61 million (21.70 million ha) in 1975; that is, from 33 percent of the area under corn in 1960 to 80 percent of the corn acreage in 1975.[6]

Apart from soybeans, however, wheat, oats, barley, sorghum, and alfalfa all play an important *subsidiary* role in parts of the central Corn Belt, and assume *primary* importance in various areas along its fringes. This corn-grain-grass rotation not only operates in the interests of soil fertility, but it also serves to spread the

[6]Fraser Hart explains the soybean's popularity (J. Fraser Hart, "The Middle West," *Annals* of the Association of American Geographers, vol. lxii (1972), p. 268):

"The high-protein soybean must be considered something of a miracle crop, and it certainly is a relatively new one to the Middle West, because data on soybeans were not even published in the U.S. Census of Agriculture until 1929. The crop is a leguminous soil-enricher if it is grazed, cut for hay, or plowed under for green manure, but much of its nitrogen is transferred from its root nodules to its beans if the beans are allowed to ripen. Oil crushed from the beans is an ingredient of shortening, margarine, and other food products, and it has numerous industrial uses; the residual meal is an excellent concentrated feed for livestock. . . . "

The U.S. Department of Agriculture, not an organization that normally gushes over mere crops, adds in its 1975 Yearbook, *That We May Eat* (p. 225): "By 1973, soybeans had become our Number 1 cash crop, the leading export commodity, the major alternative crop of midwestern and southern farmers, the world's most effective producer of protein per acre, and the hope of starving millions for a better diet.''

farm's labor requirements over a longer summer season, an important consideration in an area where, as we have seen, most farms are operated by their owners, with only family labor.

4. Livestock in the Corn Belt. We shall not understand the agriculture of the Corn Belt without a clear statement of its last and most basic feature: in terms of farm activity and farm income, it is not a Corn Belt at all but a Meat Belt. Three-quarters of the Belt's farm income is derived from the sale of animal products, and it is to this that the cropping is geared. Even when the farmer does sell his corn in the sack rather than on the hoof, it is highly probable that the buyer merely requires it to feed to other stock within the region.

This intensive and well-integrated livestock farming takes several forms. Apart from the dairy farming and poultry-keeping which, as in other regions, are common here wherever there is a market to be found, the Corn Belt farmer may both raise his own stock and also act as fattener and finisher of stock bought from farmers further west. In either case his output is destined for the meat-packers in the Corn Belt cities.

Pigs, which are the principal livestock product of the Belt, are raised wholly within it, and the hog pasture is a standard feature of its farms. But beef-cattle raising is rather more complex in that the Corn Belt farmers have acted as intermediaries for many years, buying stock from the dry ranges of the West and fattening them in the Belt. Range cattle normally did not have the "finish" required by the meat-packers, nor could the range support them all year round. Thousands of cattle therefore passed through the Corn Belt farms each year, in much the same way that, in an earlier period, the Connecticut Valley served as a finishing area for cattle raised further north in New England or the famous Meath pastures in Ireland fatten stock from the west of the country.

This practice still continues in the Corn Belt, but the volume of the transit movement has been reduced. Thanks to changes in farm techniques and land use in the drier West (changes which we shall consider in a later chapter), much more range stock is being not only fattened but also slaughtered in the West. Improved pastures produce better beef, and reservoirs and irrigation projects save the ranchers from the need to sell off stock in dry years.

The numbers of cattle finished in the Corn Belt therefore vary from year to year, and so, necessarily, do prices. Such price fluctuations, whatever their cause, constantly raise for the farmer the question of whether it will be more profitable to sell his output as grain or as meat. His decision will be governed partly by the comparative state of prices for the two types of product (which in turn probably reflects government support policy), and partly by such local considerations as freight rates to the nearest main market. Around Chicago, for example, there are curious anomalies in the rate pattern, and certainly there are parts of the Corn Belt which year after year ship grain rather than meat.

It is, however, precisely because the Corn Belt farmer has the option of producing grain or meat in addition to the other advantages he enjoys, that he has been able to build up over the years a high standard of living that may well be envied by his colleagues who farm in less favored regions.

THE SOUTHERN MARGINS

The southern margin of the Corn Belt is marked by the increasingly broken terrain that heralds the approach to the Ohio and Missouri rivers. Here at its southern limit the cover of glacial drift is patchy; the streams flowing south have cut down into it, and the loss of fertility and of smoothness is clearly reflected in a decline in both prosperity and intensity of cultivation in southern Indiana and Illinois and in northern Missouri.

Beyond the Ohio, in Kentucky, the same trend continues. Relief is more pronounced; woodland and rough grazing appear more frequently. With the transition from the fertile till plains to the wooded uplands of Kentucky, and with increasing distance from the main markets of the Midwest, agriculture on the Corn Belt pattern gives way to mixed farming of a less intensive type, with increasing amounts of pasture, grading off into what is

virtually subsistence farming in the most remote areas.

South of the Missouri much the same conditions apply. Where the land rises to the Ozarks the proportion of farmland under cultivation declines, and woodland and pastures replace crops. Once again the remote hill farms support little more than subsistence agriculture and the Ozark hillsmen share the problems and the reputation of those in the Appalachians, whom we shall encounter in the next chapter. Like Appalachia this is an area of declining population, of poverty (with twice as many families beneath the family income level which serves as the national poverty threshold, as for the nation as a whole), and of low land values and small investments in its farms.

In general, then, this southern edge of the Interior is an area of increasing physical limitation. But it also embraces some agricultural lands of a higher quality. Apart from the superbly fertile alluvia of the Mississippi Valley bottomlands, the most notable of these are associated with the limestone areas of Kentucky and Tennessee—the Bluegrass and the Nashville basins.

When the first migrants struggled through the Cumberland Gap and along Boone's Wilderness Road in the last years of the eighteenth century, they were spurred on by reports of an area of incredible fertility beyond the hills. This was the Bluegrass country of Kentucky, where the limestone core of an eroded dome has weathered to form soils that support a rich grassland. Today, as a hundred and fifty years ago, this region has a great agricultural reputation—for the racehorses it breeds; for its dairy and beef cattle and its tobacco; for the splendour of its stud farms, with their pillared facades and white fences. Less spectacular, but basically similar in its pasture-corn-livestock farming, is the basin in Tennessee, with its famous dairy herds of Channel Island stock. Focused on Lexington and on Nashville respectively, these two basins form islands of prosperity in the broad zone of "general farming" that stretches across the United States south of the Ohio.

The cash crop of much of this general farming area of Kentucky and Tennessee is tobacco,

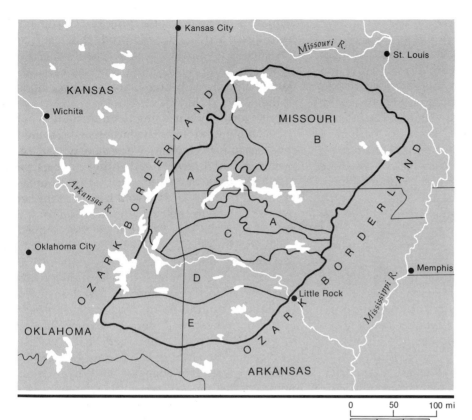

Fig. 14-2. Physical subdivisions of the Ozark region: A = Springfield Plateau, B = Salem Plateau, C = Boston Mountains, D =Arkansas Valley, E = Ouachita Mountains. Lakes and reservoirs are also shown (in grey). These represent an important part of the resource base for a naturally poor region, since they contribute to its attractiveness for tourists.

a crop whose cultivation over recent years has come to be so closely controlled by a system of government quotas that possession of the right to market it enhances the selling value of the farm; the purchaser must pay for the acreage allotment along with the land.[7] West of the Mississippi the southern margin of the Corn Belt sees a change from the intensive livestock production based on feed crops which characterizes the Belt north of the Missouri to a land use that is little more than subsistence agriculture in the heart of the Ozarks. The Springfield Plateau forms a kind of transition zone, beyond which lie the forested mountains with their poor soils and physical conditions unfavorable for farming. Natural pasture replaces

[7] M. Prunty, "Land Occupance in the Southeast," *Geographical Review*, vol. xlii, 439–61. "The only device open to a newcomer [wishing to grow tobacco] is to purchase a farm that has traditionally grown the crop under allotment, but he finds that the allotment . . . has value far beyond the customary value of the land . . . . The crop probably serves as the best agricultural example of a new brand of determinism—political determinism" (p. 450).

the planted fodder crops of the Corn Belt and accounts for more than half the farmland. Although, in the past, farmers in the northern Ozarks have raised pigs and dairy cattle, there is in evidence a swing to the production of beef cattle and poultry, the marketing of which presents less problems. Farm activity has been steadily declining, both in area and in numbers of farms.

The remaining specialty crops of the region are fruits, especially grapes and apples. But many of the farmers rely less on the cash income brought in by the fruit crop than on other employment. Since more than half of the area of the Ozarks is under forest, work in the lumber industry is an obvious alternative to work on the farm. Even in this respect, however, possibilities are limited, for much of the forest is non-commercial, and most of it is composed of slow-growing hardwoods. Tourism offers better prospects, but there is a steady emigration out of the hills which tells its own story.

If the controlling influences on the southern margins of the Corn Belt are those of relief and soils, the western limits are governed by climate. Here there is no topographic obstacle to terminate the Belt: the lowland of the Interior continues with scarcely a break to the foot of the Rockies, and the all-important drift cover extends far out over the Great Plains. But there is a gradual decrease of precipitation which, on the one hand, enforces a less intensive type of farming and, on the other hand, obliges the farmer to replace corn by a crop better adapted to the drier conditions—in practice by wheat or sorghum.

The agricultural transition on this edge of the Corn Belt takes place in two stages:

1. On the western borders of Iowa and Missouri, wheat (the second crop of much of the western Corn Belt) becomes the dominant grain crop, with sorghum accompanying it in the south, especially in Kansas, and alfalfa, oats, or corn in the north. This change in crop emphasis is essentially a precautionary one, made as the limits of secure corn growing are reached; it makes little difference to the form of the farm economy which, although based on less intensive land use, remains dependent on livestock production.

2. With further decrease in precipitation, the intensive livestock raising of the Corn Belt is no longer possible. Here there is a change to cash-grain farming, and wheat growing becomes the dominant agricultural activity. West of this second zone of transition, which runs through the eastern Dakotas and eastern Kansas, lie the Spring and Winter Wheat belts, separated by the western extremity of the Corn Belt (see Fig. 6–1).[8]

The Wheat Belts (the distinction between which is simply a question of latitude and consequently of the date of sowing the crop) have been described as "the end product of a sort of destructive evolution which was impressed upon the European farming types as they advanced into the sub-humid and semiarid lands of the New World."[9]

It is worthwhile pausing to understand what this comment implies. The farmers who settled the Agricultural Interior were men whose experience had been gained either in eastern North America or in Europe; that is, in areas of mixed farming. This mixed farming they set out to practice in their new homes—say in the humid central Corn Belt. But as they moved westward into drier areas what happened was that one by one the various elements in the mixed-farming economy—the alternative crops and the livestock population—proved unsuited to the new conditions and had to be dropped, until only wheat (with perhaps barley, flax, or sorghum in support) remained of the variety with which the farming had begun. Indeed, on the driest (western) edges of the Wheat Belt a point in the process was reached where the only alternative to wheat growing was to leave the ground fallow, but advances in farm techniques have made possible some retreat from this ultimate of "destructive evolution."

Farming in the Wheat Belts is, in fact, becoming more like that of the remainder of the Interior—more variegated, with less dependence on a single crop and with a larger livestock population. Nevertheless, it still possesses a number of distinctive features. For one thing, farms are larger; a section or two sections is the normal size. The wheat farms generally occupy the smooth interfluves of the plains, while the valleys are given over to irrigated crops and the rougher lands to grazing. The main contrast with the rest of the Interior, however, is a social one: where farmers limit themselves to cereals and do not incorporate livestock in their operations, labor requirements can be reduced to a few days at the beginning and end of the season, and this makes possible a type of non-resident, "suitcase" farming which leaves the farmer free to spend most of the year elsewhere. The Wheat Belt

---

[8]The explanation of this curious break in the Wheat Belt seems to be (1) that there is a climatic no-man's-land between the two halves, where winters are too cold for winter wheat and summers are too hot for spring wheat; so that neither can be grown, and (2) that in eastern Nebraska, climatic and relief conditions permit the growing of corn further to the west than elsewhere—as far west, in fact, as the fringe of cultivation, where the grazing areas begin; so that there is no need for a transitional belt of another crop.

[9]S.N. Dicken, *Economic Geography*, D.C. Heath, Boston, 1955, p. 175.

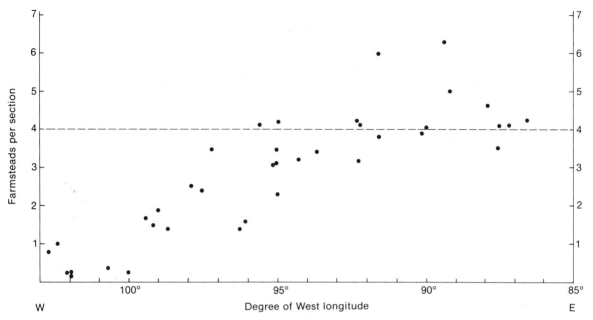

Fig. 14-3. Farm settlement in the Interior: Diagram of a map exercise on U.S. Geological Survey 1:24,000 topographic maps along a line from western Indiana to eastern Colorado. On each map (approx. 48 sq mi or 124 sq km) farmsteads per sq mi were counted. There is, of course, no assurance that all the farmsteads are today (a) occupied and (b) farmed as separate units: the reverse is likely to be the case. Nevertheless, the farmsteads exist and the diagram emphasizes the pervasive influence in the Interior of U.S. land legislation based on the quarter-section of 160 acres, giving 4 farmsteads per sq mi (2.6 sq km). See also p. 109. This density persists far out to the west where, however, increasing aridity leads to a thinning out of farmsteads.

farmer therefore often has only a slender attachment to his land.[10]

A further point of contrast between the Wheat Belts and the Corn Belt is that, while the agricultural markets of the latter lie within the Belt, those of the former do not. Much of the Spring Wheat Belt is in Canada, and only one-quarter to one-third of the Canadian wheat crop is consumed within the country, let alone within the sparsely settled wheatlands themselves. The produce of the Wheat Belts travels, in the first instance, to Winnipeg, Kansas City, or Minneapolis and from there in part to Montréal, Baltimore, or Houston and on to foreign markets.

On these western margins of the Interior, however, it is generally true to say that,

[10]On this, see W.M. Kollmorgen and G.F. Jenks, "Suitcase Farming in Sully County, South Dakota," *Annals* of the Association of American Geographers, vol. xlviii, (1958), 27–40 and refs. In Manitoba the author met a university student who claimed that, thanks to the arrangement of the Canadian academic session, he could operate his family's 640-acre (259.1 ha) wheat farm without misssing a lecture at the university. Meanwhile, students in other lands unproductively miss lectures without raising a single blade of wheat as they do so.

whereas formerly the Corn Belt and the Wheat Belts were strikingly dissimilar, they have in recent years been growing more alike. So, for that matter, have the Wheat Belts and the former grazing regions of the Great Plains, as we shall see in Chapter 18. There is a trend everywhere apparent in the western Interior toward a more mixed farming: only the intensity of input found in the central Interior falls off as one approaches its western margins.

THE NORTHERN MARGINS—
THE WESTERN GREAT LAKES AREA

On its northern edge the Corn Belt gives place to the Hay and Dairy Belt, which stretches from Minnesota in the west to Nova Scotia in the east.[11] Increasing remoteness, rougher terrain, poorer soils, and summers too cool to ripen corn all contribute to this transition. On

[11]The Corn Belt has a number of small outliers on its northern edge, in places where the soil is rich and relief is smooth, such as the Janesville and Arlington prairies in southern Wisconsin. These areas have a livestock-owning pattern more like that of the Corn Belt, and sell off large amounts of animal feeds.

Wisconsin: The Driftless Area. Although doubt has been recently cast on the validity of this name (*see* p. 16), there is no question that the area contains many water-formed features and a generally rougher relief than its surroundings. The picture shows Gibraltar Rock in Columbia County. *(Wisconsin Natural Resources Dept.)*

the positive side the local markets for milk in the Great Lakes cities and the national market for butter and cheese make the Dairy Belt a vital part of the Agricultural Interior and a no less logical adaptation to market conditions than is the "Meat Belt" further south. Corn loses importance in comparison with hay and oats, dairy cattle replace beef cattle and pigs, and the ratio of farmland to forest and improved land decreases rather rapidly northward; but the basic relationship between cropping and livestock remains unchanged. Hay, oats, and corn, all grown for fodder, occupy

over 90 percent of the cropland area; the corn is cut green and made into silage, and livestock products form the principal item of farm income.

Yet the prosperity and apparent stability of farming in today's Dairy Belt conceal a checkered story of sequent occupance. Wisconsin grew wheat before it became "America's Dairyland," and some of the region's early farm production catered to long-vanished markets to the north, rather than to those in the lakeshore cities of today. In fact it might be argued that stability on the northern edges of the Dairy

Belt, in the North Woods of Minnesota, Wisconsin, and Michigan, has not yet been achieved.

Farm settlement in Wisconsin serves well to illustrate these changes. During the first phase of agricultural land use, between 1835 and 1880, Wisconsin was a wheat state. The northern focus of North American wheat production, whose movement we have followed from New England (see p. 103), passed across Wisconsin between 1850 and 1880. Wheat was a crop well suited to the circumstances of the early settlers, but their farming was entirely unscientific, and so a constant need for fresh land drew them northwestward across the state and on into Minnesota. Peak acreage was reached in 1878; by 1905 it had dropped to a negligible figure. The wheat boom was over, and in the south farmers had already begun to see where their more permanent profit lay—in dairying.

But meanwhile another phase had intervened to postpone the coming of stability. This was the lumber boom in the North Woods. The opening of the dry, treeless West in the 1870s and 1880s led to a great demand for timber, a demand which the Great Lakes area could meet. Northward the lumbermen led the way, clearing ground for the farmers who would follow to grow their suppies. Disregarding or burning all but the particular timber they sought, they cut their way through the area between 1875 and 1905, and then, as abruptly, left for the mountains of the West. The farmers who had settled the North Woods (like their neighbors who had followed the copper miners into Upper Michigan a few years earlier) found themselves virtually marooned in wilderness without local markets; the state governments found themselves left with the cutover land.

The third phase of occupance has been marked by two processes—the establishment of commercial dairying in the southern Great Lakes area, and the retreat of the farm frontier in the north. The western half of the Dairy Belt has become North America's greatest surplus-producing are for dairy products. The area is divided fairly clearly into those parts which produce fluid milk for urban markets—as southeast Wisconsin, for example, serves Chicago and Milwaukee—and the remoter areas where absence of such markets encourages the manufacture of butter and cheese. Most important of these is the butter region of western Wisconsin and adjacent parts of Iowa and Minnesota. Half of all the cheese produced in the United States is manufactured in Wisconsin, with the descendants of European cheesemakers still producing the cheese of their homelands. So great is the milk surplus of these areas that, apart from shipping a large share of the nation's butter and cheese, they have produced enough to act as a milk "reservoir" to supply fluid milk to other regions and cities where a rapid rise in population has created a temporary shortage locally. In this way, Wisconsin has at various times had a daily "milk run" by tanker truck to Phoenix in Arizona 1750 mi (2800 km) away, and to Florida.

Farm organization in the western Dairy Belt does not differ greatly from that in the Corn Belt. Farms are generally family operated, in the 150–to–200 acre (61–81 ha) range, and the standard dairy herd consists of no more than 40 head. As the delivery point for farm produce the local creamery or cheese factory replaces the grain elevator and the stockpens at the railway station. Because of the cooler summers and rougher terrain, however, permanent pasture is more widespread than in the Corn Belt (in Wisconsin, for example, it accounts for two-fifths of the farmland), and the area under crops is considerably smaller.

Some of these crops, however, form local specialities. The Door Peninsula, jutting out into Lake Michigan, is famous for its cherry orchards, and there is a small fruit belt here, comparable to the larger ones on the Michigan side of the lake and the southern shores of Lake Ontario. The proximity of the lake tends to hold down temperatures in the spring and acts against early blossoming and so against frost damage (see Fig. 14-4), while the summer is prolonged at the other end of the growing season. Then in the Central Sand Plain of Wisconsin, an area where cultivation was until

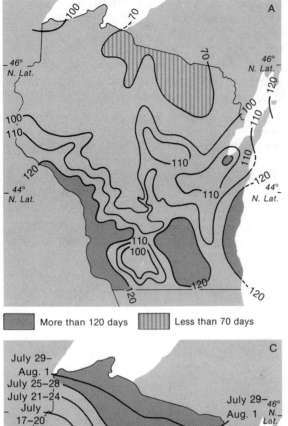

More than 120 days | Less than 70 days

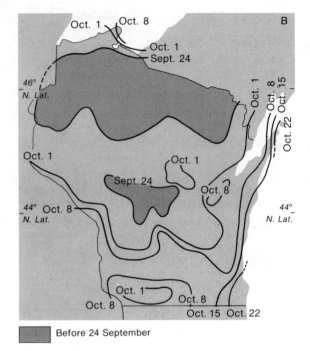

Before 24 September

After July 28

Fig. 14-4. Climatic features of Wisconsin: (A) the normal annual growing season for cultivated plants (i.e., the period between the last killing frost in spring and the first in autumn). (B) The date of the first autumn frost, 1925–49. (C) The average dates of reaching a total of 1000 growing-degree days above a base of 50°F (10°C). This map gives a measure of how quickly an area warms up in the early summer. Note the "hang-back" of the Door Peninsula, which keeps the fruit back in the spring and minimizes risk of frost losses.

quite recently restricted to cranberry bogs, the use of sprinkler irrigation has brought into being a region whose special crop is beans and whose landscape has been largely transformed from a level and monotonous heath to one of farms known locally as the "golden sands," so prosperous has it become.

Meanwhile, the northern margin of the Dairy Belt has advanced into the North Woods and retreated again. Once the stimulus of the lumbermen's demand for farm produce was removed, farming on the Superior Upland or on the devastated cutover land generally proved uneconomical. Consequently, there has been a

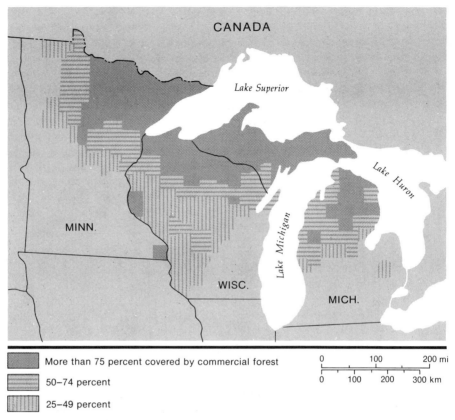

Fig. 14-5. Forest areas of the Northern Great Lakes Region: Viewed from the other aspect of the land-use pattern, this is a map of the northern margin of the Hay and Dairy Belt.

■ More than 75 percent covered by commercial forest

▨ 50–74 percent

▥ 25–49 percent

0   100   200 mi

0   100   200   300 km

steady out-migration from the area: in the decade 1950–60, for example, the net migration was 10 percent, and in the 20–24 age group was as high as 61 percent. In the same period the number of farms fell by 38 percent, and many of the remaining farmers supplemented their incomes with work off the farm.[12] Today, by far the largest money-maker here in the north is tourism; it was first stimulated in the 1880s by the region's railroads and each weekend in summer nowadays thousands of city people from as far away as Chicago drive or fly north to lakeside cabins, and the old farmers' supply centers and lumber towns have found a new life as resorts.[13]

[12]U.S. Department of Agriculture, *Agricultural Economics Report No. 108*, U.S. Government Printing Office, Washington, D.C.

[13]There is also a growing winter-sports industry and a brief but hectic period in November when the North Woods are full of deer hunters and wise nonhunters stay indoors. In 1967, as a typical year, Wisconsin issued over half a million licenses for the short deer season: over 100,000 deer were killed and 24 hunters died, mostly from exposure or heart attack.

Rather than provide at great expense the services required by outlying northern farms, local governments have used powers they possess under a zoning law of 1923 to close whole sections of the North Woods to agriculture. Here, then, is one American frontier where for reasons both of marketing difficulty and administrative economy a planned withdrawal has taken place—a withdrawal which, in these days of agricultural surplus and intense competition, represents an understandable response to economic conditions. It is thus possible to trace, running through the northern parts of Minnesota, Wisconsin, and Michigan, a *northern* limit to the Dairy Belt, the result of both physical handicaps and remoteness from markets (see Fig. 14-5).

THE NORTHERN MARGINS—
SOUTHERN ONTARIO

The peninsula of southern Ontario, between the Great Lakes and the edge of the Laurentian Shield, forms a true part of the Agricultural

243

Interior, although a part which lies in Canada, thanks to the incidence of the international boundary. Judged by most of the criteria we have already discussed, the southwestern tip of Ontario—the Essex Peninsula—belongs to the Corn Belt. Much of the rest of the area falls within the Dairy Belt; then to the north of the zone of dairying there is a belt of mixed farming, and at the edge of the Shield commercial agriculture ends abruptly.

Peninsular Ontario is structurally a continuation of the Central Lowland, with the Paleozoic formations meeting the Shield along a line from Georgian Bay to the Thousand Islands on the St. Lawrence. Most of the peninsula's surface features, however, are of glacial origin. During the Wisconsin glaciation two lobes of ice occupied the approximate positions of the present Lakes Huron and Ontario–Erie, pressing southward and encircling southern Ontario. When the ice retreated, it left behind a legacy of morainic clays and sands on the flanks of the peninsula, while much of the center was covered by till plains and morainic hills. Thus the general effect of glaciation was favorable to an agricultural future; especially on the southeastern edge of the area, where settlement was later to concentrate, the morainic slopes and lacustrine plains of the present-day lakeshores offered fertile soils for farming.[14]

Climatic conditions also favor agriculture. The presence of the Great Lakes on two sides of the triangle of southern Ontario has a marked modifying influence on the region's climate. The peninsula has a smaller seasonal temperature range than areas to the east and west of it; so that winters are warmer and the growing season is longer. Indeed, the lakeshore in the extreme southwest of Ontario and around the Niagara Peninsula has the unusually long frost-free period for this latitude of 170–175 days.

Favored in its soils and climate, southern Ontario has become eastern Canada's largest

area of relatively intensive agricultural land use. With little land excluded from farm use for reasons of climate or physique, and with suitable market outlets available to and—thanks to the international boundary—secured for the Ontario farmer, a pattern of close settlement has developed that is quite unlike that of French Canada below the Thousand Islands but bears a marked similarity to that of the Corn Belt and southern Dairy Belt. In intensity of settlement as in layout the southern Ontario pattern is midwestern rather than Laurentian, gridiron rather than linear.

But here as elsewhere on the margins of the Agricultural Interior, there is a general decline in the intensity of land use toward the fringes—in this case, from southwest to northeast. It is not a regular progression, because of the variety of soil quality among the glacial deposits of the peninsula. These deposits are patchy and infertile, but some of them have been put to surprisingly intensive use. In Norfolk County, for example, infertile sands now support fields of tobacco and one of the highest levels of farm income per unit of area in the whole of Canada. At Bradford, Dutch immigrants have turned valley marshes into a fair replica of a polderland and grow vegetables intensively. A shortening growing season and increasing distance to market do, however, impose added burdens on the farmers as one moves north. The Essex Peninsula, as we have already seen, possesses a number of characteristics of the Corn Belt: 70 percent of the farmland is in crops, and in terms of areas occupied, soybeans have moved into the lead ahead of corn, just as in some other parts of the Belt's fringes (see p. 235). In the peninsula of southern Ontario as a whole, hay and oats occupy between them 65 percent of the cropland; hay, oats, and mixed grains account for over 80 percent. These crops provide the basis for livestock farming, but with a general contrast between dairying in the more southerly and more accessible regions and beef-cattle raising toward the fringes. The better soils, milder climate, and urban growth of southern and southwestern Ontario are sufficient to explain this contrast, a contrast which during the past decade or so has also begun to make itself felt in the diverging trends in farm income between

[14]Some 53 percent of southern Ontario is covered by soils in capability classes 1, 2, and 3; i.e. by soils suitable for most field crops. For most of peninsular Ontario southwest of a line from Toronto to Goderich, the figure is in excess of 80 percent.

the inner and outer areas. While the inner, or southerly, area has seen intensification of land use and the increasing cultivation of cash crops—tobacco has already been mentioned as an example—the outer area has seen declining farm incomes, abandonment, and the kind of conversion of former farmsteads to country residences which we have noted elsewhere on the fringes of agriculture, for example, in New England.

Besides the Essex Peninsula, one other small area of southern Ontario stands out as exceptional in its agriculture—the fruit-growing region of the Niagara Peninsula. The southern shores of the Great Lakes are favored, thanks to the presence of these great bodies of water, with a long growing season and with markedly reduced frost risks, even as compared with areas only a few miles inland. As a result these shores are the location of several important fruit-growing areas, such as those in southwestern Michigan and on the southern side of Lakes Ontario and Erie; but none shows a more detailed or more complete adjustment to local conditions than that on the north-facing shore of Lake Ontario, west of Niagara. The cuesta edge lies a mile or two back from the shore, and at its foot are peach orchards. On the crest of the ridge are acres of grapes. Pears, plums, and cherries are also grown in the district.

Since there is a tendency, as we have already seen, for fruit- and vegetable-growing in North America to become more specialized and localized in the face of competition, it is probable that these lakeshore fruit districts will become more rather than less pronounced in the future. The Niagara region, however, faces competition of a quite different kind—competition for space. It lies on the lakeshore at a point where roads and railways converge to circle the end of the lake and within reach of the suburban sprawl of both Hamilton to the west and St. Catherine's to the east. As a result, housing and highways have cut seriously into the valuable peach orchards at the scarp foot, and a considerable acreage has been lost. There is plenty of space for the fruit belt to spread inland, but the microclimate away from the lakeshore, which is naturally quite different, is less favorable for soft fruits.

Southern Ontario forms an agricultural region which, like the Corn Belt, is to a considerable degree self-contained in that its farmers' markets lie largely within it. Some 70 percent of the farm output is sold either in the peninsula, in the many thriving towns supported by its relatively intensive agriculture, or in the Montréal district. Compared with those parts of Canada whose agriculture is geared to the export trade, peninsular Ontario possesses an enviable freedom from marketing problems and a useful degree of economic balance in its activities.

THE EASTERN MARGINS

The eastern limit of the Corn Belt is generally taken to lie in western Ohio. South of Lake Erie there lies the dead-level plain now occupied by the Maumee River, but formerly part of the bed of a larger Great Lakes system. This plain is today splendidly farmed by a population predominantly German in origin, and it may be taken as a convenient terminal point. Eastward from here the land rises gradually to the plateaus of the Appalachians; rivers are deeply incised and the local relief becomes more pronounced. To the east, too, there lies the heavy industry region of Ohio and western Pennsylvania, whose urban markets exercise a powerful influence on farm production. This eastern margin of the Interior is therefore characterized, on the one hand, by a decrease in the amount of land in crops but, on the other, by a close adaptation to local market conditions.

The resulting pattern shows a marked similarity to that which has developed under comparable conditions on the Middle Atlantic coast, with dairying widespread over the uplands, and intensive concentrations of truck farming at strategic supply points near the cities. As in southern Ontario, the only significant variation of this pattern occurs along the shores of Lakes Ontario and Erie, where a fruit- and vegetable-farming area extends the full length of the lakeside, famous both for the orchards of the Finger Lakes in upper New York State and for the greenhouses around Cleveland.

Iron ore mine on the Mesabi Range, Minnesota. *(American Iron & Steel Institute)*

The Industrial Interior

The continental Interior contains a large proportion of all North America's industry. It is, in fact, precisely the combination of intensive agriculture and widespread industrialization that gives the region its character and that underlies its prosperity. The eastern half of the Interior is also the western half of what has become known as the Manufacturing Belt. Even beyond the limits of this Belt, although the industrial centers are more widely dispersed, the manufactures they support form no less vital a part of the midwestern economy.

It has already been suggested that if we wish we can visualize the agricultural pattern of the Interior as forming a kind of trend surface, domelike in shape, whose highest points (whether they are to be represented by indices of farm income or of input intensity) are to be found in the central Corn Belt. We can now attempt the same sort of characterization of the Industrial Interior. This time the type of surface is quite different. It consists of a fairly even gradient, trending downward from east to west; that is, from more industrialized to less industrialized areas. At a certain point going westward the trend surface reaches zero

level, but west of this point it has outliers—islands of industrial development detached from the main body. This industrial trend surface, or rather, the area which it covers, has been given the name of Manufacturing Belt. But what we must notice is that it was not created by a single movement. Certainly, it is largely the product of a single process, but that process has comprised a series of movements. The stability which the name Manufacturing Belt suggests is belied by its history. What has happened is that in North America industry, like population, has tended to move from east to west—but in several waves rather than a single motion. In other words our trend surface consists of a number of layers.

Why is this? Industry first developed on a large scale in New England and around the port cities of the East. From there it spread to the coal fields of Pennsylvania and Ohio. Subsequently, it developed in areas which were accessible to the movement of coal, either on the Atlantic seaboard or along the water routes of the Interior—the Ohio River and the Great Lakes shores. And then it kept on spreading, even though it was now moving further away from its coal supplies. It continued to spread in this way (1) because population—that is, markets—continued to build up in the West and Southwest; (2) because agricultural production ws increasing in the West and, eventually, diminishing in the East; and (3) because beyond a certain point in space and time—roughly speaking, the Mississippi River after the First World War—it was being attracted toward *new* energy sources which were in process of replacing coal—oil and natural gas in the Southwest.

This notion of a spread of manufacturing across the Interior enables us to make a first classification of American industries on the basis of their mobility. We can distinguish four classes:

1. Industries that have never moved from their original locations. For them there has been no "spread." Anchored perhaps by their dependence on skilled labor or by family control, they remain to this day in the East. An excellent example is provided by the manufacture of small arms. It has often been said that the West was won by the Colt revolver, but the Colt itself was manufactured not in the west but in New England, along with the famous Springfield rifle.

2. One industry, at least, moved partway and then stopped. This was the steel industry. As we have already seen in Chapter 7, the steelmakers' base in the great period of expansion and frontier advance after the Civil War was Pittsburgh. From there the industry spread, in the period 1880–1901, to the cities of the Great Lakes. But there it stopped, halted by the application of Pittsburgh Plus (see p. 135). Between 1901 (the founding date of United States Steel Corporation) and the Second World War there was almost no westward expansion for steel. The steelmakers' investment in their eastern mills was too large for them to abandon; instead, they chose to impose on the industry an artificial standstill. Only since 1941 has westward spread been resumed.

3. Some industries have moved west and are still moving. Among these, the clearest examples are to be found among the agriculture-based industries. When the Agricultural Interior was first opened up, the farmer's base, both for equipment supply and for processing of farm produce, was in the East. The long west-to-east haul for grain or livestock and the return flow of farm supplies were basic—and costly—elements in the North American economy. Over the years, however, this group of industries has followed the farmers westward, more than keeping pace with the agricultural frontier, and so meeting the flow of farm produce ever closer to its source. In the 1850s the meat-packing industry, for example, was centered in Cincinnati, a city to which it was drawn because of good communications, local salt supplies, and availability of banking and financing services.[15] In the Civil War years, however, Chicago (by then the focus of an increasing number of railway lines) replaced Cincinnati in importance. Then in the 1880s and more definitely after the First world War, Chicago began to lose ground relative to cities still further west, such as Omaha and Kansas City.[16] Finally, the years since 1950 have seen the growth of a truly western meat-packing industry in the vicinity of the western ranges themselves—for example, in Utah and the Colorado Piedmont.

4. Some industries in the Interior today have no previous history of location in the East, for the simple reason that they are late arrivals on the technical scene and first came into being in their present Interior location. The most obvious examples are in the petrochemical and pharmaceutical fields, but they also include branches of electrical engineering and electronics. Such industries are to be found in the Interior because of market opportunity or for ease of access to raw materials, or because they

[15]Cincinnati became known as "Porkopolis." About the year 1848 a traveler recorded his opinion that the city was "the most *hoggish* place in the whole world."

[16]It is perhaps possible to date the completion of this move westward from Chicago by the fact that on 22 June 1959, *Time* magazine reported that the last of the "Big Three meat-packers was closing down its Chicago operations and leaving the world's Ex-Hog Butcher" (the reference was to Carl Sandburg's powerful poem *Chicago*). The explanation of the move is to be found partly in improved transport and refrigeration, partly in changes in procedure by the packers, whose buyers now buy on the farm and not at the stockyard, and partly in improved western land use, which enables farmers to fatten and finish stock further west than formerly, often on beef feedlots.

were developed by and from the region's own resources, human and material.

If we wish we can express this pattern of manufacturing in another way. At any given point in the eastern Interior, an observer gifted with long life and infinite patience could have watched successive groups of industries spreading past him from east to west in the century between 1850 and 1950. First would come the supply and processing industries of the agricultural frontier: milling and meat-packing and the supply of farm tools and a few simple consumer goods to the frontier population. Then would come a second wave of more sophisticated manufactures, catering to the needs of a population now grown in numbers and more financially secure: these could only spread west as and when the market could sustain them. Next there would spread past our observer the capital-equipment industries, supplying the means of transport and the machinery needed by plants already established—machinery which in the past had been shipped into the region from the East. And finally the observer would note the growth, in situ, of a new brand of industry, one unrelated to the specific needs or resources of the region; a class of national producers who had simply selected the Interior as a favorable location from which to meet the sophisticated requirements of today's consumers for all kinds of aids to modern living.

Supposing that our observer had stationed himself at Chicago, he could have followed this sequence of events and their impact on the growth of the city's manufacturing. In the first two decades after Chicago was founded in 1833, it built mills and breweries and packed meat under contract to the U.S. Army. No major iron-using industry was yet present, nor did such industries develop until after 1870. But the period from 1850 to 1870 saw the emergence of the meat-packing industry as the giant of the city, with the Union Stockyards (opened in 1865) and the spread of refrigeration beginning to give shape to the industry. Second to meat-packing in this period was the production of men's clothing for the farmers along the frontier.

Between 1870 and 1900, Chicago passed through a period of industrial expansion and consolidation. Meat-packing, clothing, and furniture-making emerged as the "big three" in this period, the last of these a by-product of the Great Lakes lumber boom of the 1880s. By 1900 Chicago had become the world's largest producer of upholstered furniture. Only now did the city's industry acquire a basis of steelmaking: by the end of this period, iron and steel ranked fourth among Chicago's manufactures.

Between 1900 and the First World War, iron and steel moved into the lead, the new mills rising south of the city around Calumet and Gary. Clothing, although the second industry of Chicago, was declining and so, too, as we have already seen, was meat-packing. But the city was now building machinery and equipping a good share of the nation's railway system, and after 1914, it moved into the position of national manufacturing center which it has occupied ever since. In 1974 its leading industries, measured in terms of gross sales of manufactured goods, were (1) primary metals, (2) food products, (3) fabricated metal products, and (4) electrical machinery and equipment.

In the 1950s, with new industrial areas developing elsewhere in the continent, it seemed as if the Interior was reaching the industrial saturation point under the existing conditions. In these circumstances, the opening of the St. Lawrence Seaway played a vital role in altering the situation of the region; it provided just the stimulus necessary to trigger another phase of industrial development, by bringing the Great Lakes, their ports, and their factories into direct touch with the outside world. The Seaway also made it possible to replace the diminishing flow of high-grade iron ores from Lake Superior with ore from Labrador. Whatever the next phase in American industrial development may prove to be, the Interior enjoys the advantage of a strategic, central location within the United States, easy access to all other regions, and a huge home market in which to sell its products.

So diverse and so numerous are the industries of the Interior that it will perhaps be useful to attempt a rough classification into three groups. The first groups consists of industries associated directly with agriculture—milling, meat-packing, and the supply of farm equipment. The second group consists of various

Pittsburgh: A mill district in 1941. Note the "staircase"
street on the steep valley side, and the industrial smog in
the background, around the mills. *(Library of Congress)*

heavy industries, whose locations are related to mineral deposits. Pre-eminent among these is, of course, the iron and steel industry, but the group also includes manufactures of glass, brickware, and chemicals. The third and largest group is made up of an assortment of medium and light industries whose presence may be explained in several ways: (1) Some of them are steel-using industries (such as the automobile industry) located within reach of their materials. (2) Others represent an overspill from more crowded industrial areas further east—industries which have resettled in the less densely occupied western end of the Manufacturing Belt. (3) Almost all are industries for which the Belt is a highly important market, either in the sense that they are supply industries (the manufacture of machine tools is an example) or consumer-goods industries attracted by the dense concentration of population in the industrial areas.

In various parts of the region, one or another of these groups tends to predominate—the heavy industry group in eastern Ohio and western Pennsylvania, for example, and the agricultural industries group in the western half of the Interior. Thanks to their special advantages of position, the Great Lakes ports, particularly Chicago, characteristically possess industries representing all three groups. In the years since 1940, however, as the areas of intensive manufacturing have spread westward, it is the third group—of "assorted" industries—which has contributed most to the expansion.

THE HEAVY INDUSTRY AREA OF PENNSYLVANIA AND OHIO

The industrial area which extends along the valleys of the upper Ohio and its tributaries owes much of its growth to the existence of the Appalachian coal field, but something also to the personal influence of past generations of industrialists. It is to be found in an area ill suited to the purposes of heavy industry—in narrow, winding valleys that cut into the northern part of the Appalachian Plateaus. While the combination of horizontal coal seam and steep valley wall aids the miner, and the river system serves both for transport and for industrial water supply, these advantages are seriously offset by industrial congestion in the smoke-filled valleys, where there is neither room for expansion nor attraction, in an era of "clean" industry, for the notoriously mobile American worker to settle.

So great, however, was the initial advantage of proximity to the great Appalachian coal field that this area is not only one of the most important steel-producing regions in the world, but it is also the center of North America's manufacture of glass and clay products. Within the area are localities specializing in one or another of these types of industry: 35 percent of the industrial workers of Youngstown are engaged in primary metal production, and 38 percent of those in Akron produce rubber goods, while the valley of the Kanawha in West Virginia has been described as "the Ruhr of the United States chemical industry."

At the heart of this great industrial concentration stands the city of *Pittsburgh* (2,334,000). Half of Pittsburgh's industrial workers are engaged in primary metal production, while a further one-quarter produce machinery and steel goods of various kinds. As a steel city, its main natural advantage was that of location at the junction of the Allegheny and Monongahela rivers—at the hub of the upper Ohio routeways and close to the Appalachian coking coals. Yet it was not situation alone that made Pittsburgh what it is. To explain its ascendancy we must recall a historical coincidence: in the years after the Civil War of 1861–5 three things were happening simultaneously. The first was that the demand for steel, especially steel for railways, was rising as the West was opened to settlement. The second was that the Bessemer process for making steel was introduced, as a result of which steel could be produced both more cheaply and more quickly than ever before. The third element was the appearance in Pittsburgh of Andrew Carnegie, an industrial wizard who, by his bold application of the Bessemer process, and by his ability to appreciate the economic realities of steelmaking, came rapidly to dominate the industry. Securing an alliance with Henry Frick, whose comparable talents had given him control of the coke-making phase of the industry (then centered at Connellsville, 50 mi (80 km)

The Pittsburgh heavy industry region: Industrial plants and railway tracks fill the floor of the Monongahela Valley near East Pittsburgh, Pennsylvania.

southeast of Pittsburgh), Carnegie made Pittsburgh and steel into synonyms before selling out in 1901 to the newly formed United States Steel Corporation. Thus by the conjunction of location, timing, and personal initiative, Pittsburgh became the center of the steel industry, and its steel men imposed on the industry as a mark of their hegemony the "Pittsburgh Plus" arrangement that lasted until 1924 and itself assured the continuance of the regime.

Since the end of the Second World War, however, Pittsburgh has both changed in appearance and done its best to change its public image. The most striking evidence of these changes has been the transformation of the area within the junction of the Allegheny and Monongahela rivers (the point at which the original Fort Duquesne and the later Fort Pitt stood) from a slum to an open space fringed with impressive new structures, the whole

forming a "Golden Triangle." Several steel mills and railway yards close to the city center have been removed, leaving the principal steel mills of the present city upstream on the Monongahela. Pittsburgh is no less involved in steelmaking than formerly, but today the city is primarily interested in the control and administration of the industry rather than in the output of its products. The headquarters of United States Steel appropriately dominate the Golden Triangle, but there are a number of other major American companies who also make their headquarters here—firms like the Aluminum Company of America (ALCOA) and Heinz food products. After New York, Chicago, and perhaps Los Angeles, Pittsburgh is the most important corporate headquarters in the United States.

But changing the city's image has not been easy. The deeply entrenched valleys of the

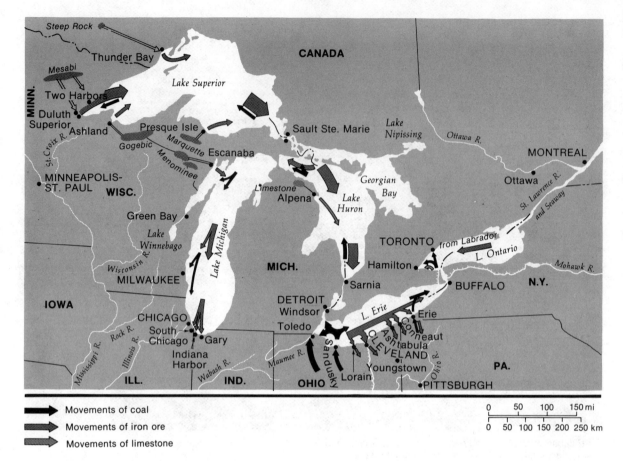

Movements of coal

Movements of iron ore

Movements of limestone

0   50   100   150 mi

0   50 100 150 200 250 km

Fig. 14-6. The Great Lakes: Cities and commerce. The arrows indicate lakeborne traffic in coal, iron ore, and limestone, and the thickness of the arrow is roughly proportional to the weight of each movement. In recent years the total amount of ore moving down the Lakes has been about twice as large as the reverse movement of coal. With the development of the Labrador ores, iron ore now moves up from Montréal as well as down from Duluth.

region and the steep slopes make urban development patchy and crosstown movement difficult. It has proved hard to attract new employment, and the population of the S.M.S.A. has been falling since 1960. What has been done to the Golden Triangle needs to be done to much of the remainder of the city, and the thirty-year campaign to reduce smoke and air pollution needs to be accompanied by an equally vigorous campaign to bring in new industries. But both these tasks are herculean in their extent. Pittsburgh was too successful for too long at making steel easily to switch over to other activities.

From Pittsburgh, the ribbons of industrial development stretch out along the valley floors of the Ohio system, south and east into the coal field and north and west toward other manufacturing centers. Youngstown (543,000) and Wheeling–Steubenville are the principal steel cities, while a number of smaller centers, such as East Liverpool, produce clayware or glassware, much of it for use in the industries of the area. Further south, in West Virginia, the output of the Kanawha Valley ranges from heavy chemicals, such as ammonia and caustic soda, to synthetics for the plastics and textile industries, and includes also steel alloys, glass, and synthetic rubber. To the northwest between Pittsburgh and Lake Erie are Akron and Canton with their satellites. Canton is a steel-goods city and Akron holds, with little fear of challenge, the title of "rubber capital of the world."

Like New England and like Old England, the industrial area of the upper Ohio is suffering today the disadvantages of its early pre-eminence. Inevitably its relative importance waned, with the change to newer sources of

252

power; with the lack of space for expansion; with the competition of new and more efficient producers further west who have profited by its experience; with the abolition of "Pittsburgh Plus." Changes in industrial techniques have killed some of its activities, such as the coke-making at Connellsville, and structural unemployment is a recurrent problem. But in spite of these difficulties, it remains the greatest industrial concentration of the continent. The attachment of its industries to coal and clay, the wealth of labor skill at its command, and the enormous investment that has gone into its heavy industries are all factors which are resistant to change and which should assure the area of a continuing importance.

THE CITIES OF THE GREAT LAKES

The six great cities that lie on the shore of the Great Lakes—Chicago, Milwaukee, Detroit, Cleveland, Buffalo, and Toronto—are the home of some eight percent of the population of Anglo-America. They are both ports and transport centers, both industrial cities and commercial headquarters. Their size and activities derive in part from their position along the route by which Appalachian coal and Lake Superior or Labrador ore move to meet each other, and in part from their relationship to their hinterlands, which stretch far into the

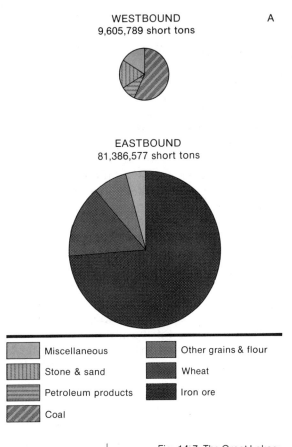

WESTBOUND   A
9,605,789 short tons

EASTBOUND
81,386,577 short tons

Miscellaneous   Other grains & flour

Stone & sand   Wheat

Petroleum products   Iron ore

Coal

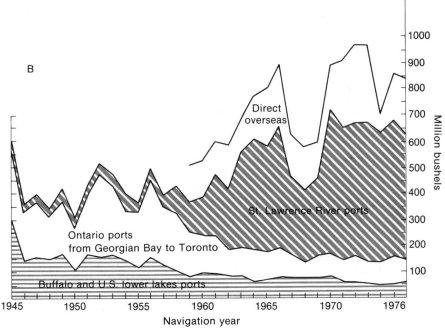

B

Fig. 14-7. The Great Lakes: Aspects of freight traffic. (above) Traffic eastbound and westbound through the Soo Canals, United States and Canadian sides, in 1976. (left) Grain receipts, 1945–76, at selected groups of ports. Before the opening of the St. Lawrence Seaway, most grain from the upper Lakes was trans-shipped at ports on Lake Huron or Lake Erie and travelled onward overland. The effect on this grain traffic of the opening of the Seaway is clearly seen in the diagram.

Agricultural Interior. With the opening of the St. Lawrence Seaway, they have added to their other functions that of being ocean ports and can now capture, for part of the year at least, some of the foreign trade formerly funnelled through Montréal, New York, or Baltimore.

To these six metropolitan centers must be added a number of smaller cities—Erie and Toledo, Hamilton and Windsor—whose functions are more limited; they are port and manufacturing cities along the coal and iron route. Their existence and their growth underline the fundamental importance to the regional economy of this movement of ore and coal, which totals over 100 million tons annually and makes up a large proportion of the Lakes' cargoes.

For more than a hundred years, this tremendous flow of raw materials has moved between the ports of Lakes Superior and Michigan, where the iron ore is loaded, and cities further south. From the Upper Lakes the flow of iron ore divides roughly into three—to the Chicago area, to the ports of Lake Erie, and through these ports to the Pittsburgh area. It has been matched by a return flow of coal which, however, is considerably smaller in quantity (see Fig. 14-6).

Since 1960 this simple two-way movement has been complicated by the fact that the Superior ores are running out, and that Labrador iron ore is in part replacing them. This ore, of course, travels *westward* across the Lakes, using the Seaway, and arrives at Hamilton or Cleveland in the same way as Superior ore. (The Pittsburgh area, however, is supplied in part by ore moving from Labrador via the Atlantic coast ports.) On the Lake Erie shore the principal receiving ports are Cleveland, Conneaut, Erie, and Ashtabula. The return flow of coal, however, shows a different pattern; the greater part of it (some 15 million tons) passes throuh Toledo and a smaller amount (5 million tons) through Sandusky.

What has happened is that as the center of Appalachian coal production has shifted southwestward into West Virginia and Kentucky, so the shipping route has increasingly favored the western Lake Erie ports over those further east in the Cleveland area. The result is that this whole line of ports suffers from a one-way traffic system, with receipts exceeding shipments by twenty to one at Cleveland, and an opposite unbalance in the ratio of three to one at Toledo in 1974.

Before we consider each of these cities of the Great Lakes in turn, it is of interest to notice that they have a number of features in common. That this should be true is not surprising when we recall that they share a common situation on a lakeshore and a common history as well—brief as urban histories go but representing a shared response to the technical stimuli and transport needs of their era.

The series of maps and explanatory comments which make up Figure 14-8 deal in simplified form with this common history. It is a history which had its effective beginnings in 1825, when the opening of the Erie Canal from the Hudson River brought the first major flow of traffic to the Great Lakes. Pre-existing settlements—forts and mission posts—or simple creek mouths became the sites of cities: portages and canals linked these anchorages with other river systems. In the following decades, while each of these cities felt the effect of local conditions upon its growth as an individual, all of them shared the stimulus of major developments: the opening of the Soo Canal in 1855; the spread of the steel industry between 1880 and 1900; the exploitation of the Mesabi ores after 1890; the opening of the enlarged Welland Canal in 1931; the changes brought about by the St. Lawrence Seaway after 1959. In view of their situation, the most formative events in the lives of these cities were those that brought changes in the sphere of transport, by water or by rail. All of them had to provide space for port installations, railway yards, and stockpiles (where the winter's supply of ore or coal could be dumped). All of them were involved in bulk traffic. All of them provided the necessary space, in part, by reclamation along the lakeshore, and each of them at some time in its history has found itself cut off from the lake by the spread of industry or the sprawl of railway lines; so that it has had to fight, consciously and not always successfully, to establish the principle of the lake as amenity and not merely as lifeline. These cities

254

Fig. 14-8. CLE-RON-KEE-O, the model of a Great Lakes city. Its story in maps:

1. *1815–40.* The natural setting: a marsh-fronted lakeshore at the mouth of a creek entrenched in old beach ridges. Anchorage at creek mouth; fort, trading post, and bridge.
2. *1840–55.* A canal parallels the river, replacing the old portage route over the watershed. Earliest railroad follows the lakeshore, with yards on reclaimed shore fill and drawbridge over river mouth, which is progressively widened for larger vessels. Fort disused; may be resurrected in tourist-orientated twentieth century.
3. *1855–80.* Railroad development; more yards and connections inland. Soo Canal (opened 1855) is one cause of increasing lake traffic which, with the trend to larger vessels, leads to construction of the first harbor works. Industry along the riverside and in the valley bottom. Commercial area growing toward the railroad station.
4. *1880–1900.* Steel industry arrives, with consequent increase in bulk cargoes handled and enlargement of the harbor. Ore stockpile is needed during winter closure of the Lakes. Grain traffic from lakehead is also increasing; elevators and flour mills at trans-shipment point. The growing city now effectively cut off from the lakefront by railroad or industrial belt. Large vessels impeded upriver by low-level bridges; the city constructs the first viaducts over the valley. Canal falls into disuse.

5. *1900–40.* New traffic in petroleum products catered for by harbor extension. Reclamation beyond railroad belt for parks or further industrial sites. The C.B.D. prevented from achieving necessary enlargement by the barriers of river bluffs, railroad belt, and industrial areas. Old low-level bridges are removed to give shipping access to docks upriver; increasing road traffic requires new viaducts. Important decisions about future amenity are called for but are shelved on account of the Depression of the 1930s. Several fine new public buildings date from the New Deal's public works program, but no geographical changes in the layout of the city.
6. *1950–present.* Declining importance of railroads leads to the elimination of many tracks in valuable central areas, while yards are re-sited outside the city. Dwindling passenger traffic leads to closure of the main railroad station; the site is redeveloped. Main railroad route now bypasses the city center, and suppression of several tracks makes possible a long-overdue expansion of the C.B.D. The city regains its lakeshore after being cut off from it for a century. But plans for replacing an old railroad by a new freeway lead to fears of a new barrier between city and lake: heated debate in the city council. More infill of the lakeshore, earmarked for recreational space, marina, etc.; no more industry to be permitted here. But pollution reduces the attractiveness of the lake for recreation. Opening of the St. Lawrence Seaway (1959) gives the city a new role as a foreign trade port.

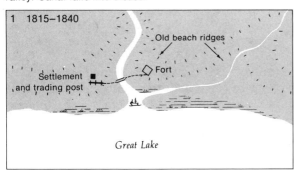

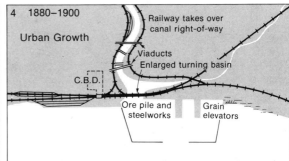

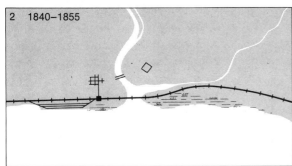

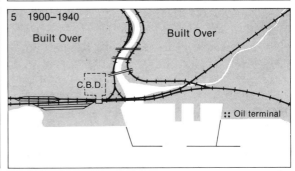

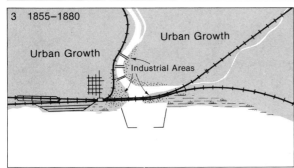

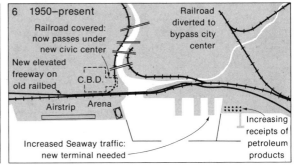

arose in an era of railway expansion, steelmaking, and industrial laissez-faire; an era when it must have appeared self-evident that the industries and transport lines serving them were the most important features in the life of the city and therefore entitled to priority in the competition for space. They have now to adjust to life in an era of road building, smoke abatement, pollution controls, and urban planning. It is these changes and the problems they raise that are sketched in Figure 14-8.

Most easterly of the Great Lakes cities is *Toronto* (2,803,101), the metropolis of the Ontario Peninsula and the great rival of Québec's Montréal. Lacking the advantages of a strategic location like that of Montréal or Chicago, Toronto nevertheless fulfils something of the role of both. It is Canada's leading manufacturing center and the commercial hub of that part of the Interior that lies within Canada. In spite of an absence of industrial raw materials, its manufacturing—both that based on agriculture and that in the category of assorted light industries—is highly diverse; if we include the towns of its immediate hinterland such as Oshawa and Oakville, where General Motors and Ford have plants, the range is wider still. Industrial employment in Toronto is over 300,000; the province of Ontario, of which Toronto is the hub, has almost exactly one-half of the manufacturing employment in Canada and more than one-half of the value added by manufacture. Commercially, the importance of its banks and insurance companies is felt not only in Ontario but throughout the nation: it handles more than 40 percent of the country's bank credits. In particular it is the financial base of the northern mining industry, the prime force in the present economic development of the Canadian Northlands. As a port, it has experienced a rapid expansion since the Seaway was opened: in terms of foreign trade tonnage it now ranks with Québec.

In the great postwar immigration into Canada, Toronto has been the primary goal of the new arrivals. Rather like New York in the period before 1914, it is a gateway city; it is filled with groups of diverse national backgrounds, many of whom are in transit, in the sense that they will move on in due course to other cities

further into the Interior. Meanwhile, however, they give the city (which outsiders used to consider very British and a little dull) a much more vivacious and cosmopolitan atmosphere not, perhaps, wholly approved of by the older core of English, Scots, and Irish residents.[17]

Forty miles west of Toronto is *Hamilton* (529,000), Canadian counterpart of the United States steel cities on the Lake Erie and Lake Michigan shores. It is a matter for conjecture whether Hamilton, which grew by drawing both ore and fuel from United States sources, would ever have developed as it has were it not for the presence of the international boundary. But this question becomes almost monotonous when we are considering Canadian industrial development; Hamilton exists and flourishes, and the new conjunction of circumstances that brings ore from Labrador through the St. Lawrence Seaway increases Hamilton's advantages without disturbing its strong position in the large, protected Ontario market.

The western end of Lake Ontario is in any case one of the most favored locations in North America for industrial development. Traffic through the Great Lakes converges upon the Niagara River and its bypass, the Welland Canal. Eastward runs the route via the Mohawk valley to the Hudson and New York; the Erie Canal, which made the valley route famous, is now replaced in importance by multiple railway lines and a freeway. The northern end of the Appalachian coal field lies less than 100 mi (160 km) to the south, and in the heart of the region is to be found its prime resource, the power of the Niagara Falls, exploited jointly by Canada and the United States. It comes as no surprise, therefore, to find that on the Canadian side of the Niagara frontier there has developed an urban-industrial shoreline zone which must soon be continuous all the way from Niagara to the eastern side of Toronto. Besides Toronto and Hamilton, the zone contains such other cities as St. Catherines and Oshawa.

On the United States side of the frontier, this strategically located industrial area is

---

[17]In round figures the "old core" contains some 1.1 million inhabitants; there are also 300,000 Italians, 250,000 East Europeans, and 100,000 Germans.

dominated by *Buffalo* (1,331,000). Goods brought east by the water route through the lakes are transferred there to the land routes which lead to the Atlantic coast, and at the point of transfer there have sprung up a wide variety of industries. Lying as it does on the iron ore route, Buffalo is a steel and machinery city, but its outstanding industrial feature is that it is the continent's largest flour-milling center. An arrangement which equalizes the railway freight rates on grain and on flour makes it equally suitable to mill the grain anywhere between the farmer and the baker, and thanks to its location Buffalo has established a dominant position in the industry. However, the opening of the Seaway was a threat to Buffalo perhaps more than to any other city, for the grain it milled formerly left the water route at this point and travelled by rail to the Atlantic coast. Now it must be reloaded into ships that are going on past Montréal to the sea, and the unique advantage of its position has been lost.

The power potential of the Niagara Falls has given Buffalo's manufacturing another facet. It has attracted to the banks of the Niagara River many industries that require access to large supplies of power—such as chemical manufacture and aluminum. Like the Kanawha in West Virginia and the St. Clair between Lake Huron and Windsor, the short Niagara River flows through a veritable "Chemical Valley."

The principal business of the ports situated along the southern shore of Lake Erie is, as we have already seen, the handling of iron ore and coal moving to and from Pittsburgh and West Virginia, and their manufactures are related to this advantageous position astride the industrial artery. In detail the sites of these ports have been decided by harbor possibilities and by the existence of valley routes connecting with the interior. It was this route factor—the linking of the Cuyahoga River to the Muskingum and thus to the Ohio by a canal in 1834—that gave *Cleveland* the initial advantage which has enabled it to become the great city of the Erie shore.

The natural advantage, however, was short-lived. The mouth of the Cuyahoga is narrow and winding, the harbor works were for long neglected, and, as the Great Lakes freighters grew larger, the problem of entering the port became more serious (and more expensive) and business was lost to neighboring ports. To some extent, therefore, the development of Lorain and of Conneaut may be regarded as an overflow from Cleveland made necessary by the limitations of the latter's site. In the meantime, however, Cleveland, now a city of 1.98 million inhabitants, has developed a list of industries which is long even by the standards of a Great Lakes city, ranging from steel to paints and from motor vehicle assembly to men's wear. Its record in manufacturing indeed does credit to the home base of the late John D. Rockefeller, who set out from Cleveland to capture North America's oil industry in the 1860s and who made the city for a short period the refining center of the continent. 12 percent of the industrial labor force are engaged in making automobiles, 8 percent in iron and steel manufacture, and 28 percent make various other types of machinery.

No city on the Erie shore, however, can compare in location with *Detroit* and *Windsor*, at the western entrance to the lake. Here, where the Detroit River forms a passage half a mile wide between Lake St. Clair and Lake Erie, is an unrivalled position from which to tap the flow of lake traffic. Yet Detroit took only a small share in the traffic of the Great Lakes, and made little attempt to develop its port (perhaps because of the narrowness of the passage at this point on the Detroit River). It required other influences to set it on its way to becoming the great city of 4.4 million inhabitants which it is today—the genius of Henry Ford and the growth of a nationwide road network.

Detroit is the fifth largest industrial city in the United States, after New York, Chicago, Los Angeles, and Philadelphia. Like other southern Michigan cities within its orbit—Flint, Lansing, and Pontiac—it depends very heavily on the motor vehicle industry, which is spread all over this region as far west as Kalamazoo and which gives direct employment to a third of Detroit's industrial workers. This is a high percentage for so large a city (although it does not compare with smaller

Cleveland: Collision Bend. The lower section of the Cuyahoga River winds sharply, and with the growth in size of
vessels serving the steel mills and factories upstream, navigation has become increasingly difficult. In spite of action
being taken to cut away the inside of the bend, this particular corner has proved a serious hazard. The photograph is
taken from the Terminal Tower; that is, virtually from the
center of the city. (John H. Paterson)

cities like Flint, where the proportion is 80
percent), and it is a very serious problem to
Detroit: it limits the number of different kinds
of work available and so the types of workers
who are needed. The city itself has been carrying out a huge and very necessary program of
urban clearance and renewal, but in spite of
this it is a place that other manufacturers have
tended to avoid. With its fortunes so dependent on the sale of automobiles, it is essential
that Detroit and its satellites should create and
be able to show clear locational attractions to
other types of industry in the future.

There remains for consideration the greatest
of all the urban areas of the Great Lakes Region: that which sprawls around the southern
shores of Lake Michigan and contains the
cities of Chicago and Milwaukee. From Gary
in Indiana to the northern edge of Milwaukee
is over 130 mi (210 km), and, although the

built-up area is not continuous for the whole
of this distance, the traveller along the lakefront might certainly be forgiven by anyone
but an enthusiastic Chamber of Commerce for
thinking that Milwaukee is merely one more
northern suburb of Chicago, instead of a city
of 1.4 million inhabitants lying 88 mi (140 km)
from the center of Chicago.

Milwaukee possesses that mixture of heavy
and light industry we have seen to be characteristic of the Great Lakes port cities, and in addition is one of North America's leading brewing
centers, a fact connected with the presence of a
large German element in its population. It
manufactures a range of vehicles and engines,
while nearby Kenosha is the headquarters of
one of the few automobile firms not located in
Michigan. With a first-class harbor and a hinterland that includes the most prosperous sections of the central Dairy Belt, Milwaukee has a

soundly based economy and loses nothing by comparison with Chicago, even if it is overshadowed by its great neighbor.

CHICAGO

Simply to list Chicago among the cities of the Great Lakes would be as misleading as to treat it among the cities of the Interior, for it belongs to both and yet transcends both. It lies on the Great Lakes waterway, but is also the focus of the rail routes of the continent. It functions not only as the "big city" of the Corn Belt, but also as the capital of the Midwest and the headquarters of Interior agriculture, while for many enterprises whose business is nationwide it provides a more central location for a base than does New York.

It is easy now, with the wisdom of hindsight, to point out how the southward projection of Lake Michigan and the low watershed between the Great Lakes and the Mississippi system gave an inevitable importance to the settlement at the lake head. But early visitors to Chicago were unanimous in condemning the site as unfit for habitation, and few cities have had to overcome more natural handicaps in their expansion. The city's importance grew, in fact, by stages. First it was the head of navigation for the Great Lakes emigration route to the West. In 1848 the Illinois and Michigan Canal was cut to link Lake Michigan with the Mississippi. Then in 1852 Chicago was linked by railway with New York. The coming of the railway marked its real beginnings, and when during the Civil War the choice of an eastern terminus for the new transcontinental line went to Chicago by default of its southern competitors, its future was assured. In the 1870s it was the development of the stockyards and of the clothing and furniture industries that marked its growth; in the first decade of the twentieth century it was the rise of the steel industry on the southern lakeshore. Today the metropolitan area has 7.0 million inhabitants, and is the second largest manufacturing center in North America. In terms of area, it is one of the largest urban concentrations in the world, with miles of sub-

urbs spreading unchecked over the featureless Illinois plains. By contrast, its central business district is now far too small for it, jammed between the Chicago River, the lake, and the largely disused remains of half the railway systems of the United States (see Fig. 14-9).

Chicago's heavy industry and oil refineries are concentrated close to the lakeshore on the south side of the city, where the steel town of Gary was created by United States Steel Corporation and named after its first president. The Union Stockyards also used to be on the south side, 5 mi (8 km) from the city center, and formerly the meat-packing plants were grouped about them. For the rest, industries tend to cluster along the railways radiating from the city, and especially along the "belt" (or ring) lines, which play a part of particular importance in a city where so many separate railway companies operate. This pattern calls attention to a general tendency for industry to move out from the overcrowded central districts (where the older industries, such as clothing manufacture, were situated) to the suburbs, leaving the central area—Chicago's famous "Loop"—to be cleared for much-needed road improvements or occupied by commerce. Several planned and fully equipped industrial estates have been created, such as the Clearing and Central districts, and northern and western suburbs 10 to 15 mi (16–24 km) from the city center have become industrialized.

In terms of employment, Chicago's largest industries are primary steel production and the manufacture of machinery, particularly electrical communications equipment. The city's older industries—the manufacture of clothing and furniture—still remain, although greatly reduced in their relative importance within the city. Altogether, nearly 900,000 (or 30 percent) of the city's gainfully employed workers are engaged in industry. That the absolute figure is so large is a reminder of the prominence of Chicago as a manufacturing center. That the percentage figure is no larger is equally a reminder of the importance of the city's other functions in the fields of commerce and of transport.

Chicago, like New York, suffers from an unusual number of obstacles to movement of

259

Chicago: The Loop. In the center, the tallest building is the Sears Tower, while at the left rear the tapering building is the John Hancock. At the right rear is Navy Pier and the mouth of the Chicago River. The view is looking northeast.

In the right foreground, the Eisenhower Expressway cuts through the middle of the Post Office building and crosses the South Branch of the Chicago River. *(Chicago Assoc. of Commerce and Industry)*

traffic; ironically enough, this results from its importance as a traffic center. On the flat lakeshore almost all the railways ran at ground level and crossed each other and the city streets by means of level crossings. Of the few railways which do not, the main one is the loop of elevated electric railway which gives the central business district its name. This, by contrast, runs above the street, 20 ft (6.1 m) up on steel trestles, and the streets beneath are dark, obstructed, and clangorous. Even worse, through the heart of the city runs the canalized Chicago River, traversed by a series of drawbridges. Each time these are opened—and fortunately for the motorists this is not often, since a canal cutoff has been built to enter Lake Michigan south of the city—the traffic of the business district comes to a stop. Immense sums have

been spent to solve these problems by bridging and tunnelling, for Chicago is above all a vigorous city. There has been a considerable development of the central business district north of the river, across from the Loop, with its axis along Michigan Avenue. A few blocks west of this axis is a second, along Wells Street—this time an axis of *re*development, where aging properties have been renovated and turned into Chicago's closest equivalent to Greenwich Village in New York.

But the main opportunity for the city in the 1980s is now emerging on the *south* side of the Loop. Here, as Figure 14-9 indicates, the business district was confined by a broad belt of railroad tracks and yards, feeding into no less than five terminal stations. But with the disappearance of so many passenger trains, these

260

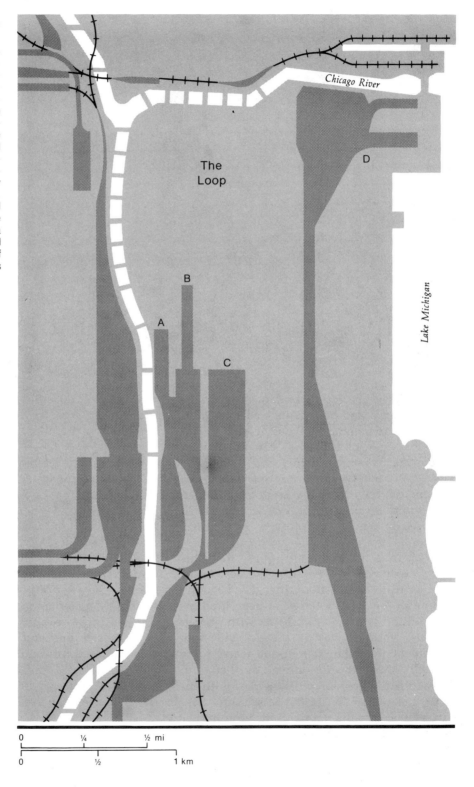

Fig. 14-9. Chicago: The city center at the peak of the railroad era, in the late 1920s. The map indicates the extent to which the railroads formed a noose around the center of Chicago, hampering expansion and distorting urban growth patterns. Nevertheless, at this period, the importance of the railroad was such that the arrangement appears unreasonable only in retrospect. By 1977, the areas marked A, C and D had been cleared of tracks, while at B the entry into once-proud La Salle Street Station had been reduced to a pair of tracks. The same area is pictured on p. 262.

The Loop

Chicago River

Lake Michigan

D

B

A

C

0   ¼   ½ mi

0   ½   1 km

Chicago: Changing land use. A view of the Loop from the south, showing the area covered by Figure 14-6, which was formerly filled with railroad tracks. By 1977, only vestiges of the tracks remained: the area was ripe for redevelopment. The Sears Tower is in the center. *(John H. Paterson)*

facilities have become redundant. Two of the terminals are dead and gone, and a third is dying. The remaining two, on the eastern and western edges of the area, can adequately handle the remaining traffic, and so there is left a vast, empty space for redevelopment, and one can only hope that so outstanding an opportunity for planned growth will be seized and used in a manner worthy of its size and position.

For there is no reason to suppose that Chicago's expansion is at an end. The new factor here, as in all the lakeshore cities, has been the coming of the Seaway, offering new opportunities in the form of a direct link with foreign markets, which should be cheaper and more convenient than the old rail-and-water route through New York or Montréal. Furthermore, Chicago is the only Great Lakes port with direct water connection to the Mississippi System, so that it is the natural transfer point between the ocean traffic using the Seaway and the waterborne commerce of the whole western interior. To serve this purpose it has enlarged its port by dredging and filling around Lake Calumet and the canal entrance that leads to the Mississippi. In 1974 the port of Chicago

handled over 20 million tons of cargoes, with additional large amounts passing through neighboring harbors like Gary and Indiana Harbor.

While this development has been occurring in the sphere of water transport, Chicago has also become the busiest air traffic center in North America. Whereas at New York, air movements are handled by three airports, the bulk of those at Chicago take place through a single field—O'Hare, on the northwestern outskirts of the city. The problem of congestion has become a serious one for, as in the heyday of railway construction, Chicago's central position within the continent and its densely populated hinterland make it the obvious meeting point for routes, both internal and international, and the buildup of traffic has reached a point where drastic measures may shortly become necessary.

Cities and Settlements of the Interior

Away from the lakeshores and across the Interior are to be found hundreds of cities and lesser centers whose similarity of appearance, regularity of spacing, and graduations of size are so striking as positively to invite the geographer to seek a general model of urban growth within the region. In studying agricultural regions and their servicing, the two basic models with which geographers have worked are Von Thünen's for land use and that of Christaller, as modified by Lösch, for service centers.[18] The first of these embodies the concept of rings of diminishing land-use intensity concentric around a central market, and the second visualizes a hierarchy of centers with overlapping hinterlands, within which various grades of service are offered.

In studying the agricultural pattern of the Interior, we have already considered something that bears a certain resemblance to the Von Thünen rings—a central zone of high intensity agriculture surrounded by areas where intensity falls away from the center. We even have near, if not at, the middle point of the central zone a great urban market—Chicago. And we can now go on to recognize that in the settlement pattern of the Interior we have a very fair approximation to the Christaller model.

The problem with most of the geographer's models is that they involve three assumptions: physical uniformity of the surface, initially uniform distribution of population, and freedom from distortion by external forces. Nowhere in the real world, of course, do these conditions obtain. But in the North American Interior and especially in the *western* Interior, they come much closer to fulfilment than they do in most other regions.

The condition of physical uniformity approaches fulfilment in the circumstance that in the Interior there are few barriers to movement, few wide variations in agricultural po-

Business Centers
First Rank ●   Fourth Rank •
Second Rank ●   Fifth Rank ·
Third Rank ●

Fig. 14-10. Business centers of the Middle West. The classification shown here, from the *National Atlas of the U.S.*, is not identical with that used in this chapter; this is because different criteria are employed. In the atlas, the criteria are precise and consist of such indices as volume of retail sales and newspaper coverage. In this chapter the criteria are broader and in part subjective, but in both cases the idea of a hierarchy of centers is strongly developed, even if precise rankings are open to discussion.

[18]The basic references translated into English are P. Hall, ed., *Von Thünen's Isolated State*, Pergamon Press, Oxford, 1966 (originally published in part in German, Hamburg, 1826); W. Christaller, *Central Places in Southern Germany*, trans. C.W. Baskin, Prentice-Hall, Englewood Cliffs, New Jersey, 1966 (originally published in German, 1933), and A. Lösch, *The Economics of Location*, Yale University Press, New Haven, Conn., 1954. There is, however, little point in the general reader going back to these original studies: they are summarized and discussed in most of the numerous books on spatial analysis and spatial model building now available.

tential, and few obstacles to maximum utilization of the surface. Such variations as exist are, on the whole, regular around the central core, and physical potential for urban growth is everywhere virtually unrestricted.

The condition of an evenly dispersed population in the initial situation was secured to a remarkable degree by the method of survey and settlement adopted across the Interior—by the uniform application of the rectangular survey grid and the land laws based on sections and quarter-sections (see p. 109). More regularly, perhaps, than anywhere else on earth the landscape of settlement in the Midwest was laid out by law—the farm roads repeating themselves at every mile, north and south, east and west, delimiting the sections, and the farmhouses lying beside the roads,

263

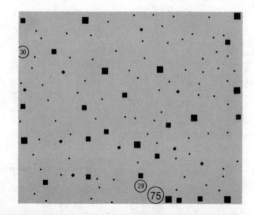

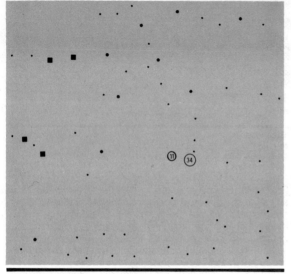

- Named hamlets under 500
- Village 500–1,000
- 1,000–2,000
- 2,000–10,000
- ㉑ Town over 10,000
  (1970 population in thousands)

```
0      10      20 mi
├───┬───┬───┬───┤
0   10  20   30 km
```

Fig. 14-11. Settlement hierarchy of the Interior: The lower ranks. Two areas are shown, on maps drawn to the same scale. One is in north-central Iowa and the other in central North Dakota. In the Corn Belt landscape of Iowa, villages and hamlets are frequent and numerous larger service centers supply the needs of a dense farming population. In the wheat country of North Dakota, the same type of functions are supplied to the much sparser farm population by smaller and fewer centers, and the villages are strung out in lines along the railroads or in the river valleys. See also Figure 14-12.

four to a section, from one horizon to the other. This regular pattern of settlement was imposed on a region with no relics from previous technologies and no remnant cultural landscapes to adapt or overlay; the region was settled, moreover, in a few short decades between 1800 and 1850; that is, in a single technological era and by two generations of settlers at most. For all these reasons the Interior provided by the end of the settlement period a pattern of uniform occupance such as could hardly be matched anywhere else in the world.

The third assumption of the model—freedom from distortion by external factors—was certainly not fulfilled in the eastern Interior, where industry became widespread, but it comes close to fulfilment in the virtually unindustrialized western part of the region. There the relationship between the service center and its consumers of services is very simple: the consumers are farmers, and no other major activity breaks the pattern; neither are there any large metropolitan areas to generate such activities. Under all these circumstances, we may well expect to find a pattern of service centers developing in a hierarchy of sizes and very close to that defined by the model.

That a hierarchy of settlements exists is empirically obvious. At the top in splended isolation is Chicago: below it are the regional metropolitan poles and below them the regional supply centers; seven or eight ranks in all, reaching down to the hamlet or the corner store. In a few areas, even the spacing of these service centers approaches the model distribution. That it generally does *not* can be explained by two or three factors. One is that it is distorted by the drainage pattern. On the largely featureless surface of the Interior and during the particular era of settlement, the only major site-factor likely to confer a decisive locational advantage on any of the hundreds of towns founded, in that optimistic age, to be the capital of the New West, was a riverbank situation in a region where the rivers formed the main lines of communication. It is no coincidence at all that every one of the Interior's cities of the second rank (which we shall later identify) began its career as a river port or portage point.

264

The second reason for distortion was that settlements in America were often founded under highly *competitive* conditions, their location in many cases based not on economic considerations but on political or even personal choice. These settlements fought each other, sometimes literally, for survival; they bribed railway surveyors and indulged in land frauds to enlarge themselves and weaken their rivals. What we have on the map, therefore, is far from being simply the product of economic principles such as least-cost location.

The third distorting factor was the tendency, over so large an area, for settlements to develop in lines along the transport routes instead of in an even distribution over the area they were servicing (see Fig. 14-11). The importance of the river and railway was so great that it easily overrode the diseconomy of a service point located on the periphery of its hinterland rather than in the center.

The place of a settlement in the hierarchy depends on its functions rather than its population. On the whole, within each rank of settlements in the Interior, the more easterly members have larger populations than those further west; that is, service functions performed in Illinois by a city of 20,000 to 30,000 may be handled by one of only 15,000 in the eastern Dakotas, or local, everyday services may be provided distributed in the west than in the east of the Interior. This brings us to the important question of how far apart we might expect service centers of a particular rank to be; what in fact are the *dimensions* of the Christaller model?

The answer is found to involve sequences of explanation that spread out from urban spacing to touch causes that are physical and legal as well as economic; they derive from land-disposal policy as well as farming system, and from original perceptions of the environment as well as contemporary transport facilities. In order to save extended discussion in the present chapter, some of the factors involved in the answer are presented in the form of a diagram (see Fig. 14-12). It must be stressed that the model applies only to a wholly agricultural region such as the western Interior where, as we have seen, there is little to complicate the basic rela-

tionship between service and those served. But the number of viable service centers must fundamentally be a function of the aggregate demand for services per unit of area, and the diagram, if read from the center outward, suggests the very large number of ingredients which go into the making of that demand.

We can now move on to discuss some of the members of the urban hierarchy in more detail. The cities of the second rank each dominate a portion of the Interior, and their poplations range in most cases from a million upward. All of them, as we have noted already, began life as river ports and it was probably their strategic location on the river system which enabled them to outgrow their lesser rivals. Into this category fall St. Louis (2,371,000), Cincinnati (1,376,000), Kansas City (1,302,000), Minneapolis-St. Paul (2,011,000), and Louisville (893,000) in the United States, while in Canada it can be argued that Winnipeg fulfils the same role and possesses a similar history.

It was the importance of the Ohio-Mississippi route as the main road to the near west which led to the settlement and early growth of Cincinnati, Louisville, and St. Louis. The falls in the Ohio River at Louisville interrupted river transport; the position of St. Louis at the junction of the Mississippi and Missouri made it the natural fitting-out point for movement westward along the Missouri; and subsequently Kansas City and Independence derived a similar advantage from their situation at the places where the overland trails left the hazardous water route and struck west for Santa Fe and Oregon. Further north the Falls of St. Anthony marked the head of Mississippi navigation and provided a focus for the growth of Minneapolis. Later came the railways to lend momentum to the rise of these cities as the natural foci of the routes of the Interior.

Cincinnati has greatly altered since its "Porkopolis" days, when it was a meat-packing and flour-milling town and one of North America's principal ports. The agricultural industries, as we have seen, moved west, but the city's proximity to the heavy industry areas of the Appalachian coal field provided the basis for a new industrial career, and today Cincinnati has a

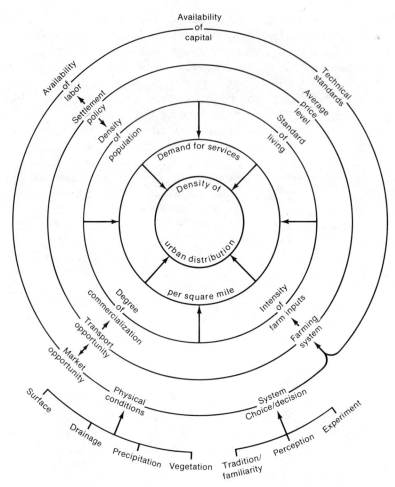

Fig. 14-12. Service centers of the Interior: Their variable spacing. Service centers are unevenly distributed over the Interior (see also Fig. 14-11). Why? A great many factors must go into the answer, and this diagram suggests what some of them are; the reader may wish to add others. The diagram should be read from the center circle outward.

well-balanced industrial structure and a world-wide reputation for its machine tools, which find a wide market in the adjacent Manufacturing Belt. *Louisville*, on the other hand, has retained the two industries for which it has long been known—tobacco processing and furniture making—as well as acquiring new industry in the form of electrical appliance manufacture, a very necessary addition since tobacco manufacturing has show little growth in recent years in the United States.

The modern city of *St. Louis* is Chicago's only close rival for the position of economic focus of the United States Interior. It is a much older settlement—it was founded by the French as a fur trading post nearly a century before Chicago was incorporated—and with its commanding position on the river system it seemed destined to be the focus of the Interior. But its commitment to the river and its traffic,

and so to the South, told against it when the railroads reached the Mississippi (see p. 149). The railroads focussed on Chicago as the riverboats had converged on St. Louis, and the railroads survived while the riverboats did not. St. Louis was left with a decaying waterfront and nothing to use it for. Only in the 1960s was a program of urban renewal started, which swept away the old commerical focus of the port and replaced it by a belt of parkland.

St. Louis is, nevertheless, a great transport center and industrial city. Much of the manufacturing is carried on in East St. Louis, on the Illinois bank of the Mississippi, or in the lower Missouri Valley, where it winds through the northern edge of the city. It builds aircraft and automobiles, brews beer, and makes clothing and hardware. It is the market headquarters for much of the produce of the southern Interior. The combination of excellent transport facilities and numerous local manufactures has given the city an important trade area that stretches not only across the southern Interior but well into the middle South.

It is interesting to notice that this group of "second-rank" cities all lie near the periphery of the Interior, adding to their functions *within* the region important connections with areas outside it. Of none of them is this more true than of the two western Interior metropolitan areas of Minneapolis-St. Paul and Kansas City. On any showing—newspaper coverage, agricultural marketing, or mail-order business— the hinterlands of these cities stretch far out into the Great Plains. They serve, in fact, both the Agricultural Interior and the Great Plains, both the intensive-farming areas of the region we are considering and the drier lands of less intensive use that lie further west. If for purposes of regional subdivision we distinguish between the Interior and the Great Plains, then these cities should, strictly speaking, be treated under both headings, for while they are located in one region, they play a part in the life of both.

Kansas City, whose beginnings date from its days as an outfitting point for the overland trails, grew up as a receiving and processing center for grain and livestock from the Corn Belt and Wheat Belt and for cattle from the ranges. This share of the nation's agricultural processing industries it has steadily increased, but it has also achieved in recent years a broader industrial base, which has changed it from a specialized to a general manufacturing city. This has been partly the result of proximity to the southwestern oil and gas fields, which have provided industrial power, and partly a product of the general westward-moving tide of industrialization, which has brought to the city numerous concerns seeking a central location within the United States.

Today, therefore, Kansas City is an outlier of the Manufacturing Belt and not merely a convenient processing point for farm produce. To use again the terms mentioned earlier (see p. 246), the most recent wave of industrialization has crossed the Interior and reached as far west as Kansas City, bringing to it sophisticated modern industries to reinforce the older

midwestern "regulars." Yet with Kansas City, as with Chicago and St. Louis, much of the city's importance derives from its roles of market and transport center. This is particularly true of the cities at the margin of the Great Plains where the next major market centers lie hundreds of miles to the west and where, in consequence, the cost of distribution or collection over the sparsely settled rangelands is exceptionally high. Thus Kansas City's wholesalers operate over an area that includes much of the Winter Wheat Belt and the southern Great Plains, and the role of its warehouses and wheat market is no less vital to the region's economy than that of its factories. As a trade center, it has the advantage of excellent rail and road services, and local opinion in Missouri is divided on the question of whether it or St. Louis can claim to rank second to Chicago among the transport centers of the Interior.

Minneapolis and *St. Paul*, the "Twin Cities" whose centers lie some 8 mi (12.8 km) apart and on opposite banks of the Mississippi, fulfil a similar role for the Spring Wheat Belt and the northern Great Plains. With three transcontinental railways running west from Minneapolis, the Cities' tributary area stretches well into Montana and is limited on the north only by the international boundary. Between the sections of the metropolitan area there is a marked "division of labor." St. Paul is a combination of state capital and railway junction, whose merchants deplore a general St. Paul habit of going to Minneapolis to shop. Minneapolis, in turn, having the waterpower of the Falls of St. Anthony at its disposal, developed the early industrial core, participated as a mill town in the Great Lakes lumber boom (see p. 241); and then settled down to a more stable career as one of the continent's flour-milling centers, with important manufactures of machinery in addition.

The cities of the third rank are, for the most part, centers whose functions tie them closely to their surrounding farmlands: their industries supply rural needs and their commerce may serve a hinterland of thousands of square miles, although always beneath the shadow of the second-rank metropolis. They vary considerably in size: the largest city which belongs to this group is Indianapolis, whose metropolitan area contains 1,144,000 inhabitants but whose functions place it in this rank. Most of the cities, however, are smaller—Des Moines (328,000) and Peoria (352,000) are more typical, although in the eastern Interior the Ohio cities, such as Dayton or Columbus, which fall into this category, have their populations and their functions enlarged by a wider spread of manufacturing employment. While many of these places are nationally known for a particular product (Peoria and Moline in Illinois, for example, are known for tractors and farm machinery) their industries are generally related to local needs; food processing and the construction of machinery are usually leaders. Their employment structure is broadly based. Characteristically, industry accounts for 30 to 35 percent of the employed workers, wholesale and retail trade for 20 to 25 percent, and finance, insurance, and real estate for 6 or 7 percent. This latter set of functions is, however, a very important one in these cities and one member of the group, Des Moines, has the highest proportion of its work force in this category—11.4 percent—of any S.M.S.A. in the nation, including New York City, where the figure is 10.5 percent.

Below the cities of the third rank, the hierarchy continues downward: cities, towns, villages, hamlets. Although the range of sizes is wide, all these settlements are concerned with the same basic set of functions: marketing, maintenance, and supply. The cities provide food-processing plants—meat-packing, flour milling, and feed preparation—while the small centers merely provide storage: grain on its way out and feeds on their way in. The cities manufacture agricultural equipment, while the small centers maintain it. It is largely a matter of scale. In the middle ranks there are also the administrative and transport functions to be fitted in—the county seat with its courthouse and lawyers' offices, or the railway division point with its maintenance crews. For settlements in their size range, these cities and towns of the Interior have a remarkably wide range of industries and services to offer. But this is, of course, a reflection of the region's economy. To supply, as many of these towns do, the farmers within a radius of 20 to 30 mi (32–48 km) with their day-to-day requirements, when those farmers operate some of the most highly mechanized farms in the world and have one of the world's highest rural standards of living, has clearly required the growth of a rather specialized type of service center.

Nevertheless, at a certain point in the lower ranks of the urban hierarchy a new question arises: that of survival. Despite the stability and prosperity at the top, the bottom of the hierarchy is somewhat precarious. Villages that once offered a range of services are today purely residential, and many small settlements are losing population.

To understand why this is so, we need to recognize the effects of two trends, already referred to in Chapter 6.

1. In the Interior, as in virtually all regions of Anglo-America, the farm population is declining in numbers. Although in this region, at least, the land remains in cultivation, the number of farms is decreasing and so, therefore, is the number of customers for such services as groceries, clothing stores, and schools. The service centers of the Interior were established for a much denser farm population than today's and, what is more, for a population whose effective range of movement was limited by its transport to horse- and cart-distances. Under these circumstances it was to be expected that service centers would develop every few miles across this agricultural region, but it must now equally be expected that, given a less numerous but at the same time more mobile population, the pattern of regional servicing will alter. There are today, in fact, *too many* service centers competing for a limited amount of business. In Nebraska, as an example, it has been calculated that in 1930 there were 230 farms for every incorporated place, but that by 1960 there were only 170— or, at a generous estimate, 800 to 900 farm-based customers. Meanwhile, however, the Department of Agriculture published a study made in neighboring Kansas, which estimated that to give the operator a net income of $7000 a year, a grocery store would require 1340 cus-

268

The Midwestern farm, the basic unit in a great productive enterprise—Interior agriculture. The livestock are the crucial factor in the production pattern; even when they are shut up in the barn, the silage towers reveal their presence. *(John H. Paterson)*

tomers, a men's clothing store, 2680, and a hardware store, about 6700. An adequate high school, it was calculated, needed a basis of some 6000 people, and only when its hinterland contained 6000 to 8000 customers could a supermarket offer the full economies of large-scale operation.[19] With the upward climb of costs and incomes it can be expected that in the smallest size of settlement fewer and fewer services will be economical. They will close, and if they *all* close, the "service" center may cease to exist and become simply a collection of residences.

2. The remaining farmers require for their operations equipment and supplies quite dif-

ferent in scale and type from those provided at the time when these service centers first developed. The technical quality of today's farming encourages the farmer to rely increasingly on the larger center: the smaller ones are likely to be bypassed, and once again they may fade out. If in practice many of them survive it may be because (whether by luck or good judgment) they come to specialize in a single type of service. The Interior farmer does not necessarily patronize one center only. He may well buy his feed in one, sell his stock in a second, buy groceries in a third, and take his wife shopping in a fourth.[20] From the farmer's

[19]U.S. Departent of Agriculture, *A Place to Live* (U.S.D.A. Yearbook), U.S. Government Printing Office, Washington, D.C., 1963, p. 181.

[20]A well-documented study of this habit, although made in an area marginal to the Interior, is in H.S. Ottoson, *Land and People in The Northern Plains Transition Area*, University of Nebraska Press, Lincoln, 1966, pp. 252ff.

point of view, what this habit produces is a kind of dispersed service center, its components scattered 10–20 miles (16–32 km) apart, which is perfectly acceptable to today's farm operator.

If, however, we exclude the influence of this modern habit, we should expect a general decline in the populations and activities of the smallest settlements, and we might guess that there might be some critical survival level of population, above which the remainder would grow. Simple observation across the Interior suggests that the critical level is at present about 1000 in the Midwest proper and perhaps 500 on the Great Plains, but that it is gradually rising. This estimate is broadly confirmed by the calculation that of 6034 urban centers whose population declined between 1940 and 1960, 3789 started the period with less than 500 inhabitants and 4709 with less than 1000. In North Dakota, for example, a state lacking a metropolitan center of even medium size, the census figures for 1950 and 1960 showed this process of change proceeding virtually undisturbed by outside forces:

North Dakota Population Changes in Villages of Less than 3000 Inhabitants[21]

Number of Villages	Size of Village (1950)	Percentage of Villages with		
		Population Decline 10%	Less than 10% Change	Population Increase 10% or more
6	2000–299	0	66.7	33.3
42	1000–1999	7.1	69.1	23.8
44	500–999	22.7	52.3	25.0
215	100–499	55.3	37.2	7.5
26	Less than 100	73.1	26.9	0

For Nebraska, Ottoson draws a line at a population of 500 and remarks, "These smallest towns seem to be dying. It is quite possible,

and even likely, that some of the towns in the 500–2000 population class are also moribund, but the group as a whole is not."[22]

However, we must not confuse activity and population: it is possible for one to decline while the other increases, as Hart and Salisbury pointed out.[23] They found that towns in the central Interior might lose their old, agriculture-orientated functions and yet gain in population, if they were located sufficiently close to a city to assume the new role of suburbs. In such villages, housing was likely to be plentiful and cheap and attractive to city people. The new role of these villages tends to show in their appearance; they look more and more like suburbs and less and less like working bases for farmers.

The Interior possesses most of the geographical advantages and almost none of the disadvantages of the other major regions of North America. If it is charged with isolationism, then it is the isolationism of economic self-sufficiency; if it is charged with monotonous uniformity, then at least it is the uniformity of a well-distributed prosperity. To leave the Interior and travel in almost any direction means to travel down the economic gradient and to enter regions whose problems are manifest in the landscape—soil erosion by wind and water, rural overcrowding or abandoned farmsteads on rugged, infertile lands. The Interior has its problems too, but they are almost all the problems of prosperity: how to dispose of its huge agricultural output; how to control the prices that farmers and industrialists are willing to pay for its land; and how to transact, within the confines of its crowded cities, the volume of business which its richness creates.

[22]Ottoson, *Land and People*, p. 251.

[23]J.F. Hart and N. E. Salisbury, "Population Change in Middle Western Villages: A Statistical Approach," *Annals of the Association of American Geographers*, vol. lv., (1965), 140–60.

[21]L.D. Loftsgard and S.W. Voelker, "Changing Rural LIfe in the Great Plains," *Journal of Farm Economics*, vol. xiv, 1113.

15

Appalachia

Negative—A Problem Region

The motorist who heads eastward out of Lexington, Kentucky, finds all the omens favorable as the Mountain Parkway carries him across the Blue Grass country toward the forested hills of the Cumberland Plateau. Following the valley of the Red River, however, the route soon becomes more winding; a single concrete ribbon replaces the double lane, and the toll gates are frequent. Nevertheless, he makes good if expensive progress until, 100 mi (160 km) from Lexington, the parkway abruptly ends. Here, he can turn either north or south into a maze of valleys followed by winding roads with potholed surfaces: the one thing he cannot do is to go straight on. He has arrived in Appalachia.

As its name suggests, Appalachia is first and foremost a physical region—that area of the United States within which the Appalachian system dictates surface, structure, and resources. As we saw in Chapter 1, the system extends in its essentials all the way into northeastern Canada, but it is to the part of the system that lies west and south of the Hudson and Mohawk corridors that the term Appalachian is generally applied. Here the breadth of the system from east to west is greatest and its westerly province in particular—the Cumber-

land and Allegheny plateaus—broadens to occupy much of northwestern Pennsylvania, most of West Virginia and eastern Kentucky, and parts of southeastern Ohio and of Tennessee. It is within these latitudes that the characteristic Appalachian topography is most clearly developed.

But these physical features alone do not account for the way in which the name *Appalachia* has become familiar to the average American in the past decade. Appalachia is today not simply the name of a physical region: it has become familiar because it carries cultural and political significance. Culturally, it stands for a world apart, whose inhabitants are generally considered to live lives unrelated to the standards and concepts of other North Americans:

Understanding the people of Appalachia must be based on the recognition that their value patterns are at variance with the value patterns found in the larger American society.[1]

Politically, its existence and its boundaries have been given form by the allocation of more than 2.5 billion dollars of funds, under the Appalachian Regional Development Act of 1965, to the region as defined for a program of pub-

---

[1]F.A. Zeller and R.W. Miller, eds., *Manpower Development in Appalachia*, Praeger Publishers, New York, 1968, p. 26.

lic works. In the American War on Poverty, Appalachia has been the primary target area.

The situation in Appalachia today is the product of forces both geographical and historical. From colonial times onward, the American's clearest consciousness of the Appalachian system has been as a barrier to east-west movement. It is true that, once across the Blue Ridge, the pioneers from the coastal settlements found in the Great Valley (occupied by the Shenandoah and Tennessee rivers and their tributaries) an easy route southwestward, but to break out of it to the west or northwest was far from simple and led into a bewildering maze of valleys and forested hills that even today baffles the stranger. Daniel Boone's famous Wilderness Road of the 1770s left the valley at the Cumberland Gap (one of the few points where a waggon trail could be carried up onto the plateau) and cut across a narrow section of the hills to reach the Blue Grass Basin. Yet between there and the Mohawk Gap far to the north, there were no easy routes and little open ground; the deeply dissected plateau virtually defied penetration, except on foot.

Whatever hindrance to movement the Appalachian system as a whole offered, therefore, the plateau province formed a kind of inner sanctuary and for that very reason attracted some of the pioneers. For the majority, however, it was an obstacle to avoid; it could neither be easily crossed nor easily cultivated. Even after a century or more of commercial timber cutting and coal mining, communications are bad. This heart of Appalachia was not simply at the end of the road to nowhere; in many cases there was no road.

Physically, then, Appalachia possesses the unity of a single geological system, but this unity is purely conceptual. Landscapes, communications, and access all vary greatly within the region, and with them, economic conditions vary also. It is probably for this reason that the concept of Appalachia as a region has been largely missing from geography texts in the past; the eastern edge of the system is linked with and forms a backdrop for the tremendous development on the Atlantic coast; the southern end of the Appalachians shares much of the character of the Old South, and the heavy industry region around Pittsburgh is normally treated as a separate entity. In fact, Appalachia can be regarded as forming part of several other regions. This leaves the non-industrial plateau as the epitome of Appalachia—the most remote, most poverty-stricken part of the region.

How has this situation arisen? Most explanations have tended to focus on the cultural aspect of development—on the way in which the people of the area, living and intermarrying in a world apart from the mainstream of American life, have either missed or resisted the march of progress. But real though this cultural isolation may be, it is possible (to judge by some of the literature on the subject) to exalt the culture-differential argument to the level of a mystique and to suggest that, given the same range of choices as other Americans, the Appalachian settlers deliberately chose a life of feuding and moonshining and idling in between the two.[2]

This was not, of course, the real situation. The sequence of developments in Appalachia has followed quite logically from principles we have already reviewed in Chapters 6 and 10. In eastern North America generally, the normal sequence of occupance has been (1) the coming of hunters and trappers; (2) the advance of the settled frontier, accompanied by subsistence agriculture; (3) a transition from subsistence farming to commercial agriculture and the rise of market-orientated production; (4) at some period after the beginning of stage (2), the growth of non-farm employment and the coming of industry.

In Appalachia, however, with severe physical limitations of climate, slope, and soils on agriculture, even subsistence farming was often impracticable: only in the "coves" and on the narrow valley floors could a few fields be cleared in the forested hills, and even these were liable to flood and soil erosion. When the time came for the critical transition from stage (2) to stage (3) in the sequence, even areas much closer to a market than Appalachia

[2]Since the settlers in question were preponderantly British in origin, this is an explanation which any British writer has a personal interest in rebutting.

Appalachian topography: The Ridge and Valley Province, looking southeast toward Harrisburg from above the Juniata River, which is visible at the lower left running "with the grain." In the center background the Susquehanna is seen breaking through the most easterly ridges to reach Harrisburg. Here in central Pennsylvania the Blue Ridge is absent, and the Ridge and Valley adjoins the Piedmont, just visible in the background. *(John S. Shelton)*

found themselves under fierce competitive pressure. The Appalachian farmers themselves stood no chance at all. Here, indeed, are value patterns "at variance with the value patterns found in the larger American society" (see p. 271). The work of Robert Coles and others has done much to make this divergence of interest clear and challenging:

You go down and sit there in the chair—we sit around in a circle all the time—and he'll be talking, the reverend, and it takes about an hour or more, but every time it happens I say to myself: here you are, Donald Samuel McCallum, and it's today and the year is 1966, or some other year, you know, and I'm here in this little church, listening to him talking, the reverend, and there's my wife, and there's my oldest son, and there's my youngest one, and these are the three boys in between, and now I've got a real sense of things. Most of the week I'm going along and I don't stop and think much at all, but by Sunday at suppertime I know when I'm living and where I'm going. . . . [3]

In the cities, the Appalachians often find it hard to obtain regular jobs. This is partly because they tend in many cases to be seasonal migrants only: after a few months in the city, they will return to the hills and to their family,

[3]R. Coles, *Migrants, Sharecroppers, Mountaineers*, Little, Brown, Boston, 1967, p. 587. This is an extract from one of Cole's remarkable trilogy under the general title *Children of Crisis*, largely made up of interview material, and more revealing than any objective work on the ethnic and cultural minorities of modern America. All three books will well repay study.

273

Appalachian landscapes: (1) A remarkable mining landscape northeast of Harrisburg, Pennsylvania, where coal has been mined along the strike of the Appalachian folds. View looking southwest. *(John S. Shelton)*

perhaps returning a year or two later to the same city. On the other hand, their irregular appearance on the labor market makes them available for the kind of temporary job that every big city generates, at low rates of pay and without any pretense of security. Since they fit all too well into this category of what might be called the labor cushion, their standard of living is generally low.[4]

On economic grounds, therefore, the area's people, if they chose to remain where they were, had little alternative but to continue in

the primitive conditions afforded by stage (1) of our sequence—or the early phases of stage (2)—until the fourth stage began, if it ever did—until the hills yielded something other than agricultural produce. *Why* they chose to remain may indeed require to be explained in cultural terms, but *if* they chose to remain, it is difficult to see what else could have happened.

In due course, the resources of the Appalachians attracted outside attention, and this largely nonagricultural region came to life economically. The first of these resources was timber, for the Appalachians possess the finest stands of hardwoods in the United States and very large stands of softwoods in addition. From the time of the Civil War onward, agents of outside timber companies were at work, buying the mountaineer's trees and often em-

[4]The best study so far available of Appalachian living conditions in the city (in this case, Chicago) is in T. Gitlin, *Uptown: Poor Whites in Chicago,* Harper & Row, New York, 1970. See also G.A. Hydland, "Social Interaction and Urban Opportunity," *Antipode,* vol. ii (1970), 68–83.

Appalachian landscapes: (2) Strip mining of coal, Kentucky. It is estimated that almost one-half of all the coal mined in the United States in recent years has come from strip-mining operations such as this rather than from underground mines. *(U.S. Bureau of Mines and the* Louisville Courier-Journal)

ploying him to cut them. The price was low and the method calamitous in its disregard for such other regional resources as soil and wildlife.

The cattle dragged or "snaked" the heavy mass of wood down the hillside to the creek, and along its rocky bank to a collecting point. There it was left, with hundreds of others like it, to await the log run.

To add to the stream's volume the mountaineers worked together to build "splash dams" at intervals along the creek. . . . When a heavy spring rain filled the rivers and sent torrents flowing over the crests of the dams, the mountaineers were ready to follow their logs to the great mills. . . .

A charge of explosives ripped out the dam nearest the head of the creek and the unleashed flood surged down in a bubbling wall onto the thousands of "sticks" cluttering the channel. . . . Like rising thunder the water and its cargo rushed downstream, gathering momentum and freight with each succeeding mile.[5]

But this destructive exploitation of the forest resource could not by its nature provide a stable or continuing basis for the regional economy of the period. Nor, it now seems,

[5]H.M. Caudill, *Night Comes To The Cumberlands*, Atlantic-Little, Brown, Boston, 1962, pp. 67–68. This remarkable book, although written with the frankest partisanship by a native of the Cumberlands (he lost two male relatives by accidents in a log-rush such as that described above), should be read by anyone with an interest in Appalachia, if only because it set off such a tidal wave of "discovery" of the region and well-meaning but sometimes wrong-headed efforts to help its inhabitants. (Caudill tells the story of this aftermath of his first book in *The Watches of the Night*, Atlantic-Little, Brown, Boston, 1976.) For Caudill's proposals for the region, see p. 286 below.

could the second of these exploitive activities, although the impact it made on the region was profounder by far and more widespread. If there is any one that feature that unites the parts of this far from uniform region, it is an involvement with coal mining. Indeed, it could be argued with fair hopes of success that the region is united by poverty precisely because it was first united by a commitment to mining. Of the eleven states affected by the act of 1965, seven were coal producers; their output in that year and in 1975 was as follows:

Coal Output (In million tons)

State	1965	1975
West Virginia	149.2	109.2
Pennsylvania	95.1*	89.3*
Kentucky	85.7	140.4
Ohio	39.3	46.2
Virginia	34.0	32.7
Alabama	14.8	22.4
Tennessee	5.9	8.1

Includes anthracite

It was in the last quarter of the nineteenth century that coal mining spread into the Appalachian valleys. In most parts of the region development waited on railway construction, although the growing industries of Pittsburgh were fed with waterborne coal. The Appalachian coal field had a number of peculiarities. One of them was that the coal underlying the plateau was in a sense too easy to mine. Much of it could be reached by opencast methods (and this was long before any question arose of restoring the mined-out surfaces, of which, at the last count, Appalachia had some 380,000 acres [153,850 ha]—80 percent of all such unreclaimed strip-mined land in the nation), while in the early period and in boom years small mines were scattered everywhere throughout the field and there was little or no incentive to organize production rationally in big mine units. Another peculiarity was that Appalachia possessed few towns. Its rural population, though large, was scattered in inaccessible cabins in the hills; consequently it was necessary to assemble mine labor and to accommodate the miners in camps run by the coal companies. While, therefore, mining profoundly

affected the physical qualities of the land, it had an equally disturbing effect on the social quality of Apppalachian life.

But at least mining represented employment, so long as the market for coal remained buoyant. When markets began to contract the extent of the region's dependence on this one resource became tragically apparent. First in the depression years of the 1930s and then in the course of the postwar rationalization of the industry, unemployment became endemic.

Not only in North America, but also in Western Europe coal producers have confronted the problems of falling demand and rising costs. They have met the situation by closing uneconomical mines and mechanizing their remaining operations. In this respect, Appalachia has not been exceptional; in fact, it has adapted to the change remarkably well, certainly more successfully than, say, the British coal fields, if we judge by sustained production and comparative cost. But what has produced the Appalachian distress has been that there is nothing else for out-of-work miners to do. Rationalization presupposes the transfer of labor to other tasks. In Appalachia, with its primitive agriculture, its sparse distribution of industry, and its services such as education and health far below average, the unemployed miner generally has only two choices—to return to his cabin in the hills and live on welfare or to leave the region altogether. In the single decade 1950–1960, over two million people chose the second alternative.

The problems of Appalachia during the decades of the 1950s and 1960s were epitomized by maps like Figure 15-1. While some parts of the Appalachian region—as defined by the act of 1965—increased their labor force by 10 or 20 percent during the 1950s, in four adjoining economic areas of eastern Kentucky the reduction in employment was between 35 and 44 percent. In adjoining West Virginia, employment in mining dropped from 134,000 to 59,000 in the same period (by 1971 it was down to 48,000), and, as an indication of how the fortunes of mining affected the life of the state, agricultural employment fell from 61,000 to 23,000. The population as a whole was reduced by 145,000.

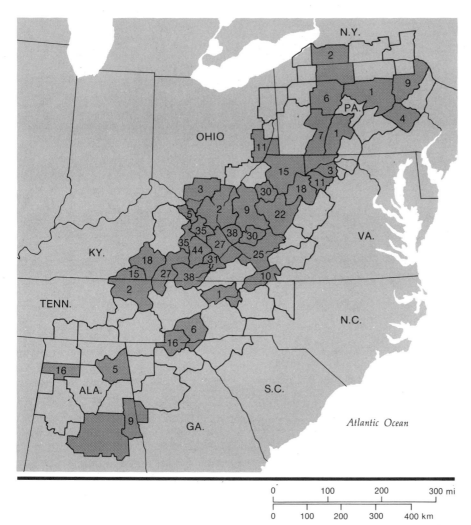

Fig. 15-1. Appalachia: Percentage decline in total employment, 1950–60. This map is of considerable historical interest because it represents the situation that John F. Kennedy became aware of while campaigning for the presidency in 1960—a situation in the Appalachian heartland so distressing that he promised to take action to remedy it if elected. The Appalachian regional program described in this chapter is his memorial. In all the areas shaded, employment fell during the decade; the percentage fall is indicated by the figure in each area. During this period, employment in the United States as a whole *rose* by 14.5 percent.

Throughout the 1960s West Virginia was losing over 25,000 people each year.

It is generally agreed that it was the plight of West Virginia which brought the problem of Appalachia to the attention of the nation. In 1960, when campaigning for the Presidency, John F. Kennedy visited the state and pledged himself to deal with the situation if elected. His memorial is the 1965 act. Meanwhile, Appalachia was growing on the consciousness of the nation in other ways. For one, an increasing number of Americans outside were finding in the region an outlet for their social awareness. In its provision of schools, health services, or dentists, the region has lagged far behind the nation; infant mortality rates, doctors per thou-

sand of the population and numbers in high school all tell the same story of submarginal conditions. Even before Kennedy discovered Appalachia, medical personnel and other volunteers were quietly giving weeks or months each year to work in the region.

The other way in which the region's problem has become known is through the out-migration of its people. Most of them look for work in the cities outside but not too far from its borders.[6] Here they form an element in the

[6]"Migrants from eastern Kentucky tend to go to the Midwest, especially to such Ohio cities as Cincinnati, Hamilton, and Dayton, whose populations are made up of sizeable numbers of persons born in Kentucky. Western West Virginia migrants generally move to central and northeast-

Rural poverty in Appalachia: A scene in Maryland. *(HUD)*

population almost as distinctive as the blacks, and they are known as Appalachians. Something of the impact of such a group on modern urban society in the United States can perhaps be judged from the following extract from an interview with a 19-year old who had arrived in Chicago two years previously from a town in eastern Kentucky with a population of 2500:

Chicago, hit's a place you can labor and work and make a livin' at. We have better things in life than we did down home. I have everything I can wish for. I still have my mother. I have my stepfather. I

have twelve good brothers and two nice sisters. And work every day an' make fine money. I eat good. I can't see anything else a man can ask for. As long as I'm workin', I figure everything'll be okay. The only thing I have against Chicago is that maybe there's too much alcoholics around here. . . . [7]

Positive—Two Approaches to Regional Development

By the beginning of the twentieth century, there was a cultural and economic differential between the Atlantic Coast cities and the Appalachian plateau which was probably greater than that between the Atlantic Coast and the

ern Ohio, to cities such as Columbus, Akron, and Cleveland. Further east in West Virginia the migrants tend to go to Pittsburgh, while still further east in the state they move to Maryland and Washington, D.C., with some going to the Midwest. . . . " N.M. Hansen, *Rural Poverty and the Urban Crisis*, Indiana University Press, Bloomington, 1970, p. 82.

[7]S. Terkel, *Division Street: America*, Avon Books, New York, 1968, pp. 128–29.

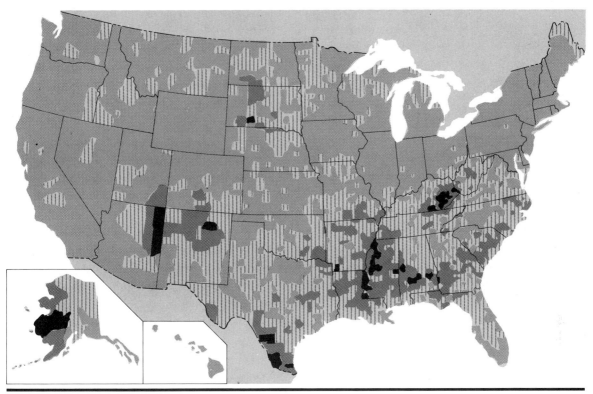

Percent below poverty level

	0–14.9		30–44.9
	15–29.9		45–60.0

Fig. 15-2. Poverty in the United States: Percentage of families with incomes below the poverty line, 1969.

mining or ranching West in the nineteenth century. It was upon this differential and the attempt to get rid of it that the Appalachian Regional Development Act of 1965 was focussed.

But those responsible for the program of the 1960s were not working in virgin territory. For inside the Appalachia defined by the act of 1965, there was a region which had been the object of an earlier plan for regional development—a plan of the 1930s that was studied and emulated the world over. It was the Tennessee Valley. The Tennessee Valley Authority (T.V.A.) had been set up in 1933 to do for the valley much the same as the regional commission for Appalachia was called upon to do for a wider area in the 1960s: relieve regional distress. In these two bodies we can, in fact, study the contrasting impact of two different

approaches to the problems of a depressed area. And considering that the earlier T.V.A was faced by much the same types of terrain, people, and economy as the later Appalachian commission, it is remarkable how little similarity there has otherwise been between them. We shall consider each of them separately, and then attempt to assess the relative success achieved by each.

The T.V.A. was initiated in 1933, at a time when the fortunes of all rural North America were at their nadir, and it was created to work in one of the most depressed areas of all. It is easy to understand, therefore, how and why it has become a symbol of progress and an example to be copied throughout the world. At a time of deep depression it showed that, with a little "pump priming" from outside, a poor

279

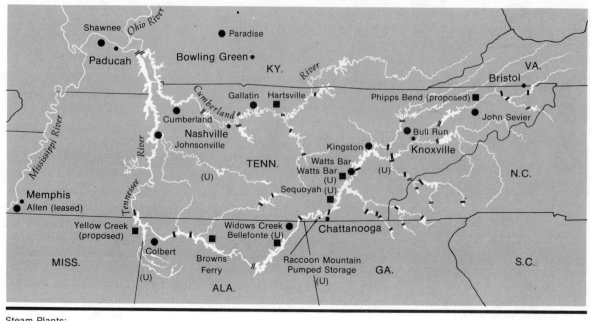

Steam Plants:

● Coal-fired   ⌇ Dams

■ Nuclear   (U)   Under Construction

Fig. 15-3. The Tennessee Valley and the T.V.A.: Dams and power plants, 1978.

and distressed region can achieve a new vitality and sense of purpose.

This being the case, it may seem strange that much of what has been said and written about the T.V.A. in the past has been hostile to it. It is necessary, in fact, to explain this hostility before considering the example which the T.V.A. offers, for otherwise the literature on the Authority is impossible to understand. The explanation is simply that, although control of the Tennessee River had been discussed by engineers for over a hundred years, the decision to create the T.V.A. was a *political* decision. It was made by Franklin Delano Roosevelt's Democratic administration in 1933, and for millions of Americans it was a decision prompted by party politics. It was therefore just as important for the Democrats to be able to show that the scheme was a success as it was for the Republicans to be able to demonstrate that it was expensive, unnecessary, or plainly unconstitutional.

The Tennessee Valley early in 1933 epitomized rural America's most pressing problems.

Low prices and uninstructed farming had undermined the valley's agriculture, and soil erosion had reached frightening proportions. Erosion affected runoff and drainage, so that the river constituted a real menace. On the one hand, its irregular flow and vast soil load made it well-nigh useless for navigation. On the other, it presented an acute flood danger to the low-lying farms and cities not only along its own course, but also on the lower Mississippi, to whose flood crests it made its contribution.

This was the background to Roosevelt's decision to create the T.V.A. Clearly the menace of the river was only a symptom of the human problems of the valley. But the approach to these problems had to be indirect. Under the Constitution, as we have seen in Chapter 3, the powers of the federal government are restricted. The President could create an Authority to control the Tennessee, on the ground that it would be removing barriers to interstate commerce; all else that he hoped for must grow out of that basic activity. Just how much might grow out of its one legitimate activity has been the great point of debate in the story of the T.V.A.

So it came about that the Authority was created with the dual mandate of flood control and navigation improvement. From the works constructed for these two purposes it was to produce and sell electric power. It was in this somewhat backhanded way that the great Tennessee power development was initiated. The T.V.A. was also given charge of a nitrate plant at Muscle Shoals, relic of an earlier project, and so entered the fertilizer business and the sphere of agricultural improvement to which it made such an outstanding contribution in the succeeding years.

The area within which the T.V.A. operates is some 40,000 sq mi (103,500 sq km) in extent. The Tennessee is formed by a number of rivers which rise in the Blue Ridge and flow into the "corrugations" of the Ridge and Valley country, where they merge to form the Tennessee proper. The main river follows the trend of the valley system to Chattanooga, where it turns west, cuts through the southern end of the Appalachian Plateau, and flows west and north to join the Ohio just before the latter joins the Mississippi. The area comprises parts of seven states.

The T.V.A. will soon have been in existence for a full half century. In pursuit of its primary objectives it has built some 20 dams (and coordinates the use of more than 20 others), and it has created for shipping a 9-ft (2.7 m) channel from Knoxville to the Ohio River, 625 mi (1,000 km) away, which in 1974 saw the passage of 29 million tons of cargoes. It operates about 25 million kw of generating capacity, with plans to double this, although the increase depends upon getting approval for the building of a number of *nuclear* plants and that, as we saw in Chapter 5, is at present uncertain. So great has been the increase in electricity demand over four decades that nowadays four-fifths of the T.V.A.'s power is generated at thermal stations, and not at the dams.

Ironically the T.V.A., which was set up to develop a new source of power—hydroelectricity—has consequently become the largest single customer for an old one—Appalachian coal. It consumes 40 million tons a year. In fact Caudill, watchful as ever over the interests of

his Kentucky miners, is severely critical of the T.V.A. for having disregarded those interests and having made long-term contracts for the purchase of coal in which, using its immense bargaining power as a customer, it drove down prices and bought from the cheapest sources, regardless of either environmental damage or miners' welfare.[8] The T.V.A. replies that its responsibility to its own customers is to supply them with electricity as cheaply as possible, whatever the energy source.

Flood damage along the river has been considerably reduced and, on a number of occasions, control of the Tennessee has lowered a flood crest further south by a few vital inches and so saved the levees. Yet it was obvious from the beginning that if the Tennessee was to be controlled, it would be necessary not only to build dams but also to penetrate to the headwaters of the river and there to rectify the conditions responsible for the floods. So the sphere of the T.V.A.'s activities widened. As a complement to the program of dam construction and nitrate production, there was initiated, with the help of the Soil Conservation Service, an anti-erosion campaign on the valley farms. Gullying was checked and trees were planted on eroded hillsides, for otherwise the newly built dams would rapidly have become silted up. This has led in turn to the T.V.A.'s participating in a detailed soil survey of its area. As a further by-product of the original construction, the Authority has joined with the U.S. Geological Survey in the topographic mapping of the valley. Finally, where dams have been built and reservoirs created, the shores have been landscaped to create parks and to encourage a growing tourist trade to the "Great Lakes of the South." At the same time it has been possible to campaign against the malaria which has for so long undermined the vitality of Southerners. Newly formed shorelines have been engineered to avoid the creation of breeding places for mosquitoes, and swamps and standing water have been sprayed.

The construction of the Tennessee navigation channel also led to an enlargement of the T.V.A.'s activities, for once it had achieved the 9-foot channel, the Authority set out to build

[8]Caudill, *Watches of the Night*, pp. 60–61.

up traffic on the route. Its economists have attracted to the river a curious assortment of cargoes and in the process have fought a number of battles over freight rates which have benefited the southeastern region as a whole.

It is in the sale of electric power that the T.V.A.'s interests have found their widest extension, for it has embarked upon a campaign to fulfil its creators' hopes by raising the whole standard of living in the valley. In this campaign the sale of cheap electricity and fertilizers, the Authority's two commercial products, is clearly of basic importance. In its widest context, therefore, the T.V.A. can be portrayed as a kind of regional fairy godmother, helping the farmers with advice and fertilizers and providing the cheap power which attracts industries to the area. Alternatively, of course, it can be portrayed as a ruthlessly undemocratic agency, whose economic dictatorship hangs over the Valley like a thundercloud. It is perhaps noteworthy that *within* the Valley the thundercloud viewpoint has steadily lost ground with the passage of time.

The 1965 Appalachian Regional Development Act, as we have noted in Chapter 8, made the first application to a specific area of the principles of regional development which had been emerging in legislation in the period since 1961. In a sense it was the first of the new regional plans and also the last of the old ad hoc arrangements which had brought into being federal schemes to aid the Tennessee and the Missouri valleys. Certainly, it could hardly be called a regional plan in the sense of being a comprehensive blueprint for the future of the region.

The act made available $1100 million of federal funds over a six-year period, to be spent on projects agreed between the federal government and the states concerned, all of whom would work together on a regional commission. While $69 million of the allocation were earmarked by the commission for health centers, and smaller amounts for erosion control, vocational training, and other projects, by far the largest share ($840 million) was set aside for road building. Four-fifths of the total federal funds were for the construction of 2000 mi (3,200 km) of "development highways."

There are two particular features of interest in this regional project. The first was the area to which it applied. The definition of Appalachia adopted by the act was a very broad one: based on rather vague criteria, it comprised 373 counties in eleven states and was in fact the "biggest" Appalachia to emerge from any of the regional studies made in the past. Its boundaries did correspond in a rough way, however, with those of the physiographic Appalachian system. What has happened is that since the regional commission was designed as a joint federal-state body, and since state governments were expected to make a contribution to projects undertaken, it was left very largely to the states to decide what was and what was not Appalachia. The thirteen southern counties of New York, for example, were left out of the region as originally delimited but were included later. On the whole, the result has been to include within Appalachia any county which, from a physiographic point of view, could claim Appalachian affinities.

The population of this region in 1960 was 17.25 million. It had grown only 2 percent in the previous decade, compared with 19 percent for the country as a whole, and its per capita income was 23 percent below the national average. But as might be expected in any region defined basically for administrative purposes, there were very wide variations within its borders. It must, for example, have come as a shock to many people to discover that most of the area where the T.V.A. had been operating for the past thirty years was included in a poverty program. On the southeast, moreover, the region ended only just short of Fulton County, Georgia—a county which includes Atlanta and contains one of the most remarkable growth-points in the nation at the present time. In the north, virtually all indices of education, income, and welfare showed a sharp rise northward from the Pennsylvania-West Virginia state line—which is hardly surprising, since this Appalachia also includes the two million people who live in the Pittsburgh conurbation.

These same indices make it clear that the Appalachian problem had its focus in eastern Kentucky and West Virginia. The dilemma of the latter was particularly acute, since it was the leading coal producer and since the distressed area covered almost the whole state. There is no non-Appalachian section which by its prosperity can balance the poverty of the problem area.[9] Eastern Kentucky, on the other hand, was statistically the most backward and the poorest section of all Appalachia. In 1966, when the average per capita income in the United States was $2963, the figure for the Appalachian portion of Kentucky was a mere $1378.[10]

Furthermore, the problem of Appalachia is essentially a rural one. The cities and towns of the region do show significant differences when tested by a number of economic and social criteria against the urban areas of the nation as a whole, but these differences certainly do not define the region clearly: they are, for example, just as great when the urban centers in all counties adjoining Appalachia are added to those within the region. In other words, it is not in the cities that the distinctive problems are to be found. But curiously enough, this does not mean that the problem primarily concerns agriculture either. Rather it is the population classified as "rural non-farm" which contains the hard core of the distressed. This element forms in Appalachia a proportion twice as high as in the nation as a whole. But it is a non-agricultural rural population because agriculture, as we have seen, has never found much place in Appalachia and commercial agriculture has almost no place at all.

We now come to the second feature of interest in the Appalachian program: the allocation of funds. Most of the original money was for highways. The hope of the planners was that the new roads would bore "development corridors" through the solid mass of this economi-

cally inert region and that, along the corridors at least, activity would be sparked off which would benefit the rest of the region. It was a variant of the "growth-pole" concept, a sort of "growth-axis."

The reasoning behind the commitment of so large an investment to the single purpose of road building was by no means clear, although it could be safely assumed that pressures on or within Congress played a part. Obviously, the coming of the new roads would yield *some* benefits: the question was whether they would be worth $800 million when they appeared, and whether they would accrue mainly to the inhabitants of Appalachia, or only to motorists in a hurry to get from, say, Washington to Chicago. There were some immediate doubters:

There are two reasons for taking the view that these development highways may not represent an effective route to economic growth. First, the highways do not attack the basic reasons behind Appalachia's lag. The second weakness . . . lies in the lack of care with which the system was planned.[11]

Nor were these doubts resolved by the midway point of the original program, when the government's auditor remarked that "limited progress has been made toward the program objective of increasing accessibility to and through the Appalachian region."[12] All that the roads could do was to give Appalachia a better chance to compete on equal terms with other regions for what they were all trying to obtain —new factories, new employment, and more tourists. But obviously the roads themselves could not guarantee any of these objectives. The main effect of the roads might, in fact, be not to bring industry into the area so much as to take people out.

There was another thing about this Appalachian program which was an obvious cause of

[9]It is worth recalling at this point that West Virginia owes its existence as a state precisely to the distinctiveness of its mountain population. Formerly a part of Virginia, it broke away during the Civil War, when Virginia joined the Confederacy, because it rejected the economic and political implications of Virginia's loyalty to the South. One feels, therefore, that there is a certain justice in taxing northern states in the 1960s to pay for a program of aid for West Virginia; had it not remained loyal to the Union in the 1860s its problems today would be less acute than they are, for it would have lowland Virginia to support and subsidize it.

[10]A detailed statistical analysis of the position in eastern Kentucky can be found in Hansen, *Rural Poverty,* pp. 89ff.

[11]J.M. Munro, "Planning the Appalachian Development Highway System: Some Critical Questions," *Land Economics* vol. xlv (1969), 160–61.

[12]Report by the Comptroller General of the United States, *Highway Program shows limited Progress toward increasing accessibility to and through Appalachia,* U.S. Government Printing Office, Washington, D.C., May 12, 1971, p. 9; see also H.L. Gauthier, "The Appalachian Highway System: Development For Whom?" *Economic Geography,* vol. xlix (1973), 103–8.

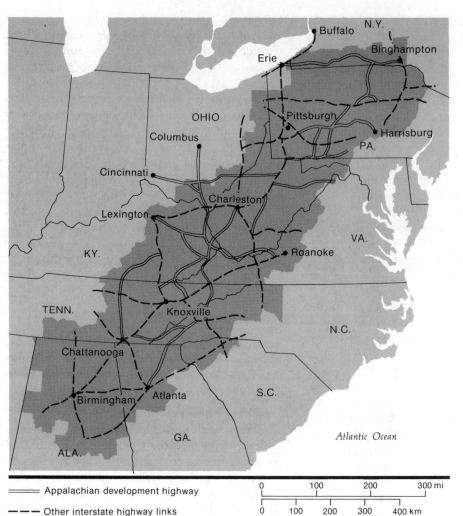

Fig. 15-4. Appalachia: The development highways.

=== Appalachian development highway

——— Other interstate highway links

| 0 | 100 | 200 | 300 mi |

| 0 | 100 | 200 | 300 | 400 km |

concern, when contrasted with that of the T.V.A. The investment in the Tennessee Valley actually *produced* something—electric power—and power is revenue-producing. The T.V.A. has paid for itself. The roads of Appalachia would directly produce nothing; infrastructure creates only the potential for revenue, not the revenue itself.

The original Appalachian program, with its $1100 million price tag, was to run for six years, but it has since been extended. It has now cost three times the original amount, and up to 1975 little more than half of the planned highway mileage had been built. By 1975, however, three other things had happened: (1) The energy crisis of 1973–74 had produced an upsurge in demand for coal and for coal miners. (2) The balance of spending on the

program had changed. Whereas roads had accounted for 80 percent of the original allocation, by 1975 highway appropriations to that date made up only 60 percent of the total funds expended; to this extent, non-highway projects had been expanded. (3) There had been some remarkable statistical reversals of earlier trends. These were slow in coming, but by 1975 they were clear.[13] An out-migration in the 1960s that averaged 100,000 a year had been replaced by a net in-migration, between 1970 and 1975, of nearly 60,000 per annum. From 1965 to 1973, Appalachia gained a million jobs, and the number of families with incomes be-

[13]They are charted in the Commission's Annual Report for 1975, U.S. Government Printing Office, Washington, D.C., 1976.

low the poverty line dropped by 41 percent. Scores of health and educational projects had been financed. After a slow start, the indirect Appalachian approach to development seemed to be bearing fruit.

Given the very large amount to be spent for better or worse on this indirect approach, there are three other problems that have to be solved in any regional development program for Appalachia. One of them is the question: should regional aid be spread uniformly or concentrated at particular points and, if concentrated, where? One sensible answer to this question is that it should be concentrated (this is the "growth pole" approach) at centers where it will have the greatest multiplier effect. However, in the United States today the fastest-growing centers are mainly metropolitan areas; indeed, Berry goes so far as to say that "the basic regional distinction is that between self-generative metropolitan America, and the hand-me-down intermetropolitan periphery, condemned to progress characterized at best by lagged emulation and second-hand growth."[14] He found that growth rates generally rose for metropolitan areas up to about one million in population, and then leveled off. But metropolitan areas are precisely what Appalachia lacks. It has therefore been necessary to choose as growth poles, or centers for regional projects, the far smaller communities with which Appalachia abounds and, when this is done, the risk of failure is far higher; the chance of "self-generative" growth is small. Choosing growth-poles by sticking a pin in the map might give just as high a rate of return.

The second problem in Appalachia is how to put to use the one asset which the region undeniably possesses—its surplus manpower. The Appalachian problem began with high unemployment; the trick is to try to change that weakness into a strength. To do so, it is necessary that labor shall be retrained. The region has not offered the *variety* of labor skills which other regions possess: an unemployed coal miner must be given *new* skills. At present, the number of workers being re-

trained is very small. To solve the problem, it has been estimated, between a fifth and a fourth of the present labor force should be enrolled in retraining programs each year.[15] A large pool of labor, adaptable, healthy and well-educated, would provide the region with a resource uniquely valuable in North America today. But with services at their present standard and welfare payments as an alternative to retraining, all this is remote from reality. "Because of the historical accident of coal, people were brought into the area. But the nature of the industry did not lead to heavy investment in the kinds of social capital which occurred elsewhere. Neither roads nor education became signifacant in Appalachia during the period of expanding economic activity."[16]

The third problem is, paradoxically, a problem of plenty, not of deprivation. Since 1973 the coal industry has seen a new expansion. Production is up and the number of miners employed increased, nationwide, from a low of 125,000 in 1969 to 195,000 in 1975. To this extent, Appalachia's problem has been solved for it. But it is solved at the cost of still further environmental damage; for example, surface mining on a larger scale than hitherto. It seems as if Appalachia can either have unemployment or suffer damage, but is bound to have one or the other, and for much of the present century has had both.

In Chapter 4, we considered this question in general, and we return here to the particular case. Environmental controls can be imposed on surface mining, given the political will and the higher cost to the producer, which will almost certainly be passed on to the consumer. The state of Pennsylvania, for example, by its Surface Mining and Reclamation Act of 1971, set high standards; it demands that the mining company submit plans for restoring the surface *before* it begins to mine, and that afterward it restores the surface to some productive use. All this is backed by a requirement that the company post a bond to guarantee fulfilment.

With such legislation in force in all the Ap-

---

[14]B.J.L. Berry, *Growth Centers in the American Urban System*, Ballinger, Cambridge, Mass., 1973, Vol. I, p. 10.

[15]Zeller and Miller, *Manpower Development,*

[16]Zeller and Miller, *Manpower Development,* p. 241.

palachian states, it should be possible to survive a crisis of prosperity as well as of adversity. The price is, however, high and the fact is that all the coal-field states do *not* have Pennsylvania-type legislation. The last thing that Appalachia wants is yet another round of destructive exploitation of its resources.

T.V.A. or Appalachian Plan— A Comparison

Both of the solutions for regional poverty which we have been considering have yielded results in their time and context—the T.V.A. in the depression years of the 1930s and the Appalachian regional plan in the 1960s, when demand for coal was low, and oil and gas were king and queen. If we try to establish which has been the *more* successful approach, then we can identify certain points of contrast, most of which might be felt to favor the T.V.A.'s style of solution: direct versus indirect approach; revenue-producing activity versus infrastructural improvement; different rates of return on capital invested. Given a very limited task, the T.V.A. has successfully expanded it to embrace many aspects of the regional economy. Given a rather broader brief, the Appalachian Commission has concentrated on a very restricted range of projects.

On the balance of these factors, it is not surprising that in 1962, before the 1965 act brought the commission into being, Caudill was advocating the creation of a Southern Mountain Authority as a solution to Appalachia's most pressing problems.[17] The analogy with the T.V.A. is clear; that was the power structure which, Caudill felt, was necessary to carry through the rehabilitation of the region. The T.V.A. is a single government-sponsored agency, with its own self-generated capital resources and its own income, while the Appalachian Commission is simply a coordinating

[17]*Night Comes To The Cumberlands,* Chap. 22.

committee which asks the appropriate government department in Washington to spend moneys held by it for individually chosen projects. It proceeds step by step and choice by choice, liable at any time to have its funds cut off by Congress.

These two regional organizations are both one of a kind; neither is duplicated elsewhere. On their comparative showing, it might be felt that there is no contest between them—the T.V.A. is the more practical and more productive arrangement. But there is a balancing factor. The T.V.A. was created in the teeth of intense political opposition. It was challenged in the courts and fought by individual interests. It produces power in competition with private power companies, and it has aroused sufficient hostility over the years to prevent the repetition of its particular formula anywhere else in the United States. There will never, it seems, be another T.V.A.

By contrast, the regional commission is a joint federal-state venture, and one which does not put government in competition with private business. It provides a formula which is politically acceptable—and so repeatable—in other regions. It offers a scrappy, piecemeal approach to regional development, but at least it is an approach unlikely to attract diehard opposition.

Whatever the form of organization, the basic problem remains that of creating in the deprived region an atmosphere of activity and hope; a state of mind in which things get done; what European planners call *animation regionale*. The T.V.A. succeeded remarkably in generating this in its early years, at least within the Valley—a new appreciation of what could be done with the resources at hand. A regional commission is ill-equipped to provide this kind of rousing leadership. Its impact must be made more quietly; this is not to say, however, that it will be less deep in the long run. Appalachia has experienced a welcome turn-around in its economic fortunes. It is now up to the commission to keep the region moving forward.

16

The South

The Old South

Between the Potomac and the Gulf Coast (the latter of which, for a variety of reasons, is best considered separately) there lies an area whose regional distinctiveness cannot be denied. It may be variously defined, and its western limit in particular is open to question, but no regional analysis could possibly overlook the Old South. This region developed a distinctive plantation economy, maintained a large black population to operate it, fought a war to preserve it, suffered the bitterness of defeat and the chaos of the aftermath and has since been struggling to regain both its regional self-esteem and its place in the nation.

It is perhaps the extent of the plantation system of the period before 1860 which gives the clearest single indication of the extent of the Old South, for it embodied both the economic and the social elements that made up the region's character. In the Civil War of 1861–65 the Confederacy drew little support from the upland areas in the Appalachians, to which the plantation system could not spread for geographical reasons. While the state of Virginia fought on the side of the South, the independent upland farmers' sympathies remained with the North, and they seceded to form the state of West Virginia. Kentucky, southern in

so many other respects, was not a plantation state and, after wavering for a time, joined the North.

However, the problem of regional definition remains. It can be resolved by suggesting that there were in fact two Souths, the Upper and Lower, which were different in character; one formed the heart of the Confederacy and the other was at best lukewarm to the cause. "The Lower South, which by 1860 encompassed almost the entirety of the Gulf and Atlantic-Coastal Plains, was a land of cotton and slavery, a land dominated economically by the plantation type of agriculture. . . . In contrast, the Upper South was primarily the domain of the slaveless yeoman farmer, an area largely devoid of cotton and the other subtropical cash crops."[1]

But define the area how we may—in terms of its former economy, its war memorials, or its black population—the South remains a reality in American life. And embedded almost equally deeply in the consciousness of the twentieth-century American is a second impression: the Old South is a depressed area. During the difficult years of the 1920s that cul-

[1]T.G. Jordan, "The Imprint of the Upper and Lower South on Mid-Nineteenth Century Texas," *Annals* of the Association of American Geographers, vol. lvii (1967), 667.

minated in the depression of 1929–32, there crystallized what became the familiar concept of the South in the American mind. The chief features of this picture may be summarized as follows:

Southern agriculture was based almost exclusively on cotton, corn, and tobacco. These crops, grown year after year on the same fields, had eaten the heart out of the land and left the soil particularly liable to erosion. Southern farmers, mostly small tenants, farmed hopelessly on in an era of low world agricultural prices and knew the despair of declining yields and gully erosion without having the means or the will to arrest the process. Farm buildings fell into disrepair, and mules did the work for which more fortunate farmers used tractors. The poverty of the white farmers was only exceeded by that of the blacks, most of whom held land as "sharecroppers,"[2] paying their rent by a fixed proportion of their crop—a crop which might disastrously glut the market one year and be stricken with blight the next.

Southern industry offered little palliative for the region's distress. With an exceptionally high regional birthrate, there was an abundance of cheap labor, and wage levels were far below the national average. New industries were slow in appearing; rather, the region's raw products were shipped north to be processed, and the population remained overwhelmingly rural.

Yet in the mid-nineteenth century this region could bear comparison with any part of the nation in respect of its wealth and of the leaders it produced in cultural and political fields. Even if we make allowance for the fact that our concept of the antebellum South is generally romanticized, the contrast with the South of the 1920s is remarkable. This is much more so when we take into account the rich resources of this region, whose natural endowment ranks it high among the regions of North America: freedom from climatic hazards, areas of fertile soils, vast timber supplies, and a variety of minerals which include the world's most strategically combined coal and iron supplies for steelmaking.

If we attempt to account for the great contrast between the 1850s and the 1920s in the Old South, we should begin by recalling that the prosperity of the earlier years was in some ways only illusory. There was soil erosion in the 1850s and earlier too, but its importance was concealed by the fact that there was always new land available in the West: abandonment of the old in favor of the new masked the seriousness of the problem. The plantation owner and his mobile labor force, the slaves, could move west if necessary—into Alabama, into Mississippi, finally into Texas—and there begin again. Then we must recall that the South's concentration on cotton resulted in an unbalanced regional economy, with industry poorly developed and even the production of food crops barely adequate for the population. Again, we must recall that the early southern prosperity was concentrated in one narrow section of the population, so that to many of its people the South's varying fortunes made no difference: they simply remained poor.

But despite all these reservations about the earlier southern prosperity, the fact remains that the Civil War was a great underlying cause of the later southern ills. The South was invaded and occupied, and physical destruction was immense. The southern ports were blockaded, and cotton exports that should have paid for industrial imports never left the quays of New Orleans. Then, in the midst of the war, came Lincoln's emancipation of the slaves. For the South it was, apart from anything else, a staggering economic blow. For generations southern landowners had been buying slaves as a form of capital investment. To abolish slavery meant the elimination of more than $3500 million of southern capital.[3] When the time for rebuilding came, the loss was acutely felt.

[2]The U.S. Bureau of the Census defines a sharecropper as a tenant who supplies nothing but his own or his family's labor: all necessary equipment is supplied by his landlord. A tenant who owns any part of the equipment (e.g. a tractor) is a *share-tenant*.

[3]L.A. Rose, "Capital Losses of Southern Slaveholders due to Emancipation," *Western Economic Journal*, vol. iii. 39–51. This sum was more than the total estimated cash value of implements, livestock and land in farms.

The end of the war in 1865 brought little relief. Military occupation, enforced liberal reforms, and southern reaction followed each other over the succeeding fifteen years. This was a period, too, when the three to four million emancipated slaves were trying to adjust to their new positions as citizens and farmers, hindered on the one hand by white prejudice (typified by the Ku Klux Klan) and on the other by ignorance of farm methods. In practice they were often forced to turn to their old masters for instruction, and many became sharecroppers.

Beyond the immediate, impoverishing effects of the war and the peace, there were other factors which foreshadowed the future weakness of the southern economy. About 1879 there began an economic revival in the South. Up to that date much of the war damage remained unrepaired; factories and port installations lay derelict. But after 1879 the North, encouraged by southern propaganda, "discovered" the South as a field of investment. Capital flowed in to repair railways and factories or to create new industries. An industrial boom resulted, but when it was over, the South was almost as firmly in northern hands financially as it had been politically in 1865. The financial hold (of which the South had by no means ceased to complain even in the 1950s) allowed the North to exploit southern lands and timber resources and has probably had other lasting effects, such as that of maintaining high freight rates between southern factories and the great market areas of the North. Since the railways were controlled by northern interests, it was possible to exclude southern goods and to enjoy undisturbed occupation of the markets.[4]

Then poverty and lack of education made themselves felt in the all-important sphere of agriculture, where the old mistake of over-specialization was repeated, this time over a wider area that included newly settled lands in the western South. Smallholders wore out their plots by persistent cultivation of the same three row crops—cotton, corn, and tobacco—either because these were the only crops they knew how to grow or, in the case of sharecroppers, because they were necessary to pay the rent. Equipment was as scarce as experience, and only labor was abundant—labor without the capital to make it productive.[5]

These, then, are some of the reasons why by 1930 the annual income per person in fifteen southern states was only 45 percent of that in the other thirty-three. The depression years after 1929 widened the differentials between the South and the rest of the nation. The deity, and the South, with its dense farm population and its marked dependence on cash crops, suffered greatly. Migration to the towns, which had provided some relief in the 1920s, was halted and in some cases reversed. The passing of the depression left the South with gigantic problems for solution; both the material problem of increasing the wealth of its people and the psychological one of throwing off the stigma of the backwardness under which it had labored so long.

To solve these problems, certain objectives would have to be realized. In agriculture, these objectives were (1) to consolidate and enlarge farm units for more efficient handling, which would mean fewer but better farmers; (2) to reduce the proportion of tenant farmers (which was 20 percent above the national average) and to deal with sharecropping which, although actually preferred by some southern tenants to a cash tenancy, was such a stimulus to the persistent production of cash crops; (3) to encourage scientific farming. Only so could the South overcome its basic handicap—low productivity. Dependence on the cotton-corn-tobacco cycle must be reduced; new techniques and

[4]The tone of these statements is intentionally vague, since the validity of the southern charges on this score has been much disputed. For a thorough examination of the problem's background, see W. Joubert's *Southern Freight Rates in Transition,* University of Florida Press, Gainesville, 1949.

[5]There was something, too, in the attitude of the Southerners to life and labor which set them apart. John Crowe Ransom expressed it as follows: "The South never conceded that the whole duty of man was to increase material production, or that the index to the degree of his culture was the volume of his material production." (Quoted by W. Nicholls in "Southern Tradition and Regional Economic Progress," *Southern Economic Journal,* vol. xxvi, 187–98.)

The South: An East Tennessee farm in 1935. This picture, showing a slope which had been unwisely but continuously cultivated under row crops, epitomizes conditions in the Old South in the years of agricultural depression. These were the conditions which the Soil Conservation Service and the T.V.A., among other government agencies, helped to relieve by spreading knowledge of erosion control and scientific farming. By the end of the 1940s such scenes could still be found in the South, but they were rare: a New South was emerging. *(T.V.A.)*

information about alternative crops must be circulated, and not only circulated but applied.

If southern agriculture was to reach these goals, it was clear that not only would many farmers have to revise their methods, but also that much of the rural population would have to cease farming and find employment elsewhere. Improvements in farming would therefore depend upon the availability of other sources of employment. Only, in fact, by matching agricultural improvement with industrial development could the southern standard of living be raised.

In industry there were, once again, certain clear objectives. (1) Fuller use must be made of local materials, agricultural and mineral. (2) Instead of shipping raw materials out of the region, the South should play a far larger part in processing its own products. It would thereby retain within its borders the additional values created by turning trees into furniture and cotton into high quality cloth, instead of seeing those values pass to northern workers. (3) The South must strive to develop its own capital resources and finance its own industry, so that it might cease to be a "colony" of the North and bargain on equal terms with other regions over such matters as freight rates and factory location. (4) New employment must be provided within the region for an unskilled rural population surplus, as the only alternative to mass emigration from the area.

From the Old South to the New: Elements of Change

Today the South presents a different picture. In almost every detail the account given in the preceding section must be modified in the

290

light of developments since 1933. For the changes that have taken place some of the credit must go to the Roosevelt administration which, taking office at the low point of the depression in 1933, enacted the New Deal measures that opened the way to recovery. In a more local sphere much of the credit goes to the Tennessee Valley Authority, established as a part of the Roosevelt program. But no one can deny that, apart from these outside forces for good, there has been remarkable revival within the South itself. It has not yet caught up with the rest of the nation, but the gap has narrowed. In 1971 average income per person in sixteen southern states was 80 percent of the average for the nation, as against 60 percent forty years earlier. A description of the South as it is today will reveal the progress made toward the objectives set out in the previous section.

THE PHYSICAL SETTING

Physically the region we are considering is not well defined, but lies mainly within two physiographic divisions—the Atlantic-Gulf Coast Plains and the Appalachian System—and extends beyond them into the Ouachita Mountains and the Eastern Transition Belt. For historical and economic reasons, its northern limit should be set across northern Virginia into central Kentucky; thence across the southern tip of Missouri (an important cotton area) into central Arkansas; and southwest to Dallas. If the present extent of cotton cultivation is taken as a guide, the region ends on the west at the boundary of the Great Plains, but definition of this western edge is difficult and not particularly profitable.

Relief and soils vary considerably within this region. The Atlantic Coastal Plain remains to a large extent what it has always been, sandy and swampy in turn, infertile and widely forest covered. Inland across the plain, altitude and fertility generally increase together, up to the Appalachian Piedmont. The southern end of the Appalachians protrudes into the heart of the region, and the main areas of both agricultural and industrial production

are grouped around it in the shape of a wide U. Within the mountains themselves much of the terrain is rough and the soil poor, but in the Ridge and Valley section, at least, fertile valleys invite settlement. West of the Appalachian Plateaus the soils of central Tennessee and Kentucky are famous, and relief beyond the plateau edge is, on the whole, gentle. Further west again lie the bottomlands of the Mississippi, where the lime-rich alluvia, once drained, have a high agricultural potential.

West of the Mississippi the Ouachitas somewhat resemble the southern Appalachians in terrain and soils, with a smaller number of fertile valley areas. Finally, at the western edge of the region, the land rises gently to the level of the Great Plains, and the yellow Ultisols of the wetter southeast give way to the Mollisols of the grasslands. The black earths of the Texas Black Prairie roughly mark the limit of the region.

Climatically the region is well favored from most points of view. Only on its western fringe is it liable to drought; everywhere else the rainfall is over 40 in. (1000 mm) per annum, and in the Great Smokies it rises to 80 in. (2000 mm). Snow seldom falls, and only in the Appalachians does the frost-free period last less than 200 days. On the other hand, much of the rain falls in heavy thundershowers, which increase the danger of erosion, while high humidity over most of the area makes for summer lassitude, and cloudiness reduces evaporation and increases leaching of the soil.

Perhaps the outstanding feature of the South's natural endowment is its forest cover. Commercial forest occupies 68 percent of the surface area of Georgia, 66 percent of Alabama, 63 percent of South Carolina and 55 percent of Mississippi. The Appalachians, the Ouachitas, and much of the coastal plain and Piedmont are forest covered; indeed, from the air it is the forest that dominates the landscape, and agriculture has rather the appearance of being carried on in forest clearings—which statistically it is. These forests represent only a remainder and a regrowth of a far greater original cover, but even after the cutting and burning of the past decades the South remains possessed of a tremendous asset—40 percent of the nation's commercial forest, including the bulk of its hardwood reserves. It produces nearly 60 percent of the United States' pulpwood. Fuel supplies are also available within the region. The Appalachian coal field extends through Kentucky and Tennessee into Alabama, and the western end of the region lies athwart the great mid-continental and Gulf oil and gas fields. Other mineral resources are numerous. Bauxite is mined in the neighborhood of Little Rock and these deposits account for over 90 percent of the United States' domestic production. Around Birmingham lie the hematite iron ore deposits that serve its steel industry. Phosphate rock is worked south of Nashville, while manganese, copper, and chromite are found in the mountains of eastern Tennessee and of the Carolinas. Finally, any account of the region's resources must include mention of the great amount of electric power, potential and developed, which is available from the rivers of this area, of which the development on the Tennessee is the best publicized but by no means the only example.

SOUTHERN AGRICULTURE

We have seen how a century of misuse left its mark on the region, in the form of eroded hill slopes, low crop yields, and dilapidated farms. Today the picture is altogether different; the scarred hillsides are covered with vegetation once more, and if many of the farms still have a tumbledown appearance, it may well be as a result of traditional carelessness about the look of the place rather than through lack of prosperity.

The main features of this change can be briefly stated. The days are long past when cotton was the leading crop of the Southeast. The cotton and corn areas have contracted, and much of their former extent is given over to a series of new and localized special crops. Meanwhile, the total area under crops has declined, and pasture has come in as a replacement. This in turn has been accompanied by a rise in the number of beef and dairy cattle. New crops have been brought in to arrest erosion and revitalize the soil, so that the old

staples can be grown on proper rotations and with less risk. Farm mechanization is increasing, while farm size has grown larger. Finally, and in view of what has been written about the historical background of southern problems, the number of tenant farmers and the total number of agricultural workers have shown a sharp decline since 1940.

For a century and a quarter before the Second World War, cotton was the mainstay of southern farm income. Although the "Cotton Belt" was probably never as compact or as continuous as the map of agricultural regions implies, it is true that, at some time or other, cotton has been grown on most of the lands in the South where there is a frost-free season of 200 days or more and where the rainfall is suitable—not less than 25 in. (625 mm) annually, or more than 10 in. (250 mm) in the autumn harvest season. However, over the years the "belt" has shifted its position. Throughout the nineteenth century it spread westward, as areas in the Southeast became infested with the boll weevil or worn out by the years of monoculture. After spreading into central Texas, however, it contracted again, and the eastern end of the belt found a new vitality. Today it seems clear that a Cotton Belt as such no longer exists. There has been a contraction into certain limited areas, where cotton is the special crop of the locality and where it is raised even more intensively, but more scientifically than before. In 1974 cotton, with sales of $1.2 billion, ranked well behind beef cattle ($2.1 billion) and soybeans ($2.07 billion) among southern farm products.

Why has this change taken place? There are a number of factors. One is that ever since 1933 cotton in the United States has been produced under a system of acreage quotas. The original object of the quota system (see p. 94) was to limit production because cotton, together with a number of other crops, was being produced in unsaleable quantities. The quota system, however, was based on acreage, not on output. It requires no great financial insight to perceive that the way to get rich under these circumstances is to raise the yield per acre. So, while the quotas cut back the cotton acreage in the South from 40 million acres

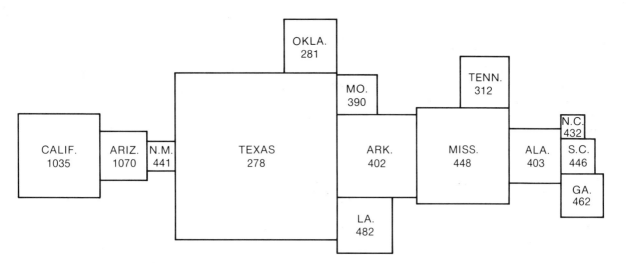

Fig. 16-1. Cotton in the United States: Each square represents a cotton-growing state, and the area of the square is proportional to the area under cotton, while the figure in the square represents the yield in lb per acre for the state. In both cases, the data is based on the average for the seasons of 1974 and 1975. Notice the relative unimportance, in present-day production, of the oldest cotton states, on the Atlantic coast.

(16.2 million ha), in 1928–32 to 14 million (5.67 million ha) in the years 1959–60, the yields doubled during the period and the total crop declined by only about one-fifth. By 1966, acreage was down to a low of 8.6 million (3.48 million ha), but it had increased again by 1975 to 9.05 million acres (3.66 million ha).

The quota system had two side effects. One was to concentrate cotton growing on the highest-yielding lands, and the other was to leave many cotton farmers with an acreage quota so small that they no longer regarded it as worthwhile maintaining the necessary equipment to work the quota acreage; and so dropped out of the business altogether.[6] At this point in the calculation another factor had to be introduced—mechanization. As recently as the 1930s there prevailed a widespread feeling that cotton cultivation was one process which *could not* be mechanized. Differences in cultural practices throughout the growing areas, consequent variations in the size and nature of the plant, and the fact that the crop did not all fruit at once—all these factors seemed to form barriers to mechanization. It was therefore assumed that the South would continue to need its enormous, mobile hand-labor force as long as it continued to grow cotton. Indeed it seemed clear that, if complete mechanization ever became a reality, the South would be saddled with a mass of unemployed workers, most of them blacks with no means of livelihood.

The reality proved to be very different. In the 1940s it became possible to complete the chain of mechanized operations and to replace the laborer at every stage. (Mechanization of weeding, for example, was as important a labor-saver as mechanization of the harvest operation.) Total mechanization cut labor requirements even more strikingly than had been predicted and than the pessimists had feared. In the Mississippi Delta, where the cultivation of a bale of cotton by mule-power and hand labor had required 155 hours, complete mechanization cut the time to 12 hours.[7] By

[6]See, for example, the evidence before the Congressional Subcommittee on Family Farms, H.R., 84th Cong., 1st sess., 7, 8, 10, 11, 13 October 1955. However, Prunty and Aiken claim that the available figures on production costs do not support the idea that any particular acreage quota is too small to be *efficient*; even a small allotment can be made to pay. (See M.C. Prunty and C.S. Aiken, 'The Demise of the Piedmont Cotton Region,'' *Annals* of the Association of American Geographers, vol. lxii (1972), 291.) It is rather that the farmer prefers to develop larger-scale production of other crops, and so may sell or lease his quota allotment to a farmer who does wish to continue in the cotton business (see p. 000).

[7]J.H. Street, *New Revolution in the Cotton Economy*, University of North Carolina Press, Chapel Hill, 1957, p. 170.

1970, 90 percent and more of southern cotton was being mechanically harvested.

Naturally, this altered the character of the operation. Large numbers of cotton growers with only a small allotment under the quota system declined to make the investment in machinery necessary to continue in the business, and their quotas have been transferred to others—generally to operators who either have accumulated larger allotments by sale or lease, or have farmlands well adapted to mechanized operations. Some of these large cotton men may rent both land and cotton acreage quotas from as many as fifty others, in order to obtain enough cropland under cotton to reap the benefits of their investment in machinery. To this type of scattered operation, the description "fragmented neoplantation" has been given.[8] Such an operation, in other words, possesses some of the managerial aspects and the size of the old-style cotton plantation, but not its compactness.

The South is still North America's great cotton-producing region as Figure 16-1 indicates. On the other hand, it is no longer the *only* one: in 1975 over 30 percent of all cotton in the United States was produced under irrigation in the Southwest, in California, Arizona, and New Mexico, where yields are twice as high as in the Southeast. Back in the older cotton regions the status of the crop has changed. From holding preeminent rank throughout the South, it has declined to become simply one specialty among half a dozen: in no southern state is it the leading item in farm receipts nor is it even the principal crop by value. The days when it accounted for over half of all southern farm income are long since gone.

This leaves unanswered the question which haunted some perceptive Southerners in the pre-mechanization era: what would become of the field hands? Their fears proved largely unfounded. Such has been the pace of change in the South that the unemployment problem has scarcely arisen. Indeed, in a few localities, farmers have been encouraged to mechanize

[8]C.S. Aiken, "The Fragmented Neoplantation: A New Type of Farm Operation in the Southeast," *Southeastern Geographer*, vol. xi (1971), 43–51.

operations because of an incipient labor shortage. The swift and peaceful transfer of this huge and otherwise unskilled labor force from its traditional occupation to new employment may well prove, in retrospect, to have been one of the outstanding social developments of twentieth-century America. In 1960, there were 8.3 million paid farm laborers in the United States, of whom 6.6 million, or 80 percent, were nonwhite. In 1975, there were only 2.9 million such laborers, of whom 1.8 million, or 62 percent, were nonwhite. If the tobacco growers succeed in emulating the cotton growers and mechanize their operations, the need for the remaining field hands will be further drastically reduced.

In order to trace the changes which have accompanied this decline in the region-wide importance of cotton, let us now return to the events of 1933. Cotton prices were poor, and the government was paying the farmers not to plant. Throughout the South thousands of acres were lying derelict, ruined by erosion and ravaged by the weevil. Further north the tobacco lands were in little better shape. The dual problem of the farmers was: what should replace the cotton crop, and could the derelict land be brought back into production? The changes in land use since that time represent, on the one hand, a search for profitable alternatives to cotton and, on the other, government-sponsored and private efforts to bring southern agriculture back into balance with its environment.

Like cotton, both corn and tobacco have, from the first, been grown in the South—corn on every farm and plot, tobacco especially in the Atlantic Seaboard states, Tennessee, and Kentucky. Like cotton, these crops remain important, but the acreage of corn has declined by a half since 1930, in spite of the introduction of new types, which have made some new areas available for planting. The acreage of tobacco is rigidly controlled by the government. Alongside them have come to prominence a series of new and profitable specializations, replacing cotton locally as a cash crop. Among the most important of these are peaches in Georgia and South Carolina, peanuts in southeast-

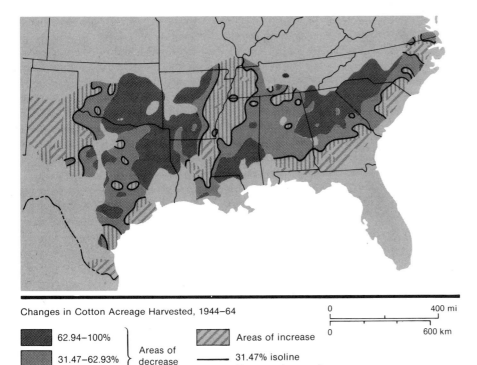

Fig. 16-2. Cotton in the South: Changes in cotton acreage, 1944–64.

Changes in Cotton Acreage Harvested, 1944–64

▓ 62.94–100%	
▒ 31.47–62.93%	Areas of decrease
▤ 0.01–31.46%	

▨ Areas of increase

— 31.47% isoline (Average decrease)

0   400 mi

0   600 km

ern Alabama and southwestern Georgia, soybeans in the Mississippi Valley, and rice in Arkansas. Perhaps the biggest of these new developments has been that of poultry farming, which yields a cash crop of broiler fowls. Poultry farming is well suited to the worn-out lands of the Southeast, since it makes little demand on the soil. The Piedmont of northern Alabama and Georgia has become the largest producing region in the nation for broilers, a food product for which demand has increased enormously in recent years. In 1975 the southern states from North Carolina to Arkansas produced 65 percent of all broilers in the United States, and Arkansas alone produced close to half a billion.

So much for the profitable alternatives to cotton. The other southern need is for an agriculture so balanced as to maintain the land in good condition. A number of new crops, such as soybeans and peanuts, not only bring profit to the farmer but nourish the soil as well. Con-

servationists have encouraged the planting of these crops either in replacement of or in rotation with the old staples. The adoption of such rotations has brought the cultivation of cotton and tobacco on to a scientifically safe level. Cotton today is typically grown on a three-year rotation with hay and legumes or grain.

But the problem of the derelict lands remained, and to these had to be added the many southern hillsides that were too steep for cultivation but were cultivated nevertheless. It was only a matter of time until they, too, were derelict. For these lands the only solution was to take them out of cultivation altogether. Between 1930 and 1960 the area under crops in the South fell by approximately 30 million acres (12.1 million ha).

Much of the land taken out of crops was closed to agriculture altogether; the rest was planted, at least temporarily, to pasture. To aid the process, a number of cover crops were imported into the South. From as far away as

Southern Agriculture
Selected Statistics—1950, 1964, and 1976

State	Number of farms (thousands)			Average farm size (acres/hectares)		
	1950	1964	1976	1950	1964	1976
Virginia	151	80	72	103/42	149/60	153/62
North Carolina	288	148	125	67/27	97/39	104/42
South Carolina	139	56	47	85/34	144/58	170/69
Georgia	198	83	73	130/53	215/87	233/94
Kentucky	218	133	124	89/36	122/49	129/52
Tennessee	231	133	124	80/32	114/46	121/49
Alabama	211	92	77	99/40	165/67	195/79
Mississippi	251	109	84	82/33	163/66	202/82
Arkansas	182	80	69	103/42	207/84	246/100
Louisiana	124	62	47	90/36	167/68	255/103

Asia came kudzu and lespedeza, crops which were felt to have fodder value coupled with the ability to cover bare, eroded ground quickly.[9]

These changes made it possible in turn to build up a livestock industry in the South. It had never been noted for cattle raising; indeed, its pastures had been poor. But the new crops and rotations formed the basis for a rise in the beef cattle population, at least; the dairy cattle industry remains to be developed.

WORKERS AND INDUSTRY IN THE SOUTH

Such basic changes in the land use of the South have naturally had their effect on labor needs and poulation distribution. All along, as we have seen, one of the main needs of the region has been to improve the man: land ratio in its agriculture, which has been far too high for efficiency. In part, this high ratio was due to the small size of southern farms, on which labor was badly underemployed. It was due also to the presence of hired farm laborers,

[9]Writing about kudzu, the outsider is entitled to feel somewhat baffled, at least when he has read J.J. Winberry and D.M. Jones, "Rise and Decline of the 'Miracle Vine'," *Southeastern Geographer*, vol. xiii (1973), 61–70. Up until about 1935, it appears, kudzu was known but little used, but when the Soil Conservation Service programs of the 1930s began, it was hailed as the South's answer to erosion. That it cut runoff and soil loss seems clear; that it had pasture value is also undeniable. Less well established are rumors that Southerners rocking in their chairs on the porch woke up to find themselves covered with kudzu vines. The peak of kudzu popularity came in the 1940s. In 1970, mysteriously, the U.S. Department of Agriculture declared it a common weed.

who made up a poorly paid labor force which worked for daily or hourly wages and which the region had to carry throughout the year.

The situation regarding farm size is shown in the following table. The changes which have been occurring in Southern agriculture have led to the elimination of many of the smaller farms, and the proportion of southern employment represented by farm workers has fallen dramatically. The South, in statistical terms, has ceased to be a rural slum. The level of living of the farmers who remained showed a welcome rise as thousands of smaller operators abandoned their meager livelihoods and moved off the land, and the tenancy which had been such a feature of the Old South had by 1970 fallen to a level below the national average.

How had these changes come about? They had obviously been necessary in the interests of agricultural efficiency and conservation, but they could only take place if some way could be found of draining off the surplus rural population. This could be done by two means—emigration out of the region or provision of other jobs within it.

In fact, these are the two means by which the changes have been brought about: two remedies for the regional dilemma which have applied in roughly equal proportions. Several million persons have emigrated to other parts of the country during the past three decades while within the region seven to eight million new jobs have been created during the same period.

Migration out of the South did not begin in 1940: it had been going on for decades and consisted of two separate streams distinguished by their color. Young white people left the South because of the limited range of opportunities offered by the region in all occupations other than farming, or because of fear of job competition from blacks at the unskilled level. Black people, drawn by news of jobs in Northern cities, moved to get away from the region where their ancestors had been slaves and where they themselves were treated as second-class citizens in so many ways. We have already noted the lure of Harlem in the early years of the century (see p. 187). The First World War saw a northward migration on a new scale, as white workers in the North left to join the armed forces, and blacks were brought in to replace them. The Second World War witnessed a return of these conditions on a larger scale. Throughout the decade of the forties, the average annual out-migration of blacks from the Old South and the border states rose to around 160,000. For the fifties and sixties the figure was only slightly less— 145,000 in each decade—although by the end of the sixties the tide was ebbing; racial violence in northern cities was a dissuader, and the crest of the migratory wave had passed. Meanwhile, the growth of the New South had been drawing back to it a small counter-flow of white managers and businessmen from outside the region. If we exclude from our calculations Florida, which drew over 1.3 million white residents during the decade, but most of them for leisure rather than for work, then the states from Virginia in the north to Texas in the southwest gained 700,000 whites and lost 1,445,000 nonwhites between 1960 and 1970. Since 1970, as we saw in Chapter 2, all the states of the South with the exception of Louisiana have recorded a net in-migration.

Had the safety valve of interregional migration not existed, the southern situation might have become very serious indeed. It is perhaps interesting to consider what the present state of the South would have been if secession had become permanent and if the transfer of southern labor to northern markets had been blocked by political barriers while the rural population went on increasing. It is under circumstances similar to these that the rural slums of the Caribbean and East Asia have come into being.

So much for those who left the region. For those who have remained, the principal change has been from agricultural to nonagricultural work, and so from rural to urban surroundings. Excluding this time the states of Virginia and Texas, where employment has been increasing for reasons only loosely connected with conditions inside the southern region, the decade 1960 to 1970 saw an increase in non-agricultural employment in the southern states of 45 percent—from 8.6 million jobs to 12.5 million. Some of this increase was in industrial employment, but the bulk of it was in professional, technical, and clerical services; that is, in sectors in which the South had traditionally been deficient. By 1969, agriculture accounted for only 4 percent of the personal income of the region.[10]

The change-over from farming to other occupations affected the whole population; indeed, it has affected the whole continent, as we have already seen. But it was most striking in the case of the blacks. In 1940, 41 percent of all employed male blacks in the South were farmers or farm laborers and so were 16 percent of the employed black women. By 1966 these figures had fallen to 16 and 2 percent respectively.

So a movement to town has taken place. In the South this movement has had a distinctive character: it has not contributed so much to the expansion of the large urban centers— there are, in any case, few of them in the South—as to the growth of the small industrial towns. It is not primarily to Atlanta or Birmingham that the workers have moved, but to the towns of the Carolina Piedmont and the Tennessee Valley. It is true that the population of Dallas increased phenomenally between 1940 and 1970, but the circumstances creating

[10]This figure and a number of those which follow are taken from the important survey by T.H. Naylor and J. Clotfelter, *Strategies for Change in the South*, University of North Carolina Press, Chapel Hill, 1975.

this situation had their origins (see p. 318) largely outside this region.

This type of urban development is to be explained in part by the character of southern industrialization. In a region where one of the main attractions to industry is the availability of labor, there is a genuine incentive to locate plants in the rural communities where the labor surplus is to be found. Furthermore, the power resources of the South are mainly electricity and oil (or gas), which allowed considerable flexibility in locating plants. It has therefore been unnecessary, and certainly southern opinion has judged it undesirable, to crowd workers into manufacturing cities; instead, the factories are located in small centers. While there is, of course, an element of risk in linking a town's employment exclusively to one or two plants, it is more than outweighed in most cases by the advantages of a garden city atmosphere and a freedom from the ills of industrial life on the nineteenth-century pattern. For this satisfactory state of affairs much of the credit must go to the planning commissions of the various states, which have encouraged the policy of rural industrialization to provide work for the rural population. Local authorities also offer a variety of inducements to suitable industries, and business groups have been active in creating local enterprises.[11]

The net result is that, apart from the Birmingham iron and steel area and the Piedmont around Charlotte, North Carolina, there is no prominent industrial area within the southern region. Industry is dispersed throughout the whole South, and only if we consider *intensity* of employment in manufacturing are the small centers, with their heavy dependence on industry, emphasized.

Nevertheless, as we saw in Chapter 5, the southeastern states have secured an impressive share of the total United Sates increase in industrial employment during the past decade, and it is worthwhile pausing to examine this phenomenon more closely, to discover what

industries are involved and why some firms have moved from other parts of the country to resettle in the South. Such an explanation in respect of the textile industry has already been attempted; a wider solution must now be sought.

Since before the Civil War the South has been noted for its manufactures of textiles and tobacco. But these traditional southern industries, though they remain important, are not primarily responsible for the expansion since 1940. This has been produced by the emergence of three other classes of industry. The first consists of branch plants of concerns producing for nationwide markets. As the southern standard of living has risen, so the consumer-goods market in the southeast has become increasingly attractive to producers, who have created local supply points to meet the growing demand. In this category fall such manufactures as those of agricultural machinery and household equipment. The second class consists of a few firms which have migrated to the South to secure a more favorable business location. They are not numerous, but a good deal has been heard of them, for political reasons. The third class consists of industries which have only recently come into existence—the aerospace and petrochemical industries are good examples—and which, in seeking new locations, chose to settle in the South.

What advantages can the South offer to attract these new industries? Electric power, oil, and gas, certainly. A growing market may be another attraction; a region with a rising standard of living. A labor force which is probably cheaper and less unionized than that of the older industrial regions, but which is also more prepared to regard working in industry as a means of gaining status rather than losing it. Under all these circumstances, it is not in the least surprising that the South has been gaining, over the past two decades, a quite disproportionate share of the new industrial jobs in the United States.

The industrial development of the South has been very varied. Forest products, cotton, tobacco, and oil have been the native raw materials: motor-vehicle assembly, aluminum smelting, and fertilizers have been brought

[11]Naylor and Clotfelter feel, however, that this tendency to decentralize industry must be pushed still further, and that industry must particularly be attracted to the smaller towns: "We are going to have to find alternatives to the urban-industrial model."(*Strategies for Change* p. 55)

into the region along with a score of other industries spilling out of the older industrial areas further north. As we have already seen, the new industries have been located typically in small towns, each of which can then claim (and does claim) to be the national focus of its industry. So Dalton in Georgia is "the nation's tufted-textile capital" (it produces some 70 percent of the tufted carpet made in the United States); Gainesville in the same state is "the nation's poultry capital," and Marietta near Atlanta was the site for the plant where Lockheed built what, up to the time of writing, is the world's largest plane—the Lockheed C-5 Galaxy—and where the company in the 1960s employed 30,000 workers to do so. By the growth of such centers as these, industrial employment in Georgia grew by 40 percent in the period 1960–70. Other industrial centers have increased in size as navigation is improved on such southern rivers as the Savannah, Chattahoochee, and Flint and water transport routes are extended.

Few areas of the South, in fact, resemble the industrial regions further north, even where the actual concentration of manufacturing employment in the South is as high as or even higher than that in the older industrial regions. One area which does, however, bear such a resemblance is the steel region around Birmingham (785,000), developed in the 1880s, originally on the initiative of the Louisville and Nashville Railroad. Here, where coal and iron ore are found within a few miles of each other, and where much of the ore, lying in formations of dolomitic limestone, is self-fluxing, is the "Pittsburgh of the South," its night skies lit by the characteristic glare of the blast furnaces. There is a well-developed railway network, and water transport has been made possible by a canal joining Birmingham to the Warrior River, which gives access to the Gulf by the way of the Tombigbee.

Unusually favored in its raw material supply and strategically placed to supply steel to the Far West as well as to the southeastern states, Birmingham's prospects at the turn of the century were bright. Their very promise, however, worked to the city's disadvantage, for the steel men of the Northeast could hardly tolerate such a challenge to their hegemony. In 1907 the bulk of the Birmingham industry passed under the control of the great interests centered in the U.S. Steel Corporation; that is, it became simply a unit in a nationwide industrial complex, whose headquarters and basing-point were in Pittsburgh. Consequently, many of its local advantages were lost.

The New South in the Nation

Students of American affairs have for so long been accustomed to treating the South as a special case economically that perhaps the best tribute which can be paid to southern progress is to record the fact that it is now possible and legitimate to treat it as part of the nation. It has its problems, but they are common to all the regions of North America—and the South, as it happens, is closer to solving them than some other regions with richer economies and longer histories of prosperity. The South may or may not have joined the Union in spirit, but as a fact of economic geography it is today inseparable from the nation. The economic issues in the modern South are not sectional but national issues. The economic goals which the nation is seeking are sought also by the South, and with a considerable degree of success. To test the truth of these statements, it is only necessary to review the familiar regional issues in American life and resource use today. Among these issues are:

1. Interregional population movements. Since the arrival of the carpetbaggers after the Civil War, almost nobody had moved *to* the South (excepting Florida); it was a place to move away *from*. In the interregional movements of the last five to ten years, the whole South has figured as a major receiving area, and some parts of it are beginning to experience the problems of urban pressure.

2. Industrial competition and adaptation. Bidding for new industry (which in turn means new jobs and new tax revenues) is a way of life in every region of North America. The South has been highly successful in attracting new industry. It is true that its long-established textile industries (which employ

some 600,000 workers) have been feeling acutely the pressure of overseas competition and have been forced into a program of modernization and self-improvement, but so have a score of other American industries: regionally, the effect of the shakeup has been beneficial after several decades of easy southern dominance.

3. Agricultural efficiency. We have already noted the problems of the American farmer, nationwide, caused by the fact that his efficiency and investment both increase, without the opportunity for a concomitant increase in the size of his farm. The problem is at its most acute in the Midwest. It exists also in the South where, as we have seen, it has been alleviated by planting new, space-saving tree and bush crops, which conserve both land and soil, and by the widespread renting of relinquished farmland and crop quotas to form Aiken's "neoplantations." In this respect, the South is no different from the rest of the nation.

4. Development of alternative employment sources. In a nation where agriculture and industry together employ a mere one-third of the labor force, all regions confront the problem of what to do for alternative employment. In this respect the South is a litle better placed than some other areas, since it has historically been deficient on the tertiary side of employment, and its proportional gains in government employees, legal and educational services, and finance have been greater than those for the nation as a whole in the past two decades.

5. Government spending. The federal government's spending and placing of contracts are influential factors in the economy of regions and states—as witness the fierce political competition to secure them. In this competition, the South has held its own in spite of such drawbacks as a lack of famous research institutes or major universities. On a per capita basis, the South gets more than its fair share of federal grants and, thanks to a number of key defense and space installations in the region, government spending has been well sustained.

6. Poles of growth. It has become apparent in the era of regional planning that one of the most significant elements in regional development is the "self-generating" growth of the metropolitan center (see p. 285). The nation contains only a limited number of such growth poles at any one time; they appear and fade as the balance of regional advantage shifts. But it is clear that in the present period the South possesses two such poles (we exclude Florida and Texas for consideration in the next chapter). One of these is Atlanta, Georgia (1,776,000). The other is not a single city, although its focus might be identified as the twelve-county area which surrounds Charlotte, North Carolina (589,000), which has come to be known as "Metrolina." Rather, it is the urban region of the Carolina Piedmont, and it includes small, flourishing cities like Greenville and Spartanburg in South Carolina, and the Winston-Salem metropolitan area (760,000) and its satellites to the north of Charlotte as well.

These two areas possess all the attributes of growth poles. Atlanta has exhibited a remarkable power of attracting business over the past two decades, while equally remarkable has been the output of research and planning initiatives for the South as a whole which have been generated by the Piedmont cities. Apart from these two, there are lesser but still striking developments within the region that attest its vitality—the growth of Memphis (853,000) as a great agricultural market and processing center, and the rise of the Tennessee Valley-towns like Knoxville, Bristol, Chattanooga, and Huntsville in the land of the T.V.A.

It is a little more than a century since Sherman took Atlanta and tore up the railroad tracks of which it was then the focus. The city he eliminated has become one of the fastest-growing in the country. Not only are its railroads in full working order; it has today a far more impressive transport role as one of the leading half-dozen airports in the world in terms of passengers handled. Because of its importance as a route center, it is used as a distributing point by many firms; in fact, warehousing and wholesaling play a larger part in the urban economy than does industry which, as we have already seen, tends to be located in smaller centers in the state. It is claimed for Atlanta that 430 of the 500 largest industrial corporations in the United States

Atlanta, Georgia, one of the United States's boom cities of
the 1970s. *(Atlanta Chamber of Commerce)*

maintain some kind of operation in the city, a
claim which could certainly not be made by
other cities of comparable size. It is one of the
largest office-space centers in the United
States, and claims to have a convention business in its hotels and halls which makes it
third or fourth in the nation. It is used as a
southeastern headquarters by a number of
agencies of the federal government, and in the
past twenty years has recaptured all the significance as a regional focus which it possessed before it fell to the Northern armies in
the tragic days of 1864.

The other major growth pole, Metrolina and
the Piedmont, is a multinucleated area of industrial cities whose principal interests are: (1)
tobacco processing, for which Winston-Salem,
Durham and, further north, Richmond, Virginia are noted (in 1975, North and South
Carolina between them accounted for more
than half of the total U.S. crop); (2) industries
based on the Appalachian forests, such as furniture-making and the manufacture of paper
and cardboard; and (3) textiles. This is the

center of the nation's cotton textile manufacture. The Carolinas contain 70 percent of the
cotton-spinning spindles of the United Sates
and a very large share of the worsted spindles
and broad fabric looms as well. The district is
also noted for its synthetic fiber mills: those at
Asheville and Roanoke are among the largest
in the world. Over 70 percent of Metrolina's
industrial employees are involved in textiles or
textile-related industries.

But we must end on a note of caution; specifically, with an answer to the question: are
there then *no* problems remaining which are
Southern rather than national in character?
There are in fact at least two, and they are
linked with each other.

The first is that although the South has
joined the nation economically, it has joined it
at the lower end. As Naylor and Clotfelter
point out in the study already quoted, it may
be true that in 1970, per capita income in the
South was 78.3 percent of the national average,

301

but the fact is that the South pulled the national average down, and in 1972 no state in the South had an income level above the national average. In 1975 Mississippi, with a personal per capita income of $4041, had less than half the income of the Alaskans ($8815)—or, if the few Alaskans are considered to be atypical, the average inhabitant of Mississippi had only 58.5 percent of the income of his opposite number in Connecticut. So there is still a lot of ground to make up.

Secondly, the Southern average is low because in large part the income of the black population is low—on the average, about 60 percent that of the whites. One of the South's greatest needs is to generate black skills and provide development capital for black businesses. The black population suffers from a chronic capital scarcity (more precisely, from a lack of black capital and a chronic reluctance of white finance to make such capital available) and unless black business can obtain the necessary investment funds, it has little chance of improving its contribution to the regional economy.

So the problems remain. It is a quarter of a century now since John Hope Franklin, himself a distinguished black historian, expressed the hope that one day the South might become so integrated into the larger life of America that it would be nothing more than "a tattoo on the arm of the nation." There has been progress, but that time has not yet come. Perhaps we can at least say, however, that now the arm *belongs* to the nation, that it is playing its part in the activity of the whole body and—who knows?—perhaps on a healthy arm a tattoo mark will in time fade away.

The Southern Coasts and Texas

The Humid Subtropical Coastlands

The southern coasts of the United States and the peninsula of Florida are subtropical in climate and vegetation. Brownsville, on the Texas-Mexico border, and New Orleans are at 26° and 30° N latitude respectively, while the southern tip of Florida—Key West—is only one degree from the Tropic of Cancer. East of the Texas-Louisiana border, no part of these coastlands has less than 45 in. (1125 mm) of rain per annum, a January mean temperature of less than 50° F (10°C), or a July mean of less than 80°F (27°C). The Florida Keys are frostless, the tip of the Mississippi Delta almost so, and the frostfree season on most of the coast is more than 270 days (although the very rarity of frost increases its economic impact when it does occur). West of the Texas border the rainfall diminishes rapidly to a coastal minimum of 24 in. (600 mm) in the extreme southwest, but the temperature conditions remain the same, and the Texas coastlands have a frost-free season of 300 days or more.

Under the climatic conditions of the humid subtropical coastlands east of the Texas-Louisiana border a luxuriant natural vegetation has developed. To these climatic conditions, however, can be added another factor, which combines with the climate to give these coasts (and with them much of peninsular Florida and southeastern Georgia) their distinctive landscape. It is the low-lying and swampy character of the terrain on this gently sloping, lagoon-fringed coast. The combination of these circumstances creates the well-known, idealized Gulf Coast landscape: tree-filled swamps, with Spanish moss festooned on the branches of oak and cypress, and winding creeks that form a maze penetrated by no one but the local fishermen and moss gatherers.

Yet this tangle of trees and water is without doubt one of the fastest-developing regions of the United States. Repeatedly, over recent years, it has provided materials for headlines in a country where competition for headlines has been intense: offshore oil fields and sulphur beds in the Gulf of Mexico; magnesium from seawater in Texas; in Florida an industrial expansion since 1946 at five times the national rate, a tourist boom that is bringing 20 million visitors a year to the state, and then the most famous earth base of the Space Age.

Certainly there was nothing in the appearance of these swamps and sandbars to encourage in the original Spanish settlers in Florida any hope of a great future for the region. Nor did the French, who founded Mobile, Biloxi, and New Orleans and occupied the Lower Mississippi territory of Louisiana early in the eighteenth century, show much interest in exploiting the resources of their new colony. Sugar and rice were the commodities for which the area became known and which were responsible for the development of a system of plantation agriculture similar to that of the Cotton Belt further inland. The Spaniards imported cattle, but the herds suffered from so many diseases that the mortality rate made progress in livestock farming slow. After the Civil War, with plantation agriculture at a standstill and the coastlands sharing the fate of the rest of the South, there was a brief and tragic lumber boom in the forests of southern pine. As late as the 1920s much of Florida remained in the condition in which Ponce de Leon had found it in 1513.

INGREDIENTS OF PROSPERITY

What, then, have been the ingredients in the rise to power of the humid subtropical coastlands? Out of a number of associated factors, it is possible to isolate five.

Soils

Once drained, the black muck soils of the coastal swamps prove, as the Louisiana plantation owners discovered, immensely fertile. The process of drainage has been a long one, and was severely set back by the Civil War, but since the 1930s it has made progress, especially in the Mississippi Delta. In Florida, where nearly a million acres (400,000 ha) of the Everglades are judged to be reclaimable for agriculture, the efforts made to drain these lands have met with repeated setbacks. With little local relief to carry off surface water and hurricane weather to breach the dikes, it was not until 1949 that a comprehensive drainage plan was finally agreed upon by the federal and local agencies concerned.

Where these soils have been drained, however, they have proved ideal, not merely for the production of the sugar and rice crops, but also for truck farming. With the advantage of its southerly position, the Gulf Coast has been able to establish itself as a principal United States producer of fresh winter vegetables and early new-season fruits. (In terms of latitude it does for the cities of the northern United States what the Canary Islands do for Northwest Europe.) The value of the vegetable crop in Florida is second only to that of the citrus crop (see below). Meanwhile, the area under sugarcane has been increasing and now comprises some 450,000 acres (182,000 ha) in Florida and Louisiana;[1] mechanical harvesting of the crop is now general.

Rice is another Gulf crop whose production has increased in recent years: in 1970 it occupied roughly half a million acres in each of the three states of Louisiana, Texas, and Arkansas and a smaller area in Mississippi. While it grows here on the Gulf under much the same physical conditions as in the paddies of Asia, there could hardly be a greater contrast than that between the production techniques of the Orient, where labor requirements are in the neighborhood of one person per acre (0.4 ha) and those of the Gulf, where the ratio is one person to 200 acres (80 ha) and the crop is harvested by combines.

[1]The raw sugar value of the U.S. crop, which was 330,000 tons in 1940, had reached 2.8 million tons by 1975, of which the eastern Gulf contributed 1.7 million tons and Hawaii the remainder. Yet it must be explained that the market for sugar in the United States is apportioned by quota between several groups of producers—the Puerto Rican, Hawaiian, Philippine, and Gulf sugarcane growers and the sugar-beet producers of the northern and western states. The quota formerly covered Cuban sugar as well, and it was the severance of links between the United States and Cuba in the 1950s which led to a rapid increase of the sugar acreage in the Gulf states as production was expanded to replace Cuban supplies. But this means that all production figures for both kinds of sugar must be read with the quota system in mind: they do not reflect potential output but are distorted by the quota.

The Everglades of Florida: A scene on the Brighton Reservation of the Seminole Indians, near Lake Okeechobee. The swamp ecology of the subtropical Everglades is today threatened by extensive drainage and reclamation schemes associated with agricultural and residential development, but on the southwestern tip of the peninsula is the protected area of the Everglades National Park. *(Florida News Bureau)*

It may seem curious to add, after describing the part played by drainage in the Gulf's new prosperity, that irrigation is of equal importance. But it is true, nevertheless, that in the drained areas supplemental irrigation is responsible for important increases in crop yields, as well as for overcoming occasional seasonal drought. Irrigation water is applied, often by sprinklers, to citrus trees, vegetable fields, and orchards.

The Citrus Fruit Industry

Included within the general topic of agriculture, but deserving a special place in this list of the forces that have built today's Gulf Coast economy, is the development of the citrus fruit industry. Oranges and grapefruit are grown over much of central Florida and in parts of Louisiana as well as further west in Texas, and citrus represents for Florida the state's most valuable crop. As with most forms of fruit growing, however, the industry has known fluctuating fortunes over the years—hurricanes, frost, and over production have all

made for price swings, so that oranges which sold for $1.89 a box in 1945–46 and $1.62 in 1949–50 brought only $0.13 in 1947–48 and $0.19 in 1951–52.

But on the whole the market for Florida citrus has certainly been enlarging one. There are two main reasons for this. One is the decline in competition offered by California. In 1940 California outsold Florida by a ratio of 5:3, but since 1945 Florida has forged ahead as acres of orange groves in southern California have disappeared in the urban explosion beneath rows of buildings (see p. 388). By 1970 Florida was supplying over three-quarters of all oranges grown in the United States, almost three-quarters of the grapefruit, and four-fifths of the tangerines. The second reason is that Florida pioneered in marketing the product which now sells most oranges—frozen concentrate. This product did not exist before 1945; it was created to meet a wartime demand, and after the war, sales mushroomed while those of fresh fruit fell off. The producers had a product which could be marketed all year round instead of only during the harvest period (November to March on the Gulf) and, provided that they had the plant to handle the crop and the means to carry the frozen stocks throughout the year, they could free themselves from many of their former market worries. What they would obviously need was capital, and this need has led to integration of producers and processers into large units, as has happened in so many other branches of fruit and vegetable production in the United States. Today only one-quarter of the Florida citrus crop is sold fresh: the other three-quarters are sold in processed forms.

Beef Cattle Production

A third feature of Gulf Coast development is, in a rather curious way, an outcome of the second. This is the rise of the eastern Gulf region as a beef cattle producer. Cattle were certainly raised here in the past; typically, the cattlemen burned off the coastal forests to obtain pasture for their stock, but the stock itself was poor. The modern industry has two bases: the introduction of a breed of cattle adapted to the region's natural conditions and the discovery of a cheap and nutritious feedstuff. In the first of these a large part has been played by Brahman cattle, first imported from India in the middle of the nineteenth century, which in various crosses have proved themselves to be hardy animals and good beef producers in both the humid and arid sections of the southern states. As the industry has become established, other breeds, particularly British animals, have been introduced. The second contributing factor has been the discovery that waste products from the citrus-processing industry can be used as cattle feed, to the mutual advantage of both the fruit processers, who have a market for their by-products, and the cattlemen, who have responded by increasing the size of their herds. In spite of the economic importance to Florida of its citrus groves and vegetable growing, by far the greater part of the state's farmland is today in pasture, while much of the farm woodland is also used for grazing. Between 1970 and 1976, the number of cattle in Florida increased by nearly 50 percent.

Fig. 17-1. Agricultural regions of Lousiana: The regions are (1) Upland cotton, dairy, and poultry, (2) Delta cotton and beef cattle, (3) Cutover pinelands, (4) Rice and beef cattle, (5) Central Louisiana mixed farming, (6) Cane sugar, (7) Eastern Louisiana dairy, truck, and mixed farming, and (8) New Orleans dairy, truck, and fruit.

Sunshine and Tourism

Basic to all these developments, however, is the one great natural advantage from which they all derive—the Gulf Coast's sunshine, which makes the region not only a leading producer of subtropical produce for a continent lying mainly in the temperate zone, but also a great resort area for the growing number of Americans who can afford to go south to dodge the winter.

The rise of the tourist industry has indeed been spectacular, particularly on the east coast of Florida, and especially around the metropolitan area of Miami, whose population of 42,000 in 1920 had risen by 1970 to 1.27 million. To turn these sandy beaches and coastal swamps into a string of thriving resort cities has involved a vast investment; vast, too, have been the rewards within the reach of those who have participated in this astonishing boom, in which sandbars, suddenly appreciated as "palm-fringed," became valuable properties almost overnight. Further west, such cities as Biloxi, Mississippi, and Pensacola, Florida, have participated in the growth

307

Florida: The citrus fruit industry. A view of orange groves in the Central Ridge District. *(Florida News Bureau)*

of the resort industry, and the Gulf Coast, like California, has become an area to which northern businessmen like to retire.

As has already been suggested, the boom in the southern resort industry must be seen as an expression of a rising standard of living, in that a growing number of Americans possess the economic freedom to move with the sun—farmers who fly their private planes south from the Wheat Belt; New York businessmen who conduct their affairs in winter by long-distance telephone. The tourist industry caters for both summer and winter traffic: August and December are both peak months. In summer the resorts do, however, suffer from one undeniable drawback and that is the threat of a hurricane. While an essential part of the hur-

ricane's unpleasantness is that its habits are unpredictable, it can be said that there is a tendency for these violent storms to be generated east of the Antilles, and for them to move west and to strike the American coast once or twice a year, in the later part of the summer. In Florida south of Lake Okeechobee, there is a general probability of hurricane damage one year out of every five. Southern builders have learned to prepare for these emergencies, but the hurricanes inevitably take a heavy toll of crops, orchards, and communication lines, while the high seas usually associated with their passage batter the coastal settlements and endanger shipping on this treacherous shore.

While the first and greatest attraction of Florida is its long coastline, not all its tourist at-

Florida's tourist traffic: The ocean front at Miami Beach. Among the 50 states, Florida and California vie with each other for first place in receipts from hotels and tourist accommodation. Miami Beach itself, however, although it has long symbolized the Florida of the vacationer, has become so intensively developed that there has been a tendency for visitors to seek less crowded tourist areas further along the coast. *(Miami Beach Tourist Development Authority)*

tractions lie along the shore. Currently, Disney World near Orlando is the South's greatest single draw (see also p. 392), but in the world of nature it is the Everglades which attract visitors—the weird maze of grass and swamp, water and wildlife which occupy the southern end of the peninsula. But here is the paradox that bedevils all the touristic "honeypots" of the western world: the more popular the attraction, the more difficult it becomes to maintain it. As larger and larger areas of Florida are built over for housing and hotels or drained for agriculture, so the delicate balance of the Everglades ecosystem becomes more difficult to preserve. The water level falls; the edges of the swamp are filled in, and roads are cut through the wilderness. Titles of books like *The Environmental Destruction of South Florida*[2] or *No Further Retreat*[3] tell their own story. In the end, if the pressures of population growth and reclamation continue, the natural can only be maintained by artificial means; one is reduced to pumping water into a swamp to keep it swampy. Longbrake and Nichols offer the following recent inventory of environmental change in the Everglades:

A gradual lowering of summer high water levels by about six feet (1.82 m) in the sawgrass Everglades. Reduction of the area of . . . the wetlands Everglades by about 50 percent.

[2]W.R. McCluney, University of Miami Press, Miami, 1971.

[3]R. Dassmann, Macmillan, New York, 1971

New Orleans in the riverboat days: An etching of the great southern port at the height of its commercial career in 1851. *(New York Public Library)*

A drastic shortening of the surface flood period . . . from six to eight months down to three or four.
A decline in the order of 80 percent of the alligator population.[4]

Along the coast, the urban sprawl continues. From Coral Gables, at the southern end of Miami, northward through the Fort Lauderdale S.M.S.A., the built-up coastline extends for virtually 100 mi (160 km) to beyond Palm Beach. There is a new Megalopolis in the making. The original focus of all this growth, however, the city of Miami itself, has been experiencing a slow-down in the last decade, while its neighbor Fort Lauderdale increased its S.M.S.A. population from a 1960 figure of 334,000 to 807,000 in 1974. This is only to be expected; as with Los Angeles (see p. 51),

growth shifts from the central city to the periphery. In the case of Miami, however, there is the complicating factor that a good deal of its recent growth (which by any standards but those of Florida has been very swift) is attributable to Cuban refugees and other Caribbean peoples, giving the Miami S.M.S.A. nearly 300,000 Spanish-speaking inhabitants, not to speak of 200,000 blacks, and bringing to the city just the kind of problems of ethnic minorities which so many of Florida's recent arrivals came south to try to avoid.

A number of the resorts along this coast are also port cities whose trade, in keeping with their situation, is mainly with the Caribbean area and South America. United States trade with Latin America forms an important proportion of the country's whole foreign commerce, and imports range from bauxite from Guyana and Surinam (bound for the aluminum plants at Alcoa, Tennessee, or at St.

[4]D.B. Longbrake and W.W. Nichols, Jr., "Sunshine and Shadows in Metropolitan Miami" in *Contemporary Metropolitan America*, ed. J.S. Adams, Ballinger, Cambridge, Mass., 1976, vol. iv, p. 49.

Louis) to bananas from the United Fruit Company's plantations in Central America. In this trade the more important participants are New Orleans, Mobile, Tampa, Jacksonville, Savannah, and Charleston.

Missile Development

The effect of the four factors we have so far considered has been to broaden greatly the base of the regional economy. The 4.5 million people who arrived in Florida between 1950 and 1975 have drawn after them industries to supply this new market and, at the same time, have provided a pool of labor for other new industries which have followed. As if this were not enough, however, the effect of the first four factors was compounded by the fifth—the establishment of defense installations in the area, and especially the missile range on Cape Kennedy (née Canaveral).

With Cuba only 90 mi (144 km) from Florida, it was to be expected that there would be conventional military activity in this corner of the United States, but the choice of location for the missile range was a pure bonus for Florida. Around the range base there gathered the housing and the plants needed to operate it. The federal government's space program brought an immense additional revenue to the state and specifically to an area which previously had almost no economic value at all. The question of whether the government will continue to maintain this base is therefore one of great importance to the communities which have so far profited from its presence.

Fortunately, there are other sources of economic activity more dependable than the space budget. One of these is forestry. There are 16 million acres (6.48 million ha) of commercial forest land in Florida and 15 million (6.07 million ha) in Louisiana, and an increasing proportion of this is in plantations. But whereas the earliest forest products of the Gulf Coast were turpentine and ship's timbers, both production and consumption are today dominated by the big paper companies, whose interest is in pulpwood. Slash pine is most commonly planted, since it grows here very rapidly and yields a quick crop of timber suitable for pulping.

Fishing is also important to the Gulf states. In 1970 these states, with Louisiana playing the largest part, accounted for more than one-quarter of the total U.S. catch by value. By weight the principal species caught is menhaden, but in terms of value shellfish contribute most to the total.

Manufacturing has gained in importance, both through the supply of consumer goods to a rapidly expanding population and through the development of industries exploiting the natural resources of the eastern Gulf. Of these latter, the pulp and paper industry has already been mentioned. Others in the same category are the production of fertilizers from the Florida phosphate beds east of Tampa and the petrochemical industries that have grown up in the Gulf ports.

NEW ORLEANS

Not everything in the Southeast is so new as the hotels of Miami or the Cape Kennedy missile range. Dominating the central Gulf Coast, today as for more than a century past, is the great port of New Orleans (1,090,000). The port statistics of recent years show New Orleans to be losing ground to its rival, Houston, and to other ports further west. But the rise in tonnage of cargo handled at the Texas ports is almost entirely accounted for by the growth of the coastwise traffic in petroleum and agricultural produce; only Houston and Corpus Christi have a significant amount of foreign trade, and in this trade pride of place is still held by New Orleans, with a considerable share going to Mobile, Tampa, and the older ports of the eastern Gulf. Thanks to its unrivalled position at the mouth of the Mississippi, New Orleans dominates foreign trade with the Southern Hemisphere, and construction of its new ship canal has further increased its advantages. In addition, oceangoing vessels can penetrate up the Mississippi a further 100 mi (160 km) inland to Baton Rouge whence the 9-foot (2.73 m) navigable channel of the Mississippi extends north to Minneapolis and (via the Illinois Waterway) to the Great Lakes, as well as giving access to the Ohio channel and navigable Tennessee.

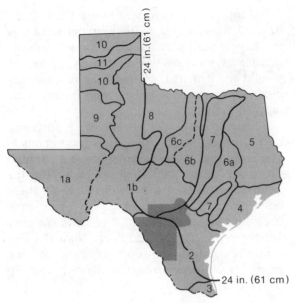

Fig. 17-2. Agricultural regions of Texas: The regions are (1) Grazing areas of (a) the High Plains and west Texas, (b) Edwards Plateau and the Central Basin; (2) Rio Grande and southern Texas plains area: grazing, irrigated vegetables, and cotton; (3) Lower Rio Grande Valley area: irrigated vegetables and cotton; (4) Coastal prairies area: cotton, rice, cattle; (5) East Texas woods area: small-scale mixed farming with considerable woodland; (6) East-central mixed farming area: livestock, including dairying, cotton, and small grains, (a) Post Oaks, (b) Grand Prairie, (c) Western Cross Timbers; (7) Black Prairie area: cotton, livestock, and poultry; (8) Low Plains: cotton, feed crops, and grazing; (9) High Plains: cotton and sorghum, (10) Panhandle wheat-sorghum area; and (11) Canadian River Brakes grazing area. The area shaded contains the Winter Garden of Texas. The continuous line marks the 24 in (600 mm) isohyet.

New Orleans' greatest days admittedly lie in the past. In the riverboat era between 1820 and the Civil War, before the westward-spreading railways established a new, safe overland link between the Midwest and the Atlantic coast, the Mississippi served as the great routeway for goods to and especially from the Interior. For all its length—down the Mississippi, through New Orleans, where transshipment took place, and around the Florida peninsula to the Atlantic ports—this route was in an economic sense a shortcut. Its importance grew as the Interior was opened up. "In the [1840s] the West had more marine tonnage than the entire Atlantic Seaboard, New Orleans alone in 1843 having twice that of New York, our greatest Atlantic port of the time." As early as 1843 the steam-

ship tonnage on the Mississippi "was nearly half that of the whole British Empire, and it multiplied sixfold in sixteen years."[5]

The year 1859–60 was long remembered in New Orleans as "the best year on the river." But in the 1850s the railways were already bringing the steamboat era to an end—even before the Civil War closed the Mississippi, and the Union blockade left the cotton bales lying and the grass growing on the quays of New Orleans. The revival of the port's commerce waited on the development of trade with Latin America and on the improvement of inland navigation. Today its trade depends on a more harmonious balance between river and ocean traffic and between water, road, and rail transport than during the picturesque but hazardous Mark Twain phase of Mississippi navigation. Meanwhile, out of its colorful past—its background of French culture and its riverboat days—New Orleans has built up a carefully preserved reputation of Old Worldliness which, in a continent where one city is much like another, is an asset worth millions of dollars annually to it in tourist traffic.

The Western Gulf Coast

West of the Sabine River, which marks the Texas-Louisiana border, rainfall rapidly diminishes, and the dense forests of the humid subtropical coast give way, first to coastal prairies with scattered woods and then to the dry rangelands that stretch to the Mexican border. Under Spanish and Mexican rule before 1836 there was little agricultural development, and the area was used only for ranching. In modern times, however, while ranching remains important, the introduction of techniques of dry farming and irrigation, together with the increase in the region's population, have brought agriculture to these drier coastlands. The type of crop grown varies with the

[5]J.T. Adams, *The Epic of America*, Atlantic Monthly Press, Boston, 1931, pp. 220–21. Mark Twain's comment on the subject was very much in character: "Mississippi steamboating was born about 1812; at the end of thirty years it had grown to mighty proportions; and in less than thirty more it was dead. A strangely short life for so majestic a creature."

availability of rain or irrigation water. In the better-watered parts of eastern Texas there has developed a characteristic combination of rice culture and cattle raising. In the central section of the state's coastlands, where rainfall is between 30 and 35 in. (750–875 mm) annually, and in the irrigated areas further west it is the cultivation of cotton and vegetables that accompanies cattle raising. In the valley of the Lower Rio Grande the irrigated sections scattered among the brush-covered ranges form an oasis area, where a very wide range of fruits and vegetables are raised. At the inland edge of this irrigated belt lie the counties that form the "Winter Garden" of Texas, noted for onions and spinach and acting, like Florida, as a supplier of fresh winter vegetables. Nearer the coast in western Texas citrus production has become widespread, and Texas, as a comparative newcomer in the competition, has made considerable headway against the older-established producers of Florida and California. Other fruits, including dates, have been introduced, and over much of the area it is possible to achieve double cropping by following winter vegetables with cotton or feed crops.

These dry Texas coastlands, like the area of southern California which they resemble and rival, suffer a major handicap to further progress in their shortage of irrigation water. With an annual rainfall of 20 to 25 in. (500–625 mm) an annual evaporation rate of 60 to 70 in. (1500–1750 mm) and a June-August mean temperature of 85°F (29°C) or more, the area is dependent on the few major rivers flowing south from better-watered regions. Like southern California, too, western Texas has to divide even this available supply between its farms and its rapidly growing industrial cities. And like southern California with the Colorado River, Texas has to share the flow of its main river, the Rio Grande, with its neighbor Mexico—and that after the farmers further upstream, in the irrigated areas of the state of New Mexico, have taken their share of its waters.

While shortage of water places a definite upper limit upon the expansion of the cultivated area, the agricultural prosperity of the southern coastlands is firmly based, nonetheless, on their special climatic character within the United States. But position is by no means the only natural advantage the region enjoys. It both contains and is surrounded by a rich variety of natural resources, whose exploitation has brought employment and, often, sudden wealth to its inhabitants, and a huge volume of transit business to its ports and cities. It is, in fact, to economic expansion in the Cotton Belt and the southern Great Plains as much as to the development of its own potential that the coast owes its new commerce and industries; as much to the mineral wealth that lies beneath the shallow waters of the Gulf of Mexico as to the mineral wealth that geological circumstances have for the present left beneath dry land.

The discovery of oil at Spindletop, near Beaumont, Texas, in 1901 presaged the opening of North America's greatest oil and gas fields. Today Texas, Louisiana, and Oklahoma rank with California as the four major oil and gas producing states of the United States; Texas alone produces more than one-third of the nation's oil, and the southwestern district contains some three-quarters of the known natural gas reserves of the nation. The fields form an almost continuous coastal belt from the west bank of the Mississippi to beyond the Mexican border. Inland they stretch in to Kansas and Arkansas; seaward the deposits extend beneath the Gulf, and their working has provided not only technical problems on a formidable scale but also a first-class political issue—the question of federal or state control of the tidelands oil.

As with oil, so with sulphur; the Gulf coastline has been merely an incidental barrier to mineral prospecting. The coastland sulphur deposits, already the largest known in the world, are being supplemented by further finds offshore from western Louisiana and eastern Texas, and this region supplies virtually the whole of North America's sulphur production.

Associated with the same subterranean domes that contain the sulphur and petroleum deposits is a third mineral, rock salt, and this, too, is mined in quantity in Louisiana. The fourth major mineral resource of these southern

Oil refining on the Gulf Coast: The catalytic cracker towers where crude oil is broken down into petroleum products. (*Sinclair Refining Company*)

the drain is so great that the life expectation of their oil and gas reserves is a matter for recurrent anxiety. Lacking alternative sources of power, they confront the situation that their primary resource is being exploited at a rate which may force them in two generations' time to import fuel once again from outside—and that it is being exploited on behalf not of the Gulf states themselves, but of other regions whose coal or waterpower reserves will last for centuries.

Conservationists in the Gulf states have been expressing concern about the depletion of their resource for many years past without attracting much attention. Suddenly, as it must now seem to them, their concern has become infectious: the whole world, let alone the United States, is conscious of the energy crisis. Oil reserves, quota systems, and new strikes have become matters of public interest and debate. Petroleum and gas supplies, so long taken for granted by the American consumer, are now seen to be precariously finite. One can only regret that it all did not happen rather earlier in the history of the petroleum industry.

But in a region where present achievements are so spectacular and where so much wealth has been created so rapidly, the general atmosphere is anything but gloomy. On the contrary, an impression of breathless progress pervades the cities of the Gulf Coast and the adjacent interior. They are an expression of the region's wealth, a wealth that might prove ephemeral but is for the present as spectacular as anything that North America can show.

Oil fields have seldom become the location of large industrial or urban centers, for their life period is too uncertain to attract the more costly forms of settlement. Where, however, some other factor creates a particularly favorable location within the vicinity of the fields, it is probable that the *combination* of circumstances will stimulate the growth of industries connected with the oil fields and create centers of importance. This is the background to the growth of the western Gulf Coast ports. They are the logical, nearby location for the refineries and chemical industries which accompany oil production. At the same time they would never have achieved such importance as ports

coastlands has already been referred to: it is phosphate rock, a resource whose significance has been steadily increasing with the spread of the fertilizer habit among American farmers. Florida is the continent's leading producer.

Yet this rich natural endowment has in turn created problems for the region, particularly in relation to oil and gas production. As the continent's principal source of these minerals, the central Gulf Coast has become the focus of a huge network of pipelines which carry its products overland to the northern states and southward to the Gulf ports for shipment to even remoter destinations. The Gulf states are primarily exporters, and only a small proportion of their output is used within the states. But

(they are almost all man-made to some extent) had it not been for their proximity to the oil fields. It is this combination of oil field and coastline (that is, of producing point and shipping point) which has brought into being the "Golden Crescent" (the Gulf coast between Brownsville in Texas and Pensacola in Florida), the location of 75 percent of the nation's petroleum processing industry.

Other influences, too, lie behind the rapid development of these cities. One of these is that since the oil fields were opened the western Gulf Coast has become, in E.A. Ackerman's phrase, "one of the foremost areas of recent capital accumulation in the nation."[6] So great has been the wealth created by the oil fields that it far exceeds any possibility of merely plowing back the profits into the industry, and the oil men have had to seek other investment outlets. These they have found in part by entering the wider sphere of national finance and in part by investing in real estate and embellishing the cities of the region.

The other important influence in the growth of these cities has been the westward spread of farming into dry Texas, which has given the western Gulf ports an agricultural hinterland. In the days of the riverboat the produce of the western Cotton Belt was funnelled through New Orleans to the outside world, and the capture and closure of the port was thus a primary objective of the Union forces. But since then, cotton production has spread west and has been supplemented, as we have seen, by other forms of farming made possible by irrigation. It has been as a result of this westward spread of cultivation and of the growth of the oil industry that the western Gulf ports have been increasing their traffic, and it is in view of these developments that both New Orleans and the Texas ports have sponsored rival projects to improve water transport in the Southwest and thus draw off its commerce, in the one case to the Mississippi and in the other to the western Gulf Coast.

While the ports of the Texas coast possess undoubted advantages of position, half a century ago they could hardly have been less suit-

[6]E.A. Ackerman, in W.G. East and A.E. Moodie, eds., *The Changing World*, Harrap, London, 1956, p. 297.

able for purposes of navigation. The alternation of sandbars and shallow lagoons along this coast has meant that almost all the ports west of New Orleans have been created only by means of costly dredging and cutting. Indeed, the two ports which handle the largest tonnage—Houston and Beaumont—both lie on the inland side of the lagoon fringe, 50 mi (80 km) from the sea, with which they are connected by deep water canals. The ports, in turn, are connected with each other by the shallower Intracoastal Waterway which, throughout much of its length, makes use of the line of lagoons that are impassable to ocean shipping. Traffic on the Waterway is building up rapidly: on the Gulf system as a whole there was an increase in ton-miles moved of 75 percent between 1960 and 1970.

Such has been the scale of these engineering works that in 1974 the United States Gulf ports from Lake Charles to Brownsville handled 200 million tons of commerce. A considerable part of this tonnage is made up of coastwise shipments of petroleum products to the Atlantic Coast, but in 1974 a contrary flow of crude oil from abroad to the Gulf Coast refineries helped to increase the traffic. Cotton was another major item in the export trade. It seems probable that in view of the growth of southwestern markets and the excellence of these ports' facilities, they will in time develop much more extensive foreign connections. Around their docks and dredged channels are to be found the new industrial concentrations of the Southwest—petroleum refineries and chemical plants; smelters for imported ores, especially bauxite; and processing plants for deriving magnesium from the waters of the sea.

Texas

The concluding section of this chapter must take account of one problem that confronts every writer who attempts to treat the geography of North America on a regional basis: what to do about Texas. If he adheres rigidly to his regional subdivisions, then this vast state, which contains one-twelfth of the land area of

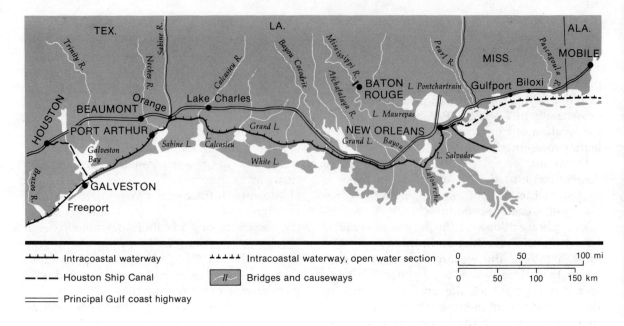

Intracoastal waterway

Houston Ship Canal

Principal Gulf coast highway

Intracoastal waterway, open water section

Bridges and causeways

0   50   100 mi
0   50   100   150 km

Fig. 17-3. Major ports along the Gulf Coast and the Intra-coastal Waterway.

the continental United States, must be divided between at least three major regions—the Great Plains, the Southeast, and the Gulf Coast.[7] But while he will have satisfied his geographical conscience in dissecting it, he will have destroyed one of the most famous—and self-conscious—realities of American society, the Texas of the Texans. That its inhabitants are Texans first, and only secondarily Americans, has become a commonplace in the nation's reckoning and the nation's humor. That the state's individualism has been heightened by national recognition of it is an equally observable fact. Expected to be separatists, the Texans set out with gusto to live up to expectations.

Beneath this phenomenon, however, there lies a certain basis of historical fact and eco-

[7]T.G. Jordan's article, "The Imprint of the Upper and Lower South on Mid-Nineteenth Century Texas," *Annals of the Association of American Geographers*, vol. lvii (1967) 667–90, establishes beyond question that in terms of settlement and historical geography, Texas should equally be subdivided into regions of distinctive character. However, neither Jordan nor anyone else can solve the problem of modern Texan unity outlined in the remainder of this section: it can only be accepted with due meekness by non-Texans.

nomic reality. Texas is the only part of the United States that was an independent republic before it joined the American Union. It was in 1835 that the 20,000 or so settlers who had entered Texas from the eastern United States revolted against the province's Mexican government; in the next year a republic was established and obtained recognition. Only after this young republic had accepted annexation by a plebiscite in 1845 did Texas become part of the United States. The conditions of its entry into the Union were such that it retained somewhat more of its state sovereignty (for example, the ownership of its public lands) than did those other western parts of the nation which began as sparsely populated territories and which only "graduated" to the rank of states after an intermediate period.

The Spanish and Mexican origins of Texan land disposal also gave it a character of its own. Some of its Spanish land subdivisions resemble those of the French in Canada and Louisiana (see Fig. 4-2) rather than the American gridiron. In any case the Mexican government was far more generous (and realistic) to the earliest arrivals than was the United States government further north; the standard grant to a head of family was one league plus one *labor*—a total of 4605 acres (1864.4 ha)—while land remained so plentiful that right up to 1898 a Texan who had none could obtain 160 acres (64.8 ha) for the asking.[8]

Here, then, is the historical background to Texan self-consciousness. As a contributing factor on the geographical side, we may note that the huge dimensions of the state (it is roughly 800 mi (1280 km) from north to south and from east to west, and there are 14 Texan acres (5.67 ha) for each inhabitant) give its people both a wide range of resources and a sense of space and self-sufficiency. Perhaps most important of all, the great southwestern oil boom of the last half century has created wealth and made available capital with an ease and speed in relation to effort expanded which can seldom have been equalled in world history. In these circumstances a belief that the dry soil of Texas possesses magical properties is perhaps understandable. Nor should the word *magical* lead us to overlook, as Cotton Mather has pointed out, the contribution of Texans to the solid business of settling the West:

It was Texans who initiated most of the great cattle drives a century ago to the northern railheads, it was Texans who pioneered the introduction of Brahma cattle in the United States, and it was Texans who were responsible for developing the first officially recognized American breed of beef cattle, the Santa Gertrudis. Texans opened most of the oil fields on the southern, central, and northern Great Plains. They initiated suitcase farming, they own and operate most of the migratory custom combines [which harvest Great Plans crops], they instituted the planting of winter wheat in the "spring wheat belt. . . ."[9]

Much of the wealth created by the oil fields has found expression, as we have already seen, in the growth of the metropolitan areas of the Southwest. Of these the largest is Hous-

ton, whose 1950 population of 806,000 had by 1974 risen to 2.2 million. We have already noted its leading position among the nation's ports; its industrial development has been no less spectacular. Within some 50 mi (80 km) of the city is produced almost one-tenth of the nation's crude oil; it has more than a dozen refineries as well as numerous plants producing chemicals and synthetic rubber; and it is the main steel-milling center of the Southwest. The availability of cheap oil and gas fuel has attracted to the area numerous other industries, among which the manufacture of mining equipment is the largest employer. As port and as industrial center, there seems no immediate reason why the meteoric rise of Houston should not continue.

Perhaps the term "rise" is not the one which best describes Houston's growth, for it has tended to expand outward rather than up. As we saw in Chapter 4, Houston is the one major city in America which will have nothing to do with zoning; its growth and its land uses are left to free market forces and it covers a huge area. This may in part explain its powerful attraction for newcomers, and especially for ethnic minorities—300,000 blacks and 150,000 Mexican Americans.

By contrast with Houston, the western metropolis of San Antonio, with a population of 980,000, derives its importance principally from the agriculture of its hinterland. East of it lie the cotton lands of central Texas; not far to the west, cultivation gives place to ranching. In a country where the general movement of agricultural produce is from west to east, however, San Antonio, like most of the cities on the margin of the dry plains, looks west rather than east.[10] Thus it was here, in 1874, that there was given the first demonstration in the Southwest of a new device to solve the ranchers' fencing problem—barbed wire—and the interests of San Antonio have been bound

[8]T.L. Miller, *The Public Lands of Texas, 1519–1970*, University of Oklahoma Press, Norman, 1972.

[9]E. Cotton Mather, "The American Great Plains," *Annals of the Association of American Geographers*, vol. lxii (1972), 237–57; quotation on p. 257.

[10]It has an additional good reason for doing so: it was the military base and capital of the Spanish and later the Mexican province of Texas, and all its early connections were with Mexico City. From San Antonio there stretched the chain of mission stations which Spain thrust out northeastward to the Red River to head off the French (see Chap. 20).

up with the rangelands, with cattle and sheep, ever since. With the westward shift of agriculture and the coming of irrigation, however, the city has also become a collecting point for the produce of an area that raises cotton, corn, and vegetables.

There remain for consideration Dallas and Fort Worth which together form an S.M.S.A. of 2.5 million inhabitants. The disparity in size between them (Dallas is almost twice as large as Fort Worth) does nothing to mitigate the intensity of the famous rivalry between these two cities, whose centers are 33 mi (53 km) apart; proximity is a stimulant to the contest. From the geographical point of view, however, it is not their competitive similarities that are of real interest, but their differences of function. For these two cities, standing as they do close to the frontier between humid East and arid West (the long-term record gives Dallas a mean annual precipatation of 33.6 in. [840 mm] and Fort Worth one of 31.6 in. [790 mm]) divide between them those relationships with both regions that Kansas City, for example, combines within a single metropolitan area.

Dallas belongs primarily to the western Cotton Belt; it is a great cotton market, and is linked with cultivation and the more humid East. Fort Worth is a cattle town grown prosperous and industrialized; it looks westward to the ranges, and its stockyards are the largest anywhere south of Kansas City. Thus the descriptions of these cities belong, properly speaking, to the separate chapters of this book on the South and the Great Plains, with the regional boundary cutting across the narrow gap that lies between them. But in reality they form one urban concentration whose functions, like those of the cities in the western Interior, link it with both East and West, and whose common possession is the quality of being Texan. Since 1974, they have shared "the world's biggest airport," situated midway between them.

As with Houston, so with Dallas and Fort Worth, it is oil that has made these market cities wealthy, while cheap fuel and the sunshine and space of Texas have brought industry to them. Dallas has developed a well-balanced structure of consumer industries and has become a clothing fashion center and regional commercial capital in the process. Fort Worth's postwar employment has been dominated by the aircraft industry, which moved to Texas, as it did to California, to profit from the availability of space, low heating costs, and the possibility of carrying out in the open air some of the industry's space-consuming operations.

Texan boasts have been loud, but the impressiveness of Texan progress over recent years cannot be denied. Although its dry western half must seem uninviting to anyone but a local enthusiast, the state has maintained a rate of population increase since 1945 that is among the most rapid in the nation. Such rapid development has been made possible by the realization of the state's greatest asset—its petroleum resources. Income has accumulated more swiftly than it could be usefully invested. Inevitably, some of the investment has been unwise, some even frivolous. But an increasing and welcome sense of maturity in the Texan attitude to the state's rich resources has been emerging and this, together with the shadow of the energy crisis which now hangs over all fuel-producing regions, should ensure that the area plays a full and responsible part in decision making in the future.

18

The Great Plains
and the Prairies

Introduction

It is one of the splendid paradoxes with which North America abounds that the region of the continent possessing the least physical distinction has been the scene of some of the most dramatic episodes in the story of its human occupance. On the smooth surface of the Great Plains, which stretch from southern Texas north to the Arctic Ocean, have occurred the continent's sharpest clashes of group interest. And while these deceptively innocent-looking grasslands have attracted successive generations of settlers, nature has provided, both above and beneath their surface, hazards which time and again have forced the settlers to recoil before an environment they have failed to tame.

For in terms of human geography the Great Plains have formed a problem region—an area which forced upon settlers, even quite recent settlers, a respect for natural conditions which even today cannot be treated carelessly. As the pioneers left the humid, fertile Midwest and moved westward across the central lowlands of North America, they were moving into an area

where the natural controls of man's activities—climate and soil—asserted themselves with increasing vehemence; a vehemence which the smoothness of relief masked but did nothing to mitigate. After a few decades of occupance the region's problems were evident to the most casual visitor; they could be seen in blizzards and in dust storms, in eroded fields and abandoned farms. They served notice that, if the plains were to be settled with any hope of permanency, it would be necessary to accept the limitations of this fierce but fascinating environment and to develop a system of land use which was truly compatible with it.

This "problem area" does not exactly correspond in extent with the physical province of the Great Plains as we defined it in Chapter 1. For the eastern edge of that province is an area of settled and generally prosperous farming which comprises the western parts of the Wheat, Corn, and Cotton belts. The regional problem is one of security against climatic hazard, for as we move west across the plains the threat of climatic accident, negligible in the Midwest, grows steadily greater, become serious after we pass the 98th or 100th meridian of

The Great Plains environment: The margin of the Plains. The uplift of the Rocky Mountains contorted the otherwise largely horizontal strata underlying the Plains and created along the base of the mountains a series of west-facing scarps representing the up-tilted edges of these Plains strata. The picture was taken southwest of Denver. *(John S. Shelton)*

longitude. Thus defined, the "problem area" covers much of western Texas, the western parts of Oklahoma, Kansas, Nebraska, and the Dakotas, and the southwestern part of the Prairie Provinces. On the west it terminates at the foothills of the Rockies, where the increasingly broken terrain removes the temptation to unwise agricultural activity. On the east and north the boundary between the problem area and the rest of the Great Plains province fluctuates year by year; it is a boundary not of relief but of risk; it differentiates between the relatively secure farming of the Agricultural Interior and the relatively hazardous business of occupying the dry plains.

The Physical Circumstances

The factors which govern the character of Great Plains settlement are primarily climatic. The plains lie in a continental interior, intermediate between the humid East and the definitely arid West, and this location governs the climatic régime.

PRECIPITATION

With the high wall of the Rockies blocking their western margin, the Great Plains depend for most of their precipitation on the northward intrusion of moist air from the Gulf of Mexico. There is thus a general decrease in the amount of precipitation from southeast to northwest across the plains; Abilene, Texas (32° N, 99° W), averages 25 in. (625 mm) per annum and Oklahoma City (35° N, 97° W) 32 in. (800 mm), while Miles City in Montana (47° N, 106° W) has 13 in. (325 mm) and Medicine Hat, Alberta (50° N, 111° W), has slightly less than this amount. In the winter season both rainfall and snowfall are light—a fact to which we must shortly return—and over the plains generally, some 70 to 80 percent of the precipitation occurs between May and September; that is, in the vital months of summer plant growth. While this rainfall régime discourages tree growth and while the rains fall at the time when evaporation rates are highest, the small quantity of moisture received by the plains does, nevertheless, arrive at the season of maximum demand for the farmer or rancher.

However, the rain-bearing Gulf air, upon whose intrusions the Great Plains depend, is not altogether reliable in its habits. As it moves northward over the continent this tropical maritime air generally trends northeast rather than northwest, with the result that the amount of rain reaching the plains, and in particular the quantity of the vital summer rains, varies greatly from year to year. Over much of the plains the mean annual variation is as much as 25 percent of the annual precipitation. This variability is greatest in the southern plains, where the rainfall is somewhat more plentiful. The dry northern plains have less precipitation, but their supply is slightly more reliable, for they lie closer to the source areas of the polar continental air, whose interaction with the humid Gulf air forces the latter to deposit its moisture.

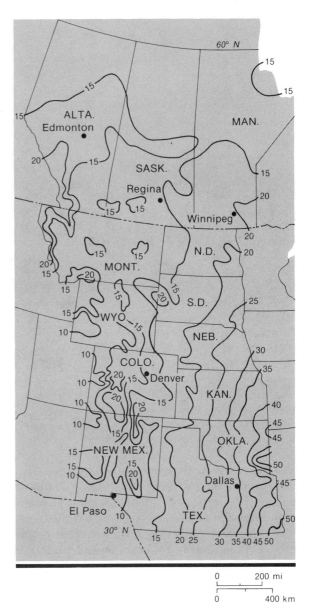

Fig. 18-1. The Great Plains and the Prairies: Annual precipitation in inches.

TEMPERATURE

The Great Plains experience the extremes of temperature characteristic of a continental interior. The northern plains on both sides of the international boundary have recorded the lowest winter temperatures experienced in any populated part of the continent—between 50° and 60° F below zero (−45° to −51° C). On the other hand, summer temperatures in all parts of the Great Plains soar to maxima of over 100° F (38° C). In rather general terms winter tem-

321

The Great Plains environment: The effect of wind erosion. A blowout hollow with core in western Nebraska about 1897. (U.S. Geological Survey)

peratures tend to vary with latitude. The southern edge of the plains has a January mean of 50° F. (10° C.), while at the Canadian boundary the figure is 0° to 5° F. (−18° to −15° C.). Summer temperatures, on the other hand, are governed partly by latitude and partly by altitude, the higher, western edge being in general cooler than the eastern edge, which is some 3000 ft (910 m) lower. However, this general pattern is disturbed by the effects of the Chinook. Dry air from the Pacific coast, which is warmer than the prevailing winter air over the plains, crosses the Rocky Mountain barrier and, descending the eastern slope of the mountains, brings a sudden and spectacular increase of temperature to the foothills and western plains—a welcome if brief break in the intense winter cold of the area.

CLIMATIC HAZARDS

But the statistics we have so far considered tell only a part of the story of the struggle with the Great Plains environment. It is not the basic climatic conditions that are the menace of the region, but the climatic hazards that accompany them. These are of four kinds.

1. Frost. Since temperatures are affected by two wholly different air masses whose influences tend to alternate over the area, the length of the frost-free season varies greatly from year to year. On the average, its length is about 100 days in the southern Prairie Provinces and 240 days in central Texas, but over a forty-year period it has varied from 129 to 181 days at stations on the Nebraska-Colorado border, and from 89 to 172 days in western North Dakota, near the international boundary.

2. Hail. The central and southern Great Plains are the area of the continent most subject to hailstorms, and, infrequent though they may be, a single storm is sufficient to do immense damage to crops.

3. Winds. The winds sweep this smooth, treeless area unchecked. There are several types of wind peculiar to the plains, and all of

them are deadly in their effects. On the southern plains the summer danger is provided by the hot winds that blow from the interior and parch the crops, while in winter this same area suffers from the visitations of the Norther, a cold wind causing sudden drops in temperature and so representing a serious frost hazard.

But the "grizzly of the Plains," in W.P. Webb's phrase, is the blizzard. In winter the principal storm tracks cross the continent from west to east, approximately in the latitude of the international boundary, but occasionally there occurs an overspill of cold air out of the north, which breaks across the storm tracks, moves southeast along the front of the Rockies, and swings out into the central Great Plains. There the storm may last for several days, while its center shifts and circles unpredictably. Apart from the immediate danger created by the wild weather, the particular menace of the blizzard is that it usually brings with it a heavy snowfall, which the wind builds up into deep drifts. On the Great Plains which, as we have already seen, generally experience little snowfall, ranchers usually leave their stock to winter outdoors. But the snowdrifts deny the stock access to food supplies, so that the animals are the chief victims of the blizzards. Serious economic loss often follows the passage of these vicious winter storms.

Quite apart from the effects of these particular winds upon temperature and humidity, however, there is the ever-present threat of wind erosion on the Great Plains. With little in the way of an obstacle above the surface and with poorly consolidated parent materials below it, the soil of the Great Plains falls an easy victim, once bared to the wind's action. In few other regions of the world does unwise cultivation receive such prompt and embarrassing publicity as when the dust storms rise to darken the skies above the Great Plains.

4. Drought. We have already seen that the principal source of precipitation for the plains is the unpredictable intrusion of moist air northwestward from the Gulf of Mexico, and that this produces wide variations in rainfall from year to year. But what complicates the problem of the settler in this area is that the years of subnormal rainfall have a tendency to occur in groups; so that it is by no means safe to assume that a year of meager rainfall will be followed by a year of compensating excess. On the contrary, the records of the past half-century show that rainfall may be above or below average for a decade at a time. In Montana, for example, during the years 1906–16 inclusive, the rainfall was above average in every single year (and was 125 percent or more of normal in six of them). Then between 1928 and 1937 inclusive, it was below the fifty-year average for eight of the ten years, and for the three years 1934–36 never exceeded 75 percent of normal.

Such a rainfall régime as this clearly increases the difficulties presented by the environment: the wetter-than-normal decade gives a false impression of humidity and fertility, and so lures the settler to the margins of possible farming. Then the drier decade that follows robs him of any possibility of tiding over from one season to the next. In other words, on the Great Plains the average rainfall figure is doubly deceptive: it conceals year-to-year fluctuations, which a resolute farmer can survive, and it also conceals decade-to-decade fluctuations, which he cannot.

In very general terms, the decade of the 1930s on the Great Plains was a bad one. Even without the general depression, which was causing acute distress throughout the nation, the drought years of 1934 and 1936 (when most of the plains had less than 75 percent of average rainfall) would have been serious; the coincidence of the events was catastrophic. The 1940s were years when rainfall was somewhat above normal, and farm yields on the Great Plains were high—happily for war-torn nations elsewhere. The 1950s, however, proved to be another decade of general rainfall deficiency; on the southern plains, farmers and ranchers suffered a succession of drought years, and many gave up hope and abandoned their holding.

But the 1960s again reversed the situation: they were a decade of generally average-to-better rainfall, and at the end of the decade the plains wore an air of prosperity which they had all too seldom displayed in the century or so since the first settlers arrived. The sequence, however, continues: the 1970s have

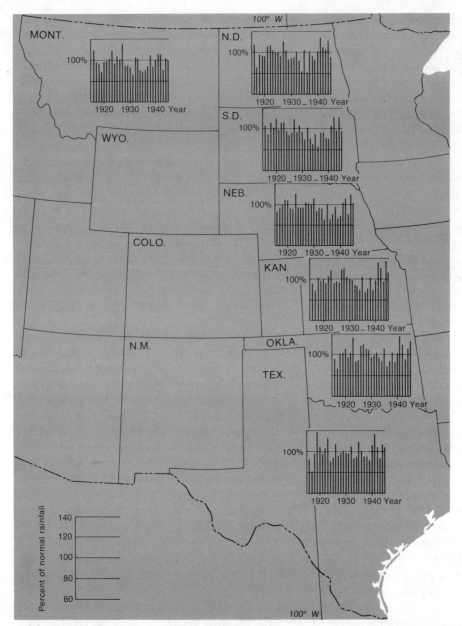

Fig. 18-2. The Great Plains: Rainfall variability. The map shows the rainfall each year from 1916 to 1945 in each of seven Great Plains states, expressed as a percentage of the forty-year average.

seen one more swing of the pendulum. The mid-seventies saw the drought area spreading eastward even into the Corn Belt. Today as we shall see, the farmers are much better prepared than their predecessors to survive drought years, but the drought years occur just the same.

SOILS AND VEGETATION

The general decline in the amount of precipitation from east to west across the Great Plains produces a fairly regular progression in the types of soil and vegetation found there. These soils fall within the general order of Mollisols and grade from Udolls in the eastern plains to Ustolls in the west and Borolls in the north: in the older terminology from black earths in the more humid east, though dark brown to brown on the dry western margins of the plains. As a result of glacial deposition over the northern part of the region, these soils are developed from a wide variety of materials, almost all re-

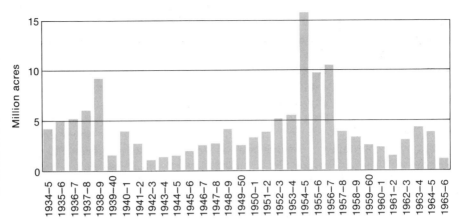

Fig. 18-3. The Great Plains: Soil damage, 1934–66. The diagram shows the area of the United States plains estimated by the Soil Conservation Service to have suffered damage, mainly by wind erosion, each season. The period begins with the latter part of the dust bowl period, but the damage done in the dry 1950s was actually greater in extent, although less publicized.

cent, but they all support a grassland vegetation whose character likewise varies with the amount of rainfall. The black soils support—or rather, supported, for most of them are now under cultivation—a tall-grass, sod-forming vegetation, while in the semiarid west, the vegetation consists of shorter grasses, which form a mat cover in the moister parts and a cover of scattered bunch grasses in the driest sections.

The soil factor which governs this progression is a layer of salts accumulated in the subsoil, beneath which is a permanently dry zone. The depth of this layer beneath the surface varies with the amount of rainfall and with the length of the "wet" season. In the black earth belt it lies between 30 and 40 in. (75–100 cm) below the surface, so that long-rooted grasses and cereals can flourish. Westward, the salt layer rises nearer the soil surface with the increasing aridity, until at the western margin of the plains it is only 8 to 12 in. (20–30 cm) down, and root development is only possible for short grasses. The point where the depth of the layer beneath the surface is 25 to 30 in. (50–75 cm) is an important dividing line: it is the line of change from black earth to brown, from tall, prairie grass to short, plains grass. In terms of human occupance it is the line that divides the eastern Great Plains from the "problem area" to the west. Lying as it does between the 98th and 100th meridians of west longitude, it is this line that accounts for the prominence of those meridians in every discussion of the settlement of the Great Plains.

But if this is the general pattern established by nature, it has been modified by man. For reasons which we must shortly consider, the "natural" vegetation of much of the Great Plains, especially in their southwestern section, is quite different today from that of a century ago. The character of the range vegetation has changed with use. In particular, changes have occurred in the balance between grasses and shrubs, and a tough, woody shrub vegetation of sagebrush or mesquite has spread over millions of acres of former grasslands, to change the appearance of the southwestern plains and increase the severity of soil erosion.

Because the character of the plains vegetation is an index of the amount, reliability, and seasonal duration of rainfall, it serves also as a guide to the areas that may safely be cultivated and to those better left under the native grass cover. Most of the tall-grass prairie has been under cultivation for several decades without serious mishap. The area covered by shorter, grama-wheatgrass associations, on the other hand, represents an agricultural margin where cultivation is risky, while the sections of the plains covered by a grama-buffalograss combination, or even more, by a mesquite-sage association, carry in their vegetation a warning which the cultivator ignores to his cost.

Land Use in the Great Plains

In the years between the end of the Revolutionary War (1783) and the 1830s the frontier of settlement in the United States spread rapidly westward across the Mississippi Valley to the eastern edge of the Great Plains. From there it jumped across 1500 mi (2400 km) of intervening plain, mountain, and desert to the Pacific coast, and not for almost half a century was progress made in filling the gap with permanent settlements. In Canada the sequence of events was comparable. Beyond the wilderness barrier of the Laurentian Shield small, farm-based colonies were planted at the eastern edge of the Great Plains (in what is now the Winnipeg area) in the decade 1810–20. But for over fifty years these struggling colonies knew little expansion; the population of Manitoba at the census of 1871 was 25,000, and the West continued to be of interest as a source not of agricultural products, but of furs and gold.

The reasons for this abrupt halt to the westward spread of settlement have become familiar to a later generation as a classic example of environmental control upon man's activities. For this was an area with an annual rainfall of 20–30 in. (500–750 mm) and a smooth surface, which in statistical theory could have been cultivated, but which, in terms of the techniques available in the 1830s, might as well have been a desert. Indeed, so hopeless did the task of settling it seem to early travellers, that the firm conviction took root that it *was* a desert, and it was treated as such, in the 1840s and 1850s, by American geography teachers and policy-makers alike. As early as 1843 some scores of pioneer farmers had decided that agricultural prospects in Oregon were better than those in the Great Plains and had made the hazardous transcontinental journey by the Oregon Trail; their reports, backed by the discovery of gold in California in 1848, encouraged others to follow. In the south the Spanish-Mexican population had been equally unsuccessful in establishing permanent settlements on the plains. If the area possessed any virtue at all, in mid-nineteenth-century eyes, it was that at least it was possible to cross it swiftly on the way to pleasanter places.

The environmental problems were threefold:

1. The area was treeless. It was not merely that to eastern minds land that would not grow trees was poor land, but also that in the 1840s there was in the West neither coal nor cheap iron and consequently no substitute for wood as a domestic necessity. There was no means of fencing land and no means of building homes; the earliest dwellings were sod houses, which were merely pits roofed with turf and a few precious timbers. The only substitute for wood as a fuel was buffalo dung.

2. The sheer dryness of the plains found the eastern farmer ill-prepared, his crops unsuited to the short wet season, and his farming techniques adapted to a more humid climate.

3. The limited supply of available water raised its own problems; rivers often flowed only seasonally, and waterholes were few and far between. Under the cheap land policies prevailing at the time, and even more under the pre-emption policy, the earliest arrivals took up the lands adjacent to the water supply, and so made valueless the waterless lands on the interfluves and away from the waterholes. Only slowly were legal measures adopted to control the use of western water, and indeed, in spite of progress made in both legislation and provision of water, the problem of waterless lands remains acute up to the present day.

The farmer who had migrated from the humid East was, therefore, simply not equipped to deal with the plains environment; in this technical sense the Great American Desert was a reality. But the pioneers in the United States (for here the story of settlement on the Canadian prairies tends to diverge from that of the United States plains and will be treated separately in a later section) had also to face another obstacle to westward progress—the Plains Indians. We have seen in Chapter 2 how the horse became available to the tribes of the Interior after the arrival of the Spaniards in Mexico. Because this gave the Indians a new mobility and in particular because the horse made it possible to hunt the buffalo which roamed the grasslands, there took place a migration of tribes from the surrounding forests to the plains, to exploit the new situation.

Thus there occurred in the Great Plains an encounter between the two groups of newcomers, the red and the white, which has become the most publicized culture clash in history. Indian resistance was ferocious, and on the western trails travel was safe only in convoy. Nowhere else, on a continent which had known a long and tragic series of Indian wars, was the struggle so bitter or the Indian strength so great as on the Great Plains.

If peace came at length, it was due partly to the development of superior fighting skills on the side of the white man, with his famous Colt revolver, and partly to the virtual extinction of the buffalo, rather than to the triumph of sedentary agriculture. The time for that had not yet come. Throughout the history of white settlement of the plains there have been two principal claimants to the grasslands—the rancher and the wheat farmer—and of the two the rancher was there first. It took time for the frontier farmers to develop the techniques necessary to bring the plains under cultivation, and while they were doing so the cattlemen lived through their heyday.

"The physical basis of the cattle kingdom was grass," says W.P. Webb, "and it extended itself over all the grassland not occupied by farms."[1] Ranching represented the most profitable means of occupying a grassland area which for the moment was useless to the agriculturalist. Its origin was in Texas, where the early settlers had already developed a type of stock raising suited to the Great Plains environment, for "in the final analysis, the cattle kingdom arose at that place where men began to manage cattle on horseback. It was the use of the horse that primarily distinguished ranching in the West from stock farming in the East."[2]

The "cattle kingdom" was built up by two processes. First, there was the process of delivering Texas cattle to eastern markets. After some groping by the Texas drovers for the best method of doing this, a pattern emerged. Cattle were driven north from the source region in Texas until the trail met the westward-thrusting railways that led to Kansas City, St. Louis, or Chicago. There the drovers sold the cattle and the buyers shipped them north and east by rail. As the railways built west across the plains in the 1870s, so the shipping points moved west also. Under these conditions the grasslands simply served as a great transit

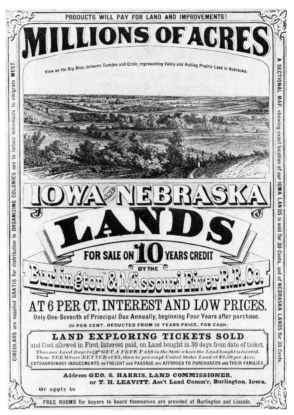

The settlement of the Western Interior: (1) One of many broadsides issued to encourage settlers to take up land in the west, in this case in Iowa and Nebraska. *(Library of Congress)*

camp, providing forage along the way for the northbound stock.

The second feature of the cattle era, however, was the spread of ranching from its original location in the southern plains until it covered the whole of the unfarmed grassland northward into Montana and Canada. Texas cattle supplied not only meat for eastern markets but stock for other western ranches. By the mid-1880s ranching had taken hold of an area which little more than a decade ago had been empty of productive activity.

Of this early, romanticized cattle era it is necessary to say that economically it was an unimproved and unimproving activity. Its basis was the natural range, open and unfenced,[3]

[1]W.P. Webb, *The Great Plains*, Ginn & Co., Boston, 1931, p. 207.

[2]Ibid.

[3]Since the grassland was still legally part of the public domain, it was illegal to fence it, although some cattlemen tried to stake claims by this means: troops were sent out to remove the fences.

327

The Settlement of the Western Interior: (2) *The Stone Boat* by Harvey Dunn. Dunn vividly recorded in a long series of paintings the lives and hardships of early settlers in the Dakotas. The "stone boat" was a sledge drawn by a team of oxen. The stones were used for building on the treeless plains. *(South Dakota State Univ.)*

the stock was almost wild, and breeding to improve the strain was out of the question. It is therefore not surprising that, once the plains began to fill up, the cattlemen had to change their ways. In the 1880s the farm frontier began at last to advance once more. Equipped with the new barbed wire, the plainsmen began legally to fence the range, the farmers to protect their crops, and the go-ahead ranchers to improve their stock. The old-style, open-range cattlemen cut all the wire they could find, but gradually they were forced either to retreat further still to the west or to accept a more sedentary life. Ranchers and farmers came to divide the ranges between them, the ranchers taking the rougher, drier western plains and the farmers the smoother and more humid east. The days of the cattle kingdom ended abruptly, as they had begun abruptly only twenty years before.

The advance of the farm frontier across the eastern part of this debatable land occurred in the 1880s, while the more westerly farmlands have been occupied in a series of advances and retreats lasting from the 1890s to the present day. The advance was made possible by a series of developments in technique and equipment which opened the plains to the cultivation of cereals. These were (1) the development of drought-resistant and frost-resistant grains, suited to conditions on the plains; (2) the evolution of dry-farming techniques, upon which such great hopes were pinned in the 1880s; (3) the mechanization of grain farming, the effect of which was to increase the area one man could cultivate, and so to make it possible for him to live by extensive farming, even when yields were low; (4) the invention of barbed wire, a cheap fencing material in place of timber, which enabled plainsmen to keep the

The Settlement of the Western Interior: (3) An early home-stead. Because of the lack of building materials on the treeless plains, early homes were often walled and roofed with sods. In the picture, the Chrisman sisters pose outside their home on Lieban Creek, Custer County, Nebraska. *(Nebraska State Historical Society)*

ranchers' cattle out of the crops and away from each other; and (5) the development of a cheap, easily erected windmill. This made it possible, on the one hand, to raise water from greater depths and in more constant supply than by hand pump; and on the other, to provide a water supply at isolated and waterless places on the grasslands, so that cattle could be fenced into separate pastures instead of crowding around the few natural water sources and trampling down the waterside areas.

In the years between 1880 and 1890, therefore, while the population of the United States rose by 25 percent, that of the Great Plains states increased by 78 percent. (If Texas, which already had over 1,500,000 inhabitants in 1880, is excluded, the increase was 110 percent.) But the 1890s were years of drought, and the advance of settlement faltered. Hundreds of those who had arrived only a few years previ-

ously to plow up the western plains left, defeated. The population of Nebraska increased by only 4000, as against an increase of more than half a million in the previous decade. Only after 1896, when there began a series of wetter years that lasted until 1910, did the westward movement again gather momentum. The early 1890s had provided a fair sample of the experiences that lay ahead of the farmers on the plains.

The newcomers planted grain; between 1900 and 1910 the wheat acreage on the southern plains increased by 600 percent. They did this in face of the difficulty of securing from the all-powerful railways satisfactory rates for transport to the flour mills, and under constant threat of catastrophe by dought, blight, and insect pests. In an area where yields of wheat might vary from 15–20 bushels per acre (37–49 per ha) in a good year to 5 bushels (12.3) or nothing in a dry one, they came to depend to a dangerous degree on this single, wholly hazardous form of livelihood. Each series of wetter years tended to obliterate the memory of the preceding drought and to deceive a fresh group of newcomers.[4]

The effects of both ranching and wheat farming on the Great Plains soon became apparent; the ranching areas began to suffer from overgrazing and the wheat areas from unwise cultivation. Because the rainfall of the plains varies from year to year, the amount of range forage available also varies, and this in turn requires that the numbers of stock grazed be adjusted to the condition of the range. But the adjustment was seldom made in time; the temptation to graze the ranges to their peak capacity is always strong, and the grasslands deteriorated in consequence. The grasses grazed by the stock declined severely and were replaced by shrubs and plants that were either less sought after or entirely worthless. As the carrying capacity of the ranges diminished, sheep and goats replaced cattle,[5] brush replaced grass, and the forces of erosion met less and less resistance to their attack. In 1936, when the famous government report *The Future of the Great Plains* was issued, it was estimated that the western ranges as a whole were 70 percent overstocked and that

their carrying capacity had been reduced by more than half in eighty years.

For this deterioration, as Chapter 4 suggests, the individual rancher was not wholly to blame. If the ranges were overgrazed, it was partly because the government, failing to appreciate in time that the institutions of the humid East would not suit the dry West, prevented the rancher from securing legally a holding adequate to provide him with a living. Marion Clawson has written of an "institutional fault line" at 98° W—that is, a line to the west of which fresh policies and laws were needed, ones adapted to the thinner scatter of resources and the possibility of using land in large blocks or in common. Before such a policy had been formulated, much of the plains had been homesteaded in 160- or 320-acre (65 or 130 ha) blocks—as if they were tall-grass prairies in Iowa or Illinois.

The results of wheat cultivation were equally serious and far more spectacular. Removal of the natural grass cover on the dry plains, especially during the days of the "dust mulch" régime described in Chapter 6, exposed the soil to powerful erosive action. That the frontier of grain farming was too far to the west needed no demonstration in dust bowl years or when low prices made production, at 5 bushels to the acre (12.3 per ha), hopelessly uneconomical. The real problem has arisen in better years—especially in the humid 1940s, when the stimulants of wartime demand and support prices made grain farming of almost any standard profitable. It is in such years as these that the challenge of conservation farming has been hardest to face and the temptation to plant more wheat the strongest. To quote Marion Clawson again, "The real problem is not to put poor wheat land into grass—the real problem is to keep it there, when unusually favorable weather and/or price years come again."[6]

Present Patterns and Problems

Today most of the plains area wears a prosperous air, and the catastrophic events of the

---

[4]For a fuller discussion of the effect of climatic variations on Great Plains wheat yields, see either "Risk in the Central Great Plains," by L. Hewes and A. C. Schmiedling, *Geographical Review*, vol. xlvi (1956) 375–87, or "Weather-Crop Relationships," by E.M. Frisby, *I.B.G. Trans & Papers*, 1951, 79–96, with additional references. In Miss Frisby's study the most important correlations established were between the yield and (1) precipitation in the pre-yield year, (2) May-plus-June precipitation in the yield year, and (3) mean July temperature in the yield year.

[5]This trend was especially marked in southern Texas, which became the main sheep-raising area of the United States. Between 1920 and 1959, while the number of sheep and lambs in the United States fell overall from 40 to 34 million, the numbers in Texas rose from 2.5 million to 6 million. Since that time the totals have fallen again, but of the 13.35 million sheep and lambs in the United States in 1975, 2.6 million, or just under 20 percent, were in Texas. Range deterioration led to an increase in the number of sheep and goats: range improvement and better stocking practices have led to their numbers falling again as they are replaced once more by cattle.

[6]M. Clawson, "An Institutional Innovation to Facilitate Land Use Changes in the Great Plains," *Land Economics*, vol xxxiv, 75.

1930s seem very remote. "The recovery of the Great Plains economy from 1938 to 1945 was as spectacular as had been its downfall," writes Bailey; it was "almost miraculous."[7] This is not to say that hard times may not come again: climatically they are quite certain to do so, if the statistics do not lie. But the Great Plains farmers today are in a far better position to cope with them than their predecessors; they have been able to outgrow both the ignorance and the fears of earlier generations.

In retrospect we can see that, given the variability of climatic conditions on the Great Plains, from year to year and from decade to decade, most of the problems which defeated so many early settlers were the result of three things:

1. Lack of reserves. When a settler homesteaded a 160-acre (64.8 ha) holding on the Great Plains, he was likely to start with minimal resources of capital and equipment and to stake everything on his success. If he was unfortunate enough to pick a dry spell in which to begin, he had nothing to fall back on (although some colonizing agencies, such as the railroads, did re-equip settlers on their own lands if they lost their first crop or two); he clung grimly to "his" land until he had nothing left and then suffered total defeat. It was this lack of reserves which caused so many personal tragedies among the first waves of settlers.

2. Lack of technical alternatives. The farming practiced by the first plains settlers was the only kind most of them knew—the mixed farming they had carried on back in the East or the Midwest.[8] But the drier conditions of the plains enforced changes of practice; yields were lower and conservation measures were necessary, and some of the midwestern crops could no longer be relied upon. To learn the new techniques and find alternative crops took time—too much time for many of the first settlers to survive until they did so. The outcome in terms of land use was likely to be either an attenuated mixed farming or an unwise concentration on wheat, neither of them a solid basis for resistance to a cycle of dry years.

3. Inflexible administrative and financial arrangements. As we have already seen, the plains were settled within a framework of law and finance that had developed in the humid East. The most obvious expression of this eastern thinking was the retention of 160 acres (64.8 ha) as the basic size of government land grant. This figure of 160 acres first appeared in legislation governing disposal of land in what is now Indiana in 1804. It was a feature of other land acts up to and including the Homestead Act of 1862, and, despite the fact that settlement had by this time reached the borders of the dry plains it was left unchanged—even after Major J.W. Powell's famous report in the late 1870s had urged the necessity for a working unit in the dry West of at least 2560 acres (1036 ha). The concept of the homestead as a holding of what might be called "eastern-family size" went unmodified in legislation virtually until 1969; in some legislation, in fact (see p. 387), it survives to the present day.

The outcome was to tie the fortunes of thousands of settlers to one particular quarter-section of land on which, in a region of climatic uncertainty, their whole future depended. It is little wonder that in the 1950s Kraenzel wrote "It is not the fact of semi-aridity that causes the difficulties in the Plains, but the fact of an

[7]W.R. Bailey, "The Great Plains in Retrospect," *Journal of Farm Economics*, vol. xlv, 1092, 1095.

[8]The movement onto the Great Plains was generally not the sort of long-distance migration which resulted in Ukrainian peasants abruptly appearing in Saskatchewan or Scandinavians in the Dakotas (although it is true that some of the colonization societies, especially in Canada, produced this effect). Most of it represented short-distance advances by farmers whose previous experience was certainly American, often gained in borderline areas. Thus in Gunnar Rolvaag's classic, *Giants in the Earth*, his heroes move only from southern Minnesota to eastern South Dakota: yet, even this short move presented difficulties of adjustment which taxed them to the limit. This book and its sequel, *Peder Victorious*, are well worth reading in this connection. By the same token, it has been calculated that in the main post-Civil War migration into Kansas (1870–90), of 526,000 new arrivals 75.3 percent were white Americans, 3.3 percent were black Americans, and only 21.4 percent were foreign-born whites: many of them, of course, would have had a previous home or homes in America.

unadapted culture that does so."[9] What was needed, then, was administrative flexibility: "Management principles for the Great Plains farmer must be such that he can shift quickly and roll with the punch,"[10] and he must have legal and financial freedom to do so.

If we consider each of these problems in turn, it becomes apparent that in most respects the Great Plains farmer or rancher of today is far better off than his predecessor. It is not so much a question of *prosperity*— although at this particular moment of time the level of prosperity is high over most of the region—as of *security* and *stability*.

1. The provision of reserves. The early settlers had nothing but their quarter-section, and there was no chance of alternative employment within hundreds of miles if their farms failed. Today's farms are large and becoming larger: they are, in fact, gradually reaching what might be called a realistic size for this region. And a sizeable proportion of them are owned by people who have interests elsewhere; that is, their stake in the land is incidental rather than vital, and they will not starve if the harvest is bad. For those who do represent the real successors of Rolvaag's "giants," there is always the possibility that in a drought year a job in a garage or workshop will provide interim employment. Thus life within the region need not again come to a standstill, as it virtually did in the 1930s.

To this factor of diminished regional dependence on the outcome of a single harvest year or series of years can be added that of increased physical reserves to tide over bad times. Past experience has taught the plains farmers to prepare for trouble in advance, and most of them today either carry or have access to a stockpile of fodder which, as with Joseph in Egypt, is reckoned in some cases to be as much as a seven-year reserve.

It was precisely the lack of such reserves that ruined the chances of earlier generations of the region's farmers. What has happened to change the situation? Today's reserves are the product in part of higher yields and also in large measure of irrigation and reservoir building—that is, reserves of produce result from creating reserves of water. To the cultivator, irrigation means a degree of freedom from climatic hazards, higher yields, and a wider choice of crops. For the cattleman, irrigated pasture and fodder crops help to overcome the perennial difficulty that the natural grass has only seasonal value, and they also provide a secure food base for stock in time of drought.

Allied to the spread of irrigation in the Great Plains has been another measure to improve water supply—the construction of small stock dams. It has been calculated that over 300,000 of these have been built on the United States plains in the past 25 years, while in Canada the P.F.R.A. has carried out a very active policy for the same purpose. Certainly these dams are a striking recent addition to the plains landscape, and they benefit the farmer not only by providing a reservoir but also by creating water supply on what may formerly have been rangeland too remote from water for stocking to be safe.

2. Improvements in agricultural techniques. A hundred years of accumulated experience of the plains environment, together with the immense technical improvement of North American agriculture, have relieved the plainsman of many of his original anxieties. He can make use today of improved strains of crop and chemical defences against pests; he knows about contour plowing and plowing at right angles to the prevailing summer wind; he can choose whether to follow recommended scientific crop rotations or to go on planting wheat when the price is good, confident that he has at his command the technical resources to rescue him if he is threatened by the sort of natural calamity that would have ruined his grandfather.

Because of the range of possibilities open to the farmer today, it has become much more difficult to generalize about the Great Plains than at any time in the recent past. The dust bowl years produced a generation which regarded the plains environment as a tiger: the Soil Conservation Service produced manuals

[9]C.F. Kraenzel, *The Great Plains in Transition*, University of Oklahoma Press, Norman, 1955, p. 287.

[10]E. Starch, "The Future of the Great Plains Reappraised," *Journal of Farm Economics*, vol. xxxi, 919.

Agriculture on the Plains: (1) The landscape of wheat farming, here seen at Wilcox, Saskatchewan. *(National Film
Board of Canada)*

and advice on tiger-taming. Today there is a
widespread confidence in the region that the
situation is under control, with the result that
areas which in the 1940s would have been regarded as too dry and too far west for safe
cultivation are now under the plow: in fact, by
choosing one's route it is possible to follow the
plow all the way from the Mississippi to the
foot of the Rockies. Yet at the same time, crop
rotations have been improved, and the old sequence of wheat-fallow-wheat-fallow has been
replaced by longer cycles in which wheat is
associated with other crops and with planted
grasses. In this respect, an interesting feature
of postwar agriculture on the southern plains
has been the expansion of the acreage under
sorghums. Sorghums combine good drought-
resistant quality with high feed value and have

often been introduced on former wheat lands,
especially in the late 1950s when the acreage
quota system obliged wheat farmers to put
their land down to other crops.[11]

Whatever may be true of the cultivated parts
of the Great Plains, however, there are also
wide areas which, although never plowed up,

[11]Sorghums were first grown in the United States on a
large scale during the Civil War, when the North found
itself suddenly cut off from the supply of southern mo-
lasses. Since sorghum juice contains sweetening, it was
hoped to use this to replace sugar for the duration of the
war. See P.W. Gates, *Agriculture and the Civil War*, Knopf,
New York, 1965, pp. 145–49. We are assured that the resulting brew tasted horrible; the experiment was quickly
dropped, and sorghums were left strictly for the livestock.
Since the late 1950s, the sorghum crop has occupied 13 to
16 million acres (5.3–6.5 million ha) each year, mainly in
Texas, Oklahoma, and Kansas.

Agriculture on the Plains: (2) *Left,* a beef cattle feed-lot near Fort Collins, Colorado. The Colorado Piedmont has become a principal location for this type of stock raising; the irrigated cropland of the Piedmont supplies the necessary feedstuffs. (*Denver Public Library Western Coll.*) *Opposite,* harvesting sugar-beets grown under irrigation. (*Dept. of Agriculture, Canada*)

are badly in need of restoration. These are overgrazed sections on which the range grasses have deteriorated beyond the point where mere respite from grazing will bring them back. In these areas the solution of plowing and reseeding the grasses has sometimes been adopted. By reseeding it has proved possible either to increase the carrying capacity of the range or to lengthen the growing season or, in some cases, to do both. Yet the reseeding process (sometimes carried out by means of aircraft) is an expensive one, and, unless previous experiment has clearly shown what type of grass will suit the area, there is a serious risk that the operation will fail.

3. Institutional arrangements. In the two ways so far described, the Great Plains farmers have gone a long way toward freeing themselves from the peculiar anxieties of their predecessors. At overcoming their third problem, inflexible institutional arrangements, they have been less successful. Most of the Great Plains area is in private hands, unlike the remoter West, where federal or local governments are often the majority landowners. Consequently, the status of the private owner and the pressures on him are of vital concern for the welfare of the region. The best recipe for

the region as a whole may well be inapplicable (or unacceptable) to the individual farmer.

Examples of the sort of pressure to which the Great Plains farmer is subject are (1) a high price for wheat, which encourages farmers to go on growing it where in some cases it would be wiser to keep land under grass; (2) the mechanization of grain farming involves the farmer in a huge outlay on machinery, and to obtain a return on his investment he needs to increase, rather than reduce, his cultivated acreage; (3) as a result of past development, most of the Great Plains region is overvalued for tax assessment purposes; so that farmers may well feel that, with the shadow of tax delinquency falling close beside them, they cannot afford to do less than press their land to the limit year after year.

What is to be done to ease these pressures? One thing is for government, banks, and creditors to recognize that, in a region of cyclic environmental change, there will be runs of good and bad years. In bad years it may be necessary to accept delay in repaying credits advanced in good ones, while tax assessments must take account of the *average* value of these lands. The other thing is to try to provide some kind of reserve of land within each dis-

trict, so that in bad years the farmer need not feel that he is trapped on his own few burnt-up acres. We have already seen that he has been successful in creating reserves of fodder and water; this would be a reserve of land.

On the Canadian Prairies, such a reserve already exists in the form of Community Pastures established under the P.F.R.A. There are over 2 million acres (810,000 ha) of these on the Prairies, and they represent an unusual and apparently satisfactory balance of interest and control between the federal government, the provinces, and the local farmers.[12] They make it possible to take account of short-term, local changes in farm needs—and that, rather than an elaborate program of government intervention which most farmers would reject out of hand, is what the region mainly requires.

[12]The provinces select and acquire the land (usually areas abandoned through tax delinquency or severe erosion). They then lease it to the federal government, which puts the area in order for receiving stock and provides services on the pasture (including, for example, bulls-in-waiting). Allocation of the grazing privilege is then made by the elected committee of a Grazing Association formed locally, and grazing is charged at a low rate per head of stock and per day. For further details see PFRA: The Story of Conservation on the Prairies, Canadian Department of Agriculture, Pub. No. 1138, 1961.

There are plenty of other areas on the Great Plains to which the community pasture idea might usefully be extended.

All the technical changes on the plains in the past thirty years have had their effect upon the region's social geography. In very general terms, economic improvement (as reflected in larger farms and increasing mechanization) has been bought at the price of social disintegration. The new land use implies a greatly reduced labor force, and in a region so lacking in cities as the American plains (the Canadian situation will be considered in the next section) the effect of reducing farm labor requirements is to provoke out-migration. In the five Great Plains states between North Dakota and Oklahoma, the decade of the 1950s saw the farm population decline from 1.9 million to 1.3 million, and this figure of 600,000 loss from the farms corresponded almost exactly with the figure for out-migration from these states (595,000) during the intercensal period 1950–60. Between 1960 and 1970 a further reduction of the farm population occurred, to 966,000, and once again the decade was marked by a heavy out-migration from the five states, amounting to some 406,000. While the years 1970–75 have apparently seen this out-migration slowed and in some of the states, reversed, it seems likely that the next census will show that the farm population continues to decline and that in-migration is due to employment other than farming.

Where farm people move into a nearby town, they may retain their old social contacts, and this is certainly the case in the Midwest, for example. But on the Plains many communities are so small to begin with that they cease to exist altogether in any social sense, and the lower levels of local government, such as school districts, become extinct; there are neither children nor schools to administer.[13] It

[13]The decline of community consciousness and communal activities on the Great Plains throws into sharper relief the communal existence of certain groups which, usually on religious grounds, have settled and now farm together in the closest social units. An example of such groups is provided by the Hutterites, communities of whom farm both in the Dakotas and on the Prairies.

may well be argued that this is a way of eliminating costly waste in the framework of government, but the effect of the changes on the generation caught in the transition is not something that can lightly be dismissed.

The fate of many small communities on the Plains and Prairies hangs in the balance. What must be particularly enervating is that fate often depends entirely on outside factors. One common example of these factors nowadays is likely to be the decision of a railway company to close an unprofitable branch line. When that happens, the grain elevators beside the tracks become redundant and the community loses one of its basic central functions. Another factor may well be the decision of the state or provincial government on the siting of public service units such as hospitals or high schools. As consolidation of these services is forced upon the government, much will depend for the community on the disposition of these central services. Some governments may consciously try to keep alive the smaller towns by distributing services as widely as possible; a hospital to one and a research institute to another, much as the original state-provincial governments allocated their first three service functions to rival communities in the early years—the capital, the university, and the jail. A neighboring government may decide to focus all such services in a single center and let its rivals die. Uncertainty is the atmosphere these communities breathe today.

We have now considered the kind of problem confronting settlers on the plains and the solutions which have been suggested for them. In the heart of the Great Plains, however, there lies an area which invites a far more comprehensive solution; a region where every known measure of conservation and agricultural adaptation could be applied as part of a unified regional plan—the Missouri River Basin. Any account of the future of the plains must necessarily include a consideration of developments in the Missouri Valley.

The basin of the Missouri embraces the whole of the northern Great Plains of the United States, south to and including northern Kansas and northeastern Colorado. Since the 1930s it has been repeatedly urged that the Missouri Valley presents a close parallel to the Tennessee Valley; that since both have suffered from natural hazards and economic distress, the problems of the Missouri Valley might yield to the same kind of bold, large-scale rescue work that has been carried out by T.V.A. These proposals have called for the establishment of an M.V.A. on similar lines and for the development of a comprehensive plan for the Missouri Valley such as the T.V.A., for all its success, never formulated.

As the outcome of these proposals, there exist today both a plan—originally known as the Pick-Sloan Plan—and a Missouri Basin Inter-Agency Committee, on which are represented departments of both the federal government and the governments of the interested states. Among the features of the plan are the construction of 150 reservoirs and some 5 million acres (2.02 million ha) of new irrigation projects; the improvement of river navigation and field drainage; and the putting into force of a land management program which would convert several million acres of cropland to grass and bring benefit to 100 million acres remaining in cultivation. Since its inception in 1944 this plan has been put into effect, step by step, as Congress voted instalments toward a cost estimated even in those far-off days as between $8000 and $9000 million.

In theory such a plan should provide the best possible solution for the problems of the Great Plains. It should make available central irrigated areas, strategically located to act as a firm base for farming and ranching; it should ensure the best disposal of the available water supply and bring additional benefits, in the form of cheap electric power or agricultural education, to isolated plainsmen. Yet it is difficult to be enthusiastic about Missouri Valley development to date. This is because while the Tennessee Valley formed an intelligible and satisfactory unit for development, the Missouri Valley does not. In reality it falls into two parts, whose natural characteristics are different and whose interests, in consequence, are opposed to each other.

The southeastern tip of the Missouri Basin receives over 40 in. (1000 mm) of precipitation per annum. Through it flows the silt-laden

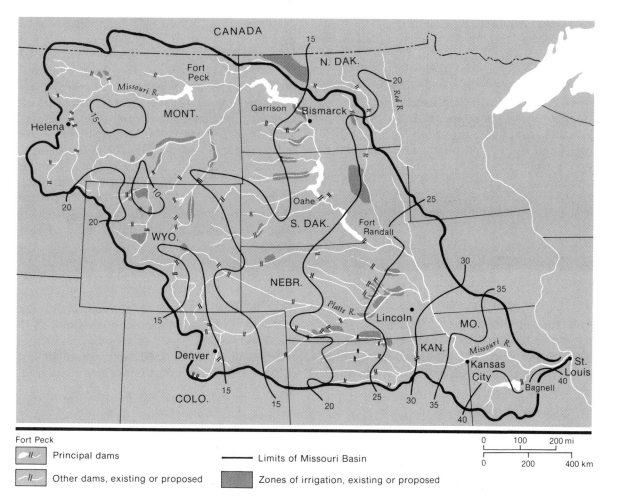

Fig. 18-4. The Missouri Valley. Solid lines represent the annual precipitation (in inches). Notice how the Missouri Basin narrows to a "funnel" at its southeastern end, thus increasing the problem of flood control.

river, often in flood and always difficult to navigate. The eastern end of the basin is interested, therefore, in flood control, in navigation improvement, and in hydroelectricity. Much of the western part of the basin, however, receives less than 15 in. (375 mm) of rain per annum, and the interests of its population are in water for irrigation and stock reservoirs. In short, the upstream section of the river has too little water and the downstream section, periodically at least, has too much.

As a result, two separate plans for the valley were drawn up, one—the Sloan Plan—by the Bureau of Reclamation, representing the interests of the dry, western section and the other— the Pick Plan—by the U.S. Corps of Engineers, whose responsibility for flood control and navigation focused its attention on the eastern section. To resolve the dilemma of choosing between two plans, which were far from being obviously compatible, the government adopted the peculiar expedient of combining the two plans, and in 1944 Congress approved a Pick-Sloan Plan (which was simply the Pick Plan united to the Sloan Plan) in what Rufus Terral has succinctly described as "a shameless, loveless, shotgun wedding."

The wedding occurred in 1944, and it was not until five years later, when the Pick-Sloan Plan had already advanced through its early stages, that the Department of Agriculture produced its parallel program of agricultural improvements. Since that time development has gone on, project by project, as funds have

337

been made available by Congress. There is no question that each of these projects has in itself been of value; nor can there be any doubt that the expenditure of several billion dollars on the Missouri Valley will enormously improve both the quality of the valley's lands and the stability of its economy. But it seems regrettable that, amid the interplay of political forces and the complications of a federal system, a truly regional solution seems likely to elude those who most desire it, for lack of a sufficient authority to impose it upon the region as a whole.

The Prairies of Canada

The Canadian part of the Great Plains region, although separated from the American part by no natural divide, must be treated individually, for in several important respects it differs from the area south of the border. These differences are best grouped under four headings.

PHYSICAL DIFFERENCES

In many respects the natural conditions of the Canadian Prairies are indistinguishable from those of the plains in the United States; there is the same generally smooth relief; the same gradual rise toward the west, interrupted by a number of low scarps; the widespread cover of glacial deposits, and a climate which resembles that of the plains to the south in its continental characteristics and its summer rainfall. But the most clear-cut feature of the American plains environment—the regular east-to-west progression from humid to arid conditions and from tall grass to desert shrub vegetation—is missing from the Canadian pattern of natural features.

On the Canadian plains, the distinctive zones of climate, soils, and vegetation, which run from north to south in the southern plains, curve to run almost at right angles to this direction through the southern part of the Prairie Provinces. Thus the better-watered plains, or subhumid prairies, form a loop round the northern end of the more arid zone (the area with 12 in. (300 mm) or less of precipitation

per annum), and the east-to-west progression which exists further south is replaced by a northeast-to-southwest progression of similar character. Statistically defined, the dry heart of the prairies is an elliptical area some 300 mi (480 km) from east to west and 200 mi (320 km) from north to south that runs across the Saskatchewan-Alberta boundary somewhat north of the Canadian border. But the better known, if cruder, definition of the dry area is under the name of Palliser's Triangle—after the surveyor who in 1857–60 presented a series of reports on the Prairies, in which he described as unfit for agricultural settlement most of Saskatchewan and Alberta between the 49th and 51st parallels. Surrounding this dry area on the northeast and north are zones of somewhat higher rainfall which correspond to the short-grass plains; between these plains and the northern forest is the zone that corresponds to the tall-grass prairie—the Park Belt, a zone that receives up to 20 in. (500 mm) of rainfall and that supports the densest rural population on the Prairies.

DIFFERENCES IN THE SEQUENCE OF SETTLEMENT

The settlement of the American Great Plains was a logical outcome of the occupation of the Mississippi Valley; the frontier of settlement moved west without a geographical break, with the ranchers in front and the farmers following behind as their means permitted. In Canada there was no such regular sequence. The first settlers on the Prairies—the Selkirk colonists of 1812–13—arrived via Hudson Bay, and many of the later arrivals had trekked north from the United States, following the Red River Valley. Between 1812 and 1870 there was virtually no westward advance; the whole of the empty West was the preserve of the Hudson's Bay Company, which discouraged agricultural colonization, and not until the Prairies were sold to the Canadian government after federation did a movement westward begin, a movement which can truly be said to have got into its stride only after the construction of the Canadian Pacific Railway in 1885.

When Prairie settlement did finally become a reality, its pattern was somewhat different from that across the border. For one thing, by the 1880s some of the technical problems of plains agriculture had been overcome and their lessons learned. In this respect, Canada reaped the benefits of experience gained the hard way in the United States: "American experience contributed greatly to the opening of the Canadian 'dry belt,' since Yankee knowledge of dry farming antedated settlement of the Canadian West. . . . Experience on the American plains was highly valued by Canadian officials in their search for suitable settlers for the West."[14]

There was in fact a mass movement across the border from the United States to Canada. It began just before 1900, at a time when the prospects of obtaining land, let alone of owning a farm of one's own, had faded in the Midwestern states almost to zero and was promoted by the Canadian government, which wanted the Prairies settled and which set up offices across the border, issuing propaganda with titles like *The Last Best West*. Between 1896 and 1914, 590,000 Americans crossed into Canada. "In truth, the movement was one of the greatest land rushes in the North American experience."[15] As Sharp remarks, "The mass migration into the Canadian West was the last advance in the long march that had begun on the Atlantic seaboard. . . . It was a movement brought about by a desire for cheap land, the same desire that had activated the earlier agrarian waves to the south."[16] The majority of the newcomers were from the northern Midwest and the Spring Wheat Belt. So alluring did Canadian land appear that the U.S. government modified its own land laws to try to offset the attraction of Canadian prospects.

But it is necessary to add that this was a transitory phase. In 1910 a drought year checked the movement, and the First World War killed it. In any case, many who crossed the border in search of land recrossed it a few years later. "Nearly two-thirds of the American residents who migrated to the Prairies returned to the United States shortly thereafter."[17]

The first phase of settlement saw two divergent lines of advance. In this phase, which lasted from 1872, soon after confederation, to about 1900, the Canadian government granted grazing leases on big areas of the dry Prairies. These leases, however, were subject to cancellation if the land was needed for agriculture; in other words, the cultivator had official priority, and the ranchers obtained security of tenure only when and where areas were declared unsuited to agriculture.

Meanwhile, the cultivators were advancing the farm frontier, and the railways were extending, northwestward along the Park Belt. They were feeling their way along what was effectively a corridor walled in by climatic boundaries—aridity to the south and frost to the north. Before they could penetrate these barriers, new varieties of wheat had to be developed (and a major breakthrough occurred when the Marquis variety became available in 1911). But even with these new varieties the climatic hazards were such that the government encouraged Park Belt farmers to practice mixed farming and not to rely too heavily on wheat. Today's agriculture in the Park Belt is the lineal descendant of this early, government-sponsored mixed farming.

When, therefore, the great boom in Prairie settlement took place in the first years of the twentieth century, it was a more restrained affair, in land-use terms, than that on the Great Plains. The distinction between ranchlands and wheatlands was clearer, and there were natural restraints on wheat growing. This did not, however, prevent some of the same mistakes being made on the Prairies. As the population of Saskatchewan and Alberta increased by 500 percent in the first decade of the century, settlers pushed out into the Triangle during a series of wetter-than-average years, displacing the ranchers. Then came the inevitable reaction: dry years followed and the farmers

[14]P.F. Sharp, "The Northern Great Plains: A Study in Canadian-American Regionalism," *Missouri Valley Historical Review*, vol. xxxix, pp. 72–73.

[15]K.D. Bicha, *The American Farmer and the Canadian West, 1896–1914*, Coronado Press, Lawrence, Kansas, 1968, p. 11.

[16]P.F. Sharp, "When Our West Moved North," *American Historical Review*, vol. lv, p. 287.

[17]Bicha, *The American Farmer*, pp. 140–1.

retreated. Around Lethbridge, as an example, the average wheat yields for the years 1911–21 were: 20, 16, 18, 6, 43, 34, 7, 5, 13, and 9 bushels per acre. It was the familiar story of advance and withdrawal: of all the lands "entered for" in this region under the Homestead Act, only about a half ever became the settlers' property. The rest were abandoned before the four-year occupance period was up.

There was one other factor in the early days which made life on the Prairies somewhat more secure than on the United States plains. The Canadian government took a more realistic view than the United States government of the size of farm needed in the dry West, and while it only offered the same 160-acre (64.8 ha) homesteads, it encouraged settlers to acquire extra land. This could usually be obtained from the railways, whose land grants gave them alternate sections over most of the best prairie land. The companies were generally glad to sell the homesteader the part of their land which adjoined his own. By the end of the Prairie boom, 70 percent of the farms were over 200 acres (81 ha) in size, and some settlers who would otherwise have been defeated by drought or frost were enabled to hold on because of their extra acreage.

For all these reasons, the pattern of land use that developed in the Prairie Provinces had somewhat more harmony than that of the plains further south. In the years since then, the difficulty of marketing the wheat crop (and the need to have, in consequence, other sources of farm income) has had the same effect of discouraging overdependence on wheat. Thus, while there are areas which, owing to their roughness or their aridity, are primarily ranching areas, the wheat areas are by no means without livestock. Oats and barley, grown mainly for stock feed, occupy 30 percent of Manitoba's cropland and 39 percent of Alberta's; in fact, Alberta raises more barley than wheat. As settlement has consolidated and, in particular, as the cities of the Prairies have increased in size, local markets for agricultural produce have grown relative to the previously dominant export market. Dairy products and meat now figure prominently in Prairie output, and certain other specializations have grown

up to offset dependence on cereals, such as the cultivation of rapeseed along the northern fringe.

In spite of the somewhat greater degree of harmony that has characterized farming in the Canadian section of the Great Plains, however, the area suffered much the same fate as did the American section in the hard years between 1930 and 1935. The conjunction of low, depression-hit prices and drought seasons during these years brought the Prairie farmers to despair and bankruptcy and obliged the federal government to intervene on their behalf. The Prairie Farms Rehabilitation Act of 1935 made available funds for restoring the ravages of drought and erosion. With the passage of time the scope of P.F.R.A. work has been extended, in parallel with the work of government agencies in the United States, to cover a program of instruction in conservation, a program of irrigation works, and, as we have already seen, administration of a system of community pastures. Small irrigation projects abound on the Prairies, while for the most part the larger schemes are to be found along the South Saskatchewan River in southern Alberta and Saskatchewan. There is no lack of irrigable lands in this area, but the estimated costs of developing them are very high.

DIFFERENCES IN SPACE RELATIONSHIPS

If the sequence of land settlement has been different on the Canadian Prairies from that on the plains of the United States, the simplest explanation of that fact lies in the difference in location of the two areas in relation to the more settled, eastern parts of the two countries concerned. In the United States, as we have seen, settlement spread westward without a break from the Mississippi to the plains because there was no geographical obstacle to such a logical extension. In Canada, on the other hand, there existed a most formidable obstacle—the southward extension of the Laurentian Shield, which interposed a barrier in the form of 1300 mi (2080 km) of forested wilderness between the settlements of Ontario and the site of the future city of Winnipeg.

When the westward spread of settlement was resumed on the Prairies in the years after 1870, it was, from the Canadian viewpoint, settlement in a world apart. A new natural environment was encountered not, as in the United States, after a period of adaptation in the subhumid eastern plains, but abruptly, and the connections of the new settlements with Canada proper were tenuous in the extreme. Many of the early settlers, in fact, were not from Canada at all but arrived either direct from Europe, by way of Hudson Bay, or from the United States (where movement northward down the fertile Red River Valley offered a less hazardous prospect than movement westward into the dry plains). Only in 1855, with the opening of the Soo Canal, was a practicable route established to link the Prairie settlements to the East. The earliest railway line into Winnipeg reached the city in 1878 from the south, and only in 1885 was the transcontinental rail link with Ontario completed. Not until the Trans-Canada Highway was completed did there exist a road link of modern standards; before that time it was easier to "cross" this part of Canada by making a southward detour into the United States. Connection across the Shield was virtually connection with a foreign country.

The break in the sequence of settlement has its effect also upon the present distribution of population and the urban pattern. We have already seen in Chapter 14 that the Great Plains of the United States lie within the hinterland of a line of cities located to the east of the region itself—Minneapolis, Kansas City, and Dallas—Forth Worth in particular. On the plains themselves there are no large cities between the 98th meridian and the Rockies except Denver, which owes more to the fertile Piedmont zone than it does to the plains and whose economic domain stretches west rather than east. Just as the surface of the Great Plains slopes east to the Missouri and the Mississippi, so the economic "gradient" runs the same way; the density of settlement increases from west to east; the products of the plains flow eastward; cattle from the ranges are fattened and finished in the Midwest; and in turn manufactured goods needed on the plains

are distributed from midwestern factories and warehouses.

The commercial situation of the Canadian Prairies is different. While there is the same contrast in density of settlement and communications network between the Dry Belt and the Park Belt as there is between the western and eastern plains in the United States, the economic "slope" ends abruptly at the edge of the Shield. The Canadian section of the Midwest, with its markets and its industries, is separated from the eastern edge of the plains by a vast area which is virtually uninhabited, and so neither provides markets nor generates traffic for the railways that cross it. Across this empty area all goods leaving or entering the Prairies must be ferried, either literally, by lake steamer or economically, in the sense that they are carried by railways whose whole maintenance cost must be borne by consumers at either end.[18]

To reduce the obstacle presented by this "ferry service," the Prairies have developed their own industries, while the United States plains remain largely non-industrial.[19] In particular, the industries which process the agricultural produce of the plains have been established further west than in the United States in order to reduce the bulk of raw materials making the long journey east. Thus it comes about that in all three of the Prairie Provinces, flour milling, meat packing, and butter and cheese making are three of the four leading industries and that processing is carried on in cities as far west as Edmonton (554,000) and Calgary (470,000), as well as in Regina, Saskatoon, and smaller centers. None

[18]As we have already seen (p. 92), the Canadian government recognized this economic fact and, changing only the simile used by the present writer, offered a "bridge" subsidy to the railways operating across the gap.

[19]Except, of course, in their most southerly parts, where the presence of the oil fields (as in the Prairies) and proximity to the Gulf coast combine to give the Texas plains some industry. It should, in fact, be explained that while what has been written about the "economic gradient" from west to east across the Great Plains holds true for most of the region, proximity of the Gulf coast to the southern end of the plains gives to that part of the region a north-to-south "gradient" of a similar kind toward the coastal cities and factories.

Winnipeg as a railroad city. When the Canadian Pacific was building the first line to the west, the small community of Winnipeg offered a broad strip of land just north of the town to the railroad company as an inducement to it to choose this route—a common practice in railroad-building days. The original strip has now become a serious obstacle to rational urban planning. Meanwhile, with the traffic of the Prairies funneling into it, Winnipeg has become even more enveloped in railroad tracks: the picture shows one of its new freight yards. *(Canadian Government Photo Centre)*

of these manufacturing cities is large by North American standards, but their significance lies in their very existence, which in turn calls attention to the isolation of this great Canadian food-producing area.

By virtue of its position, both at the foot of the Prairie slope and at the western end of the route-bridge over the Shield, the city of Winnipeg (578,000) dominates Prairie manufacturing. It is the funnel through which must pass all eastbound produce from the plains; it is the focus of the railway network; and the lake city of Thunder Bay serves, in a sense, as its outport. It is the distributing point for goods received from the East and corresponds to the supply and market cities along the Missouri and Mississippi further south. Besides its basic food-processing industries, it possesses important railway workshops and a large number of light manufactures which have grown up in the wake of Prairie development in the postwar years. Today it ranks as the Dominion's sixth industrial center, both by employment and by value of product.

The industrial development of these provinces has served the valuable purpose of providing alternative local employment for agricultural workers whom mechanization on the farms has rendered redundant and who, in the United States, must leave the Great Plains altogether to find employment. In Manitoba today industry employs more workers than agriculture, and Alberta is approaching this same situation: by this criterion, only Saskatchewan remains a predominantly agricultural province. Some 30 percent of the value added by manufacturing in the three provinces is provided by the food processing industries, but the other 70 percent is produced by a very wide variety of industrial types, such as primary metal smelting, paper manufacture, and petrochemicals.

This industrial development has served another purpose also (indeed, the development may be partly attributed to it)—the supply role in relation to the northern frontier of Canadian settlement. The nature of this frontier will be examined in Chapter 22; for the moment, we need only note that the Prairies' industries must supply both the West and the North and that on the Northlands frontier there is a continuing expansion in progress, expansion which must be equipped and maintained from the nearest available supply bases—the cities of the Prairies.

THE EXPLOITATION OF PRAIRIE OIL

The fourth factor which gives to the Canadian section of the Great Plains a distinctive character is the development of the Prairie oil fields. This is a phenomenon of the postwar years, and production has risen steadily over nearly 30 years to a 1974 level of nearly 600 million barrels per annum. It was in 1947 that the first major field came in, with strikes in the Edmonton area. In a development notable for its restraint, southern Alberta became the scene for numerous strikes; later, Saskatchewan and, to a lesser extent, Manitoba have come to share the stimulating effects of oil discovery. This was the first large-scale mineral development in the Prairies: although Alberta possesses large reserves of coal, and Saskatchewan lignite, these had never been worked on a scale much larger than the small local markets warranted. (Only in the most recent period has Alberta coal found a profitable export market—in Japan.)

The oil development therefore took place in a region whose economy was based on agriculture, ranching, and forestry. Its impact, in consequence, has been considerable. Supply industries for drilling operations and for the oil-field city populations rapidly appeared, and the cities themselves have expanded under the impact, Calgary by 101 and 43 percent respectively in the two decades of the 1950s and 1960s and Edmonton by 95 and 45 percent, drawing on a population whose drift away from the farm has been hastened by their growth. On the other hand, however, the remoteness of the Prairies from the remainder of settled North America restricts industrial growth largely to what can be marketed within the region. In other words, it is cheaper to export the oil and gas to existing manufacturing centers than to bring the industries to the oil and export its products.

But the significance of Prairie oil and gas should not be measured simply by the growth of towns and industries on the fields. It is worth noticing that this development has two other aspects. First, it is northern oil, in a continent where most previous major strikes had been made far to the south and west (the northern Alaska field had not yet come to light.) The shortage of oil supplies in the northwestern part of the continent was very strikingly brought out during the second World War, when military bases on the northern Pacific coast, especially in Alaska, had to be supplied from those same southern and western fields, several thousand miles away. The wartime governments went to the length of developing a known oil field at Norman Wells, on the Mackenzie at 65° N, and of piping the oil from there for 400 mi (640 km) over the wild Mackenzie Mountains to a refinery at Whitehorse on the Alaska Highway. What has happened in the years since then has tended to increase rather than diminish the strategic importance of the Prairie fields, and even though the North Slope fields in Alaska are now producing, there will be a large area of the Pacific Northwest which will still look to the Prairies for its supplies.

Second, this is Canadian oil. Before the opening of the Prairie fields, Canada was almost wholly dependent on imports of petroleum: eastern Canada still is. But now Canada, as we saw in Chapter 5, is a net exporter and has in the United States a neighbor most anxious not only to consume available exports but to see Canadian production increased. Undoubtedly, but for the restraints imposed on development by the provincial governments in Alberta and Saskatchewan, exploitation of the oil fields would have been more rapid and, being carried out largely by American companies, might well have been done in the urgent and wasteful manner which has so often characterized exploitation south of the border.

Yet the provinces have resisted the temptation to encourage unrestrained use of their oil reserves. A network of pipelines has been constructed which largely reflects Canada's own interests—west to the Pacific coast at Vancouver and east to Sarnia and Toronto. It is true that the latter pipeline cuts across the Great Lakes states of the United States and can supply them with petroleum products; it is true also that there is a connection southward from Alberta with the U.S. network, but the idea of a truly international pipeline "grid," an obvious policy goal in the days of plenty, has in the period of oil shortage receded further from realization. As we have already remarked, one thing the Canadians have no wish to import from the United States is an oil crisis.

There remain the Athabaska tar sands, far to the north but still within the province of Alberta. Work has been going on intermittently for many years, with the object of developing them at a competitive cost. The development centres on Fort MacMurray, and there are estimated to be 300 billion barrels for the processing. Up until now, high cost has confined development to the scale of a pilot project. But as the world price of oil rises, so the tar-sand workings become competitive with petroleum resources elsewhere. The higher the world price, the brighter the prospect for Athabaska.

The Great Plains and Prairies afford an interest to the geographer and a challenge to the North American out of all proportion to their limited variety of scenery or land use. On their eastern margin they constitute a region of the world's most highly mechanized grain farming, with all that such advanced mechanization means in terms of production costs and rural unemployment. In their western section is carried on a livestock industry which, while it may have changed in organization, is only now shaking itself free from the hazards that beset its nineteenth-century counterpart. In between these two regions of relatively consistent land use is the debatable land, with its fluctuating frontiers of settlement and cultivation; its problems of depopulation and isolation; its false hopes in the present and its possibilities for the future.

Mountain and Desert

The Region and Its Character

Where the foothills of the Rockies rise to break the monotony of a thousand miles of plains, the westbound traveller enters a region of remarkable natural splendor. From the Front Range of the Rockies to the crest of the mountains of the Pacific coastlands is some 900 mi (1440 km) along a line from Denver to San Francisco; some 400 mi (640 km) on the line from Calgary to Vancouver. Spread across this great area is a magnificent variety of scenery, a wide range of environmental conditions, and a thin scatter of natural resources available to a population whose average density is less than 5 per sq mi (2 per sq km).

Both the variety and the splendor of the region are products of the relief. It is a region where the mountain ranges—the Rockies themselves, the Uintas, the Sawtooth—occupy only a small part of the area; it is a region of plateaus also, some of which lie at altitudes—7000 ft (2130 m) or more—above the tops of the highest hills east of the Mississippi and high enough to have been glaciated. Some of its most interesting sections are the down-faulted valleys in the southwestern tip of the region—Death Valley and Salton Sea—where the earth's surface sinks to more than 200 ft (60 m) below sea level. In terms of area, this is primarily a plateau region,

but one in which the plateaus often rise steplike above one another to give the observer the impression that he is surrounded by mountain ranges.

The physical variety in turn affects the climate. While certain generalizations are possible (the frost-free season, for example, is seldom more than 120 days and is often less than 100), relief exerts the main control on temperature and precipitation, and overall description becomes impossible. The northwestern parts of the region are under the influence of Pacific coast air and have a winter-spring rainfall maximum, while the southeastern part has a summer maximum and receives much of its rain from violent thunder showers; but everywhere there are local conditions of rain and rain shadow produced by the relief. The main rain-bearing winds west of the Continental Divide blow from the Pacific, bringing 80 to 100 in. (2000–2500 mm) of precipitation, including very heavy falls of snow, to the mountains along the coast, Immediately east of these mountains there occurs a change of dramatic suddenness: the rain shadow falls across the adjoining plateaus and basins, and the dense forests of the mountain slopes are separated by only a narrow transition belt from the desert scrub of areas where annual precipitation averages 8–10 in (200–250 mm). Eastward the sur-

The desert basins: Death Valley looking south from Furnace Creek.

face rises again, and the rainfall gradually increases toward the Rockies; at their summit a precipitation of 30–40 inches (750–1000 mm) is again to be found. In a manner which is even more marked, because the west-to-east distance is shorter, the rainfall of southern British Columbia varies from 150 in. (3750 mm) in the coastal mountains down to less than 10 in. (250 mm) in the Okanagan Valley and up again to 30 in. (750 mm) or more in the eastern Cordilleras. In both Canada and the United States the Rockies cast their own rain shadow over the plains that lie to the east of them beyond their forested slopes.

Climate in turn affects vegetation, which tends to vary with both the amount of rainfall and the time and duration of the wetter season. A regular sequence of vegetation zones can be distinguished, both horizontally and vertically; that is, there is a sequence of zonal changes which generally holds true between low elevations and high and between the heart of the desert and the better-watered lands surrounding it.

The zonal changes are generally from scrub through grass and transitional woodland to forest. At one end of the scale, in the lowest and driest areas, is found desert shrub vegetation, which covers the floor of much of the Great Basin. Those parts of the area that are beds of former lakes form salt deserts where saltgrass and sage are found; for the rest, creosote bush dominates the sparse cover. From this vegetational nadir an increase in rainfall produces a sagebrush-grass combination. In the southern states there is sufficient *late summer* rain to produce semidesert grasslands which provide valuable year-long grazing. Elsewhere in the intermontane region, however, lack of summer rain restricts the growth of grasses, and the value of the vegetation for grazing purposes varies inversely with the amount of sagebrush.

Beyond the sagebrush-grass zone there is generally a belt of transitional woodland—an area where increasing rainfall encourages the growth of small, scattered trees. In the Rockies and the High Plateaus this zone is represented by the pinyon-juniper combination and is encountered generally between 4000 and 6000 ft (1215–1825 m); the trees themselves are valueless, but the grasses that accompany them provide some spring forage for stock. In California, on the slopes of the Sierras, a similar belt of transitional woodland exists at a lower elevation. It is known as chaparral. Above the transitional woodlands are the forests—open at their lower limits and so used for grazing, but becoming denser at higher elevations until they thin out into the alpine meadows above the tree line.

These introductory statements apply to the whole West between the Rockies and the mountains of the Pacific. So large an area, however, inevitably displays subregional contrasts based on either cultural or economic differences within it; therefore it seems best to isolate two of the "corners" of the region and to deal with them separately. These are the southwestern corner, with its highly distinctive cultural associations, covered in Chapter 20, and the Northwest, lying in relative isolation behind its barrier ranges, which is dealt with in Chapter 22. Both these subdivisions of the West are well recognized by geographers, but neither of them is divided from the remainder of the region by any physical change in landscape other than those gradual changes brought about by latitude. All share the quality of being "western" and the great variety of scenery and climate which forms the basis of work and recreation within the Mountain West.

Land and Livelihood in the Region

In such an area as this, where much of the land is either too dry or too rugged for settlement, the ways in which a livelihood can be secured are strictly limited. Indeed, our study of the human geography of the area can be confined to a small number of occupations. They are (1) mining, (2) ranching and lumbering, (3) irrigation farming, and (4) travel and tourism. To these should be added a fifth heading: what is sarcastically called in the West "non-use"— that is, the reservation of areas for nature and game preserves.

MINING

Many of the explorers and earliest settlers of the Mountain and Desert region were miners. Apart from the agricultural communities on the Pacific coast and at Salt Lake, miners made up the bulk of the population west of the 98th meridian in 1855. Before permanent agriculture spread further, many a mining town had reached its gaudy heyday and was already on the decline—such mining camps as Virginia City on the famous Comstock Lode in Nevada, which was discovered in 1859. At various times a town of 10,000–20,000 inhabitants up to its peak in the 1880s, Virginia City has since declined to become a ghost town with a population of 600; it remains on the maps by grace of the tourist trade alone. Few of these early mining camps have had a continuous career from their establishment until the present day; even fewer, such as Butte, Montana, have remained to become towns in their own right. The history of the western mineral industry has been one of precipitate change.

Apart from the obviously temporary character of an extractive activity, these changes have been due to several factors. One of these has been the progressive discovery of new mineral ores. Almost without exception the earliest miners were seeking gold, and so flocked to California after 1848 or to British Columbia and Colorado after 1858. After the first rush the miners came to realize that, even if a fortune was not to be made in gold, there was an expanding market for silver and lead, copper, and zinc; and this led to new beginnings in many mineralized areas which the gold seekers had too hastily abandoned.

Another and continuing factor of change has been the discovery of new uses for the rarer minerals. The exploitation of tungsten and molybdenum, for example, waited on the demand for electrical goods and tougher steels; and the use of molybdenum has brought into prominence a valley high in the Colorado Rockies, where, at the town of Climax, 11,300 ft (3436 m) above sea level on the Continental Divide, some three-quarters of the world's supply of the mineral is produced. Even more recently the continent-wide search for uranium has set off a fresh burst of prospecting and has brought to light, besides supplies of the mineral itself (notably in the region we are considering), many deposits of other minerals previously overlooked.

A third factor of change is the impact of changing techniques of mineral production, and especially the effect of enlarging the scale of production. The copper mines of upper Michigan were put out of business by the opening of mines in Montana and Utah in the 1880s, where the larger scale of working and the opportunities for open-pit mining created a decisive advantage. Much more recently there have been foreshadowed far-reaching changes in the petroleum industry; research has made commercially possible the exploitation in northwestern Colorado and southeastern Utah of oil-bearing gilsonites[1] and shales which, like the Athabaska tar sands mentioned in the last chapter, gain steadily in importance as North America and the world face a shortage of free oil.

The conjunction of these factors ensures that the one permanent feature of the western mineral industry is change. The most important features of the pattern in the 1970s can, however, be summarized briefly in relation to value of output and employment figures.

Copper is the region's most valuable single mineral: Arizona is much the largest producer, followed by Utah and New Mexico, Montana, and Nevada. In Arizona the mines are to be found in the southern and southeastern sections of the state, with Morenci as the largest center, and the copper belt extends across the

---

[1]The gilsonite is mined in Utah and pumped in the form of a slurry along a pipeline to Grand Junction in Colorado for processing.

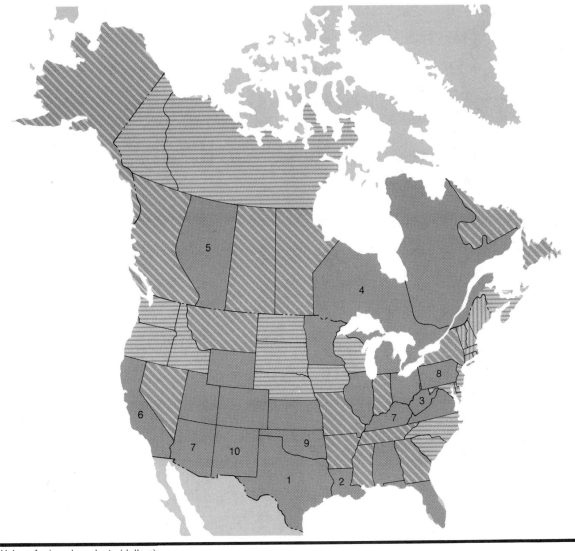

Fig. 19-1. North America: Value of mineral production by states and provinces, 1976. This is one distribution map of the continent on which the inclusion of the great empty northern territories of Alaska and Canada is both proper and necessary. But the map shows that their present development is relatively slight: much of their mineral wealth is as yet untapped. The Mountain and Desert region plays an important role in mineral production, but the oil regions contribute the greatest share of the total value. The numbers rank the leading 10 producers.

state line into New Mexico. In Utah the great open-cut mine at Bingham dominates production, and the smelters are located on the outskirts of nearby Salt Lake City. In Montana the principal source is at Butte, whose mines have been in production since 1880. For these mines the smelter is at Anaconda, some 20 mi (32 km) to the west. Copper is also mined in southern British Columbia, both on the coast and in the Interior Plateau.

The western mining industry: The Kennecott copper mine at Bingham, west of Salt Lake City, Utah. (*Salt Lake Area Chamber of Commerce*)

Zinc and Lead follow copper in value of output within the United States section of the region, while in British Columbia they are the leading minerals produced. Colorado and Idaho are the main western producers of zinc, and rank high in lead output also, together with Utah. British Columbia produces 50 percent of the zinc and almost 90 percent of the lead produced in Canada. Much of this output comes from a single mine near Kimberley and almost all of it from areas near the United States border. The ores are transported from the various mines to the great smelter at Trail, on the Columbia River. There, thanks to the centralization of smelting operations, both refined metals and a number of valuable by-products, including chemicals, are produced.

Silver, the source of many a fortune on the Comstock Lode in the 1860s and 1870s (it is estimated to have yielded minerals worth $500 million), was almost as great an early attraction as gold in the West. Today as then the mountain states of the United States dominate the output, with Idaho as the chief producer.

Ranking above silver in value of output is *molybdenum*; although production has been very largely concentrated at Climax, in Colorado, a new source has now been opened up near Taos in northern New Mexico.

Among the region's numerous non-metallic minerals, the most significant is probably *phosphate rock,* which is found over a wide area west of the Rockies and is worked extensively in Idaho to supply an ever-increasing demand for fertilizers. This same demand has encouraged the production of potash, especially at Moab in Utah; in addition the floor of the Great Basin in Utah and Nevada is rich in all kinds of salts. The region is also well supplied with *coal measures,* although exploitation of these, originally of interest mainly to the railways, has always lagged for want of wider markets. Alberta and British Columbia have now found such a market in Japan, while in the United States the western coal industry has experienced a remarkable growth in the 1970s. Originally developed to do little more than fuel passing railroad locomotives, it has come into its own (1) with the development of large-scale strip mining by modern machines, and (2) the environmentalist campaign against the higher sulphur content of coals from the longer-established eastern fields. Western production in 1975 accounted for more than 50 million tons of the 640 million mined in that year. Petroleum and natural gas are produced in New Mexico, Wyoming, Colorado, and Utah.

A few of the mining settlements have become or have given rise to genuine industrial towns in this largely non-industrialized region. Pueblo in Colorado produces steel, and Butte has become a center for agricultural processing and has acquired other industries. There is still, however, no mistaking that Butte is an old mining town; with an open mine pit hundreds of feet deep less than a mile from the city center, it would be difficult to conceal the fact, even if the spoil heaps and winding gear along the skyline did not give away its origins.

Furthermore, wartime needs in the West provided Utah with a splendid industrial exotic, in the form of the Geneva Steel Works, 35 mi (56 km) south of Salt Lake City. These mills were originally planned to supply short-term markets—rather distant markets—on the Pacific coast; they draw their coal from Price, 60 mi (96 km) away, and their iron ore from southwest Wyoming. Although the mills were therefore sited much closer to their raw materials than to their markets (which has not happened elsewhere in North America since the Duluth mills were opened in 1915), the general development of the Mountain West in the postwar period has justified their location and kept them busy.

The Second World War disclosed to Americans both the strategic importance of many minerals whose names were scarcely known to them, and also the possibility of producing almost all these minerals, at a price, in the Mountain West. In consequence of wartime need, many low-grade deposits were worked in the West, in operations which, with the re-entry of economic considerations, proved impossible to maintain. We must therefore think of part of the western mining industry as being in suspension; the deposits (and in many cases the plant) are available in case of strategic need or of a rise in price, but for the present it is simpler and cheaper to import from higher-grade sources abroad.

Not only the distribution but also the character of mining operations in the West has changed with the passage of time. Large corporations have replaced the highly individualistic operator[2] of earlier years, and this has had the

[2]The writer penned this phrase several years before discovering how gruesomely appropriate it is. A prospecting trip by Colorado miners in 1873 produced the only successful prosecution for cannibalism ever brought in a United States court. The five man expedition became trapped by winter snows in the Rockies and when spring came only one man, a certain Alfred E. Packer, emerged. Prosecution followed. Obviously, to call an industry in which an operator eats his partners "individualistic" is to err on the side of understatement.

The curious may like to know that in Packer's case, individualism did not go unrewarded. He was reprieved and lived out a blameless old age as a great favorite of the local children. Fame in due course followed. In 1968, for reasons best left unspoken, students at the University of Colorado at Boulder petitioned—successfully—to have the name of the cafeteria changed to the Alfred E. Packer Memorial Grill. Nor has the climax of his posthumous fame yet been reached. As this book goes to press, the august U.S. Department of Agriculture is itself proposing to name a Packer restaurant in his memory.

effect of increasing the stability, both geographically and economically, of the modern operations. Where the early miner worked and perhaps looked for only one mineral, the application of sciences to mining has made possible the working of mixed ores found in association; thus, with a wider range of resources to draw upon, the life of the mining community is prolonged and made more secure. The coming of the larger mining unit has also made possible new and more costly prospecting methods. It is only with the entry of the Geiger counter and the search for radioactive minerals that the western mining industry has reverted to the free-for-all of its earlier years; that once again, a century after its opening, the Mountain and Desert region has become an El Dorado for the individual treasure seeker.

RANCHING AND LUMBERING

It may not at first be apparent why two occupations so different—and in some senses so opposed in interest—as ranching and lumbering should be listed beside each other. The explanation lies in the character of the region's vegetation. In area the greatest part of the Mountain and Desert region is covered with either dry grassland or open forest, and because these grade into one another without a natural break, the use of the one affects the use of the other. In particular, since all but the densest forests are in some measure grazed by stock, the open woodland must be regarded, economically, as an extension of the grasslands.

Whatever use is made of these areas, certain considerations force themselves upon the users. (1) In the dry West the scatter of resources (and in particular of the prime resource, water) is extremely thin. In the driest of the grazing lands, 100 acres (40 ha) or more may be required to feed one head of cattle. (2) Not only are the natural resources meager, but their value is often only seasonal. Grazing in the open forest or on the alpine pastures above the tree line is possible only in summer, while the desert margins offer pasturage of a kind for a few weeks during the winter rains. This second fact, coupled with the first, means that the rancher must not only have sufficient land for

a herd of worthwhile size to graze (at a carrying rate of 100 acres [40 ha] per head) but must also have access to other grazing lands, to which he can move his stock when the seasonal forage is exhausted. Ranching in the West has always had about it an element of the Bedouin. (3) Because the value per acre of the region is so low, it is generally true that its exploitation must be multipurpose; only by combining all the values, both social and commercial, of the region can its development be made worthwhile. O.E. Baker calculated[3] that in 1924–25 the annual regional return from grazing alone was no more than 35 cents per acre (86 cents per ha). Whatever the figure is today, and considering the risks that will always attach to development in this region, it is essential to concentrate on raising the low level of return per unit area.

All these considerations point to one conclusion: in the land use of this region the decisive factor is that of land ownership. Either land must be common, and priorities in its exploitation must be left to the discretion of interested users; or it must be held in very large units, within which a system of priorities can be enforced. The first of these "solutions" was adopted in the early days of the West by simple default of any constructive alternative policy. Its effects were devastating. The second solution is the one that concerns the geographer of the 1970s. While some of the largest ranches in the western United States and the Plateau of British Columbia might qualify as "very large units," by far the largest is the 400 million-acre (162 million ha) public domain of the United States government. In all that concerns the exploitation of the Mountain West, the policies of this great landlord are of paramount importance.

Many of the problems of the Mountain and Desert region are similar to those of the Great Plains, which were discussed in the last chapter. The Great Plains, however, are largely an area of private ownership and therefore do not present an adequate opportunity to do what seems to the geographer essential—to *control*

[3]See O.E. Baker, "The Grazing and Irrigated Crops Region," *Economic Geography*, vol. vii, 325–64, and vol. viii, 325–77.

Fig. 19-2. The western United States: Seasonal land use.

100°

100°

General Range Classification

Ungrazed	Year-long range	6–9 month range
Summer range only	Winter range only	Principal irrigated areas

land use (see p. 85). But a large part of the public domain lies in the Mountain and Desert region, the dry, rugged remnant of the 1400 million acres (566 million ha) once held by the federal government. As landlord of these, North America's least promising acres, the United States government (represented by the U.S. Forest Service and the Bureau of Land Management) is free to adopt the policies best suited to the environment, subject only to recurrent political pressure to release the domain for private exploitation.

Such private use in the past resulted in overgrazing the ranges and in destruction of forest

timber. The policy of the Bureau of Land Management (which administers the rangelands) is therefore designed to improve grazing practices, and that of the Forest Service (which administers the higher, shrub- and forest-clad areas) is devoted both to grazing control and to conservation on the watersheds. It is the object of both to prevent *competitive* land use. It is this joint interest and joint control which justify our treatment of ranching and forest exploitation in the region together.

The improvement of grazing practice implies (1) restricted use and (2) enlarged reserves. As on the Great Plains, overgrazing in the past has

353

reduced the value of the ranges and has encouraged the spread of useless scrub, such as mesquite or pinyon, or the low-value cheatgrass, the enemy of every western rancher and a serious fire hazard. To reverse this process calls for better range management—management such as the government agencies try to enforce on the grazing lands of the public domain. The numbers of stock grazed must be adjusted to the varying condition of the range from month to month, and especially to the condition of the most "popular" grasses. Grazing must be deferred at the beginning of the season long enough for the range vegetation to become established and must be terminated at the end of the season in time to ensure that reserves can be built up for the next year. These principles are recognized by the progressive rancher and are enforced by the Bureau of Land Management and the Forest Service by means of grazing permits, which specify when, and in what numbers, stock may be placed on the public ranges.

This at least is the theory. Calef, in his study of the system of grazing permits in operation,[4] found that in practice the system works less well: specifically, that it is difficult to make the necessary range forecasts accurately and very difficult to get the local ranchers' committees (who advise the B.L.M. officials) to agree to reductions in numbers of stock to be grazed. The 1963 congressional hearing on the grazing law was told quite frankly by witnesses that the ranchers would not be able to cover their costs if proper stocking rates were insisted on. Actually, public lands are overgrazed and erode as well as private lands, while in some areas the ranchers do not use their grazing entitlement but hold on to their right to do so, as a means of establishing credit rating or as a reserve, "just in case."

[4]W. Calef, *Private Grazing and Public Lands,* Chicago, 1960. The Forest Service charges more for grazing on its section of the public domain, and generally succeeds in keeping a much closer control over users than does the B.L.M. This is not because of any carelessness on the part of B.L.M. officials but because the Bureau has operated for years on a shoestring, a fact which in turn can be traced to political struggles over its existence and functions. Its officials are too few and its domain too large for full efficiency.

The second task, that of enlarging reserves, is desirable not only to give greater security to the rancher, but also to reduce in amount the transhumance found to be necessary everywhere in the region, from Texas to British Columbia. While transhumance plays a vital role in a region where so much of the grazing is available only for a single season, there are obvious advantages in having as large a part as possible of the year's forage within a single area. This is particularly the case because, while the spring, autumn, and year-long grazing are to a large extent in private hands, the federal govenment, by its ownership of the highest and driest rangelands, controls much of the summer and the winter grazing.

Enlargement of reserves means the elimination of valueless vegetation on the ranges by mechanical or chemical means; the improved distribution of water for stock; and, above all, the extension of irrigated pasture and fodder crops, especially for winter feed. Thus there is a need, as on the Great Plains, for planning reserves on an area basis, with the difference that the problem presented by individual ownership of land is considerably reduced in the Mountain West.

This problem of building up adequate reserves of grazing in the West has been eased by the spread of irrigation but made more acute by afforestation of some federal and state lands formerly available for grazing. On balance, however, the West in general is much better placed today to meet the hazard of one, or even two, drought years than it was twenty years ago.

The problem of watershed control overlaps that of grazing control and is equally important, for M.H. Saunderson has suggested that, in the realistic view, the national forests of the West should be considered primarily as *water-producing* lands and the treeless ranges as *silt-producing* lands.[5] The problem is twofold. On the one hand, it is necessary to check erosion, by preventing overgrazing and unwise tree felling, in order to control runoff. On the other hand, it is necessary in a dry region such as

[5]See M.H. Saunderson, "Western Range Land Use and Conservation Problems," *Journal of Farm Economics,* vol. xxxi, 985–97.

Ranching in the West: Branding cattle in Utah. Although the scene is one generally associated with the romantic cowboy era of the nineteenth century, the photograph dates from the mid-1970s. The practices of the rancher and his hands change little with the passage of time. *(U.S. Dept. of Agriculture)*

this to reconcile conflicting claims on such water as is available. These claims may be made on behalf of irrigation; of industrial or domestic users; of power production or navigation; of sanitation or wildlife protection, and all may be countered by the demands of the engineers charged with flood control. In recent years, therefore, the Forest Service has been more concerned to conserve than to exploit its forests, to use them to regulate water supply rather than to produce revenue; and, while this policy has inevitably provoked criticism, it represents a valuable and indeed essential service to the region as a whole.

In British Columbia, where "it has been widely proclaimed that fifty cents out of every dollar spent . . . is generated by the forest industry,"[6] the problem of forest exploitation is necessarily complicated by the need to maintain timber production as well as to practice conservation measures. Here again, however, the fact that the provincial government owns over 90 percent of the forests at least gives a

[6]A.L. Farley, "The Forest Resources," in J.L. Robinson, ed., *British Columbia*, University of Toronto Press, Toronto, 1972, pp. 87–118; quotation on p. 87.

unified control over the bulk of the forest lands, and the difficulties encountered by conservationists in British Columbia are more financial than administrative. The principal question is the extent to which the province can afford the present costs of conservation in its main industry while still supporting a population which is increasing by leaps and bounds.

Against this background, then, ranching and lumbering are carried on. Ranching has spread from its original location in the Spanish Southwest to become the principal form of land use over all but the highest and most rugged sections of the region. Both sheep and cattle are raised, and, although the average size of ranch units has increased, transhumance—even if it is now motorized—is still general. Fattening is carried out in a variety of locations. In the earlier days of the industry most of the stock, like that of the Great Plains, was destined to be shipped east; there was little finishing or slaughtering within the region, and little movement of either cattle or beef to the West Coast before the Second World War. In the past two decades, however, the situation has changed in a number of ways: (1) With the increase of population on the Pacific coast, more stock has been moving west for slaughter, and the "divide" between eastward and westward movements has shifted across the region in an easterly direction. The demand for milk in the West has also greatly increased, and the region now supplies large numbers of milk cows for the "drylots" of California (see p. 388). (2) With the spread of irrigation and the general improvement in the western feed situation, fattening can now take place much more widely within the region itself; irrigated pastures will produce finished beef stock where the natural range would not, and cattle, instead of being sent east, may well be moved for fattening to an area such as the Imperial Valley of California. (3) The meat-packing industry, continuing its long westward movement, has come to the region now that more slaughter-ready animals are being produced there. Transport centers such as Ogden, Salt Lake City, and Phoenix are involved in meat-packing, as well as smaller towns like Greeley amid the irrigated lands of the Colorado Piedmont.

Lumbering and the forest-products industry are carried on in many parts of the mountains. In general the forests become denser and commercially more valuable toward the cooler north, so that lumbering increases in relative importance through western Montana and northern Idaho until in British Columbia it overrides all other occupations in its share of employment. The forests of the Rockies are composed for the most part of pine, spruce, fir, and larch, and in the United States about one-third of the forest area represents virgin growth. The lumber industry south of the border is most fully developed around such centers as Coeur d'Alene and Lewiston in Idaho and Missoula in Montana, (where the adjacent mining areas provide an immediate market for timber), but there are important outliers of the industry in the upper Colorado Basin and in the highlands of central Arizona.

In British Columbia the lumber industry grew up on the coast, where the forests are accessible and the timber is often moved by sea. The forests of the interior, however, contain huge reserves, and the industry is gradu-

ally spreading inland to tap the estimated 65 million acres (26.3 million ha) of commercial forest there. The interior now produces almost a half of British Columbia's timber, and the province has a pulp and paper industry of growing importance. The problems of British Columbia's forest products industry are discussed more fully in Chapter 22.

IRRIGATION FARMING

Farming in the intermontane areas is generally oasis farming, and the oases are for the most part man-made. Some dry farming is carried on, but the mainstay of the region's agriculture is the irrigated land, some 11 to 12 million acres (4.45–4.85 million ha) in extent. The irrigated areas include some of the highest cultivated land in the region, for example, the San Luis valley of Colorado, where irrigation waters fields lying between 7500 and 8000 ft (2280–2430 m)

Irrigation was carried on in the south of the region by the Spanish settlers, and by the Indians before them. The first major development, however, was that of the Mormon community which founded Salt Lake City in 1847 and turned its arid surroundings into some of the greenest farmlands of the West. Today it is the Snake River Plains of southern Idaho which, with the Salt Lake area, the Gila Basin of Arizona, and the Columbia Basin Project, form the main blocks of irrigated land in the Mountain West.

Irrigation, as we saw in Chapter 6, may be used in two different contexts: either to cultivate the desert or to give security to existing operations on the agricultural margins. The Mountain and Desert region contains examples of both uses. It contains hundreds of small patches of irrigated land, many of them under pasture or fodder crops like alfalfa, that provide winter feed for stock and represent a wise insurance policy for the region's farmers. It contains, too, several of the major irrigation projects of the Bureau of Reclamation and in the future will contain more. On these projects a wide variety of crops have been introduced, including fruits and vegetables, sugar beets, and in the southwestern United States, cotton. Thus there has arisen a broad distinction between the use of irrigation for livestock feeding and for growing cash crops. In either case, there is created what may be regarded as the "typical" agricultural landscape of the region— the green oasis with its irrigated cropland and pastures, surrounded by a belt of dry-farmed grain fields and encircled in turn by the brown ranges that stretch out to the horizon or up to the forest.

Although, as we also saw earlier, there are differences of opinion about the financing of irrigation in the dry West, there is unanimous agreement about its importance to the region. "Through irrigation," declared the Commission on Organization of the Executive Branch[7] of the U.S. government in 1955, "man has been able to build a stable civilization in an area that might otherwise have been open only to intermittent exploitation." For western land use to advance economically, irrigation was essential. The questions at issue are simply: who should pay for it, and how large an irrigated area is needed to build a "stable civilization"?

Among the many irrigated areas within the region, two will be described here: the Upper Colorado Project area and the Colorado Piedmont. Two others will be briefly discussed in succeeding chapters: the Gila-Salt Valley area of Arizona, which will be considered in Chapter 20, and the Columbia Basin Project, which belongs to the Pacific Northwest and so to Chapter 22.

The Upper Colorado Project is a scheme which covers not one single irrigated area but a whole river basin containing many such areas, unified by a water supply forming part of the Colorado River system. Under the Colorado River Compact (see p. 396) and subsequent agreements, each state within the Colorado basin is allocated a share of the river's annual average flow of 14 million acre-ft (175 ×

10⁸ m³). Up until the present, however, the upper basin states—Colorado, Wyoming, and Utah—have never used their full share: Wyoming, for example, has an allotment of 14 percent of the total but uses less than half of this. While California and Arizona, lower down the river, have thirstily seized upon every unused gallon of Colorado water to increase their own share, the Upper Colorado Project aims at developing and coordinating water use in the upstream part of the basin (and so adjusting use to entitlement among the states) by providing more water for the ranchers and farmers and more electric power for the industrialists of these states.

The project calls for several major dams on the Colorado and on its tributaries, some of which, like the Little Colorado, are at present waterless for much of the year. These dam sites lie deep in the canyons for which the Colorado Plateau is renowned; they are wonderful sites from the point of view of the dam builder, but less attractive to anyone concerned with drawing up irrigation water from behind them, and utterly abhorrent to nature lovers who wish to preserve the canyons in their wild state. So, while construction goes on stage by stage the argument continues—between developers and non-developers; between upper and lower basin interests, and between the United States, which possesses 99 percent of the Colorado Basin, and the sovereign state of Mexico, which owns the river's mouth and which certainly expects some water to be in the river when it eventually reaches the border (See Fig. 20-2).

The second area whose irrigation we are considering is the Colorado Piedmont. It may seem out of order to consider this example, because the Piedmont is admittedly a part of the Great Plains physiographic region. But if the irrigated farmlands belong to the Great Plains, the irrigation water is certainly supplied by the Mountain and Desert region—not only in the sense that rivers flow down to the Piedmont from the Colorado Rockies, but also in that some of the water used is Colorado River (that is, *west*-flowing) water which has been diverted and passed by tunnel under the Rockies to the east.

---

[7] It is interesting that this same commission came to the conclusion that the financial burden of the newest irrigation schemes *could not* be borne by the farmers concerned and suggested as a solution that around each scheme financed by public money an irrigation district should be formed, all of whose inhabitants, as direct or indirect beneficiaries of the scheme, should be taxed to pay for it.

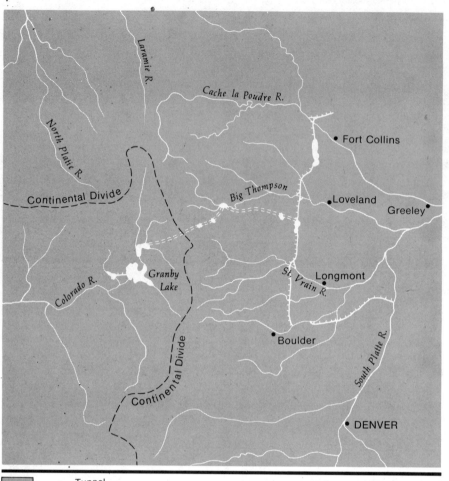

Fig. 19-3. The Colorado–Big Thompson Project: Water transfer across the continental divide from the Colorado River to the Piedmont, where population and water demand have increased very rapidly in recent years.

| | Tunnel |
| | Project canal |

0   10   20 mi
0 10 20 30 km

The Colorado Piedmont is one of the oldest irrigation districts in the West. The early schemes were small, but the area has a rapidly rising population (it is proving one of the most popular regions in the United States among the many Americans looking for "a nice place to settle"), and north of Denver cultivation is almost continuous, with the result that water has been in increasingly short supply. Eventually, all available streams on the eastern slopes of the Rockies had been tapped, and it was necessary to look further afield. Since the upper Colorado River has water to spare, the idea was conceived of breaching the watershed and meeting the ever-growing demand of the Piedmont towns and farms in this way. The latest and most ambitious of these diversions will, it is hoped, benefit not only the Piedmont

itself, but also the dry upper valley of the Arkansas (see Fig. 19-3).

The Piedmont lands are an important producing area for sugar beets, and alfalfa, beans, and vegetables are also grown. The most recent development here has been the appearance of beef cattle feedlots, on which cattle are concentrated and fed with fodder crops grown on the irrigated lands, before being sent to Denver or Greeley for slaughter.[8]

[8]The best known and most impressive of these developments is that at Greeley, where the feedlot operations of Warren Monfort are described by Cotton Mather as follows: "During World War II he was feeding 3400 head at a time. Experts were impressed by the scale of operation. Now 200,000 head are fed simultaneously or 600,000 head annually. Two million gallons of drinking water are required daily. About 400,000 tons of manure are produced

The impact of tourism and federal policy on the empty West: Interstate Highway 15 crossing southwest Utah. *(Utah Dept. of Highways)*

COMMUNICATIONS AND TOURISM

There can be few regions of the world where so large a proportion of the population is involved in the transport business as in the Mountain and Desert region. If to the running of regular communications we add the service of the millions of tourists who annually invade the region, then we account for the livelihood of almost the entire population of some areas, so that if we take as our index the income derived from such services, then we find that this fourth group of occupations in the Moun-

each year and sold to Colorado farmers. Keeping this feedlot in operation requires a total land area of approximately 25,000,000 acres to support 700,000 brood cows and bulls, to raise 600,000 yearlings to feedlot stage, and to produce 250,000 tons of silage, 365,000 tons of chopped alfalfa, 25,000,000 bushels of corn, and minor feed ingredients." The feedlots themselves, however, occupy only 800 acres. (E. Cotton Mather, "The American Great Plains," *Annals* of the Association of American Geographers, vol. lxii (1972), 237–57; quotation on 257.)

tain and Desert region fully qualifies for its place alongside the other three.

There are two main reasons for the importance of the transport industry:

1. It was transport, in the form of the western railways, that dominated the settlement period in the region, as we saw in Chapter 8. It was the railways that led the way for all but the hardiest pioneers into the West; the railways that had land to sell and the means of reaching it; that located the towns; that were, in short, the agents of civilization in the West. Their primacy was incontestable until the 1930s brought the spread of a comprehensive road network over the region.

2. As a region of sparse population and scattered resources the Mountain West has always been a geographic barrier between areas of denser population and more intensive activity; a barrier zone in which few Americans had business to transact and across which they were eager to travel as speedily as possible. But to maintain communications across an

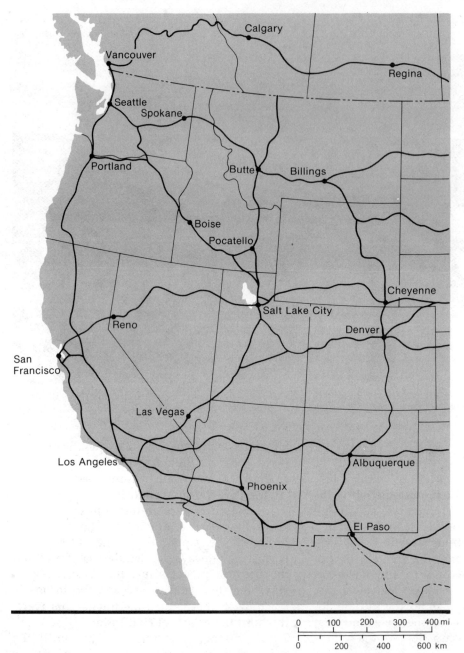

Fig. 19-4. Highways in western North America: The Interstate Highway system and the Trans-Canada Highway. Some sections of the roads are not yet built, but construction is continuing and completion is expected within a few years.

empty region requires almost as large a staff and administration as to do so across populous areas so that, although the regional population in the early years was very small, a large part of it consisted of the railwaymen who manned the division points and the lonely section posts along the tracks. The towns were located primarily for the convenience of the railways and only gradually did they develop functions that linked them with their surroundings. They were simply the piers of the transport bridges that spanned the empty West, strung out in east-west lines along the routes of the Canadian Pacific, the Union Pacific, or the Santa Fe.

When the era of road travel came in, the same pattern was repeated. The roads, built to cross the area rather than to serve local settle-

Tourism in the Mountain and Desert region: (1) Lake Louise, Alberta. *(National Film Board of Canada)*

ments—which were in any case few—ran for scores of miles through uninhabited areas. Along them therefore, there sprang up service points for motor traffic that duplicated those of the railways. What the towns were to the early railways, the "rest-stop" service clusters have become to the roads; with this distinction— that with the increase in size of the railway locomotive and especially with the coming of diesel haulage, there is less and less for the railway towns to do. Meanwhile the business of the road service-points and the number of such points is still on the increase.

The most important influence, then, on the location of settlements in this region is the re-

quirements of the transport services. Many of the larger towns are railway towns, like Ogden or Pocatello; most of the smaller ones are too. A few, by virtue of strategic location or nearness to irrigated lands, have grown to have a wider significance. The chief of these "grown-up" route centers are Spokane in the Northwest and Albuquerque in the Southwest. Albuquerque has outdone Santa Fe as a center of the southwestern region very largely because the railway which bears Santa Fe's name does not run through Santa Fe at all, but through Albuquerque (see Chapter 20).

There are two cities, however, whose influence dominates the whole of the Mountain and

Tourism in the Mountain and Desert region: (2) Lake Mead, formed on the Colorado River behind Hoover Dam. *(Las Vegas News Bureau)*

Desert region, from the Canadian border to northern New Mexico. One of these cities is Denver (1,391,000) and the other is Salt Lake City (766,000). One is in the oasis belt of the Rocky Mountain Piedmont and the other in the center of the irrigated lands at the foot of the Wasatch Mountains; the hinterland of one lies to the east of the continental divide and the other to the west. Although Denver actually lies outside the region, in all that concerns the economic activity of the Mountain West the two cities are rivals—as railway and road centers, miners' and stockmen's markets, manufacturing cities, and distribution points. Denver is the larger, but Salt Lake City, by

virtue of its religious significance for the Mormons, who have settled far and wide west of the Rockies, probably exerts the more powerful influence over its hinterland. In Canada, Edmonton and Calgary share the functions and something of the situation of Denver in servicing the mountain region.

Except on the irrigated lands, therefore, the population of the Mountain and Desert region is generally dispersed, strung out along the transcontinental routes. For all this, it is a population that probably feels itself less isolated than that of the Great Plains or the northern Great Lakes region. Its business brings it in daily contact with people who have just left

Chicago or Los Angeles, Toronto or Vancouver. High in the Rockies, or servicing the cars of motorists crossing the desert in Nevada or Utah,[9] it is in touch, if only vicariously, with the outside world.

There is, however, another antidote to isolation in the Mountain and Desert region, and that is the tourist traffic. While commercial tourism in the West may be said to have begun in 1872 with the opening of Yellowstone National Park, its modern development has been based on the automobile and the extension of the region's road network. Banff and Jasper, Yellowstone and Grand Canyon have become places familiar to millions who visit each year these products of glacial erosion, volcanic activity, or desert weathering. The distinctive cultures of the Spanish Southwest and the Indian reservations attract other thousands. Tourism has been responsible for the opening of large sections of the region which previously were both economically valueless and inaccessible. Lacking the profitable resource base of the lowlands, the mountain states have made capital out of their scenery. It is estimated that in the state of Nevada (where admittedly many tourists prefer the indoor attractions to desert or mountains) at least a quarter of the labor force is employed in serving the millions of tourists who visit the state each year and who must outnumber by 50 or 100 to 1 the resident population. Settlements have sprung up to serve and house the tourists, the largest of which is now Las Vegas, whose "metropolitan area" (a good deal of which consists of the driest of dry deserts) contained in 1974 some 320,000 people.

While Las Vegas and Reno are year-round resorts, over much of the Mountain West there are, in effect, two separate tourist industries— the summer and winter trades. In summer, with roads open at the highest elevations, the tourist traffic flows into the remotest parts of the region, by car and on horseback; only the hottest desert areas in the Southwest are closed to it. In September, however, the mountain roads begin to close, and with this closure— only the major routes are kept open—the service population withdraws, leaving whole sections of the mountains empty of inhabitants until the following spring. The winter tourist traffic then begins, making either for the winter sports centers, such as Banff, Sun Valley, or Aspen, or for the state of Arizona which, like Florida and southern California, attracts visitors by offering them a January mean temperature of 45–50°F (7°–10°C) and clear, dry weather. Then, too, is the season to explore Death Valley and the deserts of the Southwest.

Tourist facilities are constantly being improved; new settlements spring up, and new roads are cut further into the wilderness. Such roads as the Banff-Jasper Highway, the "Going to the Sun" mountain road in Glacier National Park, and the roads above the 10,000-ft (3040 m) contour in the Colorado Rockies are, besides being a testimony to engineering skill, a token of the force of modern tourism in opening the remoter West.

But it is axiomatic that in a region which relies as heavily as this one does on attractive scenery and the appeal of the wild, two things will happen. One is that the "honeypots"—the exceptional locations like Yellowstone, or the Grand Canyon—will become overloaded; that is, their popularity will destroy the very qualities which made them famous. Unless the National Park Service is prepared to operate some kind of rationing or quota system, it is difficult to see how the visitors can be kept away: success threatens to overwhelm nature. The other thing which happens is that a certain number of those who first visit these areas as tourists decide to return as settlers. The Mountain states have been experiencing a rapid rise of population; Colorado, as the best example, increased its population by 25.8 percent between 1960 and 1970, and by a further 14.7 percent between 1970 and 1975. In this case it can be said that a lead was given by the federal government, which moved a number of federal agencies

[9] Until recently, when air-conditioning in cars became a normal practice, most knowing motorists crossed the desert by night. Consequently, the transport stops were generally sleeping by day but jumping after dark. Air-conditioned vehicles have given thousands of Americans a daylight view of places like Elko and Winnemucca in Nevada, which they previously knew only as a configuration of neon signs lighting up the desert skies.

from Washington to the Denver area, and created new employment there. But in the 1970s even Wyoming and Montana, whose rates of growth had been very sluggish throughout the previous decades, have been picking up fresh population, some of it by in-migration.

So far, we have been considering the *use* of this region. Before concluding this chapter, however, we should briefly consider what has been called its "non-use."

In modern North America, with a population predominantly urban in character, there is an obvious need for the physical relief offered by recreational space and outdoor life. This felt need is given an emotional edge by the knowledge that much natural wealth and beauty has already been destroyed, and there are very strong pressure groups which urge that the preservation of parts of the West as nature reserves should be undertaken as a matter of urgent policy.

Certainly the evidence in favor of action is depressingly real. It might be imagined that to suburbanize a desert was an impossible task; yet the Americans have succeeded. Some of the most attractive,[10] and some of the most arid, parts of the West have been sold off in small lots and, with their beauty parlors and their real estate agents, these provide plenty of ammunition for the preservationists.

What has happened, of course, is that the highways which have opened up the region's splendid scenery to outside view have also had the effect of exposing that scenery to the full force of tourist traffic from a largely urban-based population for whom the weekend habit and the long vacation have become second nature. Furthermore that population enjoys a total mobility up to, say, 500 mi (800 km) at any given weekend. It has become fashionable to use this private mobility to live in the desert

and work in the city or, at the least, to own a second home out in the wilds. The rising price of desert and mountain building lots over the past decade reflects this developing life style.

The concept of "wilderness" has in these circumstances taken on for some Americans the qualities of a religion. It is a religion which already has its law—the Wilderness Act of 1964, which provides for the setting up of new reserves. One of its prophets, quoted with approval by a former Secretary of Agriculture in the United States, explains the concept as follows: "Wilderness is an anchor to windward. Knowing it is there, we can also know that we are still a rich Nation, tending to our resources as we should—not a people in despair searching every last nook and cranny of our land for a board of lumber, a barrel of oil, a blade of grass, or a tank of water."[11]

The idea of protecting and preserving nature is not new: the United States already has over 38 million acres (15.4 million ha) of national and state parks and Canada has no less than 55 million (22.2 million ha). But to press for extension of these areas is aggravating to westerners who are denied other use of the lands insulated by reservation. On these nature reserves wildlife increases, and the surrounding ranch and farmlands may suffer its depredations. What is more, such non-use, or "single use" as it is perhaps fairer to call it, contravenes the basic principle with which we began: that in the West the important economic point is that only by multiple use, the combination of all possible forms of resource value, can these lands pay for themselves. The old "single-use" problem of the West arose from such activities as wheat monoculture and overgrazing. Today's problem is different in detail, and moreover it is willed on the region from outside (for the pressure comes from city-based groups). But it is the same problem in essence: how to make the Mountain and Desert region a valued and valuable part of the nation.

[10]Two obvious examples are the shores of Lake Tahoe on the California-Nevada state line and the southern end of Oak Creek Canyon in Arizona. If there is anything to be said aesthetically in favor of these developments, it escaped the eye of the present writer. There is often, as in these cases, a clear change of landscape when one leaves the public domain (especially national forest land) and enters privately held sections.

[11]Stewart Udall, *The Quiet Crisis*, Holt, Rinehart & Winston, New York, 1963, p. 181. The quotation above has about it the logic that if Mother Hubbard will only stay away from her cupboard, she can be confident that her dog will always have a bone in reserve.

20

The Spanish and Indian Southwest

Regional Identity

Most of the statements made in the last chapter about the Mountain and Desert region apply to the whole of the great American West—statements about its economy, its emptiness, or its problems over land and water use. But it is justifiable and, in fact, necessary to look beyond the generalizations, to examine more closely the character of individual parts of this West, and the next three chapters are concerned with doing precisely that. Between them they cover the peripheries of the West, southern, coastal, and northern. In each of these three areas, individual factors combine to produce a distinctive regional character, superimposed upon the basic quality that comes from being Western.

The first of these peripheral areas is the Southwest. Its distinctiveness is accepted by regional specialists; it figures, for example, in Jensen's *Regionalism in America*[1], where it was covered by an essay of J.W. Caughey under

[1]M. Jensen ed., *Regionalism in America*, University of Wisconsin Press, Madison, 1951; 1965 edition, pp. 173–186.

the curious subtitle "An Example of Subconscious Regionalism." By this, Caughey implied that although the Southwest possesses the characteristics of a distinctive region, it had never in its history *acted*, collectively, as one—with Texans, for example, making common cause with Southern Californians over tariffs or price supports or freight rates. Of this view it is perhaps legitimate simply to comment at this point (leaving the explanation until later) that it sounds as if it was the view of a white American, probably a Californian, a long time ago: the term "subconscious" hardly describes today's mood in the Southwest.

On what grounds, then, can the singling out of a southwestern region be justified? The argument is primarily a cultural one. Within the United States this region possesses a marked concentration of two earlier cultures and their artifacts, cultures which, in contrast to the blended "American" culture that predominates over most of the remainder of the national territory, are relatively unmixed and resistant to change. These are the American Indian and the Spanish.

The Indian Southwest: A Zuni pueblo in 1879. Reproducing this picture, D'Arcy McNickle (*Native American Tribalism: Indian Survivals and Renewals*, Oxford University Press, 1973) comments: "After more than ninety years, the young man's clothing has changed, but beehive ovens still bake bread, chili still hangs to dry in the sun, and ladders are stairways." *(Smithsonian Institution National Anthropological Archives. Photo John K. Hillers)*

CULTURAL IDENTITY OF THE INDIAN LANDS

Although Indian peoples have at some time occupied the whole of the North American continent, there are valid reasons for regarding their occupance of what is now the southwestern part of the United States as in some ways the most remarkable of their achievements. Certainly that occupance is of great antiquity when contrasted to the time span during which other Indian peoples further north had occupied the lands where white men encountered them. At least since the time of Christ there have been settled Indian tribes in the Southwest; so that at the period of the first contacts with Europeans, this region of the continent was supporting the densest Indian population anywhere north of Mexico—in an area, we should note, of meager rainfall and limited resources of game. At least since the third century A.D. these Indians have been building permanent structures, reports of which lured the Spaniards northward in search of "cities" and to which they gave the Spanish name that has been attached to them ever since—pueblos. Among their other character-

istics these same Indians practiced irrigation agriculture; in a historical sense they were the forerunners of the Spaniards, the Mormons, and the Bureau of Reclamation. Finally, the southwestern region today contains by far the largest area of Indian reservations in Anglo-America: of some 50 million acres (20.2 million ha) of tribal and Indian trust lands in the United States, 20 million (8.1 million ha) are in Arizona and a further 7 million (2.8 million ha) in New Mexico (see Fig. 20-1). These two states possess an Indian population of about 170,000 and form the core of a distinctively Indian Southwest.

CULTURAL IDENTITY OF THE SPANISH LANDS

In any account of the settlement and use of the West as we know it today, however, pride of place must be given to the Spanish pioneers. It is easy for Anglo-Americans in other regions to forget that Spanish settlement of the continent predates the Pilgrim Fathers by a full 50 years. The Spanish approach was from the south, initially to the Gulf Coast and Florida (where the town of St. Augustine was founded in 1565) and then overland from northern Mexico to the Rio Grande valley. Although it is now over a century since political control of the Southwest by a Spanish-culture government in Mexico City was terminated by the treaty of Guadalupe Hidalgo (1848) and the Gadsden Treaty of 1853, the cultural influence of Spain remains. It is found in place names and architecture; it is recalled by the importance to the region of mining and ranching—both introduced by the Spaniards—and it is a part of the everyday life of at least 6 million Americans, those of Spanish-Mexican ethnic origin.[2]

The Southwest is the only large area of the United States (as opposed to inner-city districts of limited extent) where people buy groceries or offer services in a language other than English. By this criterion, Los Angeles is the largest city of Spanish culture north of Mexico City; at the 1970 census there were nearly 1.3 million persons of "Spanish heritage" in its county area, with a further 160,000 in neighboring Orange County. Other large concentrations were to be found in San Diego and in the counties east and south of San Francisco Bay. In a cultural sense the southwestern states of the United States form an area of overlap between the two macroregions of Spanish and Anglo-Saxon culture—between the "Hispano" and the "Anglo," as they have long been identified.

Within this Hispano region, whose extent we shall consider in the next section, society and landscape have been stamped with many features whose origins lie in the Spanish Empire to the south—or for that matter back in Spain.

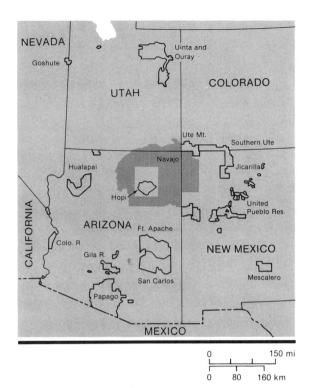

Fig. 20-1. The Southwest: Indian reservations.

---

[2]The U.S. Bureau of the Census distinguishes in the five southwestern states a population of "Spanish Heritage." This is defined (by means of a 15 percent sample) in two ways; it consists of (1) persons of Spanish language, for whom Spanish is *either* their mother tongue *or* the mother tongue of the head of the household or his wife, and (2) persons possessing a surname recognized as Spanish in a list of 8000 surnames compiled for the Bureau.

For the U.S. as a whole, the 1973 count of the population by ethnic origin recognized 10,577,000 persons of Spanish origin; these included 6,293,000 of Mexican origin and 1,548,000 Puerto Ricans (most of them settled in the cities of the northeast). To these there must then be added the Cuban exiles living mainly in Florida.

Among the elements of contrast between the colonizing work of Spain and that of its northern rivals were the Spanish attitude to the Indians, the Spanish land policy, the conscious, centralized, planned imperialism of Spain (however haphazard its application at the fringes of the empire), and the relative neglect of cultivation by the European colonists, who tended to concentrate on ranching and to depend on the native population for food crops. Even though these attitudes and habits were modified in time, their application for two and a half centuries following the first settlement (in 1598) of what is now the Santa Fe area has left a distinctive mark on these southwestern lands.

It is possible to argue that either of these cultures by itself would give the Southwest a marked regional personality. In practice the two reinforce each other in giving the area its distinctiveness, for each had taken over much from the other before any third party—in the form of the "Anglo" culture—appeared on the scene. Even after 1850, however, when the whole of the Southwest had become American

367

territory, there was a real sense in which it remained a region apart. In his perceptive analysis of the West, Meinig has pointed out the essential character of western settlement as being based on the growth of a series of nuclear areas:

Although folk colonization is always selective and uneven in area, in the East the general tide of settlement was relatively comprehensive and local nuclei and salients in the vanguard were soon engulfed and integrated into a generally contiguous pattern. . . . holding to the same scale, the pattern in the West is a marked contrast; several distinct major nuclei so widely separated from one another and so far removed from the advancing front of the East that each expands as a kind of discrete unit for several decades, only gradually becoming linked together and more closely integrated into the main functional systems of the nation.[3]

Meinig recognizes six such major nuclei and a number of minor ones. If we accept this analysis, then the Southwest is constituted by the development of two of the six nuclei— those of what he calls "Hispano New Mexico" and southern California, with three minor nuclei as links or outliers: the El Paso area, the Pheonix area, and (though outside Meinig's immediate consideration) the San Antonio nucleus in Texas. Between these nuclei and those to the north—Denver, Salt Lake City, and San Francisco—there is a cultural borderland to be crossed.

Regional Boundaries

If we accept the fact that the Southwest is a region distinguished by its cultures and isolated to a degree from its neighbors, then there is no reason to expect that it will have clearly defined boundaries. Only if the cultures themselves are related to, or depend on, environmental factors shall we find a correlation with natural conditions. Perhaps on the northwest, but there alone, can we speak of a natural boundary in the form of the Grand Canyon, a gash so wide and deep as to have formed a barrier to north-south movement which is even now bridged in only two or three places along a 350-mile (560 km) stretch in Arizona and Utah.

To what extent do environmental factors create a unity in the Southwest? Faulk argues for the unifying effect of low rainfall:

The overriding geographic feature of the Southwest is aridity. The economy of the region, the outlook of individuals, and the philosophy of the state governments are based on the limited availability of water and the fight to secure more of it.[4]

It is true that virtually the whole of the region as Faulk delimits it receives less than 16 in. (400 mm) of rainfall a year. And it is possible to argue that the Spanish Empire in Central America was essentially an empire of semi-aridity (the parallel with the Spanish Meseta is evident) and that it terminated where this ranch country gave way to more humid lands that would one day be cultivated. In Texas and Oklahoma this was approximately true. But it would be difficult to argue from this a conscious decision or causal association.

Topographically the Southwest runs across a number of the physical regions of the continent which were identified in Chapter 1. It penetrates into the southern fringes of the Rockies, and east and west of the Rio Grande it crosses the belts of plateau and lowland desert which extend south into Mexico. It spreads up over the Mogollon Rim where the latter marks the southern edge of the high Colorado Plateau, and reaches within a few miles of the Gulf of California and across the Pacific coast troughs to the sea.

A clearer idea of the extent of the region can be gained, however, from an understanding of the diffusion patterns of the two major cultures, the Indian and the Spanish.

THE INDIAN CULTURES AND THEIR EXTENSION

As we noted in Chapter 2, the Indian cultures of North America are very varied; they have

[3]D.W. Meinig, "American Wests: Preface to a Geographical Interpretation," *Annals* of the Association of American Geographers, vol. lxii (1972), 159–184; quotation from p. 160.

[4]O.B. Faulk, *Land of Many Frontiers: A History of the American Southwest*, Oxford University Press, New York, 1968, p. 3.

also no more been static in their distribution than those of the European in-comers. In the Southwest, however, we have to visualize a number of groups occupying the same lands over a period of hundreds of years, and there developing the remarkable agricultural civilization of the pueblos. They were evidently dislodged periodically by drought or invasion but they did not move far; they were sedentary peoples cultivating corn, beans, and squash, and practicing irrigation and such crafts as basket-making and pottery. They formed two relatively stable blocks, one on the southern part of the Colorado Plateau and around the headwaters of the Rio Grande (of which the Hopi and Zuni Indians represent the survivors) and the other along the border between Mexico and the United States, where such tribes as the Pimas and Papagos once enjoyed a high level of civilization, probably transmitted to them from the great culture hearths of Central America.

To the east and the northwest of these areas of relative cultural stability, conditions were much more fluid. On the eastern flank of the Pueblo Indians were the tribes of the Great Plains, for whom life was transformed in the seventeenth century by the introduction of the horse. These tribes, among whom the Comanche were to play the largest subsequent role, had always been nomads, using dogs for haulage; now, although still nomadic, they were transformed from pedestrians into equestrians. They could hunt buffalo and consequently enrich their culture with a host of new artifacts; they could also, when the time came, form a highly mobile striking-force against the Plains traders and settlers.

Northwest of the Pueblo country there began to be felt in the thirteenth century the pressure of a wave of newcomers from the far north. These migrant Indian peoples, who contrasted in every way with the sedentary Pueblo Indians, were the forerunners of the Apaches and Navajos: they came, we are told, "almost empty-handed," but they proved to be "cultural vacuum cleaners";[5] they adopted crafts and customs from the people whom

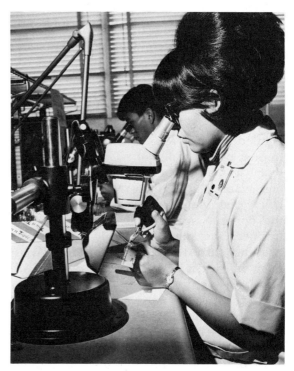

The Indian Southwest: New activities on the reservations. Inspecting modules at an electronics plant at Page, Arizona, in the northwest corner of the Navajo reservation. *(Bureau of Reclamation)*

they overran. After they had acqired some knowledge of farming and metal-working from the Pueblo Indians, they went on to learn stock raising from the Spaniards, and, when the time came to settle the Navajo on their present reservation in 1866, it was as pastoralists with stock provided by the government that they established themselves.

Whether we go back a thousand years, therefore, or consider the situation of the Indian today, we are justified in regarding this southwestern region as critical to his development and his future. Unlike the 100,000 Indians who today live in Oklahoma,[6] the southwestern peoples have a long history of occupance of the region in which they live and, in some cases, of the very lands they occupy today.

[5]A. Marriott and C.K. Rachlin, *American Epic: The Story of the American Indian*, New American Library, New York, 1970, p. 60.

[6]The point of contrast between Oklahoma and the Southwest arises from the fact that the former was established by the U.S. government as "Indian Territory," in which the remnants of a large number of tribes (eventually almost 70) could be collected, in order to clear them off lands desired for white settlement and exploitation. The two main groups so collected were (1) from the southeastern United States, a group which included the so-called Five

369

For the Spanish government, represented by a Viceroy in Mexico City, the region we are considering formed a part, but only a part, of the northern frontier of the empire. That frontier was of enormous length; as Caughey put it, "In 1789, in fact, when Washington was inaugurated President, the United States was confronted by the reality of a Spanish Southwest that began at the Georgia-Florida frontier . . . and wound up north of Nootka on the Pacific."[7] Our viewpoint for the moment is from the opposite side of this Spanish-American frontier, and under these circumstances, it need not surprise us to find that the government in Mexico was preoccupied more with holding a vast military frontier than with encouraging a colonization of new lands, which could only have the effect of straining the Spanish defenses still further. As Spain advanced north, there was a period when, because of the configuration of the North American continent, it was almost literally true that every mile of advance northward meant a doubling of the length of the frontier to be protected. To quote Caughey again:

When Spanish occupation did occur . . . in every instance it was more for the sake of erecting defences for Mexico and the Caribbean than because of the intrinsic attraction of the new lands . . . Imperial policy did not call for building up much more than a token occupation of these northern borderlands.[8]

Initially, "defenses" meant local protection against Indian hostility, such as the uprising which drove back the Spaniards from the Rio Grande valley colonies in 1680. But on the larger scale a more serious threat was posed by the French thrusting west from the Mississippi Valley and the Russians pressing south along the Pacific coast. If, as was to be the case, the

Spanish advance northward was to be three-pronged (for their advance into Arizona was halted only a short distance north of the present international boundary), then the eastern prong was designed to block French expansion into Texas, and the western prong was an effort to secure California ahead of the Russians. (Meanwhile, far away to the east in Florida, yet another chain of missions was being pushed northward to block the English, whose colonies—the Carolinas in the 1660s and Georgia in 1732—were gradually encroaching on the eastern end of the Spanish sphere of influence and threatening the oldest of all their North American settlements, St. Augustine.)

The initial expansion of the northern frontier of the empire was logical enough: it was due north up the Rio Grande into the heartland of the Indian Pueblo civilization, where Santa Fe was founded in 1610. In the late seventeenth and the eighteenth century it was the turn of the Texas frontier, while the main expansion west into California may be dated from the founding of San Diego in 1768. The general pattern of expansion was the same in each case: it was spearheaded by priests who established missions, around which they gathered Indians and where they encouraged the cultivation of gardens and fields, introducing European fruits and plants in the process. The priests were accompanied or, more usually, followed by military detachments, so that the frontier became a chain of mission stations and military posts (presidios). As colonization took place, civil settlements (pueblos) were founded. Settlement policy tended toward big land grants to ranchers, who introduced horses, cattle, and sheep from Spain and herded them over the semiarid grasslands between the islands of cultivation represented by the missions. New Mexico became famous for its sheep, while the whole culture of the cowboys as we have come to know it can be traced to Spanish origins.

Eventually the northern limits of the Spanish sphere of influence were set not so much by the advance of French or Russian colonization—the threat from both these sources proved ephemeral—as by the expansion of the young republic of the United States. Mexico gained its independence from Spain in 1821 and spent

Civilized Tribes (Cherokee, Chickasaw, Choctaw, Creek, and Seminole), who were moved to Indian Territory between 1829 and 1842, and (2) from the Great Plains after the Civil War. Plains Indians from Wyoming in the north to Texas in the south were brought together in what is now western Oklahoma.

[7]M. Jensen, ed., *Regionalism in America*, University of Wisconsin Press, Madison, 1965, p. 174.

[8]M. Jensen, *Regionalism in America*, pp. 176–77.

the first quarter-century of its life as a nation wrestling with the problem of its relations with its expansionist neighbor, independent since 1776. Already, under Spain, the problem had arisen of Anglo penetration and settlement of Texas. After 1821, traders from the Midwest began at once to appear at Santa Fe (Spain had been careful to keep them out). In California the effect of the Gold Rush of 1848 was cataclysmic for the thin veneer of Hispano culture in the center and north of the state. War and treaty came and went, and at the end Mexico had lost the whole of the Southwest. Culturally the Hispanic world had virtually lost eastern Texas and central California, for in those areas the tide of Anglo settlement had been overwhelming: California was culturally and commercially divided in two. But over the remainder of the Southwest, while the political sovereignty had changed, the cultural legacy of Spain remained to challenge or to enrich the new political masters.

The eventual international boundary between Mexico and the United States was established only in 1853. In the east it followed the Rio Grande but in the west it marched across largely unoccupied and unsurveyed land, and it owes its present course to Mexico's insistence on a land bridge between her mainland territories and Baja California and a hazy belief by some U.S. senators that the United States needed for a transcontinental route the strip of land bought by it through the Gadsden Treaty of 1853.

These, then, are the limits of the Southwest. If we now pause to enquire whether the area we have identified forms in any sense a coherent region in the life of the United States today, we have to reply in the negative: distinctive it may be; coherent it is not.

The northern border of the Spanish Empire ran in a rough arc of a circle whose center was in Mexico City, an arc extending from Texas to California. The major lines of movement radiated out from the center to the circumference, but along the circumference itself movement was difficult, slow, and infrequent. Thus the early settlements on the upper Rio Grande found their natural lines of import and export running down the river to the south; in this

sense the opening of the Santa Fe-Missouri trade route after 1821 represented an about-face for New Mexico's commerce.[9] Administratively, the only links between Texas at one end of the frontier and California at the other were via Mexico; the project for the short-lived Atlantic and Pacific Railroad (later built as the Southern Pacific) was still some decades in the future. And after the thrust of the missionaries into Arizona in the last years of the eighteenth century (their main mission of San Xavier del Bac was founded in 1700), Arizona remained a sparsely settled area of the borderlands, a gap in the frontier, and the forms of Hispanic society as they developed were quite different in New Mexico, Arizona, and California: "The date of immigration and settlement, the attendant cultural concomitants, geographic isolation, natural resources, the number and kind of Indians among whom they settled, and many other factors resulted in not one Spanish-speaking people but several."[10]

Fragmented though this Hispanic population has been, and small in its beginnings—in

[9]It is interesting to notice (as D.W. Meinig does in *Southwest: Three Peoples in Geographical Change, 1600–1970*, Oxford University Press, New York, 1971, pp. 38–40), that the idea that New Mexico's principal link would *remain* with Old Mexico rather than with the American Midwest—to reach which it was necessary to traverse the whole width of the Great Plains—underlay the first project of the railway era: the concept, initiated by *Anglo* interests, of a north-south line to be called the Denver and Rio Grande.

The railway was eventually built, but in the process it lost its planned direction and grew as an east-west stem. The first railway into northern New Mexico was the Santa Fe line, which followed the trail from Kansas City.

[10]R.W. Paul, "The Spanish-Americans in the Southwest, 1848–1900," in J.G. Clark ed., *The Frontier Challenge*, University of Kansas Press, Lawrence, 1971, pp. 31–56; quotation from pp. 33–34. See also R.L. Nostrand, "The Hispanic-American Borderland: Delimitation of an American Culture Region," *Annals* of the Association of American Geographers, vol. lx (1970), 638–61, which recognizes explicitly the border character of this region from the Hispanic (though not of course from the Indian) point of view. Nostrand includes in his borderland the southern and western two-thirds of Texas, all New Mexico, the southern one-third of Colorado and two-thirds of Arizona, and California from Yuma up through the Central Valley to north of Sacramento and thence to San Francisco. His criteria are the numbers and percentage of Spanish Heritage population by counties in 1960.

Grazing stock on the Navajo tribal range. The Navajos occupy the largest of all the United States's Indian reservations and also one of the driest. Amid the spectacular sce- nery of Monument Valley on the borders of Arizona and Utah, forage and water are both scarce. *(Utah Travel Council)*

1848 there were between 75,000 and 80,000 Spanish-speaking inhabitants of what is now the United States' Southwest—it has survived and grown and made its mark on several hundred thousand square miles of U.S. territory. The parallel with French Canada, with its 65,000 French speakers in 1763, is a suggestive one. No one would use Caughey's term "subconscious" to describe the regionalism of French Canada. The Hispanos, without the cultural protection the French Canadians enjoy in the educational and legal systems of Québec, have held their ground at least as well and, after a century and a quarter of government and education under an alien system, today show a higher level of group consciousness than probably at any time in the past.

Land and Livelihood

The Spaniards entering the Southwest brought with them their livestock and various European grain and fruit crops to add to the range of native plants cultivated by the Indians. Irrigation was known to these Indians, and to

Spain since Roman and Moorish times, so that ranching and irrigation agriculture, two of the activities which we have already seen to characterize the West as a whole, grew out of a merging of the Spanish and Indian economies. The third economic base was mining:

Every Spaniard who came north . . . no matter whether he was a soldier, a missionary, or a civilian, had some hopes of discovering mineral deposits. The dream of quick wealth . . . permeated every facet of Spanish endeavor in the provinces after they were permanently settled.[11]

In terms of minerals, the Southwest did not prove a rewarding area for Spain, as did some of those further south: the major discoveries, particularly of gold in California, came later. But it was the Spaniards who led the way in prospecting and in techniques.

These, then, have been the traditional means of livelihood in the Southwest. We must now trace their development in more recent times.

MINING IN THE SOUTHWEST

Arizona and New Mexico rank ninth and eighth respectively in value of mineral production among the states. So far as Arizona is concerned, more than 90 percent of this value is represented by copper from the southern and southeastern parts of the state. In New Mexico, on the other hand, a wide variety of minerals are mined and the oil fields of the Permian Basin of Texas extend across the state line, so that petroleum is the leading mineral by value. In a similar way the Colorado coal field extends across New Mexico's northern boundary.

The mining industry has felt the effects of strikes on the Indian reservations, strikes which have encouraged a greater awareness of the needs and potential of the Indians. Whereas they have oil, gas, coal, and ores they obviously do not have the technical means to exploit these minerals. It is to be hoped that in the future the Indians will themselves benefit to a greater degree from their resources.

RANCHING IN THE SOUTHWEST

The Spaniards introduced their livestock to the region, but it was with an influx of Anglos

after 1870 that the ranching industry developed in scale: New Mexico had only 57,000 cattle in 1870 but nearly 350,000 in 1880. The dates are significant: these were the years of the "cattle kingdom" (p. 327), and the natural rangelands of the Southwest attracted the cattlemen. It was during this same period of a decade and a half after the Civil War that the Indian tribes were "pacified" and settled on reservations. With cattle challenging sheep on the open ranges, the latter became the particular staple of the reservations, where, as the largest tribe, the Navajo built up on their arid lands after 1866 an economy based on sheep raising and weaving. The Indians thus became the heirs of a tradition of livestock raising in the New World which was, as Paul has noted, "medieval if not biblical in aspiration,"[12] while the Anglos developed the range cattle and feedlot industry of the modern Southwest. Overstocking and erosion have been serious problems on the reservations just as they have been, less justifiably, on the richer grasslands elsewhere.

IRRIGATION AGRICULTURE IN THE SOUTHWEST

Throughout the Southwest today, most crops are grown under irrigation. The Hopi Indians have developed to a fine art the techniques of dry farming, but most of the commercial agriculture of the region is concentrated in the oases. These are to be found in the valleys of the principal rivers and their tributaries—Rio Grande, Pecos, Gila, Salt. But the supply of water in these rivers is inadequate for the irrigated acreage which has been developed. The time came when the Rio Grande was reaching the border of Mexico at El Paso virtually empty of water, and the U.S. government was obliged to construct a federal storage project on the New Mexico section of the river to resolve an international argument. On the Arizona side of the continental divide the situation today is much more acute. Large-scale irrigation in central Arizona was made possible by the construction of the Roosevelt and Coolidge dams (built in 1911 and 1928 respectively), so that by the early 1930s the flow of the Gila and Salt was

[11]Faulk, *Land of Many Frontiers*, p. 79.

[12]R.W. Paul, "The Spanish-Americans in the Southwest, 1848–1900," p. 36.

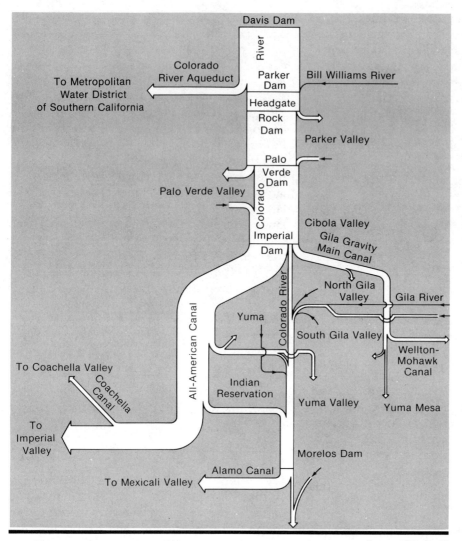

Fig. 20-2. The Colorado River: Distribution of water below Davis Dam, 1961–63. Note the very small residual flow reaching the Gulf of Mexico (bottom). This diagram should be borne in mind when considering the plans for the Central Arizona Project (Fig. 20-3), which would divert water from behind Parker Dam. The reader may wonder where the extra water is to be found. It is hoped to increase the dependable flow of the Colorado by regularizing works higher upstream—if these are not defeated at the planning stage by the conservation lobby.

fully utilized for irrigation purposes. But the demand for water continued to rise, both because of the rapid increase in Arizona's population and the remarkable postwar expansion of irrigated cotton, which in 1952 reached a peak of over 650,000 acres (263,000 ha). Effectively, Arizona was converted from a mining and ranching to a mining and cotton state.

With this conversion, the increased demand for water had to be met from the only alternative source available besides the rivers—groundwater reservoirs. It is estimated that the annual water "capital" accruing to Arizona is about 3 million acre-ft (3.67 billion m³) of which two-

thirds come from stream and river diversions and the remaining one-third from groundwater recharge. But by the mid-1960s the estimated consumption in the state was 6.5 million acre-ft (7.96 billion m³), which meant that the groundwater supplies were being drawn down at the rate of some 3.5 million acre-ft (4.28 billion m³) each year. This also means that the water table falls and that the recovery of groundwater from wells becomes increasingly expensive.

Since the peak of the cotton boom in the 1950s, the cotton acreage has fallen to less than a half of its 1952 maximum, but other crops such as winter and spring vegetables have replaced cotton, and overall demand remains unchanged. This agricultural demand, moreover, is focussed on the Phoenix oasis, where 1,172,000 of Arizona's 2.2 million population were concentrated in 1974.

We shall refer again in the next section to the growth of Phoenix. For the moment our concern is with the shortage of water in central Arizona, an area which lies within the basin of the Colorado and is subject, therefore, to the terms of the Colorado River Compact (see pp. 396 and 357). With the entire flow of the Gila and Salt already committed (see Fig. 20-2), the only way to obtain more water for Arizona is from the Colorado, and the state has been to the courts several times to try to secure more favorable treatment under the Compact. Its best hopes for the future are now pinned on its sponsorship of a scheme known as the Central Arizona Project. This is designed to tap the Colorado at Parker Dam (see Fig. 20-3) and to carry water—assuming that the water is present in the river and unclaimed by any of a number of potential litigants—to the Phoenix area, where it will reinforce the flow of the Gila and Salt rivers, and then on to Tucson. The chances of such water being regularly available will be improved if some additional storage can be provided higher up the Colorado, but this involves the construction of dams which were the object of determined opposition by the conservationist and wildlife lobbies.

As we shall see again in the next chapter, when we come to consider the water problems of southern California, the alternative to depleting still further the river or groundwater supplies is to re-allocate the existing supplies and, as a first measure, to reduce the use of water for irrigation. Of the Tucson area Wilson wrote:

Domestic, industrial, and mining uses consume 50,000 acre-feet annually, which is a substantial portion, and perhaps all, of the annual recharge. A small area of irrigated agricultural land, about 14,000 acres, uses on the average an additional 42,600 acre-feet of water annually. Agriculture in the Tucson area employs less than 1500 out of a total labor force of some 70,000. In other words, about

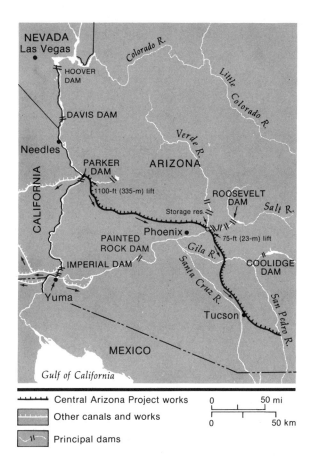

Fig. 20-3. The Central Arizona Project. The map shows the project as it will be when completed, but progress has been slow and funds have been voted by Congress only for parts of the project to date.

two per cent of the workers are supported by the use of almost half the water consumed.[13]

The question therefore becomes one not simply of a physical shortage of water supplies but of resource allocation of a scarce commodity among a number of possible uses and users.

AMENITY AND TOURISM

Shortage of water is only one aspect of the impact on the Southwest of its attractiveness to tourists and settlers in modern America. It is now twenty years since E.L. Ullman drew attention to the importance of amenity as a fac-

[13]A.W. Wilson, "Urbanization of the Arid Lands," *Professional Geographer*, vol. xii, No. 6 (1960), 7.

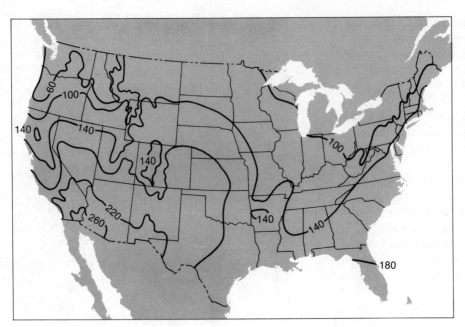

Fig. 20-4. The United States: Hours of sunshine in December. The map underlines the clear climatic attraction of the Southwest, particularly by comparison with its most obvious rival for the winter tourist trade, the state of Florida.

tor in regional growth.[14] The Southwest has been the region of the United States which has most vividly illustrated his case during the succeeding two decades. The tourist traffic began soon after the Santa Fe Railroad (which linked southern California with the Midwest in 1885) completed a branch line to the very lip of the Grand Canyon. From Albuquerque westward to Los Angeles, it gave access to one scenic marvel after another, while further to the south the Southern Pacific linked the old Spanish settlements west of El Paso. This tourist traffic has steadily increased, but it has also understandably resulted in an influx of settlers, people who have chosen the year-round enjoyment of an environment which they previously visited on vacation.

The principal amenity factors of the Southwest are its climate and its relief: the relief ensures variety of climate. Both winter and summer it possesses advantages. In the winter it far outdistances its obvious rival—Florida—in total hours of sunshine (see Fig. 20-4). Yet not only does Tucson have a January mean of almost 50° F (9.8° C) and a minimum of 77

[14]See Ullman's article under this title, *Geographical Review*, vol. xliv (1954), 119–32.

percent of possible sunshine (65 percent in Miami), but only a few miles to the northeast it has the Mt. Lemmon winter sports area. On the other hand, the plateau country offers relief from the heat of summer, with July means generally between 68° and 70° F (20–21° C) and cool nights. Relative humidities are low and the Southwest's first and continuing attraction as a home area is for those who suffer from rheumatic and bronchial complaints.

Only the spread of air-conditioning, however, has made possible the tremendous population growth within the Phoenix S.M.S.A. At Phoenix the July mean is 90° F (32.2°C) and maxima of over 100° F (37.8°C) regularly occur in the three summer months. In 1940 it was a small city of 65,000 inhabitants. By 1974 the city had long passed the half-million mark, and the S.M.S.A. had a population approaching 1.2 million. During the same period Tucson grew from 36,000 to 434,000 and Albuquerque from 35,000 to 379,000. The single decade of the 1960s brought nearly 200,000 newcomers to Phoenix and 50,000 to Tuscon. That same decade saw the emergence of Arizona as an industrial state, with the value of manufacturing coming from behind agriculture to eclipse it by 1970. The California aerospace industry has spilled over

Residential development in the Southwest: Sun City, Arizona. This 1973 photograph shows how the irrigated lands of the Phoenix oasis have been disappearing beneath a spreading rash of surburban communities laid out by developers in response to the growing popularity of the area, especially among the elderly and retired. Of Sun City, *Time* magazine reported (1 October 1973) that it "has drawn 28,000 residents (average age: 67) to a tract 16 miles northwest of Phoenix. It has . . . seven golf courses . . . Arizona's first indoor, air-conditioned shuffleboard courts, two artificial lakes, and a 7,500-seat amphitheater for plays and concerts." *(Terence Moore)*

into Arizona, and Phoenix has in addition a hot rolling mill for steel and a large food-products industry. New Mexico for its part remains one of the least industrialized states of the United States, but its now-historic connection with the early work on nuclear fission led to large government investments during and after the Second World War, and a slow but steady growth in manufacturing is occurring in Albuquerque and down-river, at El Paso, Texas.

Regional Mixture

The population of today's Southwest is made up, as we have seen, of three main components; in their order of appearance, Indian, Hispanic, and Anglo. In addition there are black minorities in most of the cities. The remainder of this chapter examines briefly the characteristics of each group and the extent to which these diverse elements have blended themselves together into a homogeneous regional population.

In the early stages of European occupance, a mixture of Spanish and Indian blood became general. The Hispanos of the Southwest today are largely the product of this mixture; their language is Spanish but their pride is much more in their Mexican and Indian background than in their shadowy connection with Spain. It might therefore be supposed that this group

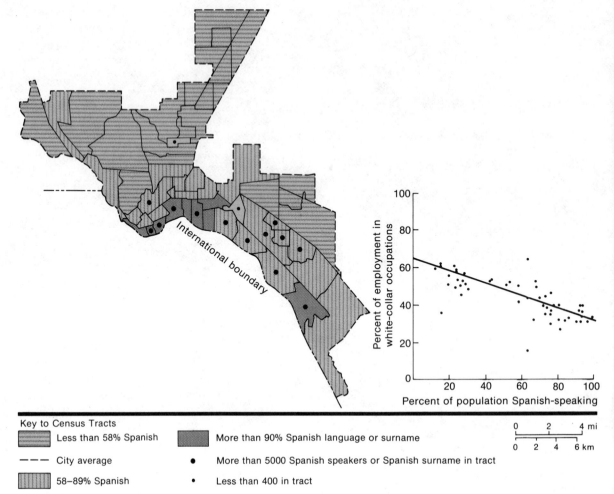

Key to Census Tracts

▨ Less than 58% Spanish	▨ More than 90% Spanish language or surname	
--- City average	● More than 5000 Spanish speakers or Spanish surname in tract	
▥ 58–89% Spanish	· Less than 400 in tract	

Fig. 20-5. A Spanish-American city, El Paso, Texas: Two facets of the character of a southwestern city with an ethnically mixed population. The map shows the distribution, by census tracts, of the Spanish-speaking population and indicates the degree of segregation of the Hispano element. The graph relates ethnic character to employment and indicates the extent to which the Hispano population is restricted (largely by educational handicaps) to blue-collar employment. The best-fit regression line is added to the graph.

would form a valuable social amalgam, reaching out to the pure Indians on one side, to the pure whites on the other. But this is far from being the case. The policy of gathering Indians on reservations set up a barrier of official segregation on one side of the "center," while further political developments erected obstacles just as formidable on the other. Those Hispanos who found themselves citizens of the United States after the 1848 treaty suffered the immediate disadvantage of a change of legal system (affecting particularly their title to land), of government in a foreign language, and of invasion by alertly commercial Anglos who quickly came to dominate all economic outlets. With no comparable commercial experience and penalized by a system foreign to them, the Hispanos were either submerged or impoverished, so that of the old Hispanic heartland Paul could later comment, "By the opening of the twentieth century the high, dry lands of rural New Mexico began to stand forth as a cultural island of poverty, illiteracy, and premodern customs."[15]

With the competitive advantage clearly in the hands of the Anglos, the scene was set for

[15]R.W. Paul, "The Spanish-Americans in the Southwest, 1848–1900," p. 37.

a deep social cleavage to develop between Anglo and Hispano. In other words, where Hispano and Indian had formed a relatively homogeneous society (although one which had certainly had its social gradations), the coming of the Anglo proved highly disruptive. For our present purposes the expressions of this disruption—or segregation, as it came to be—which chiefly concern us are those we noted when considering the relationship of the black to the white American—residential location and job opportunities. Most southwestern cities have their Mexican-American districts, which compare with the black ghetto: cities with both Hispano and black populations have two ghettos. All the census data for a city like El Paso (see Fig. 20-5) indicate clearly the effective segregation in housing and employment (and consequently income) which applies within the city. In one respect, in fact, the black is better off than the Hispano: he does not have to choose between Spanish and English. The difficulties begin in school. The five southwestern states have between them about 1.5 million Spanish-surname pupils. But education is in English; only 6 percent of the schools in the Southwest have bilingual programs and these reach in practice only some 2.7 percent of the region's Mexican-American pupils. Consequently, after 8 years of schooling, nearly two-thirds (64 percent) of the latter are classed as below their grade level in reading, compared with 58 percent of blacks and 28 percent of Anglos. Only 22.5 percent of Mexican-Americans enter college (whereas the figures for blacks and Anglos are 29 and 49 percent respectively). Only 5.5 percent complete the course.[16]

Economically, this is a very serious handicap indeed. Some occupations in the Southwest have become traditional to the Mexican-American population, such as railway track-laying and irrigation-ditch maintenance, but the obstacles to rising beyond them are formidable, and a steady immigration from Mexico of 40,000 to 50,000 persons a year ensures that there is always competition for them. To improve this depressed status in the community and broaden vocational opportunities through educational programs is the object of Chicano[17] pressure on the state and federal governments.

The same characteristics of separate, low status and growing group-awareness mark the Indians on the reservations, where 400,000 have chosen to remain up to the present time, although nowadays there is no legal obstacle to their leaving. In the Southwest the pursuit by the reservation Indians of either their traditional agriculture or their acquired pastoralism for long went on in an economic vacuum: with arid lands, few roads, and almost no elements of a modern infrastructure, they subsisted apart from the mainstream of American commercial life. Well-meaning attempts to provide employment in the kind of occupations common to the rest of the country met with little success.

Three things have acted to change this situation: the growth of tourism, the construction of roads, and the discovery of minerals on Indian lands. The product of these three factors has been a much greater awareness both of the handicaps and of the advantages of the Indian in contemporary America. The handicaps are formidable—a backlog of educational and occupational disability going back to the multiple deprivations of the Indian in the nineteenth century. The advantages are legal rights to the new-found minerals, a tender spot in the nation's conscience, and an exotic culture to draw visitors.

There is a growing self-awareness among younger Indians and it focusses on the question of treaty rights. There has been a series of court actions calling for compensation or renegotiation arising out of many of the treaties made between the tribes and the United States government, for rights to land or minerals take on a new importance when it becomes a question no longer of simply herding sheep on an arid pleateau but of a fortune in minerals or in real estate to be gained from these same dry lands, once so useless and now so coveted.

[16]All the above figures can be found in the series of reports in the Mexican American Educational Series of the U.S. Commission on Civil Rights, published in 1971 and 1972.

[17]The term *Chicano* for Mexican-American is derived from "Mexicano" and is used by choice by Mexican-Americans for increasing group consciousness among their people.

California and Hawaii

21

Introduction

California has been a name to conjure with for more than a century. Since the gold discoveries of 1848 brought in the "forty-niners," the state has seldom been out of the news for long. Yet it is probable that nothing would surprise the old-timers more, with their memories of dry grasslands and scanty food supplies, than the information that the California they knew had become the home of more than twenty million Americans, the site of great cities, and one of the world's richest agricultural areas, and that the value of the gold they so laboriously won had long since been eclipsed by that of the crops and the manufactures produced within the state.

Their surprise would probably increase on learning that the intensive development of today has spread even to those areas which to them were most forbidding. The deserts of the southern Central Valley have become an area of cotton and fruit farms, while the dry scrubland south of the Tehachapi Mountains is now the site of a conurbation whose population is more than ten million; even the Mohave Desert is now dotted with ranches, holiday homes, and service centers. Only Death Valley remains largely untamed.

For modern California is to a considerable extent the creation of the Americans who have chosen to make their homes there. In particular, it is the water engineer who has made the present measure of settlement possible, by transferring water from rugged mountains to dry plains and from rivers to irrigated fields.

The physical obstacles that confronted the pioneers were certainly formidable. To reach their new homes, future Californians had first to cross the 7000-ft (2130 m) passes of the Sierra Nevada and find their way down through snowdrifts, forests, and canyons to the Central Valley. Once they were west of the Sierras, they entered a region where the characteristic landscape consisted of grass-covered hills, lying dry and brown under the summer sun like old, wrinkled canvas, with shrub-sized trees on their higher slopes and desert scrub on the valley floors. The Mexicans, who were the first settlers of European background in California, were ranchers, and when the territory was ceded to the United States in 1848 the only agriculture was in the immediate neighborhood of the Spanish religious missions, which had been founded in the eighteenth century.

The climate of California, as we have seen in Chapter 1, is generally classified as "Mediterranean," but this is a serious oversimplification

California: The San Joaquin Valley at its southern end. The flat, irrigated floor of the valley contrasts sharply with the bare eastern slopes of the Coastal Ranges, seen in the foreground. At the left-hand edge of the photograph lies the town of Bakersfield. *(John S. Shelton)*

which conceals important differences between, for example, the northern and southern ends of the Central Valley or between the coastal hills and similar elevations at the foot of the Sierras. Along the coast mean temperatures increase and rainfall decreases with fair regularity from north to south. However, over the coastal waters of the Pacific, which are cooled by the south-flowing California Current, fog is frequent in the immediate vicinity of the coast, especially in summer. Thus San Franciscans spend many summer hours in unseasonable gloom, and the July mean temperature is held down to 59°F (15°C), giving the city an annual temperature range of less than 10°F (5°C).

In the Central Valley, conditions of both temperature and rainfall show much wider extremes; indeed, the climate is more accurately classified as continental. We may illustrate this by comparing the climatic data for three Valley stations with those for stations in the same latitude on the coast. In each of the three pairs listed in the table, the Valley station is given first with the coastal station corresponding to it following.

Climatic Data for Selected Central Valley Stations (a) and Coastal Stations (b) in California

	Growing season (days)	Av. annual precipitation in.	Av. annual precipitation mm	July mean temperature °F	July mean temperature °C
Northern End					
Redding (a)	278	37	925	82	27.8
Eureka (b)	328	37	925	56	13.3
Center					
Stockton (a)	287	14	350	74	23.3
San Francisco (b)	356	20	500	59	15.0
Southern End					
Bakersfield (a)	277	6	150	83	28.3
San Luis Obispo (b)	320	22	550	64	17.8

Rainfall diminishes from north to south through the Central Valley, and at the southern end true desert is encountered. At the same time, the eastern side, nearer the Sierras, is generally wetter than the western. Both on the coast and in the Valley the summer months are almost rainless: Bakersfield receives only 0.6 in. (15 mm) between May and September. Summer temperatures are high, and winter frosts limit the growing season in the Valley. In all this the effect of the coastal hills in shutting off marine influences is marked, for the figures given below reveal that at Stockton, inland from the only break in the hills (at San Francisco Bay), the July temperature is moderated and the growing season is lengthened by the entry of maritime air.

The coastal hills and the Sierra Nevada turn inward at their southern end to enclose the Central Valley, and south of their junction lie the plains on which Los Angeles has grown up. Such a southerly position within the state means higher temperatures and lower rainfall than on the coast further north, but the low elevation of the plains permits air from the Pacific to flow inland without hindrance. This carries the moderating influence of the ocean into southern California, but it also brings Los Angeles its now-famous smog. Maritime air spreads inland until blocked by the mountains further back, and being very stable it lies over the metropolitan area, where the exhaust fumes of millions of vehicles create below it a dense and irritating fog with a dangerously high ozone content. It is a singular climatic irony that denies to the inhabitants of the two great California cities a sight of the sun that drenches the rest of their state.

The great barrier of the Sierra Nevada lies across the path of moisture-bearing winds off the Pacific, its crestline rising from 4000–5000 ft (1230–1520 m) above sea level opposite the northern end of the Central Valley to 9000 ft (2736 m) in the south, with individual peaks thrusting above this level to 13,000–14,000 ft (3950–4260 m). Consequently it receives a very heavy precipitation which, since it falls mainly in winter, produces an annual snowfall of up to 400 in. (1000 cm). This snow cover forms an invaluable reservoir for central and southern California during the rainless lowland summer.

East of the mountains there is an abrupt decline in precipitation, reflected in a swift transition from alpine pasture through forest to scrub and desert. From the mountains only a few ribbons of vegetation run out into the basins of eastern California and Nevada, where east-flowing streams penetrate only a short distance before losing themselves in desert sinks.

The Settlement of California

Such is the region to which hundreds of thousands of Americans have migrated since 1848. The original incentive is plain: it was California's gold. The sparse population of Indians and Mexican ranchers was soon engulfed in a wave of miners and camp followers, pouring in either overland, or by sea to San Francisco, which rapidly became the commercial focus of the region. There followed a lull after this before the next wave of settlers came in with the newly constructed railways, the first of which reached California in 1869. Out of the competition between then was born the southern California boom. Heads of families were encouraged to prospect for a California home by the offer of a return ticket from Midwestern cities to Los Angeles for prices which, at the height of the rate war of March 1887 between the Santa Fe and the Southern Pacific railroads, amounted to a free ride. The railways brought a host of settlers to the dry southern plains, where commercial orange growing was established before the end of the century. By the First World War, therefore, there were two population nuclei in California, with the newer southern one rapidly overtaking the older-established region around San Francisco Bay.

Since the First World War California has experienced a continuously high rate of immigration from states further east. Over the years, however, the character of the immigrants has varied. In the 1920s, when roughly 1.25 million people moved into the state, the majority were Midwesterners of adequate means looking for new opportunities in pleasant surroundings. These newcomers tended to settle in the cities. Then came the depression of 1929–33. The

1930s again brought over a million immigrants to California, but they were of very different character from those in the previous decade. Many of them were destitute farmers from the depression-ridden, drought-hit Agricultural Interior—the "Okies" (from Oklahoma, one of the worst dust bowl areas) immortalized by John Steinbeck in *The Grapes of Wrath*. Unlike their predecessors, they sought work on the land. And fortunately for them—at least in the short term—California was looking for farm labor when the tide began to flow most strongly, in 1935. California agriculture had been dependent from the first on foreign labor—Chinese, Japanese, Filipino, or Mexican. But during the early 1930s, the state had been encouraging the repatriation of the Mexican workers. For anyone willing to accept wages at the lowest level—and the dustbowl migrants certainly fell within that category—there was field work to be had. Furthermore, these Southwesterners knew about cotton, a crop which California's farmers were planting in ever larger quantities in the late thirties. So the state absorbed this migration, too. There were probably 300,000 of them from the Southwest as a whole; 100,000 from the state of Oklahoma.[1]

The 1940s brought new circumstances—war and the growth of industry. To man the war industries, some 1.5 million people entered the state; they in turn created a market which attracted other industries. Between 1940 and 1950 the population of California increased from 6.9 to 10.6 million.

The 1950s were like the 1940s, but on a larger scale. Three million people arrived in California from other states. Most of these postwar immigrants fell into two categories. They were either elderly people returning to a warm climate or they were young and active people impressed by the possibilities and the wealth of California. Almost all of them made for the cities, for by this time the state which had attracted first miners and then farmers

was well launched on its industrial and commercial career.

The 1960s saw a continuation of the process of population increase. In the last years of the decade California overtook New York as the most populous state in the Union, an occasion for rejoicing missed by nobody in the West. By this time the census recognized fourteen S.M.S.As in the state, two of which, in southern California, grew more rapidly over the period 1960–70 than any other U.S. city except Las Vegas.

As the population of California increased, so its agriculture developed and changed. In 1848 California was cattle country; huge Mexican ranches occupied most of the lowlands. The Gold Rush created a local demand for food supplies, and, while cattle were raised in increasing numbers, there was a growing diversification to supply this market. Then in the 1870s, drought undermined the cattle industry, and for the next decade the state's farmers turned to sheep raising. The 1880s saw another change, this time to wheat growing; the ranges were plowed up, and by 1890 California had achieved the position of second wheat state in the Union.

It was in the last two decades of the nineteenth century that there began to develop the fruit growing which has brought California more permanent wealth and fame. The construction of railways in southern California made possible the shipment of fresh fruit to worthwhile markets, and the new enterprise, sedulously publicized by the railways, provoked a tremendous land boom, as we have seen, in the arid surroundings of Los Angeles, while other areas of the state developed their own fruit and vegetable specialties.

Modern California Agriculture

California today sells a greater value of farm products than any other state (Iowa and Texas are its nearest rivals). It has some 36 million acres (14.6 million ha) of farm and ranch lands, and it is the major United States producer of about 30 crops and the only state producing several of these.

---

[1]W.J. Stein, *California and the Dustbowl Migration*, Greenwood Press, Westport, Conn., 1973. It is worth adding that there was a similar, though numerically smaller migration from the northern Great Plains into the Pacific Northwest; smaller because the effects of drought were less severe further north. But a whole generation of farmers in Washington and Oregon originally started life in the Dakotas.

It is as a producer of fruit that California is now renowned, but its popular reputation as a fruit grower may make it necessary to counter at once an impression that fruit trees grow everywhere in the state, or that there is some simple reason why they do so. In reality, between one-third and two-fifths of the farm income is derived from sales of fruit and vegetables: livestock products account for about one-quarter, and the remainder is derived from sales of dairy products, crops (mainly cotton), and poultry. The fruit areas are of limited extent and well defined, each specializing in a particular crop. Localizing factors of production vary, not only for each crop, but for each intended crop use, so that peaches for canning, for example, are produced in different areas from those destined for sale as dried fruit.

What are the features of this vast agricultural enterprise? They can be briefly summarized in four categories:

1. Owing to its north-south extent and its climatic range, California produces a wide variety of crops. By guarding against the danger of frost its farmers can produce tropical crops, and by ensuring the water supply they can produce temperate-zone crops.

2. Although farm production for the state as a whole is very varied, production of individual crops is highly localized. While this tendency to local concentration can be seen as a part of a continent-wide trend toward specialization in fruit and vegetable growing (which we have already encountered in regions further east), it does of course increase the farmer's risks,[2] and in California it creates the extra complication that it makes the demand for labor highly seasonal. It is this which makes it necessary for California to use a large migrant labor force (much of it Mexican or Filipino) to harvest the fruit crops, workers who move from area to area with the harvest seasons. Although so much of the work on the

[2]In 1968, for example, when the author happened to be in the area, farmers around the small town of Moss Landing, on the coast north of Monterey, were complaining that damage amounting to a million dollars or more had been done to their crop of artichokes by mice. The significant fact is, of course, that there should be so many artichokes concentrated within mouse-range in this one area.

farms is now mechanized, the first effect of this has been to speed up the harvest process rather than to make the migrant labor force redundant. The existence of such a group, a foreign body in the community in every sense of the term, raises enormous problems on the social level, however convenient it may be for the farmer. The problems faced by these migrant workers have been brought to the attention of Americans everywhere during the past decade, as the workers' leaders have tried to organize them and to employ such techniques as urging a boycott of California grapes, lettuce, and other produce in order to obtain better conditions of labor for them.

Not only is it true that crop production in California tends to be highly localized, but the locations themselves have gradually changed in the course of time. We have already noted the decline in wheat acreage from a peak around the year 1900. Between then and now the acreage of many fruit and vegetable crops has also declined. What has been happening is a gradual concentration of each crop on the most suitable (or the most convenient) high-yield lands, so that output has in most cases increased and has more than offset the decline in acreage. Other crops then occupy the acreage released. Some impression of this dynamic aspect of California agriculture can be obtained from Figure 21-1, which shows for each of a number of crops the year in which maximum bearing acreage was attained. By contrast, the acreage of a number of other crops was still on the increase at the end of the 1960s—such crops as alfalfa, broccoli, winter carrots, onions, almonds, and walnuts.

Some of these changes were forced upon the farmer by the loss of particular farmlands through urban spread, a process which we shall later re-examine. Others of them resulted from changing tastes of American consumers— the loss in popularity, for example, of cabbage and cauliflower, or the spreading popularity of the avocado and of frozen potato products. It has therefore been quite common in California to find that specializations replace each other on the same farmlands as time goes by.

3. Development of California's special fruit and vegetable crops has resulted in a relative

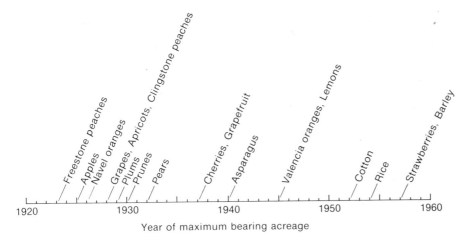

Fig. 21-1. California agriculture: Year of maximum bearing acreage for selected crops. Numerous factors are involved: changes in consumer taste; specialization and intensification; encroachment on orchard and cropland of nonagricultural land users—all these have produced wide fluctuations in acreage under particular crops.

Year of maximum bearing acreage

neglect of basic agricultural items such as stock feeds and livestock products. With a rapidly increasing population, the rising local demand for food supplies has run counter to the California habit of producing for sale outside the state. Thus while it possesses some 40 percent of the United States orchard and vineyard area,[3] and is the country's sole producer of a number of fruits and vegetables, California accounts for only 2 percent of the U.S. production of feed grains and consequently has to bring into the state a volume of imported feeds almost equal to its own production to feed its livestock.

This concentration on special crops brings us to what is perhaps the most important consideration for the California farmer—his dependence on out-of-state markets. His fruit, vegetables, and wine must be sold in highly competitive, distant markets and against the hazard of fluctuating consumer tastes. He must rely on good transport and attractive packaging if he is to out-sell rivals situated nearer the markets in the East.

4. From this last consideration we pass, logically enough, to the final feature of California agriculture—large-scale operations in production, processing, and marketing. For the success of California's speciality crops has been secured by organization, an organization taking two forms. First, market agencies have been set up to provide quality controls, selling arrangements, and bargaining power against the railways, from which they have obtained favorable freight rates on California produce moving east (see p. 92). Second, specialized crop production is dominated by two or three large firms, usually canners or processers, which effectively control the output of the individual farmer and may themselves be the principal producers of the crop. This gives rise to the now-familiar generalization that in California farming is not a "way of life" but a "business," and that the part of it which deals with speciality crops is in many ways organized more like industry than agriculture.

In the development of the whole of California's agriculture, irrigation has played a vital part. Today, with more than 8 million acres (3.3 million ha) under irrigation, California leads all other states in this respect, and projections are for a further increase, to over 9 million acres (3.7 million ha), before the end of the century.[4] While this acreage includes a large number of scattered, private enterprises, three areas outrank all others in importance. The first, and largest, is the Central Valley, the second is the Los Angeles area, and the third the Imperial-Coachella valleys in the extreme south.

[3]C.W. Olmstead, "American Orchard and Vineyard Regions," *Economic Geography*, vol. xxxii, 189–236. The maps in this article merit close study in connection with the present discussion.

[4]This figure and a number of the others which follow are taken from G.W. Dean and G.A. King, *Projection of California Agriculture to 1980 and 2000*, California Agricultural Experiment Station, 1970.

ply is badly distributed; some two-thirds are produced in the north, where remaining irrigable land is scarce, and only one-third in the southern half, where irrigable land is plentiful.

The project was designed, therefore, to transfer part of the unused flow of the Sacramento into the San Joaquin. By this means, some 650,000 acres (263,000 ha) of new lands could be irrigated, and, equally important, added security could be given to farmers already depending on the limited water supplies in the San Joaquin Valley.

The main task of water transfer is achieved by means of the Delta-Mendota Canal from the lower Sacramento to Mendota on the San Joaquin. North of Mendota, therefore, the canal water can substitute for the waters of the San Joaquin, thus making the entire flow of the latter available for use south of this point. Here a widespread system of new regulating works and canals has brought assured water supply to both old and new irrigated lands between Fresno and the Kern River at the southern tip of the valley. Altogether, the farming of some 5 million acres (2.02 million ha) has been affected by the project. Such has been its effect that the dry San Joaquin Valley now produces over 40 percent by value of the state's agricultural output from one-third of its area in farms; it has almost a half of California's land in crops, and Fresno, Tulare, and Kern counties are the three leading counties in the nation in value of farm products.

On the new farmlands of the Central Valley the Bureau of Reclamation hoped originally to encourage farmers to adopt a balanced agriculture of crops and livestock. But instead, the early years of the project were marked by a continuation of the California tendency to crop specialization. The particular feature here was the remarkable expansion of cotton acreage between 1945 (when there were 300,000 acres (121,000 ha) under cotton in the state) and 1952 (when there were almost 1,400,000 [560,000 ha]). All California cotton is grown under irrigation and, in accordance with a state law, all of it grown in the Valley is of the same variety, which has made for efficiency in research and planting, simplicity in mechanization, and yields which periodically exceed 1000 lb per acre—more than twice the na-

Fig. 21-2. Central California: Location map. (C.A. = California Aqueduct, D.M. = Delta-Mendota Canal)

The Central Valley Project of the Bureau of Reclamation has been based on a bold but simple concept. The valley is occupied by two main rivers, the Sacramento in the north and the San Joaquin in the south, the two joining to reach the sea at San Francisco Bay. Along their courses some 9 million acres (3.64 million ha) of the valley floor are irrigable; about two-thirds of this are along the San Joaquin, and one-third along the Sacramento. But to make use of this land, the valley's natural water sup-

tional average. The national quota system, which originally prompted the huge increase in cotton acreage in the 1950s, has since been responsible for something of a reduction, with replacement of cotton by other speciality crops such as vegetables, but cotton still makes periodic inroads into this acreage, and in 1974 occupied no less than 1.24 million acres (0.5 million ha).

Nor is development in the southern end of the Central Valley yet complete. The 1960s saw the launching of a further irrigation scheme, as a joint federal-state venture, which will when completed affect a large area of the west side of the San Joaquin Valley. The water supply made available by the original Central Valley Project canals has in the past decade been supplemented by the California Aqueduct (see Fig. 21-2), a state water main which surpasses the original Delta-Mendota Canal in bringing northern water to southern California. Some of this water is being diverted to recharge a falling water table and to irrigate new lands on this western edge of the Valley:

The west side of the San Joaquin Valley is a loosely defined area generally characterized by large corporate farms, mechanized cotton production, and oil fields that extends some 175 miles south from San Luis Dam near Los Banos to the Tehachapi Mountains south of Bakersfield. It has an average width of 25 miles along the western side of the Valley floor. Geologically, the area consists of a group of coalescing alluvial fans built up from deposits washed out of the coastal ranges to the west. . . . Sparsely populated and arid, the region is mainly irrigated by deep wells which are steadily exhausting the groundwater resources.[5]

By this scheme, several hundred thousand acres of the valley will either be given a new security against failing water supplies or else will receive irrigation water for the first time.[6]

[5]Dean and King, *Projection of California Agriculture,* p. 69.

[6]This area of newly irrigated lands is critical in the dispute over the federal government's policy of acreage limitation on federal benefits—in this case, irrigation water (chap. 4). In the joint federal-state scheme being described here, some of the water comes from federal sources and some is the state's. Even if the two liquids are not distinguishable in the canals, they certainly are so in law, because federal irrigation water is liable to the acreage limitation clauses of

The second important area under irrigation is in the counties that surround the city of Los Angeles. Here, on the dry alluvial fans at the foot of the San Gabriel and Santa Ana mountains, irrigation has brought into being an agricultural area whose output is truly remarkable. While the area is best known for its orange groves, other forms of production abound. Orange County once had the largest concentration of orange trees in the United States; Ventura County, northwest of the metropolis, is noted for its lemons and its vegetables (especially lima beans), and Los Angeles County itself led the nation both in total value of farm produce and in value of dairy products sold until the creep of the suburbs over its farmland forced it to yield the palm to the counties of the San Joaquin Valley.

The third main irrigated zone of California is in the Imperial and Coachella valleys. The first of these was brought to agricultural life as a private project as early as 1901, but it was swept out of existence again in 1905, when the Colorado River in flood broke its west bank, flowed into the desert, and created the Salton Sea. A new project replaced it, and this, together with the Coachella Project to the northwest, was given new security and added water resources by the opening in 1935 of the government's Hoover Dam, which controls the Colorado, and by the All-American Canal (see Fig. 21-4). Today these lands produce citrus fruits, cotton, dates, and vegetables (notably carrots and lettuce), and claim, like corresponding areas of Florida and Texas, the title of Winter Garden. A further recent development has been the growing of alfalfa, which is fed to cattle and sheep in feedlots to supply meat to the great urban markets in the southern part of the state. Most of these animals are drawn from the ranches of the Mountain and

the 1902 reclamation act, but state water is not. The legal problem of what happens when federal and state water mix is very much like that of Shylock attempting to take his pound of flesh without drawing any blood. The problem here is particularly acute, since most of the irrigated land (and the farm produce from it) is held in very large units, and if the acreage limitation rule was ever applied to it, nothing short of an agricultural revolution would be necessary. For further commentary, see Footnote 3, p. 110.

Desert region and are brought to the Imperial Valley for fattening and finishing.

California's agricultural output is one of the marvels of the American economy. As we have seen, it is essentially irrigation based: all the state's vegetables, potatoes, rice, sugar beets, and cotton are grown under irrigation, and so are almost all the alfalfa and over 90 percent of its fruit and nut crops. Without irrigation California would be (as it largely is in the non-irrigated hill country) a ranching state as in Mexican times, with cattle and sheep moving north to Oregon or east to the Agricultural Interior for fattening, rather than to the adjacent valley lands.

But now, with its booming cities providing markets and with agricultural land being swallowed up by urban and industrial growth at a rate of between 60,000 and 75,000 acres (24–30,000 ha) each year, the problem of maintaining agricultural output to feed an expanding population is a serious one. Where competition for space has become intense and where in consequence the farmer is confronted by soaring land values, the only possible method of staying in the farming business is to intensify the output per acre. For the farmer this is likely to mean a switch from extensive forms of activity, such as ranching or growing cereals, to the cultivation of specialty crops. In California this can only be done by *extending* the area under irrigation: hence the West Side extension in the San Joaquin Valley, the spread of farming in Yuma County, and the projections for an irrigated area of over 9 million acres (3.64 million ha) by the end of the century. The livestock farmer, alternatively, may switch to a kind of "urban farming" which has become especially widespread in southern California, where the pressure on space and land values is greatest—the use of the "drylot" for producing beef and milk from cattle held on feedlots; that is, on farms without the fields. By this means, some 200,000 dairy cows are kept within the Los Angeles metropolitan area alone, stall-fed on a wide range of feeds shipped into the city from the Imperial Valley and elsewhere—alfalfa pellets, citrus waste (as in Florida), and even peanuts. It is an intensive, high-yield system and it has become strongly concentrated in the southeastern suburbs of Los Angeles. Too many people want to live in southern California to leave room for the old style of farm.[7]

But, although the need to intensify farm output is evident and the means of doing it—irrigation—are at hand, the matter cannot rest there. In a state where water is a scarce commodity, the question must be asked again, as in the last chapter, whether to extend the area under irrigation is legitimate in view of the alternative demands on the limited supply, and whether, in any case, the new supplies needed can be made available at a price the farmers can afford. To this question we shall need to return later in the chapter.

California Industry

The number of employees in California's industries increased from 300,000 in 1939 to 1,600,000 in 1973. This great industrial growth was both cause and effect of the rise in California's population over the same period. Starting in 1941 the war in the Pacific created a demand for manufactured goods on the West Coast, and workers moved into the state in large numbers to meet this need. Once there, they and their families created an expanded market, and to satisfy that market after the war, manufacturers began to set up plants in the West. At the same time, the abundant labor supply provided by the immigrants, together with such local California advantages as the climate, set off a new round of industrialization, and so the process has continued.

At the start of this period of growth, it was the food processing industries that dominated California's manufacturing, giving employment to almost three times as many workers as any other group of industries. In the past thirty years, however, the manufacture of transportation equipment has taken over first place. While this grouping covers shipbuilding and motor vehicle assembly, its main component is the group of industries which began by

[7]In 1940 Los Angeles County had 320,493 acres under crops. By 1970 the figure was 88,500.

Southern California: The competition for space. Highways and suburbs have displaced many of the former citrus groves in the Ventura Lowland, west of Los Angeles. *(Calif. Dept. of Transportation)*

manufacturing aircraft in and around Los Angeles in the 1920s, and which have since grown into the giant southern California aerospace industry. This industry employs almost one-tenth of all the civilian labor force in the ten southern counties of the state and accounts for over one-third of the industrial employment there. At the 1972 Census of Manufactures, Los Angeles had 780,000 industrial employees in all, of whom 163,800 were making

transportation equipment (about 95,000 of them aircraft and aircraft parts), while the electrical and electronics group of industries accounted for a further 78,000, and other machinery 67,000. In San Diego in the same year, the transport and electrical groups employed 32,000 out of 64,000, and in Anaheim 55,000 out of 131,000. In this category of manufacturing, industries tend to "breed" other industries; aircraft bred aerospace, and aerospace in

San Francisco: Sacramento Street after the 1906 earthquake, with spectators watching one of the great fires which followed the quake. (*Arnold Genthe, California Palace of the Legion of Honor*)

turn generated a whole range of electronics, putting to civilian or consumer use the technology developed in the realm of rocketry, missiles, and space travel.

Other industries which, in conformity with national developments, have contributed to the rapid increase in the state's production are the manufacture of metal goods, machinery, and chemicals. The automobile industry, as has been its practice, has established plants near San Francisco and Los Angeles for local assembly of the motor vehicles which Californians own in such numbers; there is one car to every 1.9 persons.

This has been an industrialization for which the materials usually considered basic—coal and iron ore—are almost entirely lacking. It is true that California has a small steel production—to which the best-known contributor is the Fontana Works, built among the orange groves east of Los Angeles. But the state's coal supplies are meager, and steel output is based largely on scrap. California's more obvious natural resources are its oil fields, which are scattered widely through the southern part of the

state, and its hydroelectricity, which has been made available by the construction of the numerous flood control and irrigation schemes.

California's population at the 1970 census was 90.9 percent urban, which is the highest urban proportion for any state (cf. New Jersey 88.9; Rhode Island 87.1). Even more strikingly, it was nearly 93 percent metropolitan, and even allowing for the fact that some of California's S.M.S.As include counties which cover huge areas of desert and mountain, this figure does call attention to the drawing power, in the migration to California, of the two great conurbations: the Los Angeles lowland (including the large separate S.M.S.A. of San Diego) and the San Francisco Bay Area. It is in these areas that newcomers have settled; it is here, too, that industry tends to concentrate, and commercially one area dominates the southern part of the state as the other dominates the central and northern parts.

San Francisco achieved early prominence as the port of entry for the gold fields after 1848. Devastated by the earthquake of 1906, it lost its lead in population to Los Angeles in the decade which followed. In 1974 the San Francisco-Oakland S.M.S.A. had a population of 3.1 million, of whom about three-quarters of a million lived within the city of San Francisco proper, more than half a million across the Bay in the industrial and port city of Oakland, and the remainder in rapidly expanding bayshore communities both north and south of the older centres. At the southern end of the Bay lies the vast agglomeration of suburbs which has become the San Jose metropolitan area (1,182,000) sprawling around a small urban nucleus completely dwarfed by its growth.

The industries of the Bay area are very varied. They include shipbuilding and marine engineering, as might be expected in an area that handles half of the water-borne commerce of the United States' Pacific coast. But they also include some of the most sophisticated branches of industry in the style of the 1970s—electronics, transport equipment, and the research plants and institutes that brought these modern giants into being. Like southern New England, California offers these industries the benefit of proximity to first-class university centers, a factor which is proving a very powerful attraction to the location of modern industry on both the East and West coasts. Recent industrial growth has taken place largely along the Bay shores, much of it on reclaimed tidal lands: the San Jose S.M.S.A., for example, contains some 120,000 industrial employees, many of them working in factories which stand where only a few years ago there were orchards of apricots or salt marshes.

This last fact calls attention to the nature—and the problem—of the San Francisco metropolitan area. Its core is on the narrow, hilly peninsula between the Pacific and the Bay, where the original Spanish settlement stood, and where there remains no room for expansion. Today San Francisco proper is the commercial center—"the City" to central California—and has port facilities which handle a part, but only a part, of the waterborne commerce of the Bay Area.[8] The remainder of these

facilities and much of the industry which supports them is situated in Oakland and in lesser cities around the Bay. This means that a high proportion of San Francisco's workers live, spend their earnings, and pay their local taxes not in the city itself but across the Bay, and travel to work over the great bridges which span it.

This dispersion of the parts of the conurbation around and behind the water barriers has made San Francisco, like New York, a metropolis very sensitive to traffic problems. Although the construction of the two main bridges in the 1930s revolutionized the urban structure at that time, by the 1960s there was a clear need for a new solution to the problem of interconnection within the Bay Area. Out of this need has grown the Bay Area Rapid Transit (BART) system, the most advanced suburban transport enterprise of its kind in the world, linking the peninsula with outlying suburbs. Transit times have been so radically cut by this development that the urban area is clearly going to take on new shapes and structures in the immediate future under its impact. Whether it will help San Francisco proper with its problem of non-resident workers remains to be seen: it may merely encourage them to live further outside the city still.

Between San Francisco and Los Angeles, judged as cities, there is little comparison: San Francisco occupies one of the world's finest urban settings; Los Angeles sprawls disjointedly across 50 mi (80 km) of plains and foothills, and it is separated from the coast and from its port, near Long Beach, by a belt of suburban development interspersed with oil fields. Yet it is the southern metropolis that has outgrown the northern. This is simply a reflection of what has happened in the state as a whole: in 1900 the fourteen southern counties of California contained 25 percent of the state's population, and today the proportion is over 65 percent. The 1970 census recorded a population for the Los Angeles-Long Beach S.M.S.A. of 7.0 million, an increase of 16 percent over the figure for 1960. By southern California standards, however, this increase was modest: the main growth in the conurbation is now so far from the original core—the pueblo of Los Angeles, founded in

[8]It also has the 75,000 inhabitants of Chinatown, an important element in the urban structure and one of the leading tourist attractions of the city.

San Francisco: The city, the Bay, and the bridges from the southwest. *(San Francisco Convention and Visitors Bureau)*

1781—that it is taking place in and around secondary centers which have meanwhile themselves been designated as S.M.S.As. It was in this way that the Anaheim-Santa Ana-Garden Grove S.M.S.A., southeast of Los Angeles proper, recorded a population increase of 101.8 percent for the decade of the 1960s,[9] and by 1974 had increased a further 19 percent to an

[9]Most of this growth took place after Disneyland was opened. The German immigrants who in 1857 founded Anaheim would find today that agriculture had become dry-lot dairying and that their farmlands were occupied by the homes of over a million people and industries employing 130,000. To the list of such standard locational attractions as coal fields, water supply, or transport we can therefore now add another item: location governed by amusement park. The Disneyland recipe has now been repeated near Orlando, Florida.

estimated 1,661,000 inhabitants. As we saw in Chapter 2, the old definition of an S.M.S.A. has become inadequate in Southern California; the Bureau of the Census now recognizes a Standard Consolidated Statistical Area, covering four S.M.S.As and totaling in 1974 10.2 million inhabitants, a gain of exactly 2.5 million since 1960. For a number of years in the 1960s, migration into the five counties surrounding Los Angeles approached 200,000 a year. In retrospect, the crest of the wave seems to have occurred in 1963, a year in which 210,000 newcomers arrived.

What employment could these migrants find? For Southern California as a whole, the employment structure is not exceptional, although within the region there are local differences. Manufacturing, for example, is largely concentrated in the old industrial zone southeast of the center of Los Angeles, in the port area, and in the new southeastern suburbs. The Anaheim S.M.S.A. has the highest proportional employment in industry, wholesaling, and construction, and Oxnard-Ventura in government. Employment in services is everywhere high by U.S. standards—almost 5 percent above the national average—but this is readily explained (1) by a high average standard of living and (2) by the high proportion of elderly or wealthy people requiring such services. The construction industry is prominent everywhere in the newer suburbs. Apart from the 50,000 persons employed in "entertainment and recreation," Los Angeles has important functions in relation to the oil industry, insurance and foreign trade,[10] and has in the last ten to fifteen years challenged San Francisco's long-standing role as the banking center of the West Coast.

There is an immense variety of industries in southern California, and some of them are of considerable size: in Los Angeles, for example, there are over 60,000 workers employed in the manufacture of clothing, for the West Coast has developed its own fashions. But in terms of economic activity, nothing within the region compares with the aerospace industry and its offshoots. Natural conditions favored the early growth of an aircraft industry: in 1947, when it employed 150,000 workers throughout the United States, 65,000 of them were in the Los Angeles area. By the late 1960s, employment in the successor industries was over 450,000. But in the intervals there have been some very rapid fluctuations in this employment level.

[10]Between them the adjoining ports of Los Angeles and Long Beach handle some 50 million tons of commerce each year: in 1974 32 million tons of this was overseas trade.

The problem is twofold: (1) that so much of the output of these industries is ordered and paid for by the government and so depends on budget policy, and (2) that progress in technology is so rapid that a good deal of wastage, human or material, along the way is inevitable. When a city depends as heavily as Los Angeles does on this type of industry, then it has to learn to live with uncertainty.

This is a lesson which southern New England and southern California have had to learn. It emerges all the more clearly if we move on from Los Angeles to San Diego. Such has been the growth of Los Angeles that it is easy to overlook San Diego, 125 mi (200 km) to the south. Yet San Diego was founded before Los Angeles, has one of the world's great natural harbors (that of Los Angeles is largely man-made), and in 1974 had a population of 1.5 million, so that in any other company it would stand out as a major urban center. It grew up as a naval base, as the home port for the big southern California tuna fishing fleet, and as a place to retire to in the sun. But then came an industrial boom based on the air and spacecraft industry, and its fortunes began to fluctuate seriously. By 1957 it was estimated that more than 80 percent of the city's employment in manufacturing was in "defense-oriented industry." What this meant in local terms can be seen in the census of manufactures: in 1958, 46,000 workers were employed in the transportation equipment industries; in 1963, the figure was 13,000 and in 1972 it had risen back up to 24,000.

In Los Angeles itself, the outgrowths of air and space travel can be seen in a proliferation of electronics firms, which possess a much greater range of product and market than the original defense contracts allowed. Once again, as in the

Los Angeles Region: Percentage Increases in Population, by Counties and Decades, 1880–1970

Country	1880–90	1890–1900	1900–10	1910–20	1920–30	1930–40	1940–50	1950–60	1960–70
Los Angeles	201	69	196	86	136	26	49	46	16
Orange	—	46	74	78	93	10	66	226	102
Riverside	—	—	94	44	61	30	62	80	50
San Bernardino	227	10	102	30	82	20	75	79	36
San Diego	306	0	75	81	86	38	92	85	31
Santa Barbara	65	20	46	48	59	8	39	72	56
Ventura	98	43	28	56	91	27	63	74	89

case of the San Francisco region, this development has been related to the existence of a number of the nation's best-known universities—the "Ph.D. producers"—and to the grant of very large sums of government money for research.

Sprawling as it does over the plains which lie below and between the San Gabriel, Santa Monica, and Santa Ana mountains, the Los Angeles conurbation has developed what seems likely to become the typical urban pattern of this motor transport-electricity-amenity-planning second half of the twentieth century, much as "dark, Satanic mills" epitomized the century of the Industrial Revolution. The sequence of development has been an unusual one by earlier standards. The core of the metropolitan area—Los Angeles proper—grew around the old Spanish pueblo of that name and developed much as any other American city was developing in the early twentieth century, if at a faster rate. By the 1920s, however, there had begun the growth of separate cities located from 5 to 15 mi (8–24 km) from the original center—cities such as Pasadena, Santa Monica, Long Beach—which offered a wide range of services to the suburban population and which had the effect of drawing off both business and cultural life from the central area of the conurbation. By the end of the Second World War, central Los Angeles itself contained administrative offices, old established industries, and slums, but little else; its downtown department stores, for example, registered their peak sales in 1946. Shortly afterward, the core area suffered a further functional setback when it became the site of one of the world's largest crossroads. Meanwhile, the peripheral cities were developing suburbs and central business districts of their own. The core seemed to have become largely superfluous, and it was fashionable to refer to Los Angeles as a group of suburbs looking for a city.

But the past few years have seen a revival in central Los Angeles. One of the problems which the city confronted in developing a genuine central business district was a city ordinance severely limiting the height of buildings because of the earthquake danger. Under these circumstances it would have been diffi-

cult ever to develop the kind of concentration of business activity found in other major American city centers. However, with the progress made in building techniques, the height limit has been waived and business has responded by creating a new townscape of office blocks and dense occupance levels. City interests have also made an effort to introduce some cultural functions at the urban crossroads: the city center has improved greatly in appearance, and development has been impressive and swift along the axis that leads west from the old core—the so-called "Miracle Mile" along Wilshire Boulevard.

But whether the central area is thriving or moribund, an open-plan metropolis of this kind depends heavily on its road network, and the more so because urbanization in southern Californian style has almost entirely taken the form of separate single-family dwellings, which occupy a maximum of space and demand a maximum of service roads. The early system of streetcar lines and suburban railways built to serve the then-existing ring of towns around Los Angeles has long since withered away, and has been replaced by a network of freeways. Nowadays, new suburbs spring up along the line of an advancing freeway much as they did seventy or eighty years ago along the railway lines and the underground or subway routes around London and New York. With an apparently insatiable demand for new freeways before them and the example of San Francisco's BART system behind, Los Angeles planners are beginning to talk nostalgically about the old suburban railways and the possibility of their revival.

Los Angeles has been described as "the Ultimate City."[11] To take this title too seriously, however, would be a mistake, for it would be to deny the very lesson which this city teaches—that urban patterns change with time, technology, and standards of living, and there is never, therefore, likely to be an ultimate in the process. What *is* certain is that Los Angeles is a new kind of city and one which we may expect to see coming into existence in other parts of

[11]Christopher Rand, *Los Angeles: The Ultimate City*, Oxford University Press, New York, 1967.

Los Angeles: The city center. Because of the danger of damage to structures by earthquakes, the city for many years restricted the height of all buildings. Only with the development of new construction techniques in the past two decades has the limit been removed. *(Los Angeles Visitors and Convention Bureau)*

the world when and where conditions are similar: that is, where a community with a high standard of living and virtually unlimited space in which to spread itself, free of relict landscapes of past occupance, decides to drive itself to its work and to put a premium on the independence of the individual consumer. Such conditions are hardly yet universal in their application—and there are, no doubt, some people who are glad that they are not.

Inevitably, the question arises how long California, and especially southern California, can maintain its breakneck rate of population growth and economic development. Employment openings have so far kept up with population increase, and, although in the immediate neighborhood of the cities space is becoming a problem, settlement is continually being carried into new areas on the desert edges. The real limiting factor is water, and the real prob-

lem is to decide how best to use it. At present, one water use in the American West far outstrips all others in its demands, and that is irrigation. We saw in the last chapter that, in some areas, it is estimated that as much as nine out of every ten gallons of water withdrawn from surface or underground sources are used for irrigation, leaving only the remaining gallon for the whole range of urban and industrial uses. To cut their water bills, California's industries have introduced all manner of conservation practices, using water several times over instead of discharging it.[12] Meanwhile the state's

[12]Perhaps the best example of this conservation of water is offered by the Fontana steel works, which have reduced the amount of water required to make one ton of steel to as little as 1500 gallons. For purposes of comparison, this is about the amount of water required to raise 3 pounds of rice or a pound of cotton: a pound of beef requires some 4000 gallons.

farmers spread irrigation water on over 8 million acres (3.2 million ha).

We have seen that in the Central Valley, there is water to spare at the northern end of the Valley and a shortage at the southern end. Exactly the same is true of the state as a whole: the northern part has the water and the southern part has the greater weight of population and demand. Consequently, southern California has had to reach further and further afield for its water supplies. Its two main sources have been the Colorado River to the east and Owens Valley, 250 mi (400 km) away to the north, both of which are linked by aqueduct to Los Angeles. But the water the region can obtain from the Colorado is strictly rationed by the Colorado River Compact (see p. 357). To crowd 10 or 12 million people into a desert or semidesert area 200 mi (320 km) from a major river is to pose a problem of supply and demand that might baffle any engineer.

Since southern California is where all these people wish to live, what solution for this problem can be found? There are at present four possibilities:

1. To obtain usable water from the sea. Technically this is now possible, and pilot plants exist; the main questions here are those of cost and scale. But it seems clear that at least some of the extra supply needed in the coming decades will be provided by this means.

2. To reduce the irrigated acreage. This has already happened in the vicinity of the expanding California cities; individual farmers sell out and their irrigation water becomes available for other purposes. Yet in the state as a whole the irrigated area has never been larger than it is today, and we have already taken note of such schemes as the West Side extension in the San Joaquin Valley, which will raise the state's irrigated acreage still higher in the future.

This irrigated land is, of course, producing an important part of the United States' food supply.[13] It is also the source of California's agricultural wealth, so that it might be argued that it is contributing to the gross product of the state and should be left as it is. But this argument is a weak one, as Kelso pointed out:

Per 1000 gallons of water withdrawn per day, manufacturing in California provides 4.33 times as much personal income and produces 68 times as much product value as does farming. On the other hand, farming annually uses 8.6 times as much water per employee as does manufacturing.[14]

In other words, irrigation agriculture is not the most *productive* use of water in California, nor is it the most *remunerative*. Much of this irrigation agriculture is based on water rights which, if they were made over to a municipal or industrial user, would bring in a sizeable income in water rates. Irrigation agriculture depends on *cheap* water, and in California, water can only be cheap if its use is non-competitive. It is therefore possible to argue that the immense agricultural output of the state is marketed competitively only because the prime resource—water—is excluded from normal economic calculations of true market value. If irrigation farmers had to bid for water against other users, they would quickly be put out of business.

3. To transfer water from the northern end of the state to the southern end. This is the Central Valley Project over again on a larger scale, and it is a solution already well on the way to completion. California has constructed its State Water Project, of which the first element was

---

ines the consequences of the San Andreas fault misbehaving on an unprecedented scale and California west of the fault being drowned in the Pacific. The economic repercussions of the loss of California production on the rest of the states are then predicted to follow with almost the same speed as the earth tremor.

More prosaically, the U.S. Department of Agriculture estimates that in the United States as a whole some 10–11 percent of the nation's cropland is irrigated, and that this irrigated area produces 50 percent of all U.S. vegetables and 56 percent of all potatoes, and that it supports 58 percent of the nation's orchards.

[14]M.M. Kelso, "Theory and Practice in Public Resource Development and Allocation in the Western States," *Proceedings* of the Western Farm Economics Association, Annual Meeting, 1959, p. 7.

---

[13]Just *how* important can be judged in a highly impressionistic way by reading the last chapter of C. Gentry's *The Last Days of the Late, Great State of California*, G.P. Putnam's Sons, New York, 1968, in which the author imag-

The Owens Valley-Los Angeles aqueduct. *(Los Angeles Dept. of Water and Power)*

the Feather River Project, a $2000 million scheme for carrying several million acre-ft of water a year from the north to both San Francisco and the Los Angeles area. There is no particular reason why the state should not go on, as funds become available, to tap other northern rivers—especially rivers like the Eel—which flow west from the Coast Ranges, thus gradually involving the whole state in the business of supplying southern California with water (see Fig. 21-3).

4. To import water into the region from out-

side. Basic to all southern California's water problems is the fact that the Colorado River, nearly 1500 mi (2400 km) long and draining six states, has a mean annual flow of only 14 million acre-ft (17.5 billion m³). It has therefore been proposed that this flow might be doubled by transferring 15 million acre-ft (18.3 billion m³) of water from a river which could lose that amount and never show it—the Columbia in the Pacific Northwest. The Columbia's flow is 175 million acre-ft (214 billion m³) a year, an amount which, given all foreseeable develop-

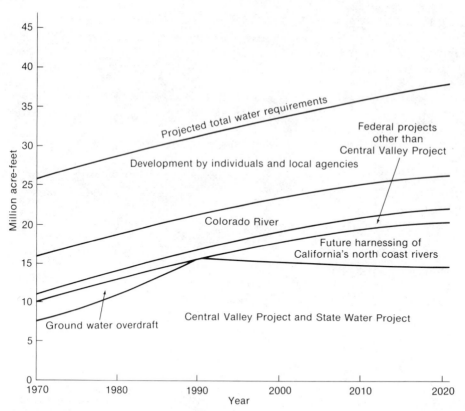

Fig. 21-3. California water supply. The problem of providing for the ever-increasing water needs of California, and especially the southern part of the state, has occupied California planners for several decades. Looking ahead to the year 2000 and beyond, the possible water sources for the needs of an increasing population are indicated by the diagram.

ments within the basin, the northwestern region could never use.

It is proposed (by the Southwest, of course) to build a north-south transfer line, and the necessary studies have already been carried out by the Bureau of Reclamation. It would admittedly be costly, and whether it will ever be built depends in part on a comparison of costs with the seawater conversion project already mentioned. But technically it is perfectly feasible; the Feather River scheme already transfers water over a distance half as great as that involved, and there is no reason why the longer transfer from the Columbia should not succeed and become the first leg of a great continent-wide water "grid." Solution of the remaining problems lies not with the engineers but with the politicians.

Hawaii

More than 2000 mi (3500 km) west of San Francisco lies the capital of the archipelago state of Hawaii, a chain of islands rising from the deep floor of the mid-Pacific in a series of low coral formations and mountainous volcanoes. Physical connection with the rest of Anglo-America there is none, but politically these islands constitute the 50th state of the United States, culturally they have been affected by America for a century and a half, and economically they play a part in the continental circulation of people and commodities. They therefore merit a place in a geography of North America and logically enough that place is after the consideration of California, the part of the continent to which they are principally linked.

The full extent of the island chain is over 1500 mi (2400 km) from end to end, or 22 degrees of longitude. But the western three-quarters consist of minute islands, many of them uninhabited, and it is within the easternmost 400 mi (640 km) that virtually the whole of the state's 6450 sq mi (16,700 sq km) are to be found, predominantly in five major islands. They lie in a southeast-northwest line in which the most easterly island, the one which is actually called Hawaii, is the largest. Most of the population, however, is concentrated on Oahu, the fourth of the five islands, where the capital of the state, Honolulu, is situated. Out of a 1975 state population of 865,000, some 700,000 lived in the S.M.S.A. of Honolulu and 350,000 in the city itself.

Small though these islands appear in the vastness of the Pacific, they are full of natural interest. Among other features, Hawaii possesses five volcanoes, the highest of which, Mauna Kea, rises to 13,796 ft (4194 m), while a second, Mauna Loa, is estimated to have discharged greater quantities of lava than any other volcano anywhere, with spectacular recent eruptions in 1954 and 1960. But in spite of these periodic outbursts there is a rich and varied flora, including a million acres (400,000 ha) of commercial forest. The variety is a product of another of Hawaii's geographical features, one which it shares with a number of other mountainous islands of the Pacific—remarkably abrupt climatic changes from one side of an island to the other. The Hawaiian chain lies in the belt of influence of the northeasterly trade winds, and each island has a windward and a leeward side. The windward side of the mountains catches the full force of the trades and the rainfall which they bring, and in at least four of the islands there are stations which record over 200 in. (5000 mm) of rainfall a year, with authenticated annual totals of well over 450 in. (11,250 mm). On the leeward side of the islands, by contrast, there are stations with long-term averages of less than 15 in. (375 mm). Honolulu itself, sheltered in the lee of the Koolau Range, has a modest 25 in. (632 mm) of rainfall; otherwise it could hardly attract tourists as it does. Temperatures vary little throughout the year; in Honolulu the January and August means are 72° and 81°F (22° and 27°C) respectively. These climatic conditions ensure a year-round tourist traffic and so, too, does the exotic vegetation and even the volcanoes, which are today sufficiently well monitored to serve rather as a kind of outsize fireworks display than as a threat to safety. Only the occasional unpredictable tsunami (tidal wave) does real damage, as in 1946 and 1960, and Hawaii can boast the longest life expec-

Fig. 21-4. Southern California: Water supply. The map shows the aqueducts which supply Los Angeles, and also the canal system which brings Colorado water to the Coachella and Imperial valleys. The problem of supply is complicated by the fact that, within the area covered by the map, there are located the highest and the lowest points in the 48 states—Mt. Whitney and Death Valley—so that relief obstacles are considerable.

tancy of any state in the Union: 73.6 years against a national average of 70.7.

The population, originally Polynesian, has become so intermingled with other stocks that the largest census component is "other races" who in 1970 formed 60 percent of the total. Japanese, Chinese, and Filipino elements have been added to a native population which at one time shrank to very small numbers through disease and tribal or partisan conflicts. The decade 1960–70 saw a net immigration into the islands of more than 50,000: the period 1970–75 one of 34,000. Part of this represented the same phenomenon which we have noted elsewhere—the search for residential amenity, especially among the retired.

Hawaii has 2 million acres (810,000 ha) in farms, but as the average farm size on these small islands is 530 acres (215 ha), much of the land is in plantation agriculture. It was to work on the plantations, especially cutting sugarcane, that many of the Asian immigrants originally came to the islands, and sugar remains the most valuable agricultual product, with pineapples—also plantation grown—second in rank. Despite a very limited industrial development, Hawaii has witnessed the same drift away from the land that the rest of the United States has experienced; between 1960 and 1970 the farm population fell by almost half.

Given its climate and its position, however, Hawaii has two sources of income on which it can comfortably rely—defense expenditures and tourism. In the days before the Second World War, these two were represented by the naval installations at Pearl Harbor, the landlocked bay just west of Honolulu made famous by the Japanese attack of December 1941, and by the cruise ships which brought wealthy tourists from the California ports. Today, the defense functions remain, although the exclusively naval role of Hawaii has been modified in an air age which, in a tragic sense, it helped to inaugurate: in 1975, the Defense payroll for the state amounted to nearly $700 million, which was more than that for New York State or Ohio. As for tourism, it has undergone a process of democratization. Fast air travel has brought the islands within reach of people who have only a week, or even a weekend, of vacation, and cheap fares have provided a tropical paradise for people of limited means. With Bermuda and the Bahamas to the east and Hawaii to the west, few Americans today need be without one.

The American involvement with Hawaii dates back to the 1820s and the arrival of a number of groups of missionaries. From that time until 1898, the American influence grew, step by step, and it was as much to resolve internal tensions as to resist the pressure of other foreign powers that in 1898 the islanders asked for annexation by the United States. The islands were created a territory in 1900 and a state in 1959.

The Pacific Northwest

The Region and its Resources

As they run northward the two great mountain chains of western North America converge upon each other, confining the narrow tip of the High Plateau Province between them. Behind this formidable double barricade some eight million Canadians and Americans live in almost complete physical isolation from the remainder of the continent. Even to the south the line of the Pacific coast troughs, which elsewhere provide a lowland route, is interrupted by the wild mass of the Klamath Mountains, which block the Oregon-California boundary and which are dominated by the huge double cone of Mt. Shasta. There is no single line of easy access into this remote corner of the continent, economically vital though it is as a major producer of timber and hydroelectricity.

Most of the population is to be found in the Pacific coast lowlands, and much of it in the line of port cities whose largest members are Vancouver (1,166,000), Seattle (1,396,000), Tacoma (398,000), and Portland (1,080,000). Inland the population is scattered, for the most part, in long streamers up the valley routes through the mountains. But circumstances of topography and history have drawn into the sphere of the Pacific Northwest two larger set-

tled areas which are really parts of the High Plateaus. One is the Columbia Basin of central Washington and southern British Columbia, the "Inland Empire" whose capital is Spokane (304,000); it is linked with the coastal region largely by grace of the Columbia River Gorge behind Portland. Of this Inland Empire the fertile, south-facing valleys of southern British Columbia form a physical part, since the Columbia and its tributary, the Kootenay, follow zigzag courses that cut across the international boundary and give a geographical unity to the interior lowlands.

The links between the Pacific coast and the second inland area—the Snake River Plains—are even more tenuous. These plains of southern Idaho are physically a part of the Great Basin of Utah and Nevada, and economically they are in some ways part of the hinterland of Salt Lake City. The Snake River itself is far from forming a bond between them and the coastal centers, for it cuts through the mountain barrier of eastern Oregon in a 5500-ft (1670 m) gorge that is all but impassable. But the plains are linked with the Pacific Northwest in the historical association of the Oregon Trail, now represented by the railway and the road which climb through the labyrinthine valleys of the Blue Mountains. As we shall shortly see,

The Cascade Range: Volcanic peaks protrude above the general crestline. Mt. Jefferson (foreground) has an elevation of 10,499 ft (3192 m). The view is northward across Oregon toward Mt. Hood. *(John S. Shelton)*

both the Snake River Plains and the Inland Empire lie on the market side of the Pacific Northwest, and their trade tends to follow the same general direction as that of the coast.

Few regions of North America present a greater variety of physical conditions than the Pacific Northwest. Though the general structure conforms to the north-south fold-and-fault pattern of the major mountain ranges, the pattern has been disturbed by widespread lava flows; the mountains of northern Oregon run from east to west; and the Columbia and Snake, once clear of the Rockies, conform to no drainage pattern but their own. While most of the terrain of the interior is rugged, the low-

lands of the Snake and the central Columbia Basin, levelled by their covering of lava, present favorable surfaces for agriculture at elevations between 500 and 3000 ft (150–900 m). British Columbia is less favored by its Fraser River; comparable low-level surfaces are scarce in the southern, populated part of the province and only appear in the Nechako Plateau around Prince George, so that agriculture in interior British Columbia is largely restricted to the "trenches" that lie between the ranges of the mountainous southeast.

The variety of climatic conditions within the Pacific Northwest has already been suggested in Chapter 1. The coastal mountains attract the

The Columbia River at Crown Point, Oregon, looking eastward. (Oregon State Highway Dept.)

continent's highest precipitation (most of it falling in winter, when snows are very heavy), while the plateau sections are semiarid or arid. Wenatchee and Yakima, in the irrigated orchard region of the western Columbia Basin, have 8.7 and 6.8 in (217 and 170 mm) of rain per annum respectively and the Okanagan Valley 10–12 in. (250–300 mm). East and south across the basin, precipitation increases to 15 and then to 25 in. (375 to 625 mm), making possible the wheat growing for which this moister section of the basin is famous.

The agricultural significance of these abrupt climatic differences may be summarized in a few general statements. (1) Agriculture in the Pacific Northwest can be divided into valley agriculture, for which the water must usually be supplied by irrigation; and plateau agriculture, where rainfall may be adequate but the frost-free season is short on account of the alti-tude. (2) Over much of the Northwest the warm-season rainfall is inadequate for crop growth (between 2 and 4 in (50–100 mm) in the central Columbia Basin), but the heavy snows of winter form a most valuable reservoir. In the interior, if not on the coast, the meltwater is released into the rivers in a manner well suited to the irrigation farmer's needs; peak flow on the Columbia usually occurs in June. (3) Because of the proximity of areas of high and low rainfall and because of the seasonal character of precipitation in the region, some areas require *both* winter drainage *and* summer irrigation to be maintained in agricultural production.

This combination of physical circumstances also contributes largely to the existence of the Northwest's three prime natural resources: forests, fisheries, and waterpower. The mountain slopes, with their heavy rainfall, are

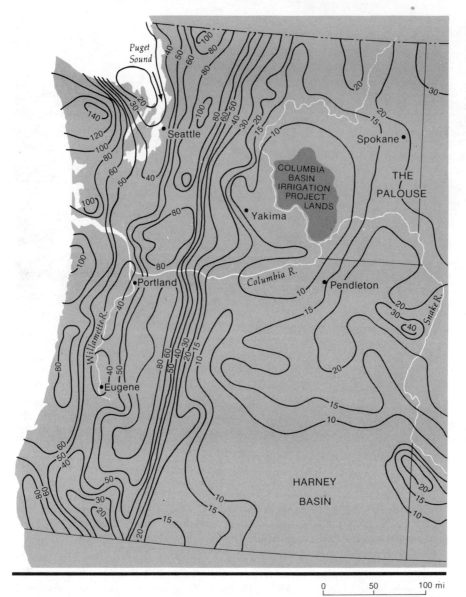

Fig. 22-1. Rainfall map of the northwestern United States: the map emphasizes the marked rainshadow effect of the Olympic Mountains over Puget Sound and of the Cascades over the deserts of the Harney and Columbia basins.

0   50   100 mi
0   50   100   150 km

clothed with the continent's principal reserves of virgin softwoods; one writer called the Northwest the "Sawdust Empire."[1]

Its salmon fisheries constitute an important element in regional income—an element of sufficient value for the depletion of the fisheries to cause acute concern and require the Canadian and U.S. governments to take in hand restoration of the salmon runs. Finally, the Columbia,

[1]See H.M. Brier, *Sawdust Empire: The Pacific Northwest*, Alfred A. Knop, New York, 1958.

Snake, and Fraser together possess a large part of the continent's hydroelectric potential. The harnessing of this potential has been progressing steadily over the past four decades: on the Columbia it dates from the general Depression, when the great dams at Grand Coulee and Bonneville were authorized as relief measures under the public works program of 1933. In British Columbia, power sites are widely scattered throughout the province and are gradually being developed as demand increases. The principal river, the lower Fraser, is not used for power generation, however, because of its importance to the salmon fisheries.

Agriculture in the Pacific Northwest

While fur traders and gold miners occupied the limelight in the first half of the nineteenth century, the first genuine agricultural settlements on the Pacific coast came quietly into being in the fertile Willamette Valley in the 1830s. The area rapidly gained in popularity, so that the 1840s saw a marked increase in the number of settlers trekking west along the Oregon Trail and the beginnings of settlement in the central Columbia Basin. In British Columbia, however, there was little agricultural development before the miners arrived in 1858. From these varied beginnings local specializations have grown, until today we can recognize four main types of farming:

1. *Dairy farming* with subsidiary poultry, fruit, and vegetable production. This type of farming occupies the main lowland areas from the Fraser Valley and Puget Sound to the southern Willamette Valley. The great urban centers of the lowlands provide markets for dairy produce, and fodder crops, irrigated and non-irrigated, occupy a large part of the cultivated land. Fruit and vegetable crops account for much of the remainder.

2. *Fruit and vegetable growing* with subsidiary dairy farming. This second type is a combination of the same elements in different proportions. Away from the principal cities the market for dairy produce is less favorable, so that in these areas the production of fruit and vegetable crops, the Northwest's main agricultural speciality, assumes major importance.

It is this type of farming which is found in the valleys that open into the central Columbia Basin. Sheltered but dry, the river and lakeside terraces provide suitable locations for irrigated orchards. The largest orchard areas are those of the Wenatchee, Yakima, and Okanagan valleys, where apples and pears are the principal fruit crops, but the range of lesser crops is very wide. It includes nuts, hops, holly grown for Christmas decorations, and little-known fruits such as youngberries and boysenberries

(named for the Northwesterners who developed them), as well as the more familiar soft fruits. From the pear orchards of the Rogue River Valley in southwestern Oregon to the apple lands of south-central British Columbia, farmers in the sheltered valleys of the Northwest have developed temperate fruits as cash crops in much the same way as the Californians in more southerly latitudes have specialized in subtropical fruits. The areas form two halves of a Pacific Coast Fruit Belt.

An equally wide range of vegetables is produced, the most important of them being potatoes, onions, beans, and peas. Potatoes are the special cash crop of the Snake River Plains. Idaho, with more than 300,000 acres (121,000 ha) under potatoes, has nearly three times the acreage of Maine, the second largest producer, and is responsible for about one-quarter of the annual United States output of the crop.

3. *Commercial wheat farming*. The eastern end of the central Columbia Basin is an area of natural grassland, the Palouse, and it forms the Wheat Belt of the West Coast. (Whitman County, in southeastern Washington, which covers the heart of this area and includes the small town of Palouse itself, is actually the largest wheat producer of any county in the United States.) On the north, east, and south it is defined by relief and terminates at the foot of the mountains (roughly on the 3000-ft (912 m) contour). On the west, as on the Great Plains, wheat farming is rendered first unwise and then impossible by diminishing rainfall toward the dry heart of the basin, with its 6–8 in. (150–200 mm) of annual precipitation. But the gently rolling surface of the Palouse, with its good grassland soils, encouraged the farmers to plow and plant wheat with dangerous abandon, and erosion has been very serious. On the other hand, it would be unfair to criticize too severely farmers who (thanks to the work done in breeding wheat by one of the most active agricultural experiment stations in the United States, that of the state of Washington at Pullman) can plant locally developed strains of wheat and harvest 70 to 75 bushels to the acre (170–185 bu per ha): the temptation to do so must be hard to resist.

Much of the Palouse wheat is grown by dry-farming methods. For some years past farmers

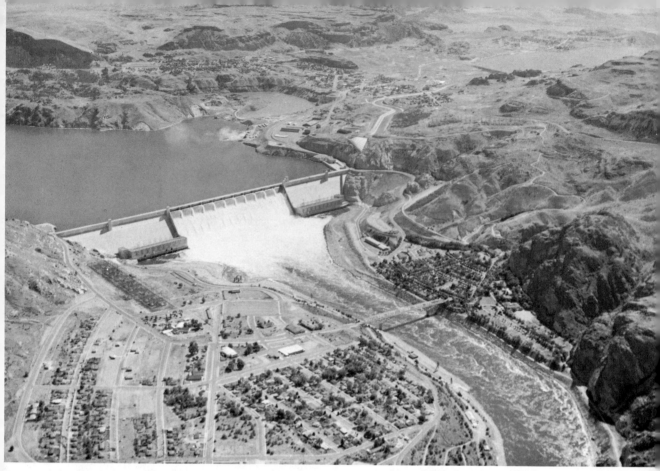

Grand Coulee Dam on the Columbia River: At the southern, or right-hand edge of the dam, pipes carry pumped water up to the canal which in turn will carry it to the equalizing reservoir in the Grand Coulee proper (right rear). See also Figure 22-2. *(Bureau of Reclamation)*

in the moister, eastern edge of the area, on the Washington-Idaho boundary, have used the fallows left by dry-farmed wheat for growing peas, which have become a local speciality. As on the Great Plains, however, the real, continuing need has been to plant more cover crops on worn wheatlands.

4. *Ranching.* On those parts of the region which are too dry for wheat and too rugged for irrigation, stock raising replaces cultivation, as it does everywhere in the Mountain West. Between the green patches of irrigated land and the tree-covered mountains, the ranges spread over much of eastern Oregon, the Snake and Columbia lowlands, and the Fraser and Nechako plateaus of British Columbia. Because of the heavy tree cover in the mountains, however, there is a more definite upper limit to the ranching zone than in other parts of the West; the high grazings are limited in extent, and

ranching in the Northwest belongs mainly to the middle altitudes.

These, then, are the four types of regional agriculture found in the Northwest. When the Columbia Basin Project for a million acres (405,000 ha) of new irrigated lands was conceived, the question naturally arose as to which of these four types of farming should be practiced on it. It was in 1952 that the first irrigation water from the Columbia flowed into an area whose annual rainfall of 8–10 in. (200–250 mm) had seemed to doom it to permanent uselessness. The scheme makes use of the waters of Lake Roosevelt, impounded behind the largest of all western dams—the Grand Coulee. Close by the dam, a former course of the Columbia River cuts across a bend that the present river makes as it turns from a westerly direction to a southerly one before joining the Snake (see Fig. 22-2). This former course, which was carved out by the waters of a Columbia swollen by ice melt-water, is the Grand Coulee, after which the dam is named.

The irrigation engineers have made use of this feature to carry water to the dry western end of the Columbia Bend. From Lake Roosevelt, water is pumped up into the Grand Coulee, which has been dammed to form a large reservoir. From this reservoir, water can be distributed with the gradient to the project land lying south of the Coulee, about a half of which has been brought into production so far. From an engineer's point of view, it is a remarkably ingenious and successful scheme.

By 1976, the project farmers were raising nearly forty different crops on an irrigable area which had been expanded to a potential 540,000 acres (219,000 ha). In the quarter-century of the project's life, there had been shifts of emphasis in farm production, and some of the earlier expectations had not been fulfilled. The forty crops included such exotics as gladioli and peppermint; the raising of beef cattle (mainly on feedlots) had sharply increased, but there had been little development of dairying. The acreage under such long-term plantings as tree fruits was steadily enlarging. However, the largest areas were occupied by alfalfa, wheat, potatoes, and sugar beet:

In the Pacific Northwest, however, and especially on fertile, irrigated lands like those of this project, it is less a question of what farmers can grow than of what they can sell. It is the market factor which dominates the life of the region: specifically, the need to market a large part of

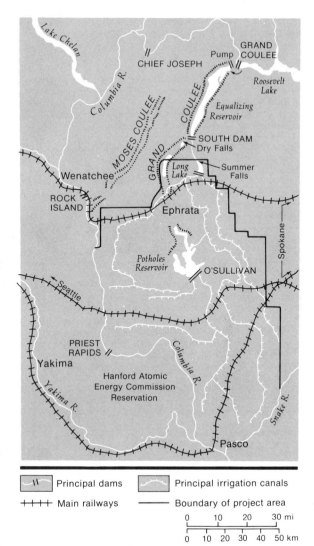

| | Principal dams | | Principal irrigation canals |
| +++++ Main railways | | — | Boundary of project area |

0   10   20   30 mi
0   10 20 30 40 50 km

Fig. 22-2. The Columbia Basin Project: Coulees are valleys cut into the surface of the lava plateau and represent former courses of the Columbia or its overflow channels. They can thus be dammed and are used for water storage.

Columbia Basin Project: Crop Areas and Values, 1966 and 1976
(1 acre = 0.405 hectares)

| | Irrigated Acreages | | Yield per Acre | | Value of Crop (millions of dollars) | |
	1966	1976	1966	1976	1966	1976
Alfalfa	137,927	133,525	5.3 tons	5.5 tons	16.1	49.8
Wheat	64,912	141,355	90.0 bu	83.0 bu	9.2	33.2
Potatoes	44,925	39,156	386.0 cwt	438.0 cwt	22.8	44.5
Sugar Beet	30,658	43,214	24.7 tons	25.0 tons	8.0	16.5
Edible Beans	26,824	19,824	18.6 cwt	20.1 cwt	3.1	4.5
Pea Seed	20,561	8,452	26.9 cwt	29.2 cwt	2.3	2.3
Corn	6,401	28,732	104.0 bu	125.0 bu	1.0	9.5
Alfalfa Seed	3,958	9,620	5.0 cwt	6.2 cwt	0.6	4.8
Total Cropland						
Irrigated	433,056	505,804			75.0	202.7

(Source: Bureau of Reclamation, Crop Production Reports, Ephrata, Wash., 1966 and 1976.)

The Columbia Basin Project: Summer Falls. This picture is included to show the *amount* of water necessary to irrigate half a million acres (200,000 ha) of farmland, for the falls are simply a natural part of the route of the main supply canal for the project, as shown on Figure 22-2. *(Bureau of Reclamation)*

their produce outside the region must dominate all planning by farmers in general in the Northwest, and by farmers of the newly irrigated lands in particular. To this problem we shall shortly return in our discussion.

Forests and Industries

Manufacturing in the Pacific Northwest is dominated by the forest-products industries. Forestry supports thousands of sawmills, from portable one-man plants to giant combinations of mill, furniture factory, and by-products industries, which in one case at least have given rise to a whole town—Longview, Washington—of 28,000 inhabitants. It chokes the smaller harbors on the coast with timber and makes its presence felt even in the heart of so

large a city as Vancouver, or Portland, where the rafts of lumber are towed down the Willamette beneath the city's bridges. In Oregon, 88,000 workers in a total labor force of 780,000 are involved in forest products industries. It provides bulk freight for the railways and part-time employment for farmers in remote valleys of the Cascades.

The Pacific Northwest, with its massive firs and pines, is essentially a sawtimber producer, and its leading forest product has until now been basic lumber rather than pulp and paper.[2] The last two or three decades have seen a great improvement in the technique of exploit-

[2] "About 70 percent of the sawn lumber produced in Canada, most of the plywood, and over one-quarter of the national production of chemical pulp comes from British Columbia forests . . . In area B.C.'s forested land comprises less than one-fifth of the national total, but it sup-

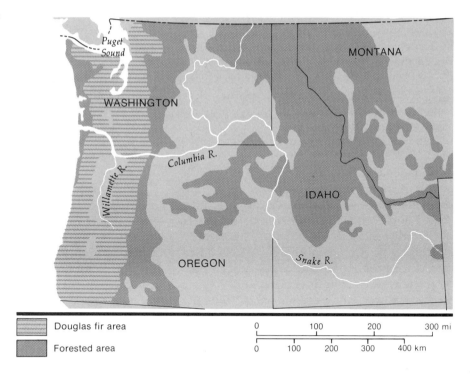

Fig. 22-3. Forests of the northwestern United States.

MONTANA

Puget Sound

WASHINGTON

Columbia R.

Willamette R.

IDAHO

OREGON

Snake R.

Douglas fir area

Forested area

| 0 | | 100 | | 200 | | 300 mi |
| 0 | 100 | 200 | 300 | 400 km |

ing the forest resource, principally (and most necessarily) in the U.S. section of the region, where the smallholders of the forest have often left a trail of desolation behind them after buying, logging off, and then abandoning their land. The practice of "tree farming" by the large firms has placed the industry on a sounder footing; and in British Columbia the provincial government exercises vigilant control. Nevertheless, the situation is serious in the best and most accessible timber areas; whatever the average cut for the region as a whole, these accessible lands continue to be worked at considerably above replacement rate. There are other hazards, too; near Tillamook on the Oregon coast an area of prime Douglas fir 300,000 acres (120,000 ha) in extent was wiped out by three separate fires between 1933 and 1945.

The size of the lumber mills varies fairly directly with the size of their hinterlands. The ports over half of Canada's remaining sawtimber volume. . . . In these respects, B.C.'s position nationally is not unlike that which Oregon, Washington, and Idaho hold in the comparable pattern of the United States." A.L. Farley, "The Forest Resource" in J.L. Robinson ed., *British Columbia*, University of Toronto Press, Toronto, 1972, p. 88.

largest plants are to be found either at tidewater locations (such as Longview), or at natural assembly points on the river system (such as Lewiston or Coeur d'Alene in Idaho), or at road centers, to which the huge logging trucks can bring the timber. In British Columbia most of the largest sawmills are to be found at the southern end of Vancouver Island or on the lower Fraser, but the interior of the province possesses hundreds of small mills, with concentrations such as those found around Prince George and in the Peace River country. As far as the young pulp and paper industry is concerned, the main concentration is at present also on the coast in the southwest of the province. This is partly a question of markets and accessibility—from the beginning the forest-products industry has used the sheltered channels between the mainland and the islands for moving log rafts to the mills—but also partly one of rate of growth of the timber. A large mill must be located where its supply of raw materials can be assured for decades ahead, otherwise there could be no justification for the capital investment involved. In the coastal forests of southern British Columbia, the rate of tree growth is much higher than in the inte-

409

rior or on the northern coast.[3] Nevertheless, it is interesting to note that several of the pulp and paper mills constructed in British Columbia in the past ten years are in the interior of the province, at locations such as Prince George and Kimberley. As collecting points these towns correspond to those already mentioned south of the border.

Two other main categories of industry are to be found in the Pacific Northwest. One of these is food processing, which deals with the output of the salmon fisheries and the region's vegetable crops. The other category is more varied and consists of industries attracted by the Northwest's electric power. Although the Northwest is rich in minerals such as silver, lead, or copper, it has little coal and imports petroleum, so that industry depends heavily on waterpower, the region's main industrial asset. In these circumstances it is not surprising to find that one of the industries which most firmly established itself here during the Second World War was light-metal smelting. Aluminum plants were established at numerous points, such as Troutdale, near Portland, and Spokane. Although the demand for these metals depended to a rather dangerous degree on defense expenditures, the industry weathered a postwar recession, and with the construction of the giant Kitimat smelter on the coast of British Columbia, the region reaffirmed its faith in it.

Apart from these regional specializations, the coastal cities possess a range of industries roughly appropriate to their size. Vancouver, the third city of Canada and the only large city on Canada's west coast, has grown impressively in the postwar years. Apart from its importance as a market and as a manufacturing center, where sawmills, paper mills, and oil refineries occupy much of the waterside, it is steadily adding to its significance as Canada's "back door"; traffic to and from the interior, including the western Prairies, is routed via the West Coast rather than the East. With the rapid rise of Canadian (not to speak of United States) trade with Japan in the past ten years, Vancouver, in common with U.S. northwestern ports, has also now a much-enlarged role in trans-Pacific trade.

[3]Farley, "The Forest Resource," p. 93.

Seattle, on Puget Sound, dominates a coastal lowland which contains a number of smaller cities, and it has outstripped Tacoma, further up the Sound, which was the original Pacific coast terminal of the first transcontinental railway to the Northwest. Seattle's industry is dominated by the Boeing aircraft company; even the lumber industries take second place here. Not that this is to Seattle's advantage, however: no major manufacturing center, not even San Diego, has experienced such ups and downs of fortune and employment as has Seattle, tied to the fluctuating output levels of the aircraft industry. During the past decade, Boeing's employment in the Seattle area has been as high as 101,000 and as low as 53,000. In both 1970 and 1971 Seattle had the highest unemployment rate of any S.M.S.A. in the nation—in each year more than double the rate for the country as a whole. Fortunately it has its service, administrative, and port functions to fall back upon, and thanks to its location and to the strategic importance of the Northlands today, it has thrived on its connection with Alaska.

The advantages enjoyed by the port of Seattle on the seaward side, however, are balanced by the limitations of its hinterland. In its rivalry with Portland for the industry and commerce of the Northwest, it suffers a severe handicap: it possesses no Columbia Gorge. Portland stands at the seaward end of the single water-level route from the interior, while behind Seattle, winter snow may pile to rooftop height in the passes. The Columbia Gorge has been of inestimable value to Portland, and even those railways which make for Puget Sound prudently provide themselves with an alternative route down the Columbia. Portland, with the Inland Empire at its back and the fertile Willamette Valley on its flank, has great commercial importance within the region. Its industries, although concentrated on lumber, pulp, and paper, also include shipbuilding, machinery, and textiles.

Basic Problems of the Pacific Northwest

Such is the geography of this isolated region beyond the mountains, a region in which frontiers of settlement are still advancing. But isolation poses economic problems, and without a consideration of those we can have little understanding of how this region fits into the geography of the continent as a whole.

There are two main economic problems. The first is that, at least until the Second World War, the Pacific Northwest possessed only "colonial" status in relation to the East. The marks of this status were (1) that the region was a primary producer whose resources were largely exploited by outside financial interests, and (2) that the "balance of trade" of the region showed a large outflow of bulky raw materials, and an inflow of manufactured goods of higher value but smaller bulk. Further, the value of the region's total "exports" was greater than its material "imports," the balance being made up by invisibles—services rendered by the East.

This "colonial" position, analogous to that of the African colonies of the European powers, was well indicated by the balance of trade drawn up in 1942 by the region's planning commission in the United States.

Balance of Trade of the Pacific Northwest States[4]
Annual Average, 1934–39

Commodity	Quantity Balance (1000s of tons)	Value Balance (1000s of dollars)
Products of Agriculture	+3600	+143,085
Animals and Products	+ 456	+ 93,366
Products of Mines	−6771	− 69,630
Products of Forests	+8285	+178,318
Manufactures and Miscellaneous	− 262	−221,798
Total	+5308	+123,341

(Source: *The External Trade of the Pacific Northwest*, Pacific Northwest Regional Planning Commission, Portland, Oregon, 1942, pp. 23 and 25.)

The figures tell their own story: a huge volume of timber and agricultural produce left the region, while a small quantity of manufactured goods entering it more than balanced, in value, eight million tons of forest products. At the same time, had the prewar Northwest not been deficient in power and fuel (the Products of Mines received were largely petroleum), the

[4]Includes the states of Washington, Oregon, Idaho, and Montana.

"export surplus" of the region would have been much larger.

The war and the postwar increase in the Pacific Northwest's population altered this situation to a certain extent, by stimulating local industries and enlarging the local market. When a region exports its raw materials to have them processed elsewhere, then the increase in value which manufacture brings is lost to that region. It is therefore possible to judge the economic progress of a "colonial" area, whether in Africa or North America, by the extent to which it is processing its own raw materials. By this criterion the Pacific Northwest has made real progress; its manufacturing is constantly increasing in range and size. Perhaps the best single indication of this is the growth of a northwestern pulp and paper industry alongside the old forest-products industry, which produced sawtimber and plywood, commodities with only a low "value added by manufacture." The greater the degree of processing, the larger is the increment of value obtained by the region from its resources.

However, the Northwest has not been so favored in this respect as some other regions. The basic need of any colonial area is capital, and capital is much more forthcoming in an area with a fast-yielding resource to exploit—oil is the obvious case—than with the much slower-yielding northwestern resources of forests and fisheries.

The second problem of the Pacific Northwest is simply that of distance from markets. It is a problem that hangs over all the region's agriculture and forestry. We have already noted that a very high proportion of the output of some agricultural items must be sold outside the region: this is inevitable because they are specialty crops produced for a national market. But to a considerable degree the same is true of such a basic product as wheat, because of the limited market afforded by the eight million people who live within the region. And what is true of agriculture is much *more* true of forest products.

Like California, the Northwest must sell in distant markets. But unlike California, the region has additional handicaps. California's produce at least has the advantage that much

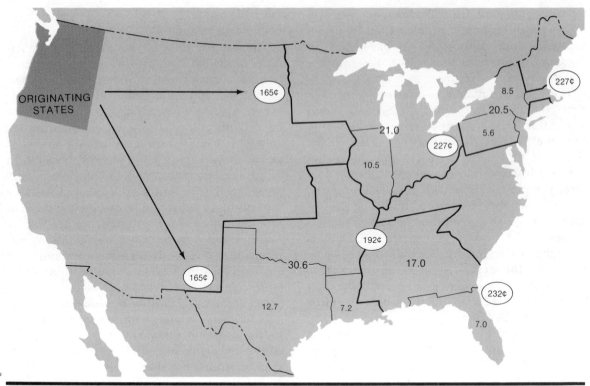

Fig. 22-4. The Pacific Northwest: The market for apples. The map shows the movement (by rail only) of apples from Washington and Oregon to their principal markets in the remainder of the United States. Note the freight rate "blanket" of 227 cents, which existed everywhere east of Ohio. (After R.J. Sampson, "Railroad Shipments and Rates" in *Pacific Northwest*, Fig. 5, Univ. of Oregon Bureau of Bus. Res., 1961.)

of it consists of crops for which the state is the only, or the major, producer in North America, so that it has a certain rarity value. But the Pacific Northwest, less favored climatically, is seeking to market produce—wheat, timber, fruit—in regions which produce or could produce these commodities themselves. To market their products, northwestern farmers must carry them past the doors of their competitors to reach the East. As an Oregonian put it to the author, "It's always bad business to carry wheat through wheat country."

Two examples may be briefly mentioned: apples and timber. British Columbia produces 40 percent of the Canadian apple crop and Washington some 20 percent of that of the United States. Growers have secured markets for these apples, in spite of distance, by attention to appearance, packaging and flavor (see Fig. 22-4). But such advantages are hard to maintain and are ill suited to hold off the challenge of growers in Ontario, Michigan, or New York, 2000 mi (3200 km) nearer their markets. The result for Washington growers has been declining sales in the East,[5] and to add to their difficulties, changes in eating habits had by 1971 reduced the U.S. per capita consumption of apples to little more than a half of what it was in 1940.

In the case of forest products the problem is the same; only the competitor is different. Washington and Oregon have to compete in the

[5]The importance of holding on to these eastern markets is indicated by the fact that the northwestern states count on selling nearly 40 percent of their fruit in the New England and Middle Atlantic states.

The Wenatchee Valley, Washington: Young apple orchards. The town of Wenatchee claims to be the "Apple Capital of the World." Most of the orchards are situated on river terraces. *(Washington State Apple Commission)*

main U.S. markets with the softwood producers of the southeastern states. To the main selling areas, the southern wood has to travel only a half or a third as far as that from the Pacific Northwest, some of which, in fact, moves via the Panama Canal to the East Coast.

In this situation it is not distance alone which tells against the Pacific Northwest, and it is certainly not lack of transport facilities, for, besides coastal shipping lines, no less than six transcontinental railroads were built through the area—more indeed than the traffic of the region makes strictly necessary.

There is also the problem of freight rates. Since, as we saw in Chapter 5, these are not based on distance alone, there is always the possibility that an adjustment of a cent or two will be ordered and that this will open or close a market to the Northwest. (This happened several times with the market for Washington grain in the southeastern states of the United States). And the general level of freight rates is also affected by the fact that a region which ships out very large quantities of lumber and wheat while importing manufactures and petroleum cannot use the same trucks or pipe-

lines in both directions. It is a region with a large number of expensive "returned empties."

What can be done to improve this situation? There are three possibilities:

1. To achieve a more favorable level of freight rates than at present. The Pacific Northwest is a region whose producers, businessmen, and newspapers are all highly "freight-rate conscious." But in this respect the region has been well served by its transport companies, for they realize that there will be no freight for them to carry unless freight rates can be held down, and they have cooperated with the shippers as fully as they could:

The Pacific Northwest, as a region, is fortunate in that its environmental surroundings and its economic base are such that its economic interests coincide with those of its serving railroads. Thus the region's geographical "disadvantage" of a location remote from many of the nation's principal consuming centers is minimized. . . . Tapering and blanket structures and holddowns keep long-haul rates on basic raw materials and some of their processed derivatives at levels which permit the region's goods to be sold in distant markets despite varying elasticities and inelasticities of demand, the avail-

413

ability of substitute products, or the existence of competing sources of supply.[6]

In other words, the carriers are doing all they can to aid the region, and there is very little more that they can do without going out of business, particularly when freight rate increases are ordered by the I.C.C. or C.T.C. and not imposed by the carriers themselves.

2. To find new markets. Considering that to reach the main North American centers, the Northwest must always market as intensively as possible, fresh outlets must be sought. It was originally hoped that these would be in Asia: the Northern Pacific, the first railway into the area, adopted a Chinese symbol as its badge, a kind of declaration of its true goal. But for many years these Asian markets proved illusory or at best unreliable. Only during the past decade has there arisen the promise of both expansion and stability in trans-Pacific trade, qualities which are now offered by the Japanese market. The Japanese economy has developed a voracious appetite for a whole range of primary products—coal from western Canada; alfalfa and wheat from the northwestern states. The growth of wheat shipments from Washington and Oregon is reflected in the following figures:

Pacific Northwest (U.S.):
White and Hard Red Winter Wheat, Inspected for
Exports
(1000s of bushels)

	1958–59	1961–62	1964–65	1967–68	1969–70
Total	83,415	107,320	138,795	195,751	167,541
Destined for Asian markets	79,671	103,884	136,398	191,674	163,919
To Japan	31,904	30,359	61,706	66,561	66,626
To India	36,307	36,670	32,243	60,051	31,315

(Source: *Washington's Wheat: Its Problems and Prospects*, Washington Agricultural Experiment Station, Pullman, Circular 531, 1971, Tables 1 and 2.)

Nearer at hand, the obvious place to look is California, with its soaring population, booming construction and lagging food supply. Here if anywhere the Northwest can find an eastern-style urban-industrial market within its reach.

[6]R.J. Sampson, *Railroad Shipments and Rates from the Pacific Northwest*, University of Oregon Bureau of Business Research, Eugene, 1961, pp. 59, 60.

3. To market new products. When the Columbia Basin Project was created, it seemed all too likely that the cultivation of a million new acres (400,000 ha) of irrigated farmland would merely add to the region's market problems by increasing its surpluses. But whatever criticism may reasonably be levelled at the project (as, for example, that the federal subsidy to its farmers is too large or that its farm units are too small), it cannot be said to have failed on the marketing side, and the reason for its success is the point to notice. We have already seen that two of the project's main crops are alfalfa and potatoes. Both are bulky products with a low value-weight ratio; both have experienced marketing difficulties in the past; in addition, potato consumption per capita in North America has been static or declining for years. Yet both crops have been successfully marketed by a simple conversion process: the alfalfa is converted into pellets (and may travel in this form as far as Japan), and the potatoes are transformed into frozen chips and slices. The result is, in effect, *a new product from an old crop.*

Indeed, it could almost be argued—although it would be unfair to press the point—that the officials who planned this great project in the 1940s have been saved from the embarrassment of unsaleable crops by the invention of products which did not even exist when their original calculations were made. The markets for these new products are highly expansible, and they typify the kind of sensible adaptation to local conditions which a remote region needs to make in the competitive agriculture of today.

We come, finally, to the special case of British Columbia. We have already referred, in Chapter 19, to the concept of an economic "continental divide," from which goods flow to the East and West coasts. In the early days of the West this divide lay, effectively, close to the West Coast, and the railways drew off western produce to the East, while their freight rates encouraged the movement. With the rise of the West in population and economic strength, however, the divide has been pushed back. In the case of British Columbia, at least, the means by which this has been done are fairly clear. On the one hand, every inducement has been

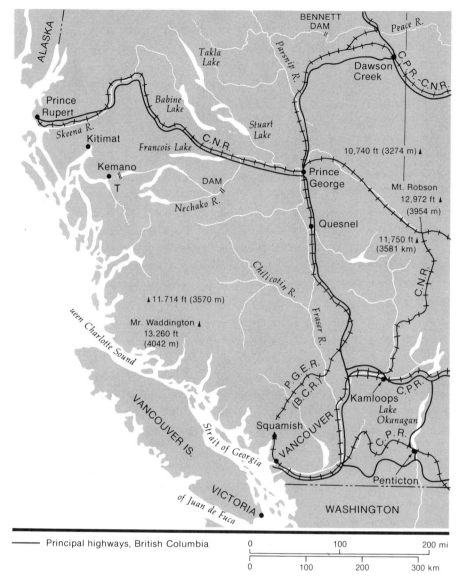

Fig. 22-5. British Columbia: Communications. The map shows how the Pacific Great Eastern Railway (now known as the British Columbia Railway) was extended to run from Vancouver to Dawson Creek and Fort St. John, thus connecting British Columbia's Peace River frontier with the Pacific. At Kemano a tunnel (T) carries the waters of the Nechako River, which has been dammed and reversed, down to the power station supplying the smelter at Kitimat.

—— Principal highways, British Columbia

0   100   200 mi

0   100   200   300 km

offered to attract commerce from the Prairie Provinces to use the "back door" of Canada, and to this the agitation about freight rates has contributed. On the other hand, the communications necessary to make this possible have been built. The Prairie oil fields and gas supplies are linked by pipeline not only to the Canadian East but also to the Pacific coast. New roads have been constructed: the Trans-Canada Highway has brought Calgary within a long day's drive from Vancouver, and provincial roads like the Hart Highway to the Peace River link Vancouver with its provincial hinterland. Perhaps the most interesting step was the completion of the Pacific Great Eastern Railway.

This line, long the butt of local humor, began at Squamish, 40 mi (64 km) by sea from Vancouver—there was no road—and ran to Quesnel, 60 mi (96 km) from Prince George, passing nothing of note on the way.

Now, however, the joke is long since dead. The line is secured at both ends to reality, and, rechristened as the British Columbia Railway, it links Vancouver firmly to the advancing frontier of settlement and mining on the Peace River, with its agriculture, its gas, and its hydroelectricity; to Dawson Creek and Fort St. John; and finally to Fort Nelson, drawing the frontier regions into the sphere of influence of the West Coast.

The Northlands

23

The Northlands of the continent, considered politically, are made up of Alaska, Yukon, and the Northwest Territories, with a total area of 2.1 million square mi (5.44 million sq km). If, however, we use the term to include all those areas which lie north of the limits of continuous settlement, then the area covered by this last great region of North America is much larger, for it includes Labrador, much of Québec, and the northern parts of Ontario, the Prairie Provinces, and British Columbia.

A number of attempts have been made by geographers to achieve a clear definition of where and what is the Canadian North. Hamelin has been the most persistent, and he has proposed that, on the basis of ten variables, it is possible to rate any location in terms of its "polaricity" or, in the case of Canada, its "nordicité."[1] This polar index may then be used to fix an arbitrary but quantitative boundary around the Northlands. In practice it might also be used for such purposes as fixing rates of pay or bonuses for workers undergoing the hardships and privations of northern employment, by relating wage rates to the scale of "nordicité." On the basis of his index, Hamelin has seen the North as divided into four zones—the Pre-North, the Middle North, the Far North, and the Extreme North (see Fig. 23-1).

A similar exercise by Gajda[2] has produced a threefold division of the North which has found some general acceptance; it distinguishes between (1) the Near North, a zone in which a good deal of settlement, including agriculture, has already taken place—the "older pioneer zone"; (2) the Mid North, with a scatter of settlements, mostly mining communities, in a "new pioneer zone," and (3) the Far North, the "zone of strategic occupation," where economic activity is absent and the only settlement is military or political in character.

Whichever of these schemes of subdivision we may adopt, or even if we revert, as we shortly shall in this chapter, to the concept of the Mid-Canada Development Corridor (mapped in Chapter 3) our interest is in recognizing that

[1] L.E. Hamelin, "Un Indice Circumpolaire," *Ann. Géographie*, No. 422 (1968), 414–30. The ten variables suggested, each of which can be scored on agreed scales to give a composite total index, are latitude, summer heat, aggregate annual cold, types of freezing and icing, total precipitation, vegetation cover, accessibility other than by air, air service, population density and degree of concentration, and measure of economic activity. A map drawn on this basis appears on pp. 424–25 of Hamelin's paper: see also Figure 23-1.

[2] R.J. Gajda, "The Canadian Ecumene: Inhabited and Uninhabited Areas," *Geographic Bulletin*, No. 15 (1960), 5–18.

The Canadian North: The midnight sun. Like northern Norway, this is a land of the midnight sun, so that although the summer and growing season both look short on the calendar, the hours of sunshine during the long days permit crops to be grown. The picture was taken at Great Bear lake, about 66°N Lat. *(National Film Board of Canada)*

within an area so huge as the Northlands, there are degrees of activity and isolation; that the onset of northern conditions is not even or consistent all along the southern edge of the region; and that the North has always been a region delimited by individual perception rather than by specific latitudes or temperatures. To a farmer successfully cultivating the Peace River prairies, "the North" may well lie beyond the provincial boundary along the 60th parallel, while to an inhabitant of the southern United States, it would appear equally self-evident that even the southern boundary of Canada along the 49th parallel is within the margins of the frigid Northlands. Watson goes so far as to say, "To speak about *the* geography of the North is nonsense; there have been as many geographies as there have been illusions."[3]

Physical Conditions

Over so large an area, physical conditions are very varied. All types of relief are to be found, while even within this area, of which the layman's impression is simply that it is cold and barren, significant differences in climate and vegetation occur. We can list here only the major physical factors that govern the use of the Northlands.

[3]J.W. Watson, "The Role of Illusion in North American Geography," *Canadian Geographer*, vol. xiii (1969), 22.

417

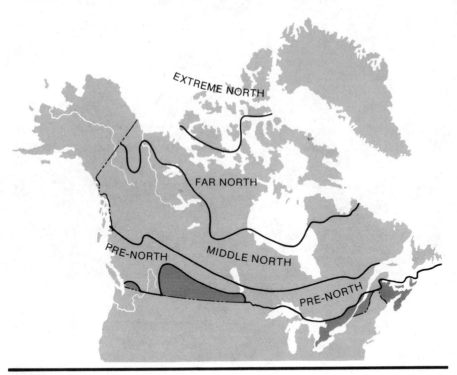

Fig. 23-1. The Canadian North and its zones.

EXTREME NORTH

FAR NORTH

PRE-NORTH

MIDDLE NORTH

PRE-NORTH

▨ Principal Canadian Ecumene

RELIEF, CLIMATE, AND SOILS

If one is thinking in terms of the physical environment, it is probably simplest to regard the Northlands as comprising two separate regions: the Northwest and the Arctic. The differences between the two are in relief, climate, and vegetation. Most of the Northwest is made up of the northward extension of the Cordillera and the Pacific Coastlands and so is mountainous, while the mainland Arctic is underlain by the Laurentian Shield and is an area of gentle relief.

As we saw in Chapter 1, the climatic heart of the American Arctic is offset somewhat to the eastern side of the Northlands. In summer the isotherms run from northwest to southeast; so that while parts of the Northwest have a short but agriculturally useful summer season, the Arctic receives much less heat in summer.

The effect of this climatic difference is seen in the vegetation of the two areas. The Northwest is a mountainous area in which (as in southern British Columbia and in Washington) lower slopes are forested and upper slopes are barren, but the Arctic is treeless tundra. The northern limit of trees, which runs diagonally across Canada from the mouth of the Mackenzie to northeastern Manitoba, forms a natural boundary between the two areas.

The soils of the Northlands are also varied. Besides the Spodosols (northern podsols) one might expect in these latitudes, there are the lacustrine clays and sands of former glacial lakes, and areas where glaciation has swept away the soil. Where drainage has been interrupted and swamps, or muskegs, have been formed, there is often a peat cover several feet thick. This must usually be stripped off, or at least reduced in thickness and drainage channels cut, before the land can be brought under cultivation.

But all soils in these high latitudes have characteristics which make their use complex and difficult. Rates of decomposition and humus formation, for example, are very slow, so that in the surface layers organic matter is held "in cold storage." Freeze and thaw are responsible for constant rearrangement of soil-making materials and, indeed, for a continuous formation

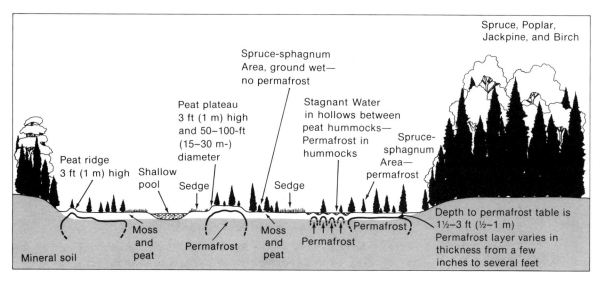

Fig. 23-2. Permafrost localities in the zone of discontinuous permafrost.

process of minor surface landforms and irregularities. Solifluction is widespread on bare surfaces of quite gentle slope, and gullying has proved to be violent when, for example, the surface is disturbed by construction.

The major soil problems in the Northlands are, however, created by the existence of permafrost. Below the surface the ground is perennially frozen to a depth which may well exceed 1500 ft (460 m) in the extreme north. At the surface a narrow layer will thaw in summer; this is known as the active zone; in the far north it has a depth of only a foot or so, but it deepens southward. The permafrost area, which is continuous in the north, becomes discontinuous in the south, consisting at its southern edge of a series of permafrost "islands." The presence or absence of permafrost depends on a number of factors of vegetation cover, aspect, or relief, some of them highly localized in their nature, as shown in Figure 23-2.[4] Thus the presence or absence of permafrost also enters into the calculations of farmers, miners, and construction engineers as a major variable in their planning.

While the existence of a permanently frozen subsurface has to be reckoned with, most of

[4]See R.J.E. Brown, *Permafrost in Canada,* University of Toronto Press, Toronto, 1970, for further details.

the problems actually arise because the active zone is *not* permanently frozen; it thaws in the summer season. One then has to deal with a surface layer which is iron hard in winter but generally soft and waterlogged in summer, for the permanently frozen subsoil impedes drainage. This seasonal contrast is of great importance to an engineer planning to construct an oil pipeline from the Alaska oil fields southward or, for that matter, to build a sewage system for a northern settlement. A cultivator has equally to reckon with the interruption of both soil drainage and leaching processes (a hardpan tends to form at the lower limit of thaw) even when he finds a soil that thaws to a sufficient depth to make crop rooting feasible.

What is the impact of physical conditions such as these on agriculture? Apart from the limitations imposed by relief and soils, it is widely assumed that the main determinant is the cold of the Northlands. But experience has shown that this is not wholly true. Although the frost-free season is very short and highly unreliable in its occurrence, some crops can nevertheless be raised in the Far North, where summer days are long, even if the summer season is short.

The two main climatic limitations are lack of summer heat and, rather surprisingly, drought. The first of these, as we have seen, marks an important difference between the Northwest and the Arctic. There are crops which can be grown on the Lower Mackenzie, beyond the Arctic Circle, which will not ripen in central Québec, 15° further south. At Dawson, in the Yukon (64°N), the mean temperature is above 50°F (10°C) for almost three months in summer, which is nearly a month longer than at Fort Mackenzie, in Québec (57°N), and only a little shorter than at Gaspé (49°N).

The second limiting factor is drought (see Fig. 1-7). Over the interior of the Northlands, precipitation is generally between 10 and 20 in. (250–500 mm) per annum; only on the Alaska-British Columbia coast does it rise to 40, or even 80 in. (1000–2000 mm). This means that the Canadian Arctic, with its cool summers, is subhumid in climate, while the Northwest is definitely semiarid, and irrigation has as much relevance for its few cultivators as concern over frost danger.

Finally, not merely the amount but also the seasonal distribution of precipitation must be borne in mind. Not only does most of the Northeast have a short, cool summer, but its 10–20 in. (250–500 mm) of precipitation arrive with a late-summer maximum, too late to be of much help to the would-be cultivator. Thus the Arctic, and in particular northern Ontario and northern Québec, suffers a triple drawback to land use: lack of soil, lack of sunshine, and lack of growing-season rainfall. Further west, in the Peace River country and the Mackenzie Valley, the amount of precipitation is no greater, and evaporation rates are higher, but the rainfall regime is of a Great Plains type and shows a growing-season maximum.

Future Prospects

In 1976 the population of the Canadian northern Territories was 64,000 and that of Alaska was an estimated 360,000. For comparison the population of all those Canadian census divisions which lie to the north of Hamelin's boundary line between his Pre-North and Middle North was 1.18 million in 1971, up from 1.03 million in 1961. While it is difficult to draw an exact comparison between the Ca-

nadian Northlands and those of the U.S.S.R., it must be recognized that the population of the latter area is many times more numerous than that of its North American counterpart.[5] Therefore, questions arise: why have so few settlers entered this great region; under what circumstances might its population increase; and is increase in its settled population essential to its future development? The final task in this book is to attempt a brief answer to these questions.

THE PAST—WHY SO LITTLE?

There is no real difficulty in answering the first of our questions if we bear in mind the conditions under which Canada has been peopled—why a population largely composed of free and individual immigrants should have chosen on the whole *not* to strike out for an area so physically harsh and lonely as the Northlands; an area which supports a native population of Indians and Eskimos amounting to a mere 100,000 or so. With few constraints to restrict their choice of settlement area, and plenty of space available, it would be surprising if many of the newcomers *had* chosen the North. The great in-migration of the years before the First World War was basically farm orientated; so, too, was the internal movement of French Canadians away from the crowded farmlands of Québec, but the Northlands repelled the farmer. On the other hand, the second great immigrant wave, in the period since 1945, flowed into a changed Canada—a country in which industry had developed, cities were booming, and the whole fabric of employment was being altered by the growth of the service occupations. Less than ever was there any incentive for the average person to settle on the fringes: the cities absorbed the immigrants, and for the few interested in farming, there were empty farms and agricultural frontiers to

[5]Such a comparison, although now out of date, was attempted by G.H.T. Kimble and D. Good, eds., in *Geography of the Northlands*, American Geographical Society, New York, 1955, p. 274. Their figures showed that in the true Arctic, the ratio of population in the U.S.S.R. territories to that in the North American was 5:1; in the Sub-Arctic it was 19:1, and in the Northlands as a whole, 18:1.

occupy even in the southernmost reaches of the country. In the absence of any constraint imposed from outside, or of an unprecedented increase in the nation's population density, Canadians would be likely to prefer comfort and community in the south to the hard and lonely life of the Northlands.

THE FUTURE—HOW MUCH?

In temperate and long-settled lands, it is normal to find that agriculture forms the basis of continuous settlement, and that other occupations grow like a pyramid from that base. But we have already noted that physical conditions limit the growth of agriculture, and, as we shall see in the next section, the overall prospects for agricultural expansion are not good. It therefore follows that the basis for continuous settlement is unlikely to exist: if it takes place at all, settlement will almost certainly *not* be continuous but concentrated—at strategic locations, along routes, or around mineral deposits. These concentrations are likely to be more and more widely spaced, northward into higher latitudes.

We must now consider the probability that development *will* occur, and see what form it is likely to take.

Agriculture in the North

Despite the dwindling significance of agriculture within the Canadian economy as a whole, it will be well to start with its prospects in the North. On the basis of the physical limitations which we have already considered, we can recognize that some regions of the Northlands offer positive prospects and that others, in the foreseeable future, offer few or none at all. In northern Québec and Ontario, for example, despite the growth of mining settlements, potentialities appear to be very slight. While the eastern Shield has adequate rainfall, it has neither soil nor summer heat. Even the Clay Belts, to which the farm frontier advanced several decades ago, are not much more favored; they are somewhat less sterile than the ice-swept surface around them, but their cultivation is not easy. Before they can be farmed

they must usually be cleared of either forest or peat, the frost danger is always present, and few crops are grown besides hay and a little grain. Further west and north the situation is different only in detail; in northern Manitoba and Saskatchewan a combined land use of forestry and tourism offers far better prospects than agriculture, and while estimates of cultivable soils run as high as 5 million acres or 2.02 million ha (along the Liard and the Slave and in the northern valleys of British Columbia), reconnaissance work has been sketchy and the climatic data on which the estimates are based are limited and suspect.[6]

Because it has no "prospects for agriculture" at all, our list does not cover the true Arctic. But it is not therefore to be forgotten. It is the home of the Eskimo, a race of hunters and fishermen who live without cultivating and who have built up a distinctive culture which their isolation and their nomadism have enabled them to preserve in its essentials down to the present.

This being the case generally along the northern frontier of agriculture, the contrast presented by the Peace River region is all the sharper. Not only does this region possess millions of acres of potentially cultivable land to add to the 5 million mentioned above; it actually has 4.5 million acres (1.8 million ha) under cultivation and forms a farming frontier at the present time. Part of the reason for the lack of agricultural progress northward elsewhere in Canada is probably that any of the few Canadians who are interested these days in pioneer farming set out automatically for the Peace. Between 1966 and 1971, while the area in farms in Canada shrank by 4.5 million acres (1.8 million ha), that in British Columbia increased by

---

[6]To show how wildly tentative such estimates can be, it is worth quoting those recorded by H.A. Johnson and H.T. Jorgenson, *The Land Resources of Alaska,* University of Washington Press, Seattle, 1963. Estimates of potential agricultural land in Alaska have been as follows: in 1940, 41.6 million acres (16.8 million ha) were thought to be cultivable; in 1946 this figure was revised downward to 2.9 million acres (1.2 million ha), and in 1954 to 0.8 million acres (324,000 ha). The actual cultivated area is minute, and Alaskan agriculture, despite growth in local population and demand (see p. 432), consists of only about 300 farms, more than half of which are too small to be commercial.

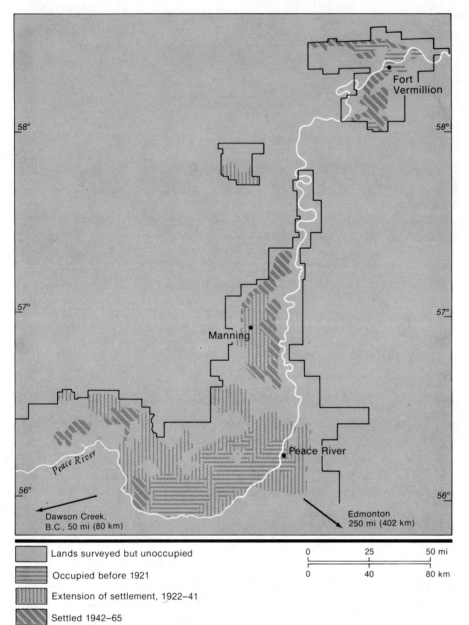

Fig. 23-3. Settlement in the Peace River country of Alberta. The map shows the enlargement of the settled area along this section of the Northland frontier from 1921 to about 1964.

Lands surveyed but unoccupied

Occupied before 1921

Extension of settlement, 1922–41

Settled 1942–65

half a million (200,000 ha), mostly along the Peace, while the Alberta section of the region saw an increase of over 700,000 acres (283,000 ha). Even more remarkable, between the censuses of 1971 and 1976 still larger increases were recorded: 641,000 acres (259,000 ha) for the British Columbia section and almost 1 million acres (400,000 ha) for Alberta.

Part of this increase is accounted for by the enlargement of existing holdings. Under the structure of provincial law it is usually possible to obtain extensions to existing farms for little more than the cost of clearing them and that, to a farmer in, say, Illinois or Iowa must sound like paradise indeed: if he can find any spare land at all, its price will be astronomical. Part of the increase in farm area on the Peace, however, represents genuine pioneering: the provinces issue several hundred homestead titles each year, and all through the region one

The Peace River region: Farmland in the Peace Valley in British Columbia. *(Government of British Columbia)*

sees the work of cutting, burning, and clearing forest going on. The southern edge of the region is fully settled: its leading crops are barley (which now occupies double the area of wheat) and rapeseed, which has proved a runaway success in the past ten years. Beyond this firm base of prosperous farms, there is a thinning out of agricultural settlement and finally the northern forests. The Peace River country is the gateway to the North.

There are, of course, special conditions here which help the farmer. In terms of soils and topography the region is an extension of the Prairies rather than a representative section of the Northlands. Relief is gentle and access

relatively easy by road and rail. The big Peace River farms operate no differently from those of the main prairie lands further south. They can thus bypass one of the main problems of the northern farmer everywhere else—how to market his produce.

Yet even along the Peace some farmers fail. They are mainly the homesteaders and they fail because they cannot survive the long initial period before they have a productive holding large enough to yield a livelihood. This has been the case with very many—perhaps the majority—of the French Canadian settlers who came in from Québec in groups, settling 40–50 acres (16–20 ha) apiece. A few produce honey

423

or work farms that others have abandoned, but the rest have left the land to seek work in the city or on oil rigs.

What are the lessons to be learned on the Peace River? First and most important, northern farming is susceptible to peculiar pressures. In the north, lands suitable for agriculture are widely scattered, mostly on old lake beds and river terraces. To the isolation of the *region* there is added, therefore, the isolation of the *homestead*. This isolation and its counterpart, cost of transport and services, are the great economic handicaps in every northern project. They have been increased by the method of settlement. Where settlement has been on a homesteading basis, each newcomer has claimed a promising quarter-section without reference to the location of other settlers; thus the cost of services is increased by the unnecessarily wide scatter of individual homesteads.

The second economic factor is the cost of settlement. In the U.S. government's Matanuska Valley Project in Alaska, the cost of clearing the ground before seeding (for much of the potentially cultivable land was under forest) was reckoned at $150 per acre ($370 per ha). Later estimates[7] have run between $200 and $300 per acre ($490–740 per ha) for simple clearance without levelling or shaping the land. Thus a problem is created similar to that faced by irrigation farmers in the dry West: that capital is required to make a start. The north suffers the additional handicap: that, whereas on irrigated lands higher yields will help to pay for the initial outlay, yields on northern lands will not be appreciably higher—indeed, they may be lower—than elsewhere.

If agricultural settlement is to develop, it must clearly be governed by certain principles. (1) Settlement should be made not at the whim of the individual cultivator, but in blocks, as the need for it arises from increasing population pressure or enlarging demand for food. Each of these blocks must be large enough to support the cost of services. (2) Just as the settlement block must be large enough to provide essential services, so the individual unit

[7]See, for example, the testimony gathered by the Sub-Committee on Research and Extension of the Committee on Agriculture, H.R., 88th Cong., 2nd sess., 1964.

must be large enough to give the settler a reasonable chance of success. We have seen how this restriction to one particular quarter-section was the ruin of many an earlier homesteader. Today in Alberta it is possible to obtain a 1000-acre (405 ha) homestead, and to lease in addition up to 5000 acres (2025 ha) of rough grazing. What is more, the residence requirements have also been made more realistic: here in the North it is accepted that many homesteaders will occupy their holdings only seasonally and that they will require the freedom to take other jobs in winter. All this the provincial government accepts as part of the necessary framework within which settlement should take place. (3) Blocks of new lands should be settled only in strict relationship to transport and to market opportunities—perhaps the clearest moral to be drawn from northern settlement thus far. In the Peace River country, that "laboratory" for northern experiments, when the first good lands were opened up early in the present century, the mistake was made of trying to grow wheat commercially at distances of 50–60 mi (80–100 km) from a railway. This proved impossible; only as the railway was carried north could this wheat compete with crops grown 10–20 mi (16–30 km) from a railway in the central Prairies.

On the other hand, the few places where agriculture has proved successful in the North have been places where a market, and in particular a *local* market, has been available. The Matanuska Valley is linked by road and rail with Anchorage, which it supplies; and after initial misjudgments were corrected, it settled down to a sensible routine of local supply of fluid milk and potatoes. The Ontario Clay Belts supply various mining and forestry communities with food. In short the only justification for expanding northern agriculture in the future, away from the frontier of continuous settlement at least, will be to supply a specific market within the locality where cultivation is possible.

Whether the provincial and federal governments ought to encourage farmers to attempt settlement even on this limited basis is very much open to question. It is even doubtful whether the provinces ought to continue to sponsor new homesteading (as opposed to enlargement of existing units) in the Peace River country, where the chances of succeeding are so much greater than elsewhere on the margins. One thing which seems clear is that *by itself* agriculture cannot support the range of services to which any sector of the Canadian population in the 1970s feels itself entitled. These services can attain an acceptable level only if other activities such as mining or forestry are present to help to foot the bill. On this ground if no other, therefore, the idea of agricultural development, independent of the growth of other economic activities, should be firmly suppressed by the governments responsible for these Northlands.

Mining in the North

To date the largest part of all northern development has been the product of mining activity. The Precambrian rocks of the Shield contain a great variety of metals; the younger formations that underlie the northern end of the Great Plains Province yield coal and petroleum, and in the western mountains lies the gold that blazed the name of Klondike round the world in the 1890s.

Some of these mineral deposits are important on a world scale—for example, the nickel-copper ores of Sudbury, Ontario, for long the source of some 90 percent of the nickel supply of the world outside the U.S.S.R.. Others are important sources of supply for the whole continent—the central Labrador iron ores, for instance, whose exploitation was referred to in Chapter 7.

In the sphere of mining, new developments occur year by year and with them new communities spring up in the Northlands. The Labrador iron ores prove now to be only a part of a long belt of ore bodies running southwest into Québec, so that the ore town of Schefferville, which has grown up at the head of the railway from Seven Islands as the principal mining community, has been followed by other similar settlements along the line of the ore workings. The old workings of the radium-uranium beds of Great Bear Lake have now

been eclipsed by large-scale operations in the Elliot Lake area on the north shore of Lake Huron, forecast to be the world's richest uranium field. In nickel production Thompson in Manitoba has become second only to Sudbury as a source of the metal.

In the Northlands as a whole, the largest number of mine openings in the past decade was in western Québec and northeastern Ontario. But perhaps the most significant developments in northern mining during the past two decades have been (1) the opening in 1964 of both operations and townsite at Pine Point on the south shore of Great Slave Lake, where the newly constructed Hay River road and railway line were available to haul out valuable lead-zinc ores (whose existence had been known for years but whose remoteness had prevented their exploitation at an earlier period), (2) the oil strikes at Prudhoe Bay on the Arctic coast of Alaska, and (3) the development of the Athabaska tar sands.

Since the 1947 strikes in the Edmonton area (see p. 137), progress in petroleum prospecting and production has been rapid. Development spread north to the Lesser Slave and Peace River fields. But between them and the North Slope of Alaska was a great leap, both geographically and technically. It was in March 1968, after several years of fruitless drilling, that oil was struck in the Prudhoe Bay area and Alaska's future, as *Time* Magazine commented, "lit up like a pinball machine." The technical problems of merely supporting the drilling crews were gigantic; those of moving the oil once it was flowing were almost insuperable. Yet in a period of increasingly tight domestic supplies there could be no doubt that the United States needed the Alaskan oil—that the problems had to be surmounted. The difficulty was to find a way of moving the oil to market which would be feasible under Arctic conditions, and Alaskan Arctic at that, which meant providing not only against low temperatures, permafrost, and the fragility of the tundra ecosystem when disturbed, but against earthquake risk as well. It took the oil crisis of late 1973 to overcome environmentalist opposition to the construction of a specially-designed pipeline, a pipeline which, four years later, began carrying oil to the warm-water port of Valdez on the southern coast.

Meanwhile, the rise in world oil prices brought exploitation of the Athabaska sands into the realm of practical economics, and this time with minimal transport difficulty, for the sands lie in the northern Peace River country around Fort McMurray, which was already accessible from the industry's Edmonton base. Their exploitation brings to the petroleum industry a new technical phase; one which, it is to be hoped, will be free from some of the grosser risks and wilder speculations of drilling for an invisible mineral underground, and missing more often than not.

In an area so huge and so little known as the Northlands, mineral discoveries are likely to continue. For example, it is a fact that the whole coastline of the Arctic Ocean—from northern Alaska east through the outermost members of the Arctic archipelago to the tip of Ellesmere Island and out to the edge of the continental shelf—is potentially oil bearing.[8] Similarly, the mineralized belt containing the Québec-Labrador iron ores extends from the present producing areas around Schefferville, Gagnon, and Wabush Lake north along the line of the Labrador Geosyncline all the way to the west side of Ungava Bay.

What is, however, principally important in our present consideration is the extent to which mining is likely to lead to long-term development in the Northlands. It is the life expectancy of the mine which matters. Tough points out that in a recent 10-year period, 82 mines *closed* in Canada: the total number of mines of all kinds operating in 1970 was about 240.[9] The question always arises as to whether the size and duration of the mining operation will justify the construction of a permanent settlement. Wherever miners have penetrated in North America this has been a question; the Mountain West, as we saw in Chapter 19, is littered with ghost towns, the remains of earlier mining communities. But there is a point of difference between the West and the North.

[8]See the maps in G. Tough, "Mining in the Canadian North," in W.C. Wonders, ed., *The North,* University of Toronto Press, Toronto, 1972, p. 88.

[9]Tough, "Mining in the Canadian North," p. 71.

Those early mining towns were built of local materials, cheaply and quickly: when the mines were exhausted it was no great loss if the settlement was abandoned, and many of them were. In some cases the whole town could be dismantled and moved to a new minehead without difficulty. There are ghost towns like these on the fringes of the Northlands also, but if we are thinking of the future, the construction of northern settlements may well involve bringing every plank and bag of cement from a thousand miles away: it will certainly involve problems of insulation, sewage, and servicing peculiar to the northern climate. Only where the life expectancy of the mine is long or where, better still, the mineralized area contains a variety of different deposits, can the construction of a "permanent" settlement be justified. In other words, mining alone is likely to provide the North in the future with little more than it does at present—a series of scattered communities whose existence begins and ends with the mine.

Hydroelectricity in the North

A further possibility of development in the Northlands arises out of the wealth of waterpower potential they possess. The impact which waterpower can make on a region's economy is already vividly illustrated by developments in areas which adjoin the Northlands on either side of the continent—the Columbia-Snake basin and the St. Lawrence Valley. In detail the impact of such development within the north itself can also be observed in the Kitimat scheme on the coast of British Columbia. Here the flow of one of the Fraser's tributaries has been reversed by damming, the water is diverted to an underground power station at Kemano, and the power generated there is transmitted to Kitimat, on one of the coast fiords, where a great aluminum smelter (see p. 410) has been brought into operation.

The next generation of projects is already in being. In the Northwest there is the Bennett Dam on the Peace River, just to the west of the Alaska Highway. In the Northeast the scheme to harness the power of the Churchill Falls in southern Labrador has now been completed

426

and contributes its 5.2 million kw capacity to the Québec grid. Beyond these schemes lie other possibilities on still more remote rivers— the Yukon and the Mackenzie and rivers around James Bay. If such possibilities are ever to be realized, the problems of financing and marketing of power will have to be overcome, and neither is likely to be easy. But it would seem certain that in a continent facing both energy shortage and pollution problems, the use of this one "clean" source of power will be extended in the future.

Apart from the brief period of construction, such schemes will not, of course, do much to increase the population of the Northlands. With improvements in transmission techniques, it is likely that nothing but power *generation* will take place in the North: *utilization* will occur in the already-settled south.

Forestry in the North

One obvious outlet for electric power within the region is the forest-products industry. Throughout the forested zone of the North there are large numbers of sawmills, and there is a discontinuous forestry frontier which is moving gradually northward as the development of access roads and water transport bring fresh areas of timber within economic range. Experience in British Columbia has shown that the forest-products industry develops a new maturity when the point is reached where it can support pulp and paper mills, for these represent the more stable, long-term element of the forest-products industry. This "take-off" point was reached in Alaska in the late 1950s, and the number of mills in the state has increased steadily since that time. The industry is a very large consumer of electric power, and offers clear growth potential in the Northlands.

While there is no doubt that the forest-products industries will expand in the future or that they will make a valuable contribution to the region in terms of employment and road-building, they will certainly not expand free from constraints. These constraints are of two kinds. One is the vigilance of conservation interests, who will be concerned to make sure (1) that great areas of forest resources are not alien-

ated to private hands without strict provisos about cutting and replanting, and (2) that the pulp industry is not allowed to pollute the northern environment.

The other constraint applies not only to forestry but to oil and mineral development also. For all of these northern products the main markets, the main financial interests involved, and the main management are not Canadian but American. There is very little doubt that the *quickest* way to open up the Northlands would be to throw the border wide open for the entry of companies and investors from the United States. The chronic lack of capital a nation of 23 million people is bound to experience when confronted with development potential on the northern scale can most simply be met by drawing on American resources.

But if this is the quickest method, it is not necessarily the one Canadians will wish to adopt. We have already seen in Chapter 7 how much of Canada's industry is owned or controlled by American firms. In the mining industry the non-Canadian share of control is over 70 percent. Against the advantages of exploitation in the immediate future, Canadians may therefore wish to balance two other considerations: (1) It is one thing to see a pulp mill or oil refinery constructed and giving employment locally, but another to know that local employment is *all* that the plant is providing; that all the value added by manufacture and the profits from the operation are being drained off outside the region and, indeed, outside the nation. (2) The resources being exploited today will, in a resource-hungry world, be worth more tomorrow and much more in ten years' time. In other words, if Canada accepts for the present a slower rate of northern development, one in line with its own capabilities, the value of its products when they are actually marketed will be that much greater. What is more they will be Canada's own, to dispose of at will. These are decisions which call for the wisdom of Solomon.

Strategic Considerations in the North

The Northlands have come into their own in the air age and with the rise of the U.S.S.R. as

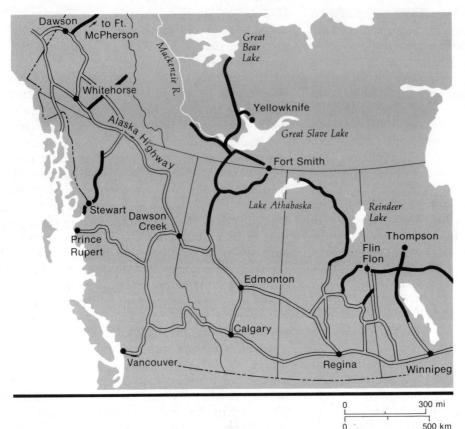

Fig. 23-4. The Northlands: The "Roads to Resources" program in western Canada. The open lines represent existing main highways and the solid lines roads being constructed under the program, some of which are already in use.

a military power on the other side of the polar wastes. The knowledge that Alaska was Russian until Seward bought it—in the teeth of fierce criticism—for $7,200,000 in 1867 is a lingering nightmare in the American mind. Members of the armed forces make up a considerable part of the population of Alaska, while the presence of numerous civilians is also attributable to strategic needs. Of these needs the wartime Alaska Highway, running northwest from Dawson Creek, British Columbia, is the most obvious geographical expression. Since the war the United States and Canada have collaborated in the construction of the continent's radar defenses against transpolar attack.

Such measures tend to open up the North, but involve little permanent settlement outside the few major bases. If, however, we extend the term "strategic" a little to cover a wider field, then the general development of northern communications, which will certainly serve strategic purposes, is likely to have the most direct effect on increasing the region's population in the future. At least the converse is true: there can be no hope of successful expansion without extension of communications, and this extension should preferably precede any attempt at further settlement.

Transport and Tourism in the North

In the early days of the North, movement was largely by water in summer and pack train in winter. The pack trains are now tractor hauled, but the same generalization still holds; the Mackenzie in particular remains the Main Street of the Northwest. To these means of movement have now been added the railways, reaching north from the St. Lawrence and the Prairies to new mining areas and the ports of Hudson Bay. While railways struggle for survival in other parts of the continent, their mileage is increasing in the Northlands.

In the Northeast the first iron ore railway from the Labrador mines to Seven Islands is now paralleled by another to Port Cartier from mines further west. New lines penetrate the Lake Mistassini area of Québec. Great Slave Lake is linked by rail with the settled lands southward. Elsewhere, roads have been built under the "Roads to Resources" program of the federal government. Four thousand miles (6400 km) of these roads have been planned with the object of opening up the widest possible range of resources in the area they serve. And one purpose which these roads will certainly serve in the future is to carry a growing tourist traffic.

Even more characteristic of the region has been the use of air transport to carry mining equipment to new projects or to assist in the export of precious metals, furs, and fish. Yet most of this northern transport network has to be laid out in acceptance of the fact that, since it is economically "strategic," its justification is not to be sought in terms of immediate financial returns, but in the long-term development which the coming of transport makes possible within the nation.

This being the case, we should adopt a realistic view of what the transport network of the future will be like. Clearly, there will never be a dense network of roads over the whole region; moreover, the tourist demand of the future will encourage the preservation of stretches of untouched wilderness as a major northern attraction. What we may expect to see is the development of particular areas, with appropriate transport routes serving them. Yet these areas will be separated from each other by empty stretches, much as the Prairies and Ontario are at present separated by the desolate north shore of Lake Superior with its single road and two lines of railway.

It is important that development should be *concentrated* in the Northlands in order to reduce the mileage of costly transport routes which would have to be maintained. Indeed, this principle of concentration holds good in all respects in northern development: with a limited amount of investment capital to spread over 2.5 million sq mi (6.47 million sq km), to

distribute it too widely would automatically be to do too little everywhere.

This is one of the considerations underlying the so-called Mid-Canada Development Corridor (see Fig. 3-1). It is a proposal for northern development, but one that recognizes the limits of the possible. It takes account of the impossibility of developing equally and simultaneously the whole of the Northlands, and so proposes to concentrate efforts on the fringe of the present ecumene; to transform the present northern frontier, dependent as it is in so many respects on the settled south, into an axis possessing its own economic strength and internal cohesion; an axis from which, if future conditions should dictate the need, a further northward advance can later be made.

THE FUTURE—HOW PERMANENT?

The last several sections of this chapter have been taken up with an assessment of the likely answers to two of the three questions with which we began: why has there been so little development in the North up to now, and under what circumstances may we expect development in the future? We now come to the third question: does development necessarily imply permanent settlement in the Northlands?

If it *does* then we must note that future settlement will probably have to be very different in character from that of the past, because the settlers themselves will be different. The lonely, rough-living prospector will be followed by the technician and scientist, and for these northerners, settlements will have to be planned in advance rather than allowed to grow up in the old, haphazard fashion of, say, a Dawson City in the gold rush days. Facilities will have to be provided and families catered for. It may well be that failure either to realize this or to provide the new type of settlement has contributed to the slowness and hesitancy of the Canadian occupance of the North. As Trevor Lloyd remarks:

The type of person who will be needed in the new north will be expensive, because he will be a technical specialist in a world where mechanization will be very advanced. He and his family will need and demand conditions as good as or better than those found in southern suburbs . . . . Such communities will be expensive, but their citizens will be well paid and able to afford them. There will be no place for the shoveller of snow or the guardian of a trapline.[10]

As Lloyd stresses, all this will be expensive. It is therefore worth pausing to consider whether it is actually necessary for "technical specialists" to "live" in the North at all. Given the long-standing attachment of the Northlands to air travel, and the speed of such travel today, it would seem reasonable to suggest that much of the truly northern development we have been considering might be carried out *without* construction of an indefinite number of miniature Torontos for the workers and their families beyond the 60th parallel. The workers would "live" in Montréal or Winnipeg and spend three or four working days a week in the North: they would be commuters on a grand scale (and some already are). The cost of commuting 500–1000 mi (800–1600 km) would be heavy, but it would not be borne by the individual, and it would be weighed against the cost of the alternative—a northern town complete with the amenities suggested by Lloyd and having a life expectancy of perhaps 25–50 years.

However, there is one other factor. Whether the technical specialist commutes in this fashion or becomes a permanent settler in the North, there is one section of the northern population which has no choice, and that is the indigenous element, which is "permanently" part of the Northlands. It is noteworthy that none of the future possibilities we have been considering offer any obvious role to the Indians or Eskimos. On the contrary, the forecast by Lloyd which we have just quoted will, if valid, have the effect of *excluding* them from the Northland's future development. We cannot leave the subject of northern prospects without pausing to ask what has created this anomaly.

In Canada as a whole the Indian and Eskimo populations represent only one percent of the total. But this proportion increases sharply as one moves north. In northern Saskatchewan it

is almost a half; in northern Québec it is over a half, and in the Northwest Territories it is 65 percent. Moreover, the fringes of this indigenous population are blurred by the existence of the Métis, or half-Indians, as a virtually separate group; their status is distinctive, but their economic condition usually approximates that of the Indian rather than the white Canadian. Both Indians and Métis in the north occupy treaty reservations, in most cases selected by the groups concerned for their potentialities as hunting-grounds. A few groups are successful cultivators; some others are marginal farmers, but the majority, insofar as they have a regular basis of livelihood, are hunters, trappers, and fisherman.

There is no particular reason why a thin scatter of such groups should not survive in their traditional life patterns in this vast wilderness, if they choose to do so. But there are two complicating factors. One is that not all these groups are scattered; there are actually some considerable concentrations of Indians in the North, a thousand, or two thousand, of them living in and around a small settlement which acts as a miniature service center at the end of a dirt road. Not all of them can hunt and fish under these circumstances; economically, concentrations like these assume the existence of other employment—in industry or service occupations. But in practice there are none. The "town" Indian lives on welfare.

To create employment for such groups of town Indians and Métis, a number of development agencies and programs have been launched. But here we come to the second complicating factor. Although it may be possible—given funds and patience—to generate secondary and tertiary employment for the Indian population in remote places such as Wabasca, or Fort Chipewyan, or Slave Lake, the *quicker* method of dealing with this problem is to train the indigenous population to find work in existing centers. Yet the first effect of training them is likely to be that the enterprising members of the community will take the earliest opportunity to leave for the south. It is unrealistic to invest in manufacturing plants in the places just named if the markets for the manufactured goods are back along the same third-class road by which the raw mate-

[10]In J. Warkentin, ed., *Canada, A Geographical Interpretation*, Methuen, Toronto, 1967, p. 590.

The Canadian North: A contrast in living quarters. On the treeless tundra, the traditional summer dwelling of the Eskimo is made of skins. The new Eskimo home is in Igloolik, N.W.T., on the shores of the Arctic Ocean. (National Film Board of Canada)

rials are brought in. The question to be decided is one that has confronted developers in many other parts of the world (Appalachia, for example)—whether to take the work to the population or to bring the population to the work. In the Northlands the case for maintaining by artificial stimulus the native population in its present harsh environment of poverty is a weak one. Yet it is certain that only in such an environment can its traditional way of life be preserved. The conclusion is a depressing one, for it is tantamount to saying that the cultures, the men and the women native to the North, have no future part to play in the development of their lands.

ALASKA

The future prospects of Alaska call for special attention, for in addition to the general factors in northern development which we have been considering, there are a number of special elements in the situation confronting the young "49th state" of the United States.

On the negative side, the physical character of Alaska is bound to hamper development. While much of the Canadian Northland is flat and open and *can* be traversed and even settled if the future so requires, the obstacles to easy movement in Alaska are immense, and the chief of these obstacles—mountains, ice fields, and deep, fiord indentations—are concentrated in the southeastern corner of the state (that is, nearest to the continental United States).

On the positive side, however, there are at least three reasons why we may expect that the rate of development in Alaska over the next decade or two will be more rapid than in the Canadian Northlands:

1. Against the lack of obvious resources in the interior of Alaska must be offset the compensation provided by the possession of a coastline and the wealth it represents. This wealth takes two main forms—fisheries and coastal forests. The fisheries, the chief of which is the salmon catch, brought in a product worth in 1974 $140 million. The coastline also gives access to more than 5.5 million acres (2.2 million

ha) of commercial forest land,[11] an area immediately available for development.

2. Alaska is a land of 586,000 sq mi (1.52 million sq km) being developed with the backing of a nation of more than 200 million people; the Canadian Northland is an area of about 2.5 million sq mi (6.5 million sq km), being developed by a nation of 23 million people. It is obvious that the resources the federal govenment of the United States could bring to bear on Alaskan development projects are vastly greater, taxpayer for taxpayer and mile for mile, than those of the Canadian government.

3. This being the case, it is doubly significant that Alaska has attained statehood, while about half of the Canadian Northlands (Yukon and Northwest Territories) remain federal dependencies. In the future it will be possible for Alaska to press for a larger share of federal spending on such projects as hydroelectric construction and defense contracts. For this time-honored political game, Alaskans have been well prepared by their years of campaigning for statehood.

But while we may agree that Alaskan development is likely to be more rapid than that of the Canadian Northlands, we are far from certain what the nature of that development will be. More than that, there is already a certain geographical impertinence implicit in treating Alaska as a single unit, as if its fate and future will inevitably be uniform. Point Barrow lies beyond lat. 71° N, while the southern tip of the state, just north of Canada's Prince Rupert, is at 55° N. From the state capital, Juneau, to the westernmost of the Aleutian Islands, is a span of more than 50 degrees of longitude—the same span as that from Portland, Maine, to San Francisco (Fig. 23-5). Even with a single state government responsible for this huge area, no one can predict, still less require, that it will be developed as a unit.

[11]Land which is (a) producing or physically capable of producing useable crops of wood, (b) economically available now or prospectively, and (c) not withdrawn from timber utilization. In Alaska this definition is important: the *total* forest area in the state is no less than 120 million acres (48.6 million ha). Much of this is too remote to meet condition (b) above, while other areas are excluded, under condition (c), by various federal measures.

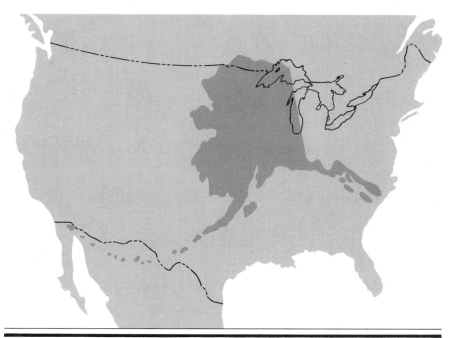

Fig. 23-5. Alaska and the "lower 48" states: A comparison of size (equal-area projection).

EQUAL AREA PROJECTION

In detail, the future of Alaska will be decided by the interplay of five separate forces: (1) the federal government, (2) the state government, (3) private development interests, (4) preservationist interests, and (5) the original population of Indians, Aleuts, and Eskimos.

The federal government is involved because it still (in some sense yet to be defined) "owns" 96.5 percent of Alaska. Its decisions are clearly critical to the area's future; in many ways much more critical than those of the state government. The pressures upon the federal departments concerned come from various lobbies in Washington but the national interest, as we saw in Chapter 5, demands as a bare minimum an energy policy and a resource policy, and it is up to the federal government to formulate these. It was Congress that ultimately authorized the Alaska pipeline, and it is in Washington that the decision must be taken as to what proportion of the nation's resources should be used or, alternatively, be sterilized by the formation of parks and preserves; that is, what proportion of its resources can a wealthy society afford to deny itself in the interests of present amenity and future reserves?

The state government is involved because when Alaska attained statehood in 1959 it re-

ceived powers of taxation and resource control, and because the federal government, as a kind of christening gift, presented it with 103 million acres (41.7 million ha) of public land, to be selected by the state itself. The selection is very far from complete; yet the state has benefited already by such windfalls as the $900 million it received from the auction of oil leases around Prudhoe Bay, and that before a single barrel of oil had actually been produced. No less than any of the other 49 states, Alaska is empowered to make laws controlling its own resources, and to press the federal government to reduce its role within the state.

Private interests are involved because journalists have long since run out of clichés about treasure chests full of resources within Alaska and, just when these clichés were beginning to sound a little too familiar and complaints were being heard that Alaska was greatly overrated (the 1964 earthquake did not exactly help) the North Slope oil fields were brought in to make good the earlier claims. Alaska *is* full of forest and mineral resources and, if they are to be exploited, there is no question of keeping commercial interests out; the only question is the extent to which either the federal or the state government may wish to control them.

433

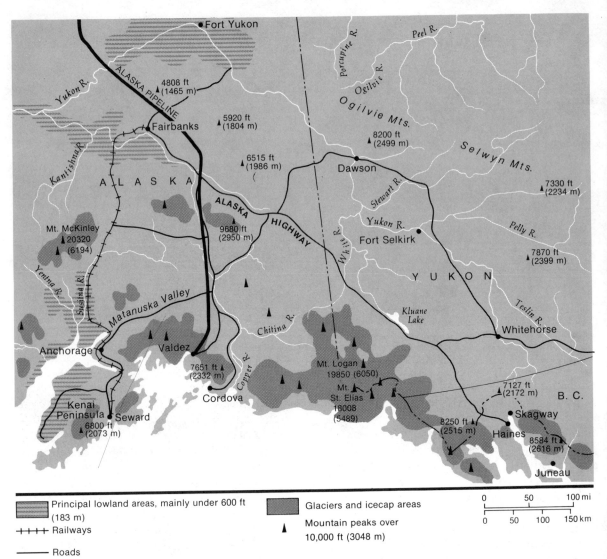

Fig. 23-6. Alaska: The mountain barricades, the routeways, and the pipeline.

Preservationist interests are involved because they see Alaska (and we are driven back again to clichés) as the Last Frontier, or the Last Chance. The word "last" implies that if the wrong policies are adopted, there will never be another opportunity to remedy them: the Unites States will simply have run out of areas to experiment upon. But just because the U.S. government still controls 96.5 percent of the land, policy enforcement should be practicable enough, if only the initial policy decision is right.

It is the preservationists' special concern that the natural equilibria in Alaska are very easily disturbed; that the tundra in particular has a natural replacement rate so slow that once the ecosystem is upset, vegetation and surface may well be destroyed. An area in which a single bulldozer or drill can cause irreparable damage obviously requires special treatment. Of equal concern to the preservationists is the wildlife of the area, and much of the argument about the oil pipeline, both before and after its construction, has focussed on 600,000 caribou, which annually migrate to their feeding grounds across the line.

Last, the native Alaskan population is involved because, while white Alaskans have tended to come and go (there was, for example, quite an exodus after the 1964 earthquake), the 60,000 natives remain: this is their true home. Not only so, but it can be argued on their behalf that they are the legal owners of Alaska; that the treaty of 1867, to which they were not a party, did not actually transfer to the U.S. government title to the land—the incoming Americans merely assumed that it did, adding one more example to a worldwide list of cases where concepts of "ownership" are differently understood by different cultures. So the native share in Alaska's wealth remains to be determined, not only in law but also in terms of real, individual improvement to what has been in the past Anglo-America's lowest standard of living.

What have gold, oil, and earthquake produced in Alaska today? Its population in 1975 was about 350,000 compared with 229,000 in 1960. But during those fifteen years, the total net migration into the state was only 36,000. The significance of this figure is that it is so small: that so many have come and gone during the period, and so few have stayed. Bearing in mind experience on earlier frontiers, we are bound to notice how much of Alaska's employment has been temporary—how much is still strictly seasonal—and how throughout the early 1970s it consistently showed the highest unemployment rate of any of the fifty states. But then again, paradoxically, for those who did have employment all was well: by 1975 average personal income per capita was also the highest for any state.

It is this curious mixture of poverty and wealth, opportunity and failure, incentive and repulsion, which makes the future of Alaska so hard to predict. Ample notice has been served on all concerned that the environment is endangered, whatever use is made of it. The main area of dispute is between those who see Alaska primarily in terms of *resource base* and those who see it as a *refuge*. We need not be surprised if there is a divergence of viewpoint

The Alaska Pipeline. The pipe is seen here on one of its insulated, above-ground sections some 85 mi (136 km) north of the terminal at Valdez. *(Alyeska Pipeline Service Co.)*

between these two groups. Among the latter group, however, there is still a second question to answer: a refuge for whom or what? For the 60,000 descendants of the original inhabitants, to use as they see fit? For world-weary Americans from other states, who may wish to keep in perpetuity one area, at least, where they can get back to the wild? Or for 600,000 caribou and sundry moose and reindeer, who should be left undisturbed and who, although they may not be able to speak for themselves, have plenty of enthusiasts to speak for them?

Before the answers to these questions can be recorded, there will have to be a seventh edition of this book.

Suggestions for Further Reading

It has become increasingly difficult, with each edition of this book, to compile a helpful list of suggested readings. There are several reasons for this. One is that the volume of literature has increased so greatly that it is beyond the powers of any single geographer to be familiar with all of it. A second is that there has been a significant increase in what might be called *local* publication; a large amount of good work is available, but in serials or formats which can only be obtained by applying to a local institution; even to hear of its existence is a task in itself. A third problem is that the center of gravity of geographical publication has shifted from regionally orientated studies to studies of methodology or technique; there are papers about the Corn Belt or Baltimore, but only as illustrations or examples of, say, a new method of statistical analysis. On the whole, this present list of readings does not include such studies but is confined to those made of the phenomena for their own sake, leaving the mnethodological studies as a bonus where and when they are found to be useful.

The fourth problem is the patchy cover of the continent afforded by the present literature, even when it is enlarged to include the popular as well as the professional papers. There are no less than six geographies of the state of California known to the writer, and geographical books and papers without number about Chicago—but not about Philadelphia or Washington, D.C. There are geographers who have made it their personal business to monitor changes and landscapes within their areas of interest—one thinks of H.F. Gregor and California agriculture, M.C. Prunty and the Old South, or T.G. Jordan and the historical geography of Texas—while other areas have no such resident watchman. In some regions, therefore, the list offered here is an exercise in barrel-scraping; in others, there is no need to go beyond a listing of the book-length literature to the individual papers, because the former is so plentiful and embodies the findings of the latter.

Thus in looking for regional analysis of any particular part of Canada one would certainly start with J. Warkentin, ed., *Canada: A Geographical Interpretation* (Toronto and London, 1968), an excellent work in every respect, and move on from there to the *Studies in Canadian Geography* (6 volumes) prepared for the International Geographical Congress in Montréal in 1972 and published by the Univ. of Toronto

Press. For the United States the sequence is less clear, however; after the general textbooks like this one, there is a "middle layer" formed by the Van Nostrand Searchlight series (which covers the principal regions, but very briefly), the state geographies—where these exist—and a few other regional studies such as J.H. Garland, *The North American Midwest* (New York, 1955) and N.N. Dodge and H.S. Zim, *The American Southwest* (New York, 1956); most of them, as it happens, written some time ago. *Regions of the United States*, ed. J. Fraser Hart (New York, 1973), contains some excellent papers but is less comprehensive than its title suggests. There are a few state geographies, but more often the state or provincial atlas forms the basic source. Something of a competition has developed over the production of these atlases in the past two decades; some are very elaborate affairs indeed, while even a sparsely populated state like Nebraska published no less than three separate atlases in 1977. For some other regions the best guide to what is going on is the area's geographical periodical: an obvious example is the *Southeastern Geographer*.

Since the fifth edition of this book was published, the Association of American Geographers' Comparative Metropolitan Analysis Project has shone light into a number of neglected corners of the urban scene in the United States by providing *A Comparative Atlas of America's Great Cities* (Minneapolis, 1976), and four volumes of *Contemporary Metropolitan America: Twenty Geographical Vignettes* (Cambridge, Mass., 1976). These vignettes are referred to again in the appropriate regional chapters in this list. In the same way, G.A. Nader, *Cities of Canada* (Toronto, 1976) offers as its second volume *Profiles of Fifteen Metropolitan Centers*.

The references that follow represent a personal selection. The present writer will be grateful for news of any important omissions.

Chapter 1

PHYSIOGRAPHY AND GLACIAL GEOGRAPHY

The basic references are W.W. Atwood's *Physiographic Provinces of North America* (Boston, 1940); W.D. Thornbury, *Regional Geomorphology of the United States* (New York, 1965), which is illustrated by some striking photographs; and C.B. Hunt, *Physiography of the United States* (San Francisco and London, 1967), which is reinforced by a new version of the same theme, *Natural Regions of the United States and Canada* (San Francisco, 1974), by the same author. The Canadian section of the continent is dealt with by J.B. Bird in *The Natural Landscapes of Canada* (Toronto, 1972). The section of the chapter on glacial geography is based largely on R.F. Flint, *Glacial Geography and the Pleistocene Epoch* (New York, 1947) and H.E. Wright and D.G. Frey, eds., *The Quaternary of the United States* (Princeton, 1965), while for Canada there is an interesting series of articles in *Cahiers de Géographie de Québec*, Nos. 8 and 10 (1960 and 1961).

CLIMATE

R.A. Bryson and F.K. Hare, eds., *Climates of North America*, vol. xi of the *World Survey of Climatology* (Amsterdam, 1973) is basic, with F.K. Hare and M. Thomas, *The Climate of Canada* (Toronto, 1973) and M. Thomas, *Climatological Atlas of Canada* (Ottawa, 1953) as back-up references for Canada and *Climate and Man*, the U.S. Department of Agriculture's Yearbook (Washington, D.C., 1941) for the United States.

SOILS AND VEGETATION

One of the best general sources covering most aspects of the biotic environment is the U.S. Department of Agriculture's series of Yearbooks (see for example *Soils*, 1957, or *Trees*, 1949). Shorter references, however, are largely confined to the introductory chapters in regional textbooks. On soil classification, see *Soil Classification: A Comprehensive System* by the Soil Conservation Service (Washington, D.C., 1960) and the U.S. Department of Agriculture's *Soil Taxonomy: A Basic System of Soil Classification* (Washington, D.C., 1975). See also R.F. Legget, ed., *Soils in Canada*, Royal Soc. Can., 1961. On forests see S. Haden-Guest and others, eds., *A World Geography of Forest Resources* (New York, 1956).

Chapter 2

A selection of recent works on the North American Indians is: H.E. Driver, *Indians of North America* (2nd ed., Chicago, 1969); A. Debo, *A History of the Indians of the United States* (Norman, Okla., 1970); A. Marriott and C.K. Rachlin, *American Epic: The Story of the American Indian* (New York, 1970); S.F. Cook, *The Population of the California Indians, 1769–1970* (Berkeley, 1976), and W.H. Oswalt, *This Land Was Theirs: A Study of the North American Indian* (3rd ed., New York, 1978).

For studies of the immigrants and the "melting pot" see M.A. Jones, *American Immigration* (Chicago, 1960); M.L. Hansen, *The Immigrant in American History* (Cambridge, Mass., 1948); *The Atlantic Migration, 1607–1860,* (Cambridge, Mass., 1951); O. Handlin, *The American People* (formerly *The Americans*) (New York, 1963); E.P. Hutchinson, *Immigrants and Their Children* (New York, 1956); and D. Ward, *Cities and Immigrants* (New York, 1971). There are many studies of particular national groups, such as R.T. Berthoff, *British Immigrants in Industrial America* (New York, 1968); H.I. Cowan, *British Migration to British North America* (Toronto, 1961); J.B. Duff, *The Irish in the United States* (New York, 1971); and Y. Ichihashi, *Japanese in the United States* (New York, reprinted 1969). See also N. Macdonald, *Canada: Immigration and Colonization, 1841–1903* (Aberdeen, Scotland, 1966).

On French Canada there is F. Mason Wade, *The French Canadians, 1760–1945* (London, 1955). See also R. Cook, *Canada and the French-Canadian Question* (Toronto, 1966) and for shorter references N. McArthur and M. Garland, "The Spread and Migration of French Canadians," *Tijds. voor econ. en soc. geog.,* 52 jaarg. (1961), 141–47; and J.P. Allen, "Migration Fields of French Canadian Immigrants to Southern Maine," *Geographical Review,* vol. 1xii (1972), 366–83.

The general history of the blacks in America is covered by J. H. Franklin, *From Slavery to Freedom* (New York, 1952) or C. Vann Woodward, *The Strange Career of Jim Crow* (New York, 3rd rev. ed., 1974). Among geographers writing about black Americans the most prominent is H.M. Rose; see his *The Black Ghetto: A Spatial Behavioral Perspective* (New York, 1972) and *Black Suburbanization* (Cambridge, Mass, 1976) and numerous published papers. There are also D. Ley, *The Black Inner City as Frontier Outpost* (Washington, D.C., 1974); G.A. Davis and O.F. Donaldson, *Blacks in the United States* (Boston, 1975); and R.T. Ernst and L. Hugg, eds., *Black America: Geographic Perspectives* (New York, 1976). On the existence of other ghetto groups, see D. Ward, "The Emergence of Central Immigrant Ghettoes in American Cities, 1840–1920," *Annals,* Assc. of Amer. Geographers, vol. 1viii (1968), 343–59.

The Canadian government's *Year Book* contains census data. Other useful references are R.T. Gajda, "The Canadian Ecumene—Inhabited and Uninhabited Areas," *Geographical Bulletin,* No. 15 (1960), 5–18, and T.R. Weir, "Population Changes in Canada, 1867–1967," *The Canadian Geographer,* vol. xi (1967), 197–215. The many volumes of the United States census are summarized in *The Statistical Abstract of the U.S.* (Washington, D.C., annually). On rural population changes see W. Zelinsky, "Changes in the Geographical Patterns of Rural Population in the United States, 1790–1960," *Geographical Review,* vol. lii (1962), 492–524. On urban population and cities the reader might start with two general works: Jane Jacobs, *The Death and Life of Great American Cities* (New York, 1961) and Kevin Lynch, *The Image of the City* (Cambridge, Mass., 1960). These may then be followed by M.H. Yeates and B.J. Garner, *The North American City* (New York, 1971) and by R.E. Murphy, *The American City: An Urban Geography* (2nd ed., New York, 1974). The large U.S. cities are featured in *Urban Atlas: 20 American Cities,* by J.R. Passonneau and R.S. Wurman (Cambridge, Mass., 1966) and *A Comparative Atlas of America's Great Cities* (Minneapolis, 1976), as well as the volumes of *Contemporary Metropolitan America: Twenty Geographical Vignettes,* ed. J.S. Adams (Cambridge, Mass., 1976); those of Canada in N.H. Lithwick, *Urban Canada: Problems and Prospects* (Ottawa, 1970); J. Jackson, *The Canadian City* (New York, 1973), and *Cities of Canada,* vol. ii (Toronto, 1976). See also A.M.

Guest, "Population Suburbanization in American Metropolitan Areas, 1940–1970," *Geographical Analysis*, vol. vii (1975), 267–83, and J.R. Borchert, "America's Changing Metropolitan Regions," *Annals*, Assc. of Amer. Geographers, vol. lxii (1972), 352–73.

On the regional balance of the U.S. population, see B.L. Weinstein and R.E. Firestine, *Regional Growth and Decline in the United States* (New York, 1978).

Chapter 3

On the working of the federal system there are a number of recent textbooks which give ample detail. On the individuality of Canada, see R.C. Harris and J. Warkentin, *Canada Before Confederation: A Study in Historical Geography* (New York, 1974) and then W.L. Morton, *The Canadian Identity* (Madison, Wisc., 1961); H. Hardin, *A Nation Unaware: The Canadian Economic Culture* (Vancouver, 1974); and E.R. Black, *Divided Loyalties: Canadian Concepts of Federalism* (Montréal, 1975). For the Mid-Canada Corridor concept a brief reference is I.G. Davies, "The Mid-Canada Development Conference," *Canadian Geographical Journal*, vol. lxxxii (1971), 2–11.

For references on the attitudes of local governments to land and resources, see the lists for Chapters 4 and 5.

On the sectionalism of the frontier, there is a huge literature generated by the work of Frederick Jackson Turner and his many later critics. On sectionalism in the South, see either W.J. Cash, *The Mind of the South* (New York, 1941) or P. Gerster and N. Cords, eds., *Myth and Southern History* (Chicago, 1974).

Chapters 4 and 5

The early history of land policy and disposal is covered by some long-established texts in the United States, such as P.J. Treat, *The National Land System, 1785–1820* (New York, 1910); B.H. Hibbard, *A History of the Public Land Policies* (New York, 1924); and R.M. Robbins, *Our Landed Heritage: The Public Domain 1776–1936*

(Princeton, 1942, etc.); more recent are V. Carstensen, *The Public Lands* (Madison, Wisc., 1963); E. Dick, *The Lure of the Land* (Lincoln, Neb., 1970); the Public Land Law Review Commission's *One Third of the Nation's Land* (Washington, D.C., 1970); and H.B. Johnson, *Order Upon the Land* (New York, 1976). For Canada see the *Canadian Frontiers of Settlement* series, ed. W.A. Mackintosh and W.L.G. Joerg (Toronto, 1934–38).

On land controls, a selection of references is: M. Clawson, *The Suburban Land Conversion Process in the United States* (Baltimore, 1971) and *Modernizing Urban Land Policy* (Baltimore, 1973); F. Bosselman and D. Callies, *The Quiet Revolution in Land Use Control* (Washington, D.C., 1972); R.R. Linowes and D.T. Allensworth, *The States and Land Use Control* (New York, 1975); R.G. Healy, *Land Use and the States* (Baltimore, 1976); and R.H. Platt, *Land Use Control: Interface of Law and Geography* (Washington, D.C., 1976).

On water needs see F.E. Moss, *The Water Crisis* (New York, 1967), C.E. Dolman, ed., *Water Resources of Canada* (Toronto, 1967), or J.S. Cram, *Water: Canada's Needs and Resources* (3rd ed., Montréal, 1973); B.H. Ketchum, ed., *The Water's Edge: Critical Problems of the Coastal Zone* (Cambridge, Mass., 1972). Lorna Barr gives a short and useful summary of the NAWAPA scheme in "NAWAPA: A Continental Water Development Scheme for North America," in *Geography*, vol. lx (1975), 111–19.

The literature on conservation has grown to enormous proportions. One of the best works by a geographer remains G.H. Smith, ed., *Conservation of Natural Resources* (4th ed., New York, 1971). Some specific aspects are covered by M. Frome, *Whose Woods These Are: The Story of the National Forests* (New York, 1962); M. Clawson, *The Economics of National Forest Management* (Baltimore, 1976); J.W. Watson and T. O'Riordan, eds., *The American Environment: Perceptions and Policies*, Part IV (London, 1976); and the report of the California Land-Use Task Force, *The California Land: Planning for People* (Los Altos, Calif., 1975). For Canada, the government maintains a most useful running file on conservation measures which is available under the title *Ecolog*.

Many of the works mentioned deal with specific government attitudes and initiatives, i.e., with the theme of Chapter 5. Freight rates, however, are separately treated; the structure of rates is discussed in several textbooks on transportation economics but for Canada in two specific works: A.W. Currie, *Economics of Canadian Transportation* (Toronto, 1954) and H.L. Purdy, *Transport Competition and Public Policy in Canada* (Vancouver, British Columbia, 1972). S.R. Daggett and J.P. Carter, *The Structure of Transcontinental Railroad Rates* (Berkeley, Calif., 1947) covers rate-making in the formative years of the West. Examples of more specific treatment by geographers are: J.W. Alexander and others, "Freight Rates: Selected Aspects of Uniform and Nodal Regions," *Economic Geography*, vol. xxxiv (1958), 1–18, and M. Fulton and L.C. Hoch, "Transportation Factors Affecting Location Decisions," *Economic Geography*, vol. xxxv (1959), 51–59.

On energy policy it is too early yet for there to be a large book list, but there are the U.S. government documents, *Project Independence: An Historical Perspective* (Washington, D.C., 1974) and H. Ashley, R.L. Rudman and C. Whipple, eds., *Energy and the Environment: A Risk-Benefit Approach* (New York, 1976). On federal spending on the economy generally see S.D. Brunn and W.L. Hoffman, "The Geography of Federal Grants-in-Aid to States," *Economic Geography*, vol. xlv (1969), 226–38, and C.E. Browning, *The Geography of Federal Outlays* (Chapel Hill, N.C., 1973).

Chapter 6

The Department of Agriculture of both the Canadian and United States governments have issued a great variety of publications and their catalogues give details of these. In addition, most states and provinces through their Agricultural Experiment Station or equivalent organization issue bulletins dealing with local agriculture, and most of them have published a bulletin with a title like *Types of Farming in . . .* which gives a detailed description of their agriculture. New directions in American farming were first traced by L. Haystead and

G.C. Fite, *The Agricultural Regions of the United States* (Norman, Okla., 1955) and E. Higbee's *American Agriculture: Geography, Resources, Conservation* (New York, 1958). On the impact of technical change on farming see also Higbee's *Farms and Farmers in an Urban Age* (New York, 1963). More recent changes can be followed in the U.S. Department of Agriculture's Yearbook for 1962, *After a Hundred Years,* and for 1970, *Contours of Change* as also in J.B. Billard, "The Revolution in American Agriculture," *National Geographic Mag.*, vol. cxxxvii (1970), 147–85.

On the subject of policy, present and future, the many works of Marion Clawson should probably be given a place of honor; see, for example, his *America's Land and Its Uses* (Baltimore, 1972) or *Policy Directions for United States Agriculture* (Baltimore, 1968). For Canada, there is the report of the government's Task Force, *Canadian Agriculture in the Seventies* (Ottawa, 1969). Both countries issue census data on agriculture every five years, but unfortunately the census dates do not coincide. On the question of whether or not to extend the area under irrigation, see V.W. Ruttan, *The Economic Demand for Irrigated Acreage* (Baltimore, 1965), or the briefer "The Panacea of Irrigation: Fact or Fancy" by L.C. Brandhorst, *Journal of the West*, vol. vii (1968), 491–509. On other specific issues see J. Fraser Hart, "Loss and Abandonment of Cleared Farm Land in the Eastern United States," *Annals,* Assc. of Amer. Geographers, vol. lviii (1968), 417–40, and parts of his *The Look of the Land* (Englewood Cliffs, N.J., 1975), and H.F. Gregor, "The Large Industrialized American Crop Farm," *Geographical Review,* vol. lx (1970), 151–75.

Chapter 7

There is a marked shortage of good recent reading on North American industry to recommend. The historical background is covered by J.G. Glover and W.B. Cornell, *The Development of American Industries* (New York, 1951) or J.B. Walker, *The Epic of American Industry* (New York, 1949), while E.B. Alderfer and H.E.

Michl, *Economics of American Industry* (New York, 1950) and S. Vance, *American Industries* (New York, 1955) are valuable for the recent past. On Canada there is B. Brouillette's series, "Les Industries manufacturières du Canada," *L'Act. Econ.*, 40 année (1964–65), 77–88, 245–87 and 505–76. Interesting attempts to delimit the manufacturing regions of the continent have been made by S. De Geer, "The American Manufacturing Belt," *Geog. Annaler*, vol. ix (1927), 233–59; V.R. Fuchs, *Changes in the Location of Manufacturing in the United States since 1929* (New Haven, Conn., 1962); W. Zelinsky, "Has American Industry Been Decentralizing?" *Economic Geography*, vol. xxxviii, (1962) 251–69; and J.L. Morrison and others, "Basic Measures of Manufacturing in the United States, 1958," *Economic Geography*, vol. xliv (1968), 296–311. On the measurement of industrial concentration and recent trends in location, see the numerous articles by A. Pred.

A selection of useful references on coal is: G.F. Deasy and P.R. Griess, "Some New Maps of the Underground Bituminous Coal Mining Industry of Pennsylvania," *Annals*, Assc. of Amer. Geographers, vol. xlvii (1957), 336–49; "Effects of a Declining Mining Economy on the Pennsylvania Anthracite Region," *Annals*, Assc. of Amer. Geographers, vol. lv (1965), 239–59; "Local and Regional Differences in Long Term Bituminous Coal Production Prospects in the United States," *Annals*, Assc. of Amer. Geographers, vol. lvii (1967), 519–33; and A.G. Ballert, "The Great Lakes Coal Trade," *Economic Geography*, vol. xxix (1953), 48–59.

On the steel industry a large number of previous references have been superseded by K. Warren, *The American Steel Industry 1850–1970: A Geographical Interpretation* (Oxford, 1973), but some articles dealing with specific regions will be found in the lists for the appropriate chapters.

The subject of petroleum and natural gas has been poorly covered in the geographical literature since the publication of W.E. Pratt and D. Good, *World Geography of Petroleum* (New York, 1950). So, too, has the textile industry; there is little to recommend. For the automobile industry, see C.W. Boas, "Locational Patterns of American Automobile Assembly Plants, 1895–1958," *Economic Geography*, vol. xxxvii (1961), 218–30, and much more recently L.J. White, *The Automobile Industry Since 1945* (Cambridge, Mass., 1971).

On the Canadian problem of American industrial ownership see the report of the Canadian government's Task Force, *Foreign Ownership and the Structure of Canadian Industry* (Ottawa, 1968).

Chapter 8

Books dealing with the picturesque early phases of North American transport are very numerous: many of the railway companies, like the Union Pacific, the Canadian Pacific, and the Santa Fe, are commemorated by histories, and the Rivers of America series (Hodge and Co.) cover early water transport. For Canada there is G.P. Glazebrook's *A History of Transportation in Canada* (2 vols., Toronto, 1964) as well as J-C. Lassard's survey, *Transportation in Canada* (Ottawa, 1957). See also R.I. Wolfe, "Transportation and Politics: The Example of Canada," *Annals*, Assc. of Amer. Geographers, vol. lii (1962), 176–90.

WATERWAYS

The St. Lawrence Seaway, both before and after its opening in 1959, has captured most of the attention of students of water transport; otherwise there is little else than D. Patton, "The Traffic Pattern on American Inland Waterways," *Economic Geography*, vol. xxxii (1956), 29–37. For the St. Lawrence and the Great Lakes, probably the best references are: A.K. Philbrick, "The Nodal Water Region of North America," *The Canadian Geographer*, vol. viii (1964), 182–87; D. Kerr, "The St. Lawrence Seaway and Trade on the Great Lakes, 1958–63," *The Canadian Geographer*, vol. viii (1964), 188–96; and A. Roemer, *The St. Lawrence Seaway, Its Ports and Its Hinterland* (Tübingen, 1971).

RAILWAYS

A great deal of information is published by and can be obtained from the Association of

American Railroads. For a geographical evaluation see W.H. Wallace's "Railroad Traffic Densities and Patterns," *Annals, Assc. of Amer. Geographers,* vol. xlviii (1958), 352–74; "Freight Traffic Functions of Anglo-American Railroads," *Assc. of Amer. Geographers,* vol. liii, (1963), 312–31; and "The Bridge Line: A Distinctive Type of Anglo-American Railroad," *Economic Geography,* vol. xli (1965), 1–38. One type of recent change in railroading is described by J.T. Starr, Jr., *The Evolution of the Unit Train, 1960–69,* Univ. of Chicago Research Paper No. 158 (1976).

ROADS

There is little literature published by geographers that deals with road transport as such; M. Helvig's *Chicago's External Truck Movements,* University of Chicago Research Paper No. 90 (1964) is one such study. One or two local studies of road routes are listed under the chapters dealing with the regions concerned. The opening of the Trans-Canada Highway was covered by E.J. Marten in *Canadian Geographical Journal,* vol. lxvii (1963), 75–91.

AIRWAYS

Geographical analyses of air transport are also scarce, but K. Sealy, *The Geography of Air Transport* (London, 1966) devotes considerable attention to North America. As specific studies there are E.J. Taafe's *The Air Passenger Hinterland of Chicago,* Univ. of Chicago Research Paper No. 24 (1952) and "Air Transportation and United States Urban Distribution," *Geographical Review,* vol. xlvi, (1956), 219–38. See also W.F. Wacht, *The Domestic Air Transportation Network of the United States,* Univ. of Chicago Research Paper No. 154 (1974).

Broader issues of network structure are raised by K.J. Kansky, *Structure of Transportation Networks,* Univ. of Chicago Research Paper No. 84 (1963), and in the analysis of traffic flows generally, E.L. Ullman's *American Commodity Flow* (Seattle, Wash., 1957) has paved the way for a number of more detailed studies.

Chapter 9

A number of the most useful references are mentioned in footnotes to this chapter. To round out the list there are the two complementary studies, R.L. Morrill and E.H. Wohlenberg, *The Geography of Poverty in the United States* (New York, 1971) and D.M. Smith, *The Geography of Social Well-Being in the United States* (New York, 1973). For the United States see also N.M. Hansen, *Intermediate-Size Cities as Growth Centers* (New York, 1971) and *Growth Centers in Regional Economic Development* (New York, 1972), and P.M. Lankford, *Regional Incomes in the United States, 1929–1967,* Univ. of Chicago Research Paper No. 145 (1973). Beyond these works lie the general field of regional science and the writings of Walter Isard and his associates, but on the impact of federal programs see J.H. Cumberland, *Regional Development Experiences and Prospects in the United States of America* (Paris, 1971) and R.H. Haveman, ed., *A Decade of Federal Anti-Poverty Programs* (New York, 1977). For Canada see D.M. Ray, *Dimensions of Canadian Regionalism* (Ottawa, 1971); R.R. Krueger and others, *Regional and Resource Planning in Canada* (Toronto and Montréal, ed. of 1970); and A.G. Green, *Regional Aspects of Canada's Economic Growth* (Toronto, 1971). On the topic of regional subdivision of North America, see J. H. Paterson, "On Writing Regional Geography" in *Progress in Geography 6* (London, 1974), 1–26.

Chapter 10

Considering the importance of this region there is an astonishing lack of published geographical work about it. R.E. and M. Murphy's *Pennsylvania* has long been out of print, and the title of W. Zelinsky's 1977 paper is significant: "The Pennsylvania Town: An Overdue Geographical Account," *Geographical Review,* vol. lxvii (1977), 127–47. It was not until 1966 that *Geography of New York State,* John H. Thompson, ed., (Syracuse) made good a grave deficiency, although it did so handsomely. On agriculture within the region there is a scatter of references: J.F. Hart, "Loss and Abandonment of Cleared Farm Land in the Eastern United States," *Annals*, Assc. of Amer. Geographers, vol. lviii (1968), 417–40, and his "The Three R's of Rural Northeastern United States," *The Canadian Geographer*, vol. vii (1963), 13–22; J.T. Cunningham, *Garden State: The Story of Agriculture in New Jersey* (New Brunswick, N.J., 1955); J.T. Lemon, "The Agricultural Practices of National Groups in Eighteenth-Century Southeastern Pennsylvania," *Geographical Review*, vol. lvi (1966), 467–96, followed by his book, *The Best Poor Man's Country* (Baltimore and London, 1972), on the same area. See also L. Durand, "The Historical and Economic Geography of Dairying in the North Country of New York State," *Geographical Review*, vol. lvii (1967), 24–47.

On the cities of the region the standard (and for long the only) work was J. Gottmann, *Megalopolis* (New York, 1961): it was summarized and reissued in a more popular form by W. Von Eckhardt as *The Challenge of Megalopolis* (New York, 1964). The individual seaboard cities are dealt with in *Contemporary Metropolitan America* (see p. 437) as follows: New York–New Jersey, vol. i, 139–216; Philadelphia, vol. i, 217–90; Baltimore, vol. ii, 1–95; Washington, vol. iv, 297–344. A few more specialized urban studies also warrant mention, such as N. Kantrowitz, *Negro and Puerto Rican Populations of New York City in the Twentieth Century* (New York, 1969) and N. Glazer and D.P. Moynihan, *Beyond the Melting Pot: Negroes, Puerto Ricans, Jews, Italians and Irish of New York City* (2nd ed., Cambridge, Mass., 1970). For the region as a whole see L.M. Alexander, *The Northeastern United States* (Princeton, 1976).

References to the Appalachian hinterland are to be found listed under Chapters 14 and 15, but the Pennsylvania anthracite field has close ties with this region; see E.W. Miller, "The Southern Anthracite Region," *Economic Geography*, vol. xxxi (1955), 331–50, and G.F. Deasy and P.R. Griess, "Effects of a Declining Mining Economy on the Pennsylvania Anthracite Region," *Annals*, Assc. of Amer. Geographers, vol. lv (1965), 239–59.

Chapter 11

Among the many analyses of the New England economy made in recent years the following may be mentioned, in order of publication: J.K. Wright, ed., *New England's Prospect, 1933* (New York, 1933); J.D. Black, *The Rural Economy of New England* (Cambridge, Mass., 1950); S.E. Harris, *The Economics of New England* (Cambridge, Mass., 1952); A.A. Bright and G.H. Ellis, *The Economic State of New England* (New Haven, Conn., 1954); R.W. Eisenmenger, *The Dynamics of Growth in New England's Economy, 1870–1964* (Middletown, Conn., 1967). On New England's location and competitive position see H.L. Green, "Hinterland Boundaries of New York City and Boston in Southern New England," *Economic Geography*, vol. xxi (1955), 283–300, and C.J. Sharer, "A New Peninsula in the New World," *Tijds. voor econ. en soc. geog.*, 57 jaarg. (1966), 73–77.

Rural change is charted in E.C. Higbee, "The Three Earths of New England," *Geographical Review*, vol. xlii (1952), 425–38; L.E. Klimm, "The Empty Areas of the Northeastern United States," *Geographical Review*, vol. xliv (1954), 325–45; and J.F. Hart, "The Three R's of Rural Northeastern United States," *The Canadian Geographer*, vol. vii (1963), 13–22, while interesting case studies of change are to be found in the classic J.W. Goldthwait, "A Town that has gone Downhill" (Lyme, N.H.), *Geographical Review*, vol. xvii (1927), 527–52, and C. Rand, *The Changing Landscape* (New York, 1968), dealing with the area around Salisbury, Conn. On the population aspects there are R.L. Ragatz, "Vacation Homes in the Northeastern United States: Seasonality in Population Distribution," *Annals*, Assc. of Amer. Geographers, vol. lx (1970), 447–55, and G.K. Lewis, "Population Change in Northern New England," also in the *Annals*, vol. lxii (1972), 307–22.

On New England's industry R.C. Estall's *New England: A Study in Industrial Adjustment* (London, 1966) is basic. See also W.H. Wallace, "Merrimack Valley Manufacturing: Past and Present," *Economic Geography*, vol. xxxvii (1961), 283–308; D. Ward, "The Industrial

Revolution and the Emergence of Boston's Central Business District," *Economic Geography*, vol. xlii (1966), 152–71; and G. Manners, "Decentralization in Metropolitan Boston," *Geography*, vol. xlv (1960), 276–85. On the urban growth of Boston, see O. Handlin, *Boston's Immigrants* (Cambridge, Mass., 1959); S.B. Warner, Jr., *Streetcar Suburbs: The Process of Growth in Boston, 1870–1900* (Cambridge, Mass., 1962); sections of D. Ward's *Cities and Immigrants* (New York, 1971); W.H. Bunting, *Portrait of a Port: Boston 1852–1914* (Cambridge, Mass., 1971), and the survey of Boston in *Contemporary Metropolitan America* (see p. 437), vol. i, 51–138.

Chapter 12

As is the case for most of the regions of Canada, it is hard to improve on the regional account in Warkentin's *Canada: A Geographical Interpretation* (Toronto, 1967) or A.G. Macpherson, ed., *Studies in Canadian Geography: The Atlantic Provinces* (Toronto, 1972). The *Canadian Geographical Journal* deals with each province in turn periodically. On the historical background the work of A.H. Clark is basic; see his *Three Centuries and the Island* (Toronto, 1959), which is a historical geography of Prince Edward Island, or *Acadia: The Geography of Early Nova Scotia to 1760* (Madison, Wisc., 1968). There is also J.B. Bird, "Settlement Patterns in Maritime Canada, 1687–1786," *Geographical Review*, vol. xlv (1955), 385–404.

A selection of studies of agriculture is: R.L. Gentilcore, "The Agricultural Background of Settlement in Eastern Nova Scotia," *Annals, Assc. of Amer. Geographers*, vol. xlvi (1956), 376–404; N.L. Nicholson, "Rural Settlement and Land Use in the New Glasgow Region," *Geographical Bulletin*, No. 7 (1955), 38–64; B. Cornwall, "A Land Use Reconnaissance of the Annapolis-Cornwall Valley," *Geographical Bulletin*, No. 8 (1956), 23–52; C.W. Raymond, "Agricultural Land Use in the Upper Saint John Valley in New Brunswick," *Geographical Bulletin*, No. 15 (1960), 65–83; and C.W. Raymond and others, *Land Utilization in Prince Edward Island* (Ottawa, 1963), or their "Land

Abandonment in Prince Edward Island," *Geographical Bulletin*, No. 19 (1963), 78–86.

Mining, manufacturing, and forestry are poorly covered in the geographical literature, but the Atlantic Provinces Economic Council has published various studies, and the *Canadian Geographical Journal* has an occasional article. An interesting comparative study is R.E. George, *A Leader and A Laggard: Manufacturing Industry in Nova Scotia, Québec and Ontario* (Toronto, 1970). By contrast the transport functions are quite well covered, beginning with the 12 volumes of the *Atlantic Provinces Transport Study* (Ottawa, 1967) prepared for the Canadian government, while among a number of shorter references there are J.A. Rayburn, "Some Factors Affecting the Movement of Foreign Traffic through Saint John," *Geographical Bulletin*, No. 7 (1955); J. Saint and M.H. Matheson, "The Hinterlands of Saint John," *Geographical Bulletin*, No. 7 (1955), 65–101; D.J. Patton, "Railroad Rate Structures, Ocean Traffic Routes and the Hinterland Relations of Halifax and Saint John," *Tijds. voor econ. en soc. geog.*, 52 jaarg. (1961), 2–13; C.N. Forward, "Railway Freight Traffic in Newfoundland," *The Canadian Geographer*, No. 10 (1957), 13–19; and C.H. Little, "Halifax—Container Port," *Canadian Geographical Journal*, vol. lxxxvi (1973), 126–33. On future prospects for the region see M.C. Storrie, "Prognosis for Atlantic Provinces," *Geographical Magazine*, vol. xliv (1972), 674–80.

Chapter 13

The major regional description of the St. Lawrence Valley is contained in a 3-volume study in French by R. Blanchard, a summary of which is represented by his *Le Canada Français* (Paris and Montréal, 1960). Material in periodicals is concentrated in the *Revue de Géographie de Montréal* (formerly the *Revue Canadienne de Géographie*), the *Cahiers de Géographie de Québec* (see for example, No. 23 (1967) devoted to "Le Saint-Laurent") and *L'Actualité Economique*. On the origins of the French system, see R.C. Harris, *The Seigneurial System in Early Canada* (Madison, Wisc., and Québec, 1966). On other aspects of French and Québec settlement see L. Beauregard, "Le Peuplement du Richelieu," *Revue de Géographie de Montréal*, vol. xix (1965), 43–74; P. Bussières, "La Population de la Côte-Nord," *Cahiers de Géographie*, No. 14 (1963), 157–92 and No. 15 (1963–64), 41–93; and S. Rimbert, "L'Immigration Franco-Canadienne au Massachusetts," *Revue Canadienne de Géographie*, vol. viii (1954), 75–85.

On the economy of Québec there are B. Brouillette, "Les Régions géographiques et économiques. . ." *Cahiers de Géographie*, No. 6 (1959), 65–84, and M. Daneau, "Evolution Economique du Québec, 1950–1965," *L'Act Economique*, vol. xli (1966), 659–92. Agriculture is covered in a series of articles by P.B. Clibbon; see, for example, those in *Geographical Bulletin*, vol. vi (1964), 5–20; *Cahiers de Géographie*, No. 15 (1963–64), 5–39, and No. 19 (1966), 55–71. See also an interesting up-to-date study, Helen E. Parson, "An Investigation of the Changing Rural Economy of Gatineau County, Québec," *The Canadian Geographer*, vol. xxi (1977), 22–31. Forestry is dealt with by A. Bédard, "Forestry in Québec, Past, Present and Future," *Canadian Geographical Journal*, vol. lvii (1958), 36–49. The electric power company, Hydro-Québec, produces maps, information, and a periodical, all of them useful sources; see also W.J. McNaughton, "Bersimis: The Development of a River," *Canadian Geographical Journal*, vol. lx (1960), 115–35. As a commentary on Fig. 13-1 in the present text, see P. Biays, *Les Marges de L'Oekoumène dans l'Est du Canada* (Québec, 1964).

On the urban geography, there are M. Yeates, *Main Street: Windsor to Québec City* (Toronto, 1975) and the relevant sections of volume ii of G.A. Nader, *Cities of Canada* (Toronto, 1976).

On the urban geography of Montréal, see the *Revue de Géographie de Montréal*, vol. xxi (1967), no. 2 (entire number); J.I. Cooper, *Montréal: A Brief History* (Montréal and London, 1969); and P. Dagenais, "La Metropole du Canada: Montréal ou Toronto?" *Revue de Géographie de Montréal*, vol. xxiii (1969), 27–37. For Québec City, see P. Camu, "Le Paysage Urbain de Québec," *Geographical Bulletin*, No. 10 (1957), 5–22. For Ottawa, see A. Coleman, *The Planning Challenge of the Ottawa Area* (Ottawa, n.d.)

Chapter 14

The basic reference on this region has long been J.H. Garland, ed., *The North American Midwest* (New York, 1955), while G. Hutton's *Midwest at Noon* (London, 1945) is still worth reading. A more up-to-date treatment is J. Fraser Hart, "The Middle West," *Annals*, Assc. of Amer. Geographers, vol. lxii (1972), 258–82. The agricultural occupance of the Interior is considered by A.G. Bogue in *From Prairie to Corn Belt* (Chicago, 1963); by L. Atherton in *Mainstreet on the Middle Border* (Bloomington, Ind., 1954); by M.P. Conzen, *Frontier Farming in an Urban Shadow* (Madison, Wisc., 1971); and by J.E. Spencer and R.J. Horvath, "How does an Agricultural Region Originate?" (dealing with the Corn Belt), *Annals*, Assc. of Amer. Geographers, vol. liii (1963), 74–92. See also J.D. Wood, ed., *Perspectives on Landscape and Settlement in Nineteenth Century Ontario* (Toronto, 1975). Agricultural patterns were considerably clarified by four articles on land use and crop combinations by J.C. Weaver appearing in *Economic Geography*, vol. xxx (1954), 1–47, *Geographical Review*, vol. xliv (1954), 175–200, 560–72; vol. xlvi (1956), 536–65. The Corn Belt economy is considered by L.P. Hoag in "Location Determinants for Cash-Grain Farming in the Corn Belt," *Economic Geography*, vol. xxxviii (1962), 1–7, and J.J. Hidore, "The Relationship between Cash-Grain Farming and Landforms," *Economic Geography*, vol. xxxix (1963), 84–89. See also J. Fraser Hart, "Field Patterns in Indiana," *Geographical Review*, vol. lviii (1968), 450–71.

For the southern margin of the Agricultural Interior, see P.P. Karan, ed., *Kentucky: A Regional Geography* (Dubuque, Iowa, 1973). For the southwestern margin see the following in *Annals*, Assc. of Amer. Geographers: J.E. Collier, "Geographic Regions of Missouri," vol. xlv (1955), 368–92; E.W. Kersten, "Changing Economy and Landscape in a Missouri Ozarks Area," vol. xlviii (1958), 398–418; and E. Joan Miller, "The Ozark Culture Region . . ." vol.

lviii (1968), 51–77. For the Dairy Belt, L. Durand produced a whole series of studies, the most recent of which are in *Economic Geography*, vol. xxxi (1955), 301–20 and vol. xl (1964), 9–33. See also G.R. Lewthwaite, "Wisconsin Cheese and Farm Type," *Economic Geography*, vol. xl (1964), 95–112. On the occupance of the North Woods the states concerned—Wisconsin, Michigan, and Minnesota—have produced a large amount of materials; in the geographical literature there is M.E. McGaugh's *The Settlement of the Saginaw Basin*, Univ. of Chicago Research Paper No. 16 (1950); see also D. Kromm, "Sequences of Forest Utilization in Northern Michigan," *The Canadian Geographer*, vol. xii, 144–57, and L. Durand, "The West Shawano Upland of Wisconsin," *Annals*, Assc. of Amer. Geographers, vol. xxxiv (1944), 135–63.

Agriculture in southwestern Ontario can be studied in L.G. Reeds, "Agricultural Regions of Southern Ontario, 1880 and 1951," *Economic Geography*, vol. xxxv (1959), 219–27; R.G. Putnam, "Changes in Rural Land Use Patterns on the Central Lake Ontario Plain," *The Canadian Geographer*, vol. vi (1962), 60–68; and R.R. Krueger, "Changing Land Uses in the Niagara Fruit Belt," *Geographical Bulletin*, No. 14 (1960), 5–24. On the fringe of the area, see also E.B. MacDougall, "An Analysis of Recent Changes in the Number of Farms in the North Part of Central Ontario," *The Canadian Geographer*, vol. xiv (1970), 125–38.

Rural population is considered by R.G. Golledge and others in "Some Spatial Characteristics of Iowa's Dispersed Farm Population," *Economic Geography*, vol. xlii, 261–72; by J.F. Hart and N.E. Salisbury in "Population Change in Middle Western Villages," *Annals*, Assc. of Amer. Geographers, vol. lv, 140–60; and in "The Dying Villages and Some Notions about Urban Growth," *Economic Geography*, vol. xliv (1968), 343–49. See also W.E. Kiefer, "An Agricultural Settlement Complex in Indiana," *Annals*, Assc. of Amer. Geographers, vol. lxii (1972), 487–506.

On the industrial life of the region, particularly the heavy industry area, many of the published studies are now out-of-date. For the steel areas it is best to refer to K. Warren, *The American Steel Industry 1850–1970: A Geographical Interpretation* (Oxford, 1973), although the Pittsburgh Regional Planning Association's *Economic Study of the Pittsburgh Region* (3 vols., Pittsburgh, Pa., 1963–64) is still worth consulting. So, too, is J.E. Wrathall, "Recent Developments in the Ohio River Valley," *Geography*, vol. liv (1969), 419–29. For the Great Lakes cities in general, see H.M. Mayer, "Metropolitan Shorelines of the Great Lakes," *The Canadian Geographer*, vol. viii (1964), 197–202; other general references are A.F. Burghardt, "The Location of River Towns in the Central Lowland of the United States," *Annals*, Assc. of Amer. Geographers, vol. xlix (1959), 305–23, and also in the *Annals*, J.S. Adams, "Residential Structure of Midwestern Cities," vol. lx (1970), 37–62. This latter theme has been well explored recently, thanks to the work of H.M. Rose on Milwaukee and the following: D.R. Deskins, "Race, Residence and Work-Place in Detroit, 1880 to 1965," *Economic Geography*, vol. xlviii (1972), 79–94; W. Bunge, *Fitzgerald: A Geography of A Revolution* (Cambridge, Mass., and London, 1971); T. Gitlin, *Uptown: Poor Whites in Chicago* (New York, 1970), and A.H. Spear, *Black Chicago: The Making of a Negro Ghetto, 1890–1920* (Chicago, 1967). In the four volumes of *Contemporary Metropolitan America*, J.S. Adams, ed., already referred to, the studies of the cities of the Interior are to be found as follows: Chicago, vol. iii, 181–283; Cleveland, vol. iii, 109–79; Detroit, vol. iii, 285–354; Minneapolis–St. Paul, vol. iii, 355–423; Pittsburgh, vol. iii, 1–59; St. Louis, vol. iii, 61–107.

Probably no city in the world has been more thoroughly analyzed by geographers than Chicago, thanks primarily to the long series of the University of Chicago Research Papers and, more recently, the Northwestern University Studies in Geography. Reference should be made to both series. The most recent additions to this literature are I. Cutler's *Chicago: Metropolis of the Mid-Continent* (Chicago, 1973) and the two volumes of C.W. Condit, *Chicago* (Chicago, 1973 and 1974), covering the periods 1910–29 and 1930–70 respectively.

For studies of Ontario's urban and manufacturing centers, see J. Warkentin, "Southern

Ontario: A View from the West," *The Canadian Geographer*, vol. x (1966), 157–71; J. Spelt, *Urban Development in South-Central Ontario* (Toronto and Montréal, 1972); N. Pearson, "Conurbation Canada," *The Canadian Geographer*, vol. v (1961); 10–17; M. Yeates, *Main Street: Windsor to Québec City* (Toronto, 1975); and relevant sections of vol. ii of G.A. Nader, *Cities of Canada* (Toronto, 1976). D. Kerr and J. Spelt produced several articles on manufacturing in Toronto and its hinterland; they are in *Geographical Bulletin*, no. 10 (1957), 5–22, and in *The Canadian Geographer*, no. 12 (1958), 11–19 and no. 15 (1960), 12–25. See also D.F. Walker and J.H. Bates, eds., *Industrial Development in Southern Ontario* (Waterloo, Ont., 1974). Two of the University of Chicago Department of Geography Research Papers deal with aspects of Toronto's urban morphology; they are by J.W. Simmons (No. 104, 1966) and R.A. Murdie (No. 116, 1969). H. McDougall, "Toronto's Waterfront Plan," *Canadian Geographical Journal*, vol. lxxxiv (1972), 2–15, is relevant to the discussion in this chapter on the model of the Great Lakes city. Also of interest is C.F.J. Whebell, "Corridors: A Theory of Urban Systems," *Annals*, Assc. of Amer. Geographers, vol. lix (1969), 1–26.

Chapter 15

Like New England, Appalachia has been subjected to intensive regional temperature-taking ever since it was declared an invalid. Thus apart from H.M. Caudill's personal analysis of the problems in *Night Comes to the Cumberlands* (Boston and Toronto, 1962), *My Land is Dying* (New York, 1972), and *The Watches of the Night* (Boston and Toronto, 1976), there are T.R. Ford, ed., *The Southern Appalachian Region* (Lexington, Ky., 1962); M.J. Bowman and W.W. Haynes, *Resources and People in East Kentucky* (Baltimore, 1963); and R.C. Langman, *Appalachian Kentucky: An Exploited Region* (Toronto, 1971), together with the works referred to in the footnotes to this chapter, and a series of government reports, such as Nos. 69 and 73 in the U.S. Dept of Agriculture's *Agricultural Economics Report* series (both dated 1965).

Parts of N.M. Hansen, *Rural Poverty and the Urban Crisis* (Bloomington, Ind., 1970) are very relevant, and there is also J.D. Photiadis, ed., *Change in Rural Appalachia* (Philadelphia, 1971). Two good short references are W. Van Royan and S. Moryadas, "The Economic Basis of Appalachia's Problems," *Tijds. voor econ. en soc. geog.*, 57 jaarg. (1966), 185–93, and R.C. Estall, "Appalachian State: West Virginia as a Case Study in the Appalachian Regional Development Problem," *Geography*, vol. liii (1968), 1–24. The Appalachian Regional Commission reports periodically, and the U.S. Government Printing Office, Washington, D.C., publishes the reports. The Appalachian road program was reviewed by J.M. Munro, "Planning the Appalachian Development Highway System: Some Critical Questions," *Land Economics*, vol. xlv (1969), 149–61. The *Southeastern Geographer* has some useful studies of the region: see, for example, J.E. Green, "The Problem of Reclamation of Derelict Land after Coal Strip Mining in Appalachia," in vol. ix (1969), 36–47, or N.G. Lineback, "Low-Wage Industrialization and Town Size in Rural Appalachia," vol. xii (1972), 1–13. For another aspect see J. Fraser Hart, "Land Rotation in Appalachia," *Geographical Review*, vol. lxvii (1977), 148–66.

On the T.V.A. see D. Lilienthal, *TVA: Democracy on the March* (20th anniv. ed., New York, 1953) which, apart from giving a founder-member's views on the T.V.A., contains a large bibliography; G.R. Clapp, *The T.V.A.: An Approach to the Development of a Region* (Chicago, 1955), and J.R. Moore, ed., *The Economic Impact of T.V.A.* (Knoxville, Tenn., 1967).

Chapter 16

A number of studies of the South were carried out in the 1930s, in the days of its worst poverty, but the new picture has been drawn successively by J.M. Maclachlan and J.S. Floyd, *This Changing South* (Gainesville, Fla., 1956); J.G. Maddox and others, *The Advancing South* (New York, 1967); T.D. Clark, *The Emerging*

South (2nd ed., New York, 1968), and T.H. Naylor and J. Clotfelter, *Strategies for Change in the South* (Chapel Hill, N.C., 1975).

Since it first appeared in the 1960s, *Southeastern Geographer* has become a major source of regional analysis and information: geographers had previously had to rely mainly on the *Southern Economic Journal*. The outstanding work on southern agriculture has been done by M.C. Prunty; see his articles, for example, in *Geographical Review*, vol. xlii (1952), 439–61; vol. xlv (1955), 459–91; and vol. liii (1963), 1–21; also (with C.S. Aiken) in the *Annals*, Assc. of Amer. Geographers, vol. lxii (1972), 283–306, and (with W.T. Mealor) in vol. lxvi (1976), 360–76. Change was also charted by J.L. Fulmer, *Agricultural Progress in the Cotton Belt since 1920* (Chapel Hill, N.C., 1950); J.H. Street, *New Revolution in the Cotton Economy* (Chapel Hill, N.C., 1957); and W. Range, *A Century of Georgia Agriculture, 1850–1950* (Athens, Ga., 1954). Fisheries off the southern coasts are dealt with by H.R. Padgett, "The Sea Fisheries of the Southern United States," *Geographical Review*, vol. liii (1963), 22–39.

The rise of industrial and urban centers can be traced in R.R. Vance and N.J. Demerath, *The Urban South* (Chapel Hill, N.C., 1955), T.A. Hartshorn, "The Spatial Structure of Socio-Economic Development in the Southeast, 1950–1960," *Geographical Review*, vol. lxi (1971), 265–83; R.E. Lonsdale and C.E. Browning, "Rural-Urban Locational Preferences of Southern Manufactures," *Annals*, Assc. of Amer. Geographers, vol. lxi (1971), 255–68; and L.F. Wheat, *Urban Growth in the Nonmetropolitan South* (Lexington, Mass. and Toronto, 1976). Urbanization in the Piedmont area is analyzed in C.R. Hoyes, *The Dispersed City: The Case of Piedmont, North Carolina*, Univ. of Chicago Research Paper No. 173 (1976), as well as in R.E. Lonsdale, "Two North Carolina Commuting Patterns," *Economic Geography*, vol. xlii (1966), 114–38, and the *Metrolina Atlas*, eds., J.W. Clay and D.M. Orr, Jr., (Chapel Hill, N.C., 1972). In *Contemporary Metropolitan America*, ed. J.S. Adams (Cambridge, Mass., 1976), the section on Atlanta is in vol. iv, 151–225.

Chapter 17

Development in this region has been very rapid, and the geographical literature has not kept up. However, on the agriculture of the Humid Gulf area there are S.H. Bederman, "The Citrus Fruit Industry in Louisiana," *Southeastern Geographer*, vol. i (1961), 1–8; W.C. Found, "The Relation of the Distribution of Citrus to Soil Type and Winter Temperature," *The Canadian Geographer*, vol. ix (1965), 63–73; W.T. Mealor and M.C. Prunty, "Open-Range Ranching in Southern Florida," *Annals*, Assc. of Amer. Geographers, vol. lxvi (1976), 360–76, and also in the *Annals*, G.A. Stokes, "Lumbering and Western Louisiana Landscapes," vol. xlvii (1957), 250–66. Fishing along the coast is covered in the *Geographical Review* by H.R. Padgett, "The Sea Fisheries of the Southern United States," vol. liii (1963), 22–39, and G.W. Schlesselman, "Gulf Coast Oyster Industry of the United States," vol. xlv (1955), 531–41. Some impression of southeastern port traffic can be obtained from J.B. Kenyon, "Land Use Admixture in the Built-Up Urban Waterfront" (of southern ports), *Economic Geography*, vol. xliv (1968), 152–77. On the issue of preservation of the Everglades and maintenance of the wildlife there, see R.F. Dasmann, *No Further Retreat: The Fight to Save Florida* (New York, 1971); W.R. McCluney, *The Environmental Destruction of Southern Florida* (Miami, 1971); and L.J. Carter, *The Florida Experience: Land and Water Policy in a Growth State* (Baltimore, 1974).

Texas was for a long while neglected by geographers, but this situation has now been rectified, at least so far as its historical geography is concerned. T.G. Jordan has made this field his own; see his *German Seed in Texas Soil* (Austin, 1966), and the series of his papers in the *Annals*, Assc. of Amer. Geographers, vol. lvii (1967), 667–90, and vol. lx (1970), 404–5, 409–27; in the *Geographical Review*, vol. lix (1969), 83–103; in *Economic Geography*, vol. xlv (1969), 63–87. A more general work on the same theme is D.W. Meinig's fine *Imperial Texas* (Austin, Tex., 1969); see also T.L. Miller, *The Public Lands of Texas, 1519–1970* (Norman, Okla., 1972).

General coverage is offered by W.T. Chambers and L. Kennamer, *Texans and Their Land* (Austin, Tex., 1963). On urban growth, see R.L. Martin, *The City Moves West: Economic and Industrial Growth in Central West Texas* (Austin, Tex., 1969) and two recent studies of Houston—D. McComb, *Houston, The Bayou City* (Austin, Tex., 1969), and G. Fuermann, *Houston: The Once and Future City* (New York, 1971). In *Contemporary Metropolitan America*, ed. J.S. Adams, New Orleans is dealt with in vol. ii, 97–216; Dallas–Fort Worth in vol. iv, 1–39; Miami in vol. iv, 41–106; and Houston in vol. iv, 107–49.

Chapter 18

Any reading list on this region must begin with W.P. Webb's classic *The Great Plains* (Boston, 1931). Of a somewhat similar character is J.C. Malin's *The Grassland of North America* (Gloucester, Mass., ed. of 1967), while the best recent short reference is undoubtedly E. Cotton Mather, "The American Great Plains" *Annals*, Assc. of Amer. Geographers, vol. lxii (1972), 237–57. The *Great Plains Journal* and the *Journal of the West* have recently come into being as useful sources on the region. For the physical background, see the references to Chapter 1 and also J.R. Borchert, "The Climate of the Central North American Grassland," *Annals*, Assc. of Amer. Geographers, vol. xl (1950), 1–39, and "The Dust Bowl in the 1970s," vol. lxi (1971), 1–22; A.H. Doerr and S.M. Sutherland, "Humid and Dry Cycles in Oklahoma in the Period 1930–1960," *Great Plains Journal*, vol. v (1966), 84–94; M.P. Lawson and Others, *Nebraska Droughts*, Univ. of Nebraska, Dept. of Geography Occasional Papers No. 1 (1972); and L. Hewes and A.C. Schmiedling, "Risk in the Central Great Plains: Patterns of Wheat Failure in Nebraska, 1931–1952," *Geographical Review*, vol. xlvi (1956), 375–87. At the same time the *perception* of the hazards created by the Plains environment has been studied; see, for example, G.M. Lewis's articles on the concept of the Great American Desert in the Institute of British Geographers, *Transactions No. 30* (1962), 75–90 and *Annals*, Assc. of Amer. Geogra-

phers, vol. lvi (1966), 33–51; see also T.F. Saarinen, *Perception of the Drought Hazard of the Great Plains*, Univ. of Chicago Dept. of Geography Research Paper No. 106 (1966); W. and J. Kollmorgen, "Landscape Meteorology in the Plains Area," *Annals*, Assc. of Amer. Geographers, vol. lxiii (1973), 424–41, and from another point of view, D.M. Emmons, *Garden in the Grasslands: Boomer Literature of the Central Great Plains* (Lincoln, Neb., 1971). This last work is published by the University of Nebraska Press, and any bibliography of the Great Plains would be incomplete without tribute paid to the publishing activity of the state university presses on the Plains, especially those of the Universities of Nebraska and Oklahoma. In the same context many of the most recent studies of the Great Plains have been published as papers in symposia on the region planned by these same universities: it is in this way that B.W. Blouet and M.P. Lawson have produced *Images of the Plains: The Role of Human Nature in Settlement* (Lincoln, Neb., 1975).

Land use in the Spring Wheat Belt of the United States was mapped by J.C. Weaver in "The County as a Spatial Average in Agricultural Geography," *Geographical Review*, vol. xlvi (1956), 536–65, while on the grazing areas a voluminous literature includes useful sections of *Grass*, the Department of Agriculture's 1948 Yearbook (Washington, D.C.); E.E. Dale's *The Range Cattle Industry* (Norman, Okla., 1960); and numerous articles in *Journal of Farm Economics*, as well as items listed under Chapter 19. Two localized studies of land use are L. Hewes, "A Traverse Across Kit Carson County, Colorado," *Economic Geography*, vol. xxxix (1963), 332–40, and A.H. Doerr and J.W. Morris, "The Oklahoma Panhandle—A Cross Section of the Southern High Plains," *Economic Geography*, vol. xxxvi (1960), 70–88. See also J.C. Malin's "The Adaptation of the Agricultural System to Sub-Humid Environment," *Agricultural History*, vol. x (1936), 118–41, and J. Hudson, "Two Dakota Homestead Frontiers," *Annals*, Assc. of Amer. Geographers, vol. lxiii (1973), 442–62.

There are a number of references dealing more especially with the social consequences of changing farming patterns on the Plains, e.g., C.D. Kraenzel, *The Great Plains in Transition* (Norman, Okla., 1955); L.D. Loftsgard and S.W. Voelker, "Changing Rural Life in the Great Plains," *Journal of Farm Economics,* vol. xlv (1963), 1110–18; O.D. Duncan, "Social Adjustments in Great Plains Agriculture," *Great Plains Journal,* vol. iii (1963), 1–8; H.W. Ottoson, ed., *Land and People in the Northern Plains Transition Area* (Lincoln, Neb., 1966); M.L. Szabo, "Characteristics of Non-Resident Farm Operators on the Canadian Prairies," *Geographical Bulletin,* vol. viii (1966), 279–303; W.M. Kollmorgen and G.F. Jenks, "Suitcase Farming in Sully County, South Dakota," *Annals, Assc. of Amer. Geographers,* vol. xlviii (1958), 27–40, and "Sidewalk Farming in Toole County, Montana, and Traill County, North Dakota," *Annals,* vol. xlviii (1958), 209–31, and I. Sotton, "Land Tenure in the West," *Journal of the West,* vol. ix (1970), 1–23. L. Hewes's *The Suitcase Farming Frontier* (Lincoln, Neb., 1973) brought together some of the results of Hewes's long involvement as a geographer with this region; no one has kept a closer eye on developments.

On group settlement on the Plains see J. Warkentin, "Mennonite Agricultural Settlements of Southern Manitoba," *Geographical Review,* vol. xlix (1959), 342–68 and, more specifically, P. Sawka, "The Hutterian Way of Life," *Canadian Geographical Journal,* vol. lxxvii (1968), 126–31, or W.G. Laatsch, "Hutterite Colonization in Alberta," *Journal of Geography,* vol. lxx (1971), 347–59.

On the Missouri Valley and its development lively opinions were expressed by R. Terral, *The Missouri Valley* (New Haven, Conn., 1947) and R.G. Baumhoff, *The Dammed Missouri Valley* (New York, 1951); see also H.C. Hart, *The Dark Missouri* (Madison, Wisc., 1957), and J.R. Ferrell, "Water in the Missouri Valley: The Inter-Agency Committee Concept at Mid-Century," *Journal of the West,* vol. vii (1968), 96–105. On U.S.–Canadian relations in the area see P.F. Sharp's various papers, beginning with his "The Northern Great Plains," *Missouri Valley Historical Review,* vol. xxxix (1952), 61–76; others of them are mentioned in the footnotes to the chapter.

For the Canadian Prairies, the physical setting and the story of settlement are both covered by vols. i and ii of the great *Canadian Frontiers of Settlement* series, W.A. Mackintosh and W.L.G. Joerg, eds. (Toronto, 1934 and 1938). A shorter reference is J.L. Tyman, *By Section, Township and Range: Studies in Prairie Settlement* (Brandon, Man., 1972). See also J.R. Villmow, "The Nature and Origins of the Canadian Dry Belt," *Annals, Assc. of Amer. Geographers,* vol. xlvi, 211–32, and F.B. Watts, "The Natural Vegetation of the Southern Great Plains of Canada," *Geographical Bulletin,* No. 14 (1960), 25–43. On Prairie settlement, see also I.M. Spry, "Captain John Palliser and the Exploration of Western Canada," *Geographical Journal,* vol. cxxv (1959), 149–84, or her book, *The Palliser Expedition* (Toronto, 1963); J.G. Nelson, "Man and Landscape in the Western Plains of Canada," *The Canadian Geographer,* vol. xi (1967), 251–64; and B.G. Vanderhill's several papers on the subject, such as those in *Economic Geography,* vol. xxxv (1959), 259–68, and vol. xxxviii (1962), 270–77. On the problems of erosion and conservation on the Prairies, see J.H. Gray, *Men Against The Desert* (Saskatoon, Sask., 1967) and the Canadian Department of Agriculture's PFRA: *The Story of Conservation on the Prairies* (Ottawa, 1961).

Chapter 19

The advance of settlement into the West is described in several excellent works, for example, R.A. Billington, *Westward Expansion* (New York, 1949); T.D. Clark, *Frontier America: The Story of the Westward Movement* (New York, 1959); and J.A. Hawgood, *The American West* (London, 1967). Problems of public policy are covered by R.M. Robbins, *Our Landed Heritage: The Public Domain* (Princeton, N.J., 1942); H.W. Ottoson, ed., *Land Use Policy and Problems in the United States* (Lincoln, Neb., 1963); S.T. Dana, *Forest and Range Policy* (New York, 1956); V.R. Carstensen, *The Public Lands* (Madison, Wisc., 1963); and the numerous works of Marion Clawson: see also the readings on Chapter 4. There are several books on the livestock industry, for example, M.H. Saunderson,

Western Stock Ranching (Minneapolis, Minn., 1950); M. Clawson, *The Western Range Livestock Industry* (New York, 1950); and E.E. Dale, *The Range Cattle Industry* (Norman, Okla., 1960). The *Journal of the West* published an entire number on "Ranching in the West," vol. xiv, no. 3 (July 1975), 1–132. The political and administrative problems connected with the industry are covered by P.O. Foss, *Politics and Grass* (Seattle, 1960); by W. Calef, *Private Grazing and Public Lands* (Chicago, 1960), and by W. Voigt, Jr., *Public Grazing Lands: Use and Misuse by Industry and Government* (New Brunswick, N.J., 1976). On the other hand, the ecological problems are dealt with by L. Ellison, "The Influence of Grazing on Plant Succession of Rangelands," *Botanical Review*, vol. xxvi (1960), 1–78; on this subject, see also the references to Chapter 20.

The relationship of irrigation agriculture to the region's economy might be studied by starting with W.E. Smythe, *The Conquest of Arid America* (New York, 1899; reissued in Seattle, 1969), one of the great "booster" documents of the irrigation movement, and then moving on to realistic modern appraisals in V.W. Ruttan, *The Economic Demand for Irrigated Acreage* (Baltimore, 1965), for example; there is also an interesting series of papers entitled "Irrigation, Conservation and Reclamation," A.B. Sageser, ed., in *Journal of the West*, vol. vii (1968), 1–105. A valuable but perhaps easily overlooked source on western land and water is the series of U.S. Geological Survey Professional Papers, a number of which deal with human as well as physical aspects of the West. See, for example, M.C. Rabbitt and others, *The Colorado River Region and John Wesley Powell*, U.S.G.S. Prof. Paper 669 (Washington, D.C., 1969.)

There is little up-to-date work on mining or manufacturing by geographers. A selection of papers on specific aspects of the West (where there is a huge tourist or popular literature) in recent geographical publications is: D.W. Meinig, "American Wests: Preface to a Geographical Introduction," *Annals*, Assc. of Amer. Geographers, vol. lxii (1972) and "The Mormon Culture Region," *Annals*, vol. lv (1965), 191–200; R. Durrenberger, "The Colorado Plateau,"

Annals, vol. lxii (1972), 211–36; and G.D. Weaver, "Nevada's Federal Lands," *Annals*, vol. lix (1969), 27–49. See also W.E. Hollon, *The Great American Desert, Then and Now* (New York, 1966). On the idea of wilderness see R. Nash, *Wilderness and the American Mind* (New Haven, Conn., 1967 and revisions).

Chapter 20

Textbooks of regional geography covering the Southwest have been C.M. Zierer, ed., *California and the Southwest* (New York, 1956) and H.S. Zim, *The American Southwest* (New York, 1955), while the region's historical geography is traced by D.W. Meinig, *Southwest: Three Peoples in Geographical Change, 1600–1970* (New York, 1971) and the general historical background by O.B. Faulk, *Land of Many Frontiers: A History of the American Southwest* (New York, 1968) or O.L. Jones, ed., "The Spanish Borderlands," *Journal of the West*, vol. viii (1969), 1–142. See also R.L. Nostrand, "The Hispanic-American Borderland: Delimitation of an American Culture Region," *Annals*, Assc. of Amer. Geographers, vol. lx (1970), 638–61 and J.F. Bannon, *The Spanish Borderlands Frontier, 1513–1821* (Albuquerque, 1974).

The climate of the region is described by R.L. Ives, "Climate of the Sonoran Desert Region," *Annals*, Assc. of Amer. Geographers, vol. xxxix (1949), 143–82, and hydrology by a number of the U.S. Geological Survey's Professional Papers; see, for example, A.G. Hely, *Lower Colorado River Water Supply—Its Magnitude and Distribution*, (Paper 486-D, Washington, D.C., 1969); by J. Humlum, who gives details of both Arizona and California projects in *Water Development and Water Planning in the Southwestern United States* (Aarhus, Denmark, 1969); by N. Hundley, Jr., in his two books, *Dividing the Waters* (Berkeley, 1966) and *Water and the West* (Berkeley, 1975); and by J.C. Day, *Managing the Lower Rio Grande*, Univ. of Chicago Dept. of Geography Research Paper No. 125 (1970). On the related problems of overgrazing, erosion, and conservation, see D.R. Harris, "Recent Plant Invasions in the Arid and Semi-Arid Southwest of the United States," *Annals*, Assc.

of Amer. Geographers, vol. lvi (1966), 408–22; W.M. Denevan, "Livestock Numbers in Nineteenth-Century New Mexico, and the Problem of Gullying," *Annals*, vol. lvii (1967), 691–703; L.S. Fonaroff, "Conservation and Stock Reduction on the Navajo Tribal Range," *Geographical Review*, vol. liii (1963), 200–223; and I.A. Campbell, "Climate and Overgrazing on the Shonto Plateau, Arizona," *Professional Geographer, vol. xxii (1970), 132–41.*

Recent works on Indian life in the Southwest include J.U. Terrell, *The Navajos* (New York, 1970) and E.G. McIntire, "Changing Patterns of Hopi Indian Settlement," *Annals*, Assc. of Amer. Geographers, vol. lxi (1971), 510–21; see also the readings for Chapter 2. There is not a great deal to recommend on mining and manufacture, apart from T.L. McKnight, *Manufacturing in Arizona* (Cambridge, Mass., 1962). The best source on Arizona's economic development is the *Arizona Review*. For New Mexico the *New Mexico Historical Review* contains a great deal that is of contemporary interest.

Chapter 21

Textbooks on the geography of California are numerous: arranged in order of appearance, a short list runs as follows: N.N. Dodge and H.S. Zim, *The American Southwest* (New York, 1955); C.M. Zierer, ed., *California and the Southwest* (New York, 1956); P.F. Griffin and R.N. Young, *California, The New Empire State* (San Francisco, 1959); D.W. Lantis and others, *California: Land of Contrast* (Belmont, Calif., 1963); D.N. Hartman, *California and Man* (Dubuque, Iowa, 1964); and R. Durrenberger, *California: The Last Frontier* (New York, 1969), while the physical features are surveyed in G.B. Oakeshott, *California's Changing Landscapes* (New York, 1971). For other materials there are *The California Geographer* and the *Yearbook* of the Association of Pacific Coast Geographers among the periodicals.

The climate of California is dealt with by R.J. Russell, "Climates of California," *University of California Publications in Geography*, vol. ii (1919–29), 73–84; J.W. James, "A Modified Köppen Classification of California's Cli-

mates," *The California Geographer*, vol. vii (1966), 1–12; C.P. Patton, "Climatology of Summer Fogs in the San Francisco Bay Area," *Univ. of California Pub. in Geography*, vol. x (1956), 113–200, and J.W. Reith, "Los Angeles Smog," *Yearbook*, Assc. of Pacific Coast Geographers, vol. xiii (1951), 24–32. For the desert areas there are E.C. Jaeger and others, *The Californian Deserts* (Palo Alto, Calif., 1955) and W.S. Lee, *The Great California Deserts* (New York, 1962).

Stages in settlement history can be traced in R.L. Gentilcore, "Missions and Mission Lands of Alta California," *Annals*, Assc. of Amer. Geographers, vol. li (1961), 46–72, and S.J. Jones, "The Gold Country of the Sierra Nevada in California," Institute of British Geographers, *Transactions No. 15* (1949), 113–39.

On population growth and the appeal of California, see E.L. Ullman, "Amenities as a Factor in Regional Growth," *Geographical Review*, vol. xliv (1954), 119–32; O.O. Winter, "The Use of Climate as a Means of Promoting Migration to Southern California," *Missouri Valley Historical Review*, vol. xxxiii (1946–7), 411–24; H.F. Gregor, "Spatial Disharmonies in California's Population Growth," *Geographical Review*, vol. liii (1963), 100–22; and J.E. Vance, Jr., "California and the Search for the Ideal," *Annals*, Assc. of Amer. Geographers, vol. lxii (1972), 185–210. For another view, also in the *Annals*, see K. Thompson's "Insalubrious California: Perception and Reality," vol. lix (1969), 50–64, and "Irrigation as a Menace to Health in California: A Nineteenth-Century View," *Geographical Review*, vol. lix (1969), 195–214.

On California's water problems the overall sources are J. Humlum, *Water Development and Water Planning in the Southwestern United States* (Aarhus, Denmark, 1969), and the two books by N. Hundley, Jr., *Dividing the Waters* (Berkeley, 1966) and *Water and the West* (Berkeley, 1975). Detail is supplied by J.S. Bain, R.E. Caves and J. Margolis, *Northern California's Water Industry* (Baltimore, 1966); H.F. Gregor, "The Southern California Water Problem in the Oxnard Area," *Geographical Review*, vol. xlii (1952), 16–36; E. Eiselen, "The Central Valley Project, 1947," *Economic Geography*, vol.

xxiii (1947), 22–31; M.E. Marts, "When Can California Join the Union?" *Yearbook*, Assc. of Pacific Coast Geographers, vol. xxiii (1961), 7–12; F. Quinn, "Water Transfers: Must the West be Won Again?" *Geographical Review*, vol. lviii (1968), 108–32; and J.F. Davis, "Some Recent Developments in the Search for Solutions to California's Water Supply Problems," *Tijds. voor econ. en soc. geog.*, 62 jaarg., (1971), 95–103.

Agriculture in California received a basic treatment in C.B. Hutchison, ed., *California Agriculture* (Berkeley, 1946), but since then a very large number of studies have been made, both by the state's agricultural services (lists and bibliography from the University of California Agricultural Experiment Station at Davis) and by geographers; among the latter, one—H.F. Gregor—has produced virtually a whole library by himself. It is best to seek further bibliographic guidance than the present list can provide, to find one's way through these large quantities of materials.

References to the San Francisco Bay area are M. Scott, *The San Francisco Bay Area: A Metropolis in Perspective* (Berkeley, 1959); R.N. Young and P.C. Griffin, "Recent Land-Use Changes in the San Francisco Bay Area," *Geographical Review*, vol. xlvii (1957), 396–405; and C.L. White and H.M. Forde, "The Unorthodox San Francisco Bay Area Electronics Industry," *Journal of Geography*, vol. lix (1960), 251–58. The Institute of Governmental Studies at the Univ. of California, Berkeley, has also published a series of studies of the metropolitan area (the F.K. Lane project). *Contemporary Metropolitan America*, ed. J.S. Adams (Cambridge, Mass., 1976) deals with San Francisco in vol. ii, 217–307 and with Los Angeles in vol. iv, 227–95.

On southern California, reading might start with the symposium, W.L. Thomas, ed., on "Man, Time and Space in Southern California," in *Annals*, Assc. of Amer. Geographers, vol. xlix (1959), pt. 2, 1–120. The *Journal of the West* then carried "The Story of Los Angeles," by Margaret Romer, in 8 sections in volumes i–iii (1962–64). This can be supplemented by R.M. Fogelson's *The Fragmented Metropolis: Los Angeles, 1850–1930* (Cambridge, Mass., 1967), which

was followed by R.D. Batman's "Orange County, California: A Comprehensive History," in the *Journal of the West*, vol. iv (1965). For San Diego, in turn, there is a 6-volume history published in the city between 1960 and 1967. See also R. Steiner, "Reserved Lands and the Supply of Space for the Southern California Metropolis," *Geographical Review*, vol. lvi (1966), 344–62, and R.E. Preston, "Urban Development in Southern California between 1940 and 1965," *Tijds. voor econ. en soc. geog.*, 58 jaarg., (1967) 237–54.

Chapter 22

The Pacific Northwest was at one time extremely well covered by geographical studies, thanks largely to the efforts of one or two men, namely, O.W. Freeman and W.A. Rockie, but much of this work is now out-of-date. However, the Agricultural Extension Service at Pullman, Washington, is one of the most active institutions of its kind in producing studies of regional agriculture, and the Columbia Basin Project has been the occasion of a number of studies; see, for example, the Bureau of Reclamation's *The Story of the Columbia Basin Project* (Washington, D.C., 1964) and G. Machinko, "The Columbia Basin Project: Expectations, Realizations, Implications," *Geographical Review*, vol. liii (1963), 185–99. Irrigation agriculture in the Willamette Valley is dealt with by R.M. Highsmith (another prolific author of regional studies) in *Geographical Review*, vol. xlvi (1956), 98–110. In regional development it is necessary to bear in mind the international character of the Columbia Basin; see on this point W.R.D. Sewell, "The Columbia River Treaty: Some Lessons and Implications," *The Canadian Geographer*, vol. x (1966), 145–56; J.V. Krutilla, *The Columbia River Treaty* (Baltimore, 1967); and D. Waterfield, *Continental Waterboy: The Columbia River Controversy* (Toronto, 1970).

On forestry within the region see W.J. Mead, "The Forest Products Economy of the Pacific Northwest," *Land Economics*, vol. xxxii (1956), 127–33, and R.L. Monahan, "Locational

Changes in the Forest Products Industries of the Pacific Northwest," *Yearbook*, Assc. of Pacific Coast Geographers, vol. xxviii (1966), 29–40. Fisheries are covered in G.W. Hewes, "The Fisheries of Northwestern North America," *Economic Geography*, vol. xxviii, 66–73, and M.E. Marts and W.R.D. Sewell, "The Conflict between Fish and Power Resources in the Pacific Northwest," *Annals*, Assc. of Amer. Geographers, vol. 1 (1960), 42–50. A selection of papers on trade and transport is J.N. Tattershall, "Exports and Economic Growth: The Pacific Northwest, 1880–1960," Regional Science Assc., *Papers*, vol. ix (1962), 215–34; E.L. Ullman, "Rivers as Regional Bonds: The Columbia-Snake Example," *Geographical Review*, vol. xli (1951), 210–25; and W.R. Siddall, "Seattle: Regional Capital of Alaska," *Annals*, Assc. of Amer. Geographers, vol. xlvii (1957), 277–84. On the settlement of the Columbia Basin the basic reference is D.W. Meinig, *The Great Columbia Plain: A Historical Geography, 1805–1910* (Seattle, Wash., 1968); see also his "A Comparative Historical Geography of Two Railnets: Columbia Basin and South Australia," *Annals*, Assc. of Amer. Geographers, vol. lii (1962), 394–413. In *Contemporary Metropolitan America*, ed. J.S. Adams (Cambridge, Mass., 1976), Seattle is dealt with in vol. iii, 425–500. Dealing with British Columbia specifically there are, apart from the volume on the province (edited by J.L. Robinson) in the series, *Studies in Canadian Geography* (Toronto, 1972), D. Kerr, "The Physical Basis of Agriculture in British Columbia," *Economic Geography*, vol. xxviii (1952), 229–39; T.R. Weir, *Ranching in the Southern Interior Plateau of British Columbia* (Ottawa, 1964); R.R. Krueger, "The Physical Basis of the Orchard Industry of British Columbia," *Geographical Bulletin*, no. 20 (1963), 5–38; and R. Hayter, "Corporate Strategies and Industrial Change in the Canadian Forest Product Industries," *Geographical Review*, vol. lxvi (1976), 209–28. On Vancouver, there is P.D. McGovern, "Industrial Development in the Vancouver Area," *Economic Geography*, vol. xxxvii (1961), 189–206. A general treatment of the city is found in W.G. Hardwick, *Vancouver* (Toronto, 1974).

Chapter 23

A number of more or less popular studies of the Northlands have been made between the publication dates of the two basic references— G.H.T. Kimble and D. Good, eds., *Geography of the Northlands* (New York, 1955) and T. Armstrong, G. Rogers and G. Rowley, *The Circumpolar North: A Political and Economic Geography of the Arctic and Sub-Arctic* (London, 1978). Somewhere in between the two categories are R.A.J. Phillips, *Canada's North* (New York, 1967) or J.K. Naysmith's *Canada North— Man and the Land*, published by the Department of Indian Affairs and Northern Development (Ottawa, 1971) or the short statement by W.C. Wonders, "Our Northward Course," *The Canadian Geographer*, vol. vi (1962), 96–105. Wonders has also edited the volume on the North in the series of *Studies in Canadian Geography* (Toronto, 1972). See also R.J.E. Brown, *Permafrost in Canada* (Toronto, 1970). On this region an interesting periodical is *The Musk-Ox: A Journal on the North*, published by the Institute for Northern Studies of the University of Saskatchewan.

Mining developments have been regularly reported by the *Canadian Geographical Journal*; there is also E.W. Miller, "Mineral Regionalism of the Canadian Shield," *The Canadian Geographer*, No. 13 (1959), 17–30 and I.M. Robinson, *New Industrial Towns on Canada's Resource Frontier*, Univ. of Chicago Dept. of Geography Research Paper No. 73 (1962). A scheme for zoning the pay of northern workers is put forward by L-E. Hamelin, "Un Système zonal de Primes pour les Travailleurs du Nord," *Cahiers de Géographie de Québec*, vol. xxxiii (1970), 309–28 and vol. xxxiv (1971), 5–27. On agriculture and its problems see P. Biays, "Problèmes de l'Agriculture marginale dans la zone pionnière de l'Est du Canada," *Cahiers de Géographie*, No. 16 (1964), 219–29, and J.R. Shortridge, "The Collapse of Frontier Farming in Alaska," *Annals*, Assc. of Amer. Geographers, vol. lxvi (1976), 583–604.

Alaska's achievement of statehood was accompanied by publication of numerous general and specific studies. Among the former there have been G.W. Rogers, *The Future of Alaska: The Economic Consequences of Statehood* (Oxford, 1962) and B. Cooper, *Alaska: The Last Frontier* (London, 1972), while the discovery of oil on the North Slope produced M.A. Adelman et al., *Alaskan Oil: Costs and Supply* (New York, 1971). Among the shorter studies see for example K.H. Stone, "Populating Alaska: The United States Phase," *Geographical Review*, vol. xlii (1952), 384–404; K.E. Francis, "Outpost Agriculture: The Case of Alaska," *Geographical Review*, vol. lvii (1967), 496–505; and W.G. Hardwick, "Changing Corridors to Alaska," *Journal of Geography*, vol. lxi (1962), 49–57. On the physical features of Alaska see C. Wahrhaftig, *Physiographic Divisions of Alaska*, U.S.G.S. Prof. Paper 482 (Washington, D.C., 1965) and H.A. Johnson and H.T. Jorgenson, *The Land Resources of Alaska* (New York, 1963).

Credits for Maps and Diagrams

1-4 From *The National Atlas of the U.S.A.*, 1970, p. 76.

1-5 After H.E. Wright and D.G. Frey, eds., *The Quaternary of The United States*, Princeton Univ. Press, 1965, p. 266, by permission.

1-10 After a map published periodically in the *Canada Yearbook*.

2-2 Data from "Population Estimates by Race, for States: July 1, 1973 and 1975," no. 67, *Current Population Reports*, U.S. Bureau of the Census, Feb. 1978.

2-3 From J.S. Adams, ed., *Contemporary Metropolitan America*, Ballinger, 1976, vol. 2, p. 266; vol. 3, p. 133; vol. 4, p. 126, by permission.

2-5 Data from "Annual Estimates of the Population of States, July 1, 1970 to 1977," no. 727, *Current Population Reports*, U.S. Bureau of the Census, July 1978.

2-6 From D.B. Longrake and W.W. Nichols, "Sunshine and Shadows in Metropolitan Miami," in J.S. Adams, ed., *Contemporary Metropolitan America*, Ballinger, 1976, vol. 4, p. 103, by permission.

3-2 After *Atlas of the Greater Lake Superior Region*, Inst. for Environmental Studies, Madison, Fig. 6-2.

4-1 From H.B. Johnson, *Order upon the Land*, Oxford Univ. Press, N.Y., 1976, Fig. 4-3.

4-5 Data courtesy Ralph M. Parsons Co.

5-2 From S. Daggett and J.P. Carter, *The Structure of Transcontinental Railroad Rates*, Univ. of Calif. Press, 1947.

6-2 From *A Century of Wisconsin Agriculture*, Wisc. Crop and Livestock Reporting Service, Bull. 290, 1948.

6-4 From *Irrigation Agriculture in the West*, U.S. Dept. of Agriculture Misc. Pub. 670, 1948, pp. 25 and 27.

6-5 From M. Clawson, *America's Land and Its Uses*, Johns Hopkins for Resources for the Future, Baltimore, 1972, Fig. 13.

6-6 After J.F. Hart, *The Look of the Land*, Prentice-Hall, Englewood Cliffs, N.J., 1975.

7-3 After H.W. Hoots, U.S. Geological Survey Prof. Paper 165, 1930, pl. 16.

9-3 From B.J.L. Berry, "The Geography of the United States in the Year 2000," in *Transactions*, No. 51, Inst. of British Geographers, 1970, Fig. 3, by permission.

11-1 From G.K. Lewis, "Population Change in Northern New England," *Annals*, Assc. of Amer. Geographers, vol. lxii, 1972, Fig. 2, by permission.

11-2 From *The National Atlas of the U.S.A.*, 1970.

12-2 Railroad data from *The National Atlas of Canada*, 4th ed., 1974.

13-1 From M. Bélanger, "Le Québec Rural," in F. Gronier, ed., *Etudes sur la Géographie du Canada: Québec*, © Univ. of Toronto Press, 1972, by permission, Fig. 3-4.

14-4 Map *A* after a map by J.Y. Wang; map *C* after a map by M.W. Burley, Weather Bureau State Climatologist, and the Wisc. Crop Reporting Service.

14-7 Based on statistics in the *Annual Report of the Lake Carriers Assc.*, 1976.

14-9 After C.W. Condit, *Chicago, 1910–29: Building, Planning and Urban Technology*, Univ. of Chicago Press, 1973, Fig. 5.

15-3 From The Tennessee Valley Authority, 1978.

15-4 From the *Annual Report* of the Appalachian Regional Commission, 1966.

16-2 After M.C. Prunty and C.S. Aiken, "The Demise of the Piedmont Cotton Region," *Annals*, Assc. of Amer. Geographers, vol. lxii (1972), 283–306, by permission.

17-2 From *Types of Farming in Texas*, Bull. 964, Texas Agricultural Experiment Station, 1960.

18-1 Data from the U.S. Bureau of Mines, "Value of Mineral Production in the U.S. and principal minerals produced in 1976," U.S. Bureau of Mines, 1978.

18-2 Data from the U.S. Dept. of Agriculture.

20-2 From A.G. Hely, *Lower Colorado Water Supply—Its Magnitude and Distribution*, U.S. Geological Survey Prof. Paper 486–D, 1969, Fig. 17.

20-5 Data from the *U.S. Census of Population, 1970*, calculation by R.A. Dearden.

21-3 After E. Hamelin, "L'Ecoumene du Nord Canadien," in W.C. Wonders, ed., *Studies in Canadian Geography: The North*, Univ. of Toronto Press, 1972, Fig. 2-2, by permission.

23-2 After E. Ehlers, *Das nordliche Peace River Country*, Tübingen, 1965, by permission.

Index

Places and physical features mentioned only once in the text, in their appropriate regional setting, are not indexed.

462

San Francisco, Calif., 1, 13, 22, 45, 57, 129, 135, 153, 367, 382, 390–91, 393
San Jose, Calif., 51, 391
Santa Fe, N.M., 149, 265, 361, 370, 371
Saskatchewan, 50, 131, 338, 339, 342, 343, 421, 430. *See also* Prairie Provinces
Scranton, Pa., 127, 177, 181, 190
Seattle, Wash., 135, 401, 410
sheep, 102, 197, 330, 355, 370, 373, 383, 387
Shield, Canadian *or* Laurentian, 6, 49, 105, 106, 142, 163, 220, 225, 227, 231, 244, 326, 340–41, 418, 421, 425
shipbuilding, 181, 189, 190, 388, 391, 410
Sierra Nevada, 13, 106, 347, 382
silver, 214, 341, 350–51, 410
Snake River, 142, 356, 401f
"Soil Bank," 94, 121
Soil Conservation Service (U.S.), 85, 94, 281, 296, 332
Soo Canal, Locks, 81, 133, 152, 254, 255, 341
sorghums, 235, 238, 333
South, The, 41–42, 43, 44, 54, 65, 68–69, 110, 134, 144, 147, 149, 150, 166, 172, 188, 201, 266, 267, 272, 287–302, 318
soybeans, 234, 235, 244, 292, 295
Spanish Americans, 47, 310, 317, 326, 356, 365–79
Spokane, Wash., 361, 401
Standard Metropolitan Statistical Area (S.M.S.A.), 51, 56, 392
steel, 96, 129, 131, 134–36, 143, 181, 190, 214, 247, 248, 250–51, 252, 255f, 351, 377, 390, 395
sugar, 102, 304, 356, 358, 388, 399, 407
"suitcase farming," 238–39, 317
sulphur, 100, 131, 132, 303, 313
"Sun Belt," 54

Susquehanna River, 16, 175, 182, 193

taconite, 133
tariffs, 68, 110
tar sands, *see* Athabaska tar sands
tenancy, farm, 110, 288, 289, 292
Tennessee, 4, 7, 65, 81, 104, 131, 142, 143, 151, 236, 271, 291, 292, 294, 297
Tennessee Valley Authority (T.V.A.), 142, 167, 279–82, 284, 286, 291, 336
Texas, 1, 6, 25, 27, 56, 81; agriculture, 104, 291, 292, 304, 312–13, 327, 330; character, 315–18; climate, 303, 312–13, 319, 368; industry, 129, 147, 341; land policy, 316–17; oil and gas, 137, 140, 146, 166, 313–14, 373; population, 43, 51, 54, 297, 318, 365; settlement, 288, 368, 370, 371; vegetation, 29, 33, 303
textiles, 65, 129, 144–45; 147, 181, 189, 190, 196, 201–2, 203, 224, 226, 298, 299, 301, 410
"tidelands," 97
tobacco, 85, 94, 129, 175, 176, 177, 200, 214, 236–37, 244, 266, 288, 289, 294, 298, 301
Toledo, Ohio, 129, 254
Toronto, Ont., 22, 49, 128, 153, 157, 162, 172, 183, 228–29, 253, 256, 343
Trans-Canada Highway, 159, 341, 415
Trenton, N.J., 174, 175, 182, 189, 190
truck farming, 175, 176, 178, 179, 189, 245, 304

uranium, 37, 425
Utah, 10, 17, 24, 36, 88, 97, 131, 247, 348–49, 351, 357

Vancouver, B.C., 50, 129, 155, 343, 401, 408, 410, 415
vegetables, 175, 176, 197, 199, 244, 245, 304, 306, 313, 356, 358, 375, 384, 387, 388, 396, 405. *See also* truck farming

Vermont, 89, 103, 199, 203. *See also* New England
Virginia, 4, 20, 43, 103, 104, 175, 176, 283, 287, 297

Washington (state), 17, 20, 31, 85, 105, 131, 142, 164, 405, 412
Washington, D.C., 43, 162, 182, 189, 190–92
water law, 79, 326, 396
water supply, 57, 79–82, 87–89, 193, 329, 373–75, 384, 388, 395–98
water transfers, 386, 396–98
Welland Canal, 152, 254, 256
West Virginia, 4, 131, 134, 230, 254, 257, 271, 276, 282, 287. *See also* Appalachia, Appalachian coal field, coal
wheat, 39, 40, 94, 95, 96, 102, 103–4, 108, 166, 176, 233, 235, 238, 240, 241, 267, 317, 327, 329, 330, 333, 334, 339, 340, 383, 384, 403, 405–6, 407, 411, 412, 414, 423, 424
Wheat Belts, 104, 105, 106, 170, 233, 238–39, 267, 319, 405
Wilderness Act (U.S.), 364
Wilderness Road, 149, 236, 272
Willamette Valley, 13, 105, 405, 410
Windsor, Ont., 147, 254, 257
Winnipeg, Man., 20, 48, 68, 129, 162, 167, 172, 239, 265, 326, 341, 342, 430
"Winter Garden," 313, 387
Wisconsin: agriculture, 103–4, 118, 224, 241–42, 243; climate, 20; legislation, 67, 79; physical, 6, 8, 15, 16, 27, 232, 239, 242; settlement, 40, 240, 241
Wyoming, 10, 50, 131, 137, 351, 357, 364

Yellowstone Park, 10, 85, 363

zinc, 214, 347, 350, 425
zoning, 58, 77–78, 79, 224, 243, 317